CULTURAL CENTRALITY
AND POLITICAL CHANGE
IN CHINESE HISTORY

Cultural Centrality and Political Change in Chinese History

Northeast Henan in the Fall of the Ming

ROGER V. DES FORGES

Stanford University Press
Stanford, California 2003

Stanford University Press
Stanford, California

© 2003 by the Board of Trustees of the Leland Stanford Junior University.
All rights reserved.

Published with the support of China Publications Subventions and the State University
of New York at Buffalo.

Printed in the United States of America
on acid-free, archival-quality paper.

Library of Congress Cataloging-in-Publication Data

Des Forges, Roger V.
  Cultural centrality and political change in Chinese history : northeast Henan
in the fall of the Ming / Roger V. Des Forges.
    p. cm.
  Includes bibliographical references and index.
  ISBN 0-8047-4044-5 (alk. paper)
  1. Henan Sheng (China)—History—16th century. 2. Henan Sheng (China)—
History—17th century. 3. China—History—Li Zicheng Rebellion, 1628–1645.
I. Title.
DS793.H5 D47 2003
951.18'026—dc21   2002011397

Original Printing 2003

Last figure below indicates year of this printing:
12   11   10   09   08   07   06   05   04   03

Typeset by Integrated Composition Systems in 10/13 and New Baskerville

For Alexander and Jessie

CONTENTS

Contents

Errata—On p. 12, the wrong map appears; the correct Map I.3 is shown below. See the other side of this sheet for a correction to Map 6.4, pp. 250–51.

MAP I.3. The Counties and Departments of Northeast Henan After 1545 CE with Their Capitals. Sources: Ya xindi xueshe 1923: 1; Tan Qixiang 1975: VII: 82–83; Mote and Twitchett 1988: Map 1.

Errata—On pp. 250–51, the wrong map appears; the correct Map 6.4 is shown below. See the other side of this sheet for a correction to Map I.3, p. 12.

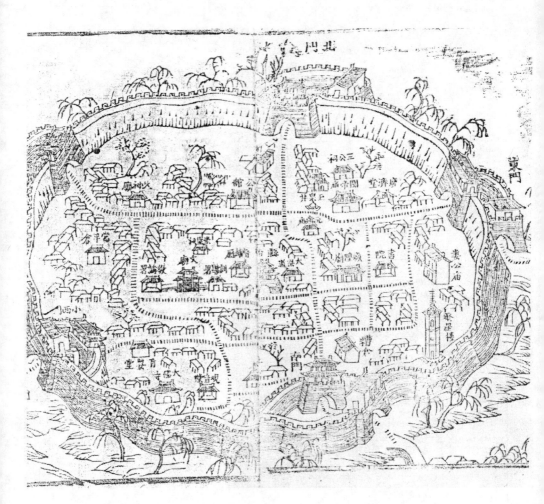

MAP 6.4. The County Town of Qi. Source: Zhu and Zhou 1788: quantukao 1b–2a.

MAPS

FIGURES

REIGNS OF THE MING DYNASTY

RULER'S GIVEN NAME	REIGN NAME AND DATES	POSTHUMOUS TEMPLE NAME
Zhu Yuanzhang	Hongwu 1368–98	Taizu
Zhu Yunwen	Jianwen 1399–1402	Huidi, Huizong
Zhu Di	Yongle 1403–24	Taizong, Chengzu
Zhu Gaozhi	Hongxi 1425	Renzong
Zhu Zhanji	Xuande 1426–35	Xuanzong
Zhu Qizhen	Zhengtong 1436–49	Yingzong
Zhu Qiyu	Jingtai 1450–56	Daizong, Jingdi
Zhu Qizhen	Tianshun 1457–64	Yingzong
Zhu Jianshen	Chenghua 1465–87	Xianzong
Zhu Youtang	Hongzhi 1488–1505	Xiaozong
Zhu Houzhao	Zhengde 1506–21	Wuzong
Zhu Houcong	Jiajing 1522–66	Shizong
Zhu Zaihou	Longqing 1567–72	Muzong
Zhu Yijun	Wanli 1573–1620	Shenzong
Zhu Changluo	Taichang 1620	Guangzong
Zhu Youjiao	Tianqi 1621–27	Xizong
Zhu Youjian	Chongzhen 1628–44	Yizong, Sizong, Huaizong, Zhuangliedi

Southern Ming

Zhu Yousong (Fu Wang)	Hongguang 6.1644–6.1645	Anzong (at Nanjing)
Zhu Yujian (Tang Wang)	Longwu 8.1645–10.1646	Shaozong (in Fujian)
Zhu Changfang (Lu Wang)	Regent Lu 6.1645	(in Zhejiang and Fujian)
Zhu Youlang	Yongli 12.1646–1.1662	(Guangdong to Yunnan)
Zhu Yuyue	Shaowu 12.1646	
Zhu Yihai	Regent Lu 8.1645–1653	

A NOTE ON TERMS, TRANSLATIONS, AND USAGES

IN ANY ANALYSIS AND ESPECIALLY IN AN INTERCULTURAL ONE, terms play significant and often determining roles. In this study, I adopt my own translations of several Chinese terms in an effort to capture the original meanings and develop a fresh line of analysis. Thus I render *zhongguo*, ordinarily translated "China," more literally as "the central state or states" to emphasize the importance of centrality and the state in the ongoing definition and redefinition of "Chineseness" and to indicate the potential pluralism in the most commonly used Chinese term for China. I translate *tianxia*, usually rendered "empire," as "the realm," "the known world," or simply "the world" to convey the idea of the borderless, universal order implicit in the Chinese term that means literally "all under heaven." From early times, China included a majority population at the center (called Hua Xia, Zhou, Qin, Han, and so on) and minorities on a gradually expanding frontier (Yi, Di, Xianyun, Xiongnu, and so on), but the majority were not always or necessarily thought superior to the minorities, nor were the minorities, despite much usage to the contrary, usually lumped together into a single entity translatable as "barbarian." In this study, therefore, I eschew any single term for foreigners, adopting instead the various terms used by the Chinese and by foreigners over time. I also distinguish clearly between the terms "Han" and "Chinese" as well as between the Han majority and frontier minorities of Ming-Qing times such as Mongols, Manchus, and Tibetans. The term "Chinese" as used here, therefore, is a capacious one that includes all of the people paying allegiance to the central state(s) of the day, from the Shang through the People's Republic/Republic. In that sense it is a political or civic term, much like the term "American" in its conventional—if notoriously too broad-brushed (the proper term would be "United Statesian")—usage for citizens of the United States who have in common only professed loyalty to a constitution.

All translations are my own unless otherwise indicated. In translating terms, I occasionally prefer to err on the side of precision even at the cost of some awkwardness. Thus I initially translate *tianming* as "the mandate of heaven and nature" to underscore the moderate transcendence of the Chinese conception of heaven as opposed to the radical transcendence of the Western concept of God. To subvert the too common conception of the Chinese ruler as an emperor and despot, I translate the terms *tianzi, huangshang,* and *huangdi* literally as "the son of heaven," "the august superior," and "the august lord." In general, I refer to the Chinese head of state as "the ruler" to encourage comparison among the many different conceptualizations of the head of state from the Shang dynasty through the People's Republic. I also translate *shenshi* as "local elite," not "gentry"; *shengyuan* as "government student," not "licentiate"; and *nongmin* as "farmers," not "peasants." I keep Kongzi, ru (or ruist) and ruism in transliteration and do not render them "Confucius," "Confucian," and "Confucianism" for reasons to be explained.

Although it is, strictly speaking, more correct to refer to a ruler by his original personal name (for example, Zhu Di) or by his posthumous temple name (Taizong or Chengzu), I have been persuaded that the reign name (such as Yongle) will be better known to readers and I therefore use it in most cases. To distinguish place names denoted by different characters that happen to be homophonous, I sometimes indicate tones by adding accents to the pinyin. For example, to distinguish the Jìn dynasties of the third through fifth centuries from the Jin dynasty of the twelfth and thirteenth, I insert a grave accent in the former case to indicate its fourth tone. In citing texts, I sometimes enter the juan number before the page number (for example, Zheng 1749: 7: 175), even when citing recent editions in which pagination is consecutive, so as to facilitate location of the quotation in question in earlier editions where pagination was nonconsecutive among juan.

PREFACE

LIKE MANY OTHER PEOPLE, the Chinese long considered themselves to be at the center of the known world. Unlike other people, the Chinese explicitly asserted their claim to centrality in the very name of their polity: *zhongguo*, the central state or states. *Zhongguo* remains the most common name for China in Chinese to this day. Like others, the Chinese often rebelled against states they considered oppressive. More frequently than others, Chinese rebels succeeded in overthrowing existing states and establishing new ones in a process they called changing the mandate: *geming*. *Geming* is still today the most common Chinese term for revolution.

In this study I explore the relationship between China's persistent quest for cultural centrality and its pronounced proclivity for periodic political change. In one common view, the Chinese insistence on locating themselves at the center of the world inhibited their interest in other cultures and resulted in political changes that had little impact on the society or economy. On the contrary, I shall suggest, the Chinese early and persistent effort to attain and maintain cultural centrality caused them to be remarkably open to their immediate peripheries and even, on occasion, to the rest of the world. Sinocentricity, in short, resulted in recurrent political change that reflected, shaped, and sometimes radically altered social and economic formations.

To understand what claims to cultural centrality involved, we shall look closely at the history of Henan province, long known as the central province (*zhongzhou*), located at the heart of the central plain (*zhongyuan*), a common synecdoche for China. To see how the quest for cultural centrality influenced and ultimately facilitated political change, we shall examine the role of Henan in the fall of the Ming dynasty in the seventeenth century, the last major shift in political authority in China prior to the twentieth century. Henan, like most Chinese provinces, acquired its name and approximate boundaries only in the Ming. Unlike most other parts of China, the region that became known as Henan had played an important role in the evolution of Chinese civilization from earliest recorded times. For this reason, Henan can serve, better than any other province, as a microcosm of all of China.

Within Henan we shall focus on the northeast region that today includes the provincial capital of Zhengzhou, the former polity-wide capital of Kaifeng, and the regional town of Xinxiang. I was first drawn to this region by the story of Li Yan, a supposed scholar from Qi county in Kaifeng prefecture, who was widely thought to have assisted the commoner rebel Li Zicheng in overthrowing the Ming in 1644. Together with some Chinese scholars, I soon found that the story of Li Yan was highly problematic. I ventured the hypothesis that he was, in fact, a composite figure, and his legend a powerful allegory for literati activities in northeast Henan and elsewhere during the fall of the Ming. To understand the full import of that allegory and to probe more deeply into the history behind it, I focused my inquiry on the region that appeared to be most germane—what I am now calling northeast Henan. The result is an effort to write what the French might call the "total history" of this region. It begins with a brief review of the geographical, topographical, meteorological, demographic, administrative, and socioeconomic *longue durée* from early times to the fourteenth century of the Common Era (CE). It then provides a much fuller analysis of the evolution of various social strata during the course of most of the Ming period (1368–1640). It culminates in a detailed narrative of the rise of Li Zicheng's alternative regime from 1640 to 1644.

A variety of rich but hitherto underexploited sources have made this study possible. New perspectives and details are revealed by a private account by a local historian, *The Outline History of the Changes in Yu*, which was written in the seventeenth century but banned in the eighteenth century. Three rebel sieges of Kaifeng city come alive in the diaries kept by the Ming defenders of the provincial capital. The thought of leading historical actors may be gleaned from official biographies, chronological biographies, and collected works, including two rare titles discovered in Tokyo and Taipei. Important local context emerges from provincial, prefectural, and county gazetteers published in several editions over three centuries. The major famine of 1593–94 and the rebel campaign of 1635 were depicted in unique illustrated works consulted in Beijing and Zhengzhou. Finally, the family backgrounds and personal experiences of key members of the local elite and middle strata are reflected in about a dozen genealogies collected with the help of Chinese officials, scholars, and descendants of late-Ming figures in the region.

In offering this account, I am building on foundations made by many other scholars. In the West, that work includes Frederick Mote's and Denis Twitchett's two volumes on the Ming in *The Cambridge History of China*, Frederic Wakeman's two volumes on the Ming-Qing transition, and important monographs by Timothy Brook, John Dardess, Jerry Dennerline, Joanna Handlin, Robert Marks, John Meskill, James Tong, Harriet Zurndorfer, and others. In China, I have learned much from the valuable research of Cao Guilin, Gu Cheng, Luan Xing, and Qin Xinlin on the Li Yan question and important work by Shen Dingping, Wang Xingya, Wei Qianzhi, and Xie Chengren on the late-Ming rebellions. My debts to many other scholars will be evident in the notes and bibliography.

In the course of three decades of teaching and research, I have become increasingly skeptical about the utility of three paradigms that have long dominated the study of Chinese history and continue to inform many accounts of the Ming-Qing period. First, modernization theory typically posits a sharp distinction between tradition, which is supposed to have characterized most of the world through most of its history, and modernity, which is thought to have originated in Europe and spread around the globe during the last four centuries. By these standards, Ming-Qing China was either traditional or early modern, depending on how close it came to experiencing social and economic changes similar to those occurring in contemporary Europe. Even many postmodernists, who often depict themselves as critical of modernity, seem wedded to it as a necessary stage and seem to find most of their inspiration in European thought. Some critics of modernization theory have noted the complex interrelationships between various traditions and various modernities and have tried to dissociate modernity from the West and tradition from the rest of the world, but even they continue to use the terms "tradition" and "modernity" and thus perpetuate their Eurocentric and teleological thrust.

Second, Marxists of various kinds divide history into the major modes of production, including feudalism, capitalism, and socialism, which they generally presume to be universal. A few postulate an even less tenable Asiatic mode of production that they consider to have originated in early times and to have persisted without significant change to today. Most adherents of this paradigm debate whether Ming and Qing China remained feudal or produced sprouts of capitalism that would have eventuated in a new mode of production had it not been for the drag of Chinese feudalism and the arrival of Western imperialism. Some "world system" theorists have challenged the Eurocentrism of the original paradigm, and a few have begun to question the assumed universality and standard sequence of the modes of production and even the role of class struggle in determining social change. But even these critics continue to assume that economic forces decisively shape—even if they do not determine—all cultural, political, and social phenomena.

Adherents of a third paradigm, "imperial China," assume that Chinese history can be best understood in terms of the relatively centralized bureaucracy that was established in the third century BCE and endured until its demise in the early twentieth century CE. They regularly describe the Ming-Qing period as "late imperial China," and debate the causes and consequences of the growth in territory, population, and commerce that is thought to characterize it. Some have questioned the power of the monarchy vis-à-vis the bureaucracy and the authority of the state vis-à-vis society and have acknowledged important differences between the Ming and the Qing. But even those scholars continue to call the Ming an empire and to compare the Qing with contemporary empires elsewhere in the world (such as the Austro-Hungarian and the Ottoman). Advocates of this perspective thereby ignore important differences among various Chinese polities from Qin to Qing, similarities between some of those polities and those that preceded the Qin and followed the Qing, and differences between what we might call Chinese culture-states and Western national-empires.

In this book, I question the assumptions and avoid the vocabularies of these paradigms. I suggest instead that we view Chinese history through the eyes of the Chinese themselves, as the result of their thought and action in light of their ever continuous but also ever changing sense of their situation in time and space. Chinese historical actors made choices not just in terms of the material conditions of the present but also in light of cultural models drawn from the past. Because those models already involved change, allusion to them often authorized change even while maintaining continuity. The pre-occupation with the past was intense and intellectual, inspired by an elite curriculum of early classics that included several histories and later histories that were thought to have embodied and exemplified classical norms. The invocation of history was also personal and popular, with much general knowledge of the past embedded in biographies that encouraged personal identification with historical individuals who had confronted similar opportunities and challenges. In assessing their own situations and evaluating the comportment of others, Chinese historical actors thought and talked in terms of specific people from the past. When the actors of a period approached a consensus on which models from the past were most relevant to their own day—as visible individuals from all walks of life in the Ming seem to have done—they produced a discourse, or a way of talking about the present that enables us to understand better why they thought and behaved as they did. History—or what happened—thus interacted in complicated and dynamic ways with historiography—or accounts of what happened—to produce patterns in the development of Chinese civilization that were both distinctive and potentially universal.

Given that northeast Henan was in some ways central to the central province—located in the heart of the central plain, a synecdoche for the central state(s)—it offers the possibility of a case study that reveals the experience of the larger Chinese polity. Once northeast Henan gained acceptance as a major cultural center in the semilegendary Xia, became a major political center in the fully historical Shang, and served as the principal site of the first fully historical political change from Shang to Zhou, it was conceptualized as a touchstone for Chinese notions of culture and change that lasted through Ming times. Even though the cultural and political as well as social and economic centers of China were often located elsewhere, the idea of this region as the primordial cultural center and locus of political change with an accompanying authority to shape social and economic forces persisted among its inhabitants and, equally important, among their neighbors. This idea, moreover, had operational consequences. Over time, people in the region and outside it kept going back to the past, or more accurately to various pasts, in search of models that would enable them to keep their cultural equilibrium while going forward into the future. In this sense, the very concept of centrality, *zhong* 中, depicted by a horizontal rectangle bisected vertically by a single straight line, was embodied in history, *shi* 史, denoted by the same character with an additional line, perhaps indicating records. Appropriate political change, inspired by past models, was seen as the key to maintaining, or reasserting, human influence over social and economic developments.

The book begins with an introduction to the history of Henan province, including its emergence as a cultural and political center in the exemplary Three Dynasties (Xia, Shang, and Zhou) and its social and economic evolution until it came to include the three prefectures of Kaifeng, Guide, and Weihui in the late Ming. It shows that the province frequently lost its cultural and political as well as social and economic centrality to other regions, including the northwest, southeast, and northeast, but nonetheless remained a viable contender for all of those forms of centrality.

The book then describes members of various social strata and groups visible in northeast Henan during the Ming and analyzes their changing thought and action over the course of three centuries. Chapter 1 examines the many royal princes, the changing sets of officials, and the state policies of river conservancy, taxation, relief, and education that first helped restore the prosperity of the region and later threatened to undermine its viability. Chapter 2 takes up the elite, defined as all those males who passed the civil service examinations and became eligible to hold office. It traces shifts in their geographical locus and professional focus that resulted in certain lineages and individuals mediating in various ways between the state and the rest of society. Chapter 3 addresses the status of women, particularly those honored for their virtue; several middle strata, including students, merchants, and military officers that increased in number and autonomy; and a small Jewish community that retained its ethnic identity even while acculturating to the Han majority. Chapter 4 approaches the masses, the vast majority of the people who rarely appeared in the records as legitimate political actors but made their influence felt in conspiracies and uprisings that grew in size and frequency during the late Ming. Although these various groups and individuals drew on different past experiences and interpreted them in diverse ways, many of them agreed on the relevance of certain stretches of the past to their own day.

As the Ming entered its final stage of decline after 1640, the rebel Li Zicheng emerged as an alternative authority. Chapter 5 chronicles Li's passage from Shaanxi to Henan in 1641, his engagement of a member of the Henanese local elite as chief advisor, his alliances with other rebels who had support in the region, and his direction of the first two sieges of Kaifeng. Chapter 6 traces the rebels' victories in many of the forty-nine counties of northeast Henan, including the ancient towns of Qi and Shangqiu, and recounts the saga of the third siege of Kaifeng, which resulted in the unanticipated destruction of the city by flood. Chapter 7 follows the rebel leader and his Henanese cohorts from the establishment of a rudimentary base at Xiangyang, Hubei, through the construction of a regional state in Xi'an, Shaanxi, to their victory over the last effective Ming monarch, who committed suicide in Beijing in April 1644. In addition to exploiting the combined effects of Ming decline and natural disasters in northeast Henan, Li Zicheng and his supporters invoked their own historical models in efforts to win popular support and legitimate their new Shun state. As it happened, the Shun was soon superseded by another state, the Qing, which also drew on various models from the past, but that is another story.

In the Conclusion, I suggest that the Ming tendency to identify with the Han and the Shun decision to emulate the Tang may be understood as parts of a larger pattern of continuity and change in thought and action in Chinese history that unfolded from early times to the present. If that pattern proves viable for China, it may also be of some use in efforts to conceptualize the place of the Chinese experience in the context of world history.

In the course of this project I have incurred many debts, and I am delighted to have this opportunity to acknowledge the most important. I am beholden, first, to my long-time mentors, Frederick Mote and Jonathan Spence, whose expertise on the Ming and Qing and commitment to understanding China in a global perspective have helped inspire this study. I am grateful to colleagues in the History Department, the Graduate Group on Continuity and Change in Asia and Africa, the Asian Studies Program, and the Program on World Civilizations, as well as to former graduate students Anne Csete, Michael Lazich, and Luo Xu, and to numerous undergraduates at the University at Buffalo for helping to make that institution a site for scholarly inquiry as well as academic productivity.

Over the years, this project has received support from many sources. The University at Buffalo Research Foundation provided two summer research grants; the National Endowment for the Humanities supplied a fellowship for study in Japan; the State University of New York Conversations in the Disciplines supported a conference on "The Rural Community and Political Change in Asia and Africa," held in Buffalo; the American Council of Learned Societies funded a workshop on "Rebellion and Revolution in North China, Late Ming to Present," held in Cambridge; the University at Buffalo-Beijing Municipal University Exchange Committee helped arrange a year of lecturing and research in China; the Faculty of Social Sciences at Buffalo funded participation in the First International Conference on Ming History held at Huangshan; the American Council of Learned Societies supported advanced study and research in Taiwan; and the Committee on Scholarly Communications with the People's Republic of China supported research during two summers in Henan. I also wish to thank the staff of the Harvard-Yenching Institute, where much of the library research was conducted, and the Weisskopfs and Worths for hospitality during several summers in Cambridge.

During four stays in China since 1976, I have enjoyed the warm welcome and invaluable assistance of numerous colleagues at many institutions, including: Qi Shirong and Xie Chengren of Capital Normal University; Fu Zhenlun and Wang Hongjun of the Chinese History Museum; Shen Dingping and Wang Yuxin of the History Institute of the Chinese Academy of Social Sciences; Dai Yi, Yang Nianqun, and Zhu Weimin of Chinese People's University; Gu Cheng of Beijing Normal University; Fan Shuhua of the Institute of Modern History and Liu Dong of the Institutes of Philosophy and Foreign Literature of the Chinese Academy of Social Sciences; Zheng Peizhen, Zuo Chunlai, and Cha Zha of the National Library of China, Beijing (I am grateful to Liu Xueting for arranging to have a copy made of the unique *Illustrated Record of Bandit Suppression* at Beijing Library); Mao Jiaqi and Chen Yixin of Nanjing University; Luan Xing of the History Institute of the Henan Academy of Social Sciences; Wang Xingya of Zhengzhou University; Li Xiaosheng, Liu Bingshan, Wang Sichao, Wei Qianzhi, Liu Shuxian, and Shirley Wood (Wu Xueli) of Henan University; Su Derong of the Mausoleum of the Lu Prince in Xinxiang; Du Baotian, Xing Shu'en, and Zhang Hefeng of the History Bureau of Qi County; and Wang Ruiping and Wang Shulin of the history and literature departments of Shangqiu Teachers College. I am especially grateful to local officials and descendants of prominent Ming-Qing lineages in Qi, Ningling, Sui, Shangqiu, and Xinxiang counties who opened their offices and homes to me and shared manuscripts and genealogies. In Taiwan, Yang Tsui-hua of the Institute of Modern History and Chang Wejen of the Institute of History and Philology of the Central Research Academy (Academia Sinica) in Nankang facilitated my use of libraries.

I also wish to thank: the late Chang Kwang-chih, William McNeill, Moss Roberts, Tu Wei-ming, and Ying-shih Yu, who have stimulated my thinking and responded to my inquiries; fellow Henan buffs Peter Seybolt, Ralph Thaxton, Odoric Wou, and Xin Zhang, whose work on more recent periods I have found instructive; colleagues Bill Atwell, Richard Chu, Jerry Dennerline, Joseph Esherick, Ted Farmer, Blaine Gaustad, Jonathan Goldstein, Joanna Handlin, the late Ray Huang, June Mei, Mary Rankin, Keith Schoppa, the late Robert Somers, Lynn Struve, Bin Wong, and Silas Wu, whose studies of related areas and periods have been most useful; and, especially, Tim Brook, James Lee, and Alison Des Forges, whose critical but constructive comments on several versions of the manuscript helped streamline the presentation.

I am grateful to China Publications Subventions and the University at Buffalo for financial support for the publication of this book, and to Muriel Bell, Janna Palliser, Anna Eberhard Friedlander, Anne Holmes, and especially Matt Stevens of Stanford University Press for their guidance in turning the manuscript into a book.

Finally, I thank other members of my immediate family, particularly Dorothea T. Des Forges and the late Sybil S. Liebhafsky and the two members of the next generation to whom this volume is dedicated. Without their enthusiastic interest and participation, I would not have been able to undertake—let alone complete—this *travail à longue haleine.*

CULTURAL CENTRALITY
AND POLITICAL CHANGE
IN CHINESE HISTORY

Introduction:
The Making of the Central Province

THE REGION KNOWN AS HENAN PROVINCE, also called the central province, owes its name and identity in part to geography and physiography. Henan, literally "south of the river," lies for the most part south of the Yellow River, which bisects the north China plain. Henan in fact constitutes a good share of that plain, also known as the central plain, the densely settled agricultural heartland of the Chinese polity. With smaller rivers flowing northeast and southeast and with mountains in the northwest, southwest, and southeast, Henan's topography resembles that of China as a whole.[1]

Henan benefits from mild temperatures and fair weather, receiving more sunlight than any other province. The average annual rainfall of seven hundred millimeters supports the cultivation of millet, wheat, sorghum, and corn. Henan is well located midway between the cold, dry winds from the north and the warm, moist monsoons from the south, but it also gets 50 percent of its annual precipitation during a relatively short period of late summer and early fall. Sharp variations in rainfall often result in floods and droughts.

Northeast Henan has recurrently flourished as part of the heavily populated and highly productive "core" of what G. William Skinner has called the north China "macroregion." Unlike other cores located in normal river valleys, however, this one is traversed by the Yellow River, which annually deposits one and a half million tons of loess soil across the central plain and into the Yellow Sea. The river thus continually builds up its own bed and must be contained by man-made dikes periodically constructed and maintained along its banks in northeast Henan and downstream. The river is known as the "suspended river" because it flows several meters above the surrounding countryside; it is also known as "China's sorrow," referring to the disastrous floods that result from neglect of its conservancy.[2]

Henan province is drained by the Wei River in the northeast, the Huai in the southeast, the Qi and Dan in the north, and the Guo and Ying in the south. In addition, smaller rivers flowing east have historically come and gone, depending in part on state policies

1

for managing the Yellow River. The region was once covered by considerable forests, but they have long since retreated in the face of agriculture. Although the province possesses deposits of copper, tin, coal, iron, and oil, their exploitation has varied wildly according to the political as well as commercial, industrial, and technological winds of change.[3]

To understand the role of this region during the Ming, we must go beyond the timeless aspects of geography, climate, topography, and natural resources to their historical aspects and to the cultural, political, social, and economic experiences of the peoples who inhabited the region. For it was the people of this region together with their neighbors who produced and reproduced the notion of cultural centrality and associated it with this region in the face of competing claims from other regions and the vicissitudes of time.

Although recurrent floods of the original He Shui (river waters), which later became known as the consolidated Yellow River, washed away most of the evidence, the region that became Henan province in the Ming was probably the home of various Paleolithic and early-Neolithic populations and cultures that provided the substrata upon which early Chinese civilization was built. In late-Neolithic times the area emerged as part of what Ho Ping-ti and Kwang-chih Chang called the "cradle" of Chinese culture or the "interaction sphere" of several neighboring cultures, including Yangshao to the west, Longshan to the east, and others further afield. During the Xia cultural horizon (traditionally 2200–1766 BCE), when the climate was warmer, the water table higher, and the flora and fauna more abundant than they would later become, the region became known as Yu, written with a character that includes the sign for elephant. According to a chapter of the *Venerated Documents*, thought to have been compiled in the seventh century BCE, Yu was the "central province" (*zhongzhou*) among the original, legendary nine, a number that privileged the concept of centrality. Northeast Henan as we have defined it may therefore be described as Yudong, or eastern Yu. During the late Xia, the people of this region developed agriculture, interacted with pastoralists, established towns (including two with names that proved durable), and may even have constructed a state (possibly with six successive capitals). Two of those putative capitals may have been located in northeast Henan.[4]

During the fully historical Shang dynasty (c. 1600–1045 BCE), Henan emerged as the prime political as well as cultural center. Four of the six capitals known as the Great City Shang were located in Henan and one of the four, Ao, was in northeast Henan near Zhengzhou, the present capital of the province. Ao flourished in the mid-Shang period when it covered 3.2 square kilometers. It was surrounded by a wall 9.1 meters high and 36 meters wide, a structure that would have taken ten thousand men eighteen years to build. Of seventy other Shang towns, thirty were in Henan, nine of which were in the northeast. Seven were located near what later became county seats, including Qi and Shang situated near towns bearing those names today. Shang capitals may have been called central state(s) (*zhongguo*), the most common and enduring name for China to this day. The location of Shang capitals in the middle of a rich (if vulnerable) alluvial plain may have allowed the concept of centrality to emerge and endure. The terms *zhonghua* (central florescence) and *zhongyuan* (central plain), which also appeared in Shang times, became common synecdoches for China.[5]

The founders of the Zhou (1045–256 BCE) originated in the west and established their first capitals in the Wei River valley, but they effected the first change of mandate (*geming*) in Chinese history in the central plain. They established a secondary capital at Chengzhou, near present-day Luoyang in Henan province. The Zhou propitiated the spirits of the Shang by enfeoffing their descendants in a state named Song, located at Shangqiu (literally, graves of the Shang). They also invoked (or manufactured) the supposed Shang replacement of the putative Xia state as a precedent for their own rebellion and established a shrine to the ancestors of the Xia royal line at Qi. Thus began the "rites of Qi and Song," or the showing of proper respect to the ancestors of the previous ruling house, which would subsequently be used to facilitate and legitimate dynastic transitions in China. Meanwhile Chengzhou, located between the Yi and Luo Rivers in western Henan, came to be called the center of all under heaven (*tianxia*), suggesting the continued cultural power of the central plain even though the primary political capital was located in the Zhou plain to the west. By the eighth century BCE, fifty of the 140 Zhou principalities were in Henan, of which five were in the northeast region.[6]

Under pressure from its western neighbors, the Zhou court moved east to Chengzhou in 770 BCE, bringing the primary political capital back to the central plain and providing a foundation for the future development of the city of Luoyang. During the Spring and Autumn period (722–481), authority in the Henan region was divided among four increasingly autonomous states, Zheng, Wéi, Song, and Chu, and the number of towns doubled from one hundred to two hundred. During the Warring States (403–221), two new states, Hán with its capital in Luoyang and Wéi with its capital at Da Liang (also called Kaifeng), joined the competition for wealth and power. The number of towns in Henan diminished to 150 while certain towns increased in size. For example, Suiyang on the Sui River was surrounded by a five-kilometer-long wall and contained more than 100,000 residents. Da Liang on the Hong Canal became an industrial and commercial hub with a population of 200,000, second only to Luoyang in the region.[7]

The Qin state (246–206 BCE) rose to power in stages. It first established itself in the west where it guarded the Zhou ancestral graves. It next extended its authority east in the name of protecting the vestigial Zhou state at Luoyang. It then asserted its control over the states of Shu and Ba in the south. Finally it won key battles in the central plain, known from this time on as "the place where the four armies must fight." The Qin maintained its capital at Xianyang in the Wei valley to the west but established a centralized bureaucratic system over the entire realm, including counties such as Da Liang and Suiyang in northeast Henan. The Qin thus brought new meaning to the concept of the "central state." Much later it would lend its name to the Western terms "China," "sinicize," and "sinicization." But the Qin itself lasted only briefly and altered neither the concept nor the location of the central plain.[8]

The founding of the succeeding Han dynasty revealed the increasingly complex interaction of the central plain and the other regions of China. Rebels against the Qin originated in the central plain and on its southern and eastern borders, but they overthrew the Qin by taking its capital at Xianyang in the Wei valley. The subsequent civil war among contenders for the mandate was fought largely in the central plain, but the victors followed the Zhou and Qin in establishing their capital in the Wei valley at the city they named Chang'an (long peace).

Although the Han established its political center in the Zhou plain, it extended its administration (consisting of principalities, commanderies, and counties) to the central plain as well as to many new areas beyond the Qin realm. It divided the region east of the pass into the single princedom of Liang, the two commanderies of Henei and Henan, and some 150 counties. It thus asserted closer control over the central province than any previous polity had and more control than the Ming would assert a millennium and a half later (when the region, now more heavily populated, would be administered by only one hundred counties).

The Han benefited from a warmer climate and established a long period of peace and order that resulted in the spread of agricultural technology and food surpluses supporting a population of sixty million. Twenty-five percent of that Han population inhabited the region that would become Henan province. According to the historian Sima Qian, seven of China's largest cities were located in the area. We lack precise population figures for the northeast region, but the Henei, Henan, and Yingchuan commanderies boasted 200,000 households each. After the wars that attended the rise and fall of Wang Mang's Xin dynasty (9–23 CE) and took a large toll on the population, the rebels who restored the Han arose in Nanyang, in southern Henan. They won victory in part by taking the "key economic area" of Henei, and they established their capital at Luoyang. The Later Han faced a cooler climate and governed less effectively, but according to the census of 140 CE, the population recovered to fifty million, some 21 percent of whom lived in Henan.[9]

After the fall of the Han, China entered a long period of domestic strife and foreign invasion in which Henan continued to contend for a central role. During the Three Kingdoms (220–280 CE) the Wei state established its capital at Luoyang but had to contend with the rival Shu-Han and Wu. During the Jìn (265–419) and North and South dynasties (425–589), frontier minority states in the north claimed legitimacy through control of the central plain that contained remnants of the capital cities of previous dynasties; states in the south based their authority on their "ethnic" identity as descendants of Han subjects. During this period, southern Henan was usually named after the legendary Yu, northern Henan after the Warring States principality Liang, and western Henan after the Han commandery Henan. While the major towns of northeast Henan succumbed to repeated civil wars, Luoyang revived under the frontier minority state of the Northern Wei (386–534). Located near the White Horse and Shaolin temples associated with the arrival of Buddhism in China, Luoyang became a major center of the faith that had originated in India and was now spreading through East and Southeast Asia.[10]

The northwestern Xianbei aristocrats who reunified China in the Sui dynasty (581–618) drew on Zhou and Han precedents to establish their primary capital at Daxingcheng in the Wei valley. But they had risen to power with the help of Han literati from the central plain, and they established a secondary capital at Luoyang. Luoyang became a major metropolis, surrounded by a 27.5 kilometer-long wall and containing 220,000 households, more than ever before and for a long time after. Warmer temperatures and renewed order restored China's population to the near–Han level of forty-five million, 18 percent of which lived in Henan. The towns of northeast Henan flourished; Xingyang, for example, resumed its Han role as a major granary and became the most densely populated commandery in the region. The Sui constructed one major canal through Kaifeng, Qi, and Shangqiu to the Huai and another through Xinxiang to the Bohai gulf, using them to transfer grain from the southeast to the northeast. Whether by design or by chance, northeast Henan was a principal beneficiary.[11]

When the Sui attempted to extend central administrative control beyond its means, other northwestern aristocrats revolted and eventually defeated other rebels in the central plain to establish the Tang (618–907). The Tang, too, made its capital in the west, at Chang'an, but it also reconstructed Luoyang. It maintained the canal system linking the southeast with the northeast that continued to benefit the economy of Henan. The Tang applied the name Henan both to the prefecture that included Luoyang and to a circuit that included parts of the northeast region, thus confirming the Han-initiated association of the term with the area while leaving open its precise location. During the Tang, the east-west canal was naturalized as the Bian River; Bian and Song, towns along its banks, became two of the most densely populated departments in China. By the late Tang, Bianzhou emerged as a major commercial center comparable to Yangzhou and Hangzhou in the lower Yangzi valley.[12]

After the decline and fall of the Tang and during the Five Dynasties–Ten Kingdoms period (907–960), Bianzhou maintained its commercial role and became the capital of the Liang. It was thereafter the capital of the series of dynasties, the Later Tang, Later Jin, Later Han, and Later Zhou, that arose in the central plain and that reached ever further back into history for names by which to assert their authority over all under heaven. Although none succeeded in reunifying the realm, let alone in expanding its borders in the manner of the Han and Tang, their persistent political ambitions, based in part on Bianzhou's prosperity, may be as historically significant as the more widely noted shift of China's demographic, commercial, and industrial centers to the lower Yangzi valley. That region, called *Jiangnan* (south of the river) as if to mimic *Henan* in the north, now established itself as a major cultural and political center (as it had long seemed likely to become) as well. But it remained riven by mountains and divided into ten kingdoms that posed no major political challenges even to minor and evanescent dynasties located in the central plain. The supposed shift of the center of Chinese civilization from the Yellow to the Yangzi River valley associated with Naito's "modern China," Elvin's "medieval economic revolution," and the "late imperial China" paradigm was neither as extensive nor as definitive as is sometimes thought.[13]

In any case, the Song state (960–1279), with its capital in Bianzhou (960–1126), came closest to reunifying the realm inherited from the Tang. Named after the early Zhou fief established for the descendants of the Shang and the late Zhou state that had hosted peace conferences in the Spring and Autumn and Warring States periods, the Song dynasty now restored northeast Henan to its status as the political center of China for the first time since the Shang. The Song actually constructed two capitals in this region, Bianzhou (the Eastern Capital) and Yingtian (the Southern Capital), as well as two capitals elsewhere, Luoyang (the Western Capital) and Daming (the Northern

Capital). Among these cities, Bianzhou was clearly preeminent, central to both Kaifeng prefecture and the capital route, and it was surrounded by counties bearing names that will become familiar to us in the Ming. Despite a cooler climate, agriculture flourished to support an unprecedentedly large population of 100 million by 1083. To be sure, Henan's share of the Song total was only some 12 percent, continuing a decline in relative demographic importance that dated to the Later Han and that reflected, in part, the polity's expanding frontiers. But the northeast region of Henan probably increased its share of both provincial and polity-wide demographic totals in the Song; Kaifeng prefecture alone boasted about one million people.[14]

During the first half of the Song era, later dubbed the Northern Song (960–1126), Kaifeng was also the commercial and industrial center of a Chinese polity that approached the size and exceeded the wealth of the Tang. The city was a transportation hub linked by the Bian River to the northwest and southeast, the Jinshui to the west, the Huiminhe to the southwest, the Caihe to the south, and the Guangjihe to the northeast. Some county towns became major transshipment centers; others specialized in manufacturing (for example, porcelain). Endowed with cheap transportation and supported by three dozen market towns, Kaifeng established an iron and coal industry that was preeminent in the world (despite major Indian achievements) until the industrial revolution in Britain in the eighteenth century. Concomitant developments in culture, politics, and society and the three inventions (printing, fire powder, and the compass) have led some historians to portray Song China as the first modern society in the world.[15] Although that analysis involves a subtle form of Eurocentrism and teleology—modernity is defined according to European standards and considered to be the destiny of the entire world—it does highlight the prosperity of China when northeast Henan was once again its preeminent social and economic as well as cultural and political center.

Unable or unwilling to translate wealth into power, however, the Song that aspired to reestablish the frontiers of the Tang was hemmed in by the Khitan Liao (907–1125) in the northeast and the Tangut Xixia (1032–1227) in the northwest before being driven from the central plain by the Jurchen Jin (1115–1234). The Jin was no more successful than its predecessors in its efforts to rule the large realm inherited from the Tang, and it was much less benign in its governance of northeast Henan. When Jin forces took Kaifeng in 1126, they burned the city and cut the dikes of the Yellow River, thereby destroying the northern end of the Bian River. The Jin also located its primary capital at Yanjing, beginning a practice that would shift the political center of China northward, where it remains to this day. Though the Jin named Kaifeng its Southern Capital, the city's erstwhile social and economic roles were largely assumed by the Jiangnan city of Hangzhou, which became the capital of the Southern Song (1126–1279), the rump state that controlled only south China. Northeast Henan's loss of its political and economic centrality was confirmed when the Yellow River burst its dikes in 1194 and shifted its course from the northeast to the southeast, destroying the Bian River and wiping out eight market towns. One more positive Jin legacy in northeast Henan was in nomenclature: the division of the region into Kaifeng and Guide prefectures, the names and approximate locations of which were to reappear in the Ming.[16]

When Mongol forces relying on superior mobility overcame the Jin in 1234, they devastated most of the counties of Henan north of the Yellow River. They subsequently exploited what remained in the region in order to subdue the Southern Song. During the Mongol Yuan dynasty (1279–1368), the population of Henan plummeted to an estimated 800,000 people in 1330, a mere 1.34 percent of the some sixty million Chinese counted as Yuan subjects. Many drowned in the frequent flooding of the Yellow River, and survivors were left homeless and forced to labor on the dikes. Kaifeng shrank to the size of the Song period inner city, and its population declined to between 100 and 300 thousand. The city lost its function as a transportation hub, and nearby market towns disappeared or were replaced by stations, camps, or garrisons. The region was further eclipsed when the Yuan used the now southward flowing Yellow River to construct the Grand Canal that linked the capital at Dadu (present-day Beijing) with the southern metropolis of Hangzhou. The Yuan nonetheless tapped into the charisma of centrality by establishing around Dadu an enormous central province (*zhongshu sheng*) that included the part of Henan lying north of the Yellow River, which it named the Weihui Route. The dynasty applied the name Henan to another large province that included the rest of northeast Henan, subdivided into prefectures, including one named Guide. Northeast Henan thus became part of the core, however empty, around which the Yuan constructed what was arguably the most extensive polity in Chinese history.[17]

In reaction to Yuan overexpansion and exploitation, the rebel Zhu Yuanzhang rose in the central plain to establish the Ming in 1368. The Ming reorganized the realm into thirteen (later fifteen) provinces and several military regions (See Map I.1). Most of the provinces, including Henan, assumed names and boundaries that have lasted with few changes to today. Adopting the name "Henan" from previous administrative units located south of the Yellow River, the Ming now applied it for the first time to a province that also included territory north of the river. This practice resulted from the southward shift of the Yellow River and from a policy of establishing administrative units that crossed natural boundaries such as rivers and mountains. Henan, with only 147,090 square kilometers, was one of the smaller Ming provinces, but it vied with neighboring Huguang for geographical centrality and the highest number of contiguous provinces. Located between the Yellow and Huai Rivers and between mountains and plains, Henan harbored the crossroads between the north-south and east-west trunk lines of the Ming courier system.[18]

The Ming initially divided Henan into seven prefectures and one department. The founder initially considered establishing his capital in Kaifeng and thus made that prefecture extremely large, including thirty-nine counties and four departments. When he finally decided to keep his capital at Nanjing and his son moved the primary capital to Beijing, Kaifeng was reduced to a provincial capital. In 1545 Kaifeng prefecture gave up eight eastern counties and one department to a new prefecture, Guide. Meanwhile Weihui prefecture had been established north of the river. Thus were constituted by the late Ming the three prefectures of Kaifeng, Guide, and Weihui that formed the region we are calling northeast Henan (See Map I.2). Kaifeng, with thirty counties and four departments, remained the largest prefecture at 30,725 square kilometers. Guide prefecture, with eight counties and one department, was next with 10,629 square kilometers. Weihui, with six counties, was last with 3,572 square kilometers (See Map I.3).[19]

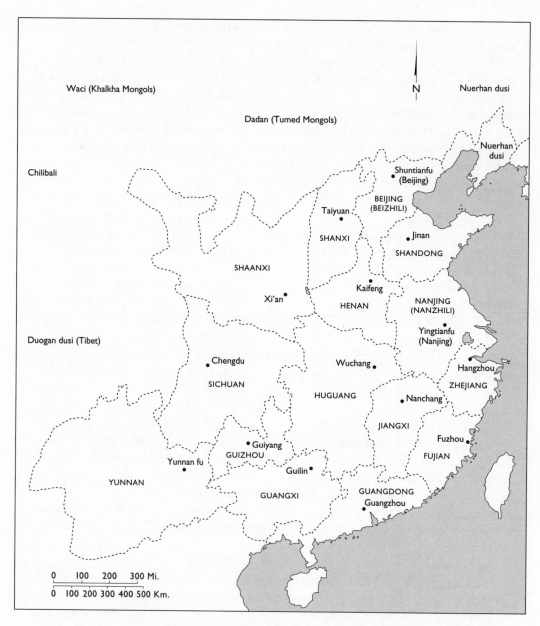

MAP I.1. Provinces and Territories of the Ming with Provincial Capitals. Sources: Herrmann 1964: 56; Geelen and Twitchett 1974: xiii; Tan Qixiang 1982: VII: 38–39; Lin and Chen 1983: 80; Mote and Twitchett 1988: Map 1.

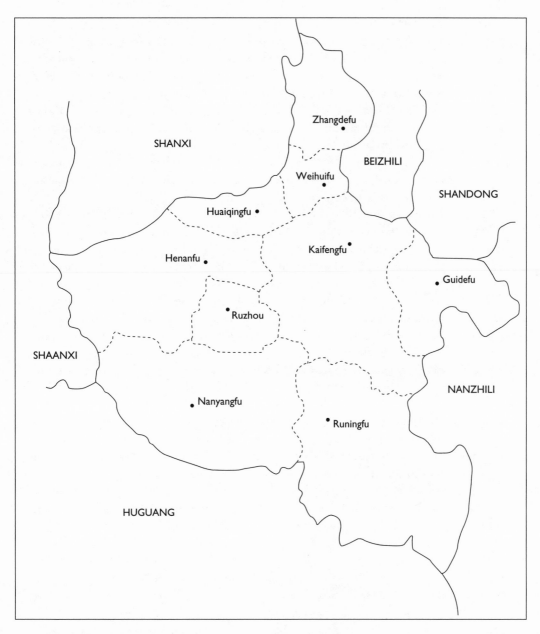

MAP I.2. The Northeast Region After 1545 CE with Prefectural Capitals. Sources: Ya xindi xueshe 1923: 1; Tan Qixiang 1975: VII: 82–83; Mote and Twitchett 1988: Map 1.

Despite the cooler climate that persisted from the fourteenth through the mid-six-teenth centuries, the Ming restoration of peace and order and its revitalization of agriculture and commerce resulted in the recovery of China's population to sixty to eighty-five million by 1400 followed by a doubling or even tripling of that to 120–260 million by 1600. Henan shared in this demographic renaissance, doubling and perhaps almost tripling its population from 1.9 million in 1381 to 5.2 million in 1578. According to Shui-yuen Yim, famine relief statistics suggest that Henan's total population may actually have reached fifteen or even twenty million by 1600. Henan's population therefore seems to have equaled about 10 percent of that of China as a whole. The population of the northeast region of Henan also grew during the Ming, perhaps doubling to some 2.2 million persons or 40 percent of the provincial total by 1573.[20]

Within northeast Henan, population was concentrated in certain prefectures, counties, and departments by the late Ming. Looking simply at registered population, we find that Kaifeng and Weihui prefectures averaged nearly fifty thousand persons per county and department while Guide counted little more than twenty-five thousand per comparable units. Within each prefecture, registered population was also concentrated in certain counties and departments. In Kaifeng, for example, the capital county of Xiangfu as well as Qi county and Yu department each boasted more than 100,000 registrants. Among the three prefectures, ten counties and four departments had more than fifty thousand while thirty-two had less than fifty thousand. Considering gross population density (registered population divided by total territory), we find eight counties, including Xiangfu and Qi in Kaifeng and Xinxiang in Weihui, to have more than one hundred persons per square kilometer while the rest of the counties and departments in Weihui and Suizhou in Guide had more than fifty persons. Twenty-two counties, including Shangqiu in Guide, had less than fifty persons per square kilometer. To this extent, Xiangfu, Qi, and a few adjacent counties in Kaifeng plus Xinxiang in Weihui constituted part of the demographic core of the region in the late Ming.[21]

The Ming restored the agricultural economy by encouraging military and civilian households to cultivate fallow land. As early as 1392, a cadastral survey showed 880 million mu of arable land in China, a figure that may be accurate if military lands (the extent of which was a carefully guarded state secret) are taken into account. Henan province, repopulated in part by colonists from the relatively poor northwest and the overpopulated southeast, claimed 144.9 million mu of registered land by 1392, second only to much larger Huguang, twice as much as Shandong, and three times as much as Shanxi. Although some military land was never recorded and some dropped from the registers over time, much continued to be counted, and the amount on the books in Henan actually increased over time. The total amount of civilian land in China, including that in the hands of officials and the people, increased 50 percent from 400 million mu in 1400 to 600 million mu in 1580 while the amount in Henan increased 100 percent or more from forty-two million in 1502 to 95–105 million in 1581. In northeast Henan, registered land in Kaifeng prefecture tripled from less than ten million mu in 1482 to more than thirty million mu in 1556 while that in Weihui nearly doubled from less than 1.7 to more than three million over the same period. Thus land on the books in this region increased some 350 percent over the course of the Ming, keeping up with—if not exceeding—population growth and constituting 42 percent of the cultivated land in the province. Within the region, moreover, the amount of registered land correlated positively with the amount of registered population. Xiangfu and Qi, for example, were high in both while Shangqiu was low in both. Even so, Qi county and five counties of Weihui prefecture were, by these measures, relatively land-short. Given the well-known discrepancies between the amounts of land that were registered and those that were actually cultivated in this region as in the rest of Ming China, however, we cannot draw any firm conclusions about the extent and incidence of population pressure (See Map I.4).[22]

The Ming state took advantage of the growth in registered population and land to impose moderate tax increases of which both Henan and the northeast region paid their fair share. For example, when total state revenues increased from 26,638,642 shi (one shi equaled 72.6 kilograms) in 1578 to 28,170,343 shi in about 1600, Henan's contribution increased from 2,380,759 shi, or 9 percent of the original total, to 2,751,970 shi, or 10 percent of the new total. The three prefectures of northeast Henan together paid 1,131,100 shi of taxes by about 1600, equal to 41 percent of the provincial total at that time. The tax burden was also rather equitably distributed within the region. For example, the counties with the largest registered populations and land, such as Xiangfu and Qi, had the largest quotas of *ding*, originally defined as adult males subject to a service tax and understood in the late Ming as a tax calculated on the basis of population and land and payable in cash. Given the well-known gap between nominal tax quotas and actual levies in Ming China, it is impossible to arrive at a general statistical quantification of the actual late Ming tax burden in this region as elsewhere. It would appear, however, that the formal taxes in this region before 1600 were relatively light. In 1578, for example, the provincial tax indicated above had been paid on 74,157,951 mu of registered land, yielding an average of .032 shi per mu. That was less than the average for China in that year (.038), less than the low ideal set by the Ming founder (.035), equal to that of Shanxi, and higher only than that of Huguang (which paid a very low .009 shi per mu). As of 1600, therefore, Ming taxes were perhaps neither too heavy, as suggested by the well-known end-of-dynasty scenario, or too light, as is sometimes argued in recent scholarship, but just about sufficient to sustain law and order without exploiting the people. This conclusion is consistent with recent judgments that the Ming was "the most successful major government in the world of its time" and that it presided over the flourishing of the "north China macroregion" among others.[23]

In sum, the region that became Henan province in the Ming dynasty emerged as the prime cultural center of China in the semilegendary Xia period, stood out as the principal political center in the fully historical Shang, and became the main locus of change in the transition to the much respected Zhou. From the beginning, its position of cultural centrality implied receptivity to influences from all sides as well as creativity in synthesizing those influences into a coherent whole with universal significance. Henan's role as a locus of cultural interaction was evident again in the North and South Dynasties when the region became a principal site for the acceptance, transformation, and diffusion of Buddhism. The central province soon shared its political preeminence

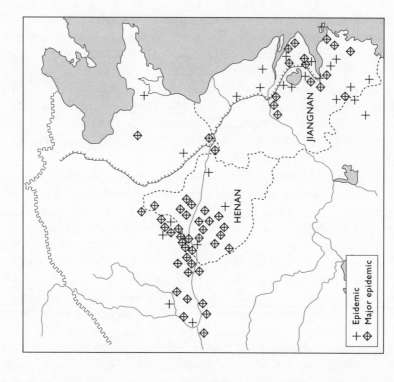

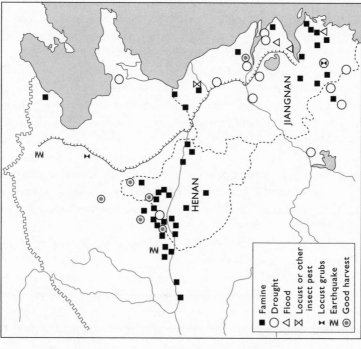

MAP 1.3. The Counties and Departments of Northeast Henan After 1545 CE with Their Capitals. Sources: Ya xindi xueshe 1923: 1; Tan Qixiang 1975: VII: 82–83; Mote and Twitchett 1988: Map 1.

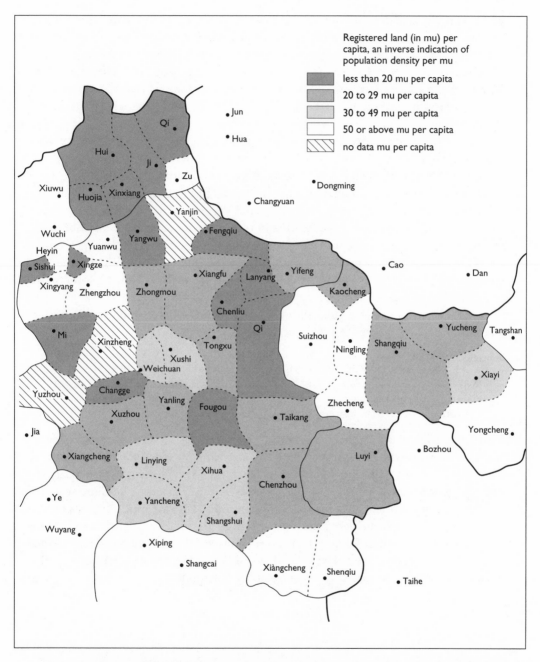

MAP I.4. Population Density in the Late Ming as Reflected, Inversely, in the Amount of Registered Land Per Capita. Sources: Tian, Sun, and Asiha 1735: 21–22; Perkins 1969: 16, 222–31; Ray Huang 1974: 164, 301; Liang 1980: 220–21, 332–33, 364; Cong 1985: 11; Wang Xingya 1984b: 37–42; Chao Kang 1986: 81–85; Gu Cheng 1986: 193–213; Gu Cheng 1990: 200, 204, 207, 216–17; Twitchett and Mote 1998: 433.

with other regions, such as the Wei valley including Chang'an, Jiangnan including Hangzhou, and the north China plain including Beijing, but it continued to help legitimate those other centers, to produce secondary capitals such as Luoyang, and to reclaim political preeminence in the Eastern Zhou, Eastern Han, late Tang, and Northern Song. The province was early on known as the place where the "four armies" had to fight and where scholars periodically appeared to advise commoner rebels in their quests for the mandate to rule.

During the Ming dynasty, the cultural and political center of China was presumably in the north, in Beijing, while the social and economic center was arguably in the south, in Jiangnan. Henan province, however, maintained its claim to centrality in several ways. It remained near the geographical center of the Ming polity, drew its name from several different previous administrative units, and continued to be called the central province. Trends in its population, land, and taxes were quite representative of those of Ming China as a whole. Within the province, the northeast region was geographically off center, but it was culturally, politically, socially, and economically central. The people of the province and of this region had good reason to be politically loyal to the Ming, but they also possessed a firm cultural foundation from which to evaluate that polity as it evolved over time. Their thought and action would depend in part on what Pierre Bourdieu has called the *habitus*. In his words:

> The *habitus*, a product of history, produces individual and collective practices—more history—in accordance with the schemes generated by history. It ensures the active presence of past experiences, which, deposited in each organism in the form of schemes of perception, thought and action, tend to guarantee the 'correctness' of practices and their constancy over time, more reliably than all formal rules and explicit norms. . . . [24]

Given Henan's role as a recurrent center of China and the northeast region's similar role in the province, the residents may have felt "the active presence of past experiences" with greater intensity and believed in the "'correctness' of practices and their constancy over time" with greater fervor than other Chinese. To the extent that the Chinese polity exhibited a "fractal" quality in which similarly irregular patterns appeared at its center and among its constituent parts, their perspectives on the "robust processes" of the Chinese past may also have been quite representative of those of Ming Chinese in general.[25] At the very least, their views suggest hypotheses that can be tested against the data from other regions as well as from the polity at large.

ONE

The State

THE MING STATE GOVERNED NORTHEAST HENAN in part through a political nobility consisting of younger sons of the rulers enfeoffed in estates outside the capital. It also managed a bureaucracy that by world standards seemed large and articulated, but in per capita terms was actually small and undifferentiated. The Ming nobility began with political and military authority, came to exert symbolic and cultural influence, and finally developed into a social and economic burden on society. Ming administration similarly evolved from an original structure to several sets of new offices, and officials developed policies on river conservation, tax reform, famine relief, and public education. For over two centuries, the Ming governed a growing population well, only later confronting problems, chiefly financial, that proved to be insurmountable.

Princes

As early as 1353, the rebel Zhu Yuanzhang received advice to model himself after the Han founder Liu Bang, who reputedly excelled in the art of "using men." Zhu, who founded the Ming and adopted the reign name Hongwu, believed that the Yuan, like the Qin, had been overcentralized. He therefore followed the Han example and kept his eldest son as heir apparent in the capital while enfeoffing his younger sons in the provinces. His goal was to exclude the princes of the blood from the politics of the capital and to give them military responsibilities in the field. To this end he bestowed on them high ranks, annual stipends of fifty thousand shi of grain, large expense accounts, imposing residences, and military guards numbering from three thousand to nineteen thousand. To maintain control, he required them to make annual visits to Nanjing. Princes had to get royal approval for military decisions, register their troops with the court, and accept supervision by central government forces.[1]

A prime case in point was Hongwu's fifth son, Zhu Su, who was named the prince of Zhou and enfeoffed in Kaifeng in 1381. He cooperated with the Ming general Xu

Da to establish a fortified estate on the site once occupied by the royal palace in the
Northern Song. In 1403 he and his brothers came under suspicion when their eldest
brother, the heir apparent, died and their nephew Zhu Yunwen ascended the throne.
Modeling himself on the second Han reign, the new ruler sought to reduce the authority of his uncles and began by dismissing Zhu Su. In 1404 Zhu Su's elder brother Zhu
Di, the prince of Yan, revolted to avoid being deposed. In a brutal three-year civil war,
Zhu Di dethroned Zhu Yunwen, erased his reign from the record, and established himself as ruler with the reign name Yongle. Zhu Su was restored to his post in Kaifeng,
where he enjoyed an annual stipend of twenty thousand shi (double the emerging norm)
and received extraordinary presents. When Yongle, modeling himself on Han Wudi,
undertook his own plan to curtail the authority of the princes, Zhu Su again came under
suspicion. In 1420, he was charged with treason by one of his own guardsmen, stripped
of most of his troops, and reduced to a mere symbol of Ming authority in Kaifeng.[2]

Thwarted in politics, the prince of Zhou channeled his energies into other pursuits.
He wrote a book entitled *Plants that Can Save One from Starvation*, which analyzed 414
herbs found in the Kaifeng area, 276 of which had never been described. This work,
which appeared over six decades prior to any comparable botanical work in Europe,
was a major contribution to surviving the famines that periodically ravaged the region.
Zhu Su, like other princes, also helped to repopulate northeast Henan by fathering fourteen sons and ten daughters. His eldest son, Zhu Youdun, who had taken responsibility for Zhu Su's alleged crimes and allowed him to survive, devoted himself to painting,
calligraphy, and drama. He later abandoned the Ming practice of encouraging noble
consorts to commit suicide at the death of their spouses. Another descendant, Zhu Mujie,
collected and catalogued over four thousand books and headed the Zhou princedom's
school from 1577 to his death nine years later. He wrote commentaries on the five classics (the *Poetry, Documents, Changes, Rites,* and *Spring and Autumn Annals*), edited the Henan
provincial and Kaifeng prefectural gazetteers, and celebrated 138 Henanese scholars
in his *Record of Personalities of the Central Province during our August Dynasty.*[3]

Although the total number of younger sons of rulers who were enfeoffed subsequently diminished, an increasing percentage was assigned to Henan. Two other sons
of Hongwu were established in Nanyang and Henan prefectures, and a son of Yongle
was enfeoffed in Zhangde prefecture. They were limited to 360 guards and allowed to
leave their estates only with permission. They were forbidden to take the civil service
examinations, hold office, or participate in commerce. In 1425 another prince was enfeoffed in Huaiqing. Zhengtong sent one son to Runing prefecture, replaced him with
another when he failed to produce an heir, and enfeoffed a third at Junzhou in Kaifeng
prefecture. Chenghua enfeoffed nine sons, including one in Weihui prefecture in 1501.
Over the course of the Ming, Henan accommodated 22 percent of the princes enfeoffed
by the dynasty and 27 percent of the princely lines that lasted through most of the dynasty
(see Map 1.1).[4]

The Ming practice of recognizing the younger sons of princes as princes of the second degree and granting their descendants lesser ranks further enhanced the proliferation of princes in Henan. The Ming princes' relative wealth and leisure combined
with their many concubines and generous stipends for progeny reportedly led to high

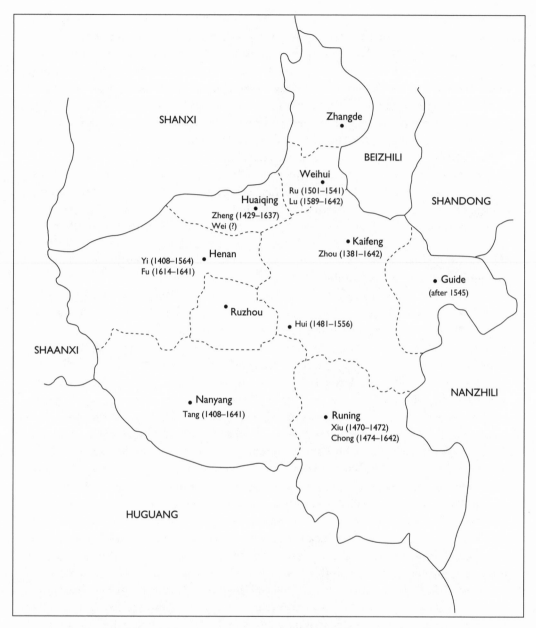

SHANXI

Zhangde
●

BEIZHILI

Weihui
●
Ru (1501–1541)
Lu (1589–1642)

SHANDONG

Huaiqing
●
Zheng (1429–1637)
Wei (?)

Yi (1408–1564)   Henan
Fu (1614–1641)   ●

● Kaifeng
Zhou (1381–1642)

● Guide
(after 1545)

Ruzhou
●

● Hui (1481–1556)

SHAANXI

NANZHILI

● Nanyang
Tang (1408–1641)

● Runing
Xiu (1470–1472)
Chong (1474–1642)

HUGUANG

MAP 1.1. Locations and Dates of Tenure of Ming Princes in Henan. Sources: Lo 1975: 28; Mei 1975: 59; Su Jinzi 1991: 41–43.

levels of fertility. Efforts to reduce offspring by controlling marriages, limiting concubines, and cutting stipends were ineffective. The number of royal clansmen in Ming
China, and especially in Henan province, grew steadily. According to incomplete statistics, while there were only fifty-eight members of the royal clan in the Hongwu reign
there were 28,840 by the end of the Jiajing reign. Henan, which began with one prince
of the first degree, accumulated 1,440 princes of many different degrees as early as 1529.
By the Wanli reign there may have been over sixty thousand royal clansmen in China
and by the end of the Ming as many as 100,000. Although we lack figures for Henan as
a whole, Kaifeng was reputed to contain 10 percent of all the nobles in China, or more
than five thousand persons. In addition to the Zhou prince, there were more than seventy princes of the second degree established in Kaifeng, forty-eight of whom were still
active in the last decades of the dynasty. According to one source, Kaifeng was home to
1,349 princes of the third through fifth degrees, 2,559 princes of the sixth through eighth
degrees, and 1,265 princesses of four different degrees. Counting spouses and children,
Kaifeng by the turn of the seventeenth century was inhabited by some twenty thousand
descendants of the Ming founder.[5]

Most nobles depended on state stipends. As their number increased more rapidly
than their individual stipends diminished, they became a financial burden. In Kaifeng
at the beginning of the Ming, a single prince received an annual stipend of twenty thousand shi, but by 1529 his 1,440 descendants were receiving annual stipends totaling
some 690,250 shi. By the Jiajing period, central and local government revenues in Henan
were less than half of what was needed to supply the stipends for princes in the province.
While Henan collected and retained only 843,000 shi in taxes per year, it was home to
nobles who consumed over twice as much, 1,912,000 shi per year. Under these circumstances, a Zhou prince, Zhu Muyang, proposed to establish a lineage school to train
young nobles to take the civil service examinations. Those who passed could hold regular posts and draw salaries in return for services rather than stipends rewarding idleness. Despite the opportunity, few princes took the examinations, and noble stipends
continued to be substantial. Princes of the lowest degree got annual stipends of two
hundred shi a year, and even cooks on their estates received 120, outranking county
magistrates who got ninety. We lack data on the numbers of princes at each level, but
incomplete figures suggest that two million shi were required to feed the clansmen in
Kaifeng at the end of the sixteenth century. Unable to supply that amount, the state cut
the stipends in half. Nonetheless, in 1613 it still had to find some 1,046,200 shi of grain
a year to support over five thousand nobles in the city. According to the Qing scholar
Gu Yanwu, Kaifeng prefecture contributed 300,000 shi, or 37.5 percent of its total annual
revenue in grain, and five other prefectures contributed lesser amounts to maintain royal
clansmen in the city.[6]

Unable to support its aristocrats, the Ming state allowed them to seek other forms
of income. Hongwu had opened the door a crack by granting the proceeds of ten thousand mu to his princes, and the princes pushed the door open further by accumulating more land illegally. For example, the Chong princedom, established in 1474,
accumulated 407,264 mu of different kinds of land in the seven counties of Runing
prefecture as well as 268,090 mu in seven other departments and counties, including

Chen and Zhecheng in Kaifeng prefecture. In the Jiajing reign, the Jing prince cited the supposed infertility of the soil in Huguang to request an enormous grant of four million mu. Although he died before obtaining that land, he arranged for local officials to collect special taxes to approximate the equivalent in rent, causing the people of at least one county to flee their homes to avoid payment.[7]

The late Ming princes' growing appetites are evident in the case of Longqing's fourth son, Zhu Yiliu, who was enfeoffed as the Lu prince at age three in 1571. Although his title derived from Lu'an prefecture in Shanxi, he was first enfeoffed in Hengzhou, Hubei, in 1589. When he argued that Hengzhou was too far from Beijing, his elder brother Zhu Yijun, ruling as Wanli, agreed to send him to Weihui, Henan, instead. The ambitious young Lu prince then seized upon the death of the Jing prince in Huguang to request the transfer of that prince's large estates to himself. Despite strong opposition from the officials and local elite of Huguang, Wanli once again indulged his brother and ordered accordingly. Five years later the surveys were completed and the Lu prince became the largest landowner among all the princes of the Ming period, with four million mu in twenty-four departments, counties, and guards located in nine prefectures of two provinces. Most of the prince's properties were in sparsely settled Huguang but some ninety thousand mu were in heavily populated Henan. According to fragmentary records, the lands in Henan included 22,600 mu in four counties of Weihui prefecture and 59,800 mu in six counties of Kaifeng and Huaiqing prefectures.[8]

The Lu prince violated the law not only by amassing lands but by engaging in business. As a youth in Beijing in 1583, he had already taken control of three stores that sold sundry items, including textiles, paper, fans, and tea. Later he took possession of other businesses, including the Yihe (just and harmonious) salt store, which consisted of two branches. One branch, located north of the Wei River, monopolized the salt trade in Weihui prefecture, handling up to fifteen thousand yin (one yin equaled two hundred jin; one jin equaled 603 grams) of salt a year and supplying six counties, including Ji, which consumed five thousand yin a year. The other branch, located south of the Wei River, defied the Ministry of Revenue to encroach on the salt trade of Kaifeng prefecture, nominally under the Changlu salt administration. This business soon expanded to provide some 100,000 yin (or twenty million jin) of salt to twenty-three outlets in Kaifeng prefecture. The Lu prince also drew unrecorded but probably substantial income from salt taxes in Sichuan province, interest on loans made to other nobles, dividends on investments managed for him by officials, and profits on sales of gold, silver, copper, iron, and porcelain.[9]

While the Lu prince accumulated new property, the Zhou princes luxuriated in old wealth. Occupying the grounds of the former royal palace of the Northern Song, they set high standards of elegance. Their estate was located near the center of Kaifeng, oriented (unlike the city) on a strict north-south axis, surrounded by a wall 2.5 li wide by 2 li long (or about six kilometers in circumference), and occupying some 12 percent of the area within the city walls. Although many Song structures had long since disappeared and some of the buildings constructed under Zhu Su in the early Ming had been dismantled, much Song-period architecture was still extant and some was still in use. Outside the Zhou estate and scattered through the southern half of the city were the

imposing residences of over forty princes of the second degree. The Zhou prince possessed a large (although unspecified) amount of land both inside and outside the city
walls, worked by 360 laborers paid by the state and by an unknown number of families
required to provide labor. The princes spent their leisure hours visiting the one hundred temples in the city and patronizing seventy troupes of actors that performed in
periodic festivals.[10]

The Lu prince's estate in Weihui was built on the substantial base of a previous
princely establishment, but Wanli wanted more extensive quarters for his brother. He
granted him property that occupied one-third of the space within the city walls that
were specially expanded to accommodate the prince. The prince himself later took over
other buildings within the town, thus exceeding the statutory limits on princely estates.
Total costs exceeded 400,000 taels, including 300,000 taels supplied by the central government, unspecified amounts from local administrators and the elite, and free labor
from the population.[11]

The Lu prince's son, Zhu Changfang, who succeeded in 1614, devoted himself to
cultural pursuits. He patronized the restoration of a pavilion in a local temple for housing
Buddhist sutras, collected antique pieces of calligraphy, and wrote a book explaining
their relevance to the present era. Modeling himself on the master calligrapher Wang
Xizhi of the fourth century CE, he wrote characters in many styles and inscribed seals,
samples of which remain to this day. He also painted elegant orchids, bamboo, and rocks,
and exchanged poetry with a leading Henanese scholar-official, Wang Duo. The Little
Lu Prince, as he was called, was also knowledgeable about music, especially the lute, a
stringed instrument popular since the Han. Like earlier Ming princes, Lu favored a design
that was narrower than that which had enjoyed favor in the Tang and Song, but unlike
them he developed his own particular style, which he dubbed the "Central Harmony."
This lute was supposed to produce music that would reflect and contribute to harmony
among the various seasons, festivals, and heavenly and earthly bodies. According to some
specialists, Lu's lute was inferior to those of the Tang and Song, but according to others it was superior because it incorporated new features learned from the Jesuits. In any
case, the Lu prince, who also took the characters "Central Harmony" for his courtesy
name, was said to have followed the example of Liu Xiang of the Han and Xi Kang
of the Jin by using a ruist (Confucian) method to attain the Daoist goal of nonasser-
tive action.[12]

Zhu Changfang's cultural activities included constructing ornate mausolea for his
father and one of his father's consorts. Located in Xinxiang county, the two gravesites
together covered more than 157,000 square meters. In layout, architecture, and art-
work, they compared favorably with those of Hongwu and Yongle. The prince once again
contravened regulations by constructing a separate gravesite for the princess who
had been only a concubine and by establishing a guard for the mausolea in excess of
five persons. The spirit way leading to the mausolea was modeled on previous ones, but
eight of its fourteen mythical beasts were new, perhaps reflecting influence from
African animals brought to China in the fifteenth century. Here again we see another
small but revealing instance of maintaining cultural centrality by remaining open to
the periphery.[13]

The cultural achievements of the late-Ming princes of northeast Henan entailed social costs. As resources were increasingly concentrated in the hands of the upper nobility, many in the lower ranks became impoverished, falling in some cases below the level of the ordinary population. One contemporary described Kaifeng in about 1640:

> I have seen how the members of the house of Zhou are restricted in their actions, have nothing to sell, and have no one to rely on. Some have not eaten for days; some are past thirty and are not yet married; some have been dead for over ten years and their corpses are not yet buried; some beg in the streets and marketplaces and do menial chores; some move to other districts or die by the roadside.[14]

In Weihui, the Lu prince continued the construction of his residence during a famine, providing paid work for some but imposing corvée on others. The prince left his business affairs in the hands of eunuchs who ran roughshod over local officials, demanded rents during famines, and meted out illegal punishments to tenants.

Zhu Changxun, the third son of Wanli born to his favorite concubine, Zheng Guifei, had for many years been thought to be his father's choice to succeed him as ruler. Indeed it was only in 1601 that Wanli finally agreed to name his firstborn son as heir apparent and appointed Zhu Changxun to be the Fu prince. It took thirteen more years before the prince, now aged twenty-six, finally made his way to his fief in Luoyang. His marriage had cost 300,000 taels and his palace 280,000 taels, and he still had the temerity to invoke the Jing and Lu estates to request four million mu of land. In this case, the reaction was so strong that the court was forced to grant only half that amount, but the prince still obtained enormous holdings that could not be assembled from lands in Henan and had to be sought in neighboring Shandong and Huguang. The Fu prince also demanded a share of the lucrative salt trade, further disrupting the Hedong and Huai salt administrations, impeding supplies to the northern frontier, and extracting profits from the people of Luoyang. The Fu prince's quest for affluence might have been more excusable if he had made some cultural contributions, but he apparently devoted himself to wine, women, and song, just as the demonology of dynastic cycle theory might have predicted.[15]

Administration

Ming administration also evolved over the course of the dynasty. After the founder abolished the post of prime minister in 1380, he and his successors governed through three sets of central offices, each with its own counterpart in the provinces. The first was the censorate, a distinctive organ of Chinese government since Zhou times charged with surveying the administration, a function it fulfilled in the Ming. It consisted of two censors-in-chief located in the capital and regional inspectors appointed to circuits in the provinces. The second set of offices included the six ministries—personnel, revenue, rites, troops, punishments, and works—dating from Tang times. Their counterparts in the provinces were called administration commissions and were defined geographically or functionally. The third set of posts included the five chief military commissions—center, right, left, front, and rear—with counterparts in regional military commissions in charge of the guards. Below these officials, prefects supervised departmental and county magistrates, holding offices that dated back to Qin times.[16]

In the course of the fifteenth century, the Ming established three new kinds of posts: grand secretaries, grand coordinators, and supreme commanders. Generally they were held concurrently by officials installed in other posts. Several members of the Hanlin Academy became known as grand secretaries. Although low in rank and in the degree of formality with which they were to be addressed, they regularly gained higher status and assumed other official posts. The throne sent grand coordinators to the provinces to supervise the provincial agencies of the censorate, administration commissions, and military commissions. They often held concurrent censorial and military posts and were considered the highest authorities in the provinces. Supreme commanders were endowed with military—and sometimes civil—authority over two or more provinces. Several came to exert considerable regional and sometimes polity-wide power. Because grand coordinators dominated provincial administration during the second half of the Ming, we begin our discussion with them.[17]

GRAND COORDINATORS

The first grand coordinator to be appointed was Yu Qian, a vice minister of troops who happened to be named grand coordinator of Henan and Shanxi from 1430 to 1446. His ancestors were actually from Henan province, but he had been born in Hangzhou, Zhejiang, where he received his metropolitan degree. He was appointed censor in Beijing and was active in military campaigns before becoming grand coordinator. According to his biography in the *Ming History*, he was a good official who sought the opinions of the local elders and called for a return to reliance on the li, local organizations comprising all of the inhabitants of a community. He personally supervised work on the Yellow River, built roads lined with trees and wells, and encouraged farmers to sell their surplus grain to local granaries to provide relief in emergencies. Yu won local admiration by opposing a plan to transfer responsibility for raising horses from Shandong and Beizhili to Henan. He demonstrated concern for the welfare of people in surrounding provinces by selling grain at low prices during times of dearth. He ordered local officials to accommodate 200,000 famine victims from Shandong and Shaanxi by providing grain, oxen, and land.[18]

In 1447, Yu Qian was recalled to the capital as vice minister of troops. When the Oirat Mongols captured Zhengtong in 1449, some officials proposed moving the central government from Beijing to Nanjing. They were likely thinking of the Song decision in the twelfth century to move its capital from Kaifeng to Hangzhou in response to the Jurchen assault. Having long admired the Southern Song loyalist Wen Tianxiang, who had died rather than surrender to the Mongols in the thirteenth century, Yu pointed out the disasters that had flowed from the Song decision to move the capital to the south. He argued instead for staying in Beijing and placing a regent on the throne to rule as Jingtai. Promoted under the regency to minister of troops and supreme commander of the armed forces, Yu reorganized the armies defending Beijing and called up freshly trained troops, including some from Henan, to hold back the Oirats. Yu was regarded as patriotic in public affairs and virtuous in his private life, but his strong public stands earned him enemies at court. When Zhengtong was freed and returned to power under the reign name Tianshun in 1457, Yu was charged with treason. He was tried, convicted, and publicly beheaded. With the accession of Chenghua, he was posthumously cleared of all charges and restored to his posts. In 1489, honorary arches were erected to his memory in Hangzhou and Beijing. Yu's third son, meanwhile, had taken up residence in the ancestral seat in Henan, where his descendants also settled. The *Ming History* praised Yu Qian for his statecraft in Henan. He was also included as a noted official in the provincial gazetteer and honored by the people of Kaifeng with a shrine.[19]

While Yu Qian was an exceptional official, his career reflects several general features of Ming administration in Henan. He was, first of all, a metropolitan graduate from Zhejiang, the prosperous and populous southeastern coastal province that, by the mid-Ming, ranked first among provinces in the number of metropolitan graduates it produced. Zhejiang also produced more than its share of higher provincial-level officials and was one of the two provinces that provided the most grand coordinators to Henan in the second half of the fifteenth century. Yu Qian was thus an "outsider," in accordance with the long-standing rule of avoidance by which officials were required to serve outside their home provinces. At the same time, Yu's grandfather had been from Henan and one son returned to make his home in the province. These connections may have enhanced Yu's concern for the province and contributed to his high reputation among locals. Yu Qian's case also reminds us that just as Henan exported people to other provinces, including Zhejiang, so other provinces such as Shandong sent people to Henan. Such population movements attenuated provincial identities while diversifying the population of the central province. Many of Henan's grand coordinators who hailed from Shandong and Beizhili therefore enjoyed dialectical affinities with immigrants from those provinces. Yu Qian was also exemplary of Ming grand coordinators in Henan in his effort to govern in harmony with the princes and the people and to promote domestic as well as frontier security.[20]

YELLOW RIVER CONSERVANCY

In 1471, a new appointee joined the grand coordinators, the director-general of river conservancy. The director-general also lacked staff and funds of his own and mainly coordinated existing officials at the provincial, prefectural, and county levels, but he could play important roles in proposing and executing policies. The director-general of river conservancy appeared among the first posts listed in the provincial gazetteer, an indication of the importance attached to the Yellow River in Henan.[21] But responsibility for the Yellow River in the Ming was scarcely reducible to one appointment; it involved many posts and policies dating back to long before the beginning of the dynasty.

During the first two millennia of recorded history, Chinese states had allowed the He Shui that issued from the steppe in the west to flow through many shifting channels across the central plain to the sea. From the Qin on, central states generally dredged and diked what then became known as the Yellow River and confined it to single channels entering the sea north of Shandong. They also constructed canals to connect capitals in the west with agricultural centers in the southeast and battlefields in the northeast. During the wars that attended the Jin and the Yuan, the Yellow River had shifted toward the east and split to flow in two courses, one entering the sea north of Shandong and the other running southeast to the Huai. In the late Yuan, the river entered yet a third channel toward the east and then shifted the bulk of its waters into a north-eastern channel, contributing to drought along the upper Huai and floods in Shandong. Rebels including Zhu Yuanzhang had taken advantage of those conditions to enlist the victims in armies that overthrew the Yuan and established the Ming.[22]

The Ming founder dropped his plans to make Kaifeng his capital but continued to devote considerable attention to managing the Yellow River to secure the city. During his reign, floods ravaged northeast Henan eleven times, causing extensive damage to crops, houses, and people in sixteen counties and departments. The state assisted victims by granting tax relief and distributing grain. It also tried to control the river by dredging waterways and reconstructing dikes. The state required that labor services be confined to slack seasons and requisitioned according to people's ability to provide them. It also moved the offices of Yifeng county to higher ground and transferred Kaifeng's granaries to a safer location upriver. In general, however, the Ming managed the Yellow River in such a way as to protect Kaifeng, turning down a proposal to move the city, which it described as a "princely screen for the state."[23]

When the prince of Yan seized the throne in 1403 to rule as Yongle, he undertook several large projects that impinged on the conservancy of the Yellow River. He first reoriented sea transport, originally designed to feed Ming troops advancing in Liaodong, to support the construction and provisioning of his new capital in Beijing. He oversaw the development of a river and land route from Jiangnan to Beijing in an effort to avoid heavy losses on the sea due to unpredictable winds and endemic piracy. Large boats carried grain up the Huai and Sha Rivers to Chenzhou in southern Kaifeng prefecture, transferring it to smaller vessels along waterways to the Yellow River. Larger crafts continued the transport up the Yellow River before carts carried the grain overland to the Wei River and finally boats made their way down the Wei River to Beijing. In addition, Yongle repaired and developed the Grand Canal that had been initiated in the Yuan. A minister of public works, Song Li, who happened to hail from Henan, mobilized 165,000 workers to dredge the canal in Shandong and create some thirty-eight locks, thereby completing the world's first articulated summit canal. Over time, the transport of grain from Jiangnan to Beijing shifted from the sea route to the land-cum-riverine route to the Grand Canal. Assuming that commercial advantages would have outweighed the burden of the unpaid labor required, northeast Henan likely would have benefited more from the maintenance and expansion of the land-cum-riverine route. The region undoubtedly had to contribute both funds and labor to maintain the Yellow River, the source of water for the southern sector of the canal. But the maintenance of the river also benefited northeast Henan. Song Li, for example, cooperated closely with other officials in dredging the Yellow River near Kaifeng, thereby bringing flooding under control.[24]

During the next two reigns, much of the lower Yellow and Yangzi valleys suffered a series of natural catastrophes. Northeast Henan experienced recurrent floods and droughts that damaged life and property in a dozen counties and deluged the upper canal while depriving the lower canal of water. Successive ministers of works and grand coordinators of Henan province responded by dredging the eastern bed of the Yellow River between Kaifeng and Shangqiu and building dikes and sluice gates along the northeastern channel. They granted tax relief and distributed grain to aid the victims of these disasters. They sought to forestall future catastrophes by building temples and holding annual sacrifices to propitiate the water spirits. In 1449, Beijing fell briefly to Mongol troops, underscoring the importance of the canal to dynastic security. The court then created a new post, that of general director of grain transport in charge of supervising the canal and associated waterways.[25]

When heavy rains in 1452 again caused flooding in Shandong, threatening agriculture and the Grand Canal, an assistant censor in chief proposed a plan to control the Yellow River by channeling it to the northeast. He rejected the example of Wudi of the Former Han, who had built dikes in the area that had not lasted, and invoked the model of Mingdi of the Latter Han to propose using sluice gates to coordinate the Yellow River with the Grand Canal. He also suggested relying on remnants of a Han-period "metal dike" to dredge a new channel for the Yellow River to the northeast. Mobilizing fifty-eight thousand workers for more than five hundred days, the censor supervised the recovery of hundreds of thousands of qing (one qing equals one hundred mu) of agricultural land in Shandong and ended flooding of the canal for three decades.[26]

The state also responded vigorously—if not always successfully—to recurrent flooding in Henan. It provided relief to and suspended the taxes on victims and sought to avoid flooding by dredging and diking the waterway. Officials directed workers from unaffected counties to provide assistance. Officials also moved a county seat to a safer site. When waters rose in Kaifeng city in 1461, taking the lives of "countless people," someone again proposed moving the capital. A record keeper opposed such talk, declaring that the city had been "established by the people." Even if Kaifeng were allowed to become the "habitat of fishes," he argued, it would still be necessary to control the river to allow people to live elsewhere in the plain. In 1489 a regional inspector urged repairing the dikes on the Yellow River distributaries and ending all discussion of moving Kaifeng, which, he wrote, only "agitated the people's minds." The court agreed, apparently realizing that the Yellow River would always require careful management to protect villagers as well as city folk. It then created the new post referred to above, director-general of waterways, with responsibility to coordinate all officials involved in river work.[27]

During the Hongzhi reign, debates continued over how to handle the three major distributaries of the Yellow River in Henan. In 1489, a minister of punishments reported that the river was breaking through the dikes to both north and south. He mobilized 250,000 laborers to build new dikes in the south to channel the waters through small rivers to the Huai. He also advocated building new dikes in the north to protect the canal. In 1493, a regional inspector in Henan argued that the Ming, with its capital in Beijing, unlike the Han and Song with capitals in Guanzhong and Da Liang, could not risk the Yellow River flooding to the north, where it would interfere with the canal. At the same time, it could not allow flooding in the south where it would harm the people of Henan. A vice censor in chief and supervisor of waterways won approval to dredge an eastern channel from west of Kaifeng to east of Xuzhou and to construct five hundred li of dike along the north bank.[28] These dikes formed the first sections of what soon came to be called the Taihang embankment, a massive structure that eventually traversed over one thousand li from Wuzhi county in Henan to Pei county in Nanzhili. This dike formally closed off the northeastern channels of the Yellow River.

During subsequent reigns, periodic floods continued to threaten the canal to the north and the people to the south. Some officials favored dredging the eastern channel, now called "standard," and strengthening the Taihang dike on the north bank. Their proposals were approved and carried out. Others urged dredging the Sha and Guo Rivers to drain off more water to the south but warned that excessive flows might threaten the Ming founder's ancestral graves at Fengyang. This work was authorized but proceeded slowly. After 1527, officials began promoting a plan to move the Grand Canal from the western to the eastern part of Zhaoyang Lake in Shandong and to build a new canal to connect it with the main channel further south. While this plan was under consideration, the director general of waterways supervised the building of diversionary canals along the standard channel of the Yellow River in Henan to reduce flooding both to the north and to the south. When these measures failed to prevent further floods in 1565 and 1570, work finally began to implement the plan to move the Grand Canal to the eastern bank of Zhaoyang Lake. The court dismissed alternative proposals such as reviving sea transport, rerouting the Yellow River north to enter the sea at Tianjin, building a new canal across the Shandong peninsula, and dredging the mouth of the Yellow River to accelerate its flow.[29]

During the early Wanli reign, Pan Jixun, from Zhejiang, was named to oversee the administration of the Yellow River. Pan opposed the plans to build a new channel for the river and to move the canal to the eastern part of Zhaoyang Lake. Instead, he wished to follow the strategy of Wang Jing of the Latter Han by dredging the existing standard channel and building dikes higher and closer together, thus accelerating the flow and causing the waterway to wash away its own silt. In 1571, Pan mobilized fifty thousand men to do this work. When some grain boats capsized in the canal, however, he was charged with ignoring the needs of the canal and was dismissed.

In 1578, Pan returned to the office of director general of waterways under the powerful grand secretary Zhang Juzheng. He noted that the "surplus waters of the river flood the central states" (here used to refer to the central plain) and argued that it was the state's "critical duty to maintain the dikes" and pay "special attention to Henan."[30] In 1584, when Zhang Juzheng died and was posthumously disgraced, Pan defended him and was again dismissed from office. Pan's emphasis on managing the river in Henan, however, was continued by others, including grand secretary Shen Shixing. In 1588 the court instructed the grand coordinator of Henan to assume joint responsibility for waterway affairs and to supervise three new local officials stationed along the standard course of the river in Henan. Pan returned to his post as director general of waterways and continued to argue for the importance of action in Henan, saying "no matter where the river breaks its dikes upstream, the Grand Canal is bound to be adversely affected."[31] He recommended repair and extension of the Taihang dike, construction of a stone dike at the juncture of the Qin and Yellow Rivers, and the designation of government lands along the river to support the workers. Pan's plans were approved and work began.

When another break occurred northwest of Kaifeng, causing considerable loss of life, Pan reminded the court that the Yellow River had progressively accumulated silt over the millennia and therefore tended either to stagnate or go on a rampage. He continued: "That is why management of the Yellow River is difficult and it is especially so in the central province. From the Han to the present, whenever the Yellow River has flooded it has always begun in Henan."[32] Pan recommended immediate repairs in ten counties and longer-term repairs in five. He requested permission to punish local officials who shirked their duties, and called for adequate remuneration of workers. He wrote that "river conservancy consists of preserving the dikes and preserving the dikes depends on the people." In this, his last tour of duty, Pan was increasingly short of funds; he soon sought early retirement. His request was approved in 1592 without any expressions of regret. Despite his frustrations, Pan Jixun made many important contributions to the control of the Yellow River in Henan. After his death in 1595, his publications won him a secure place in history as one of China's preeminent hydraulic engineers.[33]

During its last decades, the Ming state continued to express concern about river conservancy in Henan but lacked the resources to act. When, in 1601, the river breached its dikes in Shangqiu, the Henan grand coordinator requested that river officials be sent to survey the damage. His report was "noted" at court but when the chief grand secretary spoke about the matter to Wanli there was "no response." The president of the ministry of works called for repair of the dikes on the Sui and Bian Rivers to prevent further flooding along the southern distributaries of the Yellow River, but he mentioned no measures to relieve victims of the flood. The grand coordinator and concurrent supervisor of waterways reported that he had only thirty thousand of the million taels needed to repair the dikes, but his report elicited no reply from the court. When he notified the court a year later that he had somehow obtained 700,000 taels but still needed 300,000, there was again no reply. In 1602, the dikes broke again in Shangqiu, and this time flood waters rushed all the way north into Shandong. The grand coordinator was reportedly so upset that he died of a heart attack. Subsequent breaks at Kaifeng, Yangwu, and Suizhou elicited calls for dike repairs but none for relief, and no court response was recorded. In 1628, a censor tried to enlist local merchants in transporting materials to repair the dikes east of Dongwaxiang, but he noted that he was unable to pay well, and the merchants were not interested. He could come up with only ten thousand taels and had to obtain five thousand among the people. Clearly upset by this means of paying for "public" works, he exclaimed: "The central province is the heartland, and yet its troubles have reached this level!"[34]

While the best days of Ming river conservancy were over, the dynasty had invested enough in long-term projects to avoid disasters like those that had brought down the Yuan. A contemporary depiction of the Yellow River showed the extensive dikes on the north bank and various streams to the south running parallel to the main channel (See Map 1.2.). When the river broke through again in 1631 at Fengqiu and rushed all the way to the canal at Zhangqiu, the gap was plugged within two years and repairs were undertaken on the dikes in Yucheng and Pei. Not long-term administrative neglect but short-term military tactics would lead to breaks in the dikes in 1642 and the ensuing destruction of Kaifeng city.

MAP 1.2. Standard Channel of the Yellow River in Northeast Henan as Depicted in a Contemporary (late Ming or early Qing) Source. Source: From the private collection of Mr. Rewi Alley, origi-

TAXES

While creating new offices to supervise provinces and manage the Yellow River, the Ming relied on its original administrative structure at the provincial, prefectural, and county levels to collect taxes. Like most dynasties, the Ming raised the bulk of its revenues from a head tax, involving labor service, and a land tax, paid in grain or silver. Like the Han, the Ming based its fiscal system primarily on a healthy agricultural economy and only secondarily on commerce. The Song had taxed commerce and industry as well as agriculture to obtain annual revenues of 126 million strings of cash by the mid-eleventh century, roughly equivalent in value to as many piculs (shi) of grain in the Ming. Because the Ming state in about 1500 still contented itself with only 27 million shi of tax grain, its tax revenues were worth only about one-quarter of those of the Song. On this limited income, the Ming could support fewer than 100,000 officials earning modest salaries ranging from sixty shi for rank 9b up to 1,044 shi for rank 1a.[35] The Ming founder had established prefectural tax quotas that increased only modestly over the course of the dynasty. For example, Kaifeng's quota increased only 12 percent, from 719,300 shi of grain in the late fifteenth century to 807,900 shi in the late sixteenth century. To meet the state's demand for further increases, prefects won the approval of provincial author-

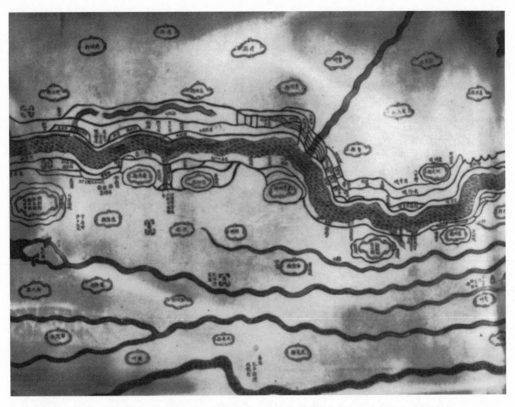

nally printed in Needham, Wang, and Lu 1971: IV: 3, Plate CCCLXII. Used with permission of Cambridge University Press.

ities to exceed their quotas and apportioned the increases among subordinate departments and counties according to their ability to pay.[36]

We can assess the Ming tax system in northeast Henan through the example of Qi county, Kaifeng prefecture, which passed down rather detailed records. Having emerged relatively unscathed from the chaos at the end of the Yuan dynasty, Qi was one of the most populous and prosperous counties in the region. In the Hongwu reign, it had 929,955 mu of reclaimed land under cultivation, of which 705,587 mu were paying annual taxes of 58,747 shi while the remaining 224,368 mu were exempt from taxes in perpetuity. In the Yongle reign, many residents of Qi county were encouraged by such tax exemptions to bring more land under cultivation, both in Qi and in neighboring counties. Meanwhile residents from neighboring counties reclaimed 140,840 mu of land in Qi. All of these newly cultivated lands came to be called "untaxed white lands." In the Xuande reign, the people of Qi refused a request from aristocratic households to turn over these lands as rent-bearing (but still tax-free) estates. The landowners' killed a prince's commandant when he tried to seize the lands, a rare documented case of direct popular resistance to landgrabbing by members of the royal clan. Called upon to mediate the conflict, the court predictably adopted a middle position beneficial to itself; it rejected the prince's claim to the land but instructed local magistrates to begin

taxing it according to the regular schedule. In 1462, the court promised a light tax schedule to people who registered lands that had previously been exempt from taxation.[37]
From then on the magistrates of Qi regularly attempted to tax all the lands of the county,
including those that had once been exempt from taxes and those held by people from
outside the county.

Beginning in the Chenghua reign, many of the yellow registers, documents containing details on land ownership in the county, were reportedly "lost in floods and fires."
Whatever the truth of those reports, landowners in Qi found it easy to hide their purchases of lands in other counties. They also circumvented contemporary state regulations by arranging to have some of their holdings in Qi registered as "white land," exempt
from taxation. According to the county gazetteer, land in Qi thus left the registers while
tax quotas remained in force, causing taxes to fall more heavily on the dwindling number of landowners actually paying them.[38] In 1528, the prefect of Kaifeng advocated a
policy of "equal taxes" (*junshui*) that required all landowners to pay at least some taxes,
so as to correct these gross disparities. His plan was opposed by powerful families in the
prefecture, causing the provincial administration to waver and finally to avoid making
a decision. Then, according to a record later inscribed in stone, the magistrate of Qi
county, Duan Xu

> recognized the extreme poverty [of the remaining taxpayers] and favored reform. He
> proposed it vigorously and soberly, spelling out his position that [taxes] should be equal-
> ized in a report of several thousand words and sending it up for approval. The grand
> coordinator reviewed it, the regional inspector forwarded it, the provincial administration
> and surveillance commissioners discussed it, and finally all were compelled to approve
> it. The Marquis [Duan] then announced the policy, fixed the measurements, delineated
> the boundaries, ranked the land by quality, distinguished among households and vil-
> lages, inspected the registers, drew up the regulations, announced them, and set the
> deadlines for collection. The provincial administration then sent [copies of] his laws to
> all seven prefectures to serve as models, praising them and writing: "Originally there
> were many quarrels over land, but this gentleman has now vigorously proclaimed reg-
> ulations. The benevolence of this capable marquis will now be the common inheritance
> of all."[39]

The court expressed its enthusiasm by promoting Duan to prefect and ordered his policies to be carried out elsewhere. In the face of entrenched landowner interests, however, it soon backed off. Only in Qi county, where Duan had established a tradition of
reform, did a successor maintain the new policy. Indeed, that magistrate suggested that
the spirit of equitable reform be extended to other realms, including military organization, horse breeding, the postal system, household registration, and public schools.[40]

In addition to pursuing the ideal of equity among landowners, the magistrates of
sixteenth-century Qi county took advantage of new opportunities to increase the revenues of the state. During the Yuan and early Ming, the Yellow River had often flowed
through Qi county. In the early sixteenth century, it was gradually shifting to the north
and to the south, leaving behind thousands of mu of uncultivated land, particularly in
the southern part of the county. At the same time, the Ming system of military colonies
was declining, as hereditary military households slipped out of state control or sold their
lands to others—both wealthy and poor—who had no military obligations. By tracking

down lands that had been fraudulently withdrawn from the registers and by taxing lands newly recovered from former riverbeds and fading military colonies, Duan and his successors succeeded in adding 1,174,046 mu of land to the tax rolls, more than doubling taxable land in the county. They also registered 102,818 mu of land owned by Qi people in neighboring counties. While the magistrates of Qi may have been exceptionally successful in collecting additional taxes, others in the province implemented the same policies. As a result, by 1556, Henan province as a whole had added some 14,080,975 mu of land to the tax rolls.[41]

Duan's equal-tax reform naturally incurred the opposition of many wealthy and powerful landowners who had previously avoided paying taxes, but the vast majority of people probably benefited from his insistence that all landowners pay their fair share. Duan failed to register all of the lands held outside the county that were potentially taxable, but he managed to get some of them on the tax rolls. He also taxed many newly cultivated lands in the county that had become available because of long-term ecological and institutional changes. Some observers have criticized Ming magistrates for "raising taxes" to win promotions; others have criticized them for "merely" equalizing the burden to win popular approval.[42] Given the long-standing Chinese ideal of low but equitable taxes and the growth in the Ming economy during the sixteenth century, one might equally well praise such officials for seeking—and to some extent attaining—efficiency and equity under changing circumstances.

During the Longqing and Wanli reigns, Qi county continued to struggle with the issue of tax equity. Some residents who owned land in neighboring counties repeatedly sued Qi magistrates who tried to tax their lands according to Qi regulations. They argued that they should pay taxes in the counties where they owned land, according to the regulations in force there. Qi county continued to use the standard mu of 240 square paces while other counties used much larger mus, of from 360 to 480 square paces. Because taxes were collected by mu, Qi's taxes would have been higher than those of other counties even if the tax rates had been the same. In fact, Qi's tax rates per mu were more than twice as high as those in many neighboring counties, averaging .0281 piculs a mu as opposed to .012 piculs elsewhere. Thus taxes on a given piece of land were often two to four times higher in Qi than in other counties. Qi magistrates nonetheless insisted on retaining the smaller mu because it was "standard"; they defended higher tax rates as necessary to meet the state quota. Magistrates of Qi county also invoked the principle that a county should be able to collect the taxes on all land held by its residents, including that located in other counties, although they never provided a rationale for this position. (Perhaps that was because they continued, quite contradictorily, to collect taxes on land in Qi owned by outsiders.) Presumably they were motivated by the fact that the amount of land held by Qi people in other counties greatly exceeded the amount held by outsiders in Qi. Whatever their pragmatism, the Qi magistrates were unable to persuade the people of Qi and other officials to accept their views. Some landowners of Qi continued to refuse to pay taxes on their land in other counties according to Qi regulations and were accordingly labeled "miscreants" in the gazetteer. Because the "miscreants" effectively resisted state authority, the magistrates of Qi were constrained to collect higher taxes from the people of Qi who owned land in their home county.[43]

During the early Wanli reign, the grand secretary and regent Zhang Juzheng, inspired by the models of the early Han and early Ming, carried out a "single register" tax reform that was popularly known by the name—homophonous in Chinese—"single whip." This reform went back to proposals of the mid-fifteenth century, called "equal service," which sought to enlist the administrative services of more people in a growing population while also spreading the burden more equitably among them. Those reforms had increased state supervision over villages and facilitated the commutation of labor service to payments in silver. During the sixteenth century, the reform broadened into an effort to eliminate the service tax and to make the land tax payable entirely in silver.

In Qi county, the changes were first proposed in 1578 by magistrate Qin Moude, a Zhejiang man, under the name "equal payment." According to the gazetteer, the reform was well received "by the people." Land taxes hitherto collected in wheat, rice, jujubes, and silk as well as those previously paid in labor, in kind, or as fees were also to be commuted to silver. When combined, all these levies became a single tax that yielded 74,461 taels of silver a year, an increase of 40 percent over the level of the early Ming. To be sure, the "single whip" reforms were not carried out as widely or fully as Zhang Juzheng had hoped. In Qi county they were subverted by unnamed opponents, and by 1584 the magistrate had retreated to a simple program of financial austerity. At the provincial level, there was a similar lack of enthusiasm for the reforms. According to Ray Huang, after the reform became polity-wide in 1580, Henan province "took one and a half years to submit its returns, which were later discovered to be simply the old data resubmitted. Though the provincial officials were reprimanded and ordered to carry out the survey again, the second report was rushed through only five months after the first was rejected." The reforms were, perhaps, too much imposed from the top down, too premature given the limited amount of silver in the economy, and too inequitable given the differential access of landowners to copper and silver specie. Yet, despite the foot-dragging, the total taxable land in Henan province increased by 28 percent from 74,157,951 mu in 1578 to 94,949,374 mu in 1581, the fourth largest provincial increase in the realm.[44] By means of such adjustments, the Ming state secured its share of the growing economy of the late sixteenth century and remained fiscally viable into the early seventeenth century.

Although the grand secretary Zhang Juzheng had been able to balance the budget, his successors faced chronic deficits due in part to Wanli's profligacy and to inflation that pushed up the cost of government. In addition, there were growing threats from Jurchen forces in the northeast and roving bandits in the northwest that increasingly required military responses (see below under Supreme Commanders). Annual military expenditures therefore increased from one million taels in the sixteenth century to four million taels by 1620, ten million taels by 1630, and twenty million taels by 1640. In an effort to meet these burgeoning expenses, the Ming state formally abandoned the policy of low and stable taxes that it had been covertly violating for some time. From 1618 to 1639, it imposed three sets of surtaxes, the *Liaoxiang* for defending Liaodong, the *Jiaoxiang* for suppressing bandits, and the *Lianxiang* for training militia. The surtaxes were imposed primarily on land and secondarily on other properties and commodities. The Ming court neither publicized these surtaxes widely nor recorded their incidence in detail as such measures would have been administratively difficult and politically counterproductive. As a result, only fragmentary evidence exists for conditions in China, Henan, and northeast Henan (see Appendix A).[45]

Incomplete statistics nonetheless permit some tentative conclusions. Even if one accepts the low rate of .0035 taels per mu for the *Liao* surtax to fund armies in the northeast, that levy alone represented an 8 percent increase in taxes for all of China. If we compare the generally accepted total receipts from all three surtaxes of 20,100,000 taels per year with the original annual tax receipts of 26,638,642, we arrive at an overall tax increase after 1639 of 78 percent. According to Ray Huang, this tax increase was made "largely illusory" by inflation. A very different picture emerges from figures that were on display at the Henan Provincial Historical Museum in Zhengzhou in 1984. According to these data, the three surtaxes taken together amounted to 24,290,000 taels of silver per year by 1639, slightly more than the total indicated by Huang.[46] The total amount of the polity-wide regular annual tax quota in shi of grain was estimated by the museum at 27,170,000 in that year, slightly more than the 26,638,642 assumed by most scholars for the late Wanli period on. Yet the museum stated that the value *in silver* of the total regular tax receipts actually declined considerably over the last decades of the Ming, from an estimated 88,930,000 taels in Wanli to 55,640,000 taels in Tianqi and only 17,760,000 taels in Chongzhen. As a result, the value of the surtaxes as a percentage of the value of the regular taxes increased phenomenally from only 6 percent (less than Huang's 8 percent) in Wanli to 14 percent in Tianqi and on to an enormous 137 percent in Chongzhen. According to this method of analysis, polity-wide taxes increased by the end of the Ming not by 78 percent but by almost twice as much. This is consistent with a conclusion arrived at independently by Guo Songyi: the three surtaxes combined ostensibly doubled the income of the Ming state after 1639.[47]

Although surtaxes were certainly imposed, it is questionable how many of them were actually collected. About one million of the five million *Liao* surtaxes on the books in 1621 were not collected and four provinces paid only 25 to 50 percent of their *Liao* quotas in 1628. Surtaxes on certain properties, such as officials' public fees in which tax collectors had personal interests, were even less likely to be collected in full. Because the *Jiao* and *Lian* surtaxes came later, when the state was even less effective, they were almost certainly never remitted according to the statutes. However, the Ming state repeatedly issued strict orders to meet quotas, punished officials who did not comply, sent special envoys out to supervise collection, and demanded payments four times a year. The state punished tardy taxpayers and increased the severity of sanctions as the years went by. Some counties were forced to pay even more than they should have. Moreover, despite the failure of the central government to secure the full amount of surtaxes, the people nonetheless often paid them. Corrupt clerks and officials often siphoned off surtaxes, as well as regular taxes, before they reached the public coffers. In addition, the surtaxes on moveable property and commerce probably caused hardship by pushing up prices and stifling production.[48]

The data for Henan province would seem to be consistent with an increased tax burden somewhere between the low one estimated by Huang and the high one estimated by the Provincial Museum. Taking the generally agreed upon figure of 94,949,374 mu of registered land in Henan and Liang Fangzhong's total of 667,422 taels of surtax actually collected from the province, we arrive at a rate of .007 taels per mu, roughly midway between the .0035 and the .009 rates discussed above. Since the surtax was a flat tax of so much silver per mu of cultivated land, Henan, as an extensively farmed province, naturally paid a large amount in surtaxes, third behind the much larger Huguang (which paid 742,476) and the much richer Nanzhili (which paid 696,552). Henan, like the rest of north China, engaged primarily in dry-land farming and thus produced lower yields per mu than the well-irrigated provinces of Jiangnan. It was therefore representative of north China in absorbing more than its fair share of the burden of the surtaxes. Henan, like Nanzhili and Shandong, also suffered from "call purchasing," the practice by which the state required people to sell grain of up to one million piculs at submarket prices and to transport it to Tianjin to supply the Ming armies. In some cases, this extra levy was regarded as worse than the surtaxes.[49]

For the situation in northeast Henan, we must be content with fragmentary data from Kaifeng prefecture. Adopting the .007 taels per mu estimated for Henan province and adjusting the number of mu under cultivation in Kaifeng prefecture in 1581 according to the 28 percent increase computed for Henan as a whole, we arrive at an estimated 270,033 taels a year in *Liao* surtaxes for Kaifeng prefecture. Unfortunately, we lack any data on Kaifeng's suppression and training surtaxes. We know only that the local historian Du Baotian has estimated that Qi county, in Kaifeng prefecture, which paid 74,461 taels of taxes in the late Ming, paid 18,861 taels in surtaxes by the end of the dynasty.[50] If correct, that represented a 25-percent increase in the tax burden of that county. While this is clearly not the 100 to 137 percent increase estimated above for China and Henan, it came on top of what was already a heavy tax burden in Qi county. Other counties of northeast Henan with lighter original tax burdens may have sustained larger percentage increases, bringing the regional average increase in taxes closer to the polity- and province-wide estimate of 100 percent.

RELIEF

If Ming officials collected taxes to keep the state solvent, they administered relief to keep the people loyal. The Ming founder Hongwu had called for the creation of four granaries in each county, and upright officials such as Yu Qian established and maintained them. In the fifteenth century, the state issued quotas for the amount of grain to be stored, and in the sixteenth century local officials established ever-normal and charity granaries to stabilize prices and provide relief. (Ever normal granaries were designed to keep grain prices from fluctuating excessively.) The state provided guidelines for the distribution of famine relief and stipulated the percentages of taxes to be forgiven under various conditions. By the late sixteenth century, however, state enforcement of those regulations had begun to wane. The state relied increasingly on the market to channel grain from surplus to deficit areas, and relief no longer kept up with disasters.[51]

The situation in northeast Henan reflected these polity-wide trends. During the first two centuries of the Ming, provincial and local officials who granted tax relief and fed the hungry were regularly honored with biographies in the gazetteer. By the third century, state funds were running low and such initiatives diminished in frequency and size. Beginning in the late 1580s, northeast Henan and eastern Jiangnan were hit by a series of droughts, floods, famines, and epidemics (see Map 1.3). In Qi county, thousands perished in a few months, and in Zhongmou, it was said that over half the people died. In 1592, heavy rains caused widespread flooding and famine in northeast Henan south of the Yellow River. According to recent studies, some forty-four of the ninety-six counties in Henan with extant gazetteers recorded famine in 1592–93. Cannibalism was reported in twenty-two counties, including five in Kaifeng prefecture and two in Guide. In Shenqiu, people were made homeless by flooding, and in Yongcheng people were ravaged by epidemic disease.[52]

Given conditions at court during the Wanli reign, the state's response was hardly predictable. Wanli had for years been locked in conflict with his officials over the appointment of an heir apparent, and he often refused to perform his most basic functions, including holding audiences and appointing officials. As it happened, however, the subsistence crisis in the central province galvanized the entire state into what would turn out to be its last effective relief program. In 1592, provincial officials in Henan granted tax relief to thirty-five affected areas and ordered local granaries to distribute grain to the needy. In 1593, the ministry of works ordered the regional inspector for Henan to prepare detailed disaster reports. The ministry of revenue permitted Kaifeng and Guide prefectures, among others, to pay their taxes in silver rather than in kind. By 1594, Wanli and his chief grand secretary, a strong opponent of the throne on the issue of the heir apparent, agreed to exempt the hardest hit areas from all tax payments and asked the ministry of personnel for suggestions on easing the food crisis. In March 1594, Wanli agreed to begin the education of his wife's eldest son, an important step toward designating him heir apparent, thus improving relations with leading officials (see Figure 1.1).[53]

It was under these propitious circumstances, in April 1594, that a secretary in the office of scrutiny attached to the ministry of punishments, Yang Dongming, a forty-six-year-old native of Yucheng county, Guide prefecture, submitted a memorial describing conditions in his home province:

> The people of the central territory [*zhongtu*] are already very poor, and current developments are extremely worrisome. I implore the August One to extend his humaneness to secure the people's livelihood [*minsheng*] and shore up the foundations of the state [*bangben*].[54]

Yang noted that he was a Henanese who had recently visited his home and was reporting what he himself had seen and heard. He attached to his report thirteen sketches that dramatized the story. The report and the attachments were later printed under the title *Album of the Famished*, a copy of which has survived in the Henan Provincial Museum in Zhengzhou.[55]

In the fifth month of the previous year (June 1593), Yang wrote, heavy rains had submerged the wheat crop, normally harvested in the spring, and prevented the planting of the millet crop, normally harvested in the fall. The first illustration depicted farmers attempting to retrieve remnants of the spring wheat crop from beneath the waves (see Figure 1.2). As the Yellow River rose and broke through the dikes, the resulting

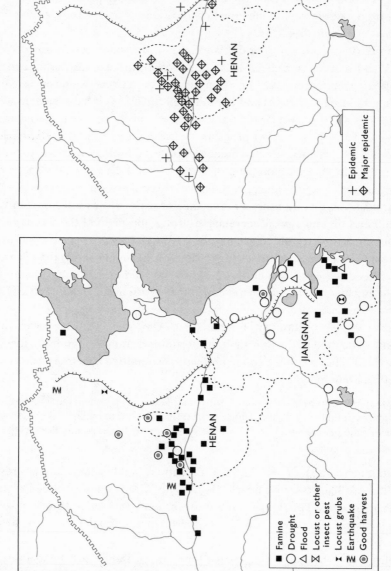

MAP 1.3. Natural Disasters and Epidemics in Northeast Henan and Jiangnan in 1588. Sources: Dunstan 1975: 54–55; Mote and Twitchett 1988: xxiv. Used with permission of *Ch'ing-shih wen-t'i* (now *Late Imperial China*) and the author.

FIGURE 1.1. Empress Wang (d. 1620) and Emperor Wanli (Zhu Yijun, 1563–1620). Source: Goodrich and Fang 1976: Plate 9, preceding p. 803. Used with permission of Columbia University Press and the National Palace Museum in Taiwan.

flood washed away homes and livestock and inundated fields (see Figure 1.3). Here Yang showed farmers saving themselves by clinging to bamboo rafts. Others fled the flood and famine regions (see Figure 1.4). Many carried small children and a few belongings, trudging through water and mud for days on end.

In the struggle for survival, families were torn apart (see Figure 1.5). In one case, a husband and wife had set out with their son and daughter, but the husband, unable to care for his family, had gone on ahead hoping to find food. His wife, too weak to carry both children, decided to leave her daughter behind. In another case, a son carried his old mother until he became so tired he could not go on. The mother then pleaded with him to go ahead to find some food to bring back to her. After he left, she dragged herself to the bank of a river, rolled in, and drowned (see Figure 1.6). When the son returned and found his mother's corpse floating in the river, he cried out and was about to throw himself into the river when he was restrained by a passerby. An observer on the bridge wept at the tragedy.

In many instances, parents were forced to sell their children in desperate efforts to insure the survival of at least some members of the family (see Figure 1.7). Here, the mother has sold both her son and her daughter to get cash to purchase a few pints of grain that will keep her alive. Sometimes parents might simply abandon the children along the road (see Figure 1.8). If a child refused to be left behind, a parent might restrain him or her, as in this scene. Yang stressed the mother's regret and the sketch depicted her weeping as she departed.

Survivors were reduced to eating the roots of wild grasses and the bark of trees mixed with certain kinds of soils (see Figure 1.9). Such measures might temporarily slacken hunger but soon caused illness and death. In some cases, whole families resorted to sui-

FIGURE 1.2. Retrieving Wheat from the Waves. Source: Yang Dongming 1688: 12b. Courtesy of the Henan Provincial Museum in Zhengzhou.

cide (see Figure 1.10). Here in the trees of an official residence, a family of seven has hung itself, leaving behind a two-year-old child with no one to look after it.

Desperate survivors sometimes consumed the corpses of those who had starved to death, cutting off the flesh and eating it raw or cooked (see Figure 1.11). Those who resorted to eating human flesh often got red eyes and feverish hearts and soon died. The corpses of those who died of hunger and cold usually had no one to bury them; they were left on the road and in moats where they were eaten by birds and dogs (see Figure 1.12). Yang added: "These are all children of the polity, relied upon as the foundation; when the least harm comes to them, our blood must run cold."

In Baofeng county, in Ruzhou a young lad took a two-year-old girl off the main road to a side lane in search of someone who would support her. A man responded and took the baby girl to his home (see Figure 1.13). When someone told the boy that the man actually took in children to eat them, he rushed back to the man's house to inquire, but he was too late. The infant had already been dismembered. Eventually, strong men driven by hunger and cold and unwilling to prey on the weak and the poor would come across the homes of the wealthy and powerful who still possessed grain and clothing. They would organize themselves into bands of ten or more and, under cover of night, knock down the doors and take the goods, sometimes burning the buildings and killing people in the process (see Figure 1.14).

FIGURE 1.3. Losing Homes and Livestock. Source: Yang Dongming 1688: 13b–14a. Courtesy of the Henan Provincial Museum.

FIGURE 1.4. Fleeing the Famine. Source: Yang Dongming 1688: 15b–16a. Courtesy of the Henan Provincial Museum.

Yang concluded:

> Recently, the nights have been like this everywhere. I am really afraid the myriad partisans will unite to plot a revolt. Starving people who have no way out will see the way the wind is blowing and will respond. When the great event occurs the central plain will be shaken. The disaster for the entire polity will be profound. If we wish to restrain the robbers and comfort the people, we must suspend taxes and distribute relief. If we open our eyes to what is happening and create a sense of hope, we can bring the situation under control in no time.[56]

Yang pleaded for action in terms that were conventional but moving:

> Your official has heard that the ruler is the father and mother of the people and the people are the children of the ruler. Now the children have nothing to rely on. How can the ruler/father bear to just sit there and watch? The ruler depends on the people for wealth and status. If he wants to protect wealth and status he cannot allow his people to starve to death. . . . to protect people is to protect the spirits of grain and soil; to neglect the people is to neglect the entire polity.[57]

With such bold words, Yang admonished Wanli to overcome his lassitude or risk losing the people who were the basis of the state.

Yang acknowledged that military expenses were growing, but he insisted that the highest priority was to forgive taxes and provide relief. In his words,

FIGURE 1.5. Leaving a Daughter Behind. Source: Yang Dongming 1688: 17b–18a. Courtesy of the Henan Provincial Museum.

> If orders to suspend the land tax are not issued, the local authorities will continue to collect them strictly. If funds are not made available from the royal treasury, people below will cease to look up to the throne with hope. If people are urged to pay their taxes when they cannot, there will be fines that will push the people into revolt. If people cease to look up with hope and the throne extends no mercy to unite their minds and hearts, then we will be forced into administering frightening punishments. If the mother cannot protect her children, how can the polity retain the support of its people?[58]

Yang warned that the state must spend 10 percent of its resources on relief immediately to avoid spending 90 percent of its resources on troops later. That was particularly true in Henan and Shandong, where education was limited and "miscreants" could mobilize many people with a single call.

Yang requested tax and grain relief on the grounds of both sentiment and power. He noted that those who opposed such policies wanted to collect resources in taxes so as to disperse them in administration; he advocated dispersing resources in relief so as to collect them in popular support. In the past, the court had issued relief worth 300,000 taels to Shaanxi and 400,000 to Jiangnan; currently, the ministries of revenue and works should each send at least 100,000 to Henan. The court should also appoint a capable and experienced official, such as Zhong Huamin, presently at the court of royal entertainment, to oversee the relief program. Yang urged the court to print his illustrations

FIGURE 1.6. A Mother's Suicide. Source: Yang Dongming 1688: 19b–20a. Courtesy of the Henan Provincial Museum.

FIGURE 1.7. Selling the Children. Source: Yang Dongming 1688: 21b–22a. Courtesy of the Henan Provincial Museum.

and forward them to the ministries for examination. He also recommended specific measures such as diverting 100,000 shi from the tributary grain system, selling it at half price as relief, and opening porridge stations to feed the starving.[59]

Yang's illustrated memorial elicited an immediate, widespread, and positive response. The Taicang vault issued 379,480 taels, the central treasury 300,000 taels, the provincial treasury twenty-five thousand taels, and the empress dowager, princesses, court officials, and the princes of Lu and Fu some 43,500 taels that, combined with numerous smaller sums, came to a total of 778,980 taels. In addition the grain tribute system diverted 100,000 shi of grain, princes and high officials donated another few thousand, and the officials of Henan province donated grain according to their salaries, with four giving one thousand shi each, five giving five hundred, and 174 giving four hundred for a total of 180,600 shi.[60]

To administer these resources, the court called in Zhong Huamin, a Zhejiang man who had distinguished himself administering relief in Shandong. Zhong reviewed a copy of Yang's memorial and was appointed investigating censor in the Henan circuit and supervisor of relief administration. He was charged with distributing the 300,000 taels of silver disbursed by the central treasury and the 100,000 shi of grain diverted from the tributary system. He was also ordered to oversee the provincial officials of Henan in administering relief to the people.[61]

FIGURE 1.8. Leaving the Children Behind. Source: Yang Dongming 1688: 23b–24a. Courtesy of the Henan Provincial Museum.

Even before leaving Beijing, Zhong issued two orders to encourage the flow of private grain into Henan. First, he suspended the usual state strategy of keeping grain prices low and allowed them to rise to entice long-distance merchants to bring grain to the province. Soon the price reached five taels a shi, and grain boats began to make their way into Henan. Next, he ordered local officials to terminate military campaigns against bandits in central Henan, allowing them to transfer troops to the Yellow River to provide security for the grain boats. As a result, vessels soon lined up "like the scales of a fish" for fifty li along the river, and the price of grain fell to a mere eight cash per shi. In the short run, this policy clearly benefited prosperous Henanese consumers as well as outside merchants. In the long run, Zhong reported, supplies increased and prices fell, making grain more readily available to everyone.[62]

Zhong first met with provincial officials in Kaifeng and then set out on horseback with six carefully chosen assistants to visit every county suffering from famine. According to Zhong's later reports, his party moved quickly, often arriving unannounced to avoid wasteful banquets and official cover-ups. He refused offers of government hospitality and ate at the officially established porridge stations to assess their quality and to share the people's hardships. He asked local residents to submit confidential appraisals of prefects' and magistrates' performances and used them as the basis for promotions and demotions. He sent prefects and magistrates into the countryside to supervise the estab-

FIGURE 1.9. Eating Grass and Bark. Source: Yang Dongming 1688: 25b–26a. Courtesy of the Henan Provincial Museum.

lishment of porridge stations and ordered subordinates to adopt emergency measures and seek approval for them later.[63]

Soon the empress and the first concubine, moved by Yang Dongming's report, sent 30,500 taels of silver to Kaifeng. Zhong reported on the effect of such royal beneficence on lower ranks of the administration.

> The scholars and people of the central province prostrated themselves, weeping in gratitude and knocking their heads on the ground until the blood flowed. They said that from ancient times there had been many instances of disbursing funds for famine relief, but they had never heard of any case of funds coming from the treasury of the women's quarters in the palace and descending all the way to the inner rooms of the poorest households. As a result, high officials suddenly contributed portions of their salaries, and upright scholars sent in money and competed to be the first in writing exhortatory documents. Is this not a rare instance of true generosity?[64]

Given such largesse from the court, Zhong did not hesitate to proffer aid to poor members of the royal clan located in what he called the "central prefecture" (Kaifeng). Citing examples of officers who lacked resources to bury their dead and of infants without means of support, he disbursed more than 22,788 taels of silver to more than 14,600 members of the royal clan. He also asked for an expansion of the quota allotted to nobles

FIGURE 1.10. A Family Suicide. Source: Yang Dongming 1688: 27b–28a. Courtesy of the Henan Provincial Museum.

in the civil service examinations. Zhong noted the plight of stipendiary students, who lived frugally in the best of times and were vulnerable during famines. He cited the case of a student in Neixiang county, Nanyang prefecture, who had accepted grain only after learning that it had been provided expressly for poor scholars.[65]

Zhong established porridge stations to feed the general population and especially the poor. Noting that half the poor people of the central province were homeless, he instructed authorities to convene the collective security managers, village heads, and elders and to select upright people to establish stations wherever they were needed. Those in legal trouble received reduced sentences if they contributed grain for relief; contributors in good standing were offered opportunities for study, awarded brevet ranks, or given state salaries. In towns, relief stations were established in official buildings or in temples. In the countryside, they were housed in new quarters made visible and attractive to the population by means of flags and signs. One section of each was set aside for storage, and three sections were for feeding the old, the sick, and women and children. No distinction was made between local residents and displaced persons or between the rich and the poor; all the starving were to be welcomed "equally." An average station was designed to accommodate two hundred people, although one was said to feed five thousand. The number of stations in the eighty-eight target counties varied according

FIGURE 1.11. Eating Human Flesh. Source: Yang Dongming 1688: 29b–30a. Courtesy of the Henan Provincial Museum.

to need; the lightly populated county of Shenqiu in southeastern Kaifeng prefecture had twenty. Efforts were made to prevent recipients from eating twice. They were required to eat on the premises to prevent hoarding and sale for profit. Each person received four-fifths of a pint of grain at each of two meals, one served between 7 and 9 A.M. and the other between 1 and 3 P.M.

According to Zhong's report, over the two-month period before the wheat crop ripened, some 22,960,912 men, women, and children in Henan were fed by such means. Citing a speech of gratitude given by an old villager at a temple, Zhong observed that while the wealthy always seemed to want more, the destitute were grateful for what they got. Zhong cited the *Great Learning*: "When wealth is collected the people disperse; when wealth is dispersed the people collect."[66] To bring the world to order, he added, the most important thing was to distribute its resources.

Zhong Huamin also extended relief to those in the countryside who were too distant, too poor, or too proud to come to the stations. He issued funds to the magistrates and ordered them to go into the countryside to distribute them to such people. Magistrates divided each county into north, south, east, and west sections and summoned the tax, security, and lecture system heads to select those in need of assistance in each section. Households were divided into the poor (who received three cash), the extremely

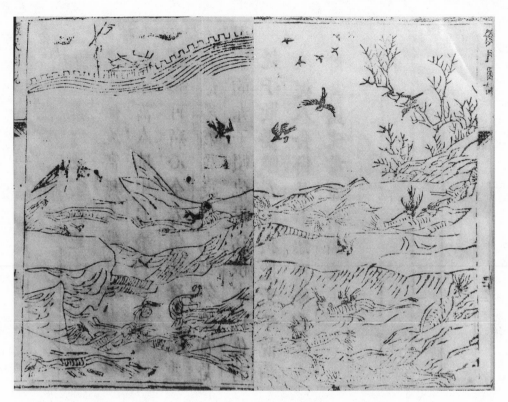

FIGURE 1.12. Corpses Being Consumed by Birds and Dogs. Source: Yang Dongming 1688: 31b–32a. Courtesy of the Henan Provincial Museum.

poor (who received five cash), and widows, orphans, and children (who received extra amounts). Those who had violated the law should be forgiven if they were repentant and provided with relief. In his report, Zhong cited the case of a man in Dengfeng county who had consumed all the available wild plants and sold his wife and children in order to survive; after receiving relief, he had been reunited with his family. Noting that many "people of the central province have survived in this way," Zhong cited the *Venerated Documents*: "Make a great bestowal on the four seas and the myriad families will happily come into allegiance." He concluded: "Our August Superior distributed relief and issued grain and the ten thousand families have joyfully come over. It is all worthy of the Way." He estimated that some 24,495,869 people in the province had benefited from the relief.[67]

Aware of the saying that after great famines come lethal epidemics, Zhong provided funds to reward people for burying corpses. He instructed subordinates to provide medicines and to assign doctors, twenty to a large county and ten in a small one. He noted the need to treat spiritual as well as physical illnesses; patients were to be nourished like transplanted trees. As in the *Venerated Documents*, officials were responsible for the people's health; in line with the thought of the Song thinker Cheng Yi, the people's injuries should be treated with care. He announced the tax reductions and suspensions widely in the countryside to prevent official fraud, and he tailored all measures to the actual condi-

FIGURE 1.13. Leaving a Toddler to her Fate. Source: Yang Dongming 1688: 33b–34a. Courtesy of the Henan Provincial Museum.

tions of each place. He discouraged litigation on all topics except relief, pointing out that it impoverished people. He prosecuted official malfeasance vigorously, but released all but the worst common offenders from prison. He provided funds to redeem family members who had been sold during the famine, discouraging those who had bought them from requiring full repayment.

According to Zhong, some 4,263 women and children were returned to their families under this program and thousands of others were returned without repayment. In Lushan county, two boys who were beneficiaries changed their family name to Huang (August) to indicate their gratitude to the ruler. Zhong remarked: "In fact, we can say that all of the children of the central province were brought back to life by the August Superior."[68]

Zhong encouraged reconstruction of the hardest hit areas by giving refugees three fen in travel expenses to return to their homes, where they were to be given subsidies to work the soil. According to reports from Xiangfu county and elsewhere, some 23,025 returning cultivators benefited from this program. Remarking that "food is the people's heaven," Zhong sent funds to magistrates to purchase seeds and oxen for free distribution to the people. In Yucheng county, Guide prefecture, Yang Dongming's hometown, Zhong noticed that people were eating mulberries. Reflecting his faith in the

FIGURE 1.14. Assaulting the Homes of the Rich. Source: Yang Dongming 1688: 35b–36a. Courtesy of the Henan Provincial Museum.

market, he criticized the "indolent cultivators" of Yucheng and instructed magistrates to exhort farmers to plant mulberries and raise silkworms. Demonstrating the bureaucratic approach, he ordered that one hundred mulberry bushes should be planted in every available mu.

Zhong also promoted the development of a local cotton industry. He noted that the central plain was "half planted with cotton" but that "all the cotton goes to merchants and the people get their clothing from trade." He cited the proverb that "if one wife fails to weave, someone is sure to be cold" to urge local officials to exhort women to produce cotton textiles. In his words,

> Your official has calculated with the village wives and elders. A wife can reel three ounces of cotton a day, so that in a month she can produce two rolls of cloth and in several months enough to clothe several people. The rest can be exchanged for money and turned into profit or used to pay taxes. But the making of textiles—spinning thread, weaving cloth—comes from hard work. The people daily use [textiles] but do not know [how they are made].[69]

Zhong ordered local officials to go to the countryside to carry out inspections, rewarding households that produced cotton thread and chastising those that did not.

To ensure that his policies became known to the people, Zhong wrote nine verses and asked local officials to put them to tunes.

> The people can get rich, can have a great culture,
> If we all work hard, and promote agriculture.
> Families big and small will all look up with respect,
> When father-and-mother officials care for their children.
>
> The rains come, the rivers roil,
> Festivals pass, we till the soil.
> If in spring plowing, no one shirks work,
> In the western suburb, there will be a good harvest.
>
> Do not quarrel, avoid penal pain,
> Do not litigate, save monetary gain.
> Outside the gate, there are fields to be planted early,
> In the towns, there's nothing to warrant frequent visits.
>
> Be a dutiful farmer, have food for your maw,
> You won't become poor, or transgress the law.
> See how the robbers are constantly on the move,
> Regretting their failure to work the land when they had it.
>
> Don't indulge in drink, or covet courtesans,
> Don't waste time gambling, or spending family fortunes.
> One spendthrift in one generation can ruin a whole clan,
> It's at the beginning that we must attend to our errors.
>
> Diligent in work, your wheat will grow faster,
> Mindful of obligations, you'll avoid the tax prompter.
> Do not wait 'til the *yamen* clerks come to your village,
> And there'll be no need for you to go to court.
>
> The five grains are ripe, the soup smells good,
> Lead wife and son, nourish parents as you should.
> Elder and younger brothers live peacefully together,
> Filial piety and cooperation are the highest abodes.
>
> In the morning supervise cultivation, in the evening education,
> Instruct sons and grandsons to realize a vocation.
> Do not laugh at the village gentlemen,
> High ministers have long issued from thatched houses.
>
> When families are happy, and the people all satisfied,
> We will reach a high point, all virtuous and gratified.
> Delighted to encounter Yao and Shun, then Tang and Yu,
> Black-haired people will sing songs of Great Peace and Equality.[70]

Zhong called for the revitalization of the two-level granary system. At the first level charity granaries should be set up and maintained by the people in each locality to store surpluses and distribute them to the needy. Magistrates should encourage each sector to use Buddhist nunneries and temples where possible to save money and to choose "individuals of good families and upright principles" to serve as managers and assistants. Whenever there was a bumper crop, households should be encouraged to store surpluses at the granaries. Records would be kept to ensure the return of comparable amounts to these households as needed. In normal times, the stored grain could be lent out to local families at 100 percent interest in kind; it was not to be lent to outsiders for cash. Those who contributed large amounts to the granaries should be rewarded. Managers and assistants who accumulated large stores over several years should be exempted from miscellaneous labor services and awarded caps and sashes (elite status).[71]

At the second level, "evernormal" granaries managed by officials would provide mutual benefits to the state and the people. In Zhong's words:

> "Evernormal" means granaries established by officials to equalize grain prices. When grain is cheap among the people, officials buy it up to raise the price. When grain is expensive, officials sell it to lower the price. The capital lies with the officials and they do not suffer losses; the benefits lie with the people and they do not incur harm.

He noted that this system had long existed in the central province but was often maintained poorly by officials; it was sometimes inoperative when it was most needed. He instructed local officials to determine the funds necessary to make the system function properly. Citing the god of agriculture, Shen Nong, he emphasized the importance of storing grain: "If you have a stone wall eighty feet high, moats five hundred feet across, and shields numbering one million, and you have no grain, you will not be able to defend yourself."[72]

Zhong called for a reformation of customs in Henan in accord with inherited rites. As he put it:

> Your official has heard that the way to manage wealth is not only to produce it but to conserve it. Many of the customs of the central province at the present time are extravagant. People borrow unlimited funds to pay respects to the spirits and turn their purses inside out to entertain guests. They build high walls and large mansions, apparently forgetting that one day they will die. They eat good food and wear new clothes, thinking only of the present moment. The wine shops are as numerous as the market places, gambling is more prevalent than working in the fields. When people encounter hardships, they cannot stand their reduced circumstances. This is all because people are extravagant and defy the rites.

Zhong believed that "people like extravagance just as water tends to flow downhill."[73]

Officials were responsible for upholding the rites to restrain the people's desires. Zhong compiled *The Essentials of the Four Rites* and instructed the administration commissioner to make copies available to local officials for distribution to the scholars and people. According to Zhong, expenses for the ceremonies of coming of age and matrimony should be restricted to obtaining a clean cap, fresh clothes, a hairpin, and a skirt. The rites for funerals and sacrifices should be limited to a thatched hut near the grave, vegetable broth, and a melon. Those who observed these minimal practices should be rewarded; those who exceeded them should be admonished. Zhong cited Mengzi: if one eats according to the season and behaves according to the rites, one's resources will never be exhausted. Seizing an opportunity to chide Wanli, whose profligacy set the tone for society, Zhong urged everyone to "respect frugality as the law of the world."[74] Only then would the current trend toward extravagance be halted and reversed.

To propagate such values in the countryside of Henan, Zhong ordered the refurbishing of the systems of collective security and village lectures. Citing Kongzi on the

Royal Way, he concluded that "when the collective security system is strong, people will be afraid to do wrong, and when the village lecture system is vital, people will be happy to do right."[75]

Upon completion of his duties in Henan, Zhong returned to Beijing and submitted a detailed report. The court was pleased with his work and promoted him to minister of the court of imperial sacrifices.[76] In 1596, he was named assistant censor in chief and grand coordinator and sent back to Henan to continue the relief work.

During his previous stint in Henan, Zhong had downplayed military action to focus on insuring the people's livelihood. Aware of bandits in the hills of Runing and Nanyang prefectures, he had issued a proclamation expressing understanding of their plight.

> The Sagely Son of Heaven is completely in sympathy with you. Unable to eat and sleep peacefully, he disbursed large funds from the royal treasury and sent me here to devise means to save you. All people have consciences, but they are also subject to the pressures of hunger and cold. Under such conditions they have no way out. Now you should spread the word: the Son of Heaven is concerned about the whole world and he has sent an official to provide relief. We little people are blessed with good fortune; we should sigh and shed tears, burn incense and pay respects to the Sagely Son of Heaven. You have all heard about the porridge stations and distribution of money; you know that they will continue until the wheat crop matures. You should immediately disperse and reform yourselves into good people. If you continue to plunder and do not see the light you will be held accountable to the laws and then you will regret it in vain. Today you can turn disaster into good fortune. If you come to your senses, you will be in heaven; if you engage in deception, you will be in hell. You must think of the ancestors who went before you and the descendants who will come after you. In the middle, you can preserve your own lives.[77]

Zhong later reported that the robbers recognized that the ruler had, through the relief program, saved their lives. They soon gave up their weapons and took up their plows. Zhong suggested that this experience reflected the truth of the saying in the *Venerated Documents* that humane government would bring peace to the people.

Returning to Henan a year later, Zhong found that court eunuchs had gone to the province and opened mines. In response, he reported, a rebel had led several thousand people in resistance. Having attended to the people's livelihood by his programs of relief and reconstruction and having warned bandits to give up their violent ways, Zhong now personally led troops to capture and behead the rebel leaders. But, to display impartial justice, he also charged seven of the mining envoys with violating the laws and put them to death. He submitted a report on the pros and cons of mining, forcefully rebuking the court for its effort to monopolize the industry. Perhaps anticipating the court's displeasure with his outspokenness, Zhong tendered his resignation. When it was refused, he asked for sick leave. Illness was often just an excuse for seeking early retirement, but in this case it seems to have been the genuine reason. On his first tour, Zhong had traveled tirelessly through Henan for two months, visiting the areas ravaged by disease and eating at porridge stations along with the masses. He may well have contracted a disease. Because the court again refused his request to retire, Zhong was still in office when he died. He was posthumously promoted to vice censor in chief, canonized as "loyal and generous," and honored as a "noted official" in the provincial gazetteer.[78]

In sum, two conscientious and energetic officials, Yang a native of northeast Henan and Zhong serving there, had mobilized the Ming administration, from the royal family down to local magistrates, to address the famine and plague of 1593. Their accomplishments certainly must have increased the prestige of the state in the eyes of the people of northeast Henan. At the same time, their reports revealed deficiencies in the administration and the failings of other officials. For the moment, honest agents of the state had invoked classical principles to manage market forces on behalf of the people. But it was clear that a less effective response in the future might well put the entire Ming order at risk.

EDUCATION

According to ruist theory, the family has the primary responsibility for education but the state also plays an important role. The Ming, like most dynasties, emphasized education as the most legitimate path to public service and the most effective means of creating a good society. Hongwu carried out the vision of Northern Song reformers by establishing a system of public schools. For the first time in Chinese history, the state systematically selected, ranked, and paid instructors, and then installed them in ruist schools at the prefectural and county levels. In 1436, the Ming regularized the appointment of educational intendants and made them responsible for supervising schools and examinations at the provincial and prefectural levels. During the fifteenth and sixteenth centuries, some officials cooperated with local wealthy families to establish private academies. In the late sixteenth century some of these institutions, such as the Donglin Academy in Jiangnan, became centers of unorthodox thought. The strict grand secretary Zhang Juzheng therefore proscribed them, although not completely effectively.[79]

During the Ming, many local officials, including prefects and magistrates in northeast Henan, gained fame by nurturing education. Prominent among them in the early seventeenth century was Zheng Sanjun, a 1598 metropolitan graduate from Nanzhili. Zheng had served as a magistrate in Beizhili as well as vice president of the board of rites in Nanjing before becoming prefect of Guide in 1610. At that time and place, the Ming system of public education was still functioning fairly effectively. In Shangqiu city, where the Guide prefectural offices were located, both prefectural and county ruist schools had been restored as recently as the Wanli period. Certain academies also persisted in northeast Henan. One at Baiquan, in Hui county, Weihui prefecture, had been restored even when Zhang Juzheng was in power. In Shangqiu, the Yingtian Academy which had been founded in the Song dynasty, was restored in the Jiajing reign. During his brief two years in Guide, Zheng Sanjun founded a new academy, named after the famous Northern Song scholar-official and reformer Fan Wenzheng (the courtesy name of Fan Zhongyan). Zheng selected over sixty promising scholars from the nine counties of the prefecture and gave them instruction in the new academy. Many of his students passed the examinations with distinction and became high officials. Zheng also gained a reputation for compassion in administering punishments and was said to have earned the respect of the people of Guide. He was promoted to assistant commissioner of education in Fujian.[80]

Zheng Sanjun thereafter pursued an illustrious career in the central government. As vice minister, first in the court of royal entertainments and then in the court of royal sacrifices, he criticized the growing power of the eunuch Wei Zhongxian. He argued that eunuch power was leading to the demoralization of the officials. In 1624, when Yang Lian, vice president of the ministry of revenue, impeached Wei, Zheng joined in the attack. Later that year, when Yang was driven from the court, Zheng took a sick leave. In 1625, he was charged with "involvement in nefarious alliances" and stripped of his office. Three years later, after the fall of Wei's party, Zheng became president of the ministry of revenue in Nanjing. He dismissed corrupt and negligent officials and worked with the ministry of troops to eliminate the false reporting of military expenditures. Zheng also proposed a 50 percent reduction in commercial taxes so as not to "burden the people." As president of the ministry of personnel in Nanjing, he dismissed seventy-eight officials. According to his biography in the *Ming History*, he made appointments based on merit rather than personal connections. He was soon promoted to president of the ministry of punishments in Beijing and was concurrently junior guardian of the heir apparent. At punishments, he inveighed against the tendency to assume guilt by association, urged subordinates to concern themselves with real issues, imposed a limit of ten days on the resolution of cases, and allowed appeals only in capital cases. All of these recommendations were approved by the new Chongzhen ruler, who was trying to discourage factionalism.[81]

Despite Zheng's probity and professionalism, he was increasingly subject to partisan pressures. His fortunes were intertwined with those of men he had known in Henan as well as with those of other powerful figures in the central administration. For example, there was Hou Xun, who had been a student of Zheng's in Shangqiu before winning his own metropolitan degree in 1616. Hou had then served as a censor and as surveillance commissioner in Guizhou before becoming identified as a member of the Donglin party. Loosely associated with the Donglin Academy in Jiangnan, this group of scholar-officials stood for the revitalization of Song ru thought in the face of challenges from Wang Yangming and his followers. It also opposed the growth of eunuch influence at court. Hou subsequently lost his post during the ascendancy of the eunuch Wei Zhongxian. After the fall of Wei, Hou was returned to office and promoted from vice minister of the court of the royal stud to vice president of the ministry of troops. Soon he became president of the ministry of revenue and worked, like Zheng Sanjun, to increase supplies to the army without raising taxes. Hou's efforts went unappreciated by the powerful grand secretary Wen Tiren, who arranged to have a censor charge him with holding up supplies for the army. Hou Xun was imprisoned, and Chongzhen was said to favor his execution. At punishments, however, Zheng repeatedly advocated leniency, incurring the charge of bending the laws to protect a fellow Donglin partisan. When Zheng favored a light sentence in an unrelated case, Chongzhen was furious. Zheng was dismissed and his name was sent to the ministry of punishments for further action. At this point, several high officials, including the supreme commander of Xuanfu and Datong, Lu Xiangsheng, who had held important military posts in Henan in the early 1630s, intervened on Zheng's behalf. Because there was no evidence that Zheng had ever received any illicit payments for his leniency, he was released after paying a fine.[82]

Zheng Sanjun's career shows how local officials developed close relationships with students and continued to patronize them in office. Such networks could operate to enhance the education and careers of talented people who might otherwise have been overlooked. They could also lead to charges of partisanship and thus contribute to the factionalism that was weakening the Ming state. Zheng Sanjun was well treated in the histories because he was thought to have belonged to the right (Donglin) party, but his form of politics was closely akin to the careerism and corruption attributed by the Donglin to its adversaries. Zheng was later to be drawn back into the maelstrom of court politics, with significant consequences (see Chapter 2).

SUPREME COMMANDERS

Zheng Sanjun's defender, Lu Xiangsheng, was a civil graduate and military official who wielded a different kind of influence over the politics of northeast Henan in the late Ming. In the original Ming system, the regional military commissioner was the chief military official in Henan who administered the guard-battalion system and played key roles in consolidating state authority in the region. According to the provincial gazetteer, however, "Henan was in the center of the world," and its garrisons had rarely seen action on the frontier. Even more than guards elsewhere, therefore, the guards of Henan gradually lost authority. By the Chongzhen reign, the three regional military commissioners were but names on the table of organization, and their guards were little more than locations on the map. Supreme commanders in charge of troops outside the guard-battalion system had long since supplanted them. The post of supreme commander had originated in the Zhengde reign when the regular military commissioners had been unable to suppress rebellions in the Beizhili-Shandong-Henan border region without calling in troops from the frontier.[83] But, according to the provincial gazetteer, the post remained empty during the succeeding century and was filled again only in the Chongzhen reign.

The post of supreme commander was created to strengthen central civilian control even while expanding regional military power. Like the directorship of river conservancy, it was a responsibility given to well-educated and high-ranking civilian officials who concurrently held other posts. Although nominally supreme, these commanders actually shared authority with grand coordinators and the other provincial and local officials. They had headquarters but no official assistants; they had to rely on private secretaries to convey their instructions to colleagues and subordinates.[84] As with other centrally appointed officials, supreme commanders could draw upon personal relationships to effect their purposes. In other words, their authority was supreme but their power depended on their personal capacities and the cooperation they could elicit from others.

As it happened, all three of the prominent supreme commanders in northeast Henan during the Chongzhen reign had previous experience in northeast Henan. The first, Lu Xiangsheng, a metropolitan graduate from Jiangnan, had served as regional inspector and censor there in the Tianqi period. A reputable scholar, Lu was also famous for his skill in martial arts and his knowledge of military strategy. Outstanding in shooting from horseback in an era when few Ming officers could, he often rode into battle at the head of his troops. He gained renown for once having fought valiantly on his feet after his mount had been shot out from under him.

Lu first confronted mounted or roving bandits in Shaanxi in 1628. Four years later he blocked their advance into northern Henan. In 1635, as grand coordinator of Huguang, he was ordered to supervise the military affairs of the five provinces of Henan, Jiangbei, Shandong, Sichuan, and Huguang. The following year he drove insurgents from Nanjing and Henan into Shaanxi and Huguang and received authority over two more provinces, Shaanxi and Shanxi. His general strategy was to build up a large, centrally controlled army and to send columns out to attack the enemy's flanks as well as its rear. In 1637, following the rise of the Manchus in northeast China, he was transferred to Shanxi as grand coordinator to lead the defense. He favored firm resistance but lacked sufficient troops and supplies. During a Manchu attack in 1638, he was among the many who were killed in battle. He was not honored by the court because his policy of strong defense against the Manchus was not in favor at the time. Eventually, however, he came to be regarded as one of the more honest and capable of the late Ming commanders. He was honored by the Fu Prince's regime in Nanjing in 1644 and accorded a biography in the *History of the Ming*.[85]

The second supreme commander of note was Yang Sichang, son of a high civil official from Huguang, Yang He, who became famous for trying to persuade the bandits in Shaanxi to return to the fold. Yang Sichang received his metropolitan degree in 1610 and served as lecturer at the prefectural school in Hangzhou and at the state university in Nanjing before being appointed director of the bureau of supplies at the ministry of revenue in Beijing. In 1622, he noted that the surtax imposed to pay for the armies in the northeast was insufficient to meet current expenses. He recommended and gained approval for further levies on guard lands, grain sales, property transactions, and pawnshops.

In 1628 Yang was posted as surveillance vice commissioner and director of education in Henan, although he apparently served too briefly to acquire any protégés. The following year he was transferred to Beijing, where he held several posts related to defense of the capital from incursions by the Jurchens, a Tungusic-speaking people who were challenging Ming authority in northeast China. When his father died in 1635, Yang returned home to observe the expected three-year (actually, twenty-seven-month) mourning period. Within a year, however, he returned to active duty at the request of the court. In cutting short the mourning period, Yang incurred criticism from the Donglin partisans and their epigonni, the Fushe, who opposed both tax surcharges and moral compromises.

In 1637 Yang was named president of the ministry of troops. He immediately proposed a strategy of bottling up the roving bandits in the central plain by stationing four armies in Shaanxi, Henan, Huguang, and Nanzhili and backing them up with six more forces in northern Shaanxi, Shanxi, Shandong, Jiangxi, Sichuan, and Jiangnan. Yang placed a subordinate in command of 120,000 troops at Yunyang in north Huguang and asked the court to supply him with 2.8 million taels of silver derived from the new surtax on the land. He promised that, if this plan were approved, he would crush the bandits within three months. To permit this focus on the internal bandits, Yang advocated a policy of peace with the Jurchen, now calling themselves Manchus, on the northern frontier. This brought him further criticism from the Donglin people, who favored a policy of resistance on the frontier. Yang's policies were nonetheless approved in Beijing, and he was promoted to the high-ranking post of grand secretary, which he held concurrently with his position as president of the ministry of troops.[86]

Yang's fortunes peaked in 1638 and immediately began to decline. In that year, the Manchus raided deeply into Beizhili and Shandong, crossing seventy counties in the space of five months. Yang called for the second surtax of 7.3 million taels to train militia to defend against the Manchus. Yang's former policy of appeasing the Manchus, his failure to prevent their devastating raids, and his request for further tax surcharges incurred a storm of criticism, especially among the Donglin people. To make matters worse, the bandit leader Zhang Xianzhong, who had supposedly surrendered in 1638, revolted again in 1639. Yang thereupon dismissed his chief subordinate, took personal command of military operations, and enlisted the assistance of another general, Zuo Liangyu, in an offensive against Zhang Xianzhong. Together, Yang and Zuo chased Zhang into Sichuan, but they failed to capture him. Yang then turned to confront the growing threat of another major bandit, Li Zicheng in Shaanxi (see Chapter 4).

The third supreme commander relevant to this story, Sun Chuanting, was from a hereditary military household in Shanxi. He had obtained his metropolitan degree in 1619 and assumed his first post as magistrate of Yongcheng county, in Guide prefecture, northeast Henan. There he gained a reputation for "nourishing talent" and "confronting local strongmen on behalf of the common people." In the words of Zheng Lian, the early Qing writer from neighboring Shangqiu whose history provides a major source for this study, Sun was "simple yet dignified, not cowed by higher officials and capable of conducting honest investigations into extraordinary matters." In one case, Sun demonstrated ingenuity and courage in tracking down and arresting a young scion of a local powerful family who had committed rape.[87]

In 1621, Sun was appointed magistrate of Shangqiu, the head county of Guide prefecture. Unfortunately the gazetteer contents itself with the clichés that he was "outstandingly talented and energetic, accomplished in civil and military matters, with great achievements beyond comparison with those of ordinary officials." That appraisal may reflect Sun's later career more than his tenure in Shangqiu. For whatever reason, Sun was singled out in the Shangqiu gazetteer as the only "noted official" in the county during the last two reigns of the Ming. In 1625 Sun was promoted to secretary in a bureau in the ministry of personnel in the capital. He soon rose to be director of the bureau to evaluate officials.[88] During the late 1620s, when Wei Zhongxian's party dominated the government, Sun retired to his home, where he stayed for nearly a decade.

In 1635 Sun was cited for his public service and named assistant prefect of Shuntian in Beizhili. Having concerned himself for some time with military strategy, he was promoted to grand coordinator of Shaanxi province with instructions to suppress roving banditry there. As we shall see in more detail in Chapter 4, Sun captured and executed the leading insurgent, Gao Yingxiang, and cooperated with officials in Henan to suppress unrest there. Sun nonetheless opposed Yang Sichang's plan, arguing that it would

impose too heavy a burden on the people without guaranteeing peace. Sun took personal responsibility for pacifying southeastern Shaanxi. When he proved unable to prevent the advance of the rebels, he was demoted, and he found it difficult to get along
with Yang Sichang's subordinates in Henan. In 1638 he was nonetheless called upon
to replace Lu Xiangsheng. He was appointed vice president of the ministry of troops
and charged with planning the defense of Beijing. The following year he was made responsible for military matters in Baoding, Shandong, and Henan. Conflict with Yang
Sichang, however, led to his dismissal from this post, and he spent the next two years
in jail.[89] As in the case of many officials in this period, Sun's imprisonment was to be
brief and followed by reappointment to high posts.

MAGISTRATES

During the Ming, county and departmental magistrates continued to constitute the front
line of Ming administration. Some historians have remarked that outstanding men tended
to serve in such posts in the early years of a dynasty but were likely to disappear from
them in later years as a dynasty lost authority. In the Ming, for example, one hundred
of the 120 model local officials in the dynastic history served between 1368 and 1435,
fewer than twenty served between 1436 and 1566, only two were in office between 1567
and 1619, and none appeared thereafter. In the third quarter of the sixteenth century,
less than two hundred of the two thousand departmental and county magistrates in China
held the highest, metropolitan degree. At first glance, this pattern seems to apply to
Henan. According to a well-informed scholar-official from Shandong, in one year of
the late sixteenth century only four of the 108 departmental and county magistrates in
Henan were metropolitan graduates. The rest were provincial graduates (sixty-two) or
state university students (twenty-eight); fourteen posts were vacant.[90] During the Ming,
metropolitan graduates were produced at the rate of only about three hundred every
third year. That tiny elite naturally preferred offices in the capital and had the means
to obtain them. Under the inattentive Wanli, many magistracies remained vacant, and
by the end of the dynasty, absenteeism in poor and dangerous counties became rife.

    This evidence fits so well with the theory of the dynastic cycle that it suggests the
possibility that it was the product of historians who have been predisposed to find talent in the early reigns of a dynasty, when it seemed to explain success, and inclined to
ignore it in later reigns, when it seemed inconsistent with failure. Although gaps in the
data for northeast Henan in the early Ming make it difficult to assess changes in the
qualifications of magistrates serving there over the course of the dynasty, fairly complete information on the late Ming indicates that many more metropolitan graduates
served as magistrates than the above samples would suggest. According to my survey of
the provincial gazetteer, an average of over 25 percent of the magistrates serving in northeast Henan from the beginning of the Wanli reign to the end of the dynasty were metropolitan degree holders. Within this period, the striking differences were not over time
but over space. In some cases, as we would expect, metropolitan graduates were concentrated in relatively powerful, populous, and prosperous counties. Thus in Xiangfu,
Qi, and Shangqiu, 100, 90, and 83 percent of the magistrates respectively were metro-

politan graduates while sparsely settled, poor, and weak counties such as Yanjin, Xingze, and Kaocheng had no magistrates with the highest degree. In other cases, however, metropolitan graduates seem to have been distributed rather impartially. For example, Chenliu in Kaifeng, Xiayi in Guide, and Hui in Weihui were not particularly prominent counties, but they all had relatively high percentages of metropolitan graduates. Perhaps that was because of their proximity to prefectural towns, or, in the case of Hui, to the famous Baiquan Academy. But some important places near major towns, such as Suizhou, had only modest percentages of metropolitan graduates while some less significant places distant from towns, such as Linying, had higher percentages. It would appear that to some extent graduates were appointed to local posts in this region by lot as was customary.[91]

The attainment of a higher degree was no guarantee of an official's honesty or effectiveness. Although a large number of metropolitan graduates held local posts in northeast Henan in the late Ming, not many magistrates were celebrated as model officials in the gazetteers. It is likely, however, that there were some upright and capable magistrates (such as Sun Chuanting) whose achievements (unlike Sun's) failed to be recorded in the histories. (There were also, alas, some honest and incompetent magistrates as well as some corrupt and capable ones, as we shall see). For example, casting our net slightly more widely we find Wang Han, who served as magistrate of Henei county, Huaiqing prefecture, in 1639–40. Although Huaiqing falls outside of northeast Henan as we have defined it in this study, it is immediately adjacent and shared a similar ecology and history. In the absence of comparable biographies of magistrates in the northeast region, the rather well-documented case of Wang Han may serve as representative of the outstanding magistrates in this region in the late Ming.

Wang Han was in several ways typical of magistrates serving in northeast Henan. First, he was from Shandong. If appointments had been strictly by lot, Shandong, as one of fourteen provinces, would have supplied Henan with only 7 percent of its magistrates. But Shandong was a populous province that produced more than its share of officials. It was also contiguous to Henan and its people spoke a dialect similar to that of the Henanese. Shandong thus supplied 14 percent of the magistrates serving in the forty-nine counties and departments of northeast Henan and the six counties of Huaiqing prefecture. Indeed, although Shandong produced fewer officials than heavily populated Zhejiang, Nanzhili, Jiangxi, or Fujian, it was the top-ranking province in providing magistrates to northeast Henan and Huaiqing in the late Ming.[92] Henei county, where Wang served, was one of eight in the region in which at least 20 percent of late Ming magistrates hailed from Shandong. Most of them, including Xiangfu, Chenliu, Qi Lanyang, Xuzhou, and Xinxiang, were among the most populous, prosperous, and powerful in the region, further underscoring a kind of "Shandong connection" in the region.[93]

Wang Han typified late-Ming magistrates in the region as well because he had to confront the controversial issue of surtaxes. In May 1640, less than a year after assuming his post, he submitted an illustrated report entitled "Sketches of a Disaster." He pointed out that Huaiqing prefecture had stubbornly remained loyal to the Yuan, causing the Ming founder to punish it by increasing its regular tax quota some 300 percent. It was therefore burdened with a basic tax quota of 330,600 shi of grain on 4,280,000 mu of cultivated land, yielding a rate of .077 shi per mu. That was indeed a high rate of taxation since Henan province as a whole was paying an average of only .032 shi per mu as late as 1578. To be sure, the tax quota for Huaiqing had barely changed over the course of the dynasty, and it is barely possible that the prefecture was actually under-taxed by the late Ming. Still, Huaiqing had much barren soil, may have achieved only modest increases in arable, and was vulnerable to flooding. Although Wang supplied no data on the impact of the late-Ming surcharges, they undoubtedly made matters worse. Wang reported in 1640 that "there is no place in northern Henan where the land is poorer and taxes heavier than in Huaiqing."

As for Henei county, it had some 1,130,000 mu of cultivated land yielding ninety-nine thousand shi of tax grain. It was thus taxed at the even higher rate of .087 shi per mu. Part of Henei was subject to the flooding of the Qin River, which regularly sub-merged several thousand mu of fertile bottom lands. Another part of the county was mountainous and had thin soils that were highly susceptible to drought. In Wang's opin-ion, "Among the six counties of Huaiqing, there is none where the land is so poor and the taxes are so heavy as in Henei." In addition, the county was burdened by onerous labor services, such as the transport of cloth to Beijing, salt to Shanxi, and grain to Beizhili. It also had special annual duties, such as breaking ice in the Yellow River to inhibit flood-ing. The three late Ming surtaxes added an estimated 24,200 taels to the county's tax burden. Assuming the Wanli conversion rate of one tael equals one shi of grain, this represented a 27 percent increase in taxes in the county. In Wang's summary, "Henei's taxes have never been as heavy as they have become today."[94]

The surtaxes were all the more disastrous because they came in the midst of eco-logical disasters reminiscent of those of the late sixteenth century. As Wang reported in 1640:

> From the sixth month of last year there have been eleven months without rain. In the past year people have suffered from floods, locusts, and drought. The drought was so bad that people could not plant the wheat and what little was planted was eaten by locusts. These conditions affected one million mu of land [90 percent of the registered land in the county]. In the winter there was no snow, and the unfledged locusts merely bided their time to come out later. Last year there was no fall planting and so this year there was no wheat crop. The poor people have consumed all of the bark of the trees and the roots of the grasses. Fathers and sons and husbands and wives have begun to eat each other. The people all have yellow jaws and swollen cheeks; their eyes are like pig's gall. The corpses of the starving are as numerous as pearls on a string. Alas! Alas![95]

As a conscientious official, Wang not only reported these conditions but took respon-sibility for them. He believed that it was fundamentally unfair for officials to survive when the people were dying. Taking a leaf from the book of Yang Dongming and Zhong Huamin, he commissioned the drafting of sixteen sketches of famine conditions to per-suade his superiors of the need for action. He remarked that the drawings accurately captured scenes he had witnessed personally but they could not transmit the accom-panying sounds, "the screams from hunger and howls from the cold." Wang noted real-istically that few rulers in history had truly loved the people, but he expressed the hope that the present ruler would follow the models of the legendary sage-kings Yao and Shun and would be pleased to learn about the actual conditions of the people. Undoubtedly aware of the court's insolvency, Wang did not request any specific action, not even tax relief. Perhaps with the same harsh realities in mind, his superiors in Henan and in Beijing made no response to his memorial.[96]

Although Wang Han was part of a Shandong connection that will require closer scrutiny, his primary loyalty appears to have been to the Ming state and to the people of Henan. He subsequently served in other key posts in the province, and his name appeared on a list of upright and capable local officials recorded by the local historian Zheng Lian.[97] His fate was to be closely associated with that of the Ming state, as will be described in Chapter 6.

Some other Shandong men who served in northeast Henan in the late Ming seem to have been less concerned about good government. Ten scholar-officials from Laiyang county, Dengzhou prefecture, in Shandong, served in Kaifeng and Guide prefectures in the Chongzhen reign. The number was perhaps not too surprising because Laiyang was among the top 13 percent of all Ming counties that together provided 49 percent of all Ming officials. But among the ten officials were two Dongs and two Songs who held office in some of the higher posts (for example, vice administration commissioner) and preferred counties (for example Qi) at the same time. Four of the ten held two posts successively in this region. These data seem to support Otto Van der Sprenkel's hypothesis that regional, familial, and political ties sometimes lay behind appointments ostensibly based on scholastic talent, administrative achievement, and the luck of the draw.[98]

The background and activities of several of these Laiyang officials strengthen this hypothesis. The metropolitan graduate Dong Sichen served as prefect of Guide in 1627 and as assistant administration commissioner and vice administration commissioner of Henan in subsequent years. In the absence of a biography or a genealogy, we cannot determine his precise relationship to Dong Sipu, a provincial graduate who served as magistrate in Xuzhou county, Kaifeng prefecture, in the 1630s. Given the shared surname and first character of their personal names, however, they must have been brothers or cousins. Sichen was certainly well placed to facilitate the appointment of his relative to a post in Henan. Whether or not the Dongs used family connections to obtain these posts, their service in the same province at the same time violated the rule of avoidance. It cannot have enhanced the confidence of Henanese that the Ming was administering the province impartially.

Also in Laiyang, Song Mei and his elder brother Song Cong belonged to a prominent lineage that traced its ancestry back to the early Ming. By the late Ming, the Songs were said by the Jiangnan historian Tan Qian to have "used their strength for generations to dominate their hometown."[99] Song Mei and his uncle won metropolitan degrees in 1625, and Song Cong obtained his metropolitan degree two years later. In 1626 Song Mei was posted to Yongcheng county in Guide prefecture while his uncle became magistrate of Qingfeng county, Daming prefecture, in neighboring Beizhili.[100] In 1627 Song Mei was rewarded for his "talent" and transferred to the more prosperous county of Qi, in Kaifeng prefecture. His elder brother, Song Cong, was simultaneously appointed magistrate of Xiangfu county, the head county in the same prefecture.

Because their uncle's post was only four counties away in southern Beizhili, Song Mei's biographer exaggerated only slightly when he remarked that "the territories of the three men were adjacent." Perhaps mindful that appointments of relatives to the same region at the same time were in violation of the rule of avoidance, the biographer hastened to add that all three counties were "well governed."[101]

The biography in the Qi county gazetteer acknowledged Song Mei's inexperience but also praised his achievements.

> Mei was young when he got his degree and some people had doubts because he lacked experience in administration. But after taking office he acquired skills and wisdom, and soon he surpassed previous administrators in transforming things to accord with the Way. People no longer dared impose their own views in the classes, and many scholars of Qi became famous after receiving his instruction. At that time, sect robbers were increasingly active, so he had walls built and moats dug. He was busy everyday preparing against attacks.[102]

Soon Song Mei was recommended by provincial authorities, and, in 1631, he was promoted supervising secretary in the office of troops in Beijing. At the same time, Song's uncle became supervising secretary in the ministry of personnel. These appointments also flouted the rule of avoidance that was intended to keep family influence out of the central administration.

The Songs apparently not only assisted each other in rising in the bureaucracy but also eliminated those who stood in their way. When Zhang Yao, a judge in Kaifeng, charged them with paying bribes to obtain their coveted central posts, his allegations were summarily dismissed. He was soon demoted four ranks to lowly assistant magistrate in strife-torn Gansu, where he eventually died at the hands of bandits.[103] When Song Mei's mother died, he made a perfunctory gesture of filial piety by going home to mourn, but he soon returned to Beijing to become supervising secretary in the office of scrutiny for justice. There he reportedly called for leniency in meting out sentences, a policy that won the throne's approval. He was promoted to a succession of vice ministerships in the court of royal sacrifices, the grand court of revision, and the ministry of works.

By 1640 Song Mei was ensconced high on the bureaucratic ladder in Beijing, but he was still not satisfied. In 1642 one of his patrons, Sheng Shun, who was a client of the chief grand secretary Zhou Yanru, took advantage of Zhou's return to power to recommend Song Mei for an appointment to the position of grand secretary. When Chongzhen ignored the recommendation, Sheng memorialized again, insisting that Song was the right man for the job. Chongzhen finally lost his patience and upbraided Sheng for permitting "private ties" to result in "excessive recommendations." When Song Mei boldly spoke up for himself in a personal audience with the throne, Chongzhen "hooted" and had him arrested and jailed.[104] In 1643 Song Mei was released from jail, allegedly after paying large bribes. He then returned to his hometown where he became involved in local defense (see Chapter 5).

Clearly, Song Mei was quite a different figure from Sun Chuanting, who had preceded him as magistrate of Yongcheng, and Wang Han, who served conscientiously in Henei while Song was climbing the bureaucratic ladder in Beijing. Unfortunately for the Ming, Dong Sichen and Song Mei were probably more typical than Sun Chuanting or Wang Han of magistrates serving in northeast Henan—and China at large—during the last years of the dynasty.

In sum, the Ming state established a nobility and elaborated an administration to govern northeast Henan effectively for two centuries before waning after 1600. The princes began with civil and military authority, evolved into cultural avatars, and only later became a social and economic burden. The administration that included a censorate dating from the Zhou, six ministries inherited from the Tang, and magistrates initiated in the Qin developed to include grand secretaries that functioned like a collective prime ministership, grand coordinators that presided over the field administration, supreme commanders to supervise various military hierarchies, and directors-general of river conservancy to manage the complex relationship between the Yellow River and the Grand Canal. The state collected light taxes and raised them gradually along with increases in population and arable land before finally imposing surtaxes to deal with external and internal challenges to its authority. It provided relief during floods, droughts, famines, and plagues before incurring fiscal deficits. It eventually relied on private contributions and market mechanisms to supplement and gradually replace public funds and administrative action. The Ming established public schools and appointed qualified magistrates from neighboring provinces before coming to accept private academies and patron-client networks that sometimes placed particular interests ahead of the common good.

The Ming paid particular attention to northeast Henan because it regarded it as the core of the central province in the heart of the central plain that had to be well governed if the dynasty was to establish and maintain its legitimacy. It enfeoffed many princes in the province, including one based in the "central prefecture" of Kaifeng who compiled a prosopography of leading scholars of the "central province." It appointed its first grand coordinator in this region and selected for the post a man whose ancestors came from the province and whose son returned there to live. The Ming emphasized the proper management of the Yellow River in the "central states" to promote the welfare of the local population as well as to service the dynastic life-line of the Grand Canal. It approved the implementation of "equal taxes" in Qi county as a model for the rest of the province, perhaps hoping the idea would take hold throughout the realm. It administered relief in the "central territory" to retain popular support in the "central plain," tolerated an old academy in Hui county and a new one in Shangqiu to nurture the local elite, and appointed supreme commanders with past experience in the region. Up to the 1630s at least, the state selected well-educated—if not always honest or capable—members of the elite from neighboring provinces to serve as magistrates in the region.

The Ming tried to govern the central province well by consciously invoking precedents from the Han and conforming to the Han style of rule. Ming Taizu followed the example of Han Gaozu in establishing his younger sons as territorial princes and his successors adopted the policies of later Han rulers in curbing their authority. The Ming relied on relatively light taxes on land combined with control over the distribution of salt for the bulk of its revenues, perpetuating a pattern established in the Han and eschewing the model of heavier taxes on commerce and industry established in the Northern Song. Officials of the Yellow River Conservancy cited positive and negative precedents from the Former and Latter Han to dike and dredge a single channel for the river and to use sluice gates to regulate its interaction with the Grand Canal. Officials confronting famine and plague cited the classics and histories to justify the provision of relief and followed the Han example of establishing ever-normal granaries to attain the ideal of "great peace and equality." It remains to be seen how the people of northeast Henan responded to these Ming efforts to reproduce selected features of the Han system under different—and ever changing—circumstances.

TWO

The Elite

THE MING GOVERNED NORTHEAST HENAN as it did other regions in concert with the elite, defined as tributary students and provincial graduates of the civil service examinations eligible to serve in office. Since the quotas for tributary students remained fixed and the number of provincial graduates from the region increased only slightly, the absolute number of elite remained constant during the dynasty. As a result, members of this stratum decreased as a proportion of the population, from about one per thousand in the first century to about .3 per thousand in the last. (See data on population in the Introduction and data on the elite in Appendix B.)

There were also important changes in the group's geographical locus and occupational focus. During the first century, Kaifeng prefecture, and especially its head county of Xiangfu, produced by far the largest number of provincial graduates. During the second century, more graduates appeared in other counties of Kaifeng prefecture, such as Yifeng, and in other prefectures, such as Guide. During this period, members of the elite achieved honor and fame through literary and philosophical activity as well as through holding public office. During the last seventy years of the Ming, certain counties (such as Qi in Kaifeng and Shangqiu in Guide) that had previously produced few graduates came to produce many. During the Ming, certain lineages were especially successful in obtaining degrees and became closely identified with the dynasty. In the late Ming, some members of these same elite lineages became increasingly disaffected from the dynasty.[1]

The First Century: Kaifeng and Xiangfu

Despite Henan's destruction in the Yuan and hardship in the early Ming, it benefited from the establishment of public schools and the implementation of regional examination quotas and did rather well in the Ming examinations. During the first century, from 1368 to 1472, Henan obtained 272 metropolitan degrees, or 7 percent of the total number awarded in this period, ranking sixth among the original thirteen provinces (see Appendix C).[2]

In this period, the large and politically central prefecture of Kaifeng produced 140 metropolitan graduates, 41 percent of the provincial total and 82 percent of the regional total. The capital county of Xiangfu, although only one of thirty-four counties in the prefecture, won thirty-five degrees, or 25 percent of the prefectural total. The county thus enjoyed a preeminence that would last during the second century of Ming rule.[3]

In Xiangfu county, the Lis, Wangs, and Zhangs were particularly successful in obtaining the metropolitan (the highest) degree. According to the provincial gazetteer, the Lis obtained seventeen, the Wangs fifteen, and the Zhangs twelve, together accounting for one-third of the total degrees awarded in the county. To be sure, the surnames Li, Wang, and Zhang are among the most common in China. In the absence of good county gazetteers and genealogies, there is no way to ascertain if they belonged to the same lineages let alone the same families. Biographies of the four most notable graduates, however, indicate that certain families succeeded in the examinations over several generations. Many of these Lis, Wangs, and Zhangs were probably part of an "aristogenic elite," the small group of interrelated families that achieved high social status in the early Ming.[4]

This hypothesis is supported by a study of twenty-three thousand officials who served at the central, provincial, and local levels during the entire Ming period. In this survey, Henan ranked eighth among fifteen provinces in the number of officials it supplied at all levels, fifth in the number of official positions held as a percentage of its population, and second in the number of central government positions it held per capita. Henan's extraordinarily high rank in participation in the central government per capita may have resulted in part from its geographical location between the two capitals of Beijing and Nanjing and its modest population in the early Ming in comparison with some other provinces. Despite Henan's overall per capita success, its share of central posts fluctuated considerably, from 17 percent in Hongwu down to 6 percent in Zhengtong, up to 24 percent in Hongzhi and down to 3 percent in Tianqi. For the whole course of the Ming, therefore, Henan emerges as a province of only moderate elite political power. According to this study, power in the central government was generally shared more equitably among the counties in the central plain than in the northwest or the south. Yet, in Henan province, officials, like metropolitan graduates, tended to come from certain counties. Xiangfu, Xiangcheng, and Qi counties in Kaifeng prefecture, together with three counties from other prefectures in the province, provided 25 percent of the total number of officials from Henan. In Xiangfu county, moreover, three surnames occupied a disproportionate number of posts: the Lis produced eleven officials holding nine offices, the Zhangs ten officials holding eleven offices, and the Wangs eight officials holding thirteen offices. These surnames' record of extensive office holding clearly stemmed in part from their success in the examinations during the first two centuries of the dynasty.[5]

The Second Century: Yifeng, Ningling, and Yucheng

During the mid-Ming, men from Xiangfu continued to get the lion's share (25 percent) of the metropolitan degrees earned in the prefecture but residents of other counties began to compete more effectively for the remaining 75 percent. Men from Yifeng, for example, obtained nine degrees (or about 4 percent). Biographies in the provincial gazetteer reveal that notables from Xiangfu continued to hold their own (with nine), but men from Yifeng got a very respectable six and those from Xinzheng got a substantial four. Men with certain surnames and those hailing from certain descent groups continued to succeed. All four of the biographies from Xinzheng, for example, were of men surnamed Gao, and two were from the same family. In Yifeng in this period (here including the Tianshun reign), two of those honored with biographies were Guos and two were Zhangs (see Appendixes C and D).[6]

YIFENG

In this middle period of the Ming, certain members of the elite went beyond office holding to gain fame for their scholarship. In Yifeng county, for example, Wang Tingxiang emerged as one of the outstanding intellectuals in Chinese history. Born into a prosperous landholding family on the newly developing north bank of the Yellow River, Wang won his metropolitan degree in 1502. He soon became friends with other prominent Henanese literati, including Li Mengyang, from Fugou county, and He Jingming, from Xinyang county. Together with four other poets, these scholars were later known as the Seven Early Masters of the Ming. They departed from the current fashion of following Song literary models by returning to the Tang for poetry and to the Han for prose.[7]

Wang's and Li's involvement in this literary group and their persistent criticism of the state hindered their official careers. Over the course of his life, Li in particular was arrested for criticizing the powerful eunuch Liu Jin, impeached for siding with his students against local officials in Jiangxi, and reduced to the status of a commoner for alleged complicity in a Ming prince's rebellion. He nonetheless lived out his life in Kaifeng and became famous as a leading poet of his day. Wang first rose to high posts by accommodating the ruler, cultivating powerful courtiers, and showing leniency to subordinates. That strategy backfired, however, when the Jiajing ruler responded to a fire by blaming himself and his subordinates for misconduct. Wang was implicated in the misdemeanors of his superiors and subordinates. When he reacted by alleging large-scale corruption among high officials, he was reduced to the status of a commoner.

While Li responded to political adversity by becoming a leading poet, Wang, whose story is more pertinent to this study, became a prominent philosopher. Unlike the Northern Song thinkers Cheng Yi and Cheng Hao, whose emphasis on pattern or principle (*li*) over material force (*qi*) had become standard in the Ming, Wang followed another Northern Song philosopher, Zhang Zai, in positing the primacy of material force. Wang doubted the Mencian tenet, widely accepted since the Southern Song, that human nature is good, and shared the alternative Xunzian acceptance of the human propensity to err, more characteristic of the Han. Wang returned to the Zhou classics to criticize the correlative cosmology that had developed in the Han and persisted into the Song and Ming. He argued that the five agents (earth, wood, metal, fire, and water) had originally been elements deemed essential to popular welfare and had only later been regarded as processes informing the cosmos. As John Henderson has noted, Wang challenged "the prevailing use of yinyang duality for interpreting such cyclical changes as the alternation of the seasons, pointing out that proximate, material causes, such as the annual movement of the sun, were sufficient to account for such phenomena." Wang denied that the eight trigrams of the *Book of Changes* had been designed to explain nature, that Shao Yong's numerology could account for the cosmic process, and that natural events were warnings directed at the ruler.[8]

While Qing sources described Wang's thought as "dissolute," and twentieth-century observers have considered it prophetic, Wang Tingxiang was also very much a man of his own time and place.[9] The Seven Early Masters' interest in Han prose and Tang poetry later influenced another literary coterie known as the Seven Later Masters of the Ming. Wang critiqued the cosmology inherited from the Former Han by drawing on the Latter Han ideas of Wang Chong and Zhang Heng. He also went beyond them by analyzing the annual difference between the paths of the sun and the moon against the stars. He addressed the problems of land accumulation, princely revolts, popular rebellion, and frontier incursions that plagued the mid-Ming by invoking the Legalist tradition of state centralization embodied in the institutions of the Qin and Han. Like Liu Zongyuan of the Tang, he opposed a radical return to decentralized administration or equal land-holding, thus influencing later thinkers such as Lü Kun and Huang Zongxi.[10]

For all his cosmological creativity, Wang articulated historiographical ideas that were in the Ming mainstream. He admired the achievements of the early sages and the three dynasties but believed that they were simply inspirational and could not be reproduced in his own day. He simultaneously entertained the possibility of progress in history, as in an evolutionary theory of ordered family relationships, and recognized constant flux in material force, arguing that each individual in each generation has to decide which changes to accept and which to reject.[11]

Like many contemporaries, Wang admired the Han founder, whom he associated with the founder of the Ming. In a passage on types of political successions, he noted that "Gaodi of the Han and our Taizu, although commoners, took power through rebellion and had nothing to apologize for." Wang recognized that the Han founder had departed from the Three Dynasties by employing more officials and ruling through laws, but he insisted that he had chosen his men wisely and thereby succeeded in establishing a long-lasting dynasty. Subsequent Han rulers had used capable subordinates to put down rebellious princes, providing a model for Ming rulers. Under Wudi, Wang acknowledged, the Former Han had overexpanded, and it later succumbed to the usurpation of Wang Mang. But the Han system of governing through hereditary headmen on the frontier remained a viable model, and Wang Mang had been succeeded by the Latter Han, enabling the Ming to aspire to similar resilience. In Wang's view, the Han had eventually come to an end through land concentration, official corruption, eunuch abuses, sectarian uprisings, and a military coup. He warned against similar trends in his own day, including what he called contemporary "Yellow Turbans" (late Han sectarians) and "Cao Caos" (late Han militarists).[12]

Wang Tingxiang, like Li Mengyang and He Jingming, was a Henanese, and one of his followers, Gao Gong, who became a powerful grand secretary, was also from Henan. But the other four members of the Seven Early Masters hailed from other provinces and Wang seems to have participated in no provincial political faction. On the contrary, one of Wang's chief critics was from Henan, one of his main political targets was a Henanese, and one of his most loyal followers was from another province. Nor did Wang accept certain legends that derived their power, in part, from their association with the central province. For example, he refused to treat the ancient River Chart (Hetu) and the Luo Book (Luoshu) as sacred prognosticatory texts; he regarded them instead as early maps of the Yellow and Luo River region. Despite his family's considerable landed estate, Wang openly criticized the concentration of landholding that, he wrote, had become particularly severe in Henan in the mid-Ming.[13]

NINGLING

During the mid-Ming, Kaifeng's percentage of the total number of metropolitan degrees awarded in the region declined slightly from 82 to 75, and Guide's edged up from 12 to 13. Within Guide, Sui department continued to get the most degrees but Ningling and Shangqiu increased their number. In Ningling, certain families dominated the examination lists, including a new one, the Lüs. Here again certain outstanding individuals pursued not only degrees and offices but broader intellectual and philosophical matters. Toward the end of this period, Lü Kun appeared in Ningling and became one of the most respected and influential thinkers of the Wanli reign.[14]

Like Wang Tingxiang, Lü Kun was not only an intellectual of transcendent importance but a man of his own time and place. Lü traced his line back to a hereditary military officer from Xin'an county, Henan prefecture, whose son had moved to Ningling. By the fifth generation, the Lüs had somehow acquired a substantial estate of two thousand mu that enabled them to prepare their sons for the examinations. Lü Kun's father, Desheng, had one cousin who became a government student, and another, named Guan (official), who was selected as a tributary student in the capital. Although appointed to office, Guan held his post for only three days before retiring to his home. One of Guan's sons came in third in the provincial examinations, but he too seems not to have pursued an official career for he was honored in the gazetteer only as a filial son.[15]

At age fifteen, Lü Kun impressed the county magistrate with his knowledge of Kongzi's *Analects*. In 1550 he began the study of history and philosophy. After marrying a woman from a modest family and studying at the home of a relative, he entered the county school. There he read medical texts as well as the classics. In 1556 he visited nearby Yongcheng county to look after some of his father's lands and made a friend whose son later became one of his students. Lü and his friend, Li Liangzhi, later compared themselves with Lian Fan and Qing Hong, famous "friends to the death" of the Latter Han.[16]

While preparing to become part of the all-male elite, Lü Kun developed an interest in the status of women. His concern had perhaps been sparked by his blind mother, who responded enthusiastically to the storytellers brought home by his father when he was only twelve. His father would later compile rhymed primers for girls as well as boys. Lü Kun was also inspired by the examples of Liu Xiang and Ban Zhao, male and female scholars of the Former and Latter Han respectively, who had written biographies of, and instructions for women. Lü tried to revive one original Han perspective by reducing the sections on "evil women" that had appeared in later editions of the Han biographies. Lü also challenged the Ming policy (see in Chapter 3) encouraging widow chastity and suicide in response to rape by promoting widow remarriage and praising women who resisted assault without sacrificing their lives. He countered the tendency to value female virtue over talent by honoring women who managed their households well and by advocating formal education for women, including instruction in their legal rights to inheritance.

Lü exemplified scholars who deplored the contemporary emphasis on money and the associated corrosion of human values. He criticized parents who arranged marriages to obtain wealth and status and who killed daughters to avoid paying dowries. He chastised greedy men who married for money and accumulated concubines, as well as jealous women who thought only about clothes. Reflecting a populism that originated in the early Ming and was celebrated by Wang Yangming and his followers, Lü avoided abstruse allusions, explained obscure characters, and included wood-block prints in his *Illustrated Models for Women*, published in 1590. While serving as an official, he drafted a primer for the instruction of the blind and encouraged them to become musicians and storytellers.[17]

While Lü expressed certain views that were radical in the context of his times, he continued to affirm family rites and went along with other contemporary trends. After passing the provincial examinations in 1561, he and his cousin were urged by his father to follow the example of Fan Zhongyan of the Northern Song by establishing a land trust to fund ancestral sacrifices and the education of kinsmen. They later designated five hundred mu as "filial and peaceful fields" for those purposes. After failing the metropolitan examination in 1562, Lü Kun began compiling a personal record titled *Groaning Words*, a work that reflected the contemporary interest in introspective autobiography. Preoccupied with editing the local gazetteer and then with mourning the death of his father, Lü did not retake the metropolitan examinations until 1571. This time he passed but he missed the final palace examinations in order to mourn the death of his mother. Only after completing such filial duties did he finally get his degree in 1574.[18]

Lü Kun's success in the examinations benefited his county, his kin, and himself. Ningling, which had produced only four metropolitan graduates in the previous two hundred years, now had a prominent spokesman. The Lüs, who were previously only at the edge of the elite, now emerged as one of the leading families in the county. Lü Kun's chief examiner was Zhang Juzheng, who became chief grand secretary and regent to the young Wanli, thus insuring patronage for Lü at the highest level. Lü soon obtained a post and established himself as a capable official. As a magistrate in Shanxi province he devised ways to control a local river without requiring onerous labor services. On the northern frontier, he invoked the experiences of Wudi of the Former Han and Ma Yuan of the Latter Han to urge principle and caution rather than force and bluster in dealing with the Mongols. He gained a reputation for probity by rebuffing a powerful member of the Shanxi elite who asked him to appoint one of his clients to a local post. Lü thereafter held several posts in the capital. When his patron, Zhang Juzheng, died in 1582 and was attacked for allegedly trying to usurp the throne on the model of the regent Yi Yin of the Shang dynasty, Lü was dissuaded by a friend, Shen Li, from speaking out in his defense. Devoting himself to his prime interest, local administration, he managed to stay in office during the bitter bureaucratic infighting of the 1580s and 1590s.[19]

In his personal life, Lü Kun came close to violating his own strictures on gender relations. He took a concubine when he and his wife were unable to produce a son. When this union, too, resulted in a daughter, Lü married her off to a government student whose father had been posted to Shaanxi, where Lü Kun had also served. Still intent on having a son, he took a second concubine with whom he had another daughter. Lü eventually married this daughter off to a government student of Guide named Shen Xuan, a relative of Lü's friend and benefactor Shen Li. Lü Kun eventually took a third concubine who finally gave birth to two sons. One of them, Zhiwei, became a government student and was married to the daughter of Yang Dongming, one of Lü's students. Lü may have believed that the husband-wife relationship was the heart of the family, but he took three concubines in order to father a son; he arranged the marriages of both sons and daughters to accord with his professional interests.[20]

During the 1580s, Lü rose to become chief of a bureau in the ministry of personnel. This post had great potential for patronage and was therefore a target in factional struggles. Lü continued to distance himself from his deceased patron, Zheng Juzheng, by criticizing his alleged policy of land equalization. He called it a utopian scheme like that of the reforming official Wang Mang, who had usurped the authority of the Former Han and established his own brief Xin dynasty (9–23 CE) that attempted to nationalize the land. Lü claimed that the policy had caused trouble in many places, including Kaifeng prefecture, before it was transmuted into a more realistic quest for equal taxes in 1583. Lü had contacts with leading Jiangnan literati, such as Zou Yuanbiao and Gu Xiancheng, who were associated with the emerging "party of the pure" (another name for the Donglin). They reportedly identified Lü as "the scholar from the central province" and were themselves at one point referred to as members of "Ningling Lü's party." When Zou and Gu came under attack in 1587, however, Lü once again escaped the line of fire, this time by obtaining a provincial post in Shandong. From 1589 to 1594, he held high provincial posts in Shanxi and Shaanxi, where he devoted himself to local administration. In 1598 his views on famine relief, personnel policy, local compacts and the like were brought together in a book entitled *Master Lü's Record of Realizing Government.* The book was widely read, revered, and sometimes even heeded; it continues to this day to be widely cited as a valuable source for the political and social conditions of that time.[21]

During these years, Lü developed his own approach to statecraft, insisting at one point "I am just a 'me.'" At the same time, he recognized the importance of keeping in

touch with his home, the central province. He gave advice on the salt administration in
Guide prefecture, corresponded with Zhong Huamin during the famine of 1593–94,
wrote biographies of local notables such as Song Xun of Shangqiu (for more on whom
see below), and authorized the reprinting and circulation of his writings by a regional
inspector in Kaifeng. While in some ways an individualist, he modestly disclaimed having all the answers and called for reliance on the opinions of many people. He advocated what he called the "Middle Way" or the "Central Path" and argued that "the mean
is without fixed form," regarding it, in Joanna Handlin's words, as "a dynamic principle that required his initiative and constant reevaluation."[22]

In 1594, Lü Kun reached the peak of his public career by assuming high posts in
the central government, but the very next year he began his descent due to personal
problems, court politics, and policy differences. His wife had died in 1592 and Lü, at
sixty, was beginning to feel his age; he repeatedly requested permission to retire on the
grounds of ill health. In August 1595, Wanli's favorite concubine, Zheng Guifei, reed-
ited Lü's *Illustrated Models for Women*, added her own preface, and, with assistance from
her brother, printed and circulated the new edition in the capital. Zheng had recently
tried to increase her son's chances of being chosen heir apparent by contributing funds
for famine relief in Henan. Now some suspected that she was using the text by the
Henanese scholar Lü Kun for the same purpose since the work included a biography
of a concubine of the Latter Han ruler Mingdi who had been promoted to empress so
that her son could become heir apparent. Such suspicions, spread by word of mouth,
probably weakened Lü's influence with many powerful officials who opposed Zheng's
ambitions. In May 1597, Lü himself brought matters to a head by submitting an eight
thousand-character memorial chastising Wanli for irresponsibility. The memorial discussed many important issues, including the growing gap between the wealthy and the
poor, and it later constituted the bulk of Lü's biography in the *Ming History*. Charac-
teristically, Wanli made no reply to the memorial, but six months later he granted Lü's
request for retirement.[23]

During the last two decades of his life at home, Lü Kun continued to deal with the
repercussions of the heir-apparent issue. When an anonymous circular accused him of
writing the *Illustrated Models for Women* to curry favor with Zheng Guifei, he pointed out
differences between his original text and the one revised and printed by Zheng's brother.
An anonymous circular provided a more detailed defense of Lü, pointing out significant
differences between Mingdi of the Han, who had lacked a legitimate heir, and Wanli of
the Ming, who had one. According to this account, the similarities between the late Han
concubine and the late Ming one were merely coincidental and had nothing to do with
the inclusion of the former in the text. A special investigation subsequently cleared Lü
of all charges and attributed them to an official who held a grudge against Lü for supposedly engineering his dismissal. Lü ignored a second anonymous circular that
renewed the charges, sensing (correctly) that Wanli was tired of the controversy. As a
result, however, Lü was never again recalled to office despite many pleas by high officials,
including his Shangqiu friend Shen Li.[24]

From his home in Ningling, Lü Kun spoke out on other controversial issues of both local and polity-wide import. He agreed that the Lu Prince might have justified his enormous landholdings on the basis of a precedent set by the Prince of Liang under Han Wudi, but he argued the Fu Prince should not expect the same treatment because it would be harmful to the state and the people. He interceded with a Yellow River intendant to reduce the burden of labor services in Guide prefecture, and he advised the prefect of Guide on how to resist exorbitant tax demands from Beijing. He acknowledged that wealthy households had taken advantage of the single whip reforms to get unfair tax exemptions, but he dismissed students' claims that exemptions he had granted for landowners had resulted in greater demands on the common people.[25] He thus played the mediating role between state and society that was expected of responsible members of the local elite.

During his last years at home in the central province, Lü repeatedly used historical references in an effort to shape local developments. In 1598, he congratulated Hou Zhipu of nearby Shangqiu for winning the metropolitan degree, alluding to the example of prime minister Yi Yin of the Shang, the dynasty that had given its name to Hou's hometown. (For more on Hou, see below). Two years later he referred to the standards of Mencius, who had once visited Shangqiu, in celebrating his patron Shen Li's seventieth birthday. He mentioned the more recent experiences of a revolt in Guide in 1553 and a conspiracy in Nanjing in 1606 in calling for repairs to the Ningling wall and other measures to save lives in a crisis. Aware of the conditions leading to the fall of the Latter Han, he worried about the future of the Ming as eunuchs and factions increasingly dominated the government. Lü followed the orthodox Song thinker Zhu Xi in attributing many of China's problems to choices dating back to the Qin, but he found other historical judgments in Zhu Xi's *Outline of the Comprehensive Mirror for Government* so dubious that he doubted that the work had been written by that sage. Lü later destroyed his critique of Zhu Xi to avoid trouble, but he did not try to hide his respect for less orthodox and even Legalist thinkers such as Guan Zhong of the Zhou and Liu Zongyuan of the Tang.[26]

Before his death in 1618, Lü Kun wrote his own epitaph, espousing a mixture of the individualism and communitarianism typical of the age. Wanli was not impressed with Lü and granted him only the usual allowances for his burial. Upon Wanli's demise in 1620, however, Lü was awarded a higher posthumous rank of president of the ministry of punishments. His study of women was reprinted many times and circulated widely in the late Ming, and his book on government became a standard reference work during the Qing. Lü's collected works were printed in 1674, when his family genealogy was compiled, and *Groaning Words*, reprinted with commentary by the Qing scholar Lu Longji, was included in the Qing *Collectanea of the Four Treasuries*. That text was influential in Japan in the late Tokugawa period, a complete edition of Lü's works was published in Japan in 1955, and a selection of his writings was printed in Beijing in 1962. While some early Qing observers put Lü in the Cheng-Zhu tradition handed down through Xin'an, the home of his ancestors, the Qing scholar Huang Zongxi placed him among less orthodox "miscellaneous" thinkers. More recently, Lü Kun has been given a niche among critical late Ming thinkers for whom "personal experiences, self-interest, and local concerns had become the center."[27] Of course, for Lü, personal experiences were also familial, self-interest included social welfare, and local concerns in Henan were, by definition, central.

Y U C H E N G

The late sixteenth century trend to act locally in northeast Henan was even more evident in the career of Yang Dongming, the author of the *Album of the Famished* and Lü Kun's sometime student and relative by marriage. Born in 1548 into a wealthy family in the poor county of Yucheng northeast of Guide city, Yang obtained his metropolitan degree in 1580, one of five during the last seventy years of the Ming (see Appendixes B and C). After serving in the central drafting office and submitting his famous memorial on the famine of 1593, he helped supervise the metropolitan examinations of 1595. Yang admired the early-sixteenth century philosopher Wang Yangming, who emphasized the unity of knowledge and action. He was close to the "party of the pure," who contended unsuccessfully for power in the 1590s. In 1595 he was demoted to the post of commissary in Shanxi, and he soon retired to his hometown. In 1620 he returned briefly to central government offices before dying in 1624. Four years later he was accorded the posthumous title of Minister of Punishments, the same honor bestowed on Lü Kun. Although famous for his memorial on famine and for his contacts with the party of the pure, he received only a brief biography in the *Ming History*.[28]

The brief mention given Yang by the dynastic history was understandable because his main achievements were in his hometown. Yang had begun to act locally in 1590, five years before his retirement, when he created a Society for Sharing Pleasure. Soon finding drinking and gossiping frivolous, the group changed its name to the Society for Sharing Goodness. It collected monthly dues and fines and used the proceeds to build roads and bridges and fund weddings and funerals. The society held drinking ceremonies to honor senior males, and Yang professed to learn even from elders who lacked formal education. In 1591 he organized a Society for Spreading Humaneness comprising thirty-one men, including nearly all the elite in the county as well as commoners. In addition to Yang and his brothers, there were clerks, state university students, government students, visitors to the town, and even country folk. Three scholars from neighboring Shangqiu, including Hou Zhigong (about whom more below), served as patrons, and forty-two members contributed six taels a month in dues. Among other activities, the society sponsored a humble doctor who lived in the hills and treated country folk.[29]

In 1595 Yang commissioned the construction of a Pavilion of Broken Willow Branches. Over the years, prominent intellectuals, including outsiders such as Zou Yuanbiao and Henanese such as Lü Kun, met there to discuss the classics and histories with hundreds of scholars. The following year, Yang organized a Society to Promote Learning. It included twenty graduates of the metropolitan examination of 1595 that he had supervised, two instructors and four assistants in the county school, dozens of local scholars, and numerous students from surrounding counties. Acting in the mode of earlier teachers such as Kongzi, Zhu Xi, and Wang Yangming, Yang recorded some of the discussions for posterity.[30]

Yang initiated other institutions that went beyond thought to action. Perhaps moved by the famine of 1594, he helped to establish a public granary in Cao county across the Yellow River in Shandong. When excessive rain and snow resulted in floods that brought another subsistence crisis to Yucheng in 1601–1602, he and his brothers created a Society to Equalize Grain Prices to prevent profiteering. The Yangs contributed one hundred taels and enlisted minor officials, government students, townsmen, and a farmer who each contributed seventy taels to buy three hundred bushels of grain for distribution to the poor. In Yucheng, Yang also supported the repair of the temple to the city god and the construction of four local shrines. When he returned to Beijing to take office in 1620, he helped establish the Shoushan Academy for scholar-officials associated with the Donglin party.[31]

Yang's long stay in Yucheng was largely involuntary, but he took advantage of the situation to contribute to the public good. He often gave public lectures; in 1596 he spoke to an audience of seventy in Xin'an, in Henan prefecture. In response to reservations expressed by scholars such as Lü Kun, who preferred to work quietly behind the scenes, Yang said that he was only an "average man" (*zhongren*) and needed periodic personal contact with other scholars to remain engaged. Like many of his contemporaries, Yang was a kind of individualist. For example, he said, "If one takes the self as the basis, then the self will be able to use the past; if one takes the past as the basis, then the self will be mired in the past." He drew creatively on history, such as on the Han institution of grain-price equalization, but he also relied on his own observations, such as those made in the neighboring county of Qi. According to Handlin, "Yang took his hometown as the center from which he extended his influence," for in managing hometown affairs he "could feel central and strong."[32] Excluded from the preeminent contemporary cultural and political center of Beijing, he fell back on the long-term cultural and political center of Henan.

The Third Century

By 1570 the elite of Shangqiu and Yongcheng counties in Guide prefecture, Qi county in Kaifeng, and Xinxiang county in Weihui played increasingly active roles in official and intellectual life. Within these four counties certain families rose to prominence and became strong supporters of the Ming. Certain individuals among them, however, became progressively alienated from the state. Their rising influence and changing attitudes contributed to the gradual decline and ultimate fall of the dynasty.

SHANGQIU

Among the counties of Guide prefecture, Shangqiu showed the most marked increase in examination success during the last seven decades of Ming rule. For the first time the county pulled ahead of Suizhou, securing 40 percent of the provincial degrees in the prefecture. Shangqiu made even greater progress in garnering metropolitan degrees, getting 23 or 25 percent of the prefectural total (see Appendixes B and C). The county also excelled in the number of its sons who were honored with biographies in the provincial gazetteer: eleven, as opposed to only three from second-ranking Suizhou. Among the most prominent Shangqiu families were the Shens, who provided a tutor to Wanli; the Songs, who boasted prominent officials in three generations; and the Hous, who produced three sets of brothers who became political leaders. The Shens exemplify families that remained largely loyal to the Ming while the Songs and Hous represent families that to varying degrees lost confidence in the dynasty.[33]

The Shens had originated in Kunshan county, in Suzhou prefecture, Nanzhili, during the late Yuan. Through service to the early Ming, they had been given hereditary military responsibilities and had moved first to Xiangfu and then to Guide. The lineage entered the elite when Shen Han won his provincial degree in 1477. Han went on to get his metropolitan degree in 1484 and served as a prefectural judge. His youngest son, Du, remained a government student, but he held a staff position in the Hanlin Academy. The Shens maintained their elite status by producing two tributary students, a provincial graduate, and an assistant magistrate. Du's eldest son, Li, won his provincial degree at nineteen. He reportedly signaled his seriousness of purpose by refusing to consort with a "fallen girl" offered to him as a reward. He also demonstrated his loyalty to the state when a bandit named Shi Shangzhao attacked Guide in 1553. Although Shi met with some sympathy in Guide, he was unable to take the town and left. Fearing that the bandit would return, Shen urged local officials to execute residents who were sympathetic to him. He also contributed family resources to help the magistrate fortify the town. When the rebel returned, he found the town well defended and did not dare attack again.[34]

In 1565 Shen Li won his metropolitan degree under the university chancellor Gao Gong, the follower of Wang Tingxiang and fellow Henanese who hailed from Xinzheng county in Kaifeng prefecture. Shen's biographer denied that he used provincial contacts on this or other occasions to advance his career, but he was certainly fortunate to receive the patronage of one of the most influential officials of the time. Although Shen had passed the examinations without great distinction (he was third in the third rank), he was selected as a bachelor in the Hanlin Academy. Soon he was called upon to lecture on the classics to the throne. Shen's principal duty was to teach Longqing, but he also tutored the heir apparent, Zhu Yijun, soon to rule as Wanli. Shen wrote poetry on a fan for Yijun, instructed him in how to mourn his parents, and advised him about aesthetics. During the 1570s when the grand secretary and regent Zhang Juzheng ran the administration with an iron fist, Shen was among the few bold enough to express criticism. When Zhang became ill and the whole court engaged in sacrifices to help ensure his recovery, Shen refused to participate. After Zhang's death, Shen became vice president of the ministry of personnel and continued to tutor Wanli.[35]

At the pinnacle of power in the 1580s, Shen Li gained a reputation for honesty and independence. He shunned contacts with eunuchs and declined to develop his own clientele, reportedly recommending meritorious officials without informing them. In 1584 he was promoted to president of the ministry of rites and concurrent junior guardian of the heir apparent. During four years at rites, Shen advocated a return to the more frugal ceremonies of previous reigns. He responded to a famine by arguing that "exalting economy and abstaining from extravagance" were the keys to "relieving the people and realizing good government." He regulated the ruler's sacrifices to concubines and the princes' respects to ancestors and vetoed requests from royal concubines and princes to enfeoff their relatives. He encouraged civility and honesty in historiography by calling for the reinstatement of the reign name Jianwen for the second Ming ruler, Zhu Yunwen, and by suggesting that Zhu Qiyu be rehabilitated as the rightful ruler during the Jingtai reign. When Wanli's third-ranked concubine Zheng gave birth to a son in 1586 and was promoted to the rank August Concubine (*guifei*), Shen was among those who requested that similar status be bestowed on the mother of his first born son who should be named heir apparent.[36]

In 1588, Shen Li found himself lacking in eunuch allies, at odds with the grand secretary, and unable to influence the increasingly headstrong Wanli. He asked to retire. His request was refused by Wanli, who still respected his old teacher and wished to make use of him in even higher offices. Placing personal pride over political power, Shen continued to request retirement. Finally he was allowed to return home where he remained for the next fourteen years. In 1601 the court reappointed Shen Li to his old post at rites and named him grand secretary, apparently recognizing that he had been remote from the capital and the partisan wrangling that had afflicted the state. Shen, however, refused because the issue of the heir apparent was still not settled. Even after Zhu Changluo was formally named heir apparent in October 1601, Shen delayed a year before returning to high posts in Beijing.[37]

Upon his return, Shen Li was caught up in a controversy over state involvement in the mining industry. The court had sent out eunuch commissioners in the 1590s to open up mines to provide revenues to fund armies against the Japanese in the northeast and the reconstruction of palaces in Beijing. The measures had proven lucrative, and the court was intent on extending them to cover rising expenditures after 1600. Shen Li reported on the harsh effects of the policy in regions he had traversed en route to the north, but Wanli, having just reaffirmed the policy, was in no mood to reconsider. Four years later, in 1606, Shen Li memorialized for the abolition of the mining commissioners on the grounds that they had driven away the spirits of the rivers and mountains without providing compensating benefits to the throne. Wanli was finally persuaded to end the policy. In another controversy, Shen Li differed with the chief grand secretary, Shen Yiguan, over the legitimacy of a prince and incurred Shen Yiguan's enmity without winning Wanli's support. When Shen Yiguan came under fire for allegedly supporting Zheng Guifei in the struggle over the heir apparent, he suspected that Shen Li was behind the charges. Shen Li also set up a screen in the secretariat inscribed with couplets exhorting Wanli to respect heaven, relieve the people, open communications, employ the qualified, and release prisoners. When Shen burned incense in front of the screen he was charged with doing incantations against the throne. An investigation concluded that he was guilty. Wanli continued to trust his former teacher, but when Shen Li asked to retire in 1606, the ruler agreed. In a memorial of thanks, Shen criticized idle government and called for clear standards. In 1610, in a memorial of gratitude for court recognition on his eightieth birthday, he continued to discuss matters of state. After he died in 1615, he was honored with the rank of grand preceptor, and canonized Wenduan (cultured and upright).[38]

Although Shen Li had scaled the peaks of late Ming scholar-officialdom, he was unable to pass the benefits on to progeny. He had two wives and three concubines but no sons. He therefore adopted a nephew who became a tributary student by inheritance, but he died young and never held any posts. Shen then adopted another nephew who never got beyond the status of government student. Shen Li's first brother became a state university student and held the post of office manager in the court of state cere- monial, but his two sons remained government students. Shen Li's second brother, also a government student, had one son who became a provincial graduate and held posts as vice magistrate and magistrate. Shen's third brother was a teacher and had six sons, including one tributary student and one university student as well as three government students. Thus a certain number of Shen Li's branch of the lineage succeeded in the lower levels of the examination system, but the branch barely maintained itself among the local elite. Other branches of the Shen descent group were even less successful in the examinations. The meager achievements of Shen Li's offspring were reflected in a biography of Shen Yu, the son of one of Shen Li's adopted sons, written by the Shangqiu literatus Hou Fangyu (see Chapter 3). Hou praised Shen Yu, who happened to have married Hou's wife's sister, as one of the few descendants of Shen Li to display literary talent.[39]

By contrast, Shen Li's fellow townsman, Song Xun, not only led his family into the elite and attained high posts but managed to pass those achievements along to other members of his lineage. Song Xun's forebears could boast only modest academic attain- ments (his father was a government student), but they enjoyed marriage ties with the Lius (likely members of one or both of two prominent lineages in the county). Xun's elder brother had become a physician in the Royal Academy of Medicine. Xun became a government student. He gained notice for resisting his classmates' request to protest the state's violation of their privileges to be exempt from labor services. If Xun was reluc- tant to assert his privileges as a government student, he actively pursued the even greater advantages associated with being a provincial graduate. He passed the examinations to attain that status in 1551, at age twenty-nine.[40]

Although Song Xun was ambitious, his loyalty to the Ming seems to have been more conditional than Shen Li's. His response to the rebellion of Shi Shangzhao in 1553, for example, was very different from Shen's. According to the Song genealogy:

> At that time, the robber Shi Shangzhao of Zhe[cheng] attacked the prefectural town, burning and plundering as he went. He had heard that master [Song Xun] was a worthy, however, and warned his subordinates not to cause him any trouble. People of the town therefore thronged to his [Song's] house to hide, and many escaped trouble in this way. Thus the master became known far and wide for his trustworthiness.[41]

"Trustworthiness," here, was clearly in the eyes of the beholders—the rebels, the pop- ulace, and the biographer. It was certainly not a quality the Ming magistrate or Shen Li would have ascribed to Song Xun. Soon thereafter Song Xun seems to have given the Ming authorities and local elite further reason to doubt his loyalties. He declined an official request to encourage villagers to raise and supply horses to the army.[42]

After passing the metropolitan examinations in 1559, Song Xun held a series of provincial posts in which he demonstrated his independence and sense of justice. As a prefectural judge in northeast Beizhili, he was said to have resisted the demands of court officials and applied the laws fairly. As surveillance commissioner in Shaanxi, he impeached eunuchs for illegal use of the twelve guards in the capital. As a prefectural surveillance commissioner in Nanzhili, he prosecuted local strongmen who had intimidated his predecessors. In the same post in Shanxi, he tracked down bandit leaders who had taken refuge in the mountains, but provided amnesty to followers who returned to their villages. He also punished forty-four men suspected of complicity with Mongol raiders, but found thirty-three others innocent and allowed them to go free. On a lighter note, he reported that a man named Li Liangyu (literally, good rain Li) in Shanxi had changed into a woman. He urged the ruler to reassert the dominance of *yang* over *yin* by promoting "gentlemen" and dismissing "petty men." The court responded by appointing Song vice prefect of the metropolitan prefecture of Shuntian. Soon he was promoted to assistant chief censor and concurrent grand coordinator of Beizhili, where he reduced expenditures for entertaining officials and culled out supernumerary troops.[43]

Song Xun, like many other Henanese scholar-officials, refused to cooperate with Zhang Juzheng. He retired from office in 1575 on the excuse of illness. His withdrawal was originally meant to be temporary, and a rescript asked him to return to office as soon as his health improved. When Zhang Juzheng failed to return home in person to mourn his father in 1577, however, Song Xun refused to greet his emissaries when they passed through Shangqiu. Song therefore became unwelcome at court and stayed in retirement until Zhang's death in 1582. At home in Shangqiu, Song joined with Shen Li in editing the county gazetteer.[44]

In 1583 Song Xun was recalled to office and served briefly in his old post in Beizhili. Arriving during a famine, he immediately distributed grain relief and then reported his actions to Beijing. This initiative annoyed court officials, who believed that he should have sought authorization before taking action, but it impressed his colleagues and won gratitude among the people. Despite tensions with court officials, Song moved into a second career as a high government official after 1586. As vice president and then president of the ministry of revenue, he confronting the growing gap between state income and expenditures. He opposed the policies of opening more mines and selling more degrees and called for the repeal of the 200,000-tael increase in taxes (called the gold-floral silver tax), collected annually since 1578. While these efforts failed, Song continued to discourage local officials from using the whip to force people to pay their taxes and instead called for reducing expenditures. He cut the subsidies to local militia by more than half, called on the wealthy to support community granaries in return for caps and sashes, urged the revival of merchant and military colonies on the frontier, and suggested cutting the Lu prince's stipends to one-third of his request. The awarding of elite status in return for grain was tantamount to the sale of degrees. The effort to cut the Lu prince's emoluments was not fully successful, but Song's intention to curb the state's quest for wealth and power at the expense of the people was clear. Indeed, his efforts combined with those of others would frustrate Zhang Juzheng's plan to transform the Ming state in line with the Legalist principles of wealth and power embodied in the Qin model of central administration and carried to a new level by

European empires using New World silver to purchase Asian products. In this respect, the Wanli reign remained true to the more ruist, and arguably more populist impulses of earlier reigns.[45]

During his five years at revenue, Song Xun also acted to benefit his home region. Facing recurrent drought and flood in north China, he urged the distribution of forty thousand taels from the palace treasury and twenty thousand piculs from Shandong granaries and other storehouses to cut market demand and therefore prices for food, bringing an end to famine in the region for three years. Song opposed the plan to transmute tributary grain into silver, arguing that it was essential to maintain grain reserves in the capital. He suggested instead reducing transport costs by moving the capital granary from Beijing to Tongzhou at the end of the Grand Canal. Song noted that many members of the guards in Guide were dying under the burden of transporting tributary grain, and he showed open partiality to his home region by suggesting that some of the burden be shifted to the guards at Linqing in Shandong. Song Xun also acted on behalf of his home province by requesting authorization for Kaifeng and Guide to purchase salt from the Changlu circuit in Shandong as well as from the Hedong circuit in Shanxi. While the impact on the Lu prince's monopoly (see Chapter 1) is unknown, this reform reportedly increased the supply of salt and reduced smuggling.[46]

In 1590 Song Xun was removed from his post at revenue, where he had blocked Wanli's thirst for wealth, and was made president of the ministry of personnel, where he opposed his ruler's quest for power. When Song's successor at revenue pointed out certain regions that regularly produced agricultural surpluses, Song urged him to withhold the information lest the throne be inclined to increase taxes and waste the additional revenue. At personnel, Song confronted officials who admired Wanli for merely ignoring critics and not punishing them. He insisted that it was not enough to tolerate criticism—the ruler should also act on it to keep problems from becoming irremediable. Song accordingly dismissed one hundred "bad officials" appointed under his predecessors and replaced them with "good people" belonging to the party of the pure. This measure was opposed by the chief grand secretary, Shen Shixing, who vetoed Song's appointments and drove many of his appointees from Beijing. During these years, it was said that Song wrote one hundred memorials that were ignored by the court. Although the number may be symbolic and exaggerated, Song was clearly frustrated for he tried to resign seven times. Wanli repeatedly refused, apparently wanting to keep him as a symbol of his tolerance; Song finally died in office in 1591. As usual, Wanli tried to compensate for his previous insouciance by mourning the passing of a loyal official. He ordered sacrifices at two altars, instructed erudites to escort the coffin home, issued four hundred taels of silver to his family, and named Song posthumously grand guardian of the heir apparent. Song Xun was honored in the county gazetteer with a biography comparing him with two prime ministers of the Tang and Song dynasties who hailed from the same county.[47]

While fully engaged in a public career, Song Xun had presided over a family that became wealthy and powerful, apparently without being greedy and abusive. He had set the example by traveling with few belongings and contenting himself with one consort with whom he had three sons. One became a tributary student by grace (in other words, because of his father's achievements). He dressed so modestly that people were not aware that he was the son of a minister, reminding a clerk in his father's office of the case of Li Gu, the modest son of a high official of the Latter Han who remained unknown to his father's associates. A grandson, who became a tributary student by favor (another form of hereditary privilege), was reputed to be lenient toward servants, understanding of tenants, and generous to relatives and neighbors. Another grandson took advantage of another hereditary degree to become vice president of the ministry of revenue. He reportedly refused an offer from one of Song Xun's clients to recommend him for a promotion, arguing that he was not the most qualified person for the post. In retirement he became a righter of wrongs, confronting wealthy and powerful families who intimidated their neighbors.[48]

Song Xun's legacy extended to one of the descendants of his father's half-brother, an ordinary farmer who accumulated enough resources to support two wives and four sons, one of whom had progeny who became scholars and officials. This man, Song Yang, carried on the family heritage by being "bright in his studies," energetic in husbandry, and diligent in commerce "in order to support his relatives." He shared his wealth with a younger brother who had squandered his part of the inheritance, and he assisted his wife's relatives in buying coffins for their dead. Song Yang and his wife (née Tian) had two sons; the elder, Zhan, "vowed to carry on the tradition" of his father's cousin, Song Xun. He ceded his share of the family property to his younger brother, lived at a subsistence level, and devoted himself to his studies.[49]

Song Zhan passed the provincial examinations in 1591, the very year Song Xun died, and became magistrate of Fushan county, in Dengzhou prefecture, eastern Shandong. There he succored victims of an epidemic disease, prosecuted local bullies, rectified the land registers, and rationalized taxes. He also revitalized the public school system and conducted judicial inquiries without using torture. Song reimbursed a woman who had spent all of her money to pay the mining tax; he then requested a reduction in the quota. When he got sick, the people of Fushan went to a nearby mountain to conduct sacrifices for him. When he suddenly died, multitudes accompanied his coffin out of Fushan and some reportedly followed it all the way to Shangqiu. While such anecdotes appeared frequently in hagiographies and cannot be taken at face value, Song Zhan seems to have been an honest official who died an untimely death. Sacrifices by the people on his behalf reminded contemporaries of the case of Zhu Yi, a worthy local official during the Latter Han who had received similar expressions of concern from the people. Unlike Song Zhan, that official had recovered, gone on to higher posts, and had eventually been buried in the county where he had served. Despite these differences, Song Zhan's biographer emphasized that the "ancient [Han] and contemporary" officials had both been honored by popular sacrifices while they were alive.[50]

Song Zhan left behind strong survivors bent on perpetuating his legacy. His father, Song Yang, maintained his frugal and modest ways, wearing the same clothes and bowing low even to his juniors. Skeptical of divination, respectful of education, and optimistic that virtue will be rewarded, he could often be found singing under a large locust tree outside the house. When Song Zhan's wife, Zhang, had reached forty without bearing a son, she had encouraged her husband to take a concubine, named Ding. Zhang respected Ding, treated her as a younger sister, and granted her authority over the household. Ding was from a rural household but was considered very capable. Her status in the family was assured when she gave birth to a son, named Quan, in 1598. Upon Zhan's death, lady Ding and her son Quan, aged six, accompanied the coffin for the several hundred li back to Shangqiu. Returning in the midst of a famine, Ding pawned her jewelry, purchased an ox, and put two trusted servants in charge of working the family lands. She turned all income over to Song Yang and his wife and provided them with the expected treats. When Song Zhan's brother died, Ding persuaded his young and childless wife Liu not to commit suicide and welcomed her into her own household.[51]

Song Quan came of age in this supportive environment. As the only son, he was under pressure to fulfill his father's unattained goals, and his mother hired a tutor to prepare him for the examinations. When he fell asleep over his books, his mother and aunt reminded him that they had refrained from committing suicide to assure his success in the world. Quan reportedly redoubled his efforts, cleared his activities with his mother, and accepted her guidance in choosing friends. When he became a government student, his grandfather, Song Yang, now ninety, publicly lauded him and declared him "our next generation." On his deathbed, Song Yang promised that his spirit would be eternally grateful to Ding for raising his grandson so well. When Song Yang died, Ding handled his funeral arrangements as she had those for Song Zhan; her "sister" Zhang; Zhan's mother, Tian; and widow Liu. In the Tianqi reign, Ding and her two "sisters," Zhang and Liu, were honored as "three chaste women in one household."[52]

Song Quan received his provincial degree in 1621 and his metropolitan degree four years later. These achievements naturally enhanced his mother's fame, but she clearly merited all the attention she received. Among other things, Ding continued to advise her son. When he was appointed to his first post as magistrate of Yangqu county, Taiyuan prefecture, Shanxi, she reminded him: "Your father was an honest official and you must keep that legacy in mind." Song Quan demonstrated his uprightness when he refused to erect a shrine to the eunuch Wei Zhongxian at the height of his influence. Although this earned Wei's enmity, Song Quan served in Yangqu for five years, surviving the powerful eunuch's tenure as well as his fall. Unfortunately, Song's biography recorded only that he conducted "an enlightened administration." A biography of his mother specifies that she reprimanded him for taking naps after lunch and setting a bad example for the people, causing him to change his habits. She also reminded him that his father had opposed excessive taxes in Shandong. Song Quan followed that precedent in protesting unwarranted levies in Shanxi. Song honored filial piety in the public domain by paying personal visits to loyal widows and filial sons. He also wrote frank letters to his superiors in Beijing, going so far as to alarm friends in the capital who feared retribution against him and themselves.[53]

Song's outspokenness, while risky under Tianqi, may have benefited his career under Chongzhen. After the transition he was promoted to be a secretary in the ministry of troops. In this post he demonstrated courage by submitting three reports impeaching the minister of personnel. He noted that provincial graduates were being routinely appointed to difficult posts in the countryside while metropolitan graduates were awarded easier jobs in the cities, thus compromising the security of the state. He identified specific instances of nepotism and cronyism that resulted in incompetent officials being given responsibilities they could not fulfill. He justified his open criticism, pointing out that he was merely articulating what others knew but were afraid to say. He mentioned his experience as an orphan raised by two women, perhaps to explain his passion for justice.[54] While the targets of Song's criticism remained anonymous, such abuses were common at the end of the Ming.

Song Quan's critique naturally antagonized the ministry of personnel, and he was soon sent back to Shanxi as surveillance vice commissioner. His mother commented wryly that his sincerity in the capital had won him a post in the provinces. Once again the record yields little about Song Quan's term in Shanxi. We learn only that he soon tired of the post and requested permission to return home "to look after his aging mother."[55] While Song clearly cared for his mother and valued her advice, she appeared to be in excellent health. Looking after her may have been a cover for other activities less acceptable to the state. In any case, his request was granted and he returned to Shangqiu. He built a home in the western suburbs where he planned to spend the rest of his life. In fact, his public career and political activities had scarcely begun.

Meanwhile, Hou Xun, introduced in Chapter 1 as a protégé of Guide prefect Zheng Sanjun, rose to similar distinction in Shangqiu during the late Ming. The founding ancestor of the Hous had come from Xiangfu at the beginning of the dynasty and had been registered as a military household of Guide. The family began its ascent in the sixth generation when Hou Jin took two wives and adopted the courtesy name Zideng (literally, son rising). He had three sons on whom he bestowed names with a common radical.[56] The first son produced a grandson named Zhipu, and the second became a tributary student and fathered a son of his own. The third son, Hou Yu, provided Hou Jin with three more grandsons, Zhigong, Zhizhong, and Zhigao, and a fourth, named Zhigu, by a concubine (see Figure 2.1).[57]

Hou Yu was a precocious child who accompanied adults during their inspections of the family fields and noted details overlooked by others. He learned many characters, assisted in managing the family, and as he grew up was generous in allocating gravesites to relatives. He later instructed his sons and, when his brother died, took responsibility for his nephew. Using agricultural metaphors to express his ambitions, he once reflected:

> I have not been able to weed the classics and plough the histories, but I have sown the seeds and expect to harvest the crops. I am determined to provide the nurturing; the results will appear not now but in my sons' generation.[58]

After Zhigong and Zhipu passed the examinations and became officials, Hou Yu maintained his modest lifestyle. He refused to use government transport to visit his son and rejected a gift of one thousand taels intended to buy leniency from his nephew. Hou Yu provided famine relief to poor clansmen and neighbors and contributed cash for the upkeep of roads, bridges, dikes, and canals. He eschewed the self-satisfied airs of many philanthropists and declined an invitation to the county drinking ceremony on the grounds that his only virtue was in yielding. When he died at age seventy-nine in 1621, he was honored for his son's achievements with the title of Grand Master and the post of administration commissioner. He was also, appropriately, given a biography in the gazetteer celebrating his own "lofty achievements."[59]

Hou Yu served as the key transformer between his family's cultivating past and its

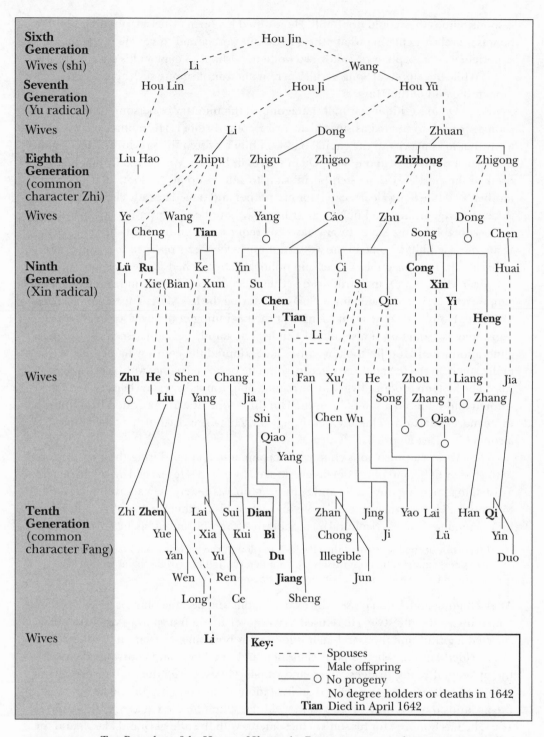

FIGURE 2.1. Two Branches of the House of Shangqiu. Data on spouses and progeny are supplied only for the sixth through ninth generations (with the exception of Li in the tenth generation). Sources: Hou Fangyue 1908; Liu and Ye 1705: 9: 304–6.

cultivated future. In the words of an acquaintance, the prominent Jiangnan scholar-painter Dong Qichang:

> In his concern for cultivation [Hou Yu] resembled Wan Shi Jun, in the extent of his virtue he was like Chen Taiqiu and Wang Yanfang, and in the quality of his family instructions he exceeded Yan Zhitui and Liu Zhongying.[60]

Wan Shi Jun, whose real name was Shi Fen, was an official from Huaiqing prefecture during the Former Han. He held a high post with a salary of two thousand shi and had four sons who became officials with the same salaries, hence the nickname—Ten Thousand Shi Lord—a play on his original name, Shi Fen. It was presumably Hou Yu's residence in Henan and the success of his four "sons" that reminded Dong of Shi Fen. Chen Taiqiu was from Xu, in Kaifeng prefecture, and served as a magistrate in Taiqiu, in Guide prefecture, in the Latter Han. He was famous for his skill in settling local disputes, and a nephew was known for his wisdom in dealing with robbers. It was perhaps Hou Yu's (or his son's) role as a local mediator in Henan that reminded Dong of those earlier figures. In both cases, Dong was almost certainly aware of—if he was not consciously embracing—the Ming conceit to be following the Han model. Yan Zhitui and Liu Zhongying were renowned authors of family instructions in the Six Dynasties, Sui, and Tang. While they had written books to guide their descendants, Hou Yu's words of wisdom were, in Dong's words, "recorded on the tablets in people's mouths."[61]

Zhizhong closely followed his father's personal style, and his biography was appropriately appended to Hou Yu's own. As a boy, he studied diligently and advanced rapidly with his elder brother Zhigong. Wishing to maintain his status as a "poor scholar," however, he stopped taking the examinations. Instead he purchased the status of a "gentleman," became a tributary student by favor, and took a minor post in the court of royal entertainments. Zhizhong apparently devoted most of his life to local and domestic matters, mediating disputes, patronizing public education, and fathering seven sons. His brother Zhigao became a state university student and produced five sons, but a half-brother Zhigu remained a mere government student and had no male progeny, a condition that was becoming exceptional in a clan that was "spreading like a melon plant."[62]

Zhigong and Zhipu fulfilled Hou Yu's ambition for degrees by passing the provincial examinations together in 1588, the first in their lineage to do so. Zhigong obtained his metropolitan degree the following year and was appointed a drafter in the secretariat. In 1597 he presided over the provincial examinations in Sichuan province, then was promoted to be director in the bureau of appointments of the ministry of personnel. When he refused to make appointments in return for gifts, he incurred the wrath of influential office seekers and was transferred to be administration vice commissioner in Huguang. Promoted to surveillance commissioner and then administration commissioner in Sichuan, he was distressed to find funds earmarked for public works going instead to princely estates. Unable to end such practices, he sought early retirement. After serving briefly at the court of royal entertainment in Beijing, he was allowed to return home to Shangqiu. There he "slept with the classics, strolled with the histories," lived like a commoner, and contributed generously to public works.[63]

Hou Zhigong was less successful in his private life. He had two wives but produced with them only one son, who, the editor of the genealogy remarked, demonstrated "courage in righting wrongs and skill in managing finances" but was unable to match his father in "pursuing justice" and ultimately "led his household to ruin." To be sure, that son became a student at the state university, married, and had one son, but he had no grandson. The lack of an heir was remedied by an adoption, but this branch of the Hous was dogged by infertility for the next two generations.[64]

Meanwhile, Zhipu's branch of the family had raised the Hous' fortunes to new heights. Zhipu obtained his metropolitan degree in 1598 and began his career as magistrate in Beizhili, where he provided, in the usual cliché, an "enlightened administration." Seven years later, he was promoted to censor. He reportedly carried out his duties vigorously, impeaching a high official whom the court had exempted from all further criticism. When one of Zhipu's close friends suggested he support the claim of Zheng Guifei's son to be heir apparent, Zhipu upbraided him, exclaiming:

> You were once a mere commoner, worried about how to get wealth and avoid poverty. Through literary talent you came to enjoy a name in the world, but now you propose to depart from the Way. And you want to drag me into the dirty water too?![65]

Opting for principle over friendship, Zhipu ended all contact with that colleague. Zhipu also roiled the court with his outspokenness and was soon sent to be surveillance commissioner in Huguang. Late in the Wanli reign he gave up that post and returned home.

Early in the Tianqi reign, Hou Zhipu was recommended by the chief censor Gao Panlong, a member of the "party of the pure," and was called back to the court to serve as chief minister in the court of the royal stud. He often studied with Gao and was considered to be a leading member of the Donglin party. In 1624 he was transferred to chief minister of the court of royal sacrifices. When the powerful Wei Zhongxian proposed to take the place of the ruler in carrying out the great sacrifices, Hou Zhipu argued that no "eunuch sorcerer" should be allowed near the throne—let alone into the place where the son of heaven maintained contact with the spirits of heaven. Wei was furious and arranged to have Zhipu dismissed. Accepting retirement, Zhipu returned home to Shangqiu.[66]

Hou Zhipu spent the last eighteen years of his life looking after his family, which included four wives. With his primary wife, named Tian, Zhipu had two sons named Xun and Ke, who, like their father and uncle, lived remarkably parallel lives. They were tutored and attended the county school together. In 1611, the Guide prefect Zheng Sanjun invited them to attend the new Fan Wenzheng Academy, where they alternated as first in the class. In 1615 they took the provincial examinations and replicated the earlier feat of their father and uncle by obtaining their degrees in the same year. The following year, Xun won his metropolitan degree; Hou Ke received his degree three years later.[67]

At this point the Hou brothers' careers diverged. Ke was selected as a bachelor in the Hanlin Academy where he lectured the ruler on the classics. Later he was put in charge of compiling the *Veritable Records* of the Wanli and Taichang reigns and served as a court diarist. When the eunuch Wei Zhongxian engineered the downfall of a minister of punishments, Hou Ke boldly recorded it, invoking Zhou models to assert that "the historian's duty is just to tell things straight." Ke openly predicted that Wei Zhongxian would become the "scourge of the elite." Although the actual events were a bit more complicated, with even Donglin members cooperating with *their* eunuch, Ke nonetheless established himself as an outspoken member of the "party of the pure."[68]

Hou Ke was courageous but he also played a few power games of his own. In 1625, as chief examiner in the metropolitan examinations, he passed Song Mei, the ambitious Laiyang man who would serve in northeast Henan before climbing the bureaucratic ladder in Beijing. Hou Ke and Song soon came under attack from Wei Guangwei, a supporter of Wei Zhongxian. Although the charges remain obscure, Hou Ke alluded to them when he acknowledged that pursuing justice was more important than seeking office. But he brushed off the criticism of Song Mei's careerism and defended him on the basis of his "talent." When Wei Zhongxian tried to buy Hou Ke's support by offering him a high post, Ke not only refused the offer but let it be known that he could not serve in high office alongside eunuchs. Wei was incensed. When a fellow townsman of Wei's learned that he was being disparaged in Hou's records, he charged Hou with membership in the Donglin party. In fact, Ke was reputed to have had a hand in drafting Yang Lian's famous memorial charging Wei Zhongxian with twenty-four crimes. Wei therefore arranged an edict dismissing Hou from his post. In frustration Hou agreed to return home quietly. But, addressing twenty-three of his students who gathered to give him a tearful send-off, he warned them that they should no longer try to be good officials but should just try to be good men.[69]

With the fall of Zhipu, Ke, and Xun, the Hous of Shangqiu became even more famous as members of the Donglin party. During the next two years they tended their gardens, wrote poetry, and drank wine, fending off agents of Wei Zhongxian who tried to persuade them to return to the capital. Ignoring his neighbors' concerns about the risks of such defiance, Hou Ke noted that Yang Lian had been killed two years earlier and that he too would be willing to die for the cause.[70] After Tianqi's death in 1627, however, Wei's party fell from power. Within a year, the eunuch and his supporters had retired from office, committed suicide, or suffered execution.

Under Chongzhen, Hou Ke was recalled to the court, first as companion and then as counselor to the heir apparent. Once again he came into conflict with the most powerful court official, now the grand secretary Wen Tiren. Wen was intent on transcending recent partisan battles and asked Hou to treat him positively in the court records. Hou refused and privately compared Wen with the much-criticized mid-Tang officials Li Linfu and Lu Qi. In 1629 Hou was promoted to advise the heir apparent; soon he was transferred to head the university in Nanjing. There he presided over nearly ten thousand students, the largest number to gather since the founding of the dynasty. According to his biography, Hou "used the ancestral system to teach the students and nurtured the spirit of scholarship to replace the quest for office." He criticized administrators who mismanaged the examinations, scholars who refused to change with the times, and opportunists who sought only office and fame. In 1630, leading members of the Donglin-related Restoration Society (Fushe) took top places in the provincial examination in Nanjing. Hou Ke was regarded as one of the society's leading patrons. Soon, however, he fell ill and retired to Shangqiu. He drank heavily and, in 1634, died prematurely at the age of forty-three.[71]

Hou Xun, meanwhile, had pursued his own career, confronting military crises in the provinces and political conflicts in the capital. Starting as a messenger in the ministry of rites, a low-ranked but highly visible entry post, in 1620 he was named an investigating censor and assigned to the Shanxi circuit. He found the northern frontier threatened by raiding Jurchen and proposed methods of supplying and training troops. In 1621 he recommended the appointment of the talented military strategist Yuan Chonghuan, who began concerted efforts to roll back Jurchen power. Hou took the Donglin position on two famous cases related to the death of the short-lived Taichang emperor and the accession of Tianqi. He thereby earned the esteem of the chief censor, Zou Yuanbiao, a leading patron and friend of the Donglin. In 1622, on Zou's recommendation, Hou was named surveillance commissioner of Guizhou province with instructions to put down a rebellion led by a Miao (or Hmong) leader, An Bangyan. Hou went in for an audience and outlined a ten-point plan to restore government control in the southwest. Arriving in Guizhou, he disciplined army officers, lifted the siege of Guiyang, and "pounded the local headmen into submission." He arranged for the reconstruction of the area and returned to Beijing, where he was awarded the noble rank of marquis. Hou was reportedly scheduled for a promotion, but, with the rise of Wei Zhongxian, he was instead dismissed.[72]

With the accession of Chongzhen in 1628, Hou Xun returned to office as a censor. He joined in calling for the punishment of officials and eunuchs who had persecuted the Donglin in the previous reign, thus incurring the enmity of the grand secretary Wen Tiren. In 1629, as Ming forces fell back from the Jurchen advance in the northeast, Hou was promoted to vice minister in the court of the royal stud. In 1630 he moved up to vice president of the ministry of troops. In this post he was responsible for the defense of Changping department, in Shuntian prefecture, which included the tombs of all of the Ming rulers except the founder. In this post, Hou came to rely on Zuo Liangyu, a general whose ability to fight and tendency to disobey were to cause Hou and the Ming much grief in years to come. In this case, Hou and Zuo helped to break the Jurchen siege of Dalinghe, thus defending Songshan and Fushan, outside Shanhaiguan. In 1631 Hou secured the throne's permission to use Portuguese cannon available from Macao. In 1632 he took charge of the armies at Tongzhou, at the head of the Grand Canal east of Beijing.[73]

In 1633, as the Jurchen put increasing pressure on Beizhili and "roving bandits" moved into Henan, Hou Xun was promoted to president of the ministry of revenue. There, as noted in Chapter 1, he faced the task of addressing exploding military expenses without imposing heavy burdens on the people. He used talented people, including Shi Kefa, a scholar-official from Xiangfu, Henan, who would play a key role in the last years of the Ming. Hou also called for the revitalization of the guard-battalion system, including the part funded by merchants, but the basic issue of taxes would not go away. While Hou hoped to lower taxes rather than raising them, many tax surcharges had already been imposed, and the grand secretary Wen Tiren requested more revenues to avoid bankruptcy. In 1635 Hou compromised and agreed to collect all back taxes and sur-charges. In 1636, when prices for food continued to rise, Hou closed the markets tem-porarily to stabilize prices. Later that year, when Hou tried to economize by cutting waste in military supplies, Wen arranged to have a censor charge him with holding up sup-plies for the army and "wronging the state." Hou was dismissed and imprisoned. Some officials advocated the death penalty, and Chongzhen reportedly favored strict pun-ishment, but, as we saw in Chapter 1, Hou Xun's former teacher, Zheng Sanjun, now president of the ministry of punishments, resisted these pressures. As a result, Hou's life was spared but he was consigned to prison where he was to spend the next six years, unable to assist the Ming in its death throes even if he had wanted to.[74]

YONGCHENG

Like the scholars of Shangqiu, those of neighboring Yongcheng were remarkably suc-cessful in obtaining provincial degrees in the late Ming. Their success rate rose from .29 per examination in the early Ming to 1.42 per examination in the late Ming. By the early seventeenth century, Yongcheng produced 16 percent of the total number of provin-cial degrees in Guide prefecture, ranking third behind Shangqiu with 40 percent and Suizhou with 32. Yongcheng made even more dramatic progress in winning metropolitan degrees, moving from none in the early and middle periods to twenty-one in the late Ming. It thus garnered 23 percent of the total, ranking second only to Shangqiu with 25 percent (see Appendixes B and C).

In Yongcheng, too, a handful of families got the lion's share of civil service degrees and gazetteer biographies. Wang Sanshan and his brother won provincial degrees in 1597, and Sanshan went on to earn a metropolitan degree in 1601. He served as a pro-vincial judge and examiner and joined Hou Xun in suppressing the Hmong revolt in Guiyang. Li Zhiyang won his provincial degree in 1603 and his metropolitan degree in 1607. He served in Cao county, Shandong, where he established village schools to teach the "sons and younger brothers of farmers." A second Li was chosen to study in Zheng Sanjun's academy, a third donated 450 mu of land for the repair of the county academy, and a fourth excelled in studies of the *Spring and Autumn Annals* and the *Book of Poetry*. A third local elite family was initiated by Lian Guoshi, who won his provincial degree in 1603 and metropolitan degree in 1616, the same year as Hou Xun. Lian served as a county magistrate and became a censor; he called for a strong defense against the Jurchen and clashed with Wei Zhongxian. As the grand coordinator of Shaanxi province, he failed to suppress banditry. In 1636 he was cashiered and exiled to Guangxi. Like Hou Xun, he was compelled to leave to others the task of looking after the family inter-ests at home.[75]

The most powerful family in Yongcheng in the late Ming were the Dings. The first generation included Ding Mouji, who supported public education and contributed one thousand strings of cash to hire braves to defend the town from bandits, and Ding Mouxun, a government student who built up the family property to six hundred mu, put thirty members of the family through school, and provided one hundred shi of grain to victims of a flood in 1603. Mouxun and a cousin, Moude, purchased places at the state university and thus brought the family to the edge of elite status. Meanwhile Ding Mouji's son, Ding Kuichu, won his provincial degree in 1612 and his metropolitan degree in 1616, the same year as Hou Xun. He served first in the ministry of revenue and in local posts in Beizhili and Shandong. He was promoted in 1632 to grand coordinator of Beizhili and soon thereafter to vice president of the ministry of troops. In 1636, Ding Kuichu failed to resist a Manchu incursion inside the wall and was cashiered and exiled. Although he managed to return from exile two years later, he did not regain a post and spent the next six years at home.[76]

Kuichu's nephew, Qirui, meanwhile, carried on the family tradition of high office. He had won his provincial degree in 1618, taking highest honors, and obtained his metropolitan degree in 1619, the same year as Hou Ke. His official career began inauspiciously. As administration vice commissioner in Shandong he handled a legal case in a way that brought him only a transfer and demotion. Appointed surveillance vice commissioner in Shaanxi, he recovered his reputation by suppressing a mutiny. He was promoted to administration commissioner in charge of the defense of the northern passes of Beizhili. In 1638 he was appointed assistant censor in chief and grand coordinator of Shaanxi with responsibility to suppress roving banditry. In 1640, on the recommendation of supreme commander Yang Sichang, he was named concurrently vice president of the ministry of troops with authority over military affairs on the northern frontier of Shaanxi.[77] Despite repeated setbacks, therefore, the Dings retained much civil and military responsibility as the Ming approached its final years. That responsibility was only to increase in the near future.

In sum, about a half dozen families in Shangqiu and Yongcheng acquired considerable social status and political influence in the late Ming. Most of them had good reason—and were well placed—to defend the dynasty from its opponents. Some of their most prominent members, however, had run into difficulties with the current administration. A few would soon begin to consider political alternatives.

Qi

Back in Kaifeng prefecture, Qi county also produced many members of the local elite in the late Ming. Whereas the county had won only 6 percent of the provincial degrees garnered by the prefecture in the early period and 8 percent in the middle period, it won over 12 percent in the late period. It thus ranked second only to Xiangfu, which remained the front runner with 25 percent. Qi's success in obtaining metropolitan degrees was even greater. Whereas in the early Ming it had obtained only 3.5 percent of the prefectural total and in the middle period only 8 percent, in the late Ming it got 16 percent, challenging leading Xiangfu with 21 percent (see Appendixes B and C). In the late Ming, Qi county also produced the largest number of sons (nine), who were honored with biographies in the provincial gazetteer, surpassing even Xiangfu (with six).[78]

As elsewhere, certain surnames were particularly predominant among the successful examination candidates. Among the thirty-one Qi men who won metropolitan degrees between 1574 and 1643, for example, there were only seventeen different surnames.

In some cases, those with the same surname belonged to the same descent groups, even to the same lineages and families. In other cases the evidence is inconclusive.[79] Among the prominent descent groups were the Lis, Hous, and Mas, who all produced members of the elite; the Mengs and Hes, who produced elite that were politically active; and the Lius, who, while generally less successful in the examinations, managed to produce the top ranking metropolitan graduate (*zhuangyuan*, or optimus) in 1634.

Two of the Lis who won metropolitan degrees in the late Ming were members of a single descent group that traced its ancestry back to the early Ming. The founder had come from Shanxi to Qi county in the Hongwu reign and established his family in Qinglonggang village in the northeastern part of the county. A descendant in the sixth generation became a student in the county school and produced two sons who became students. One of them, Li Donglu, became a tributary student and was the first member of the lineage to enter the elite. Donglu had two sons. The first, Jichun, earned his provincial degree in 1555 and his metropolitan degree the following year. He served as messenger in the ministry of rites, which took him on a mission to the Liuqiu islands. When he returned, Jichun was promoted to assistant in the seal office of the royal household department. He thereafter held a series of posts in the central government, including lecturer on the classics for the ruler. Like many other Henanese, he refused to serve under Zhang Juzheng. Instead he returned to the serenity of his garden pavilion, "Untrammeled Intimacies," where he died in 1583.[80]

Li Mouchun, meanwhile, won his provincial degree in 1579 and his metropolitan degree in 1583. His first post was magistrate in Shaanxi, where he used "the good old methods" to distribute famine relief. He was praised for his achievements but incurred the jealousy of a prefect and was demoted to teacher in Beizhili. After a brief stint as lecturer at the state university, he took charge of prisons in Zhejiang and managed finances in Guangdong. As assistant surveillance commissioner of Shaanxi and military manager for the surveillance commissioner of Shanxi, he repaired two hundred li of the frontier wall, reportedly "saving" fifty thousand taels in the process. As vice administration commissioner of Shanxi, he "recovered" eight thousand mu of pasture land that had been taken over by powerful neighbors. On visits to the capital, Li Mouchun wrote verse criticizing slackness in the administration. Finally, he too retired to his home to tend his flower garden and establish an ancestral shrine.[81]

In the ninth generation, several members of the family continued to uphold its elite status and political profile. Li Laiming obtained his provincial and metropolitan degrees and served as a magistrate in Huguang. When he resisted the demands of royal commissioners, he was criticized in the capital and soon gave up his post and returned home. A cousin, Li Laixuan, became a state university student by grace and gained a reputation as a landscape painter. Another cousin, Li Laibi, earned a provincial degree, and a third, Li Laiqing, married a daughter of the Zhou prince of Kaifeng. A member of the ninth generation, Li Laizhao produced two daughters whom he married to the Anchang and Haiyang princes in Kaifeng. As a result, Li Laizhao himself acquired noble rank and became assistant warden in the town.[82]

Subsequent generations of the Lis of Qinglonggang produced a few students but no members of the elite. For example, the tenth and eleventh generations of this branch included twenty-four students at the county, prefectural, and capital levels, a few of whom became teachers and painters of note, but none became tributary students or provincial graduates. Other branches had far fewer students.[83] Like the Shens of Shangqiu, the Lis of Qi had reached their peak in the Wanli reign, and they suffered considerable decline during the last decades of the dynasty.

The Hous of Qi county had a longer history and produced more members of the elite in the late Ming. This lineage had originated in Nanzhili in the late Yuan and had begun its ascent in the fifth generation with a member who educated his sons "to recompense the reigning sage king" by serving in office. That man's grandsons included a state university student, a popular teacher, a secretary in the Royal Academy of Medicine, and a metropolitan graduate. The graduate, Hou Yuzhao, became a major official in the Wanli reign who sided with Pan Jixun against Zhang Juzheng on river work but attempted to carry out Zhang's land equalization scheme in Shanxi, where it was reportedly popular. In the eighth generation, another metropolitan graduate reformed the granaries of the Su-Song circuit in Nanzhili, and a provincial graduate, Hou Yingyu, dealt with disease, famine, and banditry in the Taian department in Shandong. Yingyu criticized powerful eunuchs as "earringed elements," a pejorative allusion to the eunuchs of the late Han. Another metropolitan graduate in this generation stockpiled grain in Beizhili and wrote ancient-style poetry, while another provincial graduate, Hou Yinglin, declined office and became famous for his calligraphy in the style of the Jìn master Wang Xizhi. The Hous, like the Lis, produced fewer scholar-officials during the last reigns of the Ming but, with a longer history and more graduates, they were in a stronger position to weather political change.[84]

An even more venerable and accomplished lineage in Qi county were the Mas, who arrived from Shandong in the Yongle reign. They produced government students in the second generation and tributary students in the third, and, after an unexplained gap in the records, continued their upward climb in the sixth through eighth generations. In the ninth generation, the Mas reentered the elite when Ma Zhichi passed the provincial examinations in 1630 and Ma Zhifou became a tributary student by grace. In the same generation, Ma Zhifei, although a mere government student, developed a distinctive literary style and was active in poetry societies. In the tenth generation, Ma Chengde earned his metropolitan degree in 1631 and served in central and local government posts before dying prematurely in office. Ma Qi in the same generation had broad interests in literature, painting, and seals and passed the last Ming provincial examination in 1642. In addition, two dozen government students were poised to take further examinations as the Ming neared its end.[85]

While the Hous and Mas emphasized culture, the Mengs and Hes stressed politics. The Mengs could trace their lineage all the way back to Mengzi (Mencius), but they took as founder a member of the fifty-first generation who had come to Kaifeng city from Zou county in Shandong at the beginning of the Ming. During a flood in the Hongwu reign, the patriarch had left Kaifeng and made his way to Qi county, where he established himself southwest of the town. A descendant in the fifth generation had two sons who headed two branches of the family, which accumulated some wealth and status. The first acknowledged scholar was Meng Nan, in the eighth generation, who was selected as the top student in the county. He subsequently became a tributary student at the state university, spent time at the Da Liang Academy in Kaifeng, and in 1613 embarked on a career as a local official. As assistant instructor in Tangyi county, Shandong, he refused gifts and administered famine relief with particular concern for women and the elderly. As magistrate of Xiajin county in the same province, he established forty-nine congé stations to save the lives of tens of thousands during a famine. As magistrate of Xing ji county, Beizhili, he opened up lands for the landless, enforced discipline among soldiers, and reformed the transport system. One of Meng Nan's reports was so effective in moving higher officials to action that his biographer compared it with a famous memorial by Zheng Xia in the Northern Song. While apparently honest, Meng Nan was also prosperous. He had four consorts with whom he produced nine sons. When he retired, he devoted himself to teaching his sons and grandsons and the youth of other elite families.[86]

Meanwhile, the cousins Shaoyi and Shaokang in the ninth generation became provincial graduates in 1600. Shaoyi held modest posts in the provinces and in the capital, and was given a short biography as an accomplished official in the county gazetteer. Shaokang went on to secure his metropolitan degree in 1613, ranking 140th in the third class (see Figure 2.2). He began his career as a county magistrate and then took charge of the schools in Yangzhou, where he reportedly forbade the big salt merchant families from lavishing their accustomed gifts on examiners. In 1615 he tested scholars in Shanxi and was promoted to secretary—and then director—of a bureau in the ministry of troops in Nanjing. There he reportedly refused gifts offered by officers seeking promotions. As a result, when Shaokang became ill and retired, "his purse contained no excess funds." After Shaokang died, people praised his integrity and the gazetteer accorded him a biography under the category of "sincere actions."[87] While Meng Shaokang may well have been an honest official, his family was becoming both wealthy and powerful.

In the same generation, Meng Nan's son Shaoyu also joined the elite (see Figure 2.3). Born in 1580, Shaoyu earned his provincial degree in 1603, three years after his cousins got theirs, and his metropolitan degree in 1613, the same year Shaokang obtained his. Like Shaokang, Shaoyu was originally registered in Xiangfu, suggesting that the Mengs enjoyed close links with Kaifeng city. Although Shaoyu did not do as well in the metropolitan examination as his cousin, he was selected as a bachelor in the Hanlin Academy and became senior head of the household administration of Wanli's heir apparent. According to his biography in the county gazetteer, he rebuffed Cui Chengxiu, a leading supporter of the eunuch Wei Zhongxian. As a result, he came under close scrutiny and was soon obliged to ask for a leave. But finally his request was refused and he was instead promoted to vice president of the ministry of rites. Meng Shaoyu thus held high office under Wei Zhongxian, despite his biographer's best efforts to obscure that fact. With the accession of Chongzhen, Meng became a lecturer in the classics colloquium. He was soon promoted to president of the ministry of rites, served concurrently in the Hanlin Academy, and secured the throne's approval of dozens of projects. According to his biographer, however, he became disillusioned with continuing strife at court and asked to retire. The disaffection, apparently, was mutual, for his request was quickly approved. Having served when Wei Zhongxian was in ascendance, Meng Shaoyu retired

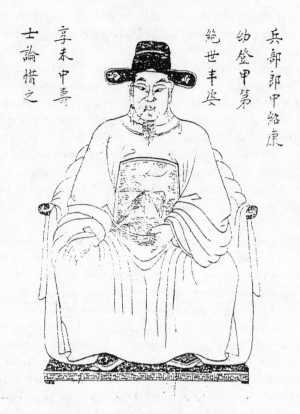

FIGURE 2.2. Director of the Ministry of Troops [Meng] Shaokang. The encomium reads: "In his youth attained the highest degree, a paragon of beauty; in his life did not reach middle age, an object of pity." Source: Meng 1990: 1: zhifang gong xiang. Used with permission of Henan University.

when his opponents returned to power. Not surprisingly, therefore, Meng would later appear on the Donglin and Fushe list of "eunuch officials."[88]

During the following decade in Qi, Shaoyu manifested ambivalence on several fronts. Finding some poor members of his descent group unable to conduct proper ceremonies, he set aside one thousand mu of land to provide rent to cover the cost. He reported in an essay that he had wanted to establish such a foundation ever since obtaining his metropolitan degree in 1613 but had needed all available resources to support himself and his immediate family. Only after holding high office in the Tianqi and early Chongzhen reigns had he acquired sufficient means to address the needs of his less fortunate relatives. Even then, he was not sure that he would be able to afford this project in the future, so he called the lands "intended (*yi* 意) fields" instead of (the usual) "charity (*yi* 義) fields." If in two decades the lands were still being used to assist needy kin, he wrote, they could be renamed "charity fields".[89] In a sense, Shaoyu was realistically describing a project that might not prove feasible, but he was also signaling that his effort to assist poor relatives was only provisional.

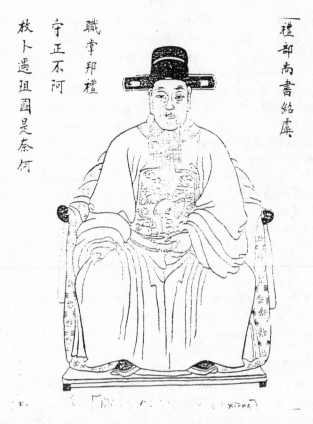

FIGURE 2.3. President of the Ministry of Rites [Meng] Shaoyu. The encomium reads: "Charged with keeping the rites of the state, he served as Guardian of Rectitude and refused to toady; in casting lots for office he encountered obstacles, leaving the state without remedies." Source: Meng 1990: 1: zongbo gong xiang. Used with permission of Henan University.

Meng Shaoyu exhibited equal ambiguity when he took over dozens of thatched houses outside the west gate of Qi to establish a Society to Solicit Literature. The purpose of the society was ostensibly to prepare young men for the examinations, but it met "even during emergencies" and may well have harbored larger political goals.[90] The Mengs actively defended the county town from banditry during the 1630s. In another essay, Meng Shaoyu noted that when banditry had broken out in villages and market towns in the Zhengde and Jiajing reigns, magistrates had considered strengthening the stamped-earth wall but had not wanted to burden the people with the labor. In 1628, however, magistrate Song Mei had decided that the county could afford the necessary several tens of thousands of taels, and he apportioned the burden among the major surnames according to the amount of land they possessed. The work had continued under Song's successor from 1632 to 1635.

In early 1635, before the work was completed, roving bandits attacked the town. Arriving suddenly on horseback, they breached the shallow moats, overwhelmed the guards at the gates, and penetrated inside the walls. A new magistrate, Shen Jiayin from

Beizhili, personally led the defense of the north gate and offered five hundred taels to residents who helped kill the attackers. Meng Shaoyu used his own money to hire braves to resist the onslaught. By such measures, the magistrate and the local elite succeeded in repelling the attack, but only with the loss of much life and property. Aware that government troops had abused the populace during the defense and fearing that the mounted bandits would return, magistrate Shen and metropolitan graduate Meng rallied members of the local elite to repair the walls and moats and prepare for another assault. Using the Han-period name for Qi county, Meng called for "firming up the local elite of Yu" and emphasized that "the hearts and minds of the masses were the most effective wall." He recommended that the big surnames already identified under magistrate Song be divided into three ranks—large, medium, and small—and assessed according to their landholdings in silver and copper to cover the expenses of strengthening the remaining 1,300 zhang of the wall.[91]

These efforts paid off when the town faced a different kind of uprising three years later. Again it was Meng Shaoyu who provided the most detailed account, revealing his continuing preoccupation with security. According to him, in 1638 when people were suffering from locusts and famine, a "crazy boy," styling himself a *shibazi* (十八子, literally, "ten eight son" or "eighteenth son," three characters that may be combined to form the family name Li 李), declared that all who believed in him would survive. Large numbers of people followed the young lad in a march on the county town and conspired to revolt with "riffraff and youths" within the walls. A new magistrate, Su Jing, rallied the population to defend the walls and ordered his troops to attack the rebels. Those who were hit were summarily killed and those who fled were tracked down. Many were caught by their white sashes and tassles, dragged into a pile, and clubbed to death. In all, several thousand were killed. Meng was contemptuous of the mere boy who issued "fallacious books" and "presumed to rebel against heaven," and he compared the magistrate Su with enlightened monarchs of the past who defended the rule of law. He nonetheless described the social causes and bloody consequences of the rebellion in a way that suggested some sympathy for the poor of Qi, caught between death by starvation and slaughter at the hands of the state. Meng noted that the sequence of events had been captured in verse and relayed through the countryside. Although the purpose of such publicity was presumably to discourage popular uprisings, its effect was also to highlight the failure of the state to alleviate the hardship of the masses and its ruthlessness in suppressing challenges to its authority.[92]

Other members of Meng Shaoyu's immediate family were also politically active. A younger brother who was said to be skilled in riding and shooting obtained a military provincial degree in 1630. Two sons became students at the county school. One of them, Jiongsu, was capable and resourceful, knowledgeable about military strategy, and skilled with the bow. In 1639 he passed the civil provincial examinations with the second highest grade, but he then decided to "abjure the common ambition of contemporaries" (in other words, to obtain the metropolitan degree). In this respect, Jiongsu may have been representative of his peers. While two Qi men had won provincial degrees in 1636 and four obtained them in 1639, not a single Qi man earned a metropolitan degree in

1637 or in 1640, the first time in nearly a century that Qi men had failed to gain a single such degree in two successive examinations. While there is an explanation for this quite apart from growing elite alienation from the Ming, it may also reflect increasing elite attention to political alternatives. Whatever his motivation, Meng Jiongsu apparently devoted his energies to the local activities already initiated by his father. The gazetteer included his short biography as an appendix to Shaoyu's own in the section on "meritorious activities."[93]

When Meng Jiongsu earned his provincial degree in 1639, he shared top honors with He Yinguang, scion of another prominent family of Qi. According to their genealogy, the Hes could trace their ancestry back to the Warring States period, but this branch more realistically claimed descent from a metropolitan graduate at the end of the Yuan. Escaping the disorders of that time, the patriarch had made his way first to Xiayi county and then, during a famine in 1374, to Qi. Subsequent generations "farmed and read," gradually accumulating enough wealth and status to become a "large household if not yet a great clan." In the fifth generation, the Hes began to adopt courtesy names.[94]

In the seventh generation, He Dengshan established the material foundations of the family. According to his biography, Dengshan was very young when the family property was divided. He therefore got little and suffered during a famine. His mother took pity on him and gave him one hundred taels, which he promptly shared with his older brothers. Dengshan worked hard raising vegetables, fruits, mulberries, and livestock and gradually purchased some land. But it was not by hard work alone, we may suspect, that he accumulated thousands of mu and "increased the family wealth several tens of times in less than a decade." Although his biography does not mention it, Dengshan must have been engaged in a fair amount of trade, money lending, and perhaps even land speculation to multiply his assets so rapidly. Some of Dengshan's wealth may also have followed rather than preceded the success of his offspring. Whatever the sources of his fortune, his biographers insist that he continued to live frugally and shared his wealth with relatives and friends.

He Dengshan used part of his wealth to support budding scholars, who of course could be good investments. When Meng Shaoyu was a government student, Dengshan provided him with lodgings. He waited until Meng became vice president of a ministry before collecting the rent. After a provincial graduate failed the metropolitan examinations, He gave him free room and board so that he could afford to prepare to retake the examinations. He extended loans to other scholars and never asked for repayment, even after they passed the examinations. He also spent his money on public works, including five hundred taels of silver and eight hundred shi of grain to help defend the town from the rebels in 1635. He was honored by the magistrate for such activities and even offered a judgeship in the guards in Beijing. He declined the post and died at age eighty-two.[95]

He Dengshan had married a woman named Ma with whom he had two sons, Chengxiang and Dongsheng. Curiously, these sons did not share a character or even a radical in their personal names, perhaps reflecting a lack of family consciousness. There

are other oddities in the records regarding these brothers. According to the genealogical table, Chengxiang became a government student while Dongsheng attained no student or degree status at all. Yet Dongsheng's biographies in the genealogy and in the
1693 and 1788 editions of the Qi county gazetteer described him as having been a
student in Guide prefecture and a tributary student, although with no indication of
time or place. In fact, Dongsheng may have spent some time as a youth in Guide, but
according to an autobiography by one of his sons in the family genealogy, he was registered in Qi, where he became a tributary student in 1642. According to this source,
Dongsheng was appointed an assistant instructor in Yangwu the following year.[96] In a
further wrinkle, the 1693 Qi gazetteer, edited by one of Dongsheng's sons, contained
a biography of Dongsheng; but the 1788 edition, edited by others, dropped most of that
biography. These anomalies suggest the possibility—perhaps even the likelihood—of
different efforts to disassociate Dongsheng from Qi and obscure his role at the end of
the Ming.

Such efforts may have resulted from Dongsheng's activities and those of his progeny. Long before 1642, he had taken three consorts and produced five sons. These sons
all shared the character *guang* (bright) in their personal names, but only the eldest,
Yinguang, shared the character *yin* (to inherit) with his cousins. This suggests a growth
in lineage consciousness but some inconsistency in the choice of names to reflect it. As
noted above, He Yinguang had won his provincial degree in 1639 with the second highest grade in his category. His poetry came to the attention of the regional inspector,
Gao Mingheng, and he was admired by two senior scholars, Wang Duo, from Mengjin
county, Henan prefecture, and Xue Suoyun, from Meng county, Huaiqing prefecture.[97]
Unlike his classmate Meng Jiongsu, He Yinguang planned to pursue the usual goals of
a metropolitan degree and an official post. Like Meng, however, He was destined to
play an unconventional political role as the Ming entered its final years.

Meanwhile, one of He Yinguang's grandfather's clients, the scholar Liu Lishun, also
became prominent toward the end of the Ming, first for his scholarship and then for
his politics. Liu issued from a much less important descent group, whose founder had
migrated from Shanxi to Henan at the beginning of the Ming. One of the patriarch's
sons had established residence in Weichuan county and another had moved on to Qi
and settled in Da Liuzhaizhuang. In the next generation, the Weichuan man's son also
moved to Qi and settled in Xihuayuanpu. In the sixth generation, a great grandson took
charge of food at the Zhou prince's establishment in Kaifeng. He had five sons whose
names were coordinated among themselves and with their cousins, suggesting growing lineage consciousness. The third son contributed grain to the state, became a minor
functionary, and had two sons. One of them, Qingyuan, studied the *Spring and Autumn
Annals* and came in first in the county and prefectural examinations. He failed the provincial examinations and became a tributary student. He then failed the routine examination that would have enabled him to hold office. Instead he made his living as a tutor.
Qingyuan had two sons, Dashun and Xingshun, by his first wife, and two more, Xiang-
shun and Lishun, by his third wife.

Liu Lishun was born in 1581, the year of his father's death. He was therefore an
"orphan" in an ambitious but ill-fated family. His eldest brother studied but failed the

upper-level examinations. The second brother became embroiled in litigation with other members of the family and had to sell off most of his inheritance to pay his debts. Lishun's mother, who became known as Dan Anren (or tranquil person Dan), organized the women of the family to spin and weave but was barely able to support her kin. As the genealogy put it, after the clerks collected the taxes there was often nothing left to eat. Aware of his mother's distress, Lishun was said to have promised her that he would study hard like the semilegendary Su Qin of the Warring States period who pricked himself with an awl to stay awake when doing his lessons. Lishun entered school at age fourteen and became a government student at seventeen. At some point, the four brothers scattered, with two living in two separate villages in Qi, a third in neighboring Tongxu county, and Lishun in the ancestral home of Weichuan. After becoming a government student, Lishun moved back to Qi and established himself in Guanhuayuan. In 1606, at age thirty-five, he earned his provincial degree with an essay on the *Book of Odes*. When he returned home to sweep his father's grave, his mother professed to be happy for the first time in her life.[98]

Liu Lishun's worries were not over, however, for the following year he failed the metropolitan examination. Although he might have settled for an educational post or some other modest office in order to support his family, he was determined to get the highest degree and continued studying full-time. Three years later he failed the examinations again, but defeat only hardened his determination, and he resolved to continue studying until he got the highest degree. Unfortunately for Liu, he would fail the examinations six more times over the next two decades while his family continued to suffer many hardships. One of his nephews died while still a student, and his wife committed suicide. Another nephew failed the examinations and retreated into self-cultivation; a third studied hard but died young, and his wife lost her will to live and died, too. When these deaths left one brother without an heir, Lishun arranged for him to adopt another brother's second son. Meanwhile, Lishun had married, but his wife died, and the funeral further depleted his resources. Liu himself took to a sickbed for several years and was unable to care for his elderly mother, who died in 1625.[99]

At this point, Liu was rescued by He Dengshan, whom he had met at a funeral when he was still a government student. After Liu passed the provincial examinations, he frequented He's house and came to know him well. Despite the difference in their ages and Liu's repeated failures in the metropolitan examinations, Liu retained He's patronage. From him he received access to old books needed in his studies, help with his wife's funeral expenses, a place in which to marry off his eldest daughter, a room in which to study without interruption, quarters in which to live rent-free with a second wife, and a coffin and guarantee of funeral expenses when he was suffering from consumption and seemed on the verge of death. Liu openly attributed his eventual recovery to He's generous assistance.[100]

During the early years of preparation for the metropolitan examinations, Liu was tutored by Luo Wenying, a fellow Qi man, client of He Dengshan, and metropolitan graduate. After Luo died in 1622, Liu taught himself and corresponded with other scholars. He also consolidated his knowledge by tutoring his eldest son, Shengzhen, who passed the provincial examinations in 1630. The following year father and son went to Beijing to take the metropolitan examinations, but they both failed. In 1634, they tried again. This time Lishun finally succeeded, on his tenth attempt, although Shengzhen failed.[101]

When the results of the metropolitan examination appeared, some officials recommended that someone else be selected as the top scholar. But the examiner, who was from Zouping, Shandong, and had once served in Henan, put forth Liu Lishun's name. Other unspecified "men from the central province" supported Liu's candidacy, arguing that he was a model of persistence. According to one account, Chongzhen disliked the literature of the day and was looking for a "great scholar of the school of *li* (pattern)" who would serve as an example for others. He therefore decided on Liu Lishun and announced to the court: "Today we have obtained a venerable gentleman of virtuous conduct." Thus, at age fifty-three, after almost three decades of effort, Liu Lishun finally became the first optimus from Qi county in almost two hundred years.[102]

From 1635 to 1639, Liu Lishun held a variety of academic posts in the central government. He began, as many top graduates did, in the Hanlin Academy. As a senior compiler, he helped collate texts such as the *Seven Military Classics*, the writings of the Cheng brothers of the Northern Song, and the *Collected Statutes of the Ming*. He also lectured at the classics colloquium, where he had direct access to the throne. After Chongzhen's first son, Cilang, reached the age of eight in 1637, Liu served concurrently as advisor to him. He thus played a role in the Chongzhen reign remarkably similar to Shen Li's role in the Wanli reign. By 1639, Liu was director of studies in Nanjing, where he influenced young scholars and helped supervise the examinations. During these years, Liu frequently attended royal audiences and influenced the formulation of policy. Yet he reportedly remained unassuming, took good care of his family, and welcomed visitors graciously.[103]

Liu took advantage of academic posts in the two capitals to express himself on philosophy. His courtesy name, Fuli (return to the rites), was taken from Kongzi's *Analects*, and he espoused Kongzi's view that the ancient dynasties of Xia, Shang, and Zhou provided the basic models of good government.[104] His personal name, Lishun, meant "to accord with the pattern," an allusion to one of the most important concepts of the Cheng-Zhu school, which was orthodox in the Ming. As one would expect of someone intent on passing the civil service examinations, Liu's thought was quite orthodox, but it was also quite broad. In his essays he cited Han theorists, such as Jia Yi and Dong Zhongshu, and he invoked Ming scholars, such as Xue Xuan and Wang Yangming. He admired the statecraft tradition of Shao Yong, the Northern Song scholar whose writings had been omitted from the canon by Zhu Xi and whose numerology was rejected by Wang Tingxiang. He acknowledged the contributions of Wang Yangming at a time when some members of the Donglin and Fushe were rejecting the thought of Wang's radical followers. Unlike Tang and Song thinkers who had traced the departure from the Way to the Qin and Han, Liu admitted the Han dynasty into the pantheon of political orders that deserved the respect of later ages. As he put it in one essay, one should pursue the ideals of the predynastic sages Yao and Shun in order to replicate the achievements of Tang, Wu, and the Han.[105]

Indeed, in essays over the years, Liu Lishun frequently expressed his admiration for the Han and insisted on its relevance to the Ming. On a visit to the Taishan temple in Shandong, he wrote "Two Items on the Comprehensive Mirror" in which he described the place of Kongzi's thought in history. The first essay focused on the role of civil officials like himself. Alluding to the famous aphorism attributed to Lu Jia by the historian Sima Qian, Liu pointed out that Han Gaozu had founded his dynasty on horseback but had ruled it with the assistance of scholars. Whereas the Qin had fallen after burning books and burying scholars, the Han had respected virtue and delighted in the Way, consequently lasting four centuries. In Liu's view, there was a "necessary" connection between the way of ruling and the longevity of the order. Pointing to implications for the Ming, he asserted: "Our dynasty has respected the rites even more than the Han did." From the sage ancestor who founded the dynasty through his successors who presided over the examination system, the Ming had put aside extravagant forms of poetry and emphasized simple, classical values. By reading the classics and examining the histories, the present ruler could select the talented and govern the world.[106]

Liu's second essay, focusing on military officers, invoked the Western Han's use of the capable general Zhou Yafu. Although Zhou was so powerful that he became a virtual hegemonist, Han Wendi used him effectively against the Xiongnu, and Jingdi relied on him to suppress the rebellion of the seven princes. Zhou Yafu was eventually arrested for corruption and died in prison, but Liu did not mention those facts. He wished to emphasize instead that since the Western Han, "respecting generals became a rite." In Liu's view, the Ming founder had observed this rite by trusting his generals, establishing a hereditary military elite, regulating military conduct, and demonstrating that "neither rites nor laws should be used onesidedly." By the Chongzhen reign, however, the Ming military had deteriorated. Officials did not trust military subordinates but hamstrung them with regulations. "Orphan generals" plundered the populace to supply their troops and decapitated people to get rewards. In short, Liu wrote, "Today's generals are different from those of ancient [Han] times and of the early Ming." Since the supervising officials were also below standard, he recommended the appointment of a single effective civilian commander in chief to make decisions and control the generals. In Liu's words, "Han Wen[di] used this method covertly; we can use it openly."[107]

Liu reportedly exemplified the ruist principle of maintaining harmonious relations with others. Some said he aspired to become a prime minister, but one of his descendants observed that Liu was never employed as a minister or grand secretary, let alone as chief grand secretary. Instead he had to compromise with chief grand secretaries such as Wen Tiren. Although Liu obtained his metropolitan degree and held his first posts under Wen, he seldom agreed with him or his supporters on policy. But because Chongzhen was intent on ending partisan conflict, Liu, unlike the Hous of Shangqiu, avoided confronting Wen. Liu was no closer to the next chief grand secretary Xue Guoguan. In 1638, Yang Sichang became grand secretary and president of the ministry of troops; the following year he was named supreme commander in north China. Yang had precisely the civilian background and military authority that Liu had prescribed to the court. Like many other Henanese, however, Liu believed that Yang's large armies and heavy surtaxes were just as threatening to local and dynastic interests as the Jurchen forces and roving bandits against whom they were raised. Liu repeatedly impeached Yang, persisting even when Yang tried to interfere with his activities at court.[108]

In March 1639, as the Ming suffered defeats by Manchus in the northeast and rebels in the northwest, Liu drafted a memorial outlining six recommendations. Since the people were becoming disaffected, officials needed to fortify the spirits of local leaders so that they would remain loyal to the state. Tax relief, food, and medicine should be supplied to survivors of assaults in towns and villages and stockpiled to prepare defenses against future attacks. Good officials should be selected and required to go to their posts to look after the common people. Armies should be disciplined to end plunder and increase their effectiveness against real opponents. Local officials who defended their towns should be promoted rapidly while those derelict in their duties should be punished severely. Finally, those who had been misled and coerced into joining rebellion should be accorded amnesty if they atoned for their errors. While Liu's recommendations were quite conventional and general, they frankly addressed current conditions and accurately anticipated future calamities.[109]

In a second memorial, entitled "A Report Respectfully Setting Forth What Was Not Discussed," Liu suggested an alternative to Yang Sichang's plan to raise large armies to confront opponents. Liu expressed anger that, while the ruler was upright, those who were supposed to serve him at court and in the country frequently lacked talent. The main problem was in motivation. "East, west, south, and north are not being transformed," he wrote, "because wealth, status, and fame are insufficient goals." Noting that the "indolent and useless allow rebel leaders to escape," he stated: "I want all officials to wash their minds and hearts and purify their motives so as to join together to sweep the land clean." Citing numerous military abuses—including the focus on salaries, changing orders, feigning compliance, and killing innocents—Liu called for the establishment of an "outstanding official" to supervise the transfer of troops from the frontier to the interior. Strongly implying that Yang Sichang was not such an official, Liu argued for raising local militia. To provide armies with supplies unavailable in the devastated countryside, the ruler should abjure banquets and finery until the end of the emergency.[110]

Liu lacked the influence necessary to gain acceptance for his recommendations, but he was free to expatiate on the place of the late Ming in the larger pattern of Chinese history. In an essay entitled "In Reading History We Must Look for the Origins of Order and Chaos," he remarked that "good government and disorder evolve in cycles." While he pitched that essay at a high level of generality, he made specific references in other works to historical personalities and events, many of them drawn from the early Han. In a funeral ode, he compared a contemporary scholar with Jia Yi, one of the leading ideologues of the early Western Han. In an essay on the examination system, he invoked Dong Zhongshu, the leading *rujia* scholar and official in Han Wudi's reign. In a congratulatory poem to a contemporary general, he alluded to the example of Zhang Qian, the commander who extended Western Han frontiers into the western regions. In a piece on the need for fiscal parsimony, he invoked the example of Bu Shi, a rich but generous farmer of Henan who contributed large sums to the Han's efforts to resist frontier incursions and to provide relief to the poor. In a funerary ode, he compared his patron He Dengshan with Fan Li, a wealthy merchant of the central state of Tao cel-ebrated by the Han-period Sima Qian as a model philanthropist.[111]

Liu Lishun also cited exemplary figures from the late Western Han and Eastern Han. In another funerary inscription, Liu compared a contemporary magistrate of Wutai county, Shanxi, with one Wang Zun, a model official of the late Western Han who hailed from Gaoyang, a region that later became part of Qi county. Liu compared Li Yutian, a magistrate of Qi in the 1630s, who later became grand coordinator of Beizhili, with Kou Xun, who pacified Henei for Guangwu, the founder of the Eastern Han. As mag-istrate of Yingchuan, just east of Henan, Kou was so popular that the inhabitants blocked the streets to prevent his transfer. In a piece on Shen Jiayin, another Qi magistrate, Liu made another allusion to the Han age.[112]

Liu also invoked exemplars from later periods. In two pieces on literature, he referred to Han and Wei standards that, he thought, the Ming had surpassed. In an essay on taxes, he mentioned both Han and Tang practices, with special attention to the reforms of Liu Yan of the Tang. In the essay on General Zhou Yafu, Liu also praised the Tang general Li Guangbi and the Ming general Xu Da for their ability to maintain discipline. In praising a fellow metropolitan graduate, Liu invoked the literary standards of the Western Han and the Northern Song. In his preface to a work by Zhang Jinyan, a fel-low metropolitan graduate from Xinxiang county, Weihui prefecture, Liu asserted that the reports it contained "were close to the sayings of Lu Jia [of the Western Han] and the writings of Donglai [Lü Zuqian of the Southern Song]."[113] To see why, we must turn to the role of that scholar-official in the late Ming.

Weihui: Xinxiang

Weihui prefecture, with only six counties, was the smallest of the three prefectures of northeast Henan and it produced the fewest local elite during the Ming. It obtained 6 percent of the metropolitan degrees of the region in the first century, increased its share to 12 percent in the second century, and fell back to only 9 percent in the last seventy years of the dynasty. Weihui's percentage of provincial degrees was equally modest, ris-ing only slightly in the second period and declining during the third. The fortunes of Xinxiang county within Weihui prefecture also fluctuated, rising from third to second place in the number of metropolitan degrees, and declining from second to third place in the number of provincial degrees (see Appendixes B and C). Nonetheless, Xinxiang was the home of Zhang Jinyan, who played a key role at the end of the Ming and whose family genealogy and official reports are available.

According to the genealogy, the Zhang patriarch arrived from Shanxi in the Yongle reign, settled in Songfo (Song Buddha) village, and became a respected elder honored at the county drinking ceremony. Over the next thirteen generations, the Zhangs remained based in Songfo village, providing a remarkable contrast to the more peri-patetic Lius of Qi. They apparently flourished through some combination of farming, study, and trade. In the sixth generation, Zhang Jinjian participated in the drinking cer-emony and married a woman named Guo. Since one set of Guos constituted the most prominent descent group in the county, this marriage may have assisted the Zhangs in their rise to elite status. In the tenth generation, Zhang Deng, nicknamed "Songfo Zhang," became famous for mediating among his neighbors. A popular saying was "people did not fear the law courts; they feared only his pure justice." Deng contributed to the repair of the Kongzi temple and the local school, won honor at the drinking ceremony, and received a tablet recognizing his "broad learning." He had two sons, Wenren (ask for humaneness) and Wenming (ask for brightness).[114]

In 1627 Zhang Wenren became a tributary student and entered the local elite. He soon came to the attention of the president of the ministry of troops, Li Hualong, from nearby Changyuan county, in Beizhili. Li described Wenren as a "great man of He and Luo," apparently referring simultaneously to his Song learning and his Henan origins. Appointed assistant instructor in the ruist school in Taikang county, Kaifeng prefecture, Wenren contributed funds to repair the literary temple, maintain ritual artifacts, and support needy students. When roving bandits besieged the town, he kept prominent families from fleeing and led students in the defense. Dressed in riding breeches and wielding short swords, they mounted the walls, drew their bows, and fired cannons to drive off the attackers. Wenren even appropriated the magistrate's seals and hunted down traitors, reportedly winning praise from the people as a "bright spirit."

Promoted to instructor in Wuzhi county, Huaiqing prefecture, Zhang Wenren led his students in demanding the punishment of a provincial commander who had long terrorized the town. His success sent tremors to the provincial capital. Wenren used his family's resources to construct a bridge over the Qin River without demanding heavy labor from his neighbors; grateful residents constructed a shrine in his honor. Wenren was promoted to prefectural judge in Beizhili, but, noting the ancient retirement age of seventy, he soon quit that post. At home in Xinxiang, he distributed grain to victims of famine and plague and enlisted the cooperation of large descent groups in bricking the county wall. In 1639 he was ordered to take charge of fortifying the towns of Henan north of the Yellow River. After his death, he was awarded honorary posts and titles and included in the county shrine to local worthies.[115]

Wenren's achievements may have facilitated the marriages of his progeny to Guo women in the next two generations. Wenren's youngest son and Wenming's second and third sons married Guos (in other words, three of the eight male offspring in the twelfth generation). Three of the eleven Zhangs in the thirteenth generation also married Guos. They included the only son of Wenren's eldest son (the main line of the senior branch) and the elder son of Wenming's eldest son (the main line of the junior branch of the family).[116]

In addition to marrying well, the Zhangs continued to seek degrees and offices. Wenren's first son was selected as a tributary student in 1634 and served as an assistant instructor in a county school. The second son purchased the status of tributary student and became director of an office in the court of royal entertainment. The third, named Jinyan, benefited from his father's instruction to obtain the provincial degree in 1621 and the metropolitan degree in 1631.[117] In so doing he secured the family's place among the local elite of Xinxiang.

Zhang Jinyan was first posted as a county magistrate in Yan'an prefecture, northern Shaanxi, where he confronted frontier raids and rural banditry. He apparently performed well and was soon promoted to magistrate of a county in Xi'an prefecture, southern Shaanxi. In this post he used mountain streams to irrigate one thousand mu of land and he raised militia to suppress banditry. In 1637 he was recommended for appointment in Beijing and went to the capital, but he had to wait a year for a post, apparently because of a surfeit of candidates as well as conflicts among factions. In 1638, Chongzhen personally intervened and included Zhang among twenty-two new appointments. Jinyan became a secretary in the ministry of revenue and was soon catapulted to the vice presidency. When his patron, the minister of personnel, was impeached for bribery, Zhang was transferred to the Hanlin Academy. He served as a compiler in the history office where he probably became acquainted with his fellow Henanese Liu Lishun. Zhang drew on his experience in Shaanxi to advise on military policy. In January 1639 he was appointed supervising secretary of scrutiny in the ministry of troops.[118]

In this censorial post from 1639 to 1641, Zhang wrote 120 reports. Two years later he selected forty-four of the best, attached his own preface and those of several friends, and printed the collection under the title *Sealed Reports from the Lentil Residence.*[119] With the publication of this volume, Zhang emerged as one of the more prominent officials to assume responsibility for events at the end of the Ming.

A censor's duty was to admonish both the throne and officials, but it was always safer to do the latter. Zhang accordingly focused on officials' failures and called for appropriate punishments. When General Xiong Wencan's policy of leniency to the rebel leader Zhang Xianzhong resulted in renewed revolt in June 1639, Zhang Jinyan joined the chorus of critics who excoriated the practice of amnesty without suppression. When the provincial capital of Ji'nan fell to Manchu raiders in August 1639, Zhang urged strict punishment of the responsible local officials. After the fall of Luoyang to Li Zicheng and Xiangyang to Zhang Xianzhong in March 1641, Zhang impeached the supreme commander Yang Sichang, contributing to the pressures that led to his suicide. Also in 1641, Jinzhou in northeast Beizhili fell to Qing forces, and Xiangcheng in central Henan surrendered to rebels. In both cases, Zhang called for rapid replacement of the responsible generals.[120]

Zhang Jinyan also proposed measures to improve the caliber of officials serving the beleaguered Ming state. He noted that many graduates of the civil service examinations were interested only in rank and fame and refused to take difficult or dangerous posts. Some of the most talented officials retired early and lived at home. Citing the Ming founder's observation that every age has talented men, Zhang urged that local officials recommend one or two outstanding men each year to serve in the central administration. This procedure, he noted, had already netted outstanding officials such as Zheng Eryang, who happened to hail from Henan. In another report, Zhang focused on the selection and training of civil and military officials, emphasizing that the problem was not a lack of talent but the difficulty of finding and using it. Opposing excessive centralization of authority, he called for widespread emulation of capable provincial officials such as "the surveillance commissioner of Yu [Henan], Gao Mingheng, who submitted detailed reports every month to keep the sage ruler informed." In a third report on recruiting military officers, he cited the cases of Guo Ziyi of the Tang and Yu Zhining of the Song to argue that capable generals could be selected though the military examination system. He sought reform in the existing system to prevent malfeasance, the conducting of more regular examinations, and the awarding of higher ranks to graduates.[121]

In several reports, Zhang acknowledged that the state had to develop an effective cavalry if it was to prevail against frontier raiders and roving bandits. Even the Song dynasty, he noted, had recognized the need to raise horses and train riders if it was to resist incursions on its borders. Yet it was the Tang, not the Song, that had shown the way. As Zhang put it: "From of old, nothing was better than the Tang system of frontier supervisorates, and nothing was worse than the Song system of security horses," that is, horses raised by the people in the interior. The original Ming system of exchanging tea from the interior for horses on the frontier had also worked well, becoming most effective in the Hongzhi reign. Unfortunately, the system had declined with the encroachment upon pasturage, the conversion of tea to silver, and the retrenchment of personnel. Zhang proposed returning to the Hongzhi system and appointing a single eminent official to serve from three to six years to carry out the reform. As in the Tang, a prime locus should be in Shaanxi, on the frontier between steppe and plain, with care taken not to drive the population into banditry.[122]

To restore order, the state should emphasize agriculture. In the wake of the 1639 Manchu raids through sixty-two counties of Shandong, Zhang submitted a report entitled "Strengthen Agricultural Work." Invoking the Yellow Lord and the sage kings Tang and Yu, he noted that "agriculture is the path to human life." To reconstruct the economy of Shandong, he recommended five measures: using punishments and rewards to encourage people to go home; working with clans and households to spur local cooperation; enlisting merchants and the military to distribute grain; forcing "scholar hegemonists" to return lands to owner-cultivators; and redirecting food now consumed at victory celebrations to hungry villagers. Evincing vintage Ming populism, Zhang concluded: "Tax revenues and local production, a flourishing state and a strong army, all depend on the myriad people."[123]

In another report, entitled "Emphasizing Agriculture and Providing Relief from Locusts," Zhang called for "sufficient food and sufficient troops." He specified:

> Only when the five grains are flourishing can gold, cowries, . . . and knives spread them around. In fact, the correct path for producing wealth lies in making grain sufficient to nourish the people of the world! . . . If the grain of this world is insufficient to nourish the people of this world, it will certainly be difficult to feed the troops of this world.[124]

Zhang was aware that these economic principles implied a certain kind of social order that was increasingly honored only in the breach. With some exaggeration he declared:

> In the past the people were divided into scholars, farmers, artisans, and merchants and that was all. . . . today many pursue office or join the army, artisans and merchants throng the highways, clerks and servants clog government offices, monks and adepts live in their refuges, tramps and vagrants put their hands in their sleeves and wander about.[125]

As a result, fields lay fallow or were only partially or ineptly cultivated, grain prices doubled every few years, and tax revenues fell short of civil—let alone military—needs. In 1639–40, drought and locusts afflicted much of China, further exacerbating these hardships.

To redress these trends, Zhang called for concerted state action:

I look to the august superior to show deep concern for the foundation of the state, to emphasize relief so that people may restore their livelihoods, and to order officials high and low to wash their minds and hearts and address the crisis by halting litigation, forbidding inveigling, forgiving taxes, lightening corvée, cleaning up prisons, alleviating oppression, burying corpses, ministering to the sick, consoling the homeless, and opening up lands—thus establishing harmony under heaven.

Where there is land but no people, lead them there. Where there are people but no land, open it up. Where there are land and people but no oxen, supply them, allowing the people to borrow at interest. Where there is water, lead it into irrigation ditches. Where there are locust larvae, collect them before they hatch. Issue grain to people to encourage them to dig pits and moats to stop the [locusts'] advance and kill them as they hatch. If all the land is opened up and all people are employed, if officials concern themselves assiduously with the people's affairs, then they can still be saved from disaster. If our thoughts really penetrate to the people, even though taxes are not collected and labor services are not obtained, the common people will work hard, have peace of mind, and not get other ideas![126]

In another report, Zhang cited precedents from the Hongwu through Jiajing reigns for policies to "restore and manage the soil" while reducing taxes by 50 percent.[127]

Zhang's overriding concern was clearly to honor classical principles to regain popular support for the Ming. In one report he cited the aphorism from the *Venerated Documents*: "Heaven sees as our people see, heaven hears as our people hear." He highlighted the factors that undercut the august superior's prestige among the people, including heavy taxes and labor services imposed on the countryside, undisciplined troops that robbed on the highways, and greedy soldiers who killed innocent bystanders to get rewards. In another report he cited the *Book of Changes* to reiterate that officials should "wash their hearts and minds" to prevent disorders. Central government officials should cease collecting taxes on mines in Beizhili, Shandong, and Henan; local officials should use the meager profits from mining to suppress banditry. The government should use the sea route to transport grain from Shandong to Tianjin because the people of Henan, Shandong, and Beizhili were too "poor and hungry" to supply grain through the canal and overland.[128]

Zhang recommended twenty-four measures to relieve famine in Henan, Shandong, and Beizhili. They included: four methods of relief, such as equalizing prices; five grants of authority, such as commissioning merchants to distribute grain; seven measures of assistance, such as providing special aid to orphans; and eight prohibitions, such as banning the hoarding of grain in a quest for high profits. Zhang noted that "adherents of the White Lotus are conniving with local robbers" in Shandong, Beizhili, Henan and Shaanxi and that "the starving people are rallying to their call, driven by their conditions of extreme poverty." Recalling that the Ming founder had strictly forbidden sect activity, Zhang advocated reiteration of the ban and severe punishment of violators. But he also reminded the court that "if we do not teach but just kill, if we do not distinguish between truth and falsehood, those accomplices who escape will leave the scene and spread rumors that we were not lenient." Even in the capital region, "reform by example" should remain the order of the day. Zhang also opposed the tax surcharges that, he said, had raised revenues from 2,120,000 to seventeen million taels a year. Rather than trying to squeeze extra resources from people decimated by famine, he suggested cutting expenditures by focusing on the training of small numbers of troops that were able and ready to fight rather than hordes that were consuming provisions without reestablishing order.[129]

While Zhang's reports drew on the full range of China's historical experience, contemporaries were particularly impressed by parallels between his essays and those of famous officials in the Han period. In his preface to the collections, Liu Lishun suggested that the reports echoed themes put forth by Lu Jia in the Han, perhaps because they emphasized civil as well as military measures. Pan Fu, the author of another preface to Zhang's reports, claimed that they were as good as those of the Han statesmen Jia Yi, Chao Cuo, Dong Zhongshu, and Gongsun Hong even if they ultimately had less impact.[130] He perhaps thought Zhang resembled Jia Yi in emphasizing agriculture and popular support, Chao Cuo in calling for strict punishment of disloyal servitors, Dong Zhongshu in seeking a stable social hierarchy, and Gongsun Hong in maintaining personal frugality and proposing practical policies.

Yet another preface to Zhang's reports by Li Eryü mentioned the sage kings Shun and Yu and then moved directly to the Han experience.

> Han scholars (*ru*) sent up their reports explaining the classics with annotations and interpretations and still had the air of friendly officials. Thus the Western Han was strong and prosperous, and one had only to be capped to earn people's respect. But government gradually became unprincipled through divisions over right and wrong and disputes over the annotations and explanations, and people came to disrespect the scholars. There was eclecticism among the hundred schools of thought and a reduction in the importance of the six arts; people lost the ability to move from the old to the new and idleness eventually turned into decadence.[131]

Li noted that Zhang had imbibed this "ruist" tradition that had persisted at Baiquan, the famous academy not far from Zhang's home, and "the public intentions of Changsha and Zhongxuan were not limited to a single age." The allusion was to Jia Yi (Changsha) of the Han, whose relevance has already been noted, and to Lu Zhi (Zhongxuan) of the Tang, a respected metropolitan graduate who confronted many rebellions. The writer also observed that Zhang's poetry "approached that of the Tang and maybe even surpassed it."[132]

Li Eryü also acknowledged, however, that Zhang Jinyan's public career was less successful than those of his predecessors in the Han and Tang. In his words,

> Changsha and Zhongxuan did not attain their goals in the Han and Tang. But at least their words were used to achieve some years of peace. The difficulties encountered by Master [Zhang Jinyan], on the other hand, were extraordinary. Now we have all of his words before us, but we cannot presume that his plans, instructions, orders, and oaths are as useful as Lu's and Jia's. There is no alternative to invoking the wise maxims and great designs that preserved the peace of the Han and Tang as we increasingly depart from the golden age of the lamented Yin and Zhou.[133]

The writer quoted Han Yu of the late Tang quoting Mencius of the late Zhou to acknowledge that empty words had no effect, but he explained that Zhang's words were all that remained.

Zhang's own brief preface reminded readers that his concern with history had preceded his tenure as censor. Alluding to the Northern Song historian Sima Guang on the ambiguities of ambition and achievement, he acknowledged that things had gone from bad to worse during his tenure but asserted that it was still worthwhile to recall his proposals. Even if some reports were excessive, he had included them in order to be true to history. Just as Zhang had used history to try to influence policy, he hoped that others would draw on his experience to make a better future.[134]

"The Four Scourges"

The above account of the elite of northeast Henan during the Ming is drawn largely from genealogies, gazetteers, and collected works, all sources compiled by members of that same elite. It therefore represents primarily the self-image of that social stratum. Yet a closer look at those sources and comparison of them with informal histories by members of other strata of society reveals a darker side of the self-appointed arbiters between state and society. In addition to scholars bent on improving the world, there were academics who sought status for themselves and their families. For every good landowner, there were others who enriched their households at the expense of relatives, demanded rent from starving tenants during famines, and engaged in usury that mired commoners in debt. For each member of the local elite who assisted the magistrate with public works and distributed food to the starving, there was another who used public funds to private advantage and hoarded grain during subsistence crises. Indeed, some members of the same elite lauded in published records belonged to families that ruthlessly pursued private interests behind the scenes. An upright scholar at court could easily turn out to be an overbearing bully at home. Some members of the elite sincerely believed that their personal and family success was well earned and even essential to the public welfare. Some undoubtedly anticipated the decline and fall of the Ming state and sought to secure the resources needed to weather the transition to a new order. However they justified their behavior, a significant and probably increasing number of the elite in northeast Henan as elsewhere were investing more energy in family welfare—and sometimes aggrandizement—during the last decade of the Ming.[135]

In September 1640, the regional inspector of Henan, Gao Mingheng, reported on four such cases. Gao was a 1631 metropolitan graduate from Shandong who had served as magistrate of two counties before being promoted to the censorate and posted to Henan in 1639.[136] He quickly emerged as an honest and energetic official who patronized promising young scholars and won praise from prominent members of the local elite, including Zhang Jinyan. Gao's original report was extensive but it has come down to us only in a fragment included in the informal history written by Zheng Lian, the early Qing government student from Shangqiu who was close enough to the elite to know them well but detached enough to criticize them discreetly. For this reason we must consider the more extensive data gleaned from gazetteers and other informal histories to get a fuller picture of the public images as well as private activities of three of the four descent groups that Gao Mingheng identified eventually as the "Four Scourges" of Henan during the last years of the Ming.

The first family was the Chus of Suizhou, a department in Guide with a favorable population-to-land ratio and a record of academic success. According to the gazetteer, a government student named Chu Cen had two sons, Taichu and Taizhen. The elder, Taichu, passed the provincial examination in 1618 and the metropolitan examination in 1625 and became an examining editor at the Hanlin Academy. His brother, Taizhen, became a tributary student and served as a magistrate in Gansu. The gazetteer mentioned no misbehavior on the Chus' part. The only hint that something might be amiss is that the editors accorded a brief biography to the tributary student Taizhen but none to the metropolitan graduate Taichu, who also held a higher office.[137]

The second family was the Fans of Yucheng. They traced their line back to the famous reformer Fan Zhongyan in the eleventh century and were more proximately descended from ancestors in the fifteenth century who earned provincial degrees, held offices, and won honor through biographies in the gazetteer. In the late Ming, the line produced Fan Liangyan, an "orphan" brought up by his mother. Fan won a provincial degree in 1612 and came to the attention of the local notable Yang Dongming (discussed in Chapter 1). He advised the magistrate on labor services, and, when the magistrate was skeptical, "prevailed on" him to accept his counsel. Fan passed the metropolitan examinations in 1616, the same year as Hou Xun, and became a messenger in the ministry of rites. Appointed a censor in Zhejiang, he submitted a report on river work in Henan that accepted the trend toward a more commercial economy by arguing that the state should purchase services from merchants rather than rely on farmers for free labor. As a censor in Zhejiang, he was regarded as a capable official, and as a surveillance commissioner in Huaiyang, Nanzhili, he gained fame for exterminating "wolves" (presumably four-legged ones). According to his biography, he was about to be promoted when he was impeached by "envious rivals" and forced into retirement. He built a garden in the western suburb of the county town of Yucheng, complete with flowers and bamboo, odd shaped stones, and a fishpond; he lived there quietly, brewing tea, warming wine, and writing poetry with his fellow literati. According to an admiring biographer, Fan Liangyan nurtured an atmosphere that was "nothing less than the spirit of . . . Liang Xiaowang," the aristocratic patron of literati in this region in the early Western Han. This also seems to have been Fan's aspiration, for he ended one of his poems with the query: "Who will succeed Xiaowang?"[138]

In the eyes of the editors of the gazetteer and of Fan himself, he was an upright scholar-official who retired to his home to enjoy his wealth during the last troubled decades of the Ming. There is evidence, however, that Fan was one of the greedier landowners of the late Ming whose ostentatious lifestyle exceeded the bounds of scholarly propriety and official sumptuary laws and constituted a burden on the rest of society. When "roving bandits" approached Yucheng in 1635, Fan urged the magistrate to mount a vigorous defense and contributed his own "special troops" to suppress the rising. When the rebels departed, he financed the repair of the walls, the moat, and a temple to Guan Di, the god of war. Such activities reveal not just loyal defense of the state but considerable personal wealth and a determination to use it to protect family interests. Even Fan's biography in the gazetteer alluded gingerly to a public relations problem. In its words,

He benefited from the privileges and suffered the resentments natural in the case of
such an old family. [But] people praised him, and the ruler examined his talents and
bestowed awards on him. Because of Master's free and easy manner, his gay extravagance,
and his outspokenness, he often confronted people and committed many excesses that
were granted improper protection. Finally he brought harm to his antagonists. [Yet]
when they memorialized the court, he was exonerated because of his well-known skill
with horses and carriages.[139]

Although this text acknowledges Fan's "excesses" and hints at his use of force to intimidate critics, it states that he was finally "exonerated" and died of an illness. The biography ends by lamenting the loss of his extensive and valuable writings in the disorders
at the end of the dynasty. Curiously enough for a man of his standing, he died without
an heir.

Whatever Fan Liangyan's "excesses," the editors of the gazetteer, who included kin,
not surprisingly regarded them as less worthy of attention than the achievements of other
members of the descent group. Of seven brothers in another elite branch of the family, two became government students, one earned his provincial military degree, and
another became assistant director of the court of royal entertainment. A fifth brother
won his provincial degree in the same year as Fan Liangyan and served as a teacher,
magistrate, prefect, intendant, and member of the Hanlin Academy. He was broadly
learned in the thought of the Warring States, the two Han, and the Song; collected tens
of thousands of books, including novels and private histories; and wrote prose, poetry,
and rules for the conduct of family members. A sixth obtained his metropolitan degree
in 1631, served in several provincial posts, wrote numerous books, rose to be vice president of the ministry of troops, and was included in the shrine to local worthies. The
seventh was only a government student, but he was purported to have "modeled himself on the ancients," to have talked his way out of trouble when bandits assaulted the
county in 1635, and to have distributed his family's grain during a famine and saved
thousands of lives. That student's merits were so extraordinary that the usual requirement of a degree was waived and he was appointed a magistrate in Beizhili, where he
reportedly acquitted himself well.[140]

The third family at issue, the Miaos of Ningling, received little attention in the county
gazetteer, but it was all positive. The immediate patriarch, Miao Wenying, was included
in the section on notable worthies and his career intersected that of the famous and
respected local notable Lü Kun. Wenying received his provincial degree in 1561 with
Lü, retired to look after his blind mother (as did Lü), and read and taught in the Hall
of the Rustic Man, where Lü once studied. From the gazetteer account, Miao Wenying's
progeny also appeared to be respectable members of the local elite. One son received
his provincial degree in 1582 and another became a tributary student and taught in
Henan and Beizhili. A grandson, Miao Sishun, became a provincial graduate in 1618
and a metropolitan graduate in 1619. To be sure, Sishun received only a spare biography despite service as a magistrate in Shanxi and Shaanxi and as a secretary and supernumerary gentleman in the ministry of troops.[141] But such perfunctory biographies were
common and there was little reason to suspect that the Miaos were anything but upright
members of the local elite pursuing a localist strategy at the end of the Ming.

The Miao genealogy predictably confirms this image, at least at first glance. It reveals that the founder had arrived in the county (from Bo, in Nanzhili) only relatively recently (in Wenying's father's generation) and that many of Wenying's progeny stayed home to read and write, manage a local temple, instruct sons, and compile the family records. They included a tributary student who could have held office but instead stayed home to cultivate bamboo, entertain scholars, and collect singing girls. Wenying's grandson, Sishun, who was a metropolitan graduate, had an official career, rising from magistrate to director of the bureau of operations in the ministry of troops, and even playing a role in Chongzhen's consolidation of authority. In 1629, however, he too returned home to attend to family matters. He set aside lands for sacrifices to the ancestors, taught his sons and grandsons, and established a Society of the Locust Tree Hall, which was said by his biographer to have recreated the atmosphere of the high Tang.[142] The Miaos were clearly withdrawing from active participation in the Ming state but, at first blush, there was little to suggest that they were abusing local society.

Surprisingly, however, the genealogy goes on to reveal that Miao Sishun did have some differences with the Ningling magistrate. Like Fan Liangyan in Yucheng, who presented himself as a spokesman of the people in re state demands for unpaid labor, Sishun styled himself as a defender of "the people" against the magistrate Meng Yanghuo. According to Miao, the magistrate who had been in office since 1637 was responsible for "bad policies" such as selling shrines and offices, forcing people to provide horses to the state, and constructing music halls in a time of famine. Unlike Fan, who had urged his magistrate to hire merchants to repair dikes, however, Miao opposed programs that required raising and spending money in a time of general hardship. He therefore "frankly remonstrated" with the magistrate and used poetry and songs to make "genial jabs" at him. Yet, despite his call for public frugality, Miao held funeral ceremonies for a deceased relative that reportedly far exceeded what was permitted by law. This brought him into direct conflict with the magistrate who "selected men from the county, armed them, and had them cause trouble." In the process, the genealogy stated elliptically, "some people were killed," and a "legal case" arose that dragged on for ten months until the magistrate "got sick and died." (The Ningling gazetteer also explicitly states that the magistrate "died of illness"—a rather unusual piece of information). At this point, the magistrate's personal servants "feared for their lives and fled," but Miao Sishun had no cause for fear and stayed at home. We may infer, perhaps, that the magistrate armed local thugs who killed people and that his subsequent "illness" had something to do with Miao's servants. But given the elliptical nature of the genealogical account, we can conclude little else about the conflict.[143]

Other accounts provide further details on these families, including their less savory activities. For example, the respected Ming loyalist and assiduous scholar Tan Qian, whose name comprised elements from the personal names of the great Han historians Sima Tan and Sima Qian, wrote *An Assessment of the Dynasty* in the early Qing. It records that in September 1638, before the Ningling magistrate Meng Yanghuo "got sick," he had arrested Miao Sishun on charges of "presuming on his influence in his hometown to protect fugitives from the law and to reap profits by illicit means."[144] Two months later, a secretary in the ministry of punishments impeached Fan Liangyan for "bending the laws for corrupt purposes" and called for his arrest.[145] In the first instance, the court case—now clearly identified as against Miao—dragged on for months, but it was magistrate Meng who succumbed first. Whether or not Miao was implicated in the magistrate's death (perhaps by poisoning at the hands of his servants), he clearly benefited from it to elude arrest. In the second instance, also, the order for the arrest of Fan Liangyan had not been carried out. It was two years later, in September 1640, that the regional inspector Gao Mingheng decided to follow up on these cases. Gao had once been a student in Suizhou, where he had personally experienced the highhandedness of the Chu family. He now put the Chus of Suizhou together with the Miaos of Ningling and the Fans of Yucheng, and added the Caos of Nanyang, another elite family that abused its neighbors, and denounced them in a report to the throne as the "Four Scourges" of Henan.

As was the wont of censorial officials, Gao minced no words:

> Today the polity is in great trouble. Rival states invade from the outside, roving bandits spread on the inside. The situation is precarious, and people's hearts and minds have grown cold with fear. I consider, however, that these are merely diseases of the skin. Although superficially harmful and not easily cured, they are still in the limbs and do not yet touch on life and death. But Henan province is the stomach, heart, and mind of the world. There are four official families in Henan that are eating away the vital organs. In Nanyang there is a certain Cao, in Suizhou Chu Taichu, in Ningling Miao Sishun, and in Yucheng Fan Liangyan and company. They all have accumulated several thousands of servants, act outrageously in the departments and prefectures, and regularly kill people for sport. They commonly seize people's lands and houses and rape their wives and daughters—the instances are too numerous to count. Little people dare not say a word, and local officials who are aware of what is going on dare not intervene. The four families have links with mounted highwaymen as well as their own assassins. If anyone dares to speak up, disaster quickly befalls his nearest kin.[146]

Gao called on the state to prosecute these cases or abandon any claim to representing the interests of the people.

Unfortunately, Gao and Zheng Lian—whose summary of Gao's report is the only version of it extant—focused on the abuses of the Caos and Chus. Perhaps that was because the Caos were outside Zheng's home region and the Chus had offended Gao personally. The Fans and Miaos, moreover, had already been brought to the court's attention, their transgressions may have been less egregious and Gao and Zheng may have been partial to them.[147] Because the Cao case is treated in the extant summary of the report in more detail, we shall begin with it to see the kinds of abuses that incurred Gao's wrath.

According to Gao, the Caos were the first family of Nanyang prefecture in the number of lands, houses, and servants. The senior Cao had once been supreme commander on the northern frontier. In retirement, he was nominally the magistrate's inferior, but in fact he had once been his teacher. The magistrate therefore had to clear everything with eight or nine Caos, and he even had to respect their servants. The magistrate was frustrated but kept his resentment to himself. One day, however, he got drunk. He was leaving his office to deal with an urgent matter when he encountered a runner dressed in black and carrying a dagger. The runner advanced and exclaimed: "Greetings from

Old Master Cao!" Angered by the man's impertinence, the magistrate shouted: "Hey! Does Nanyang belong to the Caos? This magistrate also wields a stick." With that, he knocked the runner's dagger to the ground. The runner departed and reported what had happened to Cao, embellishing the account so as to incite his master's anger. Cao called the magistrate to his house to scold him. The magistrate went but refused to apologize. Instead he warned Cao not to insult him again or he would suffer the consequences. The magistrate then left to pay his respects to the city god. Cao pursued him in his sedan chair, accompanied by many swordsmen. The magistrate swore as before, and Cao advanced and slapped his face. The magistrate cried out and threw himself to the ground, saying "Kill me! Kill me!" Many townspeople converged and clamored: "The Caos have rebelled!" The people pressed in from all sides; when Cao drew his sword to defend himself, the people seized him, beat him nearly to death, and threw him into jail. They then closed the gates of the town, seized Cao's servants, and confined them to the jail. As the magistrate was still drunk and unaware of what had happened, his secretary drafted a report and submitted it to the provincial authorities. By the time Gao saw the report, Old Master Cao had died in jail.[148]

Gao Mingheng next turned to the case of the Chus of Suizhou, in which he was particularly interested because of his previous experience. Gao had enlisted the assistance of a local military officer and prefectural clerk who had pressured one of Chu Taichu's chief advisors into reporting on his master's activities. At first the investigation revealed only the usual appropriation of lands and raping of women. But then a major conflict occurred that Inspector Gao could use to discredit the Chus. The Chus had long been coveting the lands of the neighboring Zhu Family Village, which included some one hundred households. Fearing a takeover, the Zhus enlisted the assistance of a member of the local elite, Zhang Weiyi, a former supervising secretary in the office of scrutiny in the ministry of troops. Zhang was actually related by marriage to the Chus, but he regarded them as enemies and was happy to assist the Zhus in resisting their demands. The result was daily clashes between the two camps with numerous casualties. Although aware of the conflict, officials were afraid to intervene and pretended not to know about it. Then one day the Zhangs and Zhus faced off against the Chus, and a daylong battle left most of Zhu Village consumed by fire. The Chus killed the villagers who tried to flee and threw their corpses into the fire as a means of destroying evidence. The prefect arrested Chu Taichu and authorized an investigation. A search of the village turned up many charred skeletons and a few survivors huddled in the rubble. Outraged at the greed that had led to such carnage, Inspector Gao wrote a detailed report and circulated it among the local elite.[149]

In his summary report to the throne, Gao noted that it was his duty to impeach such rapacious members of the local elite. In his words:

> I beg the sovereign to make a quick decision and implement it, to display their heads so as to assuage the grievances of the ten thousand surnames of the central plain, and to confiscate their family properties, which are sufficient to supply ten years of provisions to the nine frontier garrisons.[150]

The ministry of punishments approved the request: all four offenders were to be decapitated and their heads displayed in public places. Since Cao had already died in jail, his corpse was beheaded and his head was hung in the market place. Miao Sishun was finally arrested and escorted to Beijing for punishment, but he was killed en route by someone taking revenge. Fan Liangyan was arrested and taken to the capital, but he was deemed too old to suffer punishment. He was finally released and allowed to return home. Thus he was not exonerated, as the gazetteer claimed, but he was allowed to die of natural causes. In the end, therefore, only Chu Taichu was tried, found guilty, and executed by the state. We have no information on the confiscation of the extensive properties of these allegedly rapacious families, let alone the possibility that any proceeds were devoted to the military effort on the frontier. Given the growing debility of the Ming state and the gathering chaos in Henan, such outcomes seem unlikely.

If Gao's campaign against the Four Scourges did not stem the decline of the Ming state in the central plain, it reminded people that the dynasty still harbored a few individuals who were at least ostensibly concerned about political and social justice. Some lessons of this incident even survived the Ming. In the early Qing, Zheng Lian reflected:

> At that time [before 1640], the central province was prosperous. Most of the local elite households competed to be preeminent in amassing lands, houses, servants, and men. . . . Among these four families, the Cao and the Chu were superior and the Miao and Fan were next. They were like [the Warring States of] Teng and Xue that competed with Qin and Chu.[151]

In this violent struggle reminiscent of the Warring States, Zheng seemed to favor the lesser families, Miao and Fan, as we have seen. He was in any case aware that Gao's justice had been incomplete, for the Zhangs of Suizhou had escaped punishment or retribution. Zheng concluded that one had to be cautious in dealing with the local elite because "their fields and houses fill the land, their servants are as numerous as clouds, their power is enough to scorch your hands, and they get fierce if you so much as turn your head to look at them."[152] Zheng described his own judgment as "correcting one's speech in process," an apparent allusion to the great landowner Wang Yan, whose unlimited pursuit of private wealth was often taken as an important symbol of the social conditions leading to the demise of the Western Jin state and the rise of frontier minority regimes in the fourth century CE.[153]

In sum, a tiny elite dominated the society of northeast Henan from the beginning of the Ming to its end, but it also went through considerable changes over time. While growing only slightly in total number and thus declining as a proportion of a burgeoning population, members of the elite hailed increasingly from prefectures and counties outside Kaifeng and Xiangfu, thus providing an increasingly broad and firm base for the polity in local society. As time went on, the elite looked beyond state service, pursued intellectual inquiry, and finally turned to community action. Certain counties, and within them certain descent groups, demonstrated great success in obtaining degrees and offices. Although such families tended to identify closely with the state, some of the most successful encountered political trouble, and certain members became alienated from the government. By the end of the Ming, a few families and individuals became so devoted to defending their particular interests that officials and students joined in castigating them as inimical to both state and society.

The elite of northeast Henan regarded their region as culturally and politically central, a view that was widely shared by officials and the elite of other regions. In the early Ming, leading families in the capital county of Xiangfu dominated the provincial examination lists and held a disproportionate share of central government offices by benefiting from public schools, provincial quotas, and geographical location. In the middle period, one member of the elite challenged the Ming philosophical orthodoxy based on pattern (*li*) and emphasized a concern with material force (*qi*) that was later to become more central to Chinese thought. Another "scholar from the central province," advocated a "Middle Way" between the Ming state and the party of the pure and pursued a "Central Path" between the elite (including men and women) and commoners. Another self-styled "average man," avowedly dependent on intellectual interaction with other literati and commoners, took his hometown as a center from which to project his influence.

In the late Ming, members of the aristogenic elite in Shangqiu pursued their own paths between the state (including a powerful regent, a profligate ruler, a dictatorial eunuch, and a domineering grand secretary) and society (including the rebels, reformers, and neighbors). Two elite families in Yongcheng provided several leading civil officials and military officers, while several elite families from Qi served with the regent without becoming his clients, collaborated with the eunuch without sharing his fall, patronized less prosperous families, and produced an optimus who coexisted with a grand secretary but clashed with a supreme commander. An elite family of Xinxiang produced "a great man of He and Luo" and an outspoken censor in the ministry of troops. Finally, three elite families in Suizhou, Yucheng, and Ningling were placed among the Four Scourges who were consuming the "stomach, heart, and mind of the world" and were compared with the states that had contended for power in the same region during the Warring States period.

In the elite's efforts "to move from the old to the new," they went back to earlier Ming experience for military organization and frontier trade, to the Song for alternative philosophies and reportorial styles, to the Tang for standards of poetry and examples of statecraft, and to the Jin for models of calligraphy and the dangers of corruption. They referred repeatedly to particular exemplars from earlier periods, including Kongzi, Mengzi, Guan Zi, and Su Qin of the Spring and Autumn and Warring States periods; the Five Classics celebrating the Three Dynasties of Xia, Shang, and Zhou; and the even earlier legendary sage-kings, including the Yellow Lord, Yao, and Shun.

The elite of this region seemed to share the Ming state's tendency to identify itself with the Han.[154] They turned to the Former Han for the models of Gao Zu's plebian origins, Wendi's use of the military, and Wudi's frontier policies. They explicitly invoked—or were said by others to be reminiscent of—Lu Jia's and Jia Yi's concern for popular support, Bu Shi's and Fan Li's contributions to public welfare, and Dong Zhongshu's and Liang Xiaowang's cultural coteries. One scholar of the mid-Ming deplored the growing concentration of landholding reminiscent of the Han, although he also cited the experience of the Wang Mang interregnum to warn against radical reform. Others referred to the Latter Han for other topoi such as the model magistrate, the wise patriarch, the modest son, the cosmological skeptic, and the biographer(s) of women.

By the late Ming, some members of the elite became painfully aware of the minatory models of weak rulers, ambitious concubines, powerful eunuchs, partisan officials, religious sects, and military strongmen who together had brought an end to the Latter Han. The question remained just how far along the Ming had advanced in that Han-like administrative cycle that threatened to repeat itself by the 1640s. Answers would depend in part on the thought and action of other members of late-Ming society.

THREE

Gender, Class, and Ethnicity

WHILE A TINY ELITE MEDIATED between the state and the society as a whole, much larger groups of commoners were active in the social space between the elite and the rest of the population. Although the women who comprised half the population were excluded from the examinations and thus from the elite, some became visible because they belonged to noble and elite families and others because they exemplified certain moral virtues and were selected as models for men as well as for women. Many men—including government students, landlords, merchants, minor functionaries, military officers, and medical doctors—constituted what I shall call the middle strata of society. Several of these strata grew in size and changed in function over the course of the dynasty. Most residents of the region considered themselves—and were considered by others—to be Han Chinese, tracing their ancestry or at least their identity back to the Han period, but some—such as Christians, Muslims, and Jews—belonged to religious and ethnic minorities. Many women and members of the middle strata and minority groups possessed only minimal literacy and were barely visible in the records, but a few left traces from which their activities and sometimes even their ideas may be reconstructed.

Virtuous Women

While there are fundamental physical and sexual differences between males and females, their psychological and social attributes are increasingly recognized to be constructed variously over time and space. The resulting concept of gender can be applied not just to individuals but to the cultural, political, and social structures in which they live.[1] Students of Chinese history have come to recognize the need to uncover the hitherto largely hidden history of Chinese women and to listen to their voices in order to go beyond various stereotypes and appreciate women's accomplishments as well as their hardships.[2]

The officials, members of the elite, and other literate men who compiled most of the records of women during the Ming, prided themselves on serving the interests of the population as a whole. They therefore placed special emphasis on honoring virtuous women from commoner families, a group that might otherwise have remained completely invisible to the rest of society and to historians. The practice of honoring such women actually went back to the Han dynasty, and its revival in the Ming offers further evidence of the populism that the two dynasties had in common. During the Ming period the status of women was also increasingly influenced by practices common among the masses, such as reducing the difference between betrothal and marriage. At the same time, the virtues for which women were honored in the Ming dynasty were apparently more passive and even self-denying than those celebrated in the Han dynasty, which themselves had been less active and life-affirming than attributes praised in the Zhou.[3] This is surprising if one identifies elite ideology as the major explanation for patriarchy and assumes a linear progression in the status of women over time. But it is less difficult to explain if one acknowledges the existence of misogyny in certain strands of popular culture and hypothesizes a more complicated pattern in the development of women's status over time.[4] Here, too, the modernizationist, Marxist, and imperial paradigms do not seem to do justice to emerging patterns in the literature of women's history and in the history of women's literature.[5]

Aristocratic women in the Ming were typically drawn from the ranks of commoners and consequently enjoyed less status and authority than their predecessors in the Han and Tang or their successors in the Qing. Ming rulers restricted their wives to managing only women's affairs in the palace explicitly to prevent the emergence of powerful affinal, or "external," clans like those that had challenged royal authority in the Han. To be sure, Zhu Yuanzhang's wife, née Ma, played a role in his rise to power, and her death affected the tenor of his reign. Lady Wan rose from the status of serving woman to become the favorite concubine of Chenghua despite the death in infancy of her only son. Wanli's favorite concubine, née Zheng, exerted some political influence during his reign even though her son was never made heir apparent. Near the end of the dynasty, Tianqi's mother, née Zhang, who was originally from northeast Henan, patronized members of the Donglin party while his wet nurse, Madame Ke, cooperated with the eunuch Wei Zhongxian. Other Ming empresses and empress dowagers actively patronized religious institutions in the capital. But no Ming empress took power on her own as Empress Lü had done during the Western Han let alone declared her own dynasty as Empress Wu had declared the Zhou during the Tang. Ming Taizu and Chengzu held special examinations to select literate women to tutor palace women. The Zhou prince later selected educated women to instruct the women in his estate. But these practices were pale reflections of the civil service examinations held for women under Empress Wu.[6]

Unfortunately, extant records reveal almost nothing about these court women's views of their places in history. Two snippets of information, however, suggest some interest in precedents of the Qin and Han periods. A beautiful young serving woman was unable to meet Jiajing because she refused to bribe the female official in charge of arranging audiences. She expressed her frustration in a poem with references to the famous lovers Sima Xiangru and Wang Zhaojun of the Han. In a revealing (if possibly apocryphal) anecdote, the Empress Dowager Zhang Yi'an was said to have compared the contemporary eunuch dictator Wei Zhongxian with Zhao Gao, the prototypical, power-hungry Qin eunuch described by the Han historian Sima Qian.[7]

The status of women in elite families during the Ming varied according to circumstances but also generally fell below that of earlier times. A few loyal consorts and nurturing mothers, such as Song Quan's mother, Lady Ding, were accorded biographies in the gazetteers and thereby brought honor to their natal families, whose names they retained, as well as to their marital families, with whom they became more closely associated in the Ming. Mothers were often involved in arranging marriages, daughters were sometimes valued as social capital, and wives who had "married down" might exert considerable influence in their marital families. But marriages even in reformist families such as Lü Kun's continued to serve political, social, and economic interests. Concubines such as Lady Ding who succeeded in pleasing their mates and providing them with male progeny might exercise some influence in the family and even win the friendship of the principal wife; but in general they continued to suffer double discrimination as women and secondary consorts.

In all social strata, females were much more likely than males to suffer infanticide. This practice, which existed already in Qin times, was never sanctioned in ethics or law but persisted over the centuries and may have increased during the Ming as a mechanism for controlling fertility and avoiding the dispersion of family wealth through dowries. The Ming outlawed infanticide in 1526, stipulating that violators be exiled one thousand li from their homes. But the practice persisted as indicated by the need to issue another proscription in 1629. Since the Chinese considered children during the first year of life as not fully human, members of all social strata may have conceptualized infanticide as a form of "postnatal abortion."[8]

Increasing numbers of Han Chinese women suffered as well from the more recent practice of foot binding, a moderate form of which may have originated among court dancers of the Five Dynasties. According to recent research, the practice intensified during the Song when tight bindings crippled girls' feet. The resulting "lotus feet" were said to be common among courtesans and deemed erotic by men. Song literati who forsook the martial arts and incurred defeat at the hands of frontier minorities may have embraced foot binding as a means of ensuring their physical superiority over women. They also may have encouraged the institution to keep women at home in an era of greater mobility stemming from a burgeoning market economy. Historians have speculated that prospective wives and concubines may have bound their feet to compete with courtesans and prostitutes for their men's interest. Although foot binding was not widely discussed or openly praised as a sign of women's virtue, young women may have accepted it as a form of physical discipline in preparation for marriage, just as young men engaged in mental discipline in preparation for the examinations. Han Chinese continued the practice in the Yuan and Ming, perhaps as a sign of civilization distinguishing them from the frontier minorities who eschewed it. Even the most reformist members of the Ming elite, such as Wang Tingxiang and Lü Kun in northeast Henan, neglected to criticize it. Although most observers today agree that foot binding was an egregious symbol of patriarchy, even feminist historians acknowledge that the practice would not have endured without the complicity of generations of mothers who wove the bindings and slippers and encouraged daughters to use them to win good mates.[9]

In all social strata during the Tang and Song, daughters and widows were legally entitled to dowries and, in the absence of a male heir, to property inherited from fathers and widowers. The early Ming effectively curtailed this right by mandating, in cases of no male heir, the adoption of an heir from among a deceased father's or widower's nearest nephews. This measure represented the Kongzian emphasis on the need for all branches of a family to have male heirs; it was adopted at the expense of the Chinese state's claim to all uninherited property. It effectively excluded daughters and widows from inheriting their deceased fathers' and spouses' property and reduced them to being mere custodians of that property on behalf of heirs chosen by the fathers' and widowers' family. This decline in the ability of widows to inherit property was, however, partially balanced by an enhancement of the authority of chaste widows to reject heirs selected by their deceased husbands' families and to select heirs on the basis of sentiment as well as status.[10]

The value of widow chastity is traceable to the *Book of Rites*. It was popularized in the Han and was promoted by Tang laws designed to protect widows from pressures from marital families to remarry and thus forfeit rights to the deceased spouses' property. It was enhanced by Song emphasis on sexual purity and the Yuan canonization of exemplary cases of widow chastity that lasted twenty years. During the Ming, widow chastity became even more important as an antidote to the Mongol levirate, or the practice of widows marrying brothers-in-law, regarded by Han Chinese as incestuous. The publication of a *Discourse on Women* and the canonization of "virtuous women" during and after the Yongle reign further enhanced the ideal for the rest of the dynasty. In the sixteenth century, some women happily invoked it to resist pressures to remarry and to ward off unwanted advances. Ironically, an increase in companionate marriages, a belief that loving mates would be reunited after death, and an expectation that suicides would be exempt from the tortures of hell combined to rationalize the evolution of widow chastity into the extreme practice of widow suicide. This form of chastity seems to have begun in earnest among the Ming nobility and spread to other strata. Suicide also became increasingly honorable as a response to rape. Still, honors for suicide to avoid remarriage and rape remained exceptional during the dynasty. According to one study, the Ming celebrated three times as many cases of lifelong celibacy as of widow suicide.[11]

The situation of women in Henan province during the Ming was similarly bleak. In the early years, prominent members of the nobility began the practice of encouraging betrothed maidens to commit suicide at the death of their fiancés. After Zhu Yudun, the otherwise illustrious descendant of the Zhou prince of Kaifeng, celebrated the idea in an opera, it spread among the people along with the notion that betrothal was tantamount to marriage. According to T'ien Ju-k'ang, by 1555 Henan province had the largest number of widow suicides (108) in the realm. During the late Ming, the practice spread widely through the realm, making Henan less exceptional and more nearly typical. Indeed, widow suicide became three times more prevalent in south China than in the north. There is no way to know the extent to which the increase over time and

space reflected primarily a change in social practice or rather a change in state celebration of it resulting in fuller records. Meanwhile, the practice of cutting off pieces of
one's flesh to nourish a sick relative, a radical demonstration of self-sacrifice that dated
from the Tang, reappeared in the early Ming. This custom apparently declined later in
the dynasty among women as well as among men.[12]

Ming honoring of such female "virtues" as life-long chastity, self-mutilation to nurture parents, and suicide to avoid remarriage and rape encouraged practices that brought
sacrifice and harm to many women; but it also brought fame and status to a few individuals and their natal families. In line with the state's effort to extend education and
morality to the entire population, it first restricted honors for these virtues to women
from commoner families. Only in 1523 did it relax the regulation to allow some women
from elite families to be honored as well.[13] As a result it was primarily women from commoner families, who might otherwise never have appeared in the historical record, who
were recorded in the gazetteers as models to be emulated by men as well as women.
Because women continued to be identified by their maiden names even after marriage,
their honors were automatically shared by their natal families as well.

While Henanese women's views of these institutions during the Ming remain
largely inaccessible, the biographies of 434 virtuous women in the provincial gazetteer
shed some light on their experiences. Honored women's experiences, like those of elite
males, can be divided into three periods. During the first (from 1368–1464), the majority of honored women—thirty out of forty-eight—refused to remarry, preferring
instead to care for their parents-in-law and "orphaned" children. Far fewer—seventeen—
committed suicide; only one woman was honored for killing herself to join her fiancé
in the afterlife. While the thirty chaste widows hailed from nineteen counties, the seventeen suicides occurred in only five. Eleven of the suicides were from Xiangfu, including two in princely families. This tends to confirm the hypothesis that the Ming nobility
in Henan played an important role in inspiring the practice of widow suicide in the
early years of the dynasty. On a more positive note, no woman in this period was honored for cutting off flesh to nourish a sick relative (see Appendix E).

During the second period (1465–1572), the total number of women honored as
virtuous more than quadrupled to 205, with widows not remarrying tripling to 89, widows committing suicide quadrupling to 75, and fiancées committing suicide increasing
from one to twelve. For the first time, two women were honored for cutting off flesh to
nourish a relative. Honorees for female chastity not only increased in number but were
more widely distributed in the province. Widows who remained chaste came from thirty
counties, those who committed suicide came from twenty-seven, and the betrothed hailed
from nine. For the first time, some women were honored for committing suicide or otherwise dying honorably at the hands of rapists and bandits, revealing the increased honor
attached to those actions and, most likely, the greater incidence of violent crime (see
Appendix E).

During the third period (1573–1644), the number of widows honored for remaining chaste declined markedly while the numbers of widows who committed suicide and
betrothed who remained chaste declined less strikingly. These downward trends resulted
from the shorter time span (seventy as opposed to 100 years) and perhaps also from

imprecision (regarding dates) in the sources. The declines were also accompanied—and are perhaps partially explained—by increases in the numbers of women honored for committing suicide at the hands of bandits and for cutting off flesh to nourish an ailing relative. These increases also signaled growing social disorder. They may also have reflected the persistence of the ethics of self-sacrifice and honor in an era of rising individualism and materialism. Perhaps the increase in the celebration (and, most likely, the practice) of cutting off one's flesh to nourish a sick relative also reflected desperation during the epidemics of the 1580s and 1640s, when other treatments failed.[14]

A comparison of the distribution of female biographies with the distribution of male degrees among counties reveals a rather high correlation between the honoring of women's virtue and the recognition of men's success. Xiangfu county, the top producer of provincial graduates in Kaifeng prefecture, also printed the most biographies of virtuous women. Qi county, which produced the third largest number of provincial graduates, compiled the second largest number of women's biographies. In Guide prefecture, Shangqiu county ranked second in provincial graduates and first in biographies of virtuous women. In Weihui prefecture, Ji county produced the most graduates and the largest number of honored women. In all three prefectures, counties producing the fewest provincial graduates also tended to supply the fewest biographies of virtuous women (see Appendix F). Such correlations are readily understandable since the academically advantaged counties would have had more educated men to recommend women for recognition as well as more resources to record their activities in the gazetteers. It was also in privileged counties that elite standards of morality were most likely to have influenced commoners as they were supposed to do.

Drawing on similar correlations throughout China, T'ien Ju-k'ang hypothesized that the large and growing number of widow suicides in the mid- to late Ming may have reflected increasing frustration among government students, especially in populous and prosperous counties, who were unable to gain entry to the university or earn provincial degrees authorizing entrance into the elite. According to T'ien, government students vented their dissatisfaction and made up for their humiliation by encouraging widow suicides as an alternative form of familial prestige.[15] Indeed, the number of government students increased considerably over the Ming and students frequently submitted the recommendations of virtuous women, who were often their relatives. T'ien supports his thesis with data from counties with high rates of reported widow suicide, especially in provinces south of the Yangzi. Data from the northeast Henan counties of Chenzhou, Xihua, and Changge also appear to support this hypothesis since in those places there were few male graduates and many women honored for their virtue. In the rest of northeast Henan, however, the number of provincial degrees closely correlates with the number of women honored for virtue, suggesting an alternative hypothesis: that government students who expected to be successful in the examinations were encouraging and publicizing "virtuous" behavior on the part of their women. In this region, perhaps, students were not so much compensating for their failures as sharing their successes (see Appendix F).

The gazetteer of Xiangfu county reveals more information on the backgrounds, motivations, achievements, and categorization of "virtuous women" in this region. This county included the provincial capital of Kaifeng and accounted for the largest number of such women in the early and mid-Ming. It produced a total of fifty-eight during the entire dynasty, second only to Shangqiu county.[16]

According to this record, the Ming regulation emphasizing commoner women seems to have been observed. Of twenty-seven women honored as "loyal wives" in Xiangfu, only three were daughters and only seven were wives of identified men (that is, members of the elite, or middle strata), leaving the majority (seventeen) as daughters or wives of obscure men (that is, commoners, or members of the masses). Thus the majority of women in this county won notice and honor for themselves and their natal families through their own actions not through their natal or marital status. While the original Ming statutes had stipulated a period of fifty years of chastity to qualify for recognition, only four of these women met that requirement. Four remained unmarried for over forty years, four for over twenty, three for an unspecified "rest of their lives," and eight for unstated lengths of time. These data suggest a considerable relaxation in the criterion for awarding honors, which helps to explain the increase in the number of chaste women honored over the course of the Ming. Further, eight of the twenty-seven chaste women were praised for caring for their in-laws and children while only one was said to have disfigured herself. This suggests that many widows opted for chastity to be able to care for others, not just to gain fame for themselves.

The second category of honored women, "ardent wives," consisted of those who committed suicide at their husbands' deaths or, in one case, to save a husband's life. There were thirty-one such women, thus exceeding the number of widows who did not remarry (twenty-seven) and yielding a very rough ratio between the two groups of 1:1. This may be compared with the ratio of 1:3 found for China as a whole.[17] Assuming the record accurately reflected social practices, widows' lives were much less valued in Xiangfu than in China as a whole. At the same time, only two of the biographies included the names of fathers and only eight included the names of husbands. Thus twenty-one, or the great majority, were likely from commoner families whose social status they had materially improved through their personal sacrifices. The case of the woman who sacrificed herself to save her husband (from bandits) indicated the power of a determined and courageous woman to bring benefits to her marital family.

These biographies reveal that women often resorted to self-sacrifice under social pressure. One woman committed suicide to match her husband's filial piety, another to equal a concubine's ardency, and a third to fulfill a promise. Others killed themselves to avoid worse fates, including two to avoid drowning, six to avoid the humiliation and injury of rape, and five to avoid slaughter by bandits. Two widows committed suicide with the expectation that they would be able to rejoin their beloved spouses in the underworld. Several cases suggest the degree to which the "virtue" of suicide had been internalized by women. Two women took their lives despite their husbands' deathbed pleas, and three died by their own hand despite their families' energetic efforts to stop them. Two widow suicides involved voluntary political protests, one in the early Ming and one at its end. These cases demonstrate that women had convictions, acted on them, and were sometimes honored for it, even though it was at great cost to themselves. Some women seem to have exercised some agency in choosing the way to die. Sixteen died by the simplest and least painful way, hanging; two drowned themselves in wells to punish those left behind by fouling the drinking water; five fasted to death, using a method that was slow and painful but best designed to influence others' behavior and to invite intervention. Two widows chose death by beating their heads against their husbands' coffins in efforts to ensure immediate burial with their spouses.[18] Finally, one widow withstood repeated beatings from an aggressive suitor before committing suicide, demonstrating a determination to live as well as a willingness to die if she could not live honorably. It was to popularize that ethic—among men as well as among women—that these women's acts were celebrated in the gazetteer.

The biographies of virtuous women in the Xiangfu gazetteer reminded readers that women as well as men experienced the tensions between the values of self-sacrifice and self-realization, and between personal satisfaction and family welfare, that were characteristic of China during the late Ming—as perhaps they are of any civilization in any period. There is so far little evidence of elite women's more positive and extraordinary achievements, including writing and publication, that has been found for Jiangnan in the late Ming, but much work remains to be done. At the same time, women from all social strata in northeast Henan in the late Ming may have continued to engage in handicraft industries that were more at risk in Jiangnan, where commerce was more developed and enterprises more concentrated. In these ways, women of northeast Henan may have been more representative of the women of China as a whole during this period.[19]

Government Students

Most members of the middle ranks of Ming society made their living directly or indirectly through some combination of agriculture, industry, and commerce. They constituted not so much a distinct middle class (in opposition to an upper and lower class), as a variety of middle strata that related differently to one another and to the elite and masses over time.[20] One stratum consisted of government students who passed examinations at the county and prefectural levels, gained exemption from labor services along with two other members of their families, and received monthly stipends of one shi (133 pounds) of grain, sufficient to support three persons. These privileged commoners were well placed to represent the majority of the people (in other words, other commoners and the masses) in their dealings with the elite and the state. They were qualified to study at the state university and to take the provincial examinations, gateways to elite status and government office. As discussed in Chapter 2, some government students led their families into the elite, looked after their local interests, and cushioned their decline back into the ranks of the commoners.

Whereas the population of China probably doubled or at most tripled over the course of the Ming, the number of government students may have increased twenty times over. Thus the opportunities for literate males—estimated at 10 percent of all males in the late Ming—to become government students increased considerably over the course of the dynasty. Admissions to the university and the quota of provincial degrees, however, remained constant, so that government students' chances for entering the elite declined drastically.

This polity-wide trend was reflected in northeast Henan. There were 1,140 stipendiary (in other words, government) students produced every third year in northeast Henan. (This figure stems from a calculation using the number of schools established at the prefectural, departmental, and county levels and the number of government students allowed per school. It also factors in the reform that changed maximal quotas to minimal ones in the sixteenth century.) Thus, there was a total of approximately 22,800 government students during the last three decades of the Ming. On the reasonable assumption that there were at least as many government students who obtained their status by purchase or decree, the total rises to some forty-five thousand. Assuming the male population of that generation to be from one to three million, as many as 4.5 percent (forty-five thousand/1 million) or as few as 1.5 percent (forty-five thousand/3 million) could expect to become government students. Although there were no limits on the number of times government students could take the provincial examinations, there were only 3,600 numbered cells in the provincial examination hall at the end of the Ming. Since the number of seats was said to be inadequate to accommodate the students desiring to sit for the examinations, there were probably at least four thousand government students prepared to take the examinations at any given time. Given the quota for provincial degrees of about eighty-six per examination, the chances of getting a degree were about 2 percent.[21] In sum, to the extent that government students aspired to enter the elite, there must have been many frustrated ones in this region, as elsewhere, in the last decades of the Ming.

Government students' attitudes may well have been influenced by those of their teachers, who also had reason to become increasingly dissatisfied by the late Ming. During the early Ming, the directors and assistant directors of public schools at the prefectural, departmental, and county levels had been university students and graduates who enjoyed prestige because they were eligible for promotions to high posts in the regular civil service. After 1450, directors were increasingly drawn from the ranks of the less respected tributary students and were generally promoted, if at all, to less prestigious academic posts. In the mid-Ming, education officials who were tributary students were still allowed to take the provincial examinations; those who were provincial graduates were allowed to take the metropolitan examinations. After 1514, even metropolitan graduates began to assume teaching posts. They were permitted to keep the higher ranks they had earned according to their performance in the highest examination. During the late Ming, however, the number of tributary students who passed the qualifying examinations more than doubled from one thousand to 2,600, while the number of teaching posts remained steady at 4,200. The surplus of candidates occasioned long delays in appointments. The paucity of promotions, combined with the effects of inflation, undermined instructors' morale. Many school directors merely collected rent on school lands and did not even try to teach. By 1629 conditions were so poor that Chongzhen suggested abolishing the posts. Court officials refused, arguing that the positions were appropriate for tributary students who had devoted themselves to their studies but were too old for more demanding jobs.[22]

Changes in the selection of education officials, meanwhile, brought them into closer proximity to local society. During the early Ming, in northeast Henan as elsewhere, education officials had tended to be appointed from outside the counties, departments, prefectures, and even provinces in which they served. During the mid-Ming, the rule of avoidance was imposed even more universally and effectively for both educational officials and their assistants. During the late Ming, however, the situation changed dramatically. Perhaps 30 percent of the officials and 50 percent of their assistants were now appointed from within the province, and about 15 percent of both categories of teachers were from within the northeast region.[23]

Given their career frustrations and provincial origins, some of the educational officials of northeast Henan were well positioned to serve as patrons to their government students. As discussed in Chapter 2, local officials often took pride in the students who succeeded in the examinations under their aegis. Patron-client relations were even stronger between educational officials and students hailing from the same province. In some cases, teachers cooperated with their students in conflicts with nobles, bureaucrats, and militarists. Officials and students hailing from the same region sometimes developed political alliances.

Government students also played important roles in the literary societies that proliferated during the last decades of the Ming. Yang Dongming enlisted thirty government students in just one of the several societies he formed in Yucheng. There are no extant membership lists for Meng Shaoyu's Society to Solicit Literature in Qi. But we know that one government student from that county, Li Tingsheng, belonged to one society in Henan and joined others in Beizhili.[24] As Ming authority faded, these societies assumed political as well as literary significance. The prominent roles of teachers in forming and sustaining these organizations gave Chongzhen another reason to consider abolishing teachers' posts, thus reasserting state control. If he had had his way, however, he would merely have accelerated the flow of unemployed teachers into the maelstrom of local politics.

The vital role of government students in the literary-political societies of the late Ming may be illustrated by the admittedly extraordinary case of Hou Fangyu, who came to head the most famous literary group in northeast Henan, the Snow Garden (*xueyuan* 園) or Snow Park (*xueyuan* 苑) Society, in Shangqiu.[25] Unlike many government students, Hou Fangyu owed much of his status to birth into a highly prosperous, cultured, and politically connected family. The origins of the Snow Garden Society can be traced back to 1627 when Fangyu's grandfather Zhipu, his father Xun, and his uncle Ke, all associates of the fallen Donglin party, were living in retirement at home. At the time, Hou Fangyu was only ten years old and he was surrounded by many older and more accomplished youths. They included his elder brother Fangxia, his cousin Fangzhen, the brothers Wu Boyin and Wu Boyi, Liu Boyu, Xu Zuolin, and Jia Kaizong. The Wu brothers were poor orphans who had been taken in by a rich uncle, Liu Ge, a scion of one of Shangqiu's wealthiest families. Liu had earned his provincial degree in 1597 and engaged a tutor for his son Liu Boyu. Xu Zuolin was a descendant of a famous official of the early Ming and son of a learned teacher. He had purchased a government studentship but also studied seriously with the prefectural judge. Jia Kaizong was a free spirit who refused even to become a government student. He admired Sima Xiangru, the great poet of the Former Han, and enjoyed playing the lute, practicing swordsmanship, and traveling the countryside. Among such personalities, preeminence was neither inevitable nor predictable. Only later, when nobles, officials, and the local elite proved unable to respond effectively to contemporary challenges, would the talented Hou Fangyu step into the vacuum as a leader of this group.[26]

During the next five years, Hou Fangyu and his friends began to establish themselves as scholars. In 1628 Fangyu followed his father to Beijing and studied with the Donglin patron Ni Yuanlu. Ni taught him to "familiarize himself with the rival theories of the Warring States period and develop his own talents and only later accept the discipline of laws."[27] Two years later, Fangyu and his brothers accompanied their father to his new post at Changping, northeast of Beijing. That same year, Fangyu's uncle Ke was serving at the state university in Nanjing when the Jiangnan-based Restoration Society (Fushe) won top places in the provincial examination and held a large meeting of the students. At this time, Fangyu's father and uncle were both regarded as patrons of the society. In 1630, Xu Zuolin came in first in the Henan provincial examinations, becoming the first member of the Henan group to enter the local elite. Liu Boyu published an essay that brought the group to the attention of literati in Jiangnan. Two years later, Hou Fangyu returned to Shangqiu and placed first in the county and prefectural examinations. Wu Boyi passed the provincial examinations, becoming the second member of the society to enter the local elite.

During this time, Hou Fangyu composed three essays that revealed his identification with the Donglin and Fushe societies and his developing understanding of history. Taking a leaf from the book of Ouyang Xiu of the Northern Song dynasty, Hou distinguished sharply between parties of gentlemen devoted to justice and those of small-minded men pursuing profit. Reviewing history from the Han through the Song, however, he adopted the pessimistic view that the parties of gentlemen were often victorious in the short run but defeated in the long run. As for eunuchs, who were often the enemies of gentlemen, Hou remarked that they had been kept under control in the early Han and early Ming but greatly exceeded their legitimate roles during the late Han (and, implicitly, the late Ming). Given the Hou family's deep involvement in the Donglin and Fushe, Fangyu naturally came to regard them as parties of gentlemen while the associates of the eunuch Wei Zhongxian and of grand secretary Wen Tiren were the parties of small-minded men. In short, Hou was by family and personal inclination firmly committed to two parties of gentlemen but as a budding historian he was not optimistic about their long-term prospects.

In 1633, at age sixteen, Hou Fangyu was married to the daughter of a Shangqiu scholar-official through the good offices of his grandfather. The following year he again accompanied his father to Beijing, where he witnessed Chongzhen turn the first furrow to mark the arrival of spring. He drafted a memorial for his father, calling for revitalization of the system of military colonies established by the Ming founder in accord with policies initiated by the Former Han.[28] While his elder brother Fangxia passed the provincial examinations with the highest grade and entered the ministry of rites, Fangyu developed a reputation as a writer. Some prominent officials in Beijing had great hopes for him, evoking comparisons to Zhang Anshi of the Han, who was aware of the past, and Li Wenrao of the Tang, who managed the present. Hou Fangyu was less impressed by those in power, lamenting that no one seemed capable of leading a middynastic restoration. That same year, Xu Zuolin failed the metropolitan examinations, reportedly because his direct answers offended the chief grand secretary, Wen Tiren. In Beijing Hou met Jiangnan luminaries of the Revival Society, including Chen Zilong, Xia Yunyi, and Wu Weiye; they, in turn, came to respect the Snow Garden Society, known to them as "the group around Wu, Hou, Xu, and Liu."[29]

During the next two years, Hou Fangyu became further enmeshed in the activities of the Snow Garden and Revival Societies and had further reason to become critical of the Ming state. In 1635, he initiated correspondence with Chen Zilong, who responded with a poem alluding to the original Snow Park that had produced Sima Xiangru in the early Former Han. Later in the year, when the Revival Society leader Zhang Pu came under attack, Fangyu joined with his brother Fangxia in appealing to their father, Xun, to use his influence on Zhang's behalf. In the eleventh month, Hou Xun himself was impeached and charged with mishandling supplies for the troops. As we have seen, he was saved from execution by his erstwhile teacher Zheng Sanjun, who had become president of the ministry of punishments. But Hou Xun was consigned to prison, where he was to remain for the next six years. In the same year, 1636, Wu Boyi won his provincial degree, coming in first in his section on the classics, stirring hope in the Snow Garden Society that success in the existing system was still possible. In 1637, however, when Hou Fangyu's Jiangnan interlocutors Chen Zilong and Xia Yunyi passed the metropolitan examination, his Henan colleague Xu Zuolin failed it.[30]

In May 1639, Hou Fangyu arrived in Nanjing to enroll in the university and prepare for the provincial examinations. He was warmly welcomed by members of the Revival Society who reportedly compared him with Zhou Yu and Wang Meng, prescient strategists of the Three Kingdoms state of Wu and the Latter Qin, respectively. These analogies suggested that, far from becoming a leading official of the Ming, Hou might instead become a strategist for a successor regime. In the meantime, Hou and his friends enjoyed life. Through the good offices of his friends, Hou met a beautiful and talented courtesan named Li Xiangjun who was the belle of the Qinhuai pleasure quarters of Nanjing. He wrote poems for her and she sang for him, once giving him a fan with peach blossoms painted on it.[31]

At this point, Hou Fangyu was approached by Ruan Dacheng, an official who had served under the eunuch Wei Zhongxian and who had been publicly rebuked by the Revival Society in 1638. Because Ruan had received his metropolitan degree in 1616, the same year as Fangyu's father, who reportedly admired him, he hoped that he could enlist Fangyu's assistance against his Revival Society critics. Hou Fangyu, however, not only refused to help but invited Ruan to a public gathering at which he was once more excoriated by the Revival Society youngbloods. Hou thereby made his partisan loyalties clear and joined the large ranks of Ruan Dacheng's antagonists.[32]

In July 1639, Hou Fangyu finally took the provincial examinations in Nanjing. According to the accepted story, he passed the examinations well, but was cut from the final list for violating a taboo. A perusal of Hou's examination essays reveals that his offenses were substantive and not just oversights. In the first of five essays, perhaps reflecting anguish over his father's imprisonment, he lashed out at "high officials of the day," who certainly included the erstwhile chief grand secretary, Wen Tiren, and his current successor, Xue Guoguan. Hou followed his uncle's lead in comparing them with Lu Qi, a high official of the late Tang period who was criticized in the histories for opportunistic maneuvers at the cost of other officials and the people. In his second essay, perhaps reflecting the frustration of Xu Zuolin, who had just failed the metropolitan examination, he reminded his examiners that the Han and other dynasties had used other methods of selecting qualified personnel, including personal recommendations. He asked why such methods could not be adopted by the Ming. In his third essay, he adduced the experience of the Han to argue that the ruler was responsible for educating the heir apparent through the power of example.[33] So far, Hou's positions, although critical of the Ming court for falling short of the Han model, were not overtly hostile.

In his fourth essay, however, Hou stated flatly that the disasters of the day were domestic banditry and frontier incursions about which, he wrote, people were reluctant to speak. He continued in the sorites form of reasoning so familiar to Chinese intellectuals:

> Today, robbers arise because people are poor, people are poor because taxes are heavy, taxes are heavy because troops are proliferating, and troops are proliferating because the frontier needs protection. On the other hand, the frontier situation is bad because the troops are weak, the troops are weak because supplies are scarce, supplies are scarce because grain is not available, and grain is not available because the fields are fallow and many people have become robbers. Moreover these two calamities are likely to continue to exacerbate each other; where it will all end no one knows.[34]

Hou went on to emphasize the priority of the internal struggle over the external, but he shied away from providing any practical solutions to the dilemma. Instead he added insult to injury by alluding to the internal and external crises of earlier dynasties and asserting that he would "break with the tradition of avoiding taboos" to discuss not just the past but the present. It was most likely this direct discussion of contemporary affairs that alarmed the examiners.

If Hou Fangyu's examiners had been partial to the Revival Society, as they had been in 1637, they might have passed him to send a message to the court. But they were not and did not.[35] Xu Lintang, a Nanjing native who would later settle in Shangqiu and join the Snow Garden Society, recorded what happened:

> On the night before the list of successful candidates was posted, an assistant remarked to the chief examiner: "If this student is allowed to submit such essays, we will all certainly be blamed." Master Liao Guolin in the same office forcefully disagreed, saying: "If there is to be blame, this office wants to take full responsibility." The chief examiner delayed a long time before replying: "If we were blamed we would simply be demoted and fined. To set this student aside is really a means of protecting him."[36]

Clarifying his understanding of what had happened to Hou, Xu compared Hou to Liu Fen, a Tang scholar whose essays critical of eunuchs had caused examiners to fail him out of fear of retribution. Xu clearly believed the examiner had failed Hou simply to protect himself.

Undaunted by this rejection, Hou Fangyu continued his campaign in Nanjing against the eunuch party by forming a new group called the Broad Enterprise at the State Gate Society, a name implying sages involved in public affairs. At each meeting, members would drink wine and "chew on Ruan Dacheng." Hou and Ruan both patronized troupes of actors, and Hou wrote an allegorical biography of a famous actor to skewer another "eunuch party official." Mindful of Hou's campaign against eunuchs, contemporaries compared him with Li Ying and Fan Pang, two leading scholar-officials near the end of the Latter Han. Young, handsome, and talented, Hou indulged in wine, women, and song. He could also be arrogant and harsh, reflecting the elitism of his circle and the growing use of violence as the dynasty neared its end. For example, he reportedly once killed a cook who displeased him and threw his corpse into the Qinhuai River.[37] The scholar Huang Zongxi, among others, found Hou's merry making and bravado inappropriate at a time when his father was still languishing in jail. Hou's new society soon disbanded.

In the winter of 1639, perhaps tiring of the dissipation in Nanjing, Hou Fangyu decided to return home. At a send-off party at Taoxie Ferry, Li Xiangjun sang a "guitar song" that strongly criticized the late Han scholar Cai Yong, who although very talented had compromised his reputation by associating with the strongman Dong Zhuo. According to Hou, Li explained:

> Master's [Hou Fangyu's] talent is well known and his writings are very elegant; his cultural level is not inferior to the Court Gentleman's [Cai Yong's]. He [Cai] was good at the lute and broadly learned, a famous talent of his day. But he attached himself to Dong Zhuo and was later criticized for it. The Court Gentleman had knowledge but he did not follow up with action. The lyric transmitted by guitar is wild [in its charges against Cai], but he [Cai] was close to Dong Zhuo and that cannot be covered up. Master is strong, his steps unrestrained. He has recently been disappointed, and now we are parting, perhaps never to see one another again. I want him to continue to respect himself to the end and never to forget this Guitar Song his concubine sang! For I will never sing it again.[38]

If Li Xiangjun reached back to the late Latter Han for a cautionary tale, she may have thought about the succeeding Jin for a more positive model. Taoxie Ferry, where she sang her song, was named after a beloved concubine of Wang Xian, a scholar-recluse of the Jin period. After Hou left, Li reportedly refused all other suitors despite offers of large sums of money.[39] She apparently expected Hou to pursue a similarly principled course as he navigated the treacherous waters of late Ming politics (see Figure 3.1).

According to Hou Fangyu's retrospective account, he set out for Shangqiu in late 1639 in an optimistic mood. Bandits crisscrossed the central plain and officials attacked the Fushe, but Jiangnan still enjoyed peace, and the court still sought out pure scholars. Hou could count on support from his Fushe friends in Henan and on continuing contacts with like-minded scholars in Jiangnan. As a contemporary put it: "Scholars of the central plain had heard about those of the south; and those of the south were familiar with those of the central plain."[40] At the end of the year, back in Shangqiu, Hou sent off his friends Wu Boyi and Xu Zuolin to take the metropolitan examinations in Beijing. While Hou referred to his own recent failure in the examinations as a "liberation," he apparently continued to hope that his colleagues would succeed. In 1640, however, Wu and Xu failed the examinations and returned to Shangqiu in gloom. It was apparently at this time that Hou assumed formal leadership of the Snow Garden

FIGURE 3.1. Hou Fangyu. Source: Ye 1930: 2.

Society. He acknowledged Song Quan, the prominent scholar-official living at home in Shangqiu, as his teacher.[41]

In 1640–41 Hou and his friends did not write openly about contemporary affairs, but the historical models they chose for themselves and ascribed to each other reveal their changing attitudes. In his essay sending off Wu and Xu to Beijing, for example,

Hou referred to "the old cottage at Gaoyang," an allusion to the student Li Shiqi of Qi county, Kaifeng prefecture, who had served as an advisor to Liu Bang, founder of the Han dynasty. According to Sima Qian, Li had come to the attention of Liu after denying that he was a ruist scholar and asserting that he was only a "wine drinker of Gaoyang." By this allusion, Hou seemed to justify his dissipation and signal his aspiration to be an untrammeled hero in search of the Way that might lie outside the existing system. As discussed in Chapter 2, another scholar from northeast Henan, Li Mengyang, had initiated a mid-Ming literary trend that returned to the Han for prose and the Tang for poetry. In 1640–41 Hou's Snow Garden Society continued the literary tradition of Li Mengyang. In a preface to Wu Boyin's collected works written before 1642, Hou noted that many of the essays were rooted in the two Hans while the poetry was somewhere between Han Yu and Li Shangyin of the Tang.[42]

Hou Fangyu and his friends invoked other models from the Han past to criticize the late-Ming state. In early 1641 Hou prefaced the poetry of a fellow government student from Anhui with praise for Zou Yang and other scholars who had flourished under Xiao Wang, the younger brother of Han Wudi who had presided over the Liang kingdom in the Shangqiu region. In a later essay, Hou remarked that Jia Kaizong admired Sima Xiangru, who had also been patronized by the prince of Liang. Like Sima, Jia was a free spirit who denied that he should be judged according to standards laid down by Kongzi. Hou Fangyu also compared Wu Boyin to Sima Xiangru but noted that, unlike Sima who had become a high official in the Han, Wu was never used by the Ming state. Fangyu's cousin, Fangyue, meanwhile, was compared by contemporaries with Chen Menggong. Chen was a free spirit of the late-Western Han and Wang Mang periods who collected books, patronized "guests" (armed men), suppressed banditry, and resisted frontier incursions. Fangyue was a tributary student who had served briefly as a magistrate in Jiangsu before quitting his post and devoting himself to writing poetry and righting wrongs in his hometown.[43] Although Fangyue and his younger brother Fangyan were not members of the Snow Garden Society, they patronized their own guests and contributed to a swashbuckling atmosphere in Shangqiu at the end of the Ming.

Members of the Snow Garden Society recognized parallels, too, between the Latter Han and their own day. In a funerary inscription for the Jiangnan scholar Wu Yingji, Hou Fangyu compared their close friendship to that between Fan Zuo and Zhang Shao of the Latter Han. Fangyu praised Wu Boyi for his deep and broad learning and remarked that he "came from a place between Guo Tai and Huangfu Gui," two outspoken scholars involved in the partisan struggles of the late Han.[44] In their fascination with the late Latter Han, the Snow Garden literati seemed to be preparing themselves for the end of the Ming.

Hou Fangyu's expectation of the imminent demise of the Ming was evident in his appraisal of a contemporary, Zhang Wei. Zhang had been born into a poor family in Shangqiu but had somehow managed to accumulate a fair amount of wealth. Hoping to become a government student, he took the first set of examinations. When he failed, he cajoled his examiner into changing the grade. He then took the examinations a second time, failed again, and again tried to get the grade changed. This time he was thrown out of the examiner's office. Zhang enlisted the support of many graduates and students and caused a commotion. In the end, though, Zhang never placed, and by 1640 he was getting old and discouraged. Hou Fangyu later compared the aggressive Zhang with Ni Heng, a proud scholar active at the end of the Latter Han who refused to submit to anyone.[45] Once again, a Han habitus was invoked, this time to justify behavior that bordered on rebellion.

Hou Fangyu and his friends may even have been anticipating less centralized— though hardly better ordered—states like those that had succeeded the Han. For example, they saw clear parallels between the Jìn period and their own day. When Fangyu and Hou Yin, a clan uncle who never earned a degree but was devoted to literature, married sisters, people compared them with Ruan Xian and his uncle Ruan Ji, two of the Seven Worthies of the Bamboo Grove (*zhulin qixian*) from northeast Henan who had also married sisters. Fangyu's cousin Fangzhen published a collection of poetry titled *From the Studio of the Great Jìn.* Fangyu's preface described the scholar-official poets Wang Dao and Xie An of the Jìn as precedents for his cousin. Later, in 1646, Hou Fangyu would write that Jia Kaizong had once followed the example of Ruan Ji of the Western Jìn and remained drunk for sixty days to avoid serving in office.[46] When the (Western) Jìn was expelled from its capital in Luoyang in 317 CE by the Later Zhao, headed by a frontier minority people, the (Eastern) Jìn court established its capital in Jinling (Nanjing). Hou Fangyu was clearly impressed by the parallel to the late Ming, which had been driven from Beijing by the Manchus and subsequently established its capital in Nanjing (although less successfully than the Jìn).

The atmosphere in the Snow Garden Society in 1640 is revealed in an account of a party organized by Zhang Wei to welcome back Wu Boyi and Xu Zuolin from their unsuccessful quest for metropolitan degrees in Beijing. When Zhang had drunk enough to loosen his tongue, he proclaimed: "I am Ma Zhou! The world is in trouble, why don't they use me? But of course the world does not recognize scholars, so how can it recognize me?" According to Hou Fangyu, some guests reproached Zhang for being impolite; others said he was crazy. But Xu Zuolin exclaimed:

> You sons of wealth and nobility all depend on your fathers' and elder brothers' surpluses to stuff yourselves with meat! The world is heading toward chaos and there are no heroes who can save the situation. The likes of us can easily perish overnight. How can anyone say that Wei is crazy!?[47]

At this outburst many of the guests wept, and the party ended. In fact, by identifying with Ma Zhou, Zhang Wei was too optimistic. Ma, after all, had been overlooked by the early-Tang court and had taken to drink, but he had finally been recognized and appointed to high office. Zhang's fate and that of his friends was to be quite different.

Meanwhile in Xiangfu, another government student from an elite family, Li Guangtian, was drawn into a position of leadership in the last years of the Ming. Sources disagree over the origins of Li's family, but an ancestor seems to have been in Kaifeng by the early Ming. According to the genealogy, the Lis joined the elite in the seventh generation when one brother became a tributary student and another became a metropolitan graduate. In the ninth generation, one member of the family served briefly as a commander in a ward office in southern Beijing and then retired to live at home in Kaifeng. His son, Li Guangtian, became a government student. Although two other members of Guangtian's generation became provincial graduates and held government posts, it was Guangtian, the government student, who was to help lead the defense of Kaifeng city from rebels.[48]

Commoner Landlords

Another middle-level occupational group consisted of commoner landlords: those who acquired more land than they could work and rented out the surplus to tenants. Owner-cultivators were more prevalent in north China than in south China, but there were also some landlords in northeast Henan. According to Martin Heijdra, single-cropping and animal-drawn plowing in dry land made farms of one hundred to five hundred mu most economical in north China so that landlords there often had larger holdings than those in south China. Commoner landlords typically translated the proceeds of rent into liquid wealth and used it to buy local influence, education for their sons, and even degrees. They therefore produced most of the elite as well as other members of the middle strata. Commoner landlords must nonetheless be distinguished from elite landlords: they lacked exemptions from service and taxes and influence necessary to resist officials. In conflicts with elite landlords, commoner landlords were at a disadvantage, although their much larger numbers and, at least in the early Ming, greater collective wealth gave them a certain power that the elite could not ignore. Commoner landlords must also be distinguished from the masses, including owner-cultivators, tenants, bondservants, laborers, "serfs," and slaves, over whom they often wielded extraeconomic influence.[49]

Commoner landlords do not figure prominently in the records, but they may sometimes be glimpsed in genealogies in the generations just prior to the emergence of members of the elite. Wang Tingxiang's father took advantage of changes in the course of the Yellow River and a reduction in a prince's holdings to cultivate virgin and ownerless land. A Liu descent group in Shangqiu parlayed a hereditary guard commandership into "enormous amounts of property" through transactions "based on trust and clever schemes."[50] The Songs of Shangqiu went into trade (and probably landholding) to support their relatives. The Hes of Qi accumulated land (and probably went into business) to increase their wealth several times over in a single decade. Other landlord families, such as the Chus of Suizhou, simply appropriated their neighbors' lands by force, although that was much easier to do once they obtained degrees and entered the local elite.

The general trend toward the concentration of landholding in certain families during the late Ming was widely noted by contemporaries and has been largely accepted by historians, but systematic statistical evidence of the process is lacking in northeast Henan, as elsewhere. Even the extant figures—the two thousand mu of the Lüs of Ningling, the 100,000 mu of the Lius of Shangqiu—are difficult to interpret because the numbers of people belonging to such families remain unspecified. Two anecdotal assessments of the size and distribution of landholdings in the region illustrate the problem. Presumably referring to elite landlords, the early-Qing government student Zheng Lian of Shangqiu estimated that those in the late Ming with a lot of land had over 100,000 mu while those with little still had fifty thousand mu. Probably describing commoner landowners, the late-Ming metropolitan graduate Meng Shaoyu arrived at three more modest ranks: families with over one thousand mu, those with over one hundred, and those with over ten. Since Zheng Lian's immediate family had no degrees and reportedly had some five hundred mu of land, he clearly belonged to the commoner landlord stratum described by Meng Shaoyu. Considering that Meng's family boasted several graduates and he personally contributed one thousand mu of land to a charitable trust, his family clearly figured among the elite landlords described by Zheng Lian. Ding Mouxun's family of Yongcheng, with six hundred mu, ranked among the smaller elite landlords.[51]

While a full account of landlord income is impossible, anecdotal evidence suggests the importance of money derived from commercial agriculture. For example, a guard commander named Zhang in Qi county turned several thousand mu of his family's inherited land into a thriving farm in the middle of the fifteenth century. Some landowners sold excess grain for immediate consumption or for manufacturing spirits. Others cultivated and processed cotton, which had first appeared as a tributary item in the Han and spread in the Song and Yuan. Because cotton was more productive than silk or wool per unit of land and benefited more from various refinements in the processes of production, it was cheaper than those other fibers. The Ming founder therefore encouraged the cultivation, manufacture, sale, and taxation of cotton. He required Henan and the other four provinces of North China to submit between one and two million bolts of cotton cloth and up to one million jin of cotton each year to clothe troops on the northern frontier. Already by the end of the Hongwu reign, Henan was providing 220,000 jin of cotton a year to the central government. By the Zhengde reign, cotton was cultivated throughout the province, including all three prefectures of the northeast. During the Ming, commoners typically wore cotton clothing so that the term "cotton clothing" became a metonym for commoners and a fitting symbol of that populist age. By the late Ming, the cultivation of cotton began to compete seriously with the growing of grain in certain counties. For example, in Yanjin county, Kaifeng prefecture, half the arable land was said to be planted with cotton.[52]

According to Zhong Huamin, by the mid-Wanli reign, northeast Henan grew more cotton than it consumed locally and provided to the state. It put the surplus on the market and much of it ended up in the mills of Jiangnan. Zhong, in fact, expressed concern that people were selling their raw cotton rather than processing it for their own use, thus having to buy cloth on the market rather than manufacturing their own. Profits were flowing into the hands of the merchants who conducted the trade, resulting in an actual decline in the standard of living of some farmers who produced the crop. But some of the cash found its way into the hands of the larger landowners who could afford to put part of their land into cotton and part of their labor into processing it. In addition to the raw cotton fiber, landlords produced the by-products of seeds and oil, and, in some cases, manufactured cotton cloth. To be sure, some of the resulting fabric, such as that of Qi county, was not of sufficient quality to be used as tributary items. Some counties, such as Shangqiu, still did not list cotton among its exchanged commodities in the late Ming.[53]

The landlord families of northeast Henan sold a wide variety of other products in the towns of the region. Yucheng county sold papaya in Shangqiu, while Shangqiu marketed high quality rice "in all four directions." Linying county was famous for its soft silk thread and Yuzhou for its iron manufactures. Zhengzhou was known for its high quality rice and indigo, and Chenzhou for its fine bows and arrows. Weihui sent rice to Kaifeng city.[54]

With its many nobles, officials, and markets, Kaifeng city consumed a wide variety of products from throughout northeast Henan. Kaifeng's estimated 300,000 people annually consumed perhaps a million and a half piculs of rice, millet, and wheat. 500,000 piculs were supplied from prefectural and provincial tax receipts; the balance was purchased in two markets in the southern and western quarters of the city. Kaifeng also had eight daily produce markets that sold fresh vegetables, fruits, fish, poultry, and meat brought in from nearby counties. While much textile manufacturing was done by farm families, one entire street in Kaifeng was filled with looms that processed raw cotton and silk brought in from the surrounding countryside. Just as grain produced by farm families was grist for a dozen mills in the city, so cotton and silk fabrics woven in the countryside and market towns were dyed in a dozen shops in the city. Suizhou was known for its fine leather turbans, and the Muslims of Kaifeng produced other leather goods. One section of Kaifeng was known for making shoes, and thirty stores made hats to order. Leather tunics, hose, and trousers made in Kaifeng sold well as far away as Beijing. Firewood, medicinal herbs, mulberry paper, ramie cloth, iron implements, and even horses were sold by rural producers to urban consumers in Kaifeng.[55] Such transactions brought much silver and copper specie into the hands of landowning families, allowing them to purchase more land and increase their social standing.

The importance of the commercial economy for the landlords of northeast Henan was reflected in a negative way in the case of Zhang Wei's son. He apparently tried to trump his father's wealth by speculating in the horse market in Shangqiu and lost his fortune.[56] By the 1640s, such experiences may have been on the increase as Henanese landlords suffered along with others in a global recession.

Artisans and Merchants

The Han-period ideal of four essential occupational groups, headed by scholars and farmers followed by artisans and merchants, remained in the minds of many people of the Ming period. Under the Ming founder, artisans had been organized into one of the hereditary status groups, expected to put their talents to the service of the state. Merchants, although not a hereditary group, were subject to certain restrictions. Sumptuary laws forbade them to wear silk clothing and price controls kept them from hoarding during famines. In theory, artisans and merchants could gain social respectability only by investing their profits in land and educating their sons to take the examinations.

During the Ming, as ever, actual society diverged from the ideal hierarchy. Hereditary artisanal families soon turned to other pursuits, and merchants ignored the sumptuary laws and attained social standing on the basis of their commercial wealth. As a result of a long period of peace and order in the sixteenth century, manufacturing and commerce flourished, and the tax system was gradually monetized. The state became increasingly beholden to independent artisans and merchants for the production and distribution of commodities both for itself and for the population at large. With the resumption of foreign trade and the influx of silver during the Wanli period, many felt that artisans and especially merchants were taking over the society and threatening the inherited social norms. In the twentieth century, many historians have analyzed the growth of industry and commerce in the late Ming, and some have professed to see the sprouts of capitalism that they would have expected to grow on the model of contemporary Europe. This model raises the question of values and directs our attention not only to the effects of commercialization on artisans and merchants but also to their reactions— and those of their contemporaries—to such changes.[57]

Like women and commoner landlords, artisans and merchants usually received only passing mention in sources written by members of the elite. Fortunately, however, one scholar-official wrote expressly about merchants during the late Ming and even compared their situations in various provinces.

Zhang Han was a descendant of a landowning and commercial family of Hangzhou, Zhejiang, who became a scholar-official in the Wanli reign. His essay "On Merchants" appeared in the 1590s. Adopting the style of the Han historian Sima Qian's essay on food and commodities in the *Historical Records*, Zhang commented on the commercial status of each province in turn. He began with Beizhili, where he emphasized the importance of tributary trade from abroad. He then turned to Henan:

> South of the capital, Henan takes its place in the center of the world with Kaifeng as its capital. One can go north up the Wei and Zhang Rivers right to the edge of the capital [Beijing], or follow east along the Bian and Si Rivers to the Han and Yangzi. Land communications extend in all directions, and merchants delight in gathering here. The region is rich in lacquer, fine hemp fiber, nettle hemp fiber, ramie, cotton thread, cotton wadding, tin, wax, and leather. In ancient times the Zhou house established its capital in this province. The land is flat and expansive, the people numerous and prosperous. By custom they are thrifty and accustomed to work. Those who go east to trade in Shandong or west to trade in Sichuan and Huguang are all "men of Zhou." From Zhangde they go to Shanxi and north Zhili, and over to the place where the Yellow and Luo Rivers intersect. From Nanyang they go down the Qi and Huang Rivers to Xiangyang and Yunyang. As well, they carry on close trade with the Huai-Si region [northern Nanzhili]. Runing offers a fine example of the flourishing material life of the people and is well provided with water and land communications.[58]

In Zhang's view, the central province continued to be identified with the Zhou, perhaps because the Eastern Zhou had had its capital in Luoyang and the name Zhou had been appropriated by the Ming prince in Kaifeng. Zhang's surprisingly upbeat analysis of the economy was perhaps colored by his awareness of the prosperity of the region in the Western Han and Northern Song.

Whatever the degree of hyperbole in Zhang's description of Henan's commercial centrality in the Ming, he was correct in portraying the province as the transport center of the polity (see Map 3.1). The main road from Beijing ran south to Weihui pre-

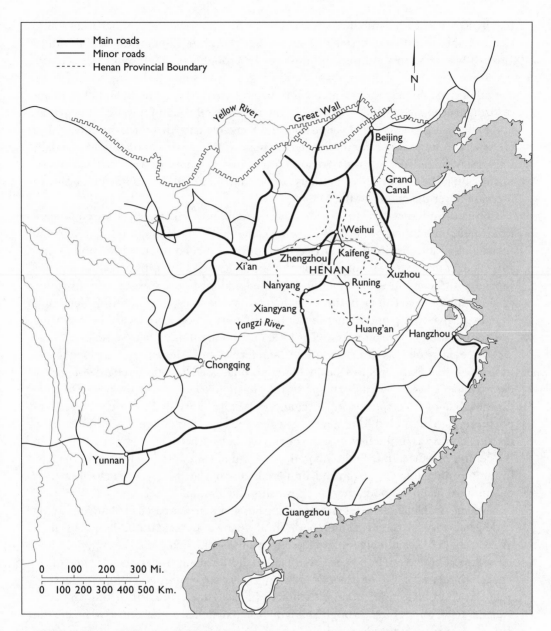

MAP 3.1. Roads of the Ming Period. Sources: Based on Wakeman 1985: following p. 27; Brook 1998: 36, map 2; Twitchett and Mote 1998: 505, 590. Used with permission from the University of California Press and the author.

fecture where it divided into three branches. The first (more minor) branch went south-east to Kaifeng, the second (major) branch went south to Zhengzhou, and the third (major) branch went southwest to Luoyang. Two roughly parallel routes then continued south, one from Kaifeng, through Runing, and on south to Huang'an in Hubei, the other from Zhengzhou through Nanyang and on to Xiangyang in Hubei. A major horizontal artery meanwhile ran from Xi'an in the west through Luoyang, Zhengzhou, and Kaifeng, and on through Qi, Suizhou, and Yongcheng to Xuzhou in the east. Within Henan, all counties were interconnected by reasonably substantial roads and had daily markets. Although market towns did not compare in size or number with what had existed in the Song, the frequency of markets in the towns and villages of northeast Henan increased over the course of the Ming.[59]

From the mid-Wanli reign, as state finances went into deficit and private commerce flourished, both officials and the local elite came to rely increasingly on merchants to recruit labor and distribute resources. River officials turned to entrepreneurs to provide labor to maintain the dikes along the Yellow River. Relief officials allowed prices to rise to attract grain to Henan and then used administrative measures to distribute grain to the starving. Fan Liangyan in Yucheng supported the policy of hiring merchants to manage river work, and Zhang Jinyan from Xinxiang concurred with the late-Ming policy of enlisting merchants as well as local elite in distributing famine relief.[60]

Since the people were thrifty and the land fertile, most Henanese continued to cultivate the soil and sell surpluses locally. One Luoyong-based timber merchant doing business in Kaifeng became wealthy and powerful enough to compete with the prince of Zhou for the affections of a courtesan. Merchants of Wuan county, in Zhangde prefecture in northern Henan, traded long-distance in tin, coal, iron, and copper. But most long-distance trade was in the hands of outside merchants "who delighted in gathering" in the central province. In the mid-Ming, the most numerous were from Jiangxi province; by the late Ming, they were from Huizhou prefecture in Nanzhili. In 1607 Huizhou merchants were said to be operating 213 pawnshops in Henan.[61]

Among the Huizhou merchants was Wang Shiqing, who was based in Shangqiu. Wang had been born into a family of merchants in Wuyuan county that traced its lineage back to the Tang. He was intelligent and liked to study, but he failed the examinations and turned to commerce. He traveled to Shaanxi and Sichuan, traded in salt and fish in Zhejiang, and patronized relatives, one of whom became a magistrate. Wang wrote acceptable verse and befriended eminent scholar-officials such as the artist Dong Qichang. Late in life he was passing through Shangqiu when he fell ill and chanced to meet Hou Zhipu. Hou reportedly advised him: "This is the center, you can make it your base." Wang accordingly took up residence in Shangqiu, returning to Zhejiang only in old age to write poetry and die at age seventy-one.[62]

Wang Shiqing was a typical scholar-merchant of the late Ming who parlayed wealth and education into relatively high status in the eyes of the elite.[63] He apparently never purchased—let alone earned—a degree, and yet he socialized with leading literati and wrote poetry. When he died, a son who was still living in Shangqiu intended to take his coffin back to Nanzhili to bury him in the ancestral plot. As a result of the military disturbances at the end of the Ming, however, he never realized his plans. In the early Qing, he asked Hou Fangyu to write an epitaph that could compensate for his lack of filial piety. Hou agreed, ostensibly to recompense an acquaintance whose melancholy he had long noticed but never before understood. In fact Hou was probably well paid for his essay. In any case, Hou wrote that Wang's son was indeed admirable since neither an unseemly quest for profit nor a superstitious belief in geomancy—but rather political disorder—had prevented him from fulfilling his filial duty. Without revealing the outcome of the son's plans, Hou celebrated both the father's commercial exploits and the son's filial intentions. He also alluded to the Han historian Sima Qian's inclusion of merchants in his *Historical Records* as if to legitimate his epitaph to Wang Shiqing.[64]

Two other cases demonstrate the close links between commercial wealth in one generation and scholarly attainment in the next. Zhang Qing of She county, Huizhou prefecture, who came to live in Xiangfu in the sixteenth century, had a son, Zhang Yizhu, who won his metropolitan degree in 1568 and held a succession of central posts. (He retired briefly during the ascendancy of grand secretary Zhang Juzheng; even the sons of merchants, it seemed, could not tolerate the profit-seeking regent.) Cao Hua, another Huizhou man, "arrived with his father to trade in Bian" and became a government student. He passed the provincial and metropolitan examinations, served as an examiner in Sichuan, and traveled widely before returning home in his old age. Although he had won his degrees as a Huizhou man and retired to an unspecified place, he was honored with a biography as a "sojourning worthy" in the Xiangfu gazetteer.[65] In these cases, immigrants to Kaifeng won civil service degrees and biographies in the local gazetteer that mention their fathers' commercial activities, which might otherwise have remained unrecorded.

A fuller view of the merchants of late-Ming Kaifeng is offered in the anonymous *Record as if in a Dream*, written in the early Qing. According to this work, merchants came from as far away as Canton, Hangzhou, Nanjing, and Beijing as well as Huizhou; traders in silk, tea, and horses hailed from neighboring Shanxi; and peddlers arrived from numerous towns in Shandong as well as from other parts of Henan. Natives of Kaifeng, meanwhile, managed a dozen prosperous pawnshops, two dozen ingot-casting shops, and hundreds of other kinds of stores. The several thousand merchants of Kaifeng thus reaffirmed commercial traditions that dated back to the Song and helped define the city.[66]

According to the *Record*, the artisans and merchants of Kaifeng organized themselves in various ways. Some artisans making the same products tended to congregate in certain streets or quarters: Bow and Arrow Street had several workshops making those items; another street had more than twenty silversmiths; the street leading from the Great Plaza to the Bell Tower had a profusion of clothing stores. Trademarks identified shops selling specific items: for example, fishes identified incense stores and iron shoes marked cobbler shops. Many merchants belonged to some 430 guilds that paid commercial taxes to the state and underwrote the expenses of the triennial provincial examinations. Wholesale marts for grain were called *hang*, suggesting some kind of state-supervised guild organization. For example, two families held state licenses to sell red ocher and green dye. Sellers of fruits and vegetables, livestock and poultry, and cotton and firewood operated in *shi* with less official supervision. While perishables were sold primarily in public markets and by private peddlers, drygoods and hardware could be found in stores scattered throughout the city. On the street that featured clothes, for example, one could find mirror shops, pawnshops, saddle-makers, a winery, a silver-ingot caster, and food stalls. Some streets bore names, such as Tinsmith Lane and Tea Leaf Lane, that had little to do with the shops that lined them in the late Ming.[67]

A few of the businesses in Kaifeng may have been managed by individuals: for example, Zhang Yingfeng's food and drink shop. Many more were owned by families, such as the Fang family portrait studio. The Yu family ran five silk stores, one west of the Drum Tower and four to the east of it. Brand name shops, such as the Helin, dealt in a wide variety of commodities. Some could be large: the Rusong store had one hundred rooms. Since these stores required a fair amount of capital and often sold goods from outside the province, June Mei has suggested that they may have been run by groups of merchants who pooled their resources.[68]

In sum, by the late Ming, artisans no longer belonged to a hereditary caste, instead producing for a market that included buyers from among the nobility and the elite as well as women, students, and landlords. Merchants no longer observed the sumptuary laws; instead, they lived in a style commensurate with their wealth and associated with the elite without having to take the examinations or even purchase degrees. Yet certain trades and professions tended to remain in family lines, and certain commercial families adopted the literati's style of life and prepared their sons to enter the elite. Some artisans and merchants were obviously somewhat literate, but they left behind no texts to indicate their values and perspectives. Fortunately, a minor functionary wrote an account that provides a fuller description of Kaifeng city at the end of the Ming.

Minor Functionaries

During the Ming, as before and after it, minor functionaries played important roles between the regular officials and the general population. They existed at all levels, from the ministries in the capital to magistracies in the countryside, and they held a wide variety of posts, from low-ranked (5a–9a) vice prefects, assistant prefects, judges, vice magistrates, and assistant magistrates to unranked police chiefs and jailers. In many prefectures and counties there were other minor functionaries, sometimes ranked and sometimes not, including station masters, patrolmen, transport officers, record keepers, clerks, and runners.[69]

Ranked and unranked assistants to prefects and magistrates held a status that was formal but low. In the gazetteers they are often listed in the section on officials, but the data are often incomplete and not easily compared. Information from ten gazetteers chosen at random reveals a few aspects of their status in the late Ming. Unlike the education officials discussed above, these assistants almost invariably continued to come from outside the province. In the areas of taxes and justice, as opposed to education, the late-Ming state made no concession to localism. Many of the assistants held minor degrees, but some were listed merely as clerks. Despite their low status, assistants could wield considerable power in the late Ming when regular officials often failed to arrive at their posts or left without notice. As in the case of local officials discussed in Chapter 1, some counties in other provinces supplied more minor functionaries to northeast Henan at certain times and places than would be expected by chance. This suggests that political networks played a role in their placement.[70]

During the early and middle Ming, clerks had been relatively few and unimportant since magistrates had dealt directly with local notables, elders, and landlords and had collected taxes and administered justice through the village-based collective systems of *lijia* and *baojia*. With the Single Whip reforms, magistrates relied increasingly upon clerks and runners to assist them in obtaining revenues and maintaining order. Clerks therefore increased greatly in number. By 1587, estimates indicated that there were four times as many clerks as there were regular officials, yielding some 100,000 clerks for the entire polity. Each county had six offices, corresponding to the six ministries of the central government, and each office was said to have had at least ten clerks. According to a report by Hou Fangyu, the number of clerks per county may have increased to several hundred by the end of the Ming. Unlike minor officials, clerks lacked degrees, were unranked, and only rarely moved up into regular offices. They were typically local residents, not just from the same province but from the same department or county where they served, and they usually inherited or purchased their posts. They received little or no salary and thus depended on gifts that shaded easily into bribes. Their jobs at the *yamen* gave them access to power and wealth beyond that of most commoners, but they lacked the social status to match and were routinely excoriated by officials and elite as corrupt and degenerate.[71]

As a government student aspiring to enter the elite, Hou Fangyu expressed the usual elite disdain for clerks. He argued that late-Ming regulations regarding clerks were inferior to those of the Han and the Tang, which had required functionaries to have some education before winning appointments to posts. According to Hou, in earlier ages clerks had been few in number, self-respecting, intent on achievement, and gentlemanly in conduct. In the Ming, however, there was no control over clerk appointments. In Hou's words,

> Villains do it, vagabonds do it, criminals do it, absconding slaves and overbearing servants of the local elite do it. These jobs are passed on to sons and grandsons or handed over to relatives and friends. With all of these types in place, where is there room for any others?[72]

In the Tang dynasty, Hou continued, officials had not been shy about dismissing incompetent clerks. Even in the early Ming an official who had once been a clerk had firmly prosecuted wayward subordinates. In recent decades, however, clerks had proliferated at all levels and usurped the authority of ranked officials and their assistants. Hou estimated that each clerk brought hardship to about one hundred people. Since there were one thousand large counties with an average of three hundred clerks each, some 300,000 clerks were adversely affecting some thirty million people. The solution, in Hou's view, was to limit the numbers of clerks allowed in offices and to require officials to enforce the regulations, not shrinking from acting strictly in the manner of the Legalists Shang Yang and Han Feizi, if necessary.

While late-Ming literati wrote about clerks, clerks rarely wrote about themselves. Fortunately, one document, the *Record as if from a Dream*, may inadvertently reveal the worldview of a minor functionary from northeast Henan. The anonymous author was certainly literate because he recorded inscriptions and produced the text with his own hand. But, unlike the Song writer Meng Yuanlao, on whose *Record of Dreaming of Liang* he modeled his work, the Ming author of this text was not highly literate. According to Chang Moulai, the Qing editor of the first printed edition of the text, the original manuscript (unfortunately no longer available) was marred by numerous stylistic errors. Unlike Meng's famous work, it did not treat all aspects of daily life but limited itself largely to material conditions. Given the wealth and precision of the data it contained on government offices and the market economy, the author was probably a minor functionary in charge of taxes or security.[73] He may have worked from written sources and interviews with survivors of the flood of 1642 to produce his highly detailed account.

As edited by Chang Moulai, *Record as if from a Dream* consists of two prefaces and ten chapters. In his preface, the author remarked on the city's central location, which had survived the many vicissitudes of history. In chapters 1 and 2, he described the two walls and five gates of the city. He explained that the west gate faced due west, to receive beneficial influences, while the four other gates—one each to the north and south, and two to the east—were constructed at an angle to contain such prosperity as might accumulate in the city. Chapters three and four described the Zhou estate located near the center of the city and the residences of the nobles dispersed throughout the city. Chapter five described the provincial, prefectural, and county offices located to the southwest of the Zhou estate. Chapters six through eight traced two sets of streets, called Dragons' Beards, that extended to the south of the Zhou estate, and then explored the streets of the central city as well as markets in the suburbs. Chapter nine took up the examination halls, located near the southwestern corner of the Zhou estate. A final chapter surveyed the annual cycle of festivals that brought the residents of Kaifeng together in the streets and temples of the city (see Maps 3.2 and 3.3).

This account, reflecting the worldview of a late-Ming minor functionary, began with the cultural and historical foundations of the city:

> Bianliang is in the part of the world known as Yuzhou. It is the central pivot between heaven and earth, the hub of eight provinces, the heart and stomach of the realm. It has been called Da Liang, Bianzhou, Bianjing, and Bianliang. It has gone through many changes over time, consolidated strong walls and deep moats, and acquired a foundation that cannot be destroyed for ten thousand years.[74]

The eight provinces included Henan as well as the seven others contiguous to it.

As described in the Introduction, the area of Kaifeng had not in fact been a major cultural, political, or commercial center during much of Chinese history. After the Shang period, it had flourished as a center mainly in periods of central government breakdown, as in the Warring States, when it was the capital of the regional states of Wei and Liang, and in the Song, when it was the capital of the Northern Song and Jin. Yet Kaifeng was located in the semilegendary central province of Yu, at the heart of the central plain, and it was the capital of Henan province in the Ming. As such, the city participated fully in the inherited culture of the central state(s), a culture that was embedded in its buildings, artifacts, and stories. Such material evidence reminded the author as well as other residents of the "active presence of past experiences" in their daily lives.

The *Record* reveals how the historical sites of Kaifeng embodied and transmitted the

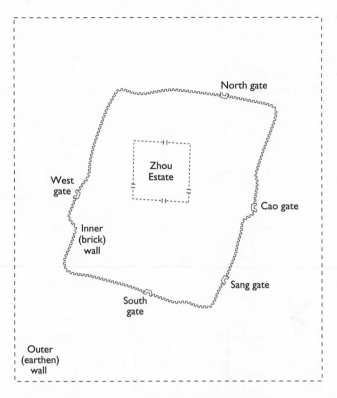

MAP 3.2. Walls and Gates of Kaifeng City in the Ming. (Shape and location of outer wall are approximate.) Source: Mei 1975: 37. Used with the permission of the author.

concept of cultural centrality. Among the government buildings southwest of the Zhou estate was a temple containing statues of Kings Wu and Cheng, founders of the Zhou dynasty who came from the west, and of their semilegendary advisor, Jiang Taigong, who hailed from the central plain. Nearby was a shrine celebrating Mengzi's visit to Liang, a trip made from the east alluded to by Lü Kun and evidence of the importance of the region in the Spring and Autumn/Warring States period. Although northeast Henan had played an important part in Cao Cao's state of Wei during the Three Kingdoms, orthodox theory since the Song held that it had been Liu Bei's state of Shu-Han in Sichuan that had been the legitimate successor to the Han. Kaifeng went along with that view, hosting numerous shrines to Guan Yu, the Shu-Han general who had been posthumously promoted to be the god of war. The antiquity and longevity of the city were embodied in the thirteen-story Youguo Temple established in the Northern Qi. The structure had been refaced in the Song with rust-colored tile and was therefore better known as the Iron Pagoda. It had survived the wars, floods, and earthquakes of the following millennium and remained the tallest structure in the city.[75]

The Tang was represented by a shrine to the Three Worthies in the southern suburb. There sacrifices were periodically conducted to the spirits of the poets Li Bo, Du Fu, and Gao Shi. Ming aristocrats, officials, and scholars often convened there to celebrate the Qingming and Chongyang festivals. A shrine to Masters Zhang Xun and Xu

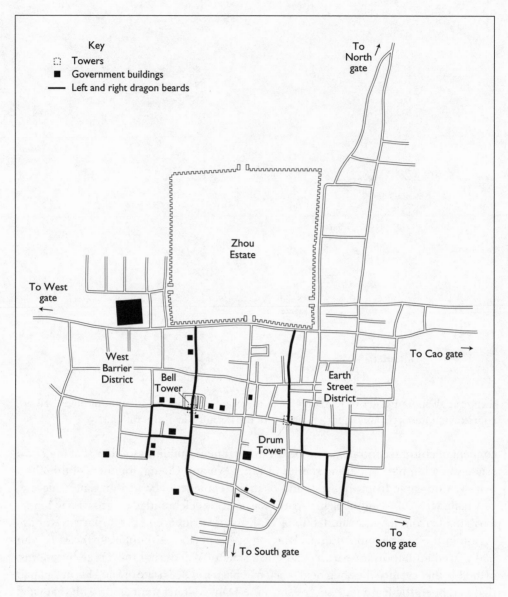

MAP 3.3. Major Streets and Districts of Central Kaifeng. Note: Symbols indicate only approximate locations; structures are not to scale. Source: Mei 1975: 45. Used with permission of the author.

Yuan, generals who had resisted the mid-Tang rebellion of An Lushan in northeast Henan, was the locus of annual sacrifices during the Ming. The site of the palace of Zhu Wen, the general who had ended the Tang and established his own Latter Liang state with his capital at Kaifeng, now included the offices of the Ming regional military commissioner. A temple nearby featured a statue of Zhao Kuangyin, the general who had established the Song with its capital in Kaifeng.[76]

The principal locus of continuity from the Song to the Ming in Kaifeng was the Zhou estate, which occupied the site of the Song royal palaces. The main entrance to the Zhou estate, the Gate of Southern Fragrance, occupied the site of the Zhengyang gate in the Song; the station where officials prepared for an audience with the Zhou prince was located where the *yamen* of supervising secretaries and investigative censors in the Song had been; and so on. Other structures in Kaifeng redolent of Song history included the residence of Li Guangtian, the late-Ming government student and imminent defender of Kaifeng, located at the site of the Song official Zhao Pu's estate; the Jade Spring Academy in the southern suburb, which offered regular sacrifices to the "Henanese" (Luoyang) thinkers, Cheng Hao and Cheng Yi, whose interpretations of Kongzi had become orthodox in the Yuan and Ming; and the residence of Meng Yuanlao, the Song author of the text on Kaifeng that was the model for the author's own.[77]

Kaifeng had of course experienced many changes from the Song to the Ming, including widespread destruction occasioned by warfare, fire, and flood during the Jin and Yuan. But the author hardly mentioned that period and instead focused on more recent events. They included modifications in the architecture of the Zhou estate that had resulted from the decision of the second Ming ruler, Yongle, to punish his brother, the first Zhou prince, for alleged conspiracy. For example, the Hall of Silver Peace inherited from the Song Forbidden City was torn down to symbolize the removal of the dragon's heart; a time-caller's tower was demolished, thus removing the dragon's eyes; and so on. A portrait of Ming Taizu was hung above the Duanli gate as if to remind the world that, as Yongle argued, the founder had chosen him as successor and would tolerate no challenge to his authority.[78]

The minor functionary and author described other sites in Kaifeng city associated with the Ming founder and the Hongwu reign. Southwest of the Zhou estate was a temple to Zhang the Immortal, an apparent reference to the Daoist Zhang Zhong who was supposed to have played a key role in Zhu Yuanzhang's rise to power. Next door there was a temple of the prefectural guardian deity containing a god of miracles who was supposed to have provided aid to Hongwu during a military campaign. The Wenshu Temple southwest of the Zhou estate was formerly the home of Tang He, one of Ming Taizu's leading generals. In the suburbs, a White Cloud Temple conducted sacrifices to the spirits of leading generals who had supported the Ming founder.[79]

The author also appraised several figures who had played significant roles during the late Ming. He admired the nobleman Zhu Mujie, who had won a provincial degree and managed a school for clansmen but criticized his grandson for continuing the aristocratic lifestyle without corresponding achievements. He remarked on the shrine to the official Yu Qian, who had left behind an iron rhinoceros designed to deter the flooding of the Yellow River. He noted the houses of members of the local elite, including the metropolitan graduate Liu Chang, who would help defend the city at the end of the Ming. Perhaps because he was a clerk and therefore a commoner himself, the author paid particular attention to commoners with notable achievements. They included Zuo Guoji, a government student and calligrapher, and Zhang Pingshan, an artist. Together with the elite poet Li Mengyang, they were described as the "Three Great Men of the Central Province." Artifacts combining their calligraphy, paintings, and verse graced several public sites in the city.[80]

The author paid less attention to the politics of the last few reigns of the Ming. He noted that when Wei Zhongxian was in power, some local officials and local elite had planned to turn the unoccupied estate of a Ming prince into a living shrine to the eunuch. When Wei fell from power, the plans were quickly scuttled, along with the estate. He recorded that the Travel Palace of the Taishan Goddess outside the northeast corner of the Zhou estate had one monk who specialized in burning incense to the royal consort Zhang. As we have seen, Zhang, who was originally from Xiangfu, patronized the Donglin toward the end of the Ming. Her father, Zhang Guoji, had mounted a plaque at the temple that read: "A Palace Full of Royal Majesty."[81]

In sum, the author shared the view of many residents of Kaifeng that they lived in one of the finest cities in the world. After describing one prince's large estate, complete with pavilions, terraces, caverns, cassia trees, flowers, lakes, bridges, waterfalls, and ponds, he concluded: "There is hardly anything that can compare with a scene like this." A plaque at the provincial administration commissioner's office read simply: "Heaven on Earth." The Kaifeng prefectural office was inscribed "Head Prefecture of the Central Plain" and the Xiangfu magistrate's office was labeled "Head County of the Central Plain." Religious establishments in Kaifeng were equally immodest. The Ancient Temple of the Three Sovereigns, which had been renovated three times during the Ming by Zhou princes, presumed itself to be "The First Ancient Temple in the World"; the Iron Pagoda was known as "The First Pagoda in the World"; and even the Daoist temple southwest of the Zhou estate, which might be expected to have followed the Daoist precept of "refusing to be first under heaven," boasted of being the "greatest of all the Daoist temples" in the region.[82] The author himself concluded his text by comparing Kaifeng with other first-ranked cities of the Ming:

> The streets and alleys, estates and mansions of princes and elite, archways and other structures were as closely packed as fish scales, and the commercial districts of the entire city were too numerous to be counted. In scale, they rivaled those of the two capitals.[83]

Although exaggerated, these assertions harked back to Kaifeng's glorious past and expressed the author's hopes for the future. In the meantime, Kaifeng could reasonably claim to be a city of the first rank. Whether it could realize that claim—or even defend itself from attack—was another matter.

The Military

The defense of Kaifeng would depend in part on another middle stratum of Ming society: military officers. The Chinese term for military officers (*shi*) used in the mid-Zhou had developed into the term for scholars in the Spring and Autumn and Warring States period. Two of the six arts of the ruist gentleman, archery and charioteering, involved the military, and the idea that scholars should be familiar with the martial arts persisted through much of Chinese history. Because the Ming had inherited the Song emphasis on central and civilian control of the military, military officers were subject to the elite rather than being part of it. But the Ming also emulated Han concern with effective defense against frontier incursions and domestic revolt, and military skill remained one path to social mobility. The status of military officers at the end of the Ming can be best described in terms of the origins and development of several layers of the Ming military institutions.

The first Ming military officers were hereditary commanders of guards and battalions that originated with the founding of the dynasty and lasted to its end. They were recruited from specially designated military families who were charged with maintaining peace and order while supporting themselves by cultivating lands granted to them by the state. After 1380, this system was headed in Beijing by five chief military commissions, each of which supervised some guards (*wei*) and battalions (*suo*) in the capital as well as others in two or more provinces. For example, the commission of the center supervised forces in Beijing as well as in Henan and Fengyang.[84]

Each province had a regional military commissioner who was responsible to Beijing for the military units in his province. The commissioner of Henan originally supervised sixteen guards, thirteen of which lasted to the end of the dynasty. Commissioners and lesser officers were theoretically recruited from the hereditary military households, but many seem to have been appointed on the basis of their military achievements. According to data in the provincial gazetteer, about half of the total number of sixty-one commissioners came from the regularly registered civilian population. Like civil officials, almost all were from outside the province; unlike them, of course, they lacked degrees.[85]

The Henan commissioner's headquarters located in Kaifeng was adjacent to the barracks of the Xuanwu guards, principal defenders of the provincial capital. Two dozen officers commanded thirty-six battalions required by statute to include some 39,200 men. When that quota had been met, there had been some truth to the inscription on an adjoining archway: "Important Garrison of the Central Plain." Five company commanders who had once defended Kaifeng had their names inscribed in characters one foot high and four inches deep in the 17.5-meter-high wall north and south of the Song gate. Although lacking degrees and even rank, these men had once been considered vital enough to Kaifeng's security to be publicly recognized in inscriptions designed to last as long as the wall. Two guards were also located in Guide prefecture, one in Shangqiu and the other in Suizhou.[86]

The second layer of the Ming military system consisted of officers appointed by the ministry of troops in Beijing; they were responsible for the actual command of troops in battle. Over time they came to include subordinate commanders attached to prefectures, departments, counties, and towns. Officers of the guard-battalion system were appointed to positions as active commanders and could be rewarded by promotions into and within the hierarchy of active commanders.[87]

During the mid-Ming, both the guard-battalion and regional commander hierarchies changed. The practice of calling up guard troops from the provinces for spring and autumn exercises in Beijing was discontinued, and troops in the interior got few opportunities for training. The policy of transferring guard soldiers from the interior to the frontier to fight under regional commanders waned; instead, troops from the frontier were increasingly transferred to the interior to combat banditry. As a result, by the late Ming, the number of guard troops on active duty in Kaifeng dwindled to a mere one thousand, causing the court to send a regional commander with six thousand troops to bolster the city's defenses. Some members of the hereditary military households succeeded in the civil service examinations and were relieved of their military responsibilities to assume civil posts. Others left—or were pushed off—the state lands they had been granted. They eventually disappeared from the registers and became unavailable for military service.

As the number of guard officers and soldiers declined, local officials gradually gave up on the hereditary system and created a third layer of the military by raising militia from among the regularly registered population. As a result, the total number of military officers of all kinds increased over six times, from an estimated thirteen thousand in the Hongwu reign to some eighty-two thousand in the Wanli reign, and the number of troops increased over three times from an estimated 1.2 million to some four million. This rate of increase exceeded that of the population as a whole and posed a challenge to a state based on limited and stable resources. In response, the Ming established the new posts of supreme commander, grand coordinator, and military intendant, designed to enhance its control over military recruitment and deployment at the regional, provincial, and local levels.[88]

During the sixteenth century, in an effort to raise the quality of military officers, the Ming established a fourth layer of military officers. New military schools in the capital trained selected members of the nobility and hereditary military families in the Four Books and the Seven Military Classics as well as in riding and shooting. These students were soon subjected to regular military examinations based on the model of the civil service examinations. By the Wanli reign, military examinations occurred triennially at the provincial, metropolitan, and palace levels, and were open to all those eligible to take the civil examinations.[89]

At the same time, in response to the monetization and commercialization of the economy, the Ming relied increasingly on a fifth layer of the military that had originated as early as 1550, hired troops drawn from the general population. To supply such troops, the ministries of troops and works and the royal household department retained control over the manufacture and distribution of weapons even while requiring provinces such as Henan to manufacture their own. Because the Ming had presided over a long period of relative peace and order, it had done little to upgrade the quality of its firearms. Manufacturing was done largely by hand, using only small amounts of metal. As a result, "cold" weapons such as bows, arrows, and shields continued to be more common on the battlefield than "hot" weapons such as rifles and cannon. While horses continued to be important in battle, the Ming had lost some 80 to 90 percent of its pasturage to Mongol pastoralists and Han cultivators by 1600. It attempted to force interior provinces such as Henan to supply horses but usually had to settle for mere monetary payments.[90]

Despite the appearance of a natural progression from one layer of the military system to another, evidence from northeast Henan suggests that the early layers often persisted and sometimes overlapped with later ones. During the sixteenth century, for example, guardsmen in Suizhou and Shangqiu continued to be active in confronting a rising tide of banditry and were rewarded for their success with promotions to commander outside the province. At the same time, Suiyang guardsmen who were less fortunate in battle could be honored in the gazetteer as "upright and devoted" members of local society.[91] The military examinations offered social and physical mobility to some men who were already part of an earlier system. A military officer from Suizhou obtained a provincial military degree and was promoted to commander in a guard. A civil provincial graduate from Qi passed the provincial military examinations and became a commander at Changping, north of Beijing.[92]

For all their mobility within the military hierarchies, military officers continued to enjoy only middling social status during the Ming. A civil metropolitan graduate from Suizhou in the early sixteenth century chastised the editors of gazetteers for paying too little attention to military men, noting that both the Han and the early Ming had produced great generals who suppressed uprisings. He called for steles to memorialize military as well as civil achievements. If guard officers were often unsung heroes, military graduates remained few. During the late Ming the polity-wide quotas for the military metropolitan examinations averaged one hundred, only one-third those for the civil metropolitan examinations.[93]

Instead of making weapons and training troops, the late-Ming state stressed building walls and maintaining peace. Kaifeng's wall was about thirteen kilometers around and about seventeen and a half meters high, while the moat was about seven meters deep and seventeen and a half meters wide. Suizhou's wall was about five and a half kilometers around and seven meters high, while the moat was over three and a half meters deep and ten and a half meters wide. Lined with brick and stone, such prefectural and departmental walls featured guard towers at the gates and on the four corners and provided bunkers for troops. Townsmen, as in Qi, recurrently repaired and upgraded county walls and were expected to defend them against banditry. The defensive, even pacific stance of the late Ming state was evident in the nicknames of Kaifeng's gates: the Cao gate was dubbed "Virtue and Harmony"; the Song, "Beautiful Views"; and even the North gate, "Distant Pacification," was described as "Winning by Moral Influence." Kaifeng city was divided into eight wards, named "Great Tranquillity," "Peace and Enterprise," and the like. It was subdivided into eighty-four localities, each of which was managed by only six persons, two heads of civil compacts and four firefighters, supported by fees paid by the residents. The regional military commission participated in manufacturing textiles as well as preparing defenses; the *Record* mentioned only one weapons manufacturer in Kaifeng.[94]

The middling status of the late-Ming military is reflected as well in the paucity of gazetteer records regarding military graduates, so incomplete in the eleven counties investigated as to allow no conclusions.[95] Individual guard officers and military graduates nonetheless continued to combat banditry as late as the 1630s. In Suizhou a guard commander, a guard judge, a battalion commander, and three company commanders "died on the front lines" in 1635 before a military provincial graduate gathered local braves and thirty men on horseback to drive a band of roving bandits from the town. That same year in Shangqiu, a military provincial graduate died fighting bandits.[96]

The case of a Liu lineage of Shangqiu shows how men with hereditary guard status also won civil and military degrees and organized braves and militia. The founder of this line had come from Nanzhili, had fought for Ming Taizu, and had been accorded hereditary military status as a commander of a guard (rank 3a) in Guide. The status of battalion commander (rank 5a) had been passed on to his descendants, including Liu Lun in the fifth generation, who parlayed it into a large fortune. Liu Lun's son won a civil provincial degree in 1558 but maintained the family's military links by marrying his daughter to the commander of the Guide guard. A grandson consolidated the family's elite status by becoming a civil provincial graduate, but he also maintained ties to the guard system by marrying a granddaughter of a Guide commander. A great-grandson became a military provincial graduate in 1618 and led able-bodied males from neighboring villages in the defense of Shangqiu from bandits in 1635. Even in the ninth generation, long after the family had succeeded in the civil examinations, another member became a military provincial graduate.[97] While the original layer of the Ming military system was formally moribund, some of its members continued to play significant military roles.

Another, unrelated Liu family of Guide was to become even more active in the military confrontations of the late Ming. According to the gazetteer, the father had come from Shanxi to trade and had settled in Yongcheng with his family. A son, Liu Chao, was tall, strong, and skilled in the martial arts. He also liked to read the *Chronicle of Zuo*, the *Discourses of the States*, and the *History of the Three Kingdoms*, records of China's early ages of division and war. In 1618 he won the highest grade in the military provincial examinations. Four years later he accompanied the scholar-official Wang Sanshan, also from Yongcheng, to his post as grand coordinator of Guizhou. Liu helped Wang break the Hmong leader An Bangyan's ten-month siege of Guiyang, but in the aftermath his troops plundered the population, fell into an ambush, and suffered heavy casualties. Because of his past achievements, Liu escaped punishment and was transferred to regional commander in Zunyi, Sichuan. In 1636 his son was named hereditary vice commander of a battalion on the frontier. Liu was dissatisfied, however, and went to Beijing in 1639 to lodge a complaint. Finding little sympathy in the capital, he returned home to Yongcheng still upset. When his Yongcheng neighbors, the scholar-officials Lian Guoshi, Ding Kuichu, and Ding Qirui rose one after the other to high civil posts charged with suppressing banditry, Liu became increasingly resentful.[98] Soon he would take dramatic action that would shape the politics of northeast Henan at the end of the Ming.

Medical Doctors

Physicians constituted another, much smaller middle stratum of late-Ming society. Medical practice extended back to the Warring States period, when the semilegendary doctor Bian Que developed a body of empirical knowledge and a holistic methodology. It developed further in the Han dynasty, when conversations between the wholly legendary Yellow Lord and his medical advisor Qi Bo were recorded in the *Yellow Lord's Classic of Cor-*

poreal Medicine. The Tang dynasty established medical examinations and appointed medical officials at both central and local levels. The Song trained 250 students in a royal medical college in Kaifeng and examined them on the classics as well as on their specialties.[99]

Interest in medicine continued at many levels in northeast Henan during the Ming. The first prince of Zhou supervised the compilation of medical treatises, including *Prescriptions for Common Ailments* and a *Materia Medica of Epidemic Diseases*. Members of the Song family of Shangqiu and the Hou family of Qi served as secretaries to the Royal Academy of Medicine. Lü Kun studied medical texts and Yang Dongming supported a rural doctor. The *Record* mentioned in Kaifeng a bureau for the people's welfare and a public hospital; the offices of two surgeons, two opthamologists, and several dentists and veterinarians; and the residences of specialists in setting bone fractures, treating wounds from beatings, and inoculating against smallpox and measles. The Kaifeng prefectural gazetteer listed medical schools, dispensaries, and clinics in its counties and departments.[100]

The Ming discontinued the Tang practice of recruiting doctors and appointing them to offices, but some physicians lived comfortably and had close contacts with officials. Many of the best known lived in Kaifeng and received biographies in the provincial gazetteer. They typically came from commoner backgrounds but acquired some literacy, decided on medicine after some dramatic personal experience, and served as apprentices under practicing doctors. They were often steeped in humanistic as well as medical texts, but they avoided the civil service examinations and devoted themselves to practicing medicine. They drew on a long tradition of cures but adopted experimental methods of diagnosis and pragmatic forms of treatment geared to the overall needs of individual patients. Good doctors were rewarded by fame, and sometimes by fortune, but rarely by power.[101]

The Kaifeng prefectural and Xiangfu county gazetteers provide five representative profiles of physicians in northeast Henan. Zhou Pu, whose family had come from Zhejiang and settled in Kaifeng at some unstated date, was bright and liked to study but contracted tuberculosis. After finding a doctor who cured him, he became his apprentice and studied medical texts including the Latter Han *Classic of Difficult Cases*. He developed a large practice, made his own special pills, and wrote several books. One of his texts provided one thousand prescriptions in verse that continued to be intoned by people in the seventeenth century. Another Xiangfu man, Li Xin, who specialized in pediatrics in the mid-fifteenth century, lived in the city and received many fine gifts from elite clientele, but he also visited rural households and earned their trust. When a prefect of Kaifeng gave Li gold to honor his contributions to society, he had it cast into a bell that he hung outside his office door. He became famous as Master Li of the Golden Bell (*jinzhong* Ligong), a rhyming phrase that reportedly remained on people's lips into the seventeenth century.[102]

Among the most honored medical doctors were those who treated patients from all ranks of society. Shi Shi, who was from a long line of doctors in Luoyang, was skilled in the "methods of the Han period." Without ever passing any examinations, he moved to Kaifeng to become director of the medical office (rank 8a) in the Zhou princedom.

In addition to caring for the prince and his many relatives, Shi cured many commoner patients before dying at age eighty-seven. Another physician, Liu Hui, who studied with a well-known doctor in Kaifeng, became famous for going on his rounds in all kinds of weather and for treating poor people free of charge. At age seventy, he was honored by local officials and appointed a public lecturer in the compact system. Zhang Pingshan, the celebrated commoner artist, was also a well-known surgeon.[103]

Because the Ming, unlike the Tang and Song, lacked public medical schools and state-administered qualifying examinations, medical expertise was largely transmitted in certain families. For example, four generations of the Zhengs of Kaifeng city were renowned for medical knowledge as well as for humanistic scholarship. The patriarch, Zheng Yi, who lived to age seventy, wrote many treatises and cured many people. His son also gained fame as a doctor, and a grandson extended the family practice to Shangqiu. One great-grandson won a provincial degree in 1624, a metropolitan degree in 1634, and served as a censor in Guangxi at the end of the Ming. He presumably had little time to practice medicine but another in the same generation continued the family tradition of medicine into the Qing.[104]

Outside Kaifeng city, notable physicians were more scarce, with many counties including no biographies of them. Even the gazetteer of populous and prosperous Qi county had but one: Li Keda, who was active in the mid- to late sixteenth century. Li was a government student who gave up his regular studies when his mother took sick. He soon turned to medical books. After many years of preparation he exclaimed, "Bian [Que] of Lu is here now!" and went out to treat the sick with good results. Li became famous for ignoring the old prescriptions and experimenting with new cures. For example, when other doctors refused to give ginseng to a woman who had just given birth and was afflicted with asthmatic coughing, Li combined the drug with sapan wood in a broth that brought her relief. For good service, he was recommended for the post of gentleman (rank 8a) in the Royal Academy of Medicine, but he never assumed the post, instead continuing his practice in Qi. When one of Li's distant relatives lost consciousness and her sons had given her up for dead, Li rescued her from the casket by applying mud to her chest and having her drink lotus-root soup. When a rumor arose that he could bring the dead back to life, he denied it, explaining that he had merely reduced a high fever that had interfered with her life force. Li treated a metropolitan graduate of Qi for dysentery and a government student for melancholia. He had many progeny, and a granddaughter married a son of the Zhou prince. Like other members of the medical middle stratum, he helped to bridge the gap between the state and the elite on the one hand and commoners and the masses on the other.[105]

A Religio-ethnic Community: The Jews of Kaifeng

According to the *Record*, there were more than one hundred religious establishments in Kaifeng during the Ming. Buddhists worshipped at thirty temples, of which the Xiangguo and Guanyin were the largest, housing more than two hundred monks and one hundred nuns, respectively. Daoists had thirty-five temples, of which the Yanqing was the largest, with sufficient staff to serve as a major hostel for visitors to the city.

Sacrifices were periodically conducted at thirty-odd temples to historical personages, including Kongzi, Guan Yu, Yue Fei, Bao Zheng, and Yu Qian.

As a former cosmopolitan capital of the Song and as a provincial capital in the Ming, Kaifeng also attracted adherents of more foreign religions. Muslims who had arrived over the long period from the Tang through Yuan lived in three separate areas of the city and may have suffered from some discrimination. Many of them specialized in tanning leather and working gold, occupations that were favored neither by Han Chinese nor by Muslims. But they were sufficiently prosperous and numerous—including several tens of thousands—to support three mosques attended by imams. During the Wanli reign, the Jesuits had arrived from Europe and Matteo Ricci had made his way to Beijing. The Jesuit Nicolas Trigault passed through Kaifeng in 1623 and Father Rodríguez de Figueredo and Brother Francisco Ferreira resided in Kaifeng from 1624 to 1642. By 1640 they had reportedly baptized over one thousand residents and had established a church to serve them. Finally, there was a community of Jews, who had established a synagogue in Li Family Lane near Earth-Market Character Street. They were only slightly larger than the Catholic community, but they had arrived much earlier and had retained their ethnic identity as well as, or even better than, the Muslims. Because the Jews were also the best documented religious group in the city, they offer the best window on issues of religion and ethnicity in northeast Henan at the end of the Ming (see Map 3.4).[106]

According to a stone inscription written in Han Chinese characters and erected at the site of the synagogue in 1489, the Israelite religion, as it was called, first arrived in Kaifeng along with seventy different families of Jews who came from India bearing Western cloth as tribute to a monarch in the Song period. The monarch reportedly welcomed the party to China (ZhongXia), encouraged them to continue their ancestral practices, and invited them to settle in Kaifeng (BianLiang). According to recent research, the Jewish immigrants were headed by a cleric named Ni-wei-ni, characters that probably represented a preliminary effort to capture the sounds of the foreign name Levi (or Levy) in Han Chinese. They arrived in 998 CE, the first year of the reign of Zhenzong, a Northern Song cosmopolitan ruler with an interest in various religions. During the following century, the Jewish community apparently thrived in the bustling Song capital of one million people, perhaps the largest and richest city in the world at that time. The community continued to prosper under the Jurchen Jin dynasty after 1127. Indeed, in 1163, the same year the Jin state moved its capital to Kaifeng, a rabbi named Liewei (another Han Chinese rendering of Levy) took charge of the religion, and a man named Andula (the approximation of Abdulla in Han Chinese) constructed a synagogue. In 1279, the same year the Mongol Yuan completed its victory over the Southern Song, the chief rabbi of the Jewish community of Kaifeng, who was probably still a Levy, reconstructed the synagogue, now called the Temple of Purity and Truth. The temple was 112.5 meters on each of its four sides and was located on the southeast corner of Earth-Market Character Street, the site it was to occupy for the next seven centuries.[107]

The Jews of Kaifeng may have benefited from being a minority ethnic group under minority (Jurchen and Mongol)- led dynasties, but they had also flourished under the majority-run Song and would do so as well under the Ming. As the stele indicated, the

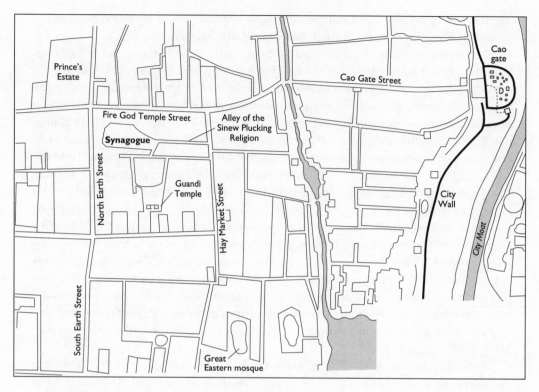

MAP 3.4. The Synagogue in Kaifeng. Source: William Charles White 1966: I.map E. Used with permission of the University of Toronto Press.

Jews, along with everyone else, were given land to cultivate by the Ming founder as part of his effort to revive the society and economy of the central plain. In the early Ming, foreigners were encouraged to marry Han Chinese and were otherwise forbidden to adopt Han Chinese surnames. These regulations were aimed mainly at controlling the Mongols and were not strictly enforced. In any case, some Jews, for whatever reason, married Han Chinese and gradually assumed Han Chinese surnames while in some cases retaining their Jewish names as well. Under Ming Taizu, the chief rabbis of the Kaifeng synagogue continued to be mainly Levys. Nine of the fourteen Manla (mullahs or rabbis) were accordingly surnamed Li (the third, and final, Han Chinese approximation of Levy). The rabbis were well versed in the Hebrew scriptures, but they also venerated their parents and the ruler, thus satisfying the expectations of the larger Chinese community of which they were increasingly a part. The Jews of Kaifeng apparently continued to circumcise their sons and refrained from eating pork, practices that they shared with Muslims and set them apart from other Chinese. But they neither practiced extensive polygamy nor forbade it, positions that they held in common with most other Chinese. (This attitude distinguished them from Muslims, who typically had many wives, and from Christians, who were limited to one.) Jews not only continued to marry Han Chinese but adopted the Han Chinese custom of calculating family descent and thus ethnic identity through the male line. Perhaps most important, the Jews of Kaifeng found many commonalities between their religious ideas and those of the Kongzians, Daoists, and Buddhists who dominated the religious life of Ming China.[108]

The case of a man named An, a common surname (perhaps rendering Hassan) among the early Jews of Kaifeng, shows how the Jews of Kaifeng became closely identified with the Ming order. According to the official *Veritable Records of the Taizong Reign*, An San, an officer in the central guard division of Henan province, "repeatedly lodged accusations against" his superior, the Zhou prince, "for plotting treason." The alleged plot, details of which are lacking, was apparently directed against the prince's elder brother, Zhu Di, who had seized the throne in a coup d'état against his nephew seventeen years earlier and ruled with a strong hand. According to the *Veritable Records*, Zhu Di (temple name, Taizong) rewarded An San for his loyalty by promoting him to assistant commissioner of the embroidered uniform guard and bestowing on him the Han Chinese name Zhao Cheng. Zhao, first in the list of the one hundred most common Han Chinese surnames, had been the name of the Song ruling lineage. Cheng meant "sincere," an allusion perhaps to the bearer's service to the Ming throne at some risk to himself. Yongle also summoned the Zhou prince to Beijing and confronted him with the allegations, forcing him to acknowledge his crimes and beg for the death penalty. The ruler finally "showed leniency" by sparing the prince's life, but he also stripped him of his guards and modified his palace.[109]

The 1489 stele at the synagogue recorded a strikingly similar case:

> An Cheng the physician in Yongle 19 [1421] received from the Ding prince of the Zhou estate a gift of incense and permission to rebuild the synagogue. In the temple was set up a tablet wishing long life to the August Ruler of the Great Ming. Then in Yongle 21 [1423], upon a memorial reporting [his] merits, he was granted the surname Zhao, appointed commissioner of the embroidered uniform guard, and promoted to assistant regional military commissioner of Zhejiang.[110]

In commenting on these cases, the American-based historian Fang Zhaoying hypothesized that, after being chastised, the prince was forced to patronize the synagogue and to allow further promotion of Zhao to a higher rank in the military system. Fang suggested that the version recorded on the stele was concocted to mask the real reason for An's enhanced status.[111] The China-based historian Li Jixian offers a second interpretation: An Cheng was a different person from An San and was a physician who had aided the Zhou prince in his important project of compiling medical materials.[112] In light of the evidence, I would hypothesize a third solution: there was only one person named An, who was both a physician and a military man and who aided the prince in his medical scholarship and later informed on him to Yongle. In this scenario, both the prince and Yongle would have rewarded An, but at different times and for different reasons. Once Yongle had promoted him and given him a Han Chinese name, the prince granted him permission to rebuild the synagogue. At the same time, the prince had Zhao Cheng promoted to a distant post in Zhejiang, where he could put his redoubtable political skills to safer use.[113]

Whatever the particulars, the An/Zhao case demonstrates the ability of a leading Jew to operate successfully in the Ming system. He not only survived one of the tricki-

est court battles of the dynasty but headed what would become one of the most prominent descent groups in the Jewish community of Kaifeng.[114]

The Jewish community of Kaifeng continued to flourish during the fifteenth century when two families with Han surnames produced sons who passed the civil service
examinations and entered the elite. Gao Nian became a tributary student in the
Xuande reign and was appointed magistrate of She county, Anhui, during the Zhengtong
reign. Since She county was the home of some of China's wealthiest merchants, Gao
may have had a good opportunity to become wealthy himself, but we learn only that he
earned merit for managing the reconstruction of the local ruist school. Ai Jun, who
won his provincial degree in 1447, became an administrator (rank 5a) in the estate of
the De prince in Shandong and served as an assistant teacher in a county in Jiangsu.[115]

While the Gaos and Ais now had the status and resources to maintain and develop
the temple, the Li family continued to provide most of the chief rabbis. Rabbis Li Rong
and Li Liang, for example, together raised funds to repair the three sections of the front
hall. In 1461 most of the temple was destroyed in a flood of the Yellow River. Ai Jing
and others successfully petitioned the provincial authorities for permission to rebuild,
and Li Rong raised more funds to refashion the temple on a grander scale. Li and others also located a copy of the Torah in another Jewish community in Ningbo and had
it brought to Kaifeng by a man named Zhao Ying. The Gaos provided funds to build
an additional three sections of the rear hall and a bethel to house the rolls of the
Pentateuch. Various Jins from Ningxia and Gansu as well as from Kaifeng purchased
more land for the synagogue and provided a stone for a stele. They also contributed a
table for offerings, a bronze censor, and a pair of vases and candlesticks. The stele of
1489 was inscribed, "Record of the Reconstruction of the Temple of Purity and Truth."
It recorded the history of the Jews of Kaifeng and celebrated their success in retaining
their own identity even while becoming Chinese and, in at least two cases, entering the
ranks of the elite.[116]

In 1512, only twenty-three years after the erection of the stele, a second inscription
was made on the back. Since there is no evidence of any intervening damage to the
temple requiring reconstruction, the explanation for the new inscription would seem
to be the appearance of new patrons, admirers, and associates of the synagogue. The
principal author of the inscription, Zuo Tang, was a metropolitan graduate. Zuo may
have been Jewish, for his surname had appeared among the Jews recorded in the stele
of 1489, and he came from Yangzhou, Nanzhili, where there was another small Jewish
community. Zuo, who was described as a pious and upright official, apparently never
held office in Henan and would seem to have had little reason to draft the inscription
if he had not been Jewish. The calligrapher probably became involved simply because
he was accompanying his father who was holding office in Henan and possessed the
necessary skill to do the inscription. The third party in the preparation of the stele, the
writer of the seal characters, probably joined the project simply as an associate of Zuo's;
he was from the same town and had passed the examinations in the same year.[117]

Whatever their precise ethnic heritage, the creators of the new inscription recorded
the Jewish community's acculturation and expanded its claims both in time and in space.
Unlike the authors of the 1489 inscription who called the synagogue a "Temple of Purity
and Truth," terms shared with Islam, these writers entitled their inscription "Record of

the Temple to Revere the Scriptures [or Classics] of the Way." It emphasized the commonalities between the Israelite religion conveyed in the Pentateuch and Kongzi's teachings embodied in the five classics. Whereas the 1489 inscription had dated the arrival of the Israelite religion in China (*ZhongXia*) to the Song dynasty, the new inscription dated the "entrance and establishment" of the faith in China (*zhongguo*) to the Han. If *ZhongXia* is read more restrictively to refer only to Henan, and *zhongguo* is taken to include all of Ming China, the dates were not contradictory but simply indicated a widening of the scope of inquiry from Henan to China. Although the Jewish community in Kaifeng had arrived in China only in Song times, there were other Jews elsewhere in China whose ancestors had arrived in Han times. The Kaifeng Jews, it seems, were now being reconceived to belong to that larger community of Jews in China. Indeed, the authors broadened their interests further to the role of Judaism in the wider world. Unlike the 1489 writers who had focused exclusively on the Jewish community in Kaifeng, these writers stated that "Adherents of this religion not only in Bian [Kaifeng] but throughout the world all revere the scriptures/classics and honor the Way."[118] While associating Judaism more closely with Han Chinese teachings and giving it a longer history in China, the writers simultaneously emphasized its relevance to other Jewish communities in the rest of the world.

Although the stele of 1512 recorded no names, it indicated that the Chinese Jews of Kaifeng were by that time distinguishing themselves as filial sons, brave soldiers, upright teachers, productive farmers, skilled artisans, and honest traders. As if to represent the Kaifeng synagogue as a center for believers from all over China, the inscription closed by praising one Jin from Yangzhou for providing a scroll of the Pentateuch, another Jin from Ningxia for reestablishing the newly recut stele in its own pavilion, and a third Jin from Kaifeng for the final editing of the inscription.[119] Thus, even as the Israelite religion acquired a longer Chinese pedigree and greater universal claims, it also established a center. According to outsiders as well as to local residents in the mid-Ming, that center was in the Kaifeng temple.

During the rest of the sixteenth century, identifiable members of the Jewish community of Kaifeng almost disappeared from the historical records. There continued to be many Zhaos, Lis, and Gaos among the tributary students and provincial and metropolitan graduates of Xiangfu county, but if they were Jews they were not so identified in gazetteers. The Kaifeng community nonetheless apparently retained its Jewish identity and continued to flourish even as Jewish settlements elsewhere in China withered and died. One key to their survival as Jews may have been continuing intermarriage among the seven surname groups into which they were now organized: Zhao, Gao, Ai, Li, Jin, Zhang, and Shi.[120]

Another sign of the continued vitality of the community was its interest in establishing outside contacts. The scholar Ai Tian (whose Hebrew name was possibly Shaphat), won his provincial degree in 1573 and traveled to Beijing in 1605 to meet the Jesuit missionary Matteo Ricci, whom he expected to be Jewish. In the first meeting, Ai mistook images of Mary, Jesus, and John the Baptist for Rebeccah, Jacob, and Esau; he also thought the twelve apostles were the twelve sons of Jacob. Ricci cleared up these misconceptions. Ai informed Ricci that he had two brothers in Kaifeng who knew Hebrew. He further reported that there were some one thousand adherents of Judaism in the city who refrained from eating pork, circumcised their male offspring, and regularly attended the synagogue, said to contain several scrolls of the Pentateuch. Ai Tian then proceeded to Baoying county in Yangzhou prefecture, where he taught for three years. At some point, he also wrote a short vertical inscription for the synagogue in Kaifeng. In 1607, Ricci sent two Chinese Christians to Kaifeng to learn more about the Jewish community there. The chief rabbi, who may have been Abishai Li, doubted the Christians' claims that Christ was the Messiah, noting that the Messiah was not expected for another ten thousand years. But he was so impressed by Matteo Ricci's erudition that he invited him to come to Kaifeng to succeed himself as chief rabbi, provided only that he agree to refrain from eating pork.

Ricci did not respond to this invitation, only one of several disappointments experienced by the community in these years. In 1608 the synagogue was damaged by fire and only one copy of the Pentateuch was saved. Soon after, the chief rabbi died and his son Jacob Li was considered unsuitable to replace him. In 1609 Ai Tian's nephew and two other young Kaifeng Jews went to Beijing in another effort to persuade Ricci to come to Kaifeng to assume the post of rabbi. But Ricci died before he could make the trip; his successor, Nicolò Longobardi, never made the trip either.[121] By renewing their invitation to the Jesuits to take over leadership of their temple, the Kaifeng Jews were going well beyond mere politeness to guests from afar. They seemed to express sincere admiration, felt also by many other Chinese, for the Jesuits' learning. They may also have shared the general Chinese assumption that all religions share a common commitment to attaining the Way.

Despite these setbacks and signs of disarray, the Jewish community of Kaifeng retained its identity. One source of stimulation may have been Jewish merchants who continued to cross the silk route through central Asia, bringing new ideas and texts. During the 1620s several rabbis and laymen wrote Judeo-Persian colophons to the Pentateuch, indicating that copies of the law were still being produced and novel commentaries added to them.[122]

By the 1640s the community was headed by a rabbi named Li Zhen (禎) (Hebrew name perhaps Jeremiah). Li may have attained his position simply on the basis of his family background and personal qualities, as had earlier commoners who assumed leadership in the Jewish community without any connection to the state. Or he may have been the same person as Li Zhen (真), who was listed in the county gazetteer as a provincial graduate of 1615 and who later served as a county magistrate. If so, it would indicate that leadership in the Jewish community was seen as compatible with service to the Ming state. Also at this time, Ai Yingkui, perhaps a son or nephew of Ai Tian, was honored with a biography in the gazetteer. He was a physician who served in the medical office of the Zhou prince. Under his courtesy name, Wensuo, he also operated a pharmacy near the synagogue.[123] As a literate commoner serving both a prince and the people, he exemplified those Jews who belonged to the middle social strata as the Ming dynasty neared its end.

In sum, the Ming exhibited both strengths and weaknesses in its handling of issues relating to gender, class, and ethnicity in northeast Henan. Consistent with its populist ethos, the polity celebrated commoner widows who remained chaste and made them models of loyalty even for elite men. But it failed to end infanticide and foot binding; it encouraged widow and betrothal suicides; and it honored—and thereby encouraged—female self-sacrifice in response to illness and assault. In dealing with government students, the Ming permitted their numbers to expand to absorb the growing number of literate males, and it allowed certain members of that stratum to exert considerable influence in the state and society. But it limited the number of degrees available to aspiring entrants to the elite and presided over the diminution in the status and resources of teachers, thus alienating the lower levels of the literate and driving them into alliances with other commoners and the masses. The early Ming kept taxes light and distributed land widely among the population, but it encouraged the commercialization of agriculture that eventually led to an increase in the number of landlords and a growing disparity between the rich and the poor. It organized artisans into a hereditary caste, and it attempted to confine profit making to merchants (and vice versa), but it eventually allowed both groups to make and sell their products to the public and failed to contain the commercialism that some thought corrosive of the ethical foundations of society. The Ming established military officers and minor functionaries to provide public security and conduct local administration, but it gradually lost control over their numbers, qualifications, and activities, and allowed them to come into conflict—and/or collusion—with the people. Finally, the Ming accommodated the small community of Kaifeng Jews, allowing them to retain their identity while acculturating to the Han majority, but it did not openly acknowledge their distinctive ethnicity or facilitate contacts with foreign coreligionists.

The data on women, various middle strata, and the Jews suggest that northeast Henan continued to aspire to cultural centrality in the Ming. Women there lacked the literary achievements of their wealthier sisters in Jiangnan, but they made sacrifices that were considered exemplary and engaged in household industry that remained more typical of the majority of women in China. Hou and his friends in the Snow Garden Society were confident enough to criticize the Ming for its deviation from the Way and were accepted as scholars of the "central plain" by Fushe associates in Jiangnan who identified themselves with the "south." A Jiangnan merchant was attracted to Guide by a local scholar who described it as "the center," and a Zhejiang scholar characterized Henan as "the center of the world with Kaifeng as its capital." The anonymous minor functionary who wrote the description of Kaifeng city observed that it was "the central pivot between heaven and earth, the hub of the eight provinces, the heart and stomach of the realm." The regional military commissioner in Kaifeng worked in a complex that publicly proclaimed itself an "Important Garrison of the Central Plain." A medical doctor who was also a painter was praised in a local inscription as one of the "Three Great Men of the Central Province." The synagogue in Kaifeng was reconstructed after a flood and later rededicated to serve as a center for the larger Jewish community that was scattered over China.

Some women, elements of the middle strata, and members of the Jewish community of northeast Henan evinced awareness of historical precedents and expressed special interest in models from the Han period. Women were inspired by Han concepts and institutions to perform acts of self-sacrifice that earned them historiographical immortality. Students commonly referred to Former Han, Latter Han, and post-Han institutions, personalities, and events to describe their aspirations, to criticize the Ming state, and to prepare for a successor government. The data on landlords, artisans, and merchants does not allow us to describe their historical views, but observers alluded to Han conditions in describing Henan's wealth and drew on Han historiographical precedents to include artisans and merchants in the record. The minor functionary who described Kaifeng city paid scant attention to the Han period and emphasized other eras during which Kaifeng assumed greater importance. But military officers and medical doctors invoked Han texts and followed Han models in addressing problems of their own day. Finally, the broader Jewish community that took Kaifeng as its center dated the arrival of their ancestors in China to the Han in an effort, conscious or unconscious, to share in the historical perspective most common among their contemporaries. In sum, all of these social groups used historical allusions, and particularly references to the Han, to advance their own views and interests. But discourse about the Han was not merely a tool in their hands; it was also a force shaping their minds. Its continuing relevance and viability would depend on the activities and views of other parts of society, including those commoners below the middle strata, the masses.

FOUR

The Masses

IN THE CHINESE POLITICAL LEXICON, the people (*min*) were logically distinct from the state, and they were usually also distinguished from the elite, minor functionaries, and military officers. But "the people" often included the women, middle strata, and minorities described in Chapter 3. To refer to the vast majority of people below the middle strata, therefore, I shall use the different word "masses" (*zhong*). The masses were the men, women, and children who cultivated the soil, herded animals, spun yarn, wove cloth, and so on. The word *zhong* dates from the Shang when it implied large numbers of common people mobilized for work, and it has continued to bear much the same meaning, while at least nominally enjoying much higher status, to the present. As used here, the term "masses" is not to be considered patronizing, as it often has been in the liberal West, or celebratory, as it was until recently in socialist China, let alone exclusively contemporary, as it sometimes is by modernization theorists.[1] During the Ming, as in most periods of Chinese (and world) history, the masses were busy coping with the challenges of everyday life. They had little time or opportunity to express themselves either collectively or as individuals. Their voices become audible in the records only occasionally in response to extraordinary political, social, and economic conditions.

Over the course of the Ming, the masses expressed their concerns most dramatically by increasing participation in collective action, including banditry, conspiracy, and rebellion. During the early period, the vast majority of people seemed to have been content to accept the state and to work peacefully to advance their lot within the existing social order. During the middle period, some became disenchanted with the existing polity and were attracted to alternatives offered by sects and rebels. In the late Ming, a substantial number, perhaps a majority, became disaffected from the state and active in movements to overthrow it. Within this linear progression, there were cycles of relative passivity and activity. Both the long-term trend and the shorter-term developments varied according to the incidence of natural phenomena, such as climate and weather, and the pattern of human activity, as manifested in politics and society. By the end of the Ming, the majority of the masses of this region were mobilized. Only a minority were able to pursue everyday life relatively undisturbed.[2]

Acceptance and/or Hope

Life in northeast Henan, perhaps even more than in China at large, was hard during the first century of Ming rule. The area had been largely depopulated by the wars and floods of the preceding century. Ming officials mobilized tens of thousands of corvée laborers to repair the dikes of the Yellow River but they were initially unable to prevent further flooding. The climate cooled during the fourteenth and fifteenth centuries, shortening the growing season and making life difficult for the vast majority who tilled the soil. The period was later characterized by the apt metaphor of winter.[3]

The masses of northeast Henan nonetheless seem to have accepted the early-Ming state because they believed that life would soon improve. Many of the residents of this region were immigrants from other heavily populated areas that offered only limited economic opportunities. In Henan they found much untilled soil and were assisted by Ming policies guaranteeing land, waiving taxes, and providing resources such as seeds, tools, and oxen. Immigration continued during the fifteenth century. 100,000 migrants came from Shanxi in 1428, 200,000 from Shanxi and Shandong in 1443, and 100,000 from Huguang in 1465. In this period, the princes made few demands, officials exerted themselves to control the river, and the state provided relief from famine. As elsewhere in this period, natural disasters in northeast Henan elicited corresponding relief programs.[4]

Low-level banditry nonetheless continued to bedevil the population, especially after the Mongol incursion of 1449 and in such regions as Sichuan and Beizhili. White Lotus sectarians revered a legendary Eternal Mother who gave birth to humankind, and they anticipated the descent of a Maitreya Buddha who would save the world. They had been active in the region before the founding of the Ming. Han Liner, based in Bozhou, Nanzhili, had proclaimed himself the Little Enlightened Prince (Xiao Ming Wang) and had led a rebellion against the Yuan. Zhu Yuanzhang had used his association with Han to enhance his own standing and outflank his rivals. Zhu eventually killed Han when he no longer needed him, but he took over his title (Ming) as the name of his new dynasty. Once in power, Ming Taizu outlawed the White Lotus and other heterodox religions he and his literati advisors regarded as subversive. Adherents of the religion, who were quite numerous in Henan and adjacent regions, thus became outlaws. While Ming Taizu's proscription of the White Lotus sect is often taken as a sign of his autocracy, he and his supporters had some reason to fear the religion. A tradition dating back to the Han held that a spiritual leader named Li would emerge as principal advisor to a good king or would become monarch himself. Since the late-Tang Liang state headed by Zhu Wen, there had been a more specific prophecy that a Li would arise to replace a Zhu. Thus the Ming ruling house of Zhu was particularly sensitive to any mass action led by a Li. As it happened, Han Liner himself had also been known by the sobriquet Master Li (*Lishi zi*). Han had followers as far afield as Shanxi and Shaanxi who traded on the family name Li to attain some status in the White Lotus religion.[5]

LIU TONG

While sectarians conspired, a more nearly secular strongman by the name of Liu Tong from Xihua, in Kaifeng prefecture, led the first rebellion against the Ming in northeast Henan. Liu had reputedly once lifted a one-thousand-catty stone lion, earning himself the nickname Liu Qianjin (thousand catty Liu). According to the gazetteer, he first plotted rebellion with a heterodox monk in 1447, but failed to realize his plan. Liu next appeared in 1464, far from home across the provincial border in Huguang, perhaps one of many Henanese refugees from floods of the Yellow River. He was now associated with one Shi Long (dragon Shi), also called Shi Heshang (monk Shi), with whom he reportedly propagated heterodox teachings (*yaoyan*) among the migrants between Jingzhou and Xiangyang. Liu and Shi were said to have attracted some forty thousand followers to their standard.[6]

Buoyed by this mass support, Liu soon proclaimed himself the Prince of Han (Han Wang). The name was logical because Liu shared the surname of the Han ruling family. He was also based in the upper Han River, which had supplied the name of the original Han dynasty, and he drew on the example of a White Lotus leader who had established a Han state in the region less than a century before. What better way to trump the Ming claim to affinity with the Han than to promise to restore the glory of the original dynasty along with its name? The Han, after all, had dealt effectively with the Xiongnu, functional "ancestors" of the Mongols who had recently humiliated the Ming in Beijing. Liu Tong soon proclaimed the reign name Desheng (virtuous victory) and seized three counties in northwestern Huguang.[7]

In 1464, stung by Liu's political challenge and alarmed by the size of his following, the Ming sent large forces against him. They drove him west, tracked him down in the mountains, and killed him along with 3,500 supporters. The Ming forces also arrested some eleven thousand others, including many youth, on charges of complicity in the rebellion. Soon they apprehended Shi Long and Liu's eldest son, who had managed to flee further west into Sichuan.[8] The Ming thus suppressed the first notable challenge to its authority by a Henanese, albeit one mounted in a neighboring province.

During the next three decades, other heterodox religious leaders named Li, who had only fleeting and indirect contacts with Henan, were charged with plotting against the state. The first, originally named Hou Dequan, was from Baoding, Beizhili. In 1476 he visited the famous Shaolin temple of warrior monks in Song county, Henan prefecture, and adopted the portentous sect name Li Zilong (dragon son of Li). He was soon arrested, charged with conspiracy, and executed. The second, Li Yuan, nicknamed Li Huzi (Li the bearded one), was originally from Xinzheng in Henan. He had participated in Liu Tong's revolt, survived its suppression, and continued to organize migrants in Huguang. He eventually proclaimed himself Prince of Peace (Ping Wang), rallied an alleged (but surely hyperbolic) 400,000 people to his cause, and extended his influence back into central Henan. The Ming reportedly sent an army of 250,000 that captured him, decapitated 640 of his adherents, and took prisoner some thirty thousand others. The third rebel leader was Li Yue, from Shanxi, who preached the White Lotus doctrines and participated in various revolts, including one led by Wang Liang in Shanxi. Although this rising was crushed in 1489 and Wang Liang was killed, Li Yue escaped and continued to proselytize in eastern Shaanxi during the Hongzhi reign. Thus ended the first century of the Ming, with northeast Henan still quite peaceful and largely free of overt opposition to the dynasty.[9]

The Rumble of Dissension

During the second century, the sounds of dissent among the masses grew louder. Cold weather persisted through most of the period, inhibiting agricultural productivity. Even allowing for the uncritical acceptance of the notion of the dynastic cycle that informs many of the sources, there were clear signs of incipient administrative decline. Monarchs increasingly came to the throne as minors and relied on eunuchs to administer the realm. Princes proliferated and demanded more resources. Officials supplemented their meager salaries with more informal income and failed to discipline subordinates for misdemeanors. Members of the elite and government students illegally extended tax exemptions to additional family members and neighbors who became private clients to avoid public obligations. Floods and droughts resulted in famines that were met by state relief in only half the cases. The number of rebellions doubled to one a year.[10]

Zhu Houzhao, who ascended the throne at age thirteen in 1505, relied heavily for the next fifteen years on the eunuch Liu Jin. Liu was intent on increasing state revenues to pay for royal building projects. Officials organized secretly in an attempt to remove Liu, but their efforts were leaked by an official, Jiao Fang, who happened to come from Nanyang, Henan. As a result, Liu consolidated his power, Jiao became grand secretary, and together they worked to increase the revenues of the state at the expense of the people.[11]

ZHAO JINGLONG

Along with administrative decline, social conditions deteriorated, giving rise to three different kinds of rebellions in northeast Henan. From 1502 to 1505, heavy rains and recurrent floods interspersed with drought and locusts resulted in widespread famine in Shangqiu and Yongcheng counties, Guide prefecture. A man named Zhao Jinglong, "using the teachings of the White Lotus to mislead the masses," gathered one thousand victims of the famine, proclaimed himself Prince of Song in the Central Plain, and assaulted the town of Guide. The rebel state was well named: Guide was the seat of the original Song state established by the Zhou for the descendants of the Shang royal line. Zhao also happened to share the family name of the founder of the more recent Song dynasty that had established a capital at Guide as well as at nearby Kaifeng. Although Zhao thus used history effectively to challenge the Ming, he apparently lacked the strong organization and popular support necessary to carry his enterprise to a successful conclusion. Instead, according to government reports, he simply "plundered Guide," "rushed" to Yongcheng, and crossed the border into Suzhou, Nanzhili. Soon a royal commissioner sent a guard commander and the magistrate of Suzhou at the head of a force to capture him along with five hundred of his followers.[12] The revolt, which lasted only a few months, was ignored by the gazetteers.

LIU LIU-LIU QI

Six years later, northeast Henan became one locus of a much larger rebellion that had its origins in neighboring Beizhili. As David Robinson has shown, this rebellion grew out of decades of endemic banditry in southern Beizhili and western Shandong that was fueled by local disputes among military and civilian households, Mongols and Han, and Muslims and non-Muslims. Powerful eunuchs in Beijing established local networks that included officials and bandits, and in their jockeying for power they used local toughs against clients of their adversaries whom they characterized as bandits. Among these local bravos were two brothers from a military household, Liu Chong and Liu Chen, who were skilled in riding and shooting and who assisted local officials in combating banditry in their home county of Wenan, in Bazhou, Beizhili. In 1510 the Liu brothers, who had paid a bribe to an agent of the powerful eunuch Liu Jin, failed to get the protection from him that they expected. Instead they were labeled bandits, and so they revolted to avoid execution. In August 1511, sporting the nicknames Liu Liu and Liu Qi (Liu the sixth and Liu the seventh), they joined together with another bravo named Yang Hu and persuaded a government student named Zhao Sui, also known as Zhao Fengzi (crazy Zhao), to serve as advisor. They declared war on the Ming and led their followers into battle in Beizhili and Shandong. At the same time, Yang Hu, Zhao Sui, and one Liu Hui (also known as Liu San, Liu the third), led forces into Henan and Nanzhili.[13]

In the fall of 1511, the rebels incorporated local bandits, grew to 100,000 strong, and assaulted the county seat of Yongcheng. In some cases, they clearly sought official acquiescence. For example, in Yucheng they reportedly burned property and released prisoners but spared the magistrate. Such gestures did not always work. In Xiayi on November 6 the assistant magistrate and instructor vowed to resist to the death and died in defense of the town. Their action was compared with that of Zhang Xun and Xu Yuan, the two generals honored at the shrine in Kaifeng for having fought to the death against An Lushan in the mid-Tang. In late November, one thousand rebels raided the prefectural town of Guide and obtained both men and mules. They were quickly driven off, however, by the local commander, who was backed by the regional military commissioner and a guard commander from nearby Bozhou (see Map 4.1).[14]

When the rebel leader Yang Hu drowned in Nanzhili, his wife assumed command of his men, suggesting the potential of certain women to assert leadership among the masses. Her ascendancy was apparently only temporary, however, for Liu San soon emerged as the new leader of this branch of the rebellion. Together with Zhao Sui, he led forces to Shenqiu, a poor county in southeast Kaifeng prefecture. Finding that the magistrate had filled in the gates with earth, the rebels dug under the walls. They killed one regional military commissioner and captured a second to take the town. They then struck north to another poor county, Luyi, in Guide prefecture, where they overcame the defenses, captured the battalion commander, and camped in the magistrate's offices. Here they won over another government student, named Chen Han, who claimed to

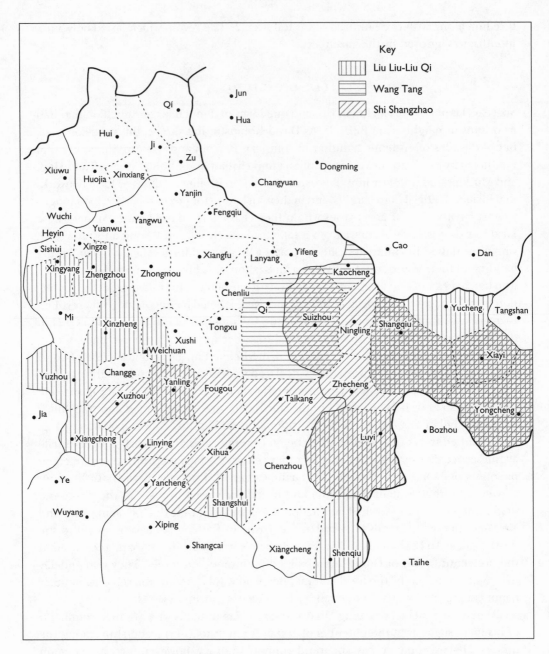

Key

- ▥ Liu Liu-Liu Qi
- ▤ Wang Tang
- ▨ Shi Shangzhao

Jun

Hua

Qí

Hui

Ji

Zu

Xiuwu

Huojia Xinxiang

Dongming

Yanjin

Changyuan

Wuchi

Yangwu

Fengqiu

Heyin
Sishui

Yuanwu

Xingze

Yifeng

Cao

Dan

Xingyang

Zhengzhou

Zhongmou

Xiangfu

Lanyang

Kaocheng

Mi

Chenliu

Qi

Suizhou

Yucheng

Tangshan

Xinzheng

Tongxu

Ningling

Shangqiu

Yuzhou

Changge

Xushi

Weichuan

Yanling

Fougou

Zhecheng

Xiayi

Jia

Xuzhou

Taikang

Yongcheng

Xiangcheng

Linying

Xihua

Chenzhou

Luyi

Bozhou

Ye

Yancheng

Shangshui

Wuyang

Xiping

Xiàngcheng

Shenqiu

Taihe

Shangcai

MAP 4.1. Sixteenth Century Rebellions in Northeast Henan. Sources: Based on data in Gu Yingtai 1658: 45; Guan and Zhang 1695: 39: 17a–18b; Liu and Ye 1705: d3: 84; Chen and Zha 1754: 31: 10a–11a; Zhu and Zhou 1788: 2: 11b; Yue, Hu, and Lü 1903: 15: 2a; Han and Li 1920: 9: 17b; Jiang and Liu 1987: 505; Robinson 1995b: chs. 4–5.

have been a secretary in the ministry of troops. Liu San adopted Chen as his son. Liu San and Zhao Sui then proclaimed themselves "chief and vice commanders entrusted by heaven to campaign and chastise." Liu identified himself with a military star and Zhao with a civil star, allusions to officers sent by heaven to serve the Song ruler in the Ming-period novel *Bandits of the Marsh.* Chen Han and another government student of Luyi nicknamed Ning Long (literally, peaceful dragon) took charge of the rebels' Eastern and Western Depots (named after the special royal judicial courts of the Ming).

Following the Ming system, the rebel leaders reorganized their army into five routes, which they subdivided on the model of the celestial mansions into twenty-eight divisions. They distributed civil titles and inscribed banners with the slogans "Three thousand brave men are going straight to You and Yan [Beijing]" and "A dragon is flying up to the throne to reopen the turbid heavens" (the latter being an allusion to a claim once made by the Ming founder). They composed songs exhorting officials to repair roads and bridges and to provide them with grain and meat; they vowed to spare all who surrendered and to destroy all who resisted.[15]

In late 1511 and early 1512, the rebels approached the towns of eastern Henan. For the most part, they encountered opposition in Runing and acquiescence in Kaifeng. When they attacked Shangcai in Runing on December 12, the magistrate, a scion of a military household, swore to resist to his death and personally led the defense. The rebels took the town, captured the magistrate, and tried to enlist him in their cause. He staunchly refused, reportedly denouncing them as "curs and swine." The rebels persisted in their appeals but the magistrate proved obdurate. They finally killed him, quartered his corpse, and hung the pieces by the four gates as a warning to others. When the rebels moved on to Shangshui, in southern Kaifeng prefecture, the magistrate, clerks, teachers, and students welcomed them. At Xiping, back in Runing again, the magistrate and his assistant offered strong resistance. When the town fell and they refused to surrender, the rebels suspended the magistrate from a flagpole and shot arrows into him until he died. The rebels encountered similarly strong resistance in Wuyang and She counties in Nanyang prefecture. When they reached Xiangcheng in Kaifeng prefecture, however, they were offered two thousand taels of silver and twenty horses and thus saw no need to attack. The contrast between Runing and Kaifeng almost certainly reflected the different political tendencies among the officials and elite located there.[16]

The rebels, too, distinguished between opponents and supporters of the eunuch Liu Jin. When Liu San and Zhao Sui arrived at Junzhou in southwestern Kaifeng, they encountered a firm defense. After several days of unsuccessful siege, some advocated putting the town to the sword. Zhao Sui reportedly vetoed this plan, arguing that the town was the home of a famous official who had been a critic of eunuch rule. Instead, the rebels withdrew and went west to capture Baofeng county. While ensconced in the county offices, the rebels received two edicts relayed by the magistrate ordering them to surrender in return for amnesty. Zhao Sui replied:

> The myriad villains are at the court, sullying all within the four seas, killing remonstrating officials and driving out senior statesmen. We demand that the August Superior decide to execute the villains in order to propitiate the world; he can then cut off the head of this official to placate the villains.[17]

As Robinson points out, Zhao was here alluding to the offer of a censor in the first year of the Zhengde reign to forfeit his own head to secure the dismissal of the eunuch Liu Jin. Apparently finding the Baofeng magistrate unsympathetic to his plea, Zhao had him killed, but he also reportedly disciplined a subordinate who mistreated the magistrate's wife. At this point, more than one hundred rebels surrendered in hopes of an amnesty, but the rebel force still included an estimated 130,000 cavalry. On February 20, 1512, Zhao Sui led this band to take Biyang county, in Nanyang prefecture, the home of Jiao Fang, the grand secretary who had collaborated closely with Liu Jin. Since Jiao was not home, Zhao confiscated his belongings, made an effigy of him, and slashed it with his sword, exclaiming that he was killing him on behalf of the world.[18] After making this appeal for the support of sympathetic officials, Zhao divided Jiao Fang's belongings among his followers.

Zhao Sui's strategy of winning over anti-eunuch officials and the masses proved insufficient to save the rebellion. The court had appointed a capable grand coordinator as military superintendent and an earl as bandit-suppressing general to lead large, seasoned forces from the northern frontier to suppress the rebellion. They offered substantial rewards to loyal officials, threatened punishment of defectors, and promised amnesty for those who surrendered. Meanwhile, Han and minority troops converged on Henan from Huguang. In March, official troops defeated Zhao Sui at Xiping, in Runing, killing over two thousand of his men and seizing numerous weapons and horses. Zhao then took Shangshui and Xihua in south-central Kaifeng prefecture. In Yanling, where the magistrate reportedly presented the rebels with gifts of silk and silver, they raided county offices and warehouses and the residence of a former minister of punishments. They then moved north and took Xinzheng but failed to take Zhengzhou, which was well defended. Passing through Xingyang and Sishui, they went west to attack Yanshi in Henan prefecture. The rebels garnered considerable support, as was recognized by the Henanese scholar Wang Tingxiang, and they won a major battle near Luoyang. But they failed to take that important town.

In April, unsuccessful in the west, the rebels circled back east to Nanzhili and reentered southern Henan. In May they suffered increasing defections and defeats at the hands of official troops and local militia. In June, the rebel leader Liu San died, reportedly after he was wounded with an arrow in his left eye. His corpse was about to be cremated when government troops arrived; they dragged it out of the fire, and decapitated it. On June 16, the rebel advisor from Luyi, Chen Han, surrendered to the Ming. He may have hoped for an amnesty but he was subsequently executed. Meanwhile Zhao Sui shaved his head to disguise himself as a monk and fled to Huguang. In July he was apprehended and sent to Beijing, where he was dismembered in the marketplace on November 7. According to one report, Wuzong so hated Zhao and other rebel leaders that he contravened the legal code and official advice and skinned their corpses to make a cover for his saddle. The report may be apocryphal, but it symbolizes the animosity incurred by the rebels' astute assault on Ming prestige in Henan. In June, Liu Liu had accidentally drowned in Huguang and in August Liu Qi was tracked down in Nanzhili and drowned. On October 6, 1512, Zhengde officially proclaimed the end of the rebellion. The largest collective action against the Ming state in the sixteenth century was over.[19]

WANG TANG

The third significant rebellion to affect northeast Henan in the early sixteenth century featured more plebian legions and less clear goals and results. This roving bandit or guerrilla-type uprising was associated with a leader, whose origins, activities, and fate remain murky. Wang Tang may have first appeared in the historical record in 1506, the initial year of the Zhengde reign, when he was described as a "big outlaw" who "plundered" Gaoyang, a market town in western Qi county, Kaifeng prefecture. But, if so, we hear nothing more of him for the next sixteen years.[20] Wang Tang next appeared in the records in 1522, the first year of the Jiajing reign, when he was identified as being from Qingzhou prefecture in Shandong. Described variously as "big robbers," "mining bandits from Yidu and Laiwu," "roving bandits of Shandong," and even "Henan bandits," Wang Tang and his followers apparently spread out from a coal mining and porcelain manufacturing town in Qingzhou and moved west to threaten the Grand Canal in late 1522. Soon they appeared in northeast Henan, where they created a stir in Xiayi, Yongcheng, and Qi. According to the Shangqiu gazetteer, "the Laiwu bandit Wang Tang crossed the river from Liangjingkou, defeated our troops, entered our territory to rob, and then led his troops to the southwest and disappeared." According to the gazetteer of Suizhou, "the roving bandit Wang Tang . . . totally defeated" the local guard troops and killed six or seven thousand people, including many women, before being "chastised in a distant suburb" and forced to flee the department (see Map 4.1).[21]

The ultimate fate of Wang Tang is unknown. The court raised troops in Beizhili, Shandong, and Henan to defeat insurgents in Kaocheng county in early 1523. It drew a lesson from the Liu Liu-Liu Qi uprising and offered amnesty to rebel bands who surrendered and cooperated in suppressing other rebels. In early March 1523, the court proclaimed the "Qingzhou miner banditry" suppressed, but there is no record of the capture of Wang Tang or his colleagues. Perhaps the state ended Wang Tang's revolt by absorbing his men into its own armies. In April 1523, the grand coordinator of Henan was forced to retire in the face of charges that many of his troops were former bandits.[22]

During the next three decades, Ming China was at relative peace, but the climate remained cool and natural disasters recurred. Jiajing gradually withdrew into a search for personal immortality and left affairs of state to the grand secretary Yan Song, who, although generally capable, was sometimes irresponsible. By midcentury, Mongols raided from the north and Japanese forces attacked from the east. The state treasury fell into deficit. Although there were efforts to raise revenues from the salt trade, there were few funds available to provide relief from the famines that periodically afflicted the Huai valley.[23]

Conditions in northeast Henan were particularly difficult. According to the gazetteer of Guide prefecture, created in 1550, there were locusts in 1529, floods in 1537, and famine and epidemics in 1539. Yongcheng county reported drought, frost, and famine in 1523, drought and disease followed by heavy rains in 1524, locusts in 1527 and 1531, drought and locusts followed by heavy rains in 1539, drought and no harvests in 1542 and 1545, and heavy rains that destroyed crops in 1547. Suizhou department reported flooding in 1546, 1547, and 1548. Even the sketchy record from Xiangfu county in Kaifeng prefecture included heavy snow in 1522, a sign of the continuing cold climate, and great famines in 1538 and 1553.[24] Local efforts at famine relief were inadequate.

SHI SHANGZHAO

It was under such conditions that Shi Shangzhao raised the standard of revolt in his native Zhecheng, one of the poorer counties in Guide prefecture. Shi belonged to a household with hereditary responsibility for producing and transporting salt. As the state administration faltered, he continued to trade in salt privately, thus earning the sobriquet salt smuggler. Shi, for his part, may have resented recent state efforts to regain control over that lucrative sector of the economy. In the spring of 1553, Shi organized a mass following that came to the attention of the magistrate. The magistrate was reluctant to resort to force and tried to persuade Shi and his assistant to cease their organizing. Shi and his men agreed in principle but in fact used the time to complete their plans for an uprising. In the seventh month they led a bold attack on the prefectural capital of Guide. According to the gazetteer of Suizhou, the prefect of Guide fled, leaving behind an assistant to lead the defense (see Map 4.1).[25]

Encouraged by the lackluster official defense of Guide but unprepared to take the town, Shi went east to Xiayi county, where he robbed the treasury and freed prisoners. He spared the teachers and students in an effort to win their support. Here again the magistrate "hid to avoid him," and many of the people did the same. Shi carried his campaign south to neighboring Yongcheng county and then returned to his home in Zhecheng.[26]

Strengthened now by recruits from elsewhere, Shi attacked the county offices of Zhecheng and drove the magistrate away. He captured one of the county's rare provincial graduates, Chen Wenshi. He proceeded south to Luyi county, where the magistrate fled and the town surrendered. At this point, the literatus Chen Wenshi refused to cooperate and committed suicide. Seemingly enraged by this overt expression of opposition from a member of the elite of his own county, Shi rushed back to Zhecheng. He went straight to his hometown, Matou, where he reportedly killed tens of thousands (that is, many). The figures were probably inflated and the identity of the victims unrecorded, but the slaughter, if true, must have severely undermined his effort to establish a base.[27]

Unable to rely on his fellow townsmen, Shi and his men assaulted counties to the north and west. In Ningling and Suizhou, they met strong resistance, perhaps because those towns were well garrisoned, had had time to prepare their defenses, and were determined to prevent massacres like the one in Zhecheng. In Taikang, however, townsmen offered gifts of wine and meat in an effort to persuade the rebels to leave the town alone. Undaunted by the opposition and encouraged by the cooperation, Shi attacked further west. At Yanling, he defeated the official troops and killed many. At Fugou, his five-thousand-man force terrified the magistrate into flight and incurred only two casualties at the hands of a militia organized by a local provincial graduate. Shi next pushed south to Xihua, where he plundered the treasury and killed "countless" inhabitants. At Xuzhou, Linying, and Yancheng, he faced stronger resistance and suffered a major defeat by government troops.[28]

This campaign proved to be Shi's last. According to the Ming prince Zhu Mujie, the state effectively mobilized the guard-battalion system, perhaps for the last time. A vice censor in chief in Beijing was put in overall charge of the campaign and instructed to cooperate with the Henan grand coordinator and surveillance commissioner. The censor personally oversaw the raising of troops, the supply of weapons, and the stockpiling of grain and fodder. He assembled the troops, admonished the officers to maintain strict discipline, warned the masses not to follow the bandits, and promised amnesty to all those who had been coerced into revolt. Officers were to reward their subordinates according to merit so as to encourage them in battle. Teams of assistant censors and assistant regional military commissioners organized five thousand troops from the Kaifeng, Suizhou, and Chenzhou guards into a central division. They also organized three thousand troops of the Zhangde guard from north Henan into a left division and two thousand troops from Nanyang, Xinyang, and Runing prefectures into a right division. The censor personally led some 1,500 crack troops from the provincial guard to provide overall direction to the campaign.[29]

In September 1553, only weeks after the rebellion began, the Ming armies converged on Xiangcheng. They then advanced eastward, capturing the rebel second-in-command and driving Shi and his force to the east. To hem in the bandits, the censor deputed an assistant to garrison Yuzhou to the west and other censors to defend Luyi, Shangqiu, and Fengyang in the east. He then sent a small detachment to follow the rebel leader. In October the Ming forces pushed the rebels out of Henan and into Nanzhili and defeated them on the Huai River northeast of Fengyang. The wily Shi fled north into Shandong, but he was soon captured and beheaded.[30] The most concerted challenge yet to Ming authority in Guide and Kaifeng ended only months after it had begun.

After the repression of these four overt uprisings, the idea of rebellion was kept alive by covert activities in neighboring areas. When Li Yue's revolt had failed, he and his nephew Li Fuda had continued to teach the White Lotus doctrines in Shaanxi. In 1512 they had revolted again but had been quickly suppressed. Li Yue had been killed, but Li Fuda had escaped. He changed his name to Li Wu, moved to Shanxi, and continued to teach the faith. One of his students, his grandson Li Tong, claimed to be descended from the Tang royal line and to have a mission to "go out into the world and bring peace to the people." Although neither man had become involved in any rebellion, they had kept alive the hope that a Li would appear to lead the world to salvation.[31]

By midcentury, a White Lotus sect leader in Beijing named Lü had one thousand students and was planning an uprising. Among tens of thousands of sect members in Beizhili, Shandong, and Henan, one Li Yinglong (Li the responsive dragon) was active in Jiyuan county, Huaiqing prefecture. According to one official report, believers in Huaiqing and Weihui prefectures had chosen Li Yinglong to be their leader. He allegedly made seals and distributed flags in preparation for an uprising on the eighth day of the fourth month of 1564. When his plans leaked out, Li fled to Shanxi, where he was later caught and executed. The following year, a Li Yingqian of Ganquan county, Shaanxi, proclaimed himself a descendant of the Tang royal family. Together with a Li Yuangong of Henei county, Huaiqing, he spread unspecified prophecies. He was charged with having contacts with bandits, making seals and flags, and conspiring to revolt in Henan. He was arrested and decapitated. The idea of establishing a Tang-like order became so prevalent in this period that it was embraced by White Lotus teachers of different surnames who did not even bother to adopt the surname Li. For example, there was a Cai Boguan in Dazu county, Sichuan, who revolted and established a Dabao reign, an apparent allusion to the Tianbao reign of the Tang. Under interrogation, Cai admitted that he too was a student of Li Tong, thus allegedly confirming the far-flung influence of the heterodox Li network in the sixteenth century.[32] Thus far, however, the Li family conspiracies were largely centered in Shanxi and Shaanxi, where the Tang royal family had originated. White Lotus activity remained at the margins of Ming authority and of northeast Henan.

Making Rebellion Central

During the late Ming, from 1570 to 1644, initially positive trends turned into negative ones, causing problems for the masses throughout China. Up to about 1620, the climate warmed up, benefiting agricultural production; but after 1620, colder weather set in that was destined to last for a century. During the first part of the period, China enjoyed a surplus in its foreign trade, resulting in an influx of silver bullion that stimulated the commercial and industrial economies. During the latter part there were recurrent downturns in the increasingly integrated world economy with depressing effects on the Chinese economy. In the early years, the powerful grand secretary Zhang Juzheng and his supporters implemented reforms to shore up state finances in an increasingly monetized economy, but the achievements were later undermined by royal profligacy, aristocratic greed, official peculation, elite self-aggrandizement, and middle strata proliferation. They were also checked by widespread official and elite opposition to Zhang's quest to increase the wealth and power of the state. As a result, the Ming faced financial difficulties and was unable to pay the newly recruited troops charged with defending the polity from frontier encroachment and internal banditry. The state began the period by providing relief for one out of every five disasters; it ended it by assisting victims in one out of eighteen subsistence crises. The average number of rebellions jumped from one to nine a year.[33]

Accordingly, northeast Henan seems to have been relatively peaceful during most of the Wanli reign. The general prosperity and reform spirit of the late sixteenth century counterbalanced the plague and famine that swept through the region in the late 1580s and early 1590s.[34] Yet the potential for various kinds of rebellions was growing. As Lü Kun put it in 1597:

> In today's world there is a specter of rebellion even though rebellion has yet to begin. . . . From of old, there have been four kinds of people who like to rebel. First are those who have no means of support, no food or clothing, whose families are in difficulties, and who consider rebelling in hopes of delaying their demise. Second are people who do

not know how to behave, who have high spirits and violent natures, who violate the laws to make life easier for themselves, who are fond of jade and silk and sons and daughters but cannot get them legitimately, and who think that if there is a rebellion they can steal what they want. Third are the people of heterodox beliefs, who combine in White Lotus associations, who spread in all four directions, whose teachers preach and attract crowds, and who will respond to and join up with anyone who calls them. Fourth, there are people without self-control, who turn petty rifts into major fights, who think only of being strong, who hope only for a change, and who take no pleasure in the existing peace in the world.[35]

Given the proliferation of such folk, Lü implied, rebellions were only a matter of time.

YANG SIJING

The seventeenth century no sooner began than a combination of the first kind of desperate people and the fourth kind of local strongmen challenged official authority in Suizhou. A minor functionary in the magistrate's office, a storehouse commissioner named Yang Sijing, allegedly developed a network of clients among the desperate (or perhaps desperadoes) of the department. Later, as head of a granary in a stockade community, he increased his following among the down-and-out. Two assistants (or henchmen) from a local family stockade were his "teeth and claws," keeping both officials and rivals at bay. In 1604 or 1605, Yang Sijing quarreled with another local tough. Unable to intimidate this antagonist as he had others, Yang finally called up one thousand of his men and sent them to crush his rival. The magistrate of Suizhou feared Yang and did nothing.

When the magistrate of neighboring Qi county heard about the case, he reported it to his superior, the prefect of Kaifeng. The prefect then informed provincial officials who instructed the military intendant of Suizhou and Chenzhou to find a way to arrest Yang and bring him to justice. When the military intendant transmitted the order, the Suizhou magistrate replied that his "right and left hands," or his clerks, were all Yang's men. Any formal decision to arrest Yang would be immediately leaked by the clerks, allowing the suspect to escape. The magistrate therefore requested the issue of a secret order to him personally to have Yang come to the departmental offices for a "discussion" of the killings. The magistrate then sent a trusted personal aide to transmit it to Yang. When the aide arrived at Yang's stockade, he encountered a dozen bodyguards with drawn swords. He somehow managed to persuade Yang to accompany him to the magistrate's office on the understanding that the magistrate thought he was innocent and wanted to settle the case quickly. When Yang arrived at the departmental office, the magistrate showered him with friendly words and sent him off to the provincial capital with an official escort of fifty men.

When the party reached Chenliu county, they were met by one thousand troops sent by the grand coordinator, who was obviously taking no chances. Yang Sijing's fame as a dangerous man was such that his arrest brought thousands of people to the streets of Kaifeng to see him. The grand coordinator remanded Yang to the jail. That night the prefect arranged to have Yang beaten in jail, where he died of his wounds. His chief accomplices in Suizhou were soon arrested and beheaded.[36] The available evidence does not indicate whether Yang Sijing was a patron of the disadvantaged, who was unjustly killed without due process of law, or a local thug who preyed on the masses and was justly eliminated. Either way, his case reveals how local strongmen could intimidate local officials into inaction and could cause provincial officials to take extraordinary measures to insure obedience if not justice.

LIU TIANXU

In the following year, 1606, a rebel of Lü Kun's third category came to light in a major court case in Nanjing. The heterodox sect leader Liu Tianxu, who had originated in Yongcheng county, Guide prefecture, had moved to Fengyang prefecture, where he had been considered a master of the religion of Non-Purposive Action. This White Lotus–related sect soon attracted over one thousand adherents. Liu moved to Nanjing, where he was known by the title "Prince Li who Opens up the Land and Settles Heaven and Earth," or, more informally, "old man Li." In 1606 he allegedly wrote an esoteric book that included the prediction that "a monarch named Li will appear in the world." He and his followers, including many government soldiers, assembled large numbers of bows, arrows, knives, and other weapons as well as red turbans and clothing. Liu was also known as the Dragon Flower Lord and King. He was said to have adopted the title Dragon Phoenix used by Han Liner at the end of the Yuan. He appointed dukes, marquis, earls, generals, and commanders, and he selected the twenty-third of the ninth month, the winter solstice, for an uprising. When the plans leaked out, Liu and his followers were arrested.[37]

The Liu Tianxu conspiracy led to a famous court case, numerous reports, and much correspondence. Liu apparently had many sympathizers and supporters among officials and the elite, and the case threatened to precipitate a major purge of the administration. In the end, the voices of moderation seem to have prevailed. Liu and six of his key assistants were executed, but the rest of his many followers were exonerated. It appears that Liu inherited the long tradition that a Li would take the throne, and he may even have believed that he was that person. According to the official records, under interrogation he claimed to be the Chen Sheng and Wu Guang of his day.[38] Whatever historical models he selected or were attributed to him, his conspiracy revealed dissidence not only among the masses but in the ranks of the bureaucracy. For that reason it was deeply unsettling to the Ming officials of the day.

XU HONGRU

Sixteen years after the quelling of Liu Tianxu's Non-Purposive Action conspiracy, Xu Hongru led a White Lotus uprising in Shandong that progressed further before it was suppressed. Its roots went back to the 1560s when one Wang Sen, from Stone Buddha village in Jizhou, Beizhili, became a disciple of Bodhisattva Lü, a fifteenth-century nun whose spirit was thought to reside in the Baoming Temple west of Beijing.[39] Wang together with a man named Gao became teachers in the "Incense Smelling Religion." By the 1590s he developed a network of evangelists and assemblies that stretched across Beizhili, Shandong, Henan, Shanxi, Shaanxi, and Sichuan. This organization alarmed the authorities, and Wang was arrested in 1595. He was soon released, however, perhaps after paying a bribe. He continued to proselytize, winning converts even among the external clan and eunuchs in Beijing. Later, one of his followers, Li Guoyong, who used charms and mantras, established a separate organization, and the two men came into conflict. The clash brought them to the attention of the authorities, and in 1614 Wang was arrested again. This time he was detained, and five years later he was executed. Leadership in the sect was assumed by his son, Wang Haoxian, and by Xu Hongru, who was from Juye county, Yanzhou prefecture, Shandong.

As the White Lotus sect continued to proliferate in the last years of the Wanli reign, the Ming once again outlawed all participation in it. Then, in March 1621, a Jurchen advance in Liaodong precipitated the flight of many refugees from the northeast into Shandong. A fear of imminent state repression and an expectation of broad mass support led Xu to plan an uprising for the midautumn festival, which fell on September 19, 1622.[40]

In fact, Xu Hongru revolted three months earlier to prevent a preemptive strike by the state. He declared himself Zhongxing Fuliedi (literally, lucky, devoted lord of the restoration) and adopted the reign name Dasheng Xingsheng (literally, greater vehicle rising to victory). He appointed princes, ministers, and military advisors. In all these ways he signaled his intention to create his own state and challenge Ming authority. Unlike his rebel predecessors, however, Xu did not appeal to Han, Song, or Tang models. His goals were apparently more transcendent on the one hand, and more reformist on the other. He established a headquarters at Liangjialou and then with surprising speed seized control of Yuncheng county west of the Grand Canal. He also took Zou, Teng, and Yi counties east of the canal. These victories gave him control of the waterway that was considered the throat of the polity. Soon the number of followers in Shandong was estimated in the tens of thousands while sympathizers throughout North China were estimated at two million. Potential allies were reported in Henan, including Gushi in the south and Yongcheng and Xiayi in the northeast. Xu was unable to take Yanzhou, however, or even his home county of Juye. As in the Liu Liu-Liu Qi revolt a little over a century earlier, the court transferred battle-hardened troops from the northern frontier to deal with this challenge from within. Under the leadership of a capable grand coordinator, they defeated rebel forces near Yanzhou, cut the road between Zou and Teng, recovered Yi, and then besieged Zou. Xu held out for three months until his forces ran out of food and surrendered. He fled on horseback but was captured and torn apart in the market place.[41]

The Ming thus suppressed the Xu Hongru rebellion before sympathizers scattered throughout the central plain could mobilize to support it. The grand coordinator responsible for the victory was promoted to grand guardian of the heir apparent. He suspended taxes in the affected counties in an effort to restore public support for the dynasty. With the defeat of Xu's rebellion, the White Lotus sect suffered a serious setback. Nonetheless, as in the case of the Yellow Turban uprising toward the end of the Han, the rebellion severely damaged the prestige of the Ming state. The Han had lasted thirty-six years beyond the Yellow Turbans; the Ming was to last only twenty-two years beyond Xu Hongru.[42]

Indeed, adherents of the White Lotus sect remained active in Shandong and Henan after 1622. In the winter of 1629, the second year of the Chongzhen reign, remnants of Xu's forces besieged Laiyang, Shandong, from all sides. The Ming regional commander who had planned the defense of the town from the coastal side was forced to transfer troops to the interior to break the siege. He finally burned down six rebel stockades and beheaded two rebel leaders to relieve the town.[43]

ZHU BINGNAN

The same year in Suizhou, northeast Henan, another survivor of the Xu Hongru revolt, one Zhu Bingnan, was arrested and charged with planning an uprising. According to a local historian, Zhu had arrived in the department some years before and had set up a dye shop to support himself. He had become wealthy and used his money to propagate the White Lotus teachings among his clientele and the public at large. According to the official report, Zhu attracted a considerable following of "villainous people" in the region between Kaifeng and Shangqiu. He and his supporters supposedly concocted a plan to enter Kaifeng city, raid the armory, and kidnap the officials of the Zhou estate and the provincial administration. Their plan had leaked out, however, and they were promptly arrested and beheaded. A brief, undated note in the Suizhou gazetteer suggests that Zhu Bingnan was planning a surprise. According to it, Zhu's followers, who numbered more than one thousand people, planned to use the pretext of presenting petitions to the magistrate of Xiangfu to stage a coup against the grand coordinator and supreme commander of the province. The note concluded that the prospect of "cruel killing and plundering did not have to await the arrival of Dashing and Cao."[44]

The charges against Zhu Bingnan may have been exaggerated to discredit the religious ideas that, it was thought, might lead to such activities in the future. Given the state's loss of face resulting from the news of even unrealized conspiracies, however, provincial officials may have had reason to fear a new millenarian uprising. They apparently accepted the bad publicity as the unavoidable cost of the campaign needed to forestall it.

LI SHENWU

In 1629 a newly appointed censor and regional inspector of Henan, Wu Sheng, rushed to Yongcheng county to investigate rumors of more sect activity. He reported that sect leaders from Guangping prefecture in Beizhili and cudgel men (armed practitioners of the martial arts) from Yanzhou prefecture in Shandong had descended on Yongcheng a few weeks before and established themselves in a village on the border with Xiayi county. Wu and his subordinates arrested the cudgel men and obtained their confessions. He then submitted a report describing one of the sect leaders. In his words,

> Li Shenwu's countenance is extraordinary. He has big ears and long hands, and there are red moles on his legs in the shape of the sun and the moon. He calls himself the Ziweixing [Purple Tenuity Constellation] and claims that a *shibazi* [literally, ten-eight-son; in other words, a Li] is going to emerge to govern the world. [His associate] and

others made contacts with bandit parties. Everyone who wanted to see Li Shenwu had to pay two taels of silver. They made and purchased weapons, kept registers of all those who came to visit, and set a date to attack Xiayi.[45]

Although the conspiracy had failed and some of the cudgel men had been arrested, Li and his assistant had escaped.

Wu went on to explain how such groups could exist in Yongcheng and even attract popular support.

> Yongcheng is on the border of the province. . . . the Lotus sect and cudgel party have many followers, and big bandits sneak into them to await an opportunity to make trouble. . . . The county's collective security system is strict and there is no reason for robbers to appear. But levies for military supplies are heavy, demands for state services are numerous, and the damages to the masses accumulate. Last summer it was hot and dry and the grain withered and burned. The people are poor and bandits arise; the people's hearts and minds are in distress.[46]

When sect leaders such as Li Zhenwu arrived from north of the river to spread their messages, therefore, "ignorant people" were "easily deceived." Fortunately, Wu continued, the cudgel men had been arrested. Otherwise, he said, Yongcheng and Xiayi might have become another Zou and Teng, an allusion to Xu Hongru's revolt in Shandong. But Wu was still dissatisfied. As he put it: "The central plain is the heart and stomach, a strategic place; how can we allow things like this to go on here?" He requested that his colleagues in neighboring provinces be ordered to apprehend the fugitives.

In a subsequent report, Wu emphasized the sectarian nature of the dissidents and described efforts to control them. As he put it,

> Recently, all of the big robbers who have been caught possessed sectarian books and used royal titles. They plundered the people in the villages, moved back and forth among towns, and bestrode whole counties and departments. Throughout an area of three to four hundred li, partisans passed clandestine signs and spread rumors that the Ziweixing was planning a big undertaking. How could they have been your ordinary, everyday villains?[47]

Fortunately, Wu continued, the collective security and militia systems had worked. They had netted sect leaders in many counties, including Li Xin in Luyi, Li Chaowang in Suizhou, and Li Shouzhi in Zhecheng. Wu praised the magistrates responsible for these arrests, including Song Cong in Xiangfu and Song Mei in Qi, writing that their vigor was worth more than one thousand troops in reducing sect activity in the region. Finally, in a third report, Wu described how he and his subordinates, including the Guide prefect Dong Sichen and the Guide judge Wan Yuanji, had tracked down Li Shenwu and arrested him in the border region between Yongcheng and Xiayi. They had quickly decapitated him and hung his head in the street to "demonstrate the force of the law." Wu expressed the hope that this would be the end of sect conspiracies in Henan.[48]

Sect preparations for rebellion apparently diminished in northeast Henan after 1630, but Wu Sheng's suppression campaign may have left an unforeseen legacy. As discussed in Chapter 1, three of the local officials who were most energetic in suppressing the White Lotus sect in Henan—Song Cong, Song Mei, and Dong Sichen—all hailed from Laiyang county in Shandong. Because Laiyang itself had recently survived a major siege led by White Lotus members, these men may have harbored more than the usual official antipathy to sectarians. Their hostility to the sect may have heightened the ferocity of their suppression, which took the lives of many sect leaders, including four who shared the surname Li. The involvement of these magistrates named Song in suppressing the rebels named Li may have influenced later accounts of the fall of the Ming in northeast Henan.[49]

GAO YINGXIANG

After 1630, roving banditry replaced sectarian conspiracies as the main form of resistance to the Ming state. Such banditry had become endemic in Shaanxi province during the late Tianqi and early Chongzhen reigns. Its causes lay partly in the long-term desiccation of the northern part of the province and the more recent shift in foreign trade from the Silk Road to the Pacific Ocean. The problems were compounded by inadequate administration typical of frontier regions and by slackening morale common to late dynastic periods. Short-term causes of trouble included Wanli's indifference and Tianqi's penury. During the 1620s, Mongols and Muslims, local gangs and unpaid soldiers, hard pressed miners and unemployed clerks, refugees from the northeast and landless farmers from the northwest, gradually coalesced into bands of mounted warriors engaging in defensive and predatory raids against each other, the state, and the masses. By 1630, roving banditry was spreading from Shaanxi into Shanxi.[50]

In 1631 roving bandits began appearing in Huaiqing prefecture, Henan. Alarmed members of the local elite called on the court to transfer Hou Xun's client, the general Zuo Liangyu, from his base in Changping, Beizhili, to Henan. In 1632 rebel forces under Gao Yingxiang, known as the Dashing Prince, appeared further north in Zhangde prefecture. In 1633 the Daming military intendant Lu Xiangsheng moved south and pushed the insurgents back to Huaiqing prefecture. Zuo Liangyu defeated rebels in Zhangde, earning a name as the head of the Zuo Family Army. He was soon promoted to regional commander. In a pattern that would become typical for him, however, he failed to follow up his victory. Instead he allowed his men to collect the women and materiel left behind by the fleeing bandits as booty. Later in the year, Zuo was defeated and lost seven thousand men. The court responded to the growing threat by appointing Xuan Mo, a 1619 metropolitan graduate from Beizhili, as grand coordinator of Henan (see Figure 4.1).[51] Xuan coordinated troops under Zuo Liangyu with forces sent from Beijing, Shanxi, and Sichuan to inflict a defeat on the rebels, driving them away from the north-south trunk road. Gao Yingxiang consolidated his control over the surviving rebel forces and advanced on Ming positions in Zhangde. He was driven back by Zuo Liangyu to the mountains of Huaiqing. By the end of 1633, the rebels reached Hui and Qí counties in Weihui prefecture, thus appearing for the first time in northeast Henan. The prince of Lu, whose estate was in nearby Ji county, called on the court to send more troops. Henan, with only 8,300 government troops, was becoming the chief battleground in the war with the insurgents.[52]

During the winter of 1633–34, Gao Yingxiang and others led over 100,000 rebels into the mountains of Wuan, She, Henei, and Jiyuan. Grand coordinator Xuan Mo sent

FIGURE 4.1. Xuan Mo Arrives to Coordinate the Defenses Against the Rebels in Northeast Henan, 1633. Source: Xuan Kangxi: 1. Courtesy of the Rare Book Room of the Beijing Library (now the National Library of China).

troops under Zuo Liangyu and others to besiege the rebels and prevent them from advancing north toward Beijing. Gao and his men therefore broke out of the siege and headed south, crossing the Yellow River that had frozen solid in the abnormally cold winter (see Figure 4.2). In 1634 Gao's forces entered Kaifeng prefecture for the first time. Simultaneously, other insurgents arrived in Henan prefecture and put pressure on Luoyang. The scholar-official Lü Weiqi, whose home was in nearby Xin'an county, appealed to the court to suspend the three tax surcharges, which, he said, were driving the people into poverty and rebellion. The court ignored this request but appointed the grand coordinator of Yan-Sui, Chen Qiyu, supreme commander of the armed forces of Shaanxi, Shanxi, Henan, Sichuan, and Huguang. This was the first such multiprovincial appointment in recent times and it reflected the court's clear recognition that roving banditry was now spreading to the center of the polity. Chen put new energy into pacifying the bandits through negotiations. He persuaded key leaders such as Gao Yingxiang to surrender in return for amnesty. Such surrenders soon proved false, however, and the bandits resumed their attacks. Chen was dismissed and was replaced by Hong Chengchou, the grand coordinator of Shaanxi, who advocated military suppression. Roving bandits retook Lushi in western Henan, and local bandits were active in Kaifeng prefecture.[53]

As Gao Yingxiang's men moved into northeastern Henan, stories began to circulate about them and their reception in the region. According to a tale recounted by a Xiangcheng man, the unidentified bandit leader who arrived in that county in southwestern Kaifeng prefecture had a black face and a curly beard and wore a red gown.

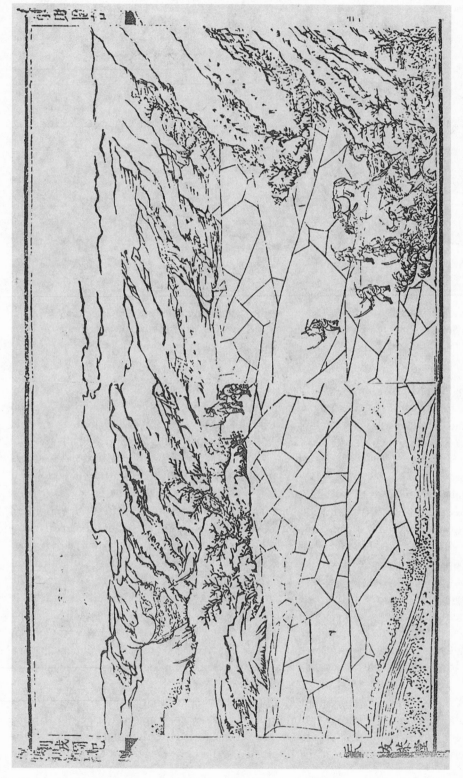

FIGURE 4.2. Rebels Crossing the Yellow River on the Ice, 1634. Source: Xuan Kangxi: 27. Courtesy of the Rare Book Room of the Beijing Library (now the National Library of China).

The magistrate was terrified and hid behind the wall. When he spied a student standing on the wall with a bow and some arrows he called out to him and asked why he was not shooting. The student then raised his bow, shot at the bandit leader, and, to everyone's amazement, killed him on the spot. The attackers then withdrew, and the student became a hero. The magistrate decided to put him in charge of training troops. When the bandits returned, the student led several hundred men out to resist them. When the bandits fled, the student and his men pursued them and fell into an ambush. The student's horse was killed from under him, and most of his men were wiped out. He managed to find his way to a tree where he stood with his bow and an empty quiver. The mounted bandits soon found him there; they galloped around him and pumped arrows into him until he died.[54] This story, featuring a curly bearded bandit, a feckless official, a naive student, and the suffering masses, could serve as a metaphor of the conflict as it spread into the central plain.

In February 1635, Gao Yingxiang led tens of thousands of men out of eastern Shaanxi into western Henan. The rebels advanced along three routes. The first went to Xingyang, Sishui, and Zhengzhou in Kaifeng prefecture. The Xingyang magistrate reportedly fled his post, and the insurgents broke through the gates and entered the town. Two provincial graduates led their families and servants to fight in the streets, killing more than thirty intruders. The rebels were more numerous, however, and soon overwhelmed the defenders, killing many. In Sishui the magistrate and a censor living at home defended the wall, resulting in casualties on both sides. During the night, the attackers dug tunnels under the walls and entered the town. The town fell and many died, including the censor. The magistrate either "changed his clothes and escaped" or was captured.[55] Xingyang and Sishui were poor counties that might have lacked the will to fight against masses of desperate people even if they had had the resources to do so. But Xingyang had long been considered a strategic town. Its fall to the rebels, the first in northeast Henan, shocked the Ming administration.

In Zhengzhou, however, the magistrate cooperated with a teacher and a member of the local elite to organize an effective defense. A townsman later recorded how it was done.

> The defenders recruited rural braves into a militia. The officers were all sons and younger brothers of the elite. Soldiers recruited from the masses accepted the wise and brave among the scholars as their leaders and called them volunteer managers. They divided up defense of the four walls among themselves and worked together against the common enemy.[56]

Political leadership and social solidarity enabled Zhengzhou to defend itself, and the rebels passed by without trying to attack. Subsequent magistrates continued the work of building "strong walls and deep moats." They made the town impregnable for the next five years despite annual drought and endemic banditry.

Gao's first column now pushed south through Chenzhou and left the region. A second column meanwhile advanced from Nanyang to attack Yancheng, in southern Kaifeng prefecture. Whether in response to this probe or independently, the Yancheng magistrate, Li Zhensheng, a Shaanxi metropolitan graduate, captured a local bandit who had adopted the name Ziweixing, suggesting the persistence of sect activity in this region.

Gao Yingxiang's third column simultaneously crossed Huaiqing, forded the Yellow River, and pushed east to Guide. The three-pronged rebel advance on northeast Henan led to a chorus of calls to reinforce Ming armies in the region. A secretary in the ministry of troops, arguing that "the security of the world depends on the central plain," reported that "seventy-two divisions" comprising two to three hundred thousand bandits were advancing toward Zhengzhou and Shangqiu. Since Zuo Liangyu and other commanders in Henan had fewer than ten thousand men, the secretary urged that troops be transferred from the entire realm to defend Henan. In the middle of the month, the president of the ministry of troops, Zhang Fengyi, and the president of the ministry of revenue, Hou Xun, a native of Shangqiu, agreed to send sixty-four thousand more troops and 780,000 taels to Henan. Undeterred, roving bandits under Gao Yingxiang and one Saodi Wang (literally, the prince who sweeps the earth) took the Ming founder's ancestral tombs in Fengyang, Nanzhili.[57]

The growth in rebel influence in northeast Henan gave rise to a story that thirteen rebel leaders had met in Xingyang on the first day of the new year, Chongzhen 8/1/1 (February 17, 1635). There they supposedly developed a coordinated strategy for seventy-two divisions that would lead to victory less than a decade later. Rebel victories at Xingyang and Fengyang were important steps in the roving bandits' march toward legitimacy, but the contention of the early-Qing writer Wu Weiye and the official *Ming History* that they were followed by a grand rebel conference in Xingyang cannot withstand close scrutiny.[58]

In the first place, Wu Weiye wrote that the meeting took place in Xingyang on the first day of the first month of the year and was in response to court discussions of plans to send major reinforcements to Henan to crush the rebellion. But Xingyang did not fall to the rebels until the *sixth* day of that month and the discussions at court were held even later. One early-Qing writer, Mao Qiling, apparently saw this problem and dropped the insistence on a specific day, writing only that the meeting took place in the first month. A second problem is that the earliest sources did not mention any rebel convocation at Xingyang. Those sources include contemporary records by participants, such as the illustrated account of bandit suppression by the Henan grand coordinator Xuan Mo; the gazetteers of Xingyang, Sishui, Zhengzhou, Kaifeng, and Henan; and early-Qing histories by Peng Sunyi, Tan Qian, and Zheng Lian. Since the supposed meeting neatly symbolized the rising fortunes of the rebellion, such sources would certainly have included it if it had occurred. A third problem is that most of the key rebel leaders who supposedly attended the meeting were busy elsewhere at the time. The Dashing General Li Zicheng was still in Shaanxi preparing to enter western Henan; the Prince Who Sweeps the Earth (Saodi Wang) was in Nanzhili preparing to seize Fengyang. A fourth problem is that most of the strategies supposedly adopted at the rebel meeting were not followed by the rebels in subsequent years. In fact, as the historians Gu Cheng and Wang Xingya have pointed out, the rebel leaders were still too disorganized in 1635 to plan any such coherent division of labor.[59]

But if the Xingyang rebel enclave never occurred, we may well ask why Wu Weiye invented it and why the *Ming History* accepted it. One answer is that the supposed meeting dramatized the fall of Xingyang, symbolized the growing strength of the rebellion, highlighted the victories of Gao Yingxiang and Saodi Wang in the central plain, and adumbrated the eventual rise of Li Zicheng to rebel leadership. The fabricated rebel conference at Xingyang in 1635 may also have served to distract attention from actual events occurring in northeast Henan that were more embarrassing to those, like Wu Weiye, who had been loyal to the Ming and hostile to the rebels (see Map 4.2).

One such event, involving official abuses and mass suffering, transpired in Shangqiu on March 5, 1635, when roving bandits arrived in Shen Family Village, apparently from the southeast. That night, the Ming regional commander attacked the rebels while they slept, causing them to flee half naked on their horses to the west. Instead of pursuing the rebels, the Ming commander followed the bad precedent of Zuo Liangyu and allowed his men to collect the clothing and armor they left behind. He then rushed back to Shangqiu to report his victory and claim his reward. At the same time, an unnamed military intendant, seeking to profit from the rout but lacking evidence to prove his participation, massacred residents of ten nearby villages to get the heads he needed. According to Zheng Lian, this atrocity gave fresh meaning to the old saying, "to borrow heads to prove one's achievements," outraging the people of Shangqiu.[60]

If Ming military abuses incurred popular wrath that benefited the rebels, local students' faith in the positive potential of social banditry led to disillusionment. When the first roving bandits appeared in Mamuji, a village in eastern Shangqiu, an old student rejected his wife's entreaties to flee, saying: "Bandits are people too, why should we flee? They only want some wine and some meat. Surely they will be satisfied with that." When the bandits arrived at his house, the student put on his hat and went out to greet them. He hardly got out a word, however, before they cut off his head. Another old student in the same village, who was known for speaking fearlessly and for cultivating flowering trees, also welcomed the bandits and fed them. The bandits were reportedly pleased and treated him like a host. When one of them tied his horse to a flowering tree and urinated on the student's porch, however, the student cursed him. When the bandits requested him to kneel and ask forgiveness for his rudeness, the student reportedly replied: "I have read books for sixty years, and you want me to bow down to bandits? My head may be cut off but my knee will not bend!" Now it was the bandits' turn to get annoyed; they promptly decapitated him and left. Many years later, the historian Zheng Lian would compare these courageous—but naive—local literati with Ji Kang, the outspoken scholar who died at the hands of militarists in the Jin period.[61]

As Gao Yingxiang's roving bandits moved from the countryside to the towns of northeast Henan, they encountered more resistance. A bandit nicknamed Yitiao Long (literally, the dragon), who occupied Zhaocunji northeast of the Ningling county seat, was soon expelled by a local Ming commander. The commander then pursued his quarry, attacking again the following night and killing and capturing many. On his way to neighboring Yucheng county to continue this bandit-suppression work, the commander fell ill and died. The people of Yucheng reportedly closed their shops and went into mourning. In Zhecheng to the south, resistance to banditry came from another quarter. A local scholar from a wealthy family contributed 1,500 taels of silver, 1,300 piculs of grain, and twenty thousand bundles of wood to construct a fort surrounded by a wall that was a kilometer and a half long and fourteen meters high. When roving bandits arrived, residents crowded into the stockade for security.

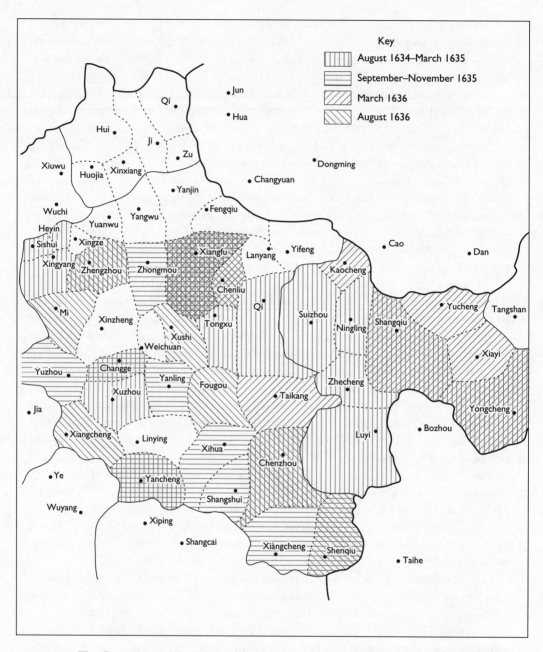

MAP 4.2. The Campaigns of Gao Yingxiang and Other Rebels in Northeast Henan, 1634–36.
Source: Based on data in Li Wenzhi 1948: 206–9.

In Xiayi county, to the east, rebel leaders appeared as personalities in their own right who could also be victims in the gathering cycle of violence and revenge. One of them, Chuangtian Wang (the prince who dashes to heaven), arrived at the town with his son, Xiao Qin Wang (the little prince of Qin), aged sixteen or seventeen, seated on horseback and garbed in red. After somehow making his way inside the town, the son pursued some residents down a narrow alley, but he was killed and his head was hung on the wall as a warning. Eyewitnesses reported that the bandits looked up at the wall and wept, revealing that they too had feelings. They then asked Buddhist and Daoist clerics to conduct a proper funeral, showing that they honored the rites. When the inhabitants of the town had been properly lulled by these events, the bandits suddenly attacked again. Several local guardsmen and a teacher led militia in resistance while seeking reinforcements from the prefecture, but relief came too little too late. The town fell to the bandits, and the guards and teacher were killed. Two townsmen later wrote poems commemorating these events. One compared the bandits with the Red Eyebrows (*chi mei*), rebel bands that had opposed the rule of the usurper Wang Mang and helped clear the way for the restoration of the Han in the first century of the common era.[62]

The Shangqiu county seat, which doubled as the Guide prefectural capital, was the main prize in this contest. It also involved the most embarrassing disaster. There were, to be sure, some colorful defenders. A former assistant regional commander from Jinzhou, Liaodong, lived in a village east of the county town and west of the market town of Jiyang. There he surrounded himself with veterans who rode horseback, went hunting, and were known in the locality as "Liao fools." When the bandits arrived and took Jiyang, the commander set up a palisade outside the village and stationed armed men to form an ambush. He sequestered women in their homes equipped with flammable powder with which to incinerate themselves should the bandits break through. When a bandit scout was apprehended, the commander told him to return to his camp, warning him that he was quite prepared to use his sword on the bandits. When one of the commander's horsemen was caught by the bandits, he persuaded the bandit leader to spare him. He was treated to a banquet, feigned drunkenness, and escaped from the rebel camp during the night.[63]

While the commander's active defense west of Jiyang succeeded, more static arrangements in nearby Mamuzhen failed. There earthen embankments proved no impediment to bandit horsemen who took the town. The inhabitants panicked and thousands were killed. According to Zheng Lian, the rebels issued proclamations against oppressive government, compiled by the scholars they captured.

On March 20 the rebels finally approached the outer walls of Shangqiu (see Figure 4.3). According to Zheng, the literati clans of Shangqiu engaged in lofty discussions, while the military rode around on their horses brandishing slack bows. Defense was left to the common people who sometimes frightened the bandits off by hurling clods of earth and rocks. When successful, the people became overconfident; but after the massacre at Mamuzhen they panicked. They tried to establish fortifications and block alleys with poles; but, according to Zheng, their efforts were child's play. When the bandits arrived at the outer wall, the military commander ostensibly led his forces to engage them. When the dust settled, however, it was clear that the "defenders" had actually plun-

FIGURE 4.3. The Rebels Attack Shangqiu, March 1635. Source: Xuan Kangxi: 48. Courtesy of the Rare Book Room of the Beijing Library (now the National Library of China).

dered the adjacent neighborhoods. With the defenders discredited, the bandits defeated them and forced them to retreat. As the defenders scattered, some bandits breached the exterior wall and plundered the town. Government troops quickly closed the gates, blocking the rest of the bandits but also foregoing further forays against the attackers. As a result, the masses outside the wall suffered the worst ravages of the siege. Zheng reported that corpses were piled in the alleys of the suburbs and on paths among the fields. Later estimates of the dead ran to ten thousand, which may be interpreted as "many." The vast majority of victims were apparently the common people, with two exceptions. One was Jia Sui, a student of the prefect Zheng Sanjun and a friend of the local writer Hou Fangyu, who had been selected as the top provincial graduate two years before. The other was a military officer who fought the bandits to repay the state for two centuries of favor to his family. Conspicuously absent from the struggle were members of elite households such as the Songs and the Hous identified with the Donglin and the Fushe. It may be more than coincidence that they were also associated with Wu Weiye, the writer whose invention of the Xingyang rebel enclave helped obscure the Shangqiu military debacle.[64]

After tarrying several days in the suburbs of Shangqiu, the rebels moved west to attack Suizhou (see Figure 4.4). The Suizhou guard, with a military tradition to uphold, established a camp in the eastern suburb. In the center they erected a flag from which they suspended a cage. In the cage they placed a single soldier with a drum, presumably to rally the defense. When the roving bandits arrived the guardsmen fought bravely, but the commander and his officers were soon killed and the foot soldiers fled. The lone drummer, left dangling from the flagpole, was promptly cut down and killed. The rebels then stormed the gate and entered the town. The inept defense of Suizhou was soon the butt of jokes that circulated widely in the region.[65]

When the rebels entered Suizhou, the magistrate was nowhere to be found. An administrative assistant from Jiangnan was in charge. The assistant abandoned his post, fled to a Buddhist monastery, and changed his garb, hoping to avoid detection. Thinking that he should further disguise himself, he asked a monk if the bandits killed clerics (*heshang*). Not understanding the man's Wu accent, the monk replied: "Of course they kill students!" (*xuesheng*). The assistant then pointed to the monk's head and asked: "Do they kill people like you? If not, I'll shave my head." Given such official irresponsibility, it was left to a local government student, Yuan Shu, to organize the defense. Yuan was the son of a metropolitan graduate who had played an important role in suppressing the White Lotus uprising in Laiyang, Shandong. When the rebels arrived, he was at home mourning the death of his father. He called for a firm defense, recruited local braves, and offered a bounty of fifty taels for every rebel head. Young stalwarts of the town competed to be the first to fight the bandits, and women and children provided them with tiles and stones for ammunition. In three days, Yuan Shu spent one thousand taels of his family's money on the defense. As a result, the attackers were isolated and had to withdraw from the town, but many people did not know they had left. Perhaps for this reason, when the grand coordinator Xuan Mo arrived with government troops to provide assistance, he reportedly mistook Yuan Shu for a bandit and killed him. Later the magistrate of Suizhou was cashiered for dereliction of duty.[66] With friends like these in Suizhou, the Ming hardly needed enemies.

During his campaign through northeast Henan in spring 1635, Gao Yingxiang assaulted other towns, including Yongcheng and Luyi in Guide and Tongxu and Xiangfu in Kaifeng, but few details were recorded. The roving bandit nicknamed Saodi Wang attacked Qi county on March 9. In an uncharacteristically hostile account, Zheng Lian recorded that his men "plundered ruthlessly, even ripping open the wombs of pregnant women and boiling their feet." Since there were several rebels who used the title Saodi Wang in these years, this man's identity is far from clear. But it is possible that he was named Li Jing and was the same rebel who had recently taken Fengyang and would eventually be captured by Wan Yuanji, a former judge with links to Guide scholars, in 1640.[67]

Meanwhile the more visible rebel leader, Gao Yingxiang, continued to unsettle Ming

FIGURE 4.4. The Battle for Suizhou. Source: Xuan Kangxi: 50. (Courtesy of the Rare Book Room of the Beijing Library (now the National Library of China).

administrators in Henan. The grand coordinator Xuan Mo responded to Gao's romp through the province in early 1635 by proposing to build up heavy forces in the central plain to keep the bandits bottled up in Shaanxi. This strategy was naturally opposed by the Shaanxi grand coordinator, Hong Chengchou, who did not wish to have the rebels confined to his region, where he would have full responsibility for suppressing them. In July, therefore, Xuan was replaced by Chen Biqian. Chen was known as a capable official, but he no sooner took office than Gao Yingxiang led another campaign across Henan in September. This thrust touched some of the same counties as previously as well as some new ones. The focus this time seemed to be on the poorer, more southern, and less well-defended counties of Kaifeng prefecture. The court responded to this challenge by making Lu Xiangsheng, the capable general with experience in the region, the new supreme commander. Lu was put in charge of the forces of five provinces and

ordered to recover control of the central plain in cooperation with Hong Chengchou. Five months later, in February 1636, Gao's rebels were in northeast Henan again, revisiting some counties and attacking fresh ones (see Map 4.2). This campaign left only four counties untouched by the bandits, but it was to be Gao's last hurrah. When he returned to Shaanxi he was captured by the grand coordinator Sun Chuanting and sent to Beijing, where he was executed.[68]

The Ming Revives, the Masses Decline

Victory over Gao Yingxiang ushered in a brief period of Ming resurgence in the central plain. Determined officials adopted an effective combination of amnesty and repression to subdue rebel challenges to Ming authority by 1640. In that year, however, natural disasters, frontier incursions, and a global recession brought increasing hardship to the masses of northeast Henan. In the next two years, the masses suffered terribly and began to mobilize in an effort to recover their fortunes.

Natural and global conditions imposed severe limitations on the state and the people. According to the basic annals of the *Ming History*, which recorded only the most notable events of the entire polity, Henan province experienced drought and locusts in 1637 (with one other province), in 1638 and 1639 (with three other provinces), in 1640 (with four other provinces), and in 1641 (with five other provinces). According to the local historian Zheng Lian, severe droughts and floods struck Kaifeng and Guide in 1636. Locusts stripped the region of plant life—attacking even clothing stored in trunks— every year from 1636 to 1640. Heavy snow fell in 1640, a local manifestation of the "little ice age" that was afflicting much of the world. After 1637, plague returned to northeast Henan, wiping out whole families and villages, reaching a peak in 1641 (see Map 4.3). At the same time, there was a marked downturn in the world economy that affected coastal and industrial China most of all but indirectly affected the interior and agriculture as well.[69]

It was in this context that the Ming attempted to reclaim its authority in the central plain. In early 1637 the court ordered the Shaanxi grand coordinator Sun Chuanting—an official with previous experience in Henan and the capture of Gao Yingxiang to his credit—to assist the Henan grand coordinator, Chen Biqian, in restoring order in the province. This effort was only partially effective, however, for unidentified roving bandits attacked Xingyang again in April. In July, Chen Biqian was removed from his post and replaced by Chang Daoli. Chang had recommended the strategy that had led to the capture of Gao Yingxiang. Still, bandits attacked Suizhou in October and Zhecheng in November. At this time, Yang Sichang, president of the ministry of troops, set a deadline for suppression of the bandits and proposed using the commanders Zuo Liangyu and Chen Yongfu to pacify Henan. In early 1638, some unspecified bandits in Xiangcheng county were wiped out. By the end of the year, Yang's choice for supreme commander, Xiong Wencan, defeated or neutralized many of the most powerful bandit leaders, including Zhang Xianzhong, Luo Rucai, and Li Zicheng.[70] The roving bandits operating out of Shaanxi seemed tamed.

As roving banditry diminished, however, sect activities increased. In early 1638, afflicted by drought and locusts and unsettled by the passage of roving bandits, numerous "unemployed people" rallied to the standard of a heterodox commoner on the border between Wu and She counties in Nanyang prefecture. The magistrate of Biyang, fearing that their influence would spread, obtained secret permission to raise militia to capture the leader and pacify the followers. The "starving people" of the prefecture promptly produced other leaders, including a county bravo and "villainous commoner." They, too, were soon suppressed but the spreading unrest augured ill for the future.[71]

It was at this point that the "crazy boy" calling himself a *shibazi* (Li) led the uprising in Qi county, Kaifeng prefecture (see Chapter 2). This revolt was quickly suppressed, but it was also made famous by verses that circulated widely in the region. Against the backdrop of a Saodi Wang (possibly named Li Jing) who attacked Qi in 1635 and a Ziweixing (probably named Li) who appeared in Yancheng the same year, the uprising of a lad styled "Li" in Qi in 1638 surely reminded contemporaries of the sectarian prophecy that a Li would take the throne. This sectarian tradition was obviously still alive—if not exactly well—in the countryside of northeast Henan.[72]

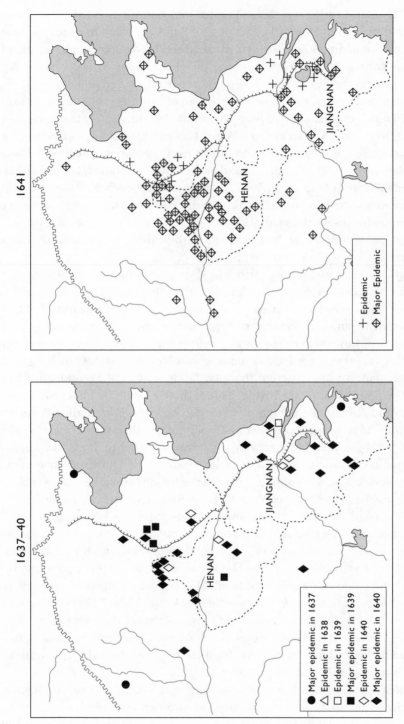

MAP 4.3. The Spread of Epidemic Disease in Henan and Jiangnan, 1637–41. Sources: Dunstan 1975: 56, 58; Mote and Twitchett 1988: xxiv. Used with permission from *Ch'ing-shih wen-t'i* (now *Late Imperial China*) and from the author.

In late 1638 and early 1639, Manchu raids into Beizhili diverted the attention of key commanders such as Hong Chengchou and Sun Chuanting from bandit suppression. The local commander Zuo Liangyu, who had accepted the surrender of many bandit leaders in Xuzhou, Kaifeng prefecture, was called away from his headquarters. Before he crossed the Yellow River in early 1639, Zuo reportedly killed one of the rebel generals who had surrendered to him on the promise of amnesty. This alarmed the other surrendered rebels in Xuzhou, who promptly revolted again. Among these generals was a Cao Wei, who was also known as Saodi Wang. Cao and his followers killed some local officials, raided the county treasury, and forced many people to go east with them. In one week they covered four hundred li and arrived in Xiayi county, Guide prefecture. Having been informed of the revolt, Zuo Liangyu pursued the rebels all the way to Guide. There he elicited some defections. He also captured some bandits and had them torn apart in the southern suburb of Guide. Zuo then returned to his base at Xuzhou. The rebel leader Cao Wei, however, had escaped. At this point, the grand coordinator of Henan, Chang Daoli, was replaced by Li Xianfeng.[73]

In 1639 the Ming court, preoccupied with Manchu expeditions into Shandong, considered two different strategies for dealing with the rebellions in Shaanxi and Henan. The first was proposed by Mao Wenbing, a 1628 metropolitan graduate from Zhengzhou, Kaifeng prefecture, and a supervising secretary in the office of scrutiny of the ministry of rites. In May or June, Mao called for the creation of small but highly trained militia in each county to provide for local defense against bandit attacks. Criticizing the policy of simple amnesty, Mao asserted that persuasion had to be accompanied by suppression. He pointed out that roving bandits had repeatedly attacked Xingyang, Zhengzhou, and Zhongmou and that local bandits had shown strength in Wu and She. Roving bandits from Shaanxi and Shanxi should not be allowed to ally with local bandits in the central province. He advocated organizing effective militia to cooperate with official troops in denying food and loot to the bandits, forcing them to surrender and reform themselves. Mao was confident that all the bandits could be won over since, as he put it, "the robbers are our people too." He commended the magistrates of Qi and Chenliu for strengthening their walls, and he encouraged the magistrates of Suizhou and Zhengzhou to do the same. He called on the populace to contribute to these efforts because, he wrote, "everyone has one's self, family, and social position" to defend. He also warned that too many militia would be as dangerous as too few: they would not be well-trained and could easily get out of hand. Mao remarked: "If servants drill and still suffer from hunger and cold, they may do unspeakable things." Local officials would also produce "bad results" if they raised militia just to enhance their wealth. Mao's observations were confirmed on June 8, 1639, when Zhang Xianzhong revolted again, discrediting the policy of amnesty, and the local commander defended Zhengzhou and relieved Heyin using militia as recommended by Mao.[74]

The court approved Mao's recommendations but hedged its bets by encouraging Yang Sichang to pursue his own, quite different, strategy. He built a massive, centrally controlled army, supported by tax surcharges and capable of confining the bandits to the central plain where they could be tracked down and exterminated. Yang envisioned a double ring of armies, with the outer one arranged around the edges of the central plain in stationary defensive positions and an inner one consisting of highly mobile and aggressive forces. He also apparently planned to absorb local militia into his grand armies. With the renewed rebellion of Zhang Xianzhong, Luo Rucai, and Li Zicheng in mid-1639, the court dismissed Xiong Wencan from his post as supreme commander and appointed Yang Sichang in his place. As grand secretary, minister of troops, and now supreme commander of armies in five provinces, Yang had the maximal authority permitted by the Ming system. Based at Xiangyang in Huguang, he was in a good position to put his strategy into effect despite opposition from other officials and the local elite of Henan.[75]

Yang Sichang developed a clear plan to suppress the rebels. Even the Shangqiu historian Zheng Lian admired his comprehensive vision and grasp of the "actual conditions." Yang courageously confronted the most powerful rebels, including Zhang Xianzhong and Luo Rucai, meanwhile depending on Zuo Liangyu to take care of Henan. In 1640 this strategy drew Yang south and west into Sichuan, where Zhang and Luo were establishing bases. Zuo Liangyu, however, intent on getting revenge against Zhang Xianzhong, ignored orders and entered Sichuan as well. Zuo won a great victory against Zhang, but failed to destroy him. Soon Zhang and Luo recovered their strength and headed east toward Huguang. Yang pursued them but failed to catch them before they took Xiangyang and killed the local Ming prince. Meanwhile Li Zicheng crossed from Shaanxi into Henan, took Luoyang on March 8, 1641, and killed the prince of Fu. With these defeats, Yang realized that his usefulness to the dynasty had ended. In April he committed suicide. In contrast, the wily Zuo Liangyu, who was at least partially to blame, took no responsibility for either setback. Instead he led his forces into Henan, where they reportedly gave fresh life to the old expression: "the bandits use a coarse comb, the armies use a fine comb."[76] Whether the Ming state revived or declined, the conditions of the masses deteriorated.

In addition to the abuses of roving bandits and undisciplined troops, the people of northeast Henan suffered from the tax surcharges imposed to pay for the military campaigns. In May 1640 Wang Han, the upright magistrate of Henei county, submitted his report on the effects of such levies on the people during a famine. Wang also submitted sixteen drawings that showed that "the corpses of those who have died of starvation are like pearls on a string." He criticized Chongzhen, "who does not ask his officials to die but instead causes his good people to die," and expressed the hope that he would "empathize from afar with the people in this calamity." Yet even Wang did not ask for tax or grain relief, and the court did not bother to respond. The Shangqiu historian Zheng Lian explained:

> To respond they would have had to disburse funds to provide relief, but there were no funds to disburse. To respond they would have had to suspend collection of the taxes, but collection could not be suspended. Even a ruler who girds his spirit to govern well can encounter periods of lawlessness. It is like the housewife who is clever but cannot cook because she has no rice. Under such conditions the ruler can only sigh deeply. It is enough to make one's material force grow cold and one's eyes stare aimlessly. When a state is about to die, the people's hearts and minds die first.[77]

Zheng Lian believed that the problem went deeper than state bankruptcy and official irresponsibility. It involved, in short, elite greed. In his words,

> In such times, the elite take the examinations to establish their status, but in their minds they are no longer true followers [of the Way]. They say they are reading the books of the sages and worthies, but they no longer know the meaning of words like humanity, justice, loyalty, and respect. Although they sit in a dignified manner and wear caps and gowns, they are busy day and night cultivating relationships and gaining fame. How can the common people have anything to do with us? We are like tigers and wolves dressed up in hairpins and robes.[78]

Here we see Zheng's ambivalence toward the elite among whom, as a government student, he clearly aspired to rank. He added that the rapacious members of that stratum would receive their punishment when their spirits came face to face with those of honest officials such as Wang Han in the Nine Springs. In fact, some of them would face judgment sooner, but it would come from the masses and their self-appointed leaders.

Some officials and members of the elite acknowledged maldistribution of wealth as the fundamental problem. In 1639, Yang Sichang remarked on the growing gap between the rich and the poor. As he put it in the time-worn cliché that nonetheless fit the actual situation: "Recently, land has accumulated in the hands of the local elite and the rich, and the poor do not have enough to stick an awl into." In September 1640 the regional inspector of Henan, Gao Mingheng, submitted his report on the "Four Scourges," the avaricious families in the heart and stomach of the realm whose abuses were "making peoples' hearts and minds grow cold" (see Chapter 2).[79] Yet neither official was able to bridge the growing gap in late-Ming society. The time had come for sterner measures at the hands of the masses.

The Mobilized Majority, The Silent Minority

By 1640, both because of and despite the devastation in their lives, the masses of northeast Henan were mobilizing in what the state and most elite considered roving banditry, what many participants probably deemed popular uprisings, and what might ultimately be judged to be mixtures of the two, with the precise proportions depending on the case.

Local rebels were above all numerous and colorful. According to Zheng Lian, our most reliable informant on that social world, after 1640

> local robbers rose like hairs on a hedgehog. There were one hundred chiefs in the one thousand li along the south bank of the Yellow River. They would suddenly rise, and just as quickly fall. Some were captured and beheaded by the military, others were absorbed into the army. For example, in Shangqiu there was Yuan Laoshan (old mountain Yuan) . . . [and others] who were not well known. Bigger and longer lasting were: in the west, Li Jiyu, Shen Jingbang . . . ; in the south, Liu Hongqi, Li Hao . . . ; in Liang and Song . . . Zhang Changtui (long-legged Zhang) . . . ; in the east, Li Zhenhai . . . etc. All of them attracted the masses to make themselves strong; they constructed forts and fought for territory. Whole prefectures and counties followed them and served as their ears and eyes, and local officials did not dare to cross them.[80]

While these local leaders used various methods and obtained different results, they were all alike in operating outside the law.

Like many others, Zheng Lian saw a direct connection between the devastation of the famine and the profusion of outlaws. Looking at his hometown, he wrote:

> Guide had recently built an outer wall and all the rich people entered it for security. That year [1640] there was a great famine. People were increasingly unwilling to sell their grain and so it became very expensive. A peck of rice or wheat cost three thousand in cash; millet cost 2,700. People ate each other: fathers consumed sons, wives consumed husbands. No one dared to travel alone on the roads or even visit nearby villages. Those who fell dead in ditches had their corpses hacked up by swarms of starving people who left only the bare bones. Officials and clerks would sometimes arrest the cannibals and even thrash them to death, but they could not stop the practice. Soon all the crafty and reckless became robbers, and there were masses of petty thieves without number. Ten thousand of them rallied to Yitiao Long, Zhang Panzi, Song Jiang, and Yuan Laoshan. The followers of Yitiao Long from Linying and Yuan Laoshan from Shouzhou were particularly numerous.[81]

According to Zheng, the local commander Gao Yuanheng was a brave and skilled fighter who often captured bandits. When the bandits saw him coming they would shout: "Here comes Dashing Gao (Gao Chuangzi)!" and flee. But Gao had only three thousand men, and the outlaws were innumerable. Although he often triumphed in battle, he dared not pursue his adversaries and so rarely succeeded in exterminating them.

What were the attitudes of these outlaws toward the officials, the elite, and the masses? Zheng Lian adduces three cases that suggest that they were ambivalent, various, and changeable. In Yuanwu county, northwest of Kaifeng across the Yellow River, one Zhang Mengxi had long been a leader of the local robbers. He would force people to do his bidding, and local officials refused to admit their inability to control him. The magistrate and prefect sat in their offices in dignity, intoning the values of humanity and justice and claiming to be mothers and fathers to the people; but actually they were betraying the people. Even the provincial grand coordinator, Li Xianfeng, who was not far away in Kaifeng, looked the other way. Such was the moral authority, Zheng wrote, of one of the top officials of the day. Given such leaders, Zheng concluded, "how could the little people avoid being poisoned at their hands?"[82] Here a bandit leader was colluding with corrupt officials to prey on the "little people." Yet the little people, Zheng hinted, were being deceived, victims of a false consciousness.

In Xiping county, Runing prefecture, southwest of Guide, the strongman was named Liu Hongqi. Liu and his brothers belonged to a "saltern" (or hereditary salt producing) household that had long since stopped working for the state and turned to producing salt clandestinely and selling it as "salt smugglers" on the open market. According to Zheng Lian, Liu disliked gowned students but believed he needed their counsel. He therefore offered them silver, hats, and robes in return for service. Students disparaged Liu as a salt smuggler, but some were lured into advising him. Liu sometimes treated his counselors well, but when they disobeyed he had them bound and beaten without mercy. All those who went before his "throne" had to bow their heads and avoid looking at him directly.[83] While Liu and the students found it difficult to work together, they apparently felt more at ease with each other than with the masses.

Yitiao Long was closer to the masses, who flocked to his banner in large numbers. According to Zheng Lian, the Yitiao Long active in the Kaifeng-Shangqiu area whose family name was Wei hailed from Linying, a poor county in Kaifeng prefecture. He appeared as early as 1635 in Ningling, Guide prefecture. In May 1639 he attacked Qi county, Kaifeng prefecture. He was driven off by Yang Sichang, whose troops reportedly caused more damage than the rebels. In November 1640, Yitiao Long marched from his home in Linying, east through Suizhou, and on to Guide. According to the gazetteer of Suizhou, his following expanded ten-fold to 100,000. Although hungry, his troops were also strong; as Zheng Lian put it, "his vanguard was sharp." The Shangqiu commander Gao Yuanheng and the prefectural judge Wang Shixiu led a force of three thousand to suppress him, but they were greatly outnumbered and were besieged on three sides by rebels and starving people. They finally avoided encirclement and forced the rebels to flee. Rather than pursuing the rebels, they simply returned to Guide to collect their rewards.[84]

Not long after, commander Gao Yuanheng died of the plague, and bandits thenceforth came to Guide "as if entering a territory without people." Yitiao Long led his band west to Qi again, where he encountered regional commander Chen Yongfu and suffered a defeat. Soon Yitiao Long, too, died of the plague and his rebel band dissolved. Thus it was a local leader of a host of the famished who encountered the most determined opposition from Ming commanders and who succumbed most quickly to their suppression campaigns. However, the ravages of the plague that killed both the Ming commander and the rebel leader was making a mockery of political victory in 1640. In some cases Guide was literally "like a territory without people."[85] Thus, while the majority of the masses in northeast Henan were mobilized by 1640, the population had shrunk considerably from that of just a few years before.

Some of the masses may have taken refuge in pockets of relative peace in the countryside, towns, and cities of the region. Others may have simply disappeared through death or flight. Whereas the majority spoke with their bodies and voted with their feet by rising in revolts, a minority—of farmers, workers, women, and servants—may have remained silent because their conditions were better, or worse.

Some farmers, for example, held on to their plots of land and continued to harvest enough to keep themselves alive, while others became tenants, hired laborers, servants, or members of a floating population of the homeless. Conditions varied by region, as evidenced by two counties of Kaifeng prefecture. In Yanjin, north of the Yellow River, farmers had devoted half their land to cotton cultivation as early as the Zhengde reign. By 1640, those who produced cotton for the market were suffering from the downturn in the textile industry while those who cultivated food crops were too few to supply the population. In Yanling, south of the Yellow River, land rents were reported to be 28 percent of the summer (wheat) crop and 37 percent of the fall (millet) crop. Rents on lands held by the nobility were even higher and were often not reduced even during natural disasters. For example, in Sishui county, in western Kaifeng prefecture, the Fu prince had appropriated thirty thousand mu of land on which he charged rent of three fen per mu. He continued to demand this rent even when the Yellow River shifted course and destroyed much of the arable. According to the gazetteer, some farmers sold rela-

tives to pay the rent and others fled to avoid punishment for nonpayment. Some cultivators who lost access to land probably perished in silence; others may have joined the
ranks of Gao Yingxiang's rebellion that took Sishui in 1635. Thereafter the conditions
of tenants probably worsened. In 1640 only elite families were reported to be in the
county seat of Qí, in Weihui prefecture. All the tenants had fled to avoid punishment
for defaulting on their rents.[86]

The fortunes of workers also varied. The best paid were perhaps those in several
textile factories in Kaifeng city that used machine looms to produce silk and cotton fabrics for wholesale and retail sales. Those workers, who were paid in specie, must have
benefited from the prosperity of the late sixteenth century but suffered from the recession in the 1630s. Piece workers and day laborers in Kaifeng, who were less fortunate
to begin with, were probably also adversely affected by the depression. Cooks in the households of nobility were paid well, but those who hired out at public markets received
only subsistence wages in the best of times and almost certainly less by 1640. Similarly,
the estimated seventy-five major troupes and twenty-five smaller companies of actors in
Kaifeng were divided into those who performed in the mansions of the well-to-do and
those who entertained members of the middle strata and masses in the towns and countryside. While the former may have benefited from the influx of landlords from the
countryside, the latter probably suffered from the depression combined with inflation
in food prices.[87] Street entertainers, temple storytellers, and diviners at the city gates
were also poor and vulnerable.

Data on women among the masses also come mainly from Kaifeng city. In general
women were dependent on men and subject to discrimination in the labor market. Some
who worked in the large-scale production of footwear may have earned decent wages
in good times but were vulnerable to any downturn in the economy. The larger number of women who took in laundry from the general population were less well paid to
begin with and probably faced unemployment by the late 1630s. Women engaged in
entertainment and prostitution, numerous in a society of arranged marriages and
sojourning males, were also divided into substrata. At one extreme, elegant courtesans
skilled in the arts of conversation, poetry, music, and dance, as well as of the bedchamber,
were often well supported. At the other extreme, streetwalkers sold their sexual favors
for a few copper coins.[88] For some entertainers, 1640 may have seen an upsurge in
business as wealthy males sought refuge in the cities. Government students such as Hou
Fangyu, who had frequented the pleasure quarters of Nanjing in 1639, may have continued such activities on a more modest scale in Guide, Kaifeng, and Weihui in 1640.
For such men and their women, that year was perhaps the calm before the storm.

As in most societies, servants were near the bottom of the social scale in Ming China,
although their lot too was varied. Some bondservants could learn to read and write, terminate their contracts, and even take the examinations, enjoying a status more akin to
tenants than to slaves. The personal retainers of nobles, officials, scholars, merchants,
and landlords sometimes became highhanded and abusive of other commoners. But
Lü Kun noted that servants in the Kaifeng-Shangqiu region were often reduced to performing menial and sometimes dangerous tasks, such as testing food for poison. In general, the living conditions of servants in northeast Henan probably deteriorated in the

shrinking economy of the 1630s and the famine and plague of 1640. Their silence should not be taken as evidence of their contentment.[89]

Still, in at least one case in Shangqiu, a servant got away with insolence. According to Hou Fangyu, the servant Guo Shang had attended his father, Hou Xun, since his youth. After Hou Xun grew up, old Guo lost interest in his work and frequently shirked his duties. Once when he was supposed to be looking after the Hous' country estate, he was found playing a lute and dallying with a woman in Luyi. When Hou Xun went to Beijing in 1627, Guo accompanied him, but his performance did not improve. Hou scolded him one day after finding him asleep on duty, but Guo simply snored more loudly, drowning out his master's voice.[90]

Some servants joined family members at the core of personal armies during the disorders of the 1630s, probably gaining status as they became indispensable to their masters' safety. When the economy slumped in 1640, many servants were undoubtedly left to their own devices to survive. Mao Wenbing, the militia organizer in Zhengzhou, had reason to worry about the consequences of hungry servants receiving military training. Indeed, at least one servant from northeast Henan was to play an important role in the rebellion of Li Zicheng that brought down the Ming (see Chapter 7).

In response to natural conditions and state policies, the masses of northeast Henan went through three distinct phases in their attitudes toward the Ming. In the early period, despite continuing cold weather and recurrent flooding, the vast majority accepted the Ming as better than anything they had experienced during the preceding century and as likely to improve conditions in the future. Sectarians nonetheless operated underground, providing potential sources of ideology and organization for disaffected elements among the masses. During the second century, declining state effectiveness, combined with growing elite and middle-strata demands for resources and cold weather, led an increasing number of the masses to participate in sect conspiracies, roving banditry, and local revolts. During the late Ming, initially favorable trends of warmer weather and a flourishing economy stimulated by an influx of silver were soon followed by accelerating administrative decline and social inequality that led to mass acceptance of—if not support for—sectarian conspiracies and roving banditry. The dynasty rallied in the late 1630s, and a minority of the masses, including some of its least favored members, likely continued to pursue their daily lives. By 1640, however, the state was in deep trouble, and the vast majority of the masses were mobilizing in anticipation of political change.

Many of those who rose to challenge the Ming in northeast Henan were conscious of living at the cultural heart of the realm and drew on past experiences to legitimate their calls for political change. The first rebel, Liu Tong, was from northeast Henan but moved to northwest Huguang to recruit followers among migrants. He took advantage of his family name and new location to proclaim a Han state, thus confronting the Ming with the specter of a more literal and potentially truer reinstantiation of the original order it claimed to revere. Sectarians in and around Henan meanwhile kept alive the idea that a sage named Li would one day rule the world, perhaps by succeeding the Zhus, who ruled it in the Ming. Zhao Jinglong similarly drew on his family name and his location in Guide to proclaim himself the prince of Song. Song was the name of the fief accorded the descendants of the Shang, the name of the state used for peace conferences in the Spring and Autumn and Warring States period, and the name of the dynasty that governed much of China in the tenth through thirteenth centuries. With varying degrees of skill and success, roving bandits from outside the region (Liu Liu-Liu Qi and Wang Tang) as well as rebels from within it (Shi Shangzhao and Li Yinglong) targeted bad officials and wooed good ones, engaged elite and student advisors, and sought mass support in the region. Meanwhile, rebels named Li claimed descent from the family that had founded the Tang a millennium earlier in Shanxi and Shaanxi provinces to the west.

After 1600 a local strongman in Suizhou was followed by a series of sectarians operating in Jiangnan, Shandong, and northeast Henan and then by mounted bandits from Shanxi and Shaanxi who conducted three campaigns into northeast Henan. Although none of these efforts succeeded in toppling the Ming, they all exposed the declining effectiveness of the state, established a trend of Li-led insurrections, and helped mobilize the population in a score of counties in northeast Henan. Through their participation in such collective actions, the masses of this region signaled their disenchantment with the Ming. They may have become skeptical about the Han discourse that had long legitimated the Ming and open to other discourses (such as that of the Tang) that could be used to justify an alternative regime.

FIVE

Rebellion In the Central Province, 1641–42

IN EARLY 1641 THE REBEL LEADER LI ZICHENG arrived in western Henan from his home base in Shaanxi. Originally driven by family hardship, later inspired by the model of the Han founder, Li soon won the support of a member of the Henanese local elite who served as his chief advisor. Together they developed a formidable mobile army comprising members of the middle strata and masses; they challenged Ming authority in several counties of western Henan and occupied Luoyang briefly. Li assumed the title Dashing Prince (Chuangwang) once held by Gao Yingxiang. He then besieged the provincial capital of Kaifeng but failed to take it and was forced to turn his attention to minor towns in the southern part of the province. Then, encouraged by a prophecy and strengthened by an alliance with another rebel leader from Shaanxi, Li Zicheng went on to further victories in south-central Henan. With a stronger base in the countryside, he mounted a second assault on Kaifeng, but once again he failed to take the town. He therefore returned once more to the countryside, where he took more towns, including Xiangcheng and Chenzhou. He then allied with another rebel leader who hailed from Beizhili and was well known to the officials and elite of northeast Henan. Together they won further victories in Kaifeng prefecture and prepared for a third assault on Kaifeng city.

Li Zicheng

As might be expected in the case of a member of the masses who rose to challenge a dynasty, accounts of the early life of the rebel leader Li Zicheng are conflicting and often unreliable. Most agree, however, that he was born in 1606, the very year, some would later note, of the death of the sectarian leader Liu Tianxu (also known as Li). Li was born in Li Jiqian village, about one hundred kilometers west of the county seat of Mizhi, in Yan'an prefecture, northeast Shaanxi province. Li and his fellow villagers claimed descent from the founder of the Xi Xia dynasty, whose ancestors were thought to have come to the region in the wake of Huang Chao's rebellion near the end of the Tang. The claim has not been verified and seems to have been asserted only later as the rebels rose to power in Shaanxi. We may speculate that the royal pedigree was designed to enhance Li Zicheng's standing in competition with the Manchu ruling family, the Aisin Gioro who equally tenuously traced their line back to the Jurchen royal family of the Jin.[1]

Whatever the status of his distant ancestors, Li Hongji, the original name of the man who became known as Li Zicheng, was born into a poor family. Members of the three previous generations had all been farmers, and some may have been responsible for raising horses for the local government. Li Hongji's elder brother, who was twenty years his senior, had produced a son, Li Guo, who was born the same year as Hongji and grew up with him. According to some early accounts, the family had sufficient resources to permit Hongji and Guo to attend the village school for a few years. According to other sources, the family was so poor it was forced to send Hongji to a local temple to survive a famine in 1616. Shades of the Ming founder Zhu Yuanzhang? Li seems to have acquired some literacy, but probably less than that of Zhu. At age twelve he reportedly became a herdsman for a Muslim widow.[2]

As he reached his teens, Li Hongji developed ambitions to transcend his circumstances. He was said to be physically strong, skilled in riding and shooting, and impressive in appearance. According to one story, while playing in a Guan Di temple with a friend, he demonstrated his strength by raising an incense burner with one hand. Borrowed from the biography of the early Ming rebel Liu Tong? It was apparently then that he changed his name to Zicheng, meaning "complete by oneself." At age sixteen, he and Li Guo reportedly studied martial arts under a master in Yan'an. Two years later they were both married. After his father died, Li Zicheng worked in a wineshop, in a blacksmith's shop, and on a farm. According to several accounts, he borrowed money from a local elite landlord named Ai and was unable to pay him back. He therefore went to Yan'an to look for a better job and, in 1627, took a position in the state courier system in Mizhi. For two years he carried mail and escorted officials, earning wages of two fen a day.[3]

Although these accounts of Li's early years seem plausible, stories of his turn to rebellion probably reflect the authors' attitudes as much as the actual events. According to the early Qing county gazetteer of Mizhi, Li's superiors in the courier service charged him with allowing a horse to die and with losing a letter. According to the early Qing authors Wu Weiye and Ji Liuqi, whose accounts of the late-Ming rebels are often dismissive and romantic by turns, Li returned from work one day to find his wife in bed with another man. He chased the man away, killed his wife, and was jailed on charges of homicide. According to the most widely accepted account, Li lost his job at the courier service when Chongzhen laid off staff in 1630 as an economy measure. Although perhaps more allegorical than literal, this account emphasizes the late-Ming state's well-known inability to pay its own personnel. Whatever the reason, Li lost his job with the government and was unable to pay the interest, let alone the principal, on his earlier loan from Ai.[4] This, at least, was the story transmitted by the Shangqiu student Zheng Lian, who was captured by the rebels, came to know them rather well, and wrote a history that is often at odds with other accounts. Whatever its degree of literal truth, the story served as an effective metaphor of the growing gap between the wealthy and poor in the late Ming and of the resulting resentment among members of the middle strata and masses.

According to Zheng Lian, whose account offers an early-Qing—northeastern-Henanese view of the matter, Li Zicheng's inability to pay his debt to Ai led him to ally with some unruly young men who ultimately clashed with the local magistrate. The disgruntled creditor first persuaded the magistrate to have Li beaten and consigned to a public *cangue* (a portable stock) without food and water. When other unemployed courier workers sneaked food to Li, Ai's personal servants intercepted them and tightened the *cangue*. A crowd then assembled and saved Li by breaking the *cangue* and spiriting him out of town. Li and his cohorts retreated to the woods nearby and fought off the pursuing government forces. The next morning they emerged from the forest shouting, causing an officer to fall from his horse and his men to break ranks and flee without their weapons. Once again we may suspect an allegory, this time dramatizing the well-known deficiencies of the late-Ming military. One night on an unspecified date, Li and his supporters attacked the town, won the allegiance of one thousand famished residents, and led them to plunder the region. Within ten days they joined together with other robbers, bestowed the title of Dashing General on Li, and formed themselves into a tightly disciplined group.[5] Thus, a former minor functionary, suffering from state retrenchment and local elite exploitation, led hungry members of the middle strata and masses in a rebellion against the state.

According to Zheng Lian, Li Zicheng and his cousin Li Guo went on to join the ranks of a larger band. When that group surrendered to the Ming, they left it to join another. In 1631, when the new rebel force was defeated by Ming troops, the Lis formed their own group, which they dubbed the "Eighth Brigade." In the next two years Li Zicheng appeared among the forces under Gao Yingxiang, the Dashing Prince, in northern Henan. Some sources credit him with taking Xiuwu county, in Huaiqing prefecture, and killing the magistrate. When another rebel leader died, Li Zicheng took over his twenty thousand men, raising his own forces to thirty thousand. In late 1633 Li followed Gao south across the Yellow River, but in the next year he went back to Shaanxi, where he remained during 1635.

Li won victories in north Shaanxi and increased his following to seventy thousand, but as his subordinates grew in number he began to suspect disloyalty from some of them. He reportedly charged one of his officers, Gao Jie, with consorting with his wife. In any event, Li's suspicions soon drove Gao and his followers to surrender to the Ming. In 1636, under pressure from grand coordinator Hong Chengchou, Li led his forces from Shaanxi to campaign in Henan. After the death of Gao Yingxiang, he went on the defensive. He moved back and forth across the mountainous borders of east and south Shaanxi and fended off troops under the Ming general Sun Chuanting. In 1639 Li suffered a defeat in eastern Shaanxi and his wife and concubines were reportedly killed. He fled into the hills between Shang and Luo counties with a handful of his closest supporters. The rebel leaders Zhang Xianzhong and Luo Rucai, who had already surrendered to the Ming in return for amnesty, encouraged Li Zicheng to join them but he refused. He apparently survived by taking to the hills and escaping official notice. He reportedly practiced martial arts and studied history, including the saga of Liu Bang, the commoner rebel who had overthrown the Qin and founded the Han.

In the summer of 1639, Zhang Xianzhong rebelled again, and Li took advantage of the distraction to break out of isolation. Soon he was in trouble again, and his closest subordinate, Liu Zongmin, suggested that they surrender to save their lives. According to one story, Li Zicheng asked Liu to divine. If their prospects were not good Liu should cut off Li's head and surrender. But the prognosis was favorable, so Liu instead killed his own wife and concubines and vowed to join Li in a fight to the death against the Ming. In late 1640, Li, Liu, and fifty other men descended from the hills of Shaanxi and prepared to enter the central plain of Henan.[6]

First Victories in Henan

Having sent scouts ahead, Li Zicheng led his small force into the central plain in late December 1640 (see Map 5.1).[7] The following month, he traversed ten counties in the southwestern part of the province, including Xichuan, in Nanyang prefecture, and Song, Dengfeng, Mianchi, Shaan, Lingbao, and Lushi, in Henan prefecture. The rebel forces attracted many new adherents from among the victims of the famine and plague that were wracking the province. In Zheng Lian's words, "When they entered Yü, it was like a tiger leaving its cage, and they became uncontrollable. . . . The starving people rallied to them in increasing numbers by the day."[8] In neighboring counties, local bandits such as Li Jiyu offered competition—but also potential alliances.

Li Zicheng's main support came from the rural masses, but he also won the allegiance of a member of the local elite, Niu Jinxing, who soon became his chief advisor (*mouzhu*). According to epitaphs recorded in the early Qing, Niu came from a long line of teachers in Baofeng county, Ruzhou department, in central Henan province. An ancestor had held the post of moral mentor (rank 7a) to the Lu prince of Shandong. Although the rank was low, such a post provided the family with the means to hire tutors to teach its youth. Jinxing therefore passed the provincial examination in 1627 and became a teacher in neighboring Lushan. At the same time, he reportedly studied divination and military strategy.[9]

Niu married and had a son, Niu Quan. When Quan came of age, Niu arranged for him to be married to the daughter of Wang Shijun, a provincial graduate of 1624 and a metropolitan graduate of 1631. Wang was from the capital county of Xiangfu and served as a ministry secretary in Beijing, so Niu may have made this match to advance his career. If so, he was to be sorely disappointed. According to elliptical stories told by one of Niu's colleagues and later by a rebel in Beijing, "there was a scandal in the boudoir." Apparently Wang Shijun had taken a cousin from his own descent group as a concubine, and Niu Jinxing revealed the impropriety when he was drunk. Wang became furious when he learned of Niu's indiscretion. In another incident, Niu was said to have gotten drunk and struck a clerk from the Baofeng magistrate's office, thus offending the magistrate. When Niu Quan's wife died, her father put pressure on the Baofeng magistrate to arrest Niu Jinxing for allegedly defaulting on his taxes and "seizing eighteen

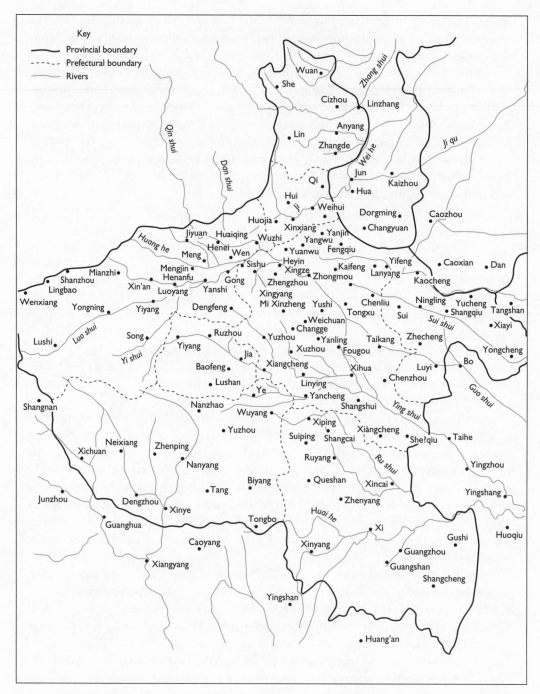

MAP 5.1. The Prefectures, Towns, and Rivers of Henan in the Late Ming. Source: Tan 1975: 82–83. Used with permission of The Chinese Map Association (Zhonghua ditu xueshe).

women." Niu may also have quarreled with the magistrate over the price of grain during a famine, but neither the date nor the details of that dispute were recorded. Whatever
the reason, the magistrate appealed to the provincial education commissioner and persuaded him to strip Niu of his elite status. He then arrested him, charged him with numerous infractions of the law, and put him in prison.[10]

According to Zheng Lian, Niu arranged to have a friend named Zhou Sheng request
a pardon from the magistrate. The magistrate, apparently sympathetic, told Zhou that
he might try to work through Liang Yungou, a metropolitan graduate from Lanyang,
to neutralize the pressure for conviction coming from Wang Shijun. In an odd maneuver, Zhou Sheng supposedly took Niu's place in prison to allow him to plead his case in
person with Liang. When Liang refused to help, Niu remained loyal to his friend and
returned to the jail in Baofeng. Although Wang had called for the death penalty, the
magistrate exercised leniency and exiled Niu to Lushi in western Henan. In December
1640, a local bandit had taken Lushi, a town with a large population of miners. Alienated
from the Ming and offered the option of rebellion, Niu seems to have joined Li Zicheng
when he passed through the county the following month. According to one story, Niu
met Li through a bandit whom he had met in jail and who was already involved with
the rebellion. According to another account, the intermediary was Shang Jiong, a medical doctor in Lushi who had already joined Li Zicheng's entourage. If the second account
is correct, it shows how a member of a middle stratum could provide a link between a
beleaguered member of the elite and a potential leader of the masses.[11]

With a base in the countryside and advised by a member of the elite, Li Zicheng
boldly assaulted the county towns of western Henan. The first target was Yiyang, on the
Luo River, thirty kilometers west of Luoyang, which was taken on January 31, 1641 (see
Map 5.1). Li killed the Ming magistrate, appointed his own official, and gave him three
thousand taels of silver "to relieve the poor and bring peace to the people." When Li
left, his newly appointed subordinate reportedly betrayed his trust by sending the money
to the Ming general Zuo Liangyu, who was stationed nearby. But Li had clearly signaled
his plan to establish a rebel administration devoted to the needs of the poor. It was soon
bruited about that the rebels "do not kill common people, they only kill officials."[12]

Li Zicheng next moved on Yongning county, some fifty kilometers further west. He
surrounded the town on February 1, used cannons against the eastern wall, and set fire
to the gate.[13] He contacted two sympathetic officials in the town, softened up the defenses
with bombardments for five days, and then led his men to enter in force. According to
Zheng Lian, the rebels met considerable opposition among town officials, local elite,
and middle strata. The magistrate refused to give up the seals, and an official living at
home was slain with his son, nephew, wives, concubines, and daughters—altogether twelve
persons. A registrar, teacher, and company commander were killed rather than surrender.
Given the social as well as political direction of the rebellion, such resistance was perhaps predictable. According to Zheng, however, some members of the masses also refused
to accept the rebel regime. In one case, the rebels attempted to carry off an attractive
young woman who was the daughter of a commoner. She refused to submit, cursed them,
and jumped off the horse several times in an effort to escape. The bandits hit her and
put out one of her eyes but she continued to resist. Finally they beat her to death.[14]

Zheng commented that the young woman's ardent loyalty reflected the influence of the ancient sage kings. It also reflected the Ming's concerted efforts to instill the ethics of loyalty, morality, and self-sacrifice among women—not to mention a woman's natural determination to avoid rape.

The rebels responded to the opposition in Yongning by imposing their own form of justice against the Ming state and its local elite. According to the gazetteer, they captured the local Ming prince, the magistrate, and more than one hundred members of the local elite and landlords and executed them outside the west gate. At the same time, they warned their men to stop raping and plundering so as to win popular support. Li Zicheng celebrated the victory in Yongning by formally adopting the title Dashing Prince, left by the late rebel leader Gao Yingxiang. He thereby signaled his intention to repeat Gao's earlier campaigns into Henan, this time with the intent of establishing permanent authority in the central province. As Zheng Lian put it, Li's adoption of the new title suggested that he wanted to be regarded as something "more than just a military man," even as he wielded arms and "rushed back and forth and hither and yon." Perhaps sensing that this description might seem too positive, Zheng added that the rebel was "as invincible as a mad dog." Whether as a liberating hero or as a rabid animal, Li took over some forty-eight villages in the counties of Yanshi, Xin'an, Baofeng, Lingbao, and Lushi. He increased his band to an estimated 100,000 and prepared for an assault on the prefectural capital of Luoyang.[15]

Li Zicheng may have expected that Luoyang would offer strong resistance. It was home, after all, to the wealthy Fu prince as well as to numerous Ming officials and officers. Alerted to the rebels' recent victories and imminent arrival, the civil and military officials of Luoyang had mobilized to defend the city. By March 1, the vice commissioner of the military defense circuit took charge at the west gate, the prefect organized resistance at the south gate, the magistrate took up a position at the east gate, the assistant prefect was at the north gate, and the regional commander and prefectural judge patrolled the streets. Fan Mengdou, a teacher in Xichuan, where the rebels had first entered Henan, had written the Fu prince asking him to use part of his fortune to win over the people and to assist the state in the crisis. Fan was aware that the princes had been forbidden to play active political and military roles since the Yongle reign, but he held up the energetic Hejian and Dongping princes of the Former and Latter Han, respectively, as models to be emulated.[16]

At the same time, Li Zicheng may have hoped for sympathy from the elite in Luoyang. In the city at this time was Lü Weiqi, a 1613 metropolitan graduate from nearby Xin'an county. Over the years, Lü had compiled a record of loyalty to the Ming combined with a certain independence. In his early career he had served as a prefectural judge in Shandong, where he had helped suppress the White Lotus sect but also demonstrated his concern for the people by contributing part of his salary for famine relief. In the 1620s he had established an academy in Xin'an to perpetuate the scholarship of the Cheng brothers of the Song and Meng Huali of the Ming, all of whom had been based in Luoyang. While embracing the orthodox philosophy of the Ming state, Lü had opposed the current administration's plan to establish a living shrine to the eunuch strongman Wei Zhongxian in Kaifeng. He had thus been barred from serving in Beijing and restricted to posts in the secondary capital of Nanjing during the 1630s. As vice president of the ministry of revenue, he had called for the collection of tax arrears, a measure with mixed implications for the people. But when the rebels had crossed the Yellow River in 1634, Lü had called for the repeal of the tax surcharges in Henan, the "mind, heart, and stomach of the realm." His hope, he wrote, was that the wealthy would not become poor, and the poor would not become rebellious. When the rebels had taken the Ming founder's tombs in Fengyang in 1635, Lü had been held responsible. He left his post and returned home to Luoyang, where he founded a scholarly group called the Yi-Luo Society. During a famine in 1637, he had appealed to the Fu prince to open his granaries to the public. When the prince had refused, Lü had shared his own family's grain with the starving. After the fall of Yiyang and Yongning, Lü appealed once more to the Fu prince to become active, this time by requesting more troops from the grand coordinator Li Xianfeng.[17] Once again, the Fu prince did nothing.

When Li Zicheng reached Luoyang in late February, he encountered less resistance from representatives of the Ming state than from members of the local elite. The regional military commander based outside the city wall had not been able to pay his troops and dared not use them against the rebels. Instead, he sought permission from the Fu prince to bring his men inside the walls. The prince refused. When Li Zicheng reached the north gate on February 28, the commander's troops mutinied, seized the vice commissioner of the military defense circuit, and opened the gate. In a single day, the rebels entered the city, captured the prefect and magistrate, and took control of the administration. The Fu prince and his son fled their palace and took refuge, appropriately, in the Temple for Welcoming Mercy. While the son fled the city, the father was captured and brought along with Lü Weiqi to the Temple to the Duke of Zhou, a fitting venue for a change of political authority. On the way, Lü Weiqi urged the prince to remember his status and to die with dignity. When the prince came before Li Zicheng, however, he wept and begged for his life. Li rebuked him, saying: "You are a prince of the blood and the richest man in the world. Yet in the midst of famine you have not been willing to share your resources to provide relief to the people." Li ordered the prince beaten forty times with the heavy stick and then had his head cut off and displayed to the public. Turning to Lü Weiqi, he said: "Ministry president Lü first asked for troops and then asked for supplies to wipe us out; what does he ask for today?" Refusing to kneel, Lü stood straight and replied: "I regret only that I have been unable to kill a single bandit to recompense the beneficence of my ruler-father. How can I be afraid to die?"[18] Thus while an infamous Ming prince surrendered, a respected member of the local elite defied the rebels. In the end both died at their hands.

Whatever Li Zicheng's disappointments in Luoyang, his political triumph was a major step toward transforming a bandit gang into a rebel force. Li made the most of the occasion, proclaiming: "These royal aristocrats oppressed the people and ignored their cold and hunger. We have therefore killed them on your behalf." He opened the prince's granary and brought out 100,000 piculs of grain to feed the multitude. According to Zheng Lian:

> From near and far the starving people carried flags and approached. People responded like flowing water, day and night without stop, numbering up to a million. The rebellion spread like a prairie fire, and no one could put it out.[19]

According to some accounts, the rebels mixed the prince's blood with that of a deer and, punning on the prince's title (*fu*; literally, lucky) and on the homophonous terms for deer and prosperity (*lu*), served it to the masses as "luck and prosperity wine" (*fulu jiu*). The rebels, in any case, now became lucky and prosperous, for they discovered several hundred thousand taels of silver in the prince's treasury. The victory at Luoyang conferred prestige on the rebels that extended throughout Henan prefecture. In Zheng Lian's view, "From this time on, wherever they passed there were no firm wills; wherever they reached there was no strong opposition."

In fact, Zheng Lian exaggerated the rebels' appeal as his own account made clear. Even in Luoyang, several members of the local elite joined Lü Weiqi in sacrificing their lives to resist rebel rule. One provincial graduate of 1624 faced north and hanged himself; a classmate refused Liu Zongmin's offer of a post and was killed, allegedly by having a hot poker thrust down his throat. The rebels did not confine their fury to the elite. When a medicine merchant from Suzhou called on his captors to return to allegiance to the Ming, he was hacked to death. Several women, including the mother of a provincial graduate, the wife of a government student, and even a fourteen-year-old girl, committed suicide rather than risk disgrace.[20] Such protests were probably exceptional and, in the case of the women, may have stemmed more from personal than political concerns. But they suggested some degree of continuing popular allegiance to the Ming and opposition to the rebels.

The victors at Luoyang lacked personnel to govern and defend the town they had won. Not trusting former Ming officials and unable to win over members of the local elite, they appointed a former Ming clerk to raise troops and secure the town. They also selected two local government students to assist with civil administration. Although these appointments were understandable, the reliance on inexperienced men of low rank was to prove ineffective.[21] Two weeks later, on March 20, two Ming assistant commanders, including Chen Yongfu, arrived from Kaifeng with three thousand troops under orders from grand coordinator Li Xianfeng to retake Luoyang. Because the bulk of the rebel army had already departed, the rebel officer and his assistants were able to raise a defense force of only five hundred men. These new recruits, unlike the old, received decent salaries of five taels of silver a month, no doubt from funds confiscated from the prince. But like their predecessors, they proved unwilling to die for the regime they purportedly served. After initial resistance, they were forced to open the gates to the government forces sent against them. The head rebel officer and more than ten other rebel functionaries were promptly executed. The former Ming officials who had surrendered or had been captured now presented themselves for punishment. According to Zheng Lian, the former magistrate who had been sheltered by the people was restored to his post pending a decision on his punishment.[22]

Although Li Zicheng's tenure in Luoyang was brief, it coincided with Zhang Xianzhong's occupation of Xiangyang and gave pause to the Ming court. Chongzhen berated himself for having failed to prevent the death of his uncle, the Fu prince. Scholar-officials criticized themselves for insufficient loyalty and paid respects to Lü Weiqi's spirit. The local historian Zheng Lian blamed the Fu prince for the disaster. As he put it, "The prince was covetous and stingy; he presided over his estate for twenty years and achieved not one praiseworthy thing." But Zheng believed that the real roots of the problem went deeper, all the way back to excessive centralization under the Qin. In his view the Han and the Tang had struck better balances between the center and localities than had the Ming under Yongle and after. Unwilling to admit that princes could be loyal and capable like Hejian and Dongping of the two Hans, the Ming state had come to supervise the principalities too strictly. As a result, the Princes Fu and Xiang "folded their hands" and allowed power to pass to the rebels Li and Zhang. In the end, Zheng opined, the Ming should have shared authority with the princes rather than allow it to fall to such "outsiders."[23]

The First Siege of Kaifeng

After taking Luoyang, Li Zicheng went east to Ruzhou, in central Henan. On March 9 he began a fierce attack on the town, and the magistrate announced that he would defend it to the death. On March 14, however, a strong wind spread a fire from a defense post along the wall of the town and the defenders panicked and fled. The rebels seized the town and killed the magistrate. Zheng Lian recorded that three women died rather than submit to the rebels, but he made no mention of any male casualties. The rebels apparently did not establish an official in Ruzhou but instead moved east along the Ru River and attacked Jia. The magistrate there had recently made a deal with a local strongman whose men had occupied the town. They now opened the gates to the rebels, ostensibly to welcome them. Finding that they were in fact planning to ambush his forces, Li Zicheng had the magistrate and strongman seized and killed. He chased the rival band from the town and appointed one of his own generals to serve as magistrate.[24]

Encouraged by these victories and aware that provincial troops from Kaifeng had gone to recover Luoyang, on March 22 Li Zicheng turned boldly north to assault the provincial capital. The rebel force comprised three thousand cavalry and thirty thousand foot soldiers, but they faced a much more formidable adversary in Kaifeng than they had in Luoyang. Having been the capital of China as recently as the Northern Song, Kaifeng still boasted imposing walls inherited from the Jin. More important, the Zhou prince, having learned from his cousin's mistakes in Luoyang, announced that he would spend his fortune to secure the city. The prince in fact made available tens of thousands of taels to reward the defenders, including fifty taels for every rebel head, thirty for other body parts, and ten for every wounded captive. The response in Kaifeng was enthusiastic. As Zheng Lian put it, "People took up their bows, arrows, swords, and lances and climbed the walls as if they were going to market." Many officials in Kaifeng also threw themselves into the defense. The regional inspector Gao Mingheng, the prosecutor of the "Four Scourges," together with the prefectural judge Huang Shu, led the defense of the west gate. The administration commissioner of the left was in charge of the east gate; the administration commissioner of the right was at the Cao gate; the prefect was in command at the south gate; and the vice prefect and controller of waterways manned the north gate.[25]

Members of the local elite, minor functionaries, and government students girded for the attack. According to Bai Yu, a clerk who kept a diary of the events, prominent members of the Kaifeng local elite who participated in the defense included Wang Shijun, Niu Jinxing's estranged relative by marriage, and Liu Chang, a metropolitan graduate of 1625 who had served as a secretary in the ministry of revenue.[26] An administrator of the Zhou estate commanded eight hundred "braves" stationed on the walls. Government students, such as Li Guangtian, rallied to the defense of the city, where they hoped one day to win their provincial degrees.

On March 22 a small rebel vanguard posing as Ming troops returning from Luoyang entered Kaifeng, but when the main rebel force arrived a few days later they confronted closed gates and walls overflowing with zealous defenders. During the first two days of the siege, the rebels suffered losses from the arrows, stones, and tiles that the defenders rained down on them. To shield themselves, they dug holes in the base of the walls. An enterprising government student in the city then constructed platforms that extended out from the walls and allowed archers to shoot back into the holes where the rebels were huddled. When a rebel attacker appeared at the wall with an impressive red shield, a government student who happened to be of the royal clan asked to be let down the wall on a rope. He fended off the rebel's attack and finally cut off his head before being hoisted back up the wall to safety.[27]

On the 26th, the capable assistant regional commander Chen Yongfu returned from Luoyang with his troops. After fierce battles in which he lost several of his officers, Chen managed to enter the city with his men through a water gate. The next day, Li Zicheng appeared below the wall to inspect conditions on the front line and was struck in the left cheek with an arrow. Since the arrow was the size of a chopstick, it penetrated only two inches; despite initial alarm, Li recovered quickly. The wound nonetheless left him blind in his left eye and earned him the nickname One-Eyed Li. Because Li was dressed like his men, his assailant probably did not know his identity. Numerous defenders on the wall had shot innumerable arrows. But when the Ming commander Chen Yongfu heard that Li Zicheng had been wounded in the assault, he unhesitatingly ascribed the merit to his son, Chen De, a junior officer in the army. This enabled Chen Yongfu to request a promotion for him, and it soon gave rise to a rumor that Chen Yongfu himself had shot the arrow that had put out Li Zicheng's eye. Once again, as in the case of the supposed rebel meeting at Xingyang in 1635, a minor event was inflated into a major incident with symbolic significance to both sides. As long ago as Liu Bang and as recently as Gao Yingxiang, heroic rebel leaders had survived arrow wounds.[28] Although eventually contributing to Li Zicheng's charisma, this hit was more immediately interpreted as a sign that assault on the provincial capital was premature. In addition, major Ming reinforcements were reportedly on their way under Yang Wenyue and Zuo Liangyu. On the next day, March 28, the rebels ended their siege.

Unable to take Kaifeng city, Li Zicheng turned his attention to smaller towns (see Map 5.2). On the very day he left the city he raced 120 kilometers to Mi, a poor county on the western border of Kaifeng prefecture. There the magistrate was determined to resist, but his defense was feeble, and Li defeated and killed him. As before, Li had no compunctions about killing magistrates who opposed him. He and his advisor Niu Jinxing, however, also tried to win over other Ming officials. When they moved west into Dengfeng, they faced a magistrate who had suppressed local rebels the year before and

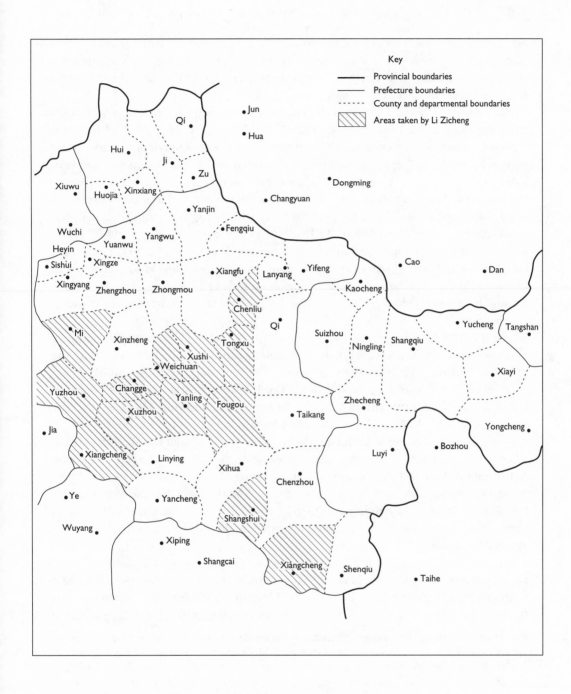

MAP 5.2. Counties and Departments of Kaifeng Prefecture Taken by Li Zicheng Between the First and Second Sieges of Kaifeng City, 1641. Sources: Based on data in Wang Xingya 1984b: 73; Xie 1986: 217–19; Zheng Lian 1749: 4: 90–96.

now led local stalwarts to defend the town. When Li learned that the magistrate was from Shaanxi, he invited him to surrender and join the rebellion. The magistrate refused, but Li persisted and sent envoys to try to persuade him. Only when the magistrate remained obdurate did Li have him put to death.[29]

Li Zicheng also reached out to local bandits and strongmen. Li Jiyu, a bravo from Dengfeng, had studied for the examinations but had failed them. He had turned to farming, joined up with some miners, and allied with a sectarian adept to lead starving people in revolt. The uprising had been suppressed and Li's wife and son had been killed along with the sect leader, but Li had somehow escaped. Later, Li had absorbed the followers of another local militarist in nearby Yu department and established himself at Jade Fort in Dengfeng. Together with another strongman from Song county, a short distance down the Yi River, Li Jiyu had raided east into Gong and Xingyang and north into Yiyang and Xin'an. He often settled disputes among rival militias and bands in the region and was known as a valiant hero to some and as a ruthless bandit to others. In early spring 1641, Li Zicheng allied with Li Jiyu, thus winning followers among the miners, sectarians, and starving people of several counties in the center of the province.[30]

At this time the Ming reshuffled its personnel in an effort to reassert its authority in Henan. When the grand coordinator Li Xianfeng returned from Luoyang to Kaifeng, the Zhou prince refused to open the gates. The regional inspector Gao Mingheng impeached Li for failure to prevent the fall of Luoyang. Cashiered by the court and ordered to await punishment, Li committed suicide in Zhengzhou. He was replaced as grand coordinator by Gao Mingheng. Chen Yongfu was rewarded for the recovery of Luoyang and the defense of Kaifeng by being promoted regional commander. His son Chen De was promoted brigade commander. With the fall of Xiangyang to Zhang Xianzhong and the resulting suicide of Yang Sichang, the court appointed Ding Qirui, the metropolitan graduate from Yongcheng county, as the new supreme commander.[31] Given Ding's experience fighting bandits in Shaanxi and his stake in protecting his home province of Henan, the court undoubtedly expected him to lead an effective defense against the rebels.

The Shaanxi rebels Zhang Xianzhong and Luo Rucai, meanwhile, continued to win victories in three counties of Nanyang and five counties and departments of Runing in southern Henan. Zhang Xianzhong was well known for his violence, but in one case the historian Zheng Lian found his men's fury understandable. According to Zheng,

> Zhang Xianzhong had a concubine who was beautiful and loved to drink. One day she got drunk and went racing on her horse and the cavalrymen who were following her could not keep up. When she reached the town of Shangcheng she was still not sober, and the patrols caught her and dragged her into town. The magistrate, a ruist, did not know what to do with her. The bandits who had been following her knelt below the wall and begged piteously, saying: "If you return her alive we will tell our general and we will never disturb the area of Shangcheng again." But the magistrate refused. The rebels then tried to redeem her with goods, but the magistrate ignored them. . . . [Instead] she was stripped and defiled by a group of monks on the parapets. Finally she was killed and her corpse was thrown over the wall. The bandits were greatly angered. They took the town, massacred for three days . . . and departed.[32]

Although perhaps apocryphal, this story reflects the idea that the rebels were not solely to blame for their excesses.

Zheng Lian, at least, had little sympathy for the officials in this case. He continued:

> Ai! What kind of defenders were they? They lost an opportunity. Why did they not fol-low the example of the Song people's treatment of Li Jiqian's mother? Having no plan like that, they used violence against violence. What they did was worse than what the bandits had done; taking the town and massacring it was quite appropriate![33]

Alluding to the Song state's leniency toward the mother of Li Zicheng's putative ances-tor Li Jiqian, Zheng criticized these late-Ming officials' harsh treatment of Zhang Xianzhong's concubine as moralistic, unimaginative, and counterproductive.

Li Zicheng, meanwhile, returned to western Henan to reassert his influence around Luoyang. He took the towns of Lushi on the upper Luo River and Lingbao on the Shanxi border. He then retreated into the mountains to escape the summer heat and train his growing forces. It was perhaps at this time that he won the services of a dwarf diviner named Song Xiance (literally, Song who contributes plans). Like the medical doctor Shang Jiong who may have helped enlist Niu Jinxing, the diviner Song was an obscure figure whose background and precise role in the rebellion remain unclear. According to some sources, he hailed from Yongcheng county and told Li Zicheng that he (Li) was the eighteenth son (*shibazi*) who was destined to take the throne. Since Yongcheng had a long tradition of White Lotus sect activity, it is quite possible that Song was "from" there, either literally or figuratively. Because Li Zicheng had yet to reach Guide, how-ever, Song must have joined the rebellion while traveling outside his hometown. In any case, Li was reportedly pleased with the prophecy and engaged Song as a second close advisor.[34]

In August 1641, Li Zicheng and Luo Rucai each experienced victories and defeats that, taken together, led them into an alliance. Early in the month, Li Zicheng evaded Ding Qirui's army advancing from the west and defeated Zuo Liangyu's forces at Xichuan in western Nanyang prefecture. At the same time, Zhang Xianzhong and Luo Rucai failed to take Eyang, in Huguang, and fell out with one another. Soon thereafter, Li Zicheng advanced on Dengzhou, in Nanyang, and then suffered a defeat at the hands of Baoding commander Yang Wenyue, who was stationed at Xuzhou, in Kaifeng. Consequently, Li and Luo were both frustrated when they met at Tang county, Nanyang prefecture. They quickly decided to join forces. Luo was older and more experienced than Li, and he was probably just as ambitious. He had adopted the nickname Cao Cao, a reference to the wily general who had risen to power in the last years of the Latter Han and whose son had administered the coup de grâce to the dynasty. But Luo also respected Li Zicheng, who had won victories in Henan and had begun to appoint local officials. Luo was therefore probably content to assume the number two spot under Li. The new allies then advanced against Dengzhou, and, although failing to take it, they gained confidence from their new solidarity. At this time, Zhang Xianzhong reportedly expressed an interest in joining the alliance. Luo sensed that a three-way alliance would not work; instead he gave Zhang seven hundred horses and urged him to go his own way. Zheng Lian suggested that Luo's solution was clever enough to earn him the right to the nickname Cao Cao.[35]

After a brief detour in Huguang, Li and Luo approached Xiàngcheng, a poor county in southeastern Kaifeng prefecture. There they confronted forty thousand troops under the Shaanxi frontier commander Fu Zonglong and the Baoding commander Yang Wenyue. In the ensuing battle, Yang retreated to the north, leaving Fu to fight alone. Fu was soon surrounded by the rebels and cut off from all food and supplies; his troops gradually disintegrated and he was captured alive. When he refused to surrender, he was taken outside the town and killed. This was the first time that an important Ming commander had been taken alive by the rebels; the event was a serious blow to Ming prestige. The rebels took Xiàngcheng and held it for ten days.[36]

After chronicling this rebel victory, the historian Zheng Lian expressed his admiration for Li Zicheng. Describing him as the most heroic of all the rebels at the end of the Ming, Zheng insisted that he had been driven to rebellion only by poverty and disappointment, "like a deer in the woods, a fish in a pot, or a wild animal in a pen." In words reminiscent of Sima Qian's appraisal of the Han founder, Zheng continued:

> His strategies were not as good as Gao Yingxiang's, his bravery was less than Luo Rucai's, and his craftiness fell short of Zhang Xianzhong's. But, illiterate though he was, he exceeded all the others in bringing out the best in the people he used. . . . When he got Niu Jinxing and used him, they were like fish rushing through the fearful waves and ravens flashing in the setting sun. They were two unfortunates who assisted each other, soaring on their wings and tumbling in flight. Their influence was unstoppable.[37]

Although exaggerated, this praise may have reflected the positive image of Li Zicheng's rebellion that was emerging at that time among some inhabitants of northeast Henan.

With the rebels advancing in northeast Henan, an otherwise obscure commoner named Wang Guoning dared to criticize Ming policies. Wang reviewed the hardships endured by the people of his native Ji county, in Weihui prefecture, a strategic juncture on the trunk line of the courier system. With descriptions of cannibalism and death rivaling those of Yang Dongming and Wang Han, Wang explained that towns were bereft of able-bodied people as a result of the drought, locusts, famine, and plague of recent years. He begged that labor requisitions be suspended and armies sent along other routes so that survivors like himself would not perish, too. Zheng Lian preserved this petition for posterity and remarked:

> Alas! At that time there were those who spoke of enduring values, not strange things, including principles that have not changed for thousands of years. "People are the basis of the state; when the basis is firm the state will be at peace." Such were the words pronounced in the *Poetry* and the *Documents*, transmitted by scholars, discussed by the elite, and listened to ad nauseam by rulers and princes. . . . But in a time of peace there are some princes, dukes, ministers, and scholars who believe and some who do not. In a time of rebellion there are those in high station and low who consider these words a deep secret. If by chance someone should mention them, the crowd sets up a clamor and laughs at their impracticality. Some cover their ears so that they do not have to hear them.[38]

Criticizing the failure of the late-Ming state to suspend taxes and provide relief, Zheng also excoriated the elite and the wealthy who refused to share their resources until forced to do so by bandits. Apparently recognizing the parallel between this plea from Ji at the end of the Ming and a manifesto from the same region at the end of the Shang, Zheng remarked: "Although we [the Ming] were not Jie and Zhou, the people regarded them [the rebels] as Tang and Wu."[39] In other words, although the late-Ming rulers were not as bad as the last monarchs of the Xia and Shang, contemporaries came to regard Li Zicheng and Luo Rucai as legitimate rebels like those who founded the Shang and the Zhou.

Having taken Xiàngcheng, Li Zicheng and Luo Rucai moved north to neighboring Shangshui on November 6, 1641. According to Zheng Lian, they encountered a firm defense mounted by two magistrates, a teacher, an official living at home, two state university students, and two government students, among others. After three days of fighting, the town fell. Both the recently dismissed magistrate and the incumbent died, the latter by throwing himself down a well "to requite the court and thank the people." The official living at home was a metropolitan graduate of 1634 who had served as a magistrate in Shanxi. Despite appeals from rebels who were themselves from Shanxi, this member of the local elite was resolved to die. The rebels obliged him by cutting his throat. All four of the students also died, at least one by suicide in which he persuaded his son to join, saying, "officials die loyally, sons die filially."[40] Clearly, there were many different, sometimes conflicting, "enduring values." Significantly, we learn nothing about the teacher. Perhaps he helped make history by accepting the rebels instead of making the histories by opposing them.

During the following two months, Li Zicheng and Luo Rucai took a total of twenty counties and departments, including one in Ruzhou, nine in Nanyang, and ten in Kaifeng. Six of those towns fell only after some officials, elite, teachers, and students resisted to the death. That was the case with Ruzhou, with Zhenping and Xinye in Nanyang, and with Yanling, Weichuan, and Chenliu in Kaifeng. In Biyang in Nanyang and Yushi in Kaifeng, whole families committed suicide rather than accept rebel rule. In Ye and Wuyang in Nanyang, the defense was mounted by military officers who had once been colleagues of the rebels Li and Luo and who had subsequently returned to the Ming fold. In both cases the former rebels fought to the death against their erstwhile colleagues. This loyalty naturally earned both men posthumous praise, titles, and sacrifices from the Ming state. Less predictably, perhaps, it won them the approval of Zheng Lian, who concluded that the former bandits' capacity for self-sacrifice proved that "bandits are people too." He added that even Li and Luo could have been won back to the Ming if they had been treated more respectfully.[41]

In three confrontations in Nanyang, members of various middle strata participated actively in resisting the rebels. In Nanyang county, a Ming general named Meng Ruhu (literally, fierce as a tiger) and the teacher in the county school held off the attack while the Ming prince of Tang tried to flee to safety. In the end they all died at the rebels' hands. In Neixiang and Dengzhou, a government student mobilized his clan to arrest and kill rebel officials. Fittingly enough, this clan was ensconced in Red Eyebrow Fort, named after the rebel band that had helped overthrow Wang Mang's Xin regime and opened the way for the restoration of the Han in the first century CE. Perhaps sensing that this fort might serve the Ming as cultural capital, the rebels demolished it. In Yu county, the local rebel Li Hao killed the militia head and wanted to take his attractive wife for himself. In a maneuver Lü Kun would have liked, the woman consented on condition that Li bury her husband according to the rites. After Li provided the proper burial, he discovered that the wife had hanged herself.[42] Such events reinforced the images of faint-hearted princes, history-minded rebels, and devoted but also clever wives.

In November 1641, Li and Luo returned to Kaifeng prefecture and began the task of taking and holding county towns. The first target was Xiangcheng in the southwestern corner of the prefecture. As the rebels approached the town, they sent a message to the magistrate requesting that he hand over his seals of office and make a present of some mules. The rebel chief advisor Niu Jinxing may also have appealed to a former student, Geng Yinggeng, who was a resident of the town. The magistrate, however, convoked the students to develop a plan. The students pointed out that when Liu Liu and Liu Qi had approached Xiangcheng in the Zhengde reign, the magistrate had made a gift of mules to avoid conflict. Now, as the much more powerful forces of Li Zicheng and Luo Rucai were coming, it would behoove the magistrate to follow that example, perhaps even to contribute funds to assist the rebels. The magistrate followed the majority opinion and issued orders not to resist the rebels. There was only one dissenter, Zhang Yongqi, and he left the town in disgust. On November 27, the town was prepared to receive the rebels peacefully.[43]

The rebel plans to take Xiangcheng peacefully went awry. According to Zheng Lian, when the rebels reached the suburbs, a government student, Li Jiexuan, confronted them and offered to teach them how to gain political legitimacy. The rebels reportedly grew impatient with him and finally threatened him with bodily harm. Li then exclaimed, "I have tried to instruct you in your duties and you still propose to raise your swords against me? You really are just bandits!" The rebels promptly stabbed him to death. Worse, according to Zheng Lian, they seized his wife and demanded that she follow them. She reportedly cursed them, shouting: "I am the wife of Li Jiexuan. How can I dishonor myself by serving bandits?" The rebels then killed her, too. Having demonstrated that they would brook no insubordination, the rebels did not enter the town at this time and instead left the area. More than a month later, on January 4, 1642, they returned and once again demanded surrender. As previously arranged, the magistrate came out to meet them with the seals of office. Acting on rumors that the magistrate had committed many vile acts in the meantime, however, Li Zicheng had him killed after accepting his surrender.[44]

Whether through misunderstandings or treachery, more violence now ensued at Xiangcheng. When the town fell, an assistant teacher who had organized some of the populace to defend the walls cursed the rebels as bandits. They retaliated by cutting out his tongue. The teacher then dipped his finger in the blood and wrote out the characters: "Exterminate the bandits!" The rebels then flew into a rage, killed the teacher, and marked his corpse with a sign: "Malicious spirit who killed bandits." Two other education officials visited Li Zicheng, apparently intent on living up to the spirit of the earlier agreement to surrender peacefully. When Li asked them why they had not come earlier, they looked at each other blankly and could not reply. Li reportedly had them killed as well. Seeing the way things were going, a government student named Li Guanglu took up his fan and a copy of the writings of Wen Tianxiang, the Song optimus who had committed suicide rather than submit to the Mongols. Li Guanglu then threw himself into the school pond and drowned. That act inspired a later encomium: "I did not hold office, but I was willing to die. I did not seek a good name, but I had a sense of shame."[45] Clearly the rebel quest for Xiangcheng was going to be more complicated than expected. It was also going to leave an important legacy. Having once more neutralized the town, however, Li and Luo left it and moved on to others.

As the rebels advanced on Xuzhou, diviners played a role in shaping its fate. In December 1641, a censor who was skilled in divination warned the Supreme Commander Ding Qirui, who was based there with some of his troops, to leave the town. Within days, Ding rushed off with his troops toward Kaifeng and Guide. At the same time, another diviner in Xuzhou predicted that the town would be safe. Thus reassured, the authorities and townspeople did little to prepare the defenses. When they learned that the rebels were coming, they sent out only a few dozen cavalry to confront them. The rebels easily ambushed the cavalry and killed them, taking the town on January 13, 1642. According to Zheng Lian, the rebels killed and plundered with abandon, sparing only the house of the local seer.[46] Perhaps they wished to thank him for his past service and encourage his future cooperation.

The rebels next went to Yuzhou, the strategic, prosperous, and populous department in western Kaifeng prefecture that had often served as the headquarters of government troops. Here they suffered many casualties at the hands of an assistant surveillance commissioner who supervised the firing of a cannon on the south wall. The attackers finally outflanked the defenders by scaling the west wall, and they soon entered the town in large numbers. They demanded the surrender of the surveillance commissioner; when he refused, they killed him. They also captured and killed the Ming prince of Yanjin, who lived in the town. Notably absent from the record, however, is any mention of resistance from other officials, let alone the local elite, the middle strata, or the masses. Despite Yuzhou's strategic and political importance, it was among the towns of northeast Henan that succumbed rather easily to Li Zicheng's growing authority.[47]

In Changge county to the east, officials and the populace played very different roles. Here the Ming magistrate surrendered to the rebels, one of the few cases of such submission thus far. Although Zheng Lian claimed not to know the magistrate's name, the gazetteer identifies him as a provincial graduate from Shaanxi.[48] From what we know of previous cases, we may suspect that the rebels appealed to him on the basis of common provincial origins. Given their recent treatment of the compliant but allegedly "bad" magistrate of Xiangcheng, however, they may also have considered the magistrate of Changge to be "good" and spared him for that reason. In any case, some prominent members of the Changge local elite as well as the local teacher and his students vowed to resist the rebels to the death. Without leadership from the magistrate or his subordinates, however, resistance proved futile. According to Zheng Lian, no fewer than 130 men died in the rebel takeover of Changge.[49]

The rebels encountered equally strong—and equally futile—resistance from both officials and the local elite in the counties of Weichuan, Yushi, and Chenliu, right up to the border of Xiangfu. But in nearby Tongxu they found a different situation that permitted a peaceful takeover. The magistrate of Tongxu, Fei Cengmou, was a tributary student from a prominent scholar-official family of Qianshan, Jiangxi. He had arrived at his post only forty days earlier, showing extraordinary sincerity and courage at a time when many magistrates were afraid to take up their assignments. When the rebels arrived, Fei selected his weapons and mounted the parapets to direct the resistance. After a few days, however, provincial reinforcements failed to arrive despite the county's propinquity to Kaifeng. Concluding that further resistance was doomed, Fei turned to the elders and said: "The supplies are gone, the clerks have fled, and there is no use incurring a massacre like that at Suiyang." The allusion, again, was to Zhang Xun's and Xu Yuan's defense of the town of Suiyang, now known as Shangqiu, against An Lushan in the Tang. Rejecting official resistance to the death as harmful to the people, Fei took up his seals of office, adjusted his cap, faced north, and jumped into a well. This suicide brought resistance to an end, and on the next day the rebels peacefully entered the town. Locating Fei's corpse, they reportedly found him looking just as he had when he was alive. Impressed by this sign of his virtue, they buried him according to the ceremonies. The people of Tongxu, having been saved by the magistrate's suicide, later honored him with sacrifices at his grave.[50]

The rebels had won various kinds of victories and different degrees of popular support and had succeeded in undermining Ming authority in many of the counties and departments of south-central Henan. They had defeated many Ming troops sent against them and had begun to appoint their own magistrates to administer the towns they had taken. In the process, Li Zicheng had assumed a new title, Great General Commissioned by Heaven to Campaign and Chastise and Manage Civil and Military Affairs.[51] Although this title suggested a certain vagueness about his ultimate ambitions, he was ready once again to tackle the daunting task of taking the provincial capital of Kaifeng.

The Second Siege of Kaifeng

The second siege of Kaifeng began on January 21, 1642, and ended on February 13. It lasted three times longer than the first but also ended in failure.

After the first siege of Kaifeng, the magistrate of Xiangfu, Wang Xie, had organized an urban militia to defend the town from future assaults. He designated each of the eighty-four wards in the city as a "community" headed by two well-to-do, upright government students responsible for providing fifty militiamen. He required the wealthiest households in the city to select, equip, train, and support the militia. Families who were worth ten thousand taels or more provided two or three militiamen; every two families worth one thousand to two thousand taels provided one to two militiaman. The entire militia, totaling 4,250 men, was divided into five battalions, one for each gate, headed by five managers who together supervised the entire system. The magistrate and the local wealthy provided the funds to pay each of the 185 community heads and their assistants one tael of silver and one length of silk. Each of the five managers received five taels of silver, one length of satin, and an official tablet.[52]

Like previous layers of the Ming military, the Kaifeng community militia was under the general direction and ultimate control of civil and military officials. At the north gate were the Xiangfu magistrate Wang Xie, the river manager, a Zhou estate functionary, and a metropolitan graduate. At the south gate were the grand coordinator Gao Mingheng and regional commander Chen Yongfu. At the Cao gate were the prefect, the regional inspector, and the judge Huang Shu. At the east gate were the administration commissioner and a military commander; at the west gate was an intendant. Among the officials and officers, the most influential were probably Gao Mingheng and Chen Yongfu, who shared responsibility for the Cao gate as well as the south gate. Playing lesser roles were leading members of the local elite such as Wang Shijun and Liu Chang.[53]

Unlike previous layers of the Ming military, the Kaifeng community militia also drew managers from among princes, local elite, and government students. At the north gate was the Yingchuan prince of the second degree; at the south gate was the Yuanwu prince's son; at the Cao gate was a provincial graduate; at the east gate was a member of the royal clan and a tributary student; and at the west gate was a government student. At the beginning of the second siege, the provincial graduate at the Cao gate was replaced by the government student Li Guangtian. He and the other government students who served as heads and assistant heads of the eighty-four communities owed their loyalty not just to the city in which they lived but also to the state that provided their stipends and, potentially, their degrees.[54]

Although improved organization and enhanced participation strengthened the defense of the city, continuing passivity among officials and local elite hampered any effort to defeat the attackers. Magistrate Wang had adopted a policy of clearing the countryside and strengthening the walls, giving the rebels almost complete freedom to operate in the area around the city. Thus Li Zicheng, at the head of an estimated thirty thousand troops and 300,000 followers, camped in the garden of the Yingcheng prince only five kilometers north of the city. Luo Rucai stationed an unknown number of troops even closer to the city, at the Fanta Temple in the southern suburb. Both Li and Luo ranged some ten kilometers in all directions around Kaifeng without fear of significant opposition. The limitations of Kaifeng's strategy of a stationary defense were evident on January 23, 1642, when several intrepid rebels posted manifestoes at the Cao gate without being caught.[55]

Responsibility for ending the siege fell primarily to government troops located outside the city. The most important force of three thousand men under supreme commander Ding Qirui had arrived in the area soon after the rebels. It was stationed outside the north gate. When Li Zicheng attacked the north gate on January 24, Ding's forces collapsed and many surrendered to the rebels. Ding sought safety in the city. The rebels then took advantage of the rout to seize the courtyard between the inner and outer doors of the gate. Some rebels even scaled the inner gate before defenders drove them back. Magistrate Wang ordered townsmen to throw burning faggots into the courtyard to stop the rebel advance. This took a heavy toll on the rebels but also on Ding's erstwhile troops that had surrendered to the rebels. At the same time, those troops failed to earn Li Zicheng's trust. Fearing they would serve as a fifth column, he called them together and had them killed. When a general named Li Goupi (dog skin Li), who had surrendered to Li Zicheng in western Henan, failed to carry out an order, Li Zicheng had him beaten. Li Zicheng's suspicions led to tighter discipline over his troops in the short run, but it would lead to trouble later.[56]

If the collapse of Ding's forces prevented any quick victory over the rebels, the solidarity among Kaifeng's militia enabled them to stave off defeat. The defenders who had driven the rebels from the inner north gate included a Qingzhen brigade under the command of a regional military commissioner named Li Yao. While holding a position in the most fundamental layer of the Ming military system, Li Yao acted also in his capacity as a Kaifeng Jew in command of a militia drawn mainly from the Muslim and Jewish communities of the city. On the second day of the siege, the rebels once again dug pits in the base of the wall to shelter themselves from the deluge of arrows and stones. In response, the Zhou estate provided reeds, and the officials provided sorghum stalks for residents to set afire and drop to the base of the wall to drive the rebels from their niches. On January 26, when the rebels dug a large hole in the northeastern section of the wall and fought their way through it, the community troops absorbed the brunt of the attack. They were soon backed up by official troops under the grand coordinator and regional commander. On January 27, these troops used cannons to counter those of the rebels, resulting in heavy casualties on both sides.[57]

The rebel siege exacerbated tensions in the social fabric of the city and may have led some residents to sympathize with the rebel cause. On the night of January 28, fires destroyed three thatched houses and threw the city into a panic. According to Li Guangtian, who kept a diary of the siege, a tenant had gotten drunk and ignited the houses by accident. The prefectural judge Huang Shu, however, feared that traitors would use the incident to weaken the defenses of the city. He had the hapless tenant beheaded to serve as a warning to others. The next day the grand coordinator ordered the judge to send three hundred members of a tenant army, previously recruited by landlord families, to assist in the defense of the northeastern section of the wall. Li Guangtian doubted that several hundred tenants would be adequate. He proposed offering one thousand in cash to residents to recruit other stalwarts, each of whom would receive one hundred in cash plus four buns. The regional inspector approved this measure. Many of the leading local elite, including metropolitan graduates Liu Chang and Zhang Wenguang, contributed to the support of the irregular troops. The sums were probably substantial since even a government student reportedly contributed five thousand taels. Meanwhile Li Guangtian and the big merchants and clans of the city provided thousands of buns a day for the troops, totaling more than 100,000 a month.[58]

In the absence of overt support from within, the rebels intensified their attacks from outside. According to the Kaifeng resident and diarist Bai Yu, on January 30, the first day of the Chinese New Year, the rebels took advantage of festivities sponsored by the Zhou prince and seized the northeast wall. In one of the fiercest battles of the siege, some insurgents managed to scale the walls, but the defenders killed them as they came over the top. Despite the great loss of life on both sides, the battle was dropped from the later accounts of the siege by Li Guangtian and Zhou Zaijun. Zheng Lian, however, mentioned it as a major assault and concluded that the defense "exceeded even that of Zhang and Xu at Suiyang."[59] Once again the famous mid-Tang defense against An Lushan in this region was invoked, this time as the standard by which to measure late-Ming resistance to Li Zicheng.

In place of Bai Yu's detailed description of this battle, other chroniclers recounted a story about the tactical use of sex. According to them, the rebels stripped some of their women (presumably captives) and thrust them forward to the edge of the moat to shout imprecations at the wall. The defending troops on the wall then mowed them down. Not to be outdone, the defenders thereupon forced indigent monks (equally powerless) to disrobe and hurl curses at the rebels. The rebels then killed the monks. According to Zheng Lian, this event became known as the confrontation between the "yin gate" and "yang gate" phalanxes. Although he included it in his history, he expressed some skepticism about its historicity. As he put it, "From the time of Chiyou to the time of Huang Chao there had been many battles, but I had never heard of this kind of battle before."[60]

During the next week, the rebels pitted their superior numbers against the city's greater wealth. For each tactic adopted by the attackers, the defenders developed a countermeasure. On January 31, the rebels constructed high towers outside the walls from which to direct cannon fire down onto the city. A government student in the city responded by constructing even taller towers inside the walls from which the defenders fired cannons down onto the rebels' towers. On February 2, when the rebels dug more holes in the wall to shelter themselves during a heavy snowstorm, Li Guangtian collected fifty taels from each pawnshop and thirty taels from each wealthy merchant to feed and clothe residents, who then shoveled snow from the walls in an effort to trap the rebels in their hideouts. When the rebels burrowed deeper into the walls, the defenders dug down from the top and dumped burning faggots onto them. When the rebels dug an enormous cavern below the Cao gate in an effort to open a passage into the city, the regional inspector offered a reward of two thousand taels to anyone who could devise techniques to counter the threat. A resident of the city used an unspecified combination of wood, powder, and water to regain control of the site and claim his reward.[61]

Because the records are all from the Ming side, they naturally provide more detailed and favorable accounts of the defense. On February 6, for example, the regional inspector sent five hundred special troops through a water gate to raid the rebel camp, taking 783 heads. On the next day, as supplies were running low, the Zhou prince contributed some wood, Li Guangtian mobilized community troops to collect more, and a university student purchased wood from private households at low prices. Li Guangtian, in his diary, acknowledged some mistakes. He also revealed that differences arose among the defenders over military tactics and perhaps over political and social issues. One of Li's cart pullers who had been captured by the rebels managed to steal a horse and make his way back to the east gate. Li favored allowing him to reenter the city and dismissed the idea that he was returning as an agent for the rebels. A Ming general at the gate, however, seized the cart puller and, before Li could intervene, had him executed as a spy.

If the defenders acknowledged their own minor errors, they emphasized major ones on the rebels' part. On February 8, Li Zicheng reportedly killed some of his own men who had gone to the wall and returned without having scaled it. Two days later he mounted a fierce attack that was repulsed by Chen Yongfu, who rallied his men with the cry: "Loyal officials are not afraid to die!" The next day the rebels dug a large hole near the northeast corner of the wall in which they placed several tens of piculs of explosive powder attached to a long fuse. When the charge went off, the stout wall withstood the blast and deflected it outward toward the rebel camp. Instead of destroying the wall, the explosion sent debris into the air that landed on the rebel troops, inflicting extensive casualties and creating chaos among the survivors. As a result of such errors, the rebels reportedly suffered thirty thousand deaths and more than three thousand injuries during the second siege of Kaifeng.[62]

In addition to setbacks reflecting the rebels' inadequate grasp of siege technology, Li Zicheng and Luo Rucai suffered from inferiority in propaganda and firepower. Encouraged by the grand coordinator to develop extraordinary measures to defend the city, a local commander took a leaf from the history of the late Yuan and secretly buried two cannons from the early Ming near the southern gate of the city. When workers ordered to undertake construction in the area "discovered" the cannons, they were said to be inscribed by Liu Ji, the Ming founder's chief strategist. This omen was trumpeted inside and outside the city and interpreted as evidence that the spirits of the dynastic founder were on the side of the defenders. Of course the "find" also served as a reminder that the Ming once had highly developed military technologies and could have them again if needed to defend the dynasty. According to Bai Yu, the defenders of Kaifeng also had one Portuguese-made cannon that they used effectively against the rebel forces whenever they approached within one and a half kilometers of the wall.[63] Whereas the early Ming cannons symbolized the defenders' link with the past, the Western one symbolized their contacts with the outside world. In both time and space, it seemed, they had an edge over the attackers.

The defenders also made much of the anticipated arrival of relief forces from outside. As early as January 31, they had announced that the Baoding commander Yang Wenyue was on the way with troops. This reassured the defenders of the city even if it did not fool the attackers. Three days later the officials in Kaifeng persuaded Zuo Liangyu to advance north from Linying to Qi county, putting him within striking distance of Kaifeng. Although the wily Zuo refused to advance further, claiming that his troops were too weak to confront Li Zicheng's, the authorities in Kaifeng used the threat of his arrival to discourage the rebels from persisting with their siege. The rebels had learned not to fear Zuo Liangyu, but they nonetheless ended their siege four days later in anticipation of the possible arrival of Yang Wenyue. They had also sustained casualties from the misuse of explosives at the northeast corner. On February 13, Li and Luo gathered their forces and headed southwest.[64]

After failing a second time to take Kaifeng city, Li Zicheng focused on driving Zuo Liangyu's forces from the region and consolidating rebel control over the outlying counties of the prefecture. He passed through Zhuxianzhen, where he looked after his wounded, and pushed south through Xihua county. Zuo Liangyu, with his usual caution, had already left Qi and was retreating south to avoid Li's advancing troops. Li caught up with Zuo in Yancheng, on the southern border of Kaifeng prefecture, and surrounded his troops. Yang Wenyue and Ding Qirui, who were nearby with their troops, beat a hasty retreat so as to avoid tangling with Li Zicheng. Li was therefore able to keep Zuo bottled up in Yancheng for eighteen days before being called away to deal with a graver threat arising in the west.[65]

After the death of commander Fu Zonglong in 1641, the court had appointed another Shaanxi official, Wang Qiaonian, to take charge of the suppression of Li Zicheng. To dramatize his hatred of the rebel, Wang secretly ordered the magistrate of Mizhi to locate and desecrate Li Zicheng's ancestral graves. Wang then took thirty thousand troops and entered Henan though Tongguan. When Wang reached Luoyang, he received an urgent appeal from Zuo Liangyu to come to his assistance against Li Zicheng at Yancheng. Wang therefore left ten thousand foot soldiers behind and rushed with twenty thousand cavalry toward Yancheng. When Li Zicheng learned that Wang was coming, he ended his confrontation with Zuo Liangyu and moved west to confront Wang. As Li had probably expected, Zuo made no effort to assist Wang but retreated farther south in the opposite direction.[66]

In Xiangcheng, Zhang Yongqi, a member of the local elite, had been the sole advocate of resistance when Li Zicheng had passed through on his way to Kaifeng. When his views were ignored by the magistrate, Zhang had quit the town, but he continued to be concerned about its defense. Now hearing that Wang Qiaonian was on his way to confront Li Zicheng, Zhang invited him to join in defending Xiangcheng from the rebels. Wang agreed, and on March 2, 1642, he entered Xiangcheng and immediately set about turning it into a base for attacking Li Zicheng. He placed three of his lieutenants at the head of most of his troops and dispatched them twenty kilometers farther east to meet Li Zicheng's forces coming from Yancheng. When Wang's forces saw Li's approaching, however, they panicked and disintegrated. Li Zicheng therefore advanced quickly toward Xiangcheng. There he was joined by the Nanyang rebel Li Hao, who had become a junior ally.[67] The scene was set for another major confrontation over Xiangcheng.

Commander Wang Qiaonian quashed all talk of compromise in the town, promised offices to all who participated in the defense, and instructed officers to cooperate closely with the populace. The four walls of the town were guarded by four regional commanders and four government students: He Qian, Zhang Hesheng, Jing Liangtian, and Zhang Xiu. Wang Qiaonian and an aide, who led the main forces to confront Li Zicheng, were assisted by two counselors who were also local government students, Liu Hanchen and Geng Yingzhang. On March 15, the rebels began their attack. As in Kaifeng, they dug holes at the base of the walls and inserted explosive powder and long fuses. The walls were less imposing than in Kaifeng, however, and the powder more carefully arranged. As a result, the explosion caused the walls to crumble. Wang Qiaonian resolved to fight to the death and threatened to kill anyone who even talked of flight. On March 17, as the town fell and rebels moved through the streets, Wang continued to resist, personally cutting down three rebels and two of his own men who tried to flee. When his strength was gone, Wang faced north, kowtowed, and tried in vain to cut his throat with his sword. He was captured and taken to see Li Zicheng.[68]

Having previously neutralized Xiangcheng with what he understood to be broad public support, Li Zicheng was furious that it had been retaken by the Ming and made into a bastion of resistance. He especially hated Wang Qiaonian who, despite a reputation for uprightness and courage, had recently dishonored his ancestral graves. When Wang refused to kneel and claimed he would turn into a malicious spirit after death and destroy Li posthumously, Li had his tongue cut out and sent him off to a suburb to be killed. Li was also angry at the member of the local elite, Zhang Yongqi, and the government students, especially the six who had played leading roles in the defense despite earlier arrangements for a peaceful transfer of power. Li ordered the arrest of Zhang Yongqi, and, when he learned that he had escaped, he authorized the execution of his kin, including nine households. Li also convoked the government students and ordered the cutting off of the noses and ears of those involved in the defense. This harsh punishment was soon inflated by rumors into amputation of their hands and feet, resulting sometimes in death. It was soon widely believed that 190 government students of Xiangcheng had suffered these punishments at the hands of the rebels. It was even said that the entire town had been put to the sword.[69]

A close reading of extant sources reveals that the provincial graduate and resistance leader Zhang Yongqi was actually captured by Luo Rucai. According to one story, he was about to be executed when a severe thunderstorm came up, leading to his release. According to another, Zhang somehow managed to conceal his identity and persuaded one of Luo's subordinates to free him. The important fact, of course, is that Zhang escaped the rebels' wrath, suggesting his limited commitment to the cause for which many others—including his entire family—had died. The survival of the hostile Zhang may also reflect the rebels' tenuous grip on Xiangcheng and its environs. Regarding the six government students most active in the defense, we know that Liu Hanchen, one of the counselors to Wang Qiaonian and a chief defender of the town, survived and that his two sons were among those mutilated by having their noses and ears cut off. The fate of the other counselor, Geng Yingzhang, is unknown, but at least two of his clansmen survived the Ming.

A subsequent list of the leading personalities of Xiangcheng included only Liu Hanchen from among the six government student leaders, although it also included two others known to be active in the resistance. It took considerable research on the part of local historians to come up with a list of loyal scholars that included the government students mutilated by the rebels. In the end, the list included only fifty-six names, not 190. Surprisingly, it did not include any of the six leaders of the resistance, although it did include some who were—and many who may have been—their clansmen. Zheng Lian, who included the list in his account, was clearly disappointed that the other 134 supposed victims of the rebels' wrath were not included. But he took comfort in the fact that the names of other heroes in history, such as "the Suiyang thirty-six," had likewise dropped from the histories. For Zheng Lian, it was enough to know that during the late Ming rebellions, Henan had been the most affected province, Xiangcheng the most damaged county, and loyal scholars the most wronged residents.[70]

Li Zicheng and Luo Rucai continued to show more interest in taking towns than in governing them. They stayed in Xiangcheng only two days and then set out to the west to recover other counties that had reverted to Ming control. On March 21, they reached Jia, where the magistrate, Li Zhenzuo, had organized the people to put up a strong defense. The rebels captured Li Zhenzuo and killed him. Li Zicheng was particularly angry at the local militia head who had killed a rebel officer previously stationed in the county. He reportedly had the man hung upside down from a tree south of the town until he died.[71]

The rebels moved on to neighboring Baofeng, home county of the advisor Niu Jinxing. The rebel Zhang Xianzhong had taken Baofeng the previous year and had killed the magistrate, a tributary student who had also been a member of the royal clan. Subsequently, the Ming had reclaimed the county and appointed a new magistrate, Zhang Renlong. Li Zicheng and Niu Jinxing took the town and captured Zhang, the most recent successor to the magistrate who had arrested Niu and exiled him to Lushi. Niu reportedly asked Zhang: "Why have you oppressed the people so badly?" Magistrate Zhang then took out one letter from Niu Quan's father-in-law, Wang Shijun, and another from Liang Yungou of Lanyang demanding that the death penalty be imposed on Niu and his son. Zhang's point seemed to be that the former magistrate had been more lenient than Niu's own relative and colleague. But Li Zicheng and Niu Jinxing had no patience for officials who continued to defend the Ming record; they promptly put magistrate Zhang to death.[72]

During late March and early April 1642, Li Zicheng and Luo Rucai restored rebel influence in several other counties and departments of Ruzhou, Runing, and Kaifeng. In Ruzhou they retook Lushan, where Niu Jinxing had once taught, and Dengfeng, where they had earlier made a deal with the strongman Li Jiyu. They then circled back southeast to take Shangcai, in northern Runing. The magistrate cut his throat to avoid a bloody battle and certain defeat. Next they went north to Xihua, in Kaifeng, where the magistrate drowned himself to save the populace from disaster. On April 8, the rebels reached Chenzhou, where the magistrate and a military intendant had mobilized the population to defend to the death. The intendant, Guan Yongjie, who claimed to be a descendant of Guan Yu, the Shu-Han general and god of war, assured his men that "It is better to die on the battleground than on the execution field." One member of the local elite, an official living at home, also vowed to die rather than submit. But many other scholars and people called on the officials to welcome the rebels, saying: "If the gates are not opened, it is the people who will be opened." When the rebels attacked they encountered resistance, and they had to burn the north gate and dig holes in the south wall to enter the town on April 11. Even then people fought in the streets. The rebels killed the magistrate, the intendant, the official living at home, and many other residents. They also suffered many casualties of their own before finally securing the town.[73]

Thus the rebels continued to encounter many different receptions in central Henan in the spring of 1642. The gap between the Ming and the people they hoped to exploit was opening only slowly and sporadically. Whether peacefully or violently, however, Li Zicheng and Luo Rucai were now able to take every county and department they approached.

The Alliance with Yuan Shizhong

At this time, Li Zicheng and Luo Rucai came into contact with another rebel leader named Yuan Shizhong, who had been active in northeast Henan for more than a year. Yuan had been born into a commoner family in Hua county, Daming prefecture, southern Beizhili, just across the border from Qi county, in Weihui prefecture, Henan. He claimed to be a country bumpkin, but his family seems to have had some land. Under conditions of famine and plague in 1640, he had appeared in Kai department as a leader of an armed band, and official documents labeled him a bandit. Arrested and then released in the fall of 1640, he led a large group of starving people into Qingfeng and Hua counties and became known to officials as a "big robber." In Hua, he defeated the local militia sent against him by the magistrate. His followers grew to several thousand and he raided further afield in Kaizhou and Jun. In late 1640, Yuan suffered defeat in Cizhou, Zhangde prefecture, Henan. In December he led a force of ten thousand in another attack on Kaizhou and was again defeated by a Ming commander sent from Zhending. The following month he was defeated a third time by the combined forces of the Zhending commander, the Daming prefectural judge, and the Hua magistrate named Li Yan. In February 1641, Yuan led his followers south across the frozen Yellow River to the poor and sparsely populated county of Kaocheng, in Guide prefecture.[74]

Yuan Shizhong arrived in northeast Henan at the same time Li Zicheng entered western Henan. Competing with many other local leaders, such as Yitiao Long at the head of a band of the starving, Yuan soon won a good reputation among the elite and middle strata of northeast Henan. As Zheng Lian later put it, "He went back and forth between Liang and Song without killing people or raping women. Among the robbers he was unusual in this respect."[75] If Yuan actually came from a family of some means, that may help to explain why he behaved from the start in ways that reassured land-holders. As Satō Fumitoshi has pointed out, he had already, by capture or persuasion, won the allegiance of a government student.[76]

In Shangqiu, Yuan would later capture another scholar, Tian Sheng, who belonged to a prominent family. Perceiving that Tian was literate, Yuan asked him his profession. Fearing for his life if he acknowledged that he was a scholar, Tian replied that he was merely a bookseller. Yuan did not believe him, but he smiled and asked him to sit down. Then one of Tian Sheng's servants spoke up, saying: "He is the offspring of a great official family, owner of many clothes, jewels, oxen, and horses." Yuan did not reply. The servant then railed at Tian, presumably for his past exploitation of the masses. Yuan merely smiled and looked at Tian. Tian was alarmed and lost color; his mouth opened but no words came out. Yuan then turned to the servant and asked him how he knew Tian. The servant replied: "I have worked for him for a long time and I know him well." Yuan then became angry and said to him: "You want me to kill your master. Although I am a bandit, I will not do that." Yuan then ordered his men to kill the servant and dismember his corpse. He continued to treat Tian Sheng respectfully as before. When Tian asked for a casket so that he could prepare his servant's corpse for burial, Yuan granted the request and praised him, saying: "You are indeed an honorable man." After recounting this story, Zheng Lian wrote: "Alas! A bandit who did not tolerate disloyalty in a servant." From this incident it was clear that Yuan Shizhong might challenge the Ming and rally the masses, but he was not about to undermine the social hierarchy that seemed as natural and legitimate to him as it did to students such as Zheng Lian.[77]

From April to June 1641, while Li Zicheng was taking his first towns in western Henan, Yuan Shizhong moved southeast into Nanzhili. In April he attacked Huoqiu, in Yingzhou prefecture, and then suddenly went to Xiao, in Xuzhou prefecture, where he captured the magistrate and then departed. In June his followers reportedly grew to 100,000, and he was active in the region of Fengyang and Si. He then traveled from Su to Bo in Mengcheng, where he picked up further support among miners. His numbers may have grown to as many as 200,000, and his influence reportedly "shook the whole region of Fengyang." Soon Yuan entered Bo and confronted the combined forces of the eunuch commander Lu Jiude, the supreme commander Zhu Dadian, and the regional commander Liu Liangzuo. The Ming forces were armed with cannons, and Yuan suffered a major defeat. Many of his men deserted. Yuan pretended to surrender and escaped with several hundred of his cavalry. In subsequent months, he cooperated with Zhang Xianzhong and local rebels in raids in Taihe county, in Ying department, Fengyang prefecture.[78]

By feigning surrender and making alliances, Yuan Shizhong worked to rebuild his forces in the Henan-Nanzhili border region. In early March 1642, he returned to an offensive against the state. His forces appeared in Runing prefecture, and he personally led an assault on Luyi, in southern Guide. He besieged the town for eight days but failed to take it. Yuan then moved north to attack Zhecheng, also in Guide, and succeeded in taking the external wall. He besieged the town for nearly two weeks, however, without taking it. On March 23 he moved on to Ningling, where he lit fires at the four gates, but he was not able to take that town either. Soon thereafter Yuan's cavalry appeared in Kaocheng, the county on the Yellow River where he had first entered Henan more than a year before. Having achieved little of permanent value in Henan, he may have contemplated crossing the river and returning to his home. At this point, however, he heard that Li Zicheng and Luo Rucai had taken several counties in central Henan, including Chenzhou. He therefore decided to stay in Henan and went west to join forces with them.[79]

Both the time and the place of Yuan Shizhong's alliance with Li Zicheng merit attention. Some early Qing historians, such as Tan Qian, put it in May; others, such as Wu Weiye, gave no date. Recent scholarship shows, however, that it occurred in the middle of April. As for the place, some early observers, such as Peng Sunyi, wrote that it happened "between Chen and Cai." This expression is rather vague: It could refer to many different places in the Ying River valley between Chenzhou and Shangcai. In fact, recent scholarship suggests that the alliance was made in Taikang county, north of Chenzhou, not south of it. Although technically inaccurate, however, the expression "between Chen and Cai" was metaphorically significant. It alluded to the famous passage in the *Analects* about Kongzi's getting into trouble when traveling between the states of Chen and Cai. Although the meaning of the original passage is obscure, the allusions to it in accounts of Yuan Shizhong were probably intended to indicate that he was having difficulty until he agreed to join with Li Zicheng and Luo Rucai. Wang Xingya has obliquely suggested as much by denying that Yuan was, in fact, in trouble on the eve of the alliance. Wang argues that Yuan may have had as many as 200,000 followers at the time. Yet the figure of 200,000 was probably an exaggeration even for the period when Yuan had been doing well in Nanzhili in the summer of 1641. Several sources gave him only 100,000 followers at that time. Since then Yuan had been badly defeated in Nanzhili and had been unable to take a single county town in Henan. It seems clear that Yuan was the weaker party in this alliance from the beginning. As Zheng Lian put it: "Li Zicheng was called the old headquarters, Luo's bandits were called Cao's Battalion, and Yuan's bandits were called the Little Yuan's Battalion." Yuan's junior partnership in the alliance was reflected in the nickname for his forces.[80]

Nonetheless, Li Zicheng, Luo Rucai, and Yuan Shizhong each brought some strengths to the alliance. Li and Luo had originated among the masses and had successfully recruited from the masses. They both ranged widely over several provinces and used siege warfare to take towns. Yuan Shizhong contributed his good reputation among the elite and middle strata of northeast Henan, his flexibility in dealing with the state, and his interest in establishing a political base. Working together, the three might be able to achieve the victories that had eluded them as individuals.

The advantages of the alliance became evident in the rebel assault on Taikang that began on April 18. Li Zicheng approached the east and west gates, Luo Rucai the south gate, and Yuan Shizhong the north gate. The magistrate, who had recently been transferred from Shangqiu, and a member of the local elite, who had once held office in Shaanxi, organized the defense. The rebels used explosives to blow large holes in the walls and took the town on April 21. Li Zicheng killed the uncooperative magistrate, but he honored the local literatus for having been a "good official in Shaanxi" and offered to spare him if he surrendered. As it happened, the scholar refused and was killed; the families of the magistrate and local elite, including more than twenty people, committed suicide.[81] Although the rebels increasingly offered amnesty to the local elite, they still could not compel them to accept it.

From Taikang the rebels moved northeast into Suizhou, the one-time locus of the Ming military in the region. Here the rebels expended even greater effort to win broad support. Their task should have been eased by the flight of the magistrate and his subordinates, who wished to avoid choosing between surrender and death. But Li Mengchen, a 1627 metropolitan graduate from Suizhou who had held offices in Beijing, heard that the rebels were taking counties in northeast Henan and rushed home to mount a defense of his hometown. Calling together his relatives, he announced: "Our lineage has received favors from the state for generations, so we must live and die with the town. Anyone who flees I will kill with my own hand." Although Li was addressing only his immediate kin, his example apparently inspired and intimidated others to stay and fight.

When the rebels arrived on April 20, Li Mengchen was on the wall with his nephew supervising the defense. The rebels broke through the south gate and sent out patrols, one of which accosted Li's party from behind. Learning the identity of Li Mengchen, the rebel troops said: "We have heard about you; if you come with us, you will not be harmed." Li refused the offer and tried to jump from the wall to kill himself. He was seized and taken to see Luo Rucai. When he refused to kneel, Luo asked him what he wanted. Li replied: "As a former high official, I wish only to die." Luo replied, "There is no reason to do that." He then turned to Li's nephew and said: "Take your men and throw a protective cordon around the Li compound." Suddenly realizing that his own nephew was in league with the rebels, Li demanded: "How come they talk to you as if you were a member of their family?!" Luo's chief advisor then held a banquet for Li Mengchen and spoke to him about the advantages of joining the rebellion. Li responded by dashing his cup to the ground in anger. Luo's advisor sighed and left. That evening,

Luo Rucai ordered his men to guard Li Mengchen closely and announced he would send him home on the next day. That night Li resolved to take his own life. His nephew tried to dissuade him on the grounds that his family and town both needed him and the rebels could be accommodated. But Li was adamant. He told his nephew to look after his grandmother, offered him his handkerchief as a memento, and then used it to strangle himself. When Luo Rucai learned what had happened, he ordered the execution of Li's defiant followers. At the same time, he tried to win public approval by instructing Li's nephew to take his corpse home and give it a decent burial.[82]

Yuan Shizhong had more success with another member of the Suizhou local elite, Tang Xuan. Tang was a metropolitan graduate of 1637 who had served as magistrate of Kaizhou, in Beizhili, when Yuan had been active there. Indeed, Tang was the very magistrate who in 1640 had imprisoned Yuan and then released him on promises of good behavior. Tang had given Yuan a parting gift of money, hoping that he would stay out of trouble in the future. When Suizhou fell to the rebels, Tang happened to be at home mourning the death of a parent. Yuan immediately sent agents to his house and had him brought to the rebel headquarters. Instead of demanding that Tang kneel, Yuan threw himself to the floor. His voice choking, he cried: "Shizhong has become a bandit again! He is really mortified before his master!" Yuan not only refrained from taking his benefactor's life but also persuaded him not to commit suicide. Indeed, Tang apparently cooperated with the rebels, for Zheng Lian reported that "many people in the department relied on this to avoid harm." In any case, Tang survived the rebel tenure in Suizhou. He continued to serve the Ming and was later posted to Beizhili, where he died resisting the Manchus.[83] Thus Yuan clearly assisted Li Zicheng in winning literati support in Suizhou.

Despite the rebels' commitment to social reform, they apparently made no attempt to target the Chu family, a branch of which, according to Gao Mingheng, had long oppressed their neighbors. Nor did they go after the Zhang family, who had escaped prosecution despite their alleged atrocities. Further, neither the Chus nor the Zhangs appear to have laid down any lives to defend the Ming and resist the rebels. In addition to Li Mengchen, discussed above, there were only two other members of the local elite— another official living at home and a local teacher—recorded in the gazetteer as having died resisting the rebels.[84] In Suizhou, at least, the rebels appeared more interested in gaining elite support than in leading the masses to rectify elite abuses. The elite, in turn, were generally more interested in saving themselves than in defending the Ming.

Two days later, on April 22, the rebels advanced to the neighboring county of Ningling. The magistrate was absent and the minor functionaries were nowhere to be seen. Even a professor who had been temporarily in charge of the town had fled. It was left to a teacher, a tributary student from Huaiqing prefecture, to direct the defense at the south wall. When the rebels entered the town through the west gate, townsmen rushed the teacher to safety, intent on saving his life. The teacher, however, did not wish to live. He found an excuse to duck into a temple, where he hanged himself.[85] With the teacher's demise, the defense of the town crumbled. No metropolitan graduate died in the defense, and only one provincial graduate died at the end of the Ming.

When the rebels entered Ningling, only a few lesser members of the local elite and middle strata continued to resist. The most prominent was Lü Zhenzhi, a member of the eighth generation of Lü Kun's lineage. Lü was a tributary student who had been a teacher in Baofeng and Yancheng counties and a professor in Runing prefecture. Contemporaries compared him with Hu Yuan, one of the leading Confucian teachers of the Northern Song. He had cooperated with the military and the people in repairing the walls of the town and had vowed to die if the town fell to the rebels. When he was captured, he refused to submit. Aware of his ancestor's good reputation, the rebels reportedly "esteemed" Zhenzhi for his "uprightness" and set him free. He nonetheless kept his vow and hanged himself. Links to Lü Kun and comparisons with Song teachers were evident in other cases. A son of a student of Lü Kun who stayed in Ningling to look after his mother died at the hands of the rebels. A teacher, who was compared with pedagogues of the Northern Song, later died in Guide.[86]

Two well-to-do commoner-scholars of Ningling also resisted the rebels. Lu Congtai, who had once heard Lü Kun lecture, had devoted himself to study even though he never won a degree. When Yuan Shizhong had attacked Ningling, Lu had contributed several tens of piculs of grain to support braves to defend the county walls. When Li Zicheng and his allies arrived, Lu went to the wall to assist in the defense but found that most people had fled. He returned home and prepared to commit suicide but was dissuaded by a servant. When Li Zicheng's forces came to demand grain at sword's point, Lu refused and cursed them. The rebels became angry, tied him to a tree, and shot arrows into him until he died. His biographer praised him for having the tongue of Yan Zhenqing, the famous calligrapher who had led forces against An Lushan in the mid-Tang. In this case the mid-Tang model may have been largely in the biographer's mind, but in another instance it seems to have inspired the historical actor himself. Li Xueshu was the son of a tributary student and himself a passionate student of history who admired Yan Zhenqing for having lived up to his ideals in opposing An Lushan. In the Wanli period, Li had contributed funds for repairing the county wall and had been awarded a cap by the local teacher. When Li Zicheng came, he reportedly cursed him and died.[87]

Family political and economic interests influenced the response of some elite families of Ningling to the rebellion. The Qiaos were a prominent local elite family with a stake in the Ming and reasons to fear a rebel victory. At the end of the Ming when a local bandit had led a crowd to threaten the town, Qiao Hongqi, a government student who had read the military works of Sun Zi and Wu Qi, led more than twenty stalwarts to capture the bandit and put him to death. When Li Zicheng arrived, Qiao was away, studying in Beijing with Liu Lishun, the optimus from Qi county. But Qiao's relatives were present and active. Qiao Sheng, for example, was among those who escorted the teacher from the town and tried to dissuade him from committing suicide. The Qiao males perhaps regarded Li Zicheng's rebellion as too likely to succeed to oppose it unconditionally; none is listed among prominent resisters. Their private sentiments, however, may have been expressed by two women surnamed Qiao and one woman married to a Qiao. These three constituted half of the devoted wives and daughters of Ningling who died resisting the rebels.[88]

If support for the rebels came mainly from the poor, and opposition came largely from the rich, class interests by whatever definition did not always determine rebel policies or popular responses. The rebels in Ningling, for example, paid no particular attention to the Miaos, at least one of whom was considered to be among the most rapacious landlords in the province. Nor is there evidence that the Miaos were particularly active in opposing the rebels. Once again, the rebels seemed more interested in securing political power than in achieving social justice and the Miaos more concerned with protecting family interests than with ensuring dynastic survival. Indeed, according to the Miao genealogy, Henglun, a clan nephew of the alleged reprobate Miao Sishun, "as a youth was captured by the rebels and went off with them, later returning." This incident indicates that many members of local elite families survived the rebellions, contrary to the impression given by some observers, including even Zheng Lian, who was himself a survivor. The incident also hints at a generational split between youth who tended to join the rebellion and elders who tended to oppose it.[89]

In sum, Li Zicheng first arose as a mounted bandit in Shaanxi and then established himself as the principal leader of a broad-based rebellion in the central province of Henan. He won support among disaffected members of the local elite such as Niu Jinxing and middle strata such as Song Xiance as well as among the masses devastated by famine and plague. With their help, he began to take county towns, overthrow princes, and besiege a provincial capital. After his first failure to take Kaifeng city, he allied with the Shaanxi rebel Luo Rucai and chased hostile magistrates and local elite from numerous county seats in Kaifeng prefecture. After the failure of the second siege of Kaifeng, he allied with the Beizhili rebel Yuan Shizhong and took several more counties in Kaifeng and Guide. By spring 1642, therefore, he had numerous bases from which to approach the prefectural town of Guide, the county town of Qi, and, once more, the provincial capital of Kaifeng.

In the contest for the central province, the rebels, their opponents, and historians invoked or alluded to various incidents and models from the past and interpreted them in different ways to define and explain their often distinct but sometimes convergent courses of action. Significantly, many began with the Han model that had long been so important to the Ming and its supporters. Li Zicheng at first identified himself with Liu Bang, the commoner–founder of the Han. Like Liu, Li survived an arrow wound, which may have won him charisma among his followers, and demonstrated skill in using men, which may have appealed to literati. Others, such as Ming officials and like-minded historians, may have associated Li Zicheng more with Xiang Yu, the rebel who overthrew the Qin but committed military excesses, such as a massacre at Xiangcheng that cost him the mandate. One contemporary scholar appealed to the Fu prince to follow the example of energetic Han princes by contributing actively to the defense of Luoyang, and a local historian blamed the prince for failing to follow that advice. Those who thought the Ming was finished looked to the Three Kingdoms for inspiration. The rebel Luo Rucai took the nickname Cao Cao from the famous general who defended the Latter Han but also positioned his son to overthrow it. A purported descendant of Guan Yu, the general who died on behalf of the (Shu-)Han state, gave his life in defense of the Ming against the rebels.

Although Han models remained important in many minds, Li Zicheng and his adversaries followed a trend already evident among the masses and turned increasingly to the Tang as a template for their own day. Li Zicheng's political ambitions were purportedly encouraged by new versions of the same *shibazi* prophecy that had inspired Li Yuan to found the Tang one thousand years earlier. Li most likely made the same offer of fictive kinship widely used by the Tang founders in allying with the local strongman Li Jiyu, appealing to the scholar Li Jiexuan, and wooing the official Li Mengchen. Those who remained loyal to the Ming looked instead to the mid-Tang suppression of An Lu-shan's rebellion for guidance in responding effectively to Li Zicheng's uprising. One magistrate alluded to the carnage that had resulted from Zhang Xun's staunch defense of Suiyang in the mid-Tang to justify his suicide as a measure to save the people of his county from similar destruction. One student reportedly invoked Yan Zhenqing's all-out resistance to An Lushan as an inspiration for his firm opposition to Li Zicheng. A local historian compared the second Ming defense of Kaifeng favorably with Zhang Xun's defense of neighboring Suiyang.

The growing interest in various Tang models, differently interpreted, did not preclude attention to later experiences. A local literatus invoked a Song precedent, the death of Wen Tianxiang when confronting the Mongols, to explain his decision to die rather than submit to rebels, and a local historian cited another Song precedent, the treatment of Li Jiqian's mother, to criticize a Ming magistrate's mistreatment of a rebel leader's concubine. Even more recent history was relevant as students in Xiangcheng cited a previous Ming magistrate's accommodation of the rebels Liu Liu-Liu Qi to justify a similar arrangement with Li Zicheng. But it was the Tang topoi, manifold and contested though they were, that had the greatest potential in the minds of those who wished to challenge the Ming and replace it with another, equally legitimate, new order.

SIX

Stalemate in Northeast Henan, 1642

IN LATE APRIL 1642, Li Zicheng and his allies challenged Ming authority in four towns in northeast Henan that had deep cultural significance as well as current political value. The first was Shangqiu, where the Shang royal house had been enfeoffed by the Zhou and where several influential families resided in the late Ming. The next was Xiayi, named for the earliest semilegendary dynasty and dominated by a single prominent family in the late Ming. The third was Qi county, where putative descendants of the Xia had been enfeoffed by the Zhou and where, in the late Ming, elite families coexisted uneasily with sectarians. The fourth was Kaifeng city, sometime capital of the Liang state, capital of the Northern Song, and the provincial capital in the late Ming that had already weathered two rebel sieges (see Map 6.1). Taken together, these towns naturally brought to mind the Three Dynasties (Xia, Shang, and Zhou) that had produced the archetypes of cultural centrality and political change, as well as later dynasties, including the Han, Tang, Liang, and Song, that had represented variations on those original themes. The Ming, the rebels, and the local residents contended for these towns in part by appealing to various historical precedents, including some from the Tang, that they interpreted differently in accordance with their particular interests and aspirations.

The Battle for Shangqiu

In the spring of 1642, Shangqiu was in the midst of a feud between Ming officials and the local elite. According to the local historian Zheng Lian, the dispute had arisen because "the local elite had been reared in tranquility and had grown accustomed to the atmosphere of Jiangzuo (literally, the left bank)." In other words, like many scholar-officials of the Eastern Jìn, the local elite families of Shangqiu had devoted themselves to enjoying life and had ignored the gathering storm. They sent their servants to overawe local officials, who then found it necessary to engage strongmen to enforce their writ. In early 1642 the Guide prefect backed his clerks in a conflict with local scholars, finally arrest-

MAP 6.1. Counties and Departments of Northeast Henan Taken or Neutralized by the Rebels Between the Second and Third Sieges of Kaifeng, 1642. Source: Based on data in Zheng Lian 1749: 5: 112ff.

ing six of them and stripping them of their ranks. The scholars reacted by wailing at the Kongzi temple and demonstrating at the prefect's office. The prefectural judge resolved the crisis by persuading the prefect to punish his clerks, but the literati became even more presumptuous. According to Zheng, they jeopardized the unity and security of the town.[1]

The Shangqiu magistrate, Liang Yizhang, a thirty-seven-year-old metropolitan graduate from Shuntian, Beizhili, had arrived at his post only the year before. He tried to end the conflict by imposing martial law. He ordered the local elite and students to assist in preparing the defense of the town and asked the metropolitan graduate and former official living at home, Song Quan, to help defend the south gate. When Liang conducted an inspection and found Song absent from his post, he arrested him and announced he would be punished for breaking the rules. Song made a superficial confession, but Liang refused to free him. Song then arranged secretly with members of the Snow Garden Society to stage a public protest. Local government students, including Hou Fangyu, met at the home of the provincial graduate Wu Boyi and decided to demonstrate when the magistrate visited the temple on April 13. When Liang pleaded illness and cancelled his visit, Hou and his friends postponed the demonstration. But, in Zheng Lian's words, the officials and scholars of Shangqiu continued to act "like enemy states."[2]

When Chenzhou fell to the rebels, magistrate Liang went to the prefect's office to plan for the defense of Shangqiu. More than one hundred government students seized the occasion to surround the prefectural offices and demand Song Quan's release. That evening the magistrate mobilized his supporters, including one Hou Xing and his cohorts, who rushed to the prefect's office on horseback, bows drawn and shields held aloft. In the resulting confrontation, "arrows fell like rain and many government students were wounded." One of them, He Guang, was struck in the forehead and died. The crowd then dispersed, allowing the magistrate to return to his office in his sedan chair. That night he sent Hou Xing and others to Kaifeng to report on what had happened. The next day, local public opinion, no doubt carefully shaped by the students, sided with He Guang's aggrieved family. As a result, magistrate Liang was forced to release Song Quan from jail. He then confined him to house arrest in a thatched hut to do penance for his alleged misdemeanors. Meanwhile, Taikang fell to the rebels and Suizhou came under attack.[3]

As the rebels approached Shangqiu, magistrate Liang assumed responsibility for the defense of the town. Flamboyant, vigorous, and given to drink, he dressed in martial garb, carried a sword and a bow, and rode horseback at the head of a host of loyal attendants. He had earlier demonstrated his resolve by chasing a local bandit to Ningling, capturing him, and bringing him back to Shangqiu to be beheaded in the marketplace. Since the prefect was ineffective, Liang cooperated with the assistant prefect, Yan Zekong, a Shandong provincial graduate who had helped suppress the Xu Hongru rebellion. After Li Zicheng took Ningling, Liang asked Yan and the judge to help defend Shangqiu to the death. In his words:

> The bandits' influence is on the rise and they may arrive any day. The masses have no one to lead them, the orders we give are not consistent, and no one is prepared to mount

a defense. If people are killed there will be no one to take responsibility. Formerly, when Zhang and Xu defended Suiyang, the command was unified so the defense endured a long time. Only you can arrange this.[4]

Impressed by Liang's invocation of the famous mid-Tang precedent of stalwart resistance against rebellion that had occurred in Shangqiu, the others replied: "Defense of the town is a heavy responsibility; people with few talents cannot assume it, only a great official can undertake it." They forthwith ceded their authority to Liang and made him head of a compact to defend the town.

With no princes and few officials, Shangqiu depended on military officers, the local elite, and government students for its defense. According to Zheng Lian, magistrate Liang served as general manager and conducted periodic inspections, "just as in the story of Suiyang." Assistant prefect Yan guarded the west gate along with Shen Shi, a tributary student (see Map 6.2).[5] The metropolitan graduate and Donglin member Zhou Shipu manned the southwest water gate, assisted by a regional military commissioner. The metropolitan graduate Song Quan, now apparently rehabilitated, was charged with defending the south gate, assisted by another regional military commissioner. The judge led the defense of the east gate along with Xu Zuolin, the provincial graduate and member of the Snow Garden Society. Two military commissioners cooperated in the defense of the southeast water gate. One government student, assisted by a military commissioner, was in charge of the north gate, while others patrolled the walls at the head of groups of ten residents each. The population was mobilized to provide cannons and catapults, compound bows and crossbows, spears and lances, and food and clothing. Those found derelict in their duties were fined. On the third offense, they were put outside the wall with their families.[6]

On April 23, the defense of Shangqiu was seemingly bolstered by two columns of troops from outside. The first consisted of seven hundred cavalry and one thousand foot soldiers under a vice commander named Zhang Yu, an old acquaintance of assistant prefect Yan Zekong. The second included several hundred men under Li Hao, the strongman of Nanyang said to have been sent by Chen Yongfu of Kaifeng to assist in the defense. Looking for all the help he could get, Liang Yizhang welcomed both groups. He stationed Zhang's men on the west wall and Li's on the north. The following day, many people from the countryside and suburbs flocked to the city seeking protection. The gates were then shut and blocked with large piles of earth. By evening tens of thousands of rebels surrounded the city. They included Li Zicheng in the southwest, Luo Rucai in the north, and Yuan Shizhong in the northeast.

The rebels discovered that the magistrate would not negotiate and so immediately began their assault. They deployed catapults to hurl huge boulders that crushed all in their path and plowed deep into the earth. Foot soldiers armed with swords, shields, and picks attacked the inner wall, dislodging bricks and stones and inserting jugs of explosive powder into the holes. When the powder was ignited, it blew up long sections of the wall and set fire to nearby wooden structures. Despite magistrate Liang's strict discipline and bold words, many defenders were terrified and lacked the will to fight. The brunt of the defense was actually borne by the outsider Zhang Yu, whose seasoned troops refused to be intimidated.

The next day heavy rains demoralized the defenders, and they failed to respond as

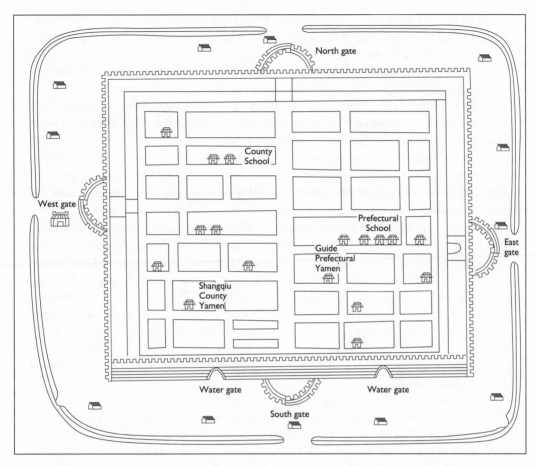

MAP 6.2. The Prefectural Town of Guide. Source: based on map in Chen and Zha 1754: shou 1b–2a.

the rebels used ladders to scale the walls. According to Zheng Lian, who was in the town, a rebel with a curly beard and red attire suddenly appeared at the northeast corner of the wall. Perhaps reminded of the famous Curly-Bearded Stranger reputed to have helped found the Tang, many defenders were reportedly paralyzed with fright. Only Zhang Yu advanced boldly, confronting the rebel leader, and finally skewering him with his spear. When the curly-bearded rebel fell to the ground, however, his body reportedly shook the earth, further alarming defenders on the wall. When another rebel leader reached the parapets some paces to the south, the defending townsmen scattered. Again the intrepid Zhang Yu rushed into the breach, but this time he received no assistance and failed to capture the rebel. Suddenly the men under Li Hao changed their clothes and began shouting the same slogans as the rebels, including: "The town has fallen!" Perhaps embarrassed at the gross intelligence failure, even Zheng Lian did not openly acknowledge what now became apparent: Li Hao's troops were imposters, presented as government troops but secretly allied with the rebels. Zheng noted cryptically: "the town then fell."[7]

Because magistrate Liang had ordered all-out resistance, many had already died trying to defend the town and many more would die in the aftermath. Liang himself, however, reacted to the fall of the town by throwing his seals of office into a well and sneaking out through a water gate. Indeed, Liang fled all the way to Huai'an in Nanzhili before finally being recognized and arrested by Shi Kefa, the local Ming commander. Shi sent Liang back north to expiate his crimes by donning white apparel and serving in the front ranks of the Ming armies opposing the rebels.[8] Meanwhile, the flight of the magistrate had left the people of Shangqiu leaderless. It also no doubt weakened whatever loyalty they may still have felt toward the Ming.

The total number of casualties in Shangqiu will never be known, but it is clear that it was large. The civil and military officials in the town were among the first to die. Assistant prefect Yan Zekong fell on the battlefield and was hacked to death; his wife and two daughters hanged themselves in the *yamen*. The judge Wang Shixiu was captured and refused to surrender. When three townsmen described him as a "good official" and offered to die in his stead, the rebels killed them along with Wang. Wang's wife, who had returned to her native place and thus escaped the carnage, committed suicide out of loyalty to her husband and the Ming. Even the wife of the feckless magistrate Liang hanged herself in her house after instructing a servant to burn it down. Assistant commander Zhang Yu had fought hard before being captured. The rebels admired his bravery and urged him to accept their authority. But Zhang reminded them that he was the younger brother of a famous general and was not about to submit to "bandits." He was decapitated on the spot. Other casualties included three clerks, four teachers, ten regional military commissioners, and five battalion commanders.[9]

Many members of the local elite also gave up their lives in defense of Shangqiu. The most prominent was Zhou Shipu, the metropolitan graduate and former president of the ministry of works who had shared responsibility for guarding the southwest gate. According to the county gazetteer, at least five other Zhous, including at least one provincial graduate, two tributary students, and two government students—all in Shipu's generation—died in the battle. Zhou's wife and concubine drowned themselves.[10]

Shen Shi, who had helped defend the west gate, was only a tributary student who had held a modest post as gentleman in the ministry of works. But he was also a descendant of the royal tutor Shen Li. Although Shen Li's progeny included few members of the elite, the family had continued to accumulate extensive property. Members were thus natural targets of any rebellion. Casualties in this family included one tributary student and one university student by purchase. They also included ten government students listed in the gazetteer and nineteen others listed in the genealogy. At least seven women married to Shens and five Shen women married to others perished at this time.[11]

The Hou clan also lost many members in 1642. Among them was Hou Zhizhong, the tributary student by grace who had purchased an office in the court of royal entertainment and given one thousand taels to the local school (see Figure 2.1, page 86). Four of Zhizhong's sons, a grandson, two nephews, their sons, and a nephew also died at this time.[12] In Hou Zhipu's branch of the family, the victims included two sons and a grandson and numerous women. Hou Zhipu's widow, née Tian, nearly eighty, refused to flee, cursed the rebels, and was killed. One of Hou Zhipu's female cousins had married a local government student named Liu Hao who had died the previous year. They had had a daughter who later married her distant cousin Hou Xie, half-brother to Hou Xun and Hou Ke. Liu Hao's widow was seized by the rebels and ordered to grind grain for them. She refused, saying she did not know how. When the rebels waved a sword at her, she exclaimed: "Even if I knew how, I would not do it for bandits!" The rebels then dragged her off to a camp where other captives were being held. There she met her son-in-law Hou Xie, who did not acknowledge her, apparently for fear that they would all be recognized as members of an elite family. When her captors asked her to identify Hou Xie, she refused, saying: "I don't recognize him, why do you ask?" The rebels then tied her to a tree and shot at her until she died. Her daughter, who was the wife of Hou Xie, and the wife of Hou Xie's half-brother Shu had both refused to flee in order to look after their mother-in-law, Tian. They were killed with her. Hou Xie's concubine and the widow of Hou Fangyu's eldest brother, Fanglai, also perished in 1642.[13]

Hou Ke's eldest son, Hou Fangzhen, a member of the Snow Garden Society, was another victim of the rebel victory in Shangqiu in 1642. Other members of the society also perished. Xu Zuolin, the provincial graduate and frustrated candidate for the metropolitan degree who had defended Zhang Wei at his homecoming party, was said to have "died at the hands of the troops." As for Zhang Wei, eyewitnesses reported that he was assaulted by a rebel and severely wounded in the face, but he kept walking, holding his jaw with one hand and wiping blood from his beard with the other. Finally he was attacked from behind and killed by another rebel. A third member of the society, Liu Boyu, the scion of the wealthy Liu family and a government student, jumped in a well and drowned. Finally, Wu Boyi, the nephew of Liu Ge who had won his provincial degree in 1636 but failed the metropolitan examination in 1640, also died in the battle of Shangqiu, according to Kong Shangda, a classmate from Taikang county, who witnessed his demise.[14] For these four members of the society, Xu Zuolin's warning at the party in 1640 had proved to be prophetic.

The total number of people who died during the fall of Shangqiu was probably large. According to the gazetteer, 100,000 or even 200,000 died in the town in 1642. In 1694 a magistrate discovered more than one thousand skeletons in a mass grave east of the town wall. He identified them as victims of 1642, but he did not specify whether their killers were rebels or government troops.[15] It is quite possible that casualties were high among commoners who lacked the means of defending themselves. However, the population of Shangqiu county had been estimated at only 250,000 in 1573. It had subsequently grown by natural increase and the influx of refugees, but it seems highly unlikely that anything like 50 percent of the residents succumbed as a result of the rebel takeover. Even local elite families such as the Shens and Hous, who were probably prime targets of the rebels, lost only small percentages of their total numbers.

The editors of the 1705 edition of the county gazetteer were content to explain the massacre of hundreds, perhaps thousands, in Shangqiu by the "cruelty" of the rebels. They compared Li Zicheng's troops to those of the Qin who were reported to have killed 400,000 prisoners of war after the battle of Changping in 260 BCE.[16] The Shangqiu historian Zheng Lian provided some graphic examples of rebel cruelty.

Zheng also offered two other quite credible—if rather contradictory—explanations of the extent of the massacre. First, after the initial order to resist to the death was followed by the sudden fall of the town through trickery and the flight of the magistrate, many people were traumatized and saw no point in further resistance. Describing hundreds of residents who had tried to flee only to be captured and put in a camp surrounded by rebel cavalry, Zheng wrote:

> The mass of them simply knelt down with their necks extended waiting to be killed, and not a single person dared to flee. The horn sounded, the swords and lances were raised, and not a single person walked out of line or tried to escape. They went to their death one after the other without the least resistance. Several tens of thousands [read many] captives prostrated themselves and died, and the corpses piled up one on top of the other like a hill. Ai! This is what the ancients called building a mound with the bodies of the dead to demonstrate one's merit. Having witnessed this, I learned the power of this practice. When a state is dying, it happens naturally. It does not take much human effort and the bodies just pile up.[17]

By "the power of this practice," Zheng presumably referred to its efficacy in intimidating people. Drawing on his own experience, Zheng added: "When the people of the town were being massacred, I was fifteen years old. I was in Cao's [Luo Rucai's] camp and I saw many people killed and no one even tried to escape." In some cases, the captives did not realize their fate was to die until it was too late to resist. In others, even government students kept quiet in hopes of not offending the rebels. As Zheng put it: "I did not see many who roundly condemned the bandits before dying."

Zheng's second explanation for the high mortality in Shangqiu was that many people, including otherwise undistinguished members of the masses, offered courageous—even reckless—resistance and thus incurred the wrath of the rebels. Zheng reported that even young students, not yet on stipends, railed at the rebels and were cut down. He personally witnessed many cases of women who refused to surrender and resisted rape often at the cost of their lives. In one case a young woman refused to go along with one rebel and almost succeeded only to have her head cut off by another rebel who was passing by. Another woman who refused to follow the troops was killed along with her three-year-old child. In a third case a woman who resisted a gang rape and injured one of her assailants was brutally tortured to death without relenting. Zheng concluded his litany of inhumanity by emphasizing the courage of the women who resisted to the death. As he put it, "People's natural dispositions are bestowed by heaven without distinctions between the base and the noble, the stupid and the worthy," and, he strongly implied, men and women.[18]

Zheng Lian's "natural dispositions" certainly included resistance to banditry. But among those who had called most loudly for resistance and even among those who died at the hands of the rebels there were some who contributed surprisingly little to the defense of the town. The flight of the bombastic and hypocritical magistrate, of course, did much to undermine the townsmen's respect for the Ming and their will to resist the rebels. But even some members of the local elite and middle strata in Shangqiu who ended up casualties of the conflict had tried their best to avoid choosing between the two parties and death. Some apparently tolerated rebel rule, at least to a certain extent and for a certain time.

Several members of the Hou family, for example, adopted middle positions between passive acceptance and bold resistance. Although the Hous had enjoyed wealth and status during the late Ming, their most illustrious member Hou Xun had spent the last six years in jail, and his clan uncle Hou Zhizhong had long since eschewed the examinations and preserved his status as a poor scholar. Zhizhong was known as a philanthropist, but he apparently contributed nothing to the defense of the town. Indeed, according to his biography, when the rebels entered Shangqiu, he mounted a donkey and rode out of the north gate. Other officials and scholars had themselves lowered over the walls with ropes in a similar effort to escape the carnage. Although understandable, this strategy was neither heroic nor uniformly successful. Hou Zhizhong was finally captured and taken to a rebel camp. When he refused to submit, he was killed.

Hou Xun's nephew Hou Fangyan led armed "guests" in raids on rebel camps to rescue members of the family, and he lived to tell the story. His brother Hou Fangzhen, however, apparently played no prominent part in the defense of the town. Indeed, according to his biography, after the town fell, "people did not know where he had gone." It was only later that "someone arriving from among the bandits announced that 'Fangzhen has cursed the bandits and died.'"[19] As in the case of Zhizhong, the records do not provide details of Fangzhen's capture and ensuing death.

Two other government students tried in vain to get along with the rebels. Yang Youwen, a good horseman from a prominent family, was captured by the rebels and treated as a brother. He drank with them and played the finger-guessing game, but he made the mistake of winning too often. One rebel challenged him to bet his head on the next round. At first Yang refused, but he finally consented. When he lost, he tried to back out of the agreement, but the rebels refused to let him go. They cut off his head and departed. Cui Zhihuai, who was described as having round eyes, a curly beard, a noble face, and a strong body, was mistaken by the rebels for commander Chen Yongfu, who some had expected to come from Kaifeng to rescue Shangqiu. Cui denied that he was the general who was rumored to have put out Li Zicheng's eye. He added that he was a "flowering talent," not just a "rough common person." By boasting about his status, Cui may have tried to impress the rebels; perhaps he even meant to offer them his services. But the rebel leader said: "No matter whether he is Chen or not, chop him up!" In his account, Zheng Lian implied that Cui might well have survived if he had not been mistaken for Chen.[20]

The clerks of Guide also responded variously to the rebels. A registrar in a guard had been given no responsibility to defend the walls, but he fought in the streets until he was captured. He then cursed the bandits and was slain. Zheng remarked that this clerk was morally superior to some high officials who "hid in the grass and begged for their lives." A clerk in the county office, however, actively cooperated with the rebels, pointing out officials and scholars, such as Wu Boyi, who were then killed. The clerk's effort to ingratiate himself with the rebels failed. He was among the first of the informers to be killed by them.[21]

Other members of the Shangqiu elite and middle strata, including some charged with defending the town, also managed to survive. The most notable example was the scholar-official living at home, Song Quan, who had been posted at the south gate. Neither the gazetteer nor Zheng's history includes any information on Song's activities after the rebels arrived. It is only in Song's longer "family biography" in the genealogy that we find the following startling information:

> In 1642 when the bandits took Guide, one of them was given the authority to protect his [Song's] home, and declared: "We former Jin [Shanxi] people want to recompense Master for his previous favors." As a result, several thousand men and their wives sought safety there.[22]

Although quite surprising in its immediate context, this passage makes eminent sense in light of the Song family history and the rebels' mode of operation. Song Quan's grandfather's cousin Song Xun, after all, had played a very similar role as protector of family and neighbors during the Shi Shangzhao rebellion in 1553. Song Quan himself had reportedly conducted an "enlightened administration" during his five years as magistrate in Shanxi and had later returned there as surveillance vice commissioner. He was thus a prime target for rebels determined to win "good officials" to their standard. The rebels were probably also aware of Song Quan's quarrel with the Shangqiu magistrate who had ordered the uncompromising defense of the town. It is therefore not surprising that Song Quan made peace with them and he and his clientele were left unharmed. As a result of his understanding with the rebels, Song Quan was allowed to lead his beloved mother out of the besieged town and across the Yellow River to safety in Cao county, Shandong.

Although only one source described Song Quan's extraordinary deal with the rebels in Shangqiu, that source was the Song genealogy, which was unlikely to have manufactured an incident implicating one of the family's most respected members in a rebellion that ultimately failed to found an enduring new order. Moreover, data from other sources are consistent with evidence from the genealogy. Two of the four men and one woman surnamed Song recorded by the Shangqiu gazetteer as having died in 1642 belonged to a different branch of the Song lineage, and the other two men and the woman do not appear in the Song genealogy at all. Finally Zheng Lian's list of the residents of Shangqiu who died defending the town included no men or women from the Song genealogy.[23]

Some members of the Hou family died in 1642, but many more survived the disaster. Hou Xie, who was the younger half-brother of Hou Xun and Hou Ke, the uncle of Hou Fangzhen and Hou Fangyan, and a sometime student at the university in Nanjing, might have been expected to contribute something to the defense of the town. Instead, as indicated in his brief encounter with his mother-in-law, he devoted his energy to saving his own life. Indeed, Xie survived the deaths of his half-brothers Shu and Lü; his father's first wife, Tian; his own wife, Liu; his concubine He; and his mother-in-law, Hou. Hou Xie was the only remaining male in the ninth generation of this branch of the family who might have taken responsibility for assisting members of the Snow Garden Society. If he did, however, it can only have been by persuading them to accommodate themselves to rebel authority.[24]

By one means or another, in any case, some younger members of the society survived the battle of Shangqiu. When Wu Boqie was treated as an official by the rebels, he reportedly denied it, adding, "Even though I am not an official, how can I follow you and become a bandit?" Although this response approximated the "cursing of the bandits" that ordinarily resulted in death, it was apparently mild enough for the rebels to continue to hope that Wu would eventually accept their authority. According to Wu's biography in the gazetteer, he was last seen being "hustled away" by the rebels, and "it was not known what became of him." Another member of the society, Jia Kaizong, as well as its leader, Hou Fangyu, also survived the fall of Shangqiu to the rebels.[25]

Xiayi and Other Counties

In contrast to Shangqiu, neighboring Xiayi surrendered to the rebels and escaped their wrath. According to Zheng Lian, the rebels sent only one hundred cavalrymen to Xiayi, and they "did not kill people or smash walls" but instead "called on the scholars and people to bring the magistrate's seals and have a discussion." When the town surrendered without a fight, Li Zicheng held a banquet for the residents. Apparently still angry over the unnecessary carnage in Shangqiu that had damaged his image, the rebel leader upbraided his generals in front of the guests, saying: "You did not obey my orders and you bothered the little people. You were disloyal to those above you and pitiless to those below you." He then ordered the beheadings of the culpable officers on the spot and continued his meal as if nothing had happened. This sudden discipline caused Li's remaining subordinates to turn white with fear. Li then reassured the scholars and people of Xiayi of his good intentions and bestowed on them several head of oxen. Ten days later he left for the west.[26]

Zheng Lian is the only source for this account, raising the question of its historicity. Zheng may have simply recorded a rumor, perhaps even one planted by the rebels to counteract the bad publicity stemming from the massacre at Shangqiu and to suggest they had learned from their mistakes. He may have transmitted the story to justify his own decision to endure captivity among the rebels or to demonstrate the benign influence of Yuan Shizhong, who, he claimed, "did not kill people." It is equally possible, however, that Zheng Lian had witnessed the peaceful takeover of Xiayi and recorded events that were ignored or suppressed by other writers. The gazetteers of Xiayi county and Guide prefecture recorded the activities of bandits dating back to Liu Liu/Liu Qi and resistance to banditry as late as 1641. Surely they would have recorded rebel attacks and popular resistance in 1642 if there had been any. Moreover, the late-Ming and early-Qing gazetteers did not normally record peaceful takeovers by rebels, so it is not surprising that they did not record this one.[27]

If Xiayi surrendered peacefully to Li Zicheng, it may have been due at least in part to the stand taken by Peng Shunling, a leading member of the local elite. Xiayi produced relatively few members of the elite during the Ming, although in the latter part of the period it improved its performance somewhat to rank fourth in provincial degrees and fifth in metropolitan degrees among the nine counties of the prefecture (see Appendixes B and C). In the lightly populated county, a few descent groups—the Zhangs, Wangs, Guos, Jias, and Pengs—appeared most often in the examination lists. Among them the Pengs were perhaps the most influential, and among the Pengs one branch stood out.

The Pengs of Xiayi entered the elite when a father and son won provincial degrees

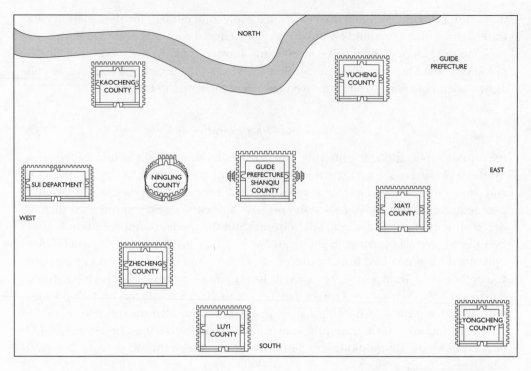

MAP 6.3. The Counties and the Department of Guide Prefecture. Source: Based on Chen and Zha 1754: Guidefu zongtu.

in the Jiajing reign, and the son became an official in the Wanli reign. It flourished when two grandsons became metropolitan graduates, pursued official careers, and earned biographies in the gazetteer. In the next generation, however, the family's fortunes dipped. Peng Yaoyu, a tributary student, repeatedly failed the provincial examination, reportedly because he insisted on writing in the Han and Tang styles instead of in the Song style favored by the Ming state. He held no office but wrote essays and poetry criticizing tax surcharges and other state policies. His nephew, Shunling, also remained a tributary student but gained prominence in the greater Guide literary circle that included Shen Li, Hou Xun, and Hou Fangyu, all in Shangqiu, and Lian Guoshi in Yongcheng. While retaining their wealth in land, the Pengs were unsuccessful in obtaining degrees or offices, and they expressed their frustrations and criticism through literature. With the disaster in Shangqiu, they may have favored a more conciliatory response to the rebels, perhaps hoping to protect the town and improve their own position. In the absence of a powerful magistrate, they may have determined the response of Xiayi to the rebels.[28] In any case, they survived the rebel occupation intact and were well placed to play important political roles in the near future.

Even before taking Shangqiu, the rebels had attacked Kaocheng, where they had destroyed office buildings, disciplined government students, and distributed relief grain (see Map 6.3). But neither contemporary sources nor recent scholarship reveal anything about rebel activities in the remaining counties of the prefecture: Yucheng, Zhecheng, Luyi, and Yongcheng.[29] Perhaps they assumed that their victory in the prefectural capital would at least neutralize those subordinate counties. In Yongcheng, at least, that would not be the case.

Having taken Shangqiu and Xiayi in Guide prefecture, Li Zicheng turned his attention to key towns in Kaifeng prefecture. By the end of April, he was in Yifeng county, which straddled the Yellow River. Most of the officials and elite and many of the people had already fled across the river to the north. A tributary student led local stalwarts in mounting the walls of the town and flinging stones at the attackers. According to his biography, the student feared the loss of seals and papers stored at the magistrate's office and decided to fight to the death. The biographer said that the man's heroic defense had saved the magistrate's office from destruction and would have saved the town if other members of the elite had offered their support. The gazetteer also recorded an incident in which a rebel soldier tried to rape a young woman who was nursing a baby and ended up killing them both.[30] Otherwise, it seems, the county fell to the rebels with little resistance and little loss of life.

The Fall of Qi

Moving southwest, the rebels could anticipate more serious resistance in the populous and prosperous county of Qi. A series of strong magistrates had governed the county and cooperated with members of the local elite to repair the walls and organize militia during previous rebel attacks in 1635, 1638, and 1640 (see map 6.4). During the second siege of Kaifeng in January and February, the town had served as the base for the Ming general Zuo Liangyu. After Zuo retreated to the south, however, the authorities and elite in Qi had adopted a strategy that, despite past preparations, left the town wide open to attack. In early April, the magistrate, a Beizhili metropolitan graduate named Lü Xiru who had been appointed in 1641, learned that the rebels were approaching nearby Chenzhou and expressed doubts that Qi would be able to resist. He consulted with a leading member of the local elite, Meng Shaoyu, who apparently agreed. Instead of organizing a local defense, therefore, Lü and Meng concocted a plan of "joining with Bian" (He Bian). According to this plan, the magistrate would go to the provincial capital of Kaifeng (also known as Bian) to work out a coordinated defense of the entire region. It is unclear whether the initiative for this plan came from the magistrate or the local elite, but it may have had something to do with the Meng family's close ties with Kaifeng (see Chapter 2).[31]

Lü and Meng feared that the provincial authorities would not approve of the magistrate leaving his post when a rebel attack seemed imminent. Meng Shaoyu therefore asked his son, Meng Jiongsu, the provincial graduate of 1639, to go to Kaifeng to persuade the grand coordinator Gao Mingheng to summon the magistrate to Kaifeng.[32] Meng Jiongsu, in turn, invited his classmate He Yinguang, whose writings were reportedly admired by Gao Mingheng, to accompany him on this mission. According to his biography in the gazetteer, He Yinguang hesitated, suspecting—reasonably enough—that the strategy was a cover for the flight of the magistrate. He finally went along, however, perhaps because he considered the magistrate useless in any case or perhaps because he saw an opportunity to clear the county of Ming authority and to make a deal with the rebels. In Kaifeng, He and Meng met with the regional inspector Su Jing,

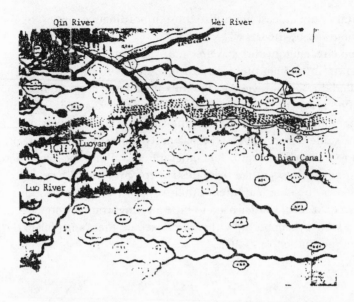

MAP 6.4. The County Town of Qi. Source: Zhu and Zhou 1788: quantukao 1b–2a.

a 1636 metropolitan graduate from the Andong guard in Nanzhili. As magistrate of Qi from 1638 to 1641, Su had won respect by crushing the *shibazi* uprising in 1638 and distributing relief during the famine of 1640.[33] Su agreed with Meng and He's plan and issued an order to magistrate Lü to proceed forthwith to Kaifeng. On April 9, with neighboring Chenzhou under rebel siege, Lü Xiru opened the gates of Qi to leave for the provincial capital. Whatever the motives of the magistrate and local elite, Lü's departure precipitated the flight of many residents. They saw it as a sign that there would be no effort to defend the town from the rebels, a judgment that would prove to be correct.[34]

Whatever the original purpose of Qi's strategy of uniting with Kaifeng, the ultimate result was the sudden and peaceful surrender of the county to Li Zicheng's forces four weeks later on May 10. According to the cryptic notice in the gazetteer, "Zicheng took the town, stayed for a day, and left." To be sure, there were some casualties prior to, during, or after that day. The gazetteer, however, attributed them to "local robbers" who, it said with considerable hyperbole, "took advantage of the opportunity to enter the town, burning and plundering it until nothing was left." Unfortunately, the gazetteer did not identify the "local robbers," nor did it specify the victims of their plunder. Given the treatment of Yuan Shizhong elsewhere in the gazetteer, we may suspect that the term *local robbers* referred to his men. The gazetteer also records, with unfortunate imprecision, that ten men died in clashes with bandits "during the Chongzhen reign." The men listed were all government students, with nine different surnames. The two who shared a surname were Mengs. Their personal names indicate they were from the ninth and tenth generations of the descent group that produced Meng Shaoyu and Meng Jiongsu, but they do not appear in the extant genealogy, perhaps because they were very distant relatives.[35]

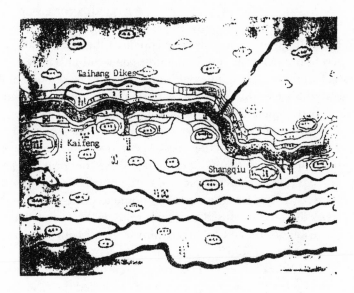

Other genealogies suggest that few died in the rebel takeover of Qi county. Among the Hes, for example, only three males were recorded as dying in 1642. Two of them were government students in the eighth generation, very distant cousins of He Yinguang's father, He Dongsheng. They were captured by Yuan Shizhong and died after refusing to accept his authority. The third was He Yinzhen, another government student and a slightly nearer cousin of He Yinguang. He Yinguang had apparently left town with his father and younger brother before the rebels arrived, thus demonstrating how the policy of "joining with Kaifeng" had the effect of legitimating the flight of the better-off, bolder (or more timid) members of the lineage. The policy left others behind to suffer (or enjoy) the consequences. In another elite descent group of Qi, the Hous, so many members of the ninth and tenth generations left town that the editor of the genealogy openly acknowledged the gaps in his records. Among those who were recorded, an unusual number died young or without issue, but only one was killed by rebels at some unspecified time and place. In addition, three members of the tenth generation were "captured" by the rebels: one never came back; a second returned and gained fame in Shaanxi for his martial skills; and the third returned, won high degrees, and later held office in the Qing.[36]

Responses to the rebels in Qi varied not only among social strata and generations but also between town and countryside and even between one village and another. Roving bandits and rebels had tended to find their first niches in the countryside, as in 1635 and 1641, and in some sense they represented the interests of the rural poor against those of the urban rich. By the time they began taking over towns in northeast Henan in 1642, therefore, they probably already dominated much of the countryside. Yet their control was by no means complete, and they continued to encounter resistance among some of the better-off elements in the countryside.

In northeast Qi, for example, the Qins were a large descent group that had one base in the village of Xifei. Like so many others in this region, they had arrived from Shanxi in the early Ming, multiplied over the course of the dynasty, and produced at least one prosperous branch by its end. In the ninth generation, a provincial graduate, Qin Mengxiong, had served as a gentleman in the ministry of revenue in Beijing and as a tax intendant in Shanxi, where he had earned a biography as a noted official. At home, Mengxiong had a reputation for distributing his wealth among relatives and neighbors, but he was not about to share it more widely. He and his sons constructed a fort called Xifeizhai and cooperated with the magistrate in opposing banditry in 1635 and 1638. During the famine of 1640, the Qins helped drive the local rebel Yitiao Long from the area. In 1642, when many people fled to the north of the Yellow River rather than confront the rebels, Qin Mengxiong stayed home to protect the family property. He was captured by the rebels, refused to submit to them, and was killed. In recognition of his loyalty, he was posthumously named minister in the court of royal ceremonies and chamberlain for the royal stud.[37]

While the Qins of Xifeizhai resisted the rebels vigorously but in relative isolation, their neighbors, the Lis of Qinglonggang, may have supported the rebels quietly but in good company. As discussed in Chapter 2, the Li Yue branch of the lineage had produced noted officials in the eighth generation and scholars in the ninth generation but only students, teachers, painters, and highly marriageable daughters in the tenth generation. With no members of the local elite, the Lis fell back into the ranks of commoners from which they had only recently emerged. At the end of the Ming, in the ninth and tenth generations, three males left the area, four were lost, two died young, and eighteen lacked progeny. Information on others was missing due to the disturbances. Some may have fled to avoid the conflict, some may have been killed, and some may have joined the rebellion. According to oral traditions in Qi county, Li Zicheng garrisoned some of his troops at Qinglonggang and may have attracted some of the local Lis into his movement, perhaps citing the shared surname if not similar goals. Although the participation of any of the Lis of Qinglonggang in the rebellion remains to be documented, some local residents believe that the Qins and Lis of this area have never subsequently intermarried because they were on opposite sides of the late-Ming rebellion.[38]

Although the struggle in northeast Qi suggested persistent loyalty to the Ming among the elite and possible acceptance of Li Zicheng among the masses, two members of the middle strata in the county seat strove to fashion a political position somewhere in the middle. Meng Shaoyu's half-brother, Meng Shaoqian, who had won his military provincial degree in 1630, seems to have wielded considerable influence in the town after the rebels arrived. Also active at this time was Su Gengsheng, a scion of a Ming hereditary ru household who enjoyed a high reputation among students at the county school for his excellent memory and broad learning. According to Su's biography in the gazetteer, Li Zicheng no sooner arrived in Qi than he called together thirty government students and asked for their advice. Su boldly asserted that the Ming still had the mandate. He suggested that Li would be wise to return to the fold and assist the state in suppressing banditry. He further specified that Li should follow the example of Zhu Wen, a rebel general who had first joined Huang Chao in revolt against the late-Tang state and later surrendered to the Tang and assisted it in suppressing Huang Chao. The Tang had rewarded Zhu by establishing him as a prince of the regional state of Liang (based in Kaifeng). The Liang had eventually inherited the mandate when the Tang collapsed of its own accord. This scenario offered Li Zicheng a middle-term victory with his own state based at Kaifeng. But it also implied a short-term surrender to the Ming and a long-term failure to establish an enduring, polity-wide dynasty. Li Zicheng was reportedly displeased with Su's "defeatist" advice and considered killing him on the spot.[39]

Li Zicheng finally spared Su's life and kept him as another symbol of literati support for his movement, but he ignored his counsel and continued to rely on Niu Jinxing as his chief advisor. It was perhaps on Niu's advice that Li decided once again to confront Ming authority in Kaifeng, the town that was being so staunchly defended by Niu's nemesis Wang Shijun, among others. As part of the effort to isolate the city, Li sent several hundred cavalry east to take Lanyang county. Niu reportedly participated in that campaign. He ordered the rebel troops to besiege the house of Liang Yungou, the scholar-official who had refused to come to his aid in his quarrel with Wang Shijun. Finding the house abandoned, Niu ordered it burned to the ground. He spared the rest of the town, perhaps hoping that it might be persuaded to join the campaign against Kaifeng.[40]

Meanwhile back in Qi, Yuan Shizhong suddenly refused to join in the attack on Kaifeng. According to Zheng Lian, Yuan had resented from the beginning his position as junior partner in the alliance with Li Zicheng and Luo Rucai. As time wore on, Yuan came to believe that his men were being used as vanguards in costly attacks on towns and were suffering more than their fair share of casualties. In addition, the Ming official Yang Wenyue had reportedly urged Yuan to keep his distance from Li Zicheng and promised to reward him with an amnesty. Yuan, who was famous for his willingness to compromise, may also have been attracted to Su Gengsheng's cautious and circuitous route to political victory, especially as contrasted with Li Zicheng's stubborn insistence on yet another frontal assault on the heavily defended provincial capital. Whatever Yuan's reasons, only days after the combined rebel victory in Qi, he gathered his forces at night and hurried away to the east. Having counted heavily on Yuan's assistance to take Kaifeng, Li Zicheng was naturally outraged and alarmed. He immediately set out in pursuit of Yuan with his own forces, now including Su Gengsheng and other students from Qi. Li's goal was apparently to bring Yuan back into the fold or to punish him for leaving it. Li was unable to catch up to Yuan in Zhecheng or Luyi, however, and finally sent his nephew Li Guo to pursue him to Bozhou. Li Zicheng meanwhile took advantage of the campaign to strengthen his influence in southern Guide and Nanzhili. His forces drove off the magistrate of Zhecheng, forced the magistrate of Luyi to commit suicide, and captured the magistrate of Bozhou, who was brought back to Luyi for execution.[41]

Although Li Zicheng was unable to win back his erstwhile ally Yuan Shizhong, who remained at large with one hundred loyal cavalry, he and his subordinates continued to court the literati of northeast Henan. In Zhecheng, a local government student named Chen Tianqing fell into the hands of one of Li Zicheng's deputies, whose nickname was Liu Lihua (literally, the tile is slippery). When Liu learned that Chen was a scholar, he confided that he was also from a "good family" who read books. He explained that he had become involved in the rebellion and was unable to leave because there had been no offers of amnesty since the fall of Luoyang. He warned Chen that it was dangerous to escape because the rebels would kill him if they encountered him again. He counseled him to wait for an opportune moment and promised that he would not try to stop him if he tried to leave. From this incident, Zheng Lian, who was probably still a captive of the rebels at this time, concluded that there were many good people who had been coerced into the ranks of the rebellion.[42] This judgment, of course, rationalized his own sojourn with the rebels. But it also revealed that there were rebel leaders with some education who remained with the movement because the Ming made no credible offers of amnesty and offered no guarantee of security for those who left.

Li Zicheng also gained the allegiance of Shen Wandeng, a strongman from Yiyang county, in Ruzhou, who apparently believed that the rebels had a brighter future than the Ming. Li Zicheng and Luo Rucai, after all, dominated many towns in Guide and Kaifeng prefectures and boasted some 100,000 battle-hardened infantry, thirty thousand cavalry, and hundreds of thousands of other adherents. They therefore turned their attention once again to assaulting the provincial capital, which they hoped to make the base for their movement to overthrow the Ming.[43]

The Third Siege of Kaifeng

On May 29, 1642, Li Zicheng and Luo Rucai moved their forces into position outside the walls of Kaifeng. Having twice failed to take the city and knowing that its defenses would be stronger than ever, they adopted the new strategy of cutting it off from outside supplies. Bai Yu wrote in his diary that the rebel strategy was to force the inhabitants of the city to fast—as the Shang loyalists Bo Yi and Shu Qi had fasted on Shouyang hill at the beginning of the Zhou dynasty. Although the analogy seems rather strained, the comparison of the late Ming to the late Shang by one of its defenders was hardly propitious. Li Zicheng's main force camped at Yanlizhai, west of the dike that encircled the city and about ten kilometers from the main wall, taking up an area some seven and a half kilometers across. Luo Rucai and his troops were stationed nearby at Hengdipu (see Map 6.5).[44]

Within the city, the grand coordinator Gao Mingheng and the judge Huang Shu had begun planning for a long siege by stockpiling grain and weapons. At first they hoped to mount an offensive; they sent out three battalions to attack the rebels before they could get settled. These troops were badly defeated, however, and by the end of the first week they retreated to the city. Kaifeng thereafter concentrated on a more passive defense.[45]

The rebels, meanwhile, built up their supplies and deprived the defenders of food by harvesting the wheat from fields surrounding the city. When the city residents went out to collect as much grain as they could, they engaged in small skirmishes with the rebels. On the whole, however, both sides avoided direct confrontations since each was sure that its policy of persistence—in siege and in resistance—would prevail in the end. On June 15, a state university student who had worked for the Shangqiu magistrate and had been captured by the rebels made his way from the rebel camp to one of the gates of Kaifeng. There he was recognized by the prefect and welcomed to the city. This

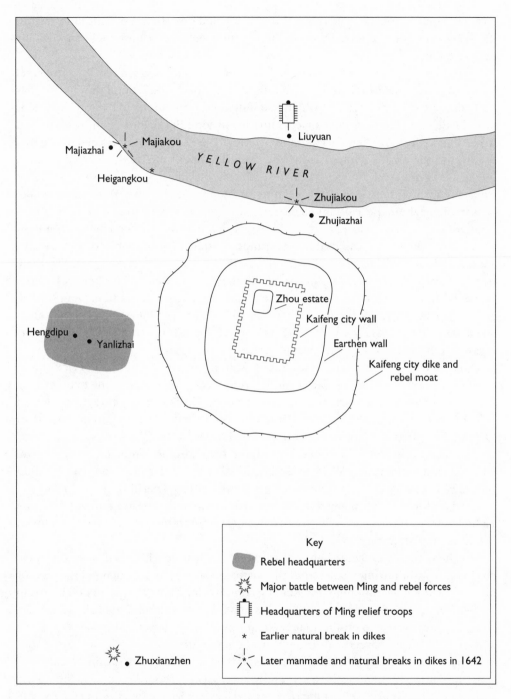

Key

Rebel headquarters

Major battle between Ming and rebel forces

Headquarters of Ming relief troops

Earlier natural break in dikes

Later manmade and natural breaks in dikes in 1642

MAP 6.5. Kaifeng City During the Third Rebel Siege, Showing the Locations of Ming and Rebel Forces in the Surrounding Area. Sources: Based on map in Xie 1986: 195; modified in accordance with research by Professor Wei Qianzhi, communicated to the author by letter, September 4, 1997.

local elite informant provided officials with a detailed description of conditions within the rebel camp that reportedly strengthened their belief that they could successfully defend Kaifeng.[46]

The passive defense of Kaifeng freed the rebels to send detachments west to expel Ming authority from other counties, thus tightening the noose around the city. In early June, they attacked Zhengzhou, which had long used local militia to defend itself. This time the defenses failed, and the magistrate tried to commit suicide by cutting his throat. According to the gazetteer, the common people prevented this and escorted him across the river to the north. While crossing the river, the magistrate tried to drown himself, but he was again saved. Arriving in Yuanwu, the magistrate encountered many refugees from Zhengzhou; he soon found meaning in life by looking after them. Meanwhile, back in Zhengzhou, the assistant magistrate, two members of the local elite, several government students, an instructor in the local guard, and several women died rather than surrender to the rebels. Unfazed by continuing resistance, presumably from those with a strong stake in the Ming order, the rebels moved on to Xingyang, Xingze, and Xinzheng (see Map 6.1). In Xingyang a government student roundly cursed the rebels as "dogs and pigs" and was killed. In Xinzheng the magistrate chose death rather than surrender. In Xingze, however, the officials and people who might have opposed the rebels had already fled across the river.[47] Li's forces thus took all three counties, greatly reducing the likelihood that any relief would arrive in Kaifeng from that quarter.

Shaken by the renewed rebel assault on Kaifeng and continuing rebel victories in neighboring towns, the Ming court ordered troops to advance on Kaifeng to relieve the siege. From Shanxi it sent the regional commander, Xu Dingguo, whose home was in Taikang and who was perhaps thought to have a particular interest in the defense of Kaifeng. But when Xu's troops confronted rebel forces at the Qin River, they promptly collapsed and withdrew. The court also ordered the supreme commander Ding Qirui, Baoding commander Yang Wenyue, and regional commander Zuo Liangyu, all still in central Henan, to lead their legions north to relieve Kaifeng. Learning of this, Li Zicheng ordered his forces to burn any remaining wheat in the fields around Kaifeng. On June 12 he led three thousand cavalry twenty kilometers south to Zhuxianzhen to confront the advancing Ming forces.[48]

In the battle of Zhuxianzhen, Li Zicheng demonstrated his strategic and tactical prowess. By withdrawing troops from the siege of Kaifeng, he had opened the way for his most formidable opponent, the Kaifeng commander Chen Yongfu, to raid his camp and collect the supplies stored there. Li was unable to prevent that setback, but he successfully maneuvered to ensure that Chen Yongfu did not advance further and attack him in the rear. He forged a document in the name of Zuo Liangyu and shot it into Kaifeng on an arrow. It said that defenders of the city should stay within its walls and leave the battle with Li Zicheng to his (Zuo's) forces. Grand coordinator Gao Mingheng and other officials either fell for the ruse or used it as a rationale for avoiding the responsibility to pursue Li Zicheng. In any case, they refrained from sending troops out to attack the rebel forces. Having secured his rear, Li Zicheng seized the higher ground around Zhuxianzhen, forcing the larger but slower Ming forces to occupy adjoining valleys and swamps. Sure of their strength, the rebels cut off the Ming troops' water supply and blocked their escape routes. They then went on the offensive, attacking their opponents before they could dig in.

After six days of battle with heavy casualties on both sides, strains began to appear among the Ming commanders. Hailing from Yongcheng in Guide, Ding Qirui wanted to support the defenders of Kaifeng. Ding lacked strong forces of his own, however, and had little knowledge of military matters. Zuo Liangyu had both hardened troops and military experience, but, as so often in the past, he refused to advance. Once again he appeared unwilling to risk his forces in support of a state that had imprisoned his patron and that seemed unlikely to deliver the supplies he needed to keep his forces in the field. Zuo was also annoyed that some of his cavalry had become mixed into Ding's forces and could not be recovered. During the night of June 19, therefore, Zuo broke camp and retreated all the way south to Xiangyang, in Huguang. Ding's and Yang's forces thereupon collapsed and Ding fled to Runing while Yang went to Guide.[49]

The rebels' victory at Zhuxianzhen was a major step forward in their campaign to discredit the Ming in northeast Henan. Thousands of Ming soldiers now joined the rebel camp with their mounts and arms. On June 25, Li Zicheng returned to the suburbs of Kaifeng and authorized Niu Jinxing to draft a new appeal to the city to surrender. Signed by "The Great General Li Commanded by Heaven to Proclaim Justice and Manage Civil and Military Affairs," the document lofted into the city read:

> Be it known to the civil and military officials, clerks, troops, and people in the city that Ding Qirui and Zuo Liangyu have been defeated by our army and have fled in all directions. Relief from north of the river has also been cut off. You are all now fish in a barrel and will not be able to last for long. If you open the gates and surrender, all of your past transgressions will be pardoned. Civil officials and military officers will be employed as before. To establish harmony with heaven, not a single person will be killed. If you compound your crimes by hoping for retribution and prolong the resistance, our army will treat you as nothing more than food for the river fish even though it values life and hates killing. Be careful not to commit a mistake that you will later have cause to regret.[50]

In the form in which it was preserved, at least, Li's appeal was rather prosaic, relying mainly on simple promises and bald threats and bereft of the historical analogies that might have swayed the minds of the defenders. Zheng Lian, who may still have been a captive in the rebel camp, later denounced it with surprising vehemence as "demonic words that could not change anything." Yet Zheng also compared Ding Qirui's impetuosity at Zhuxianzhen with that of Xiang Yu, the late Qin rebel who had fought in a similar fashion at the battle of Julu against Liu Bang, the future founder of the Han.[51] Given Li Zicheng's sometime identification with Liu Bang and Zheng Lian's previous comparison between Li and Liu, it seems likely that Zheng was signaling once more that many people in northeast Henan were beginning to regard Li Zicheng as another vigorous commoner who was gradually acquiring the mandate to rule.

The defenders of Kaifeng did not reply to Li Zicheng's appeal, but the Ming court expressed its alarm by cashiering Ding Qirui and Yang Wenyue and ordering their arrest. It also responded to a request from the Zhou prince in Kaifeng and appointed three former magistrates, Wang Xie of Xiangfu, Wang Han of Henei, and Su Jing of Qi, to be inspecting censors of the army. Their first responsibility was to determine appropriate punishments for the three commanders who had fled the scene of battle at Zhuxianzhen. Soon the court ordered the imprisonment of Ding and the employment of Yang pending a decision on punishment. In fact, Ding withdrew to his home in Yongcheng, where he lived in disgrace but perhaps not in confinement. Yang continued to oppose—and negotiate with—the rebels.[52]

To deal with the crafty Zuo Liangyu, the court turned to his patron, Hou Xun. Hou was still in jail, but his sons had never ceased seeking his release. In October 1641, Zhou Yanru, who was partial to the Donglin and Fushe people, had become chief grand secretary in Beijing. In 1642, the regional military commander Liu Zeqing, a native of Cao county, Shandong, just across the Yellow River from Shangqiu, became involved in the effort to free Hou. Liu had a love-hate relationship with the Hous, but he now called for Hou Xun's release. On July 13, the court finally freed Hou and appointed him censor, vice president of the ministry of troops, and supreme commander of all forces responsible for suppressing the rebellions.[53]

In the context of late-Ming politics, Hou Xun's rise from political prisoner to supreme commander was not extraordinary. Many officials had experienced similarly rapid and extreme shifts in fortune, including Hou's neighbor Ding Qirui, who had just traveled the reverse course from supreme commander to house arrest. The Ming court had good reasons for appointing Hou Xun to this post at this time. As a native of Shangqiu, where several members of his family had been killed by rebels, Hou could be expected to remain loyal to the Ming and unsympathetic to Li Zicheng. As a patron of the military commanders Xu Dingguo in Shanxi and Liu Zeqing in Shandong, Hou should be able to obtain their assistance in rescuing Kaifeng from the rebel siege. As the long-standing patron of General Zuo Liangyu, Hou Xun might be able to bring that talented but unpredictable officer back under central and civilian control. In addition, as an acquaintance of Sun Chuanting, who had once served as magistrate of Shangqiu and who was now commander in Shaanxi, Hou might be able to help the court persuade him to go to the aid of Kaifeng.[54]

Hou Xun assumed his duties as the new supreme commander with only a few personal troops based at Liuyuan (willow garden), the residence of the Taikang earl Zhang Guoji on the north bank of the Yellow River (see Map 6.5). Realizing that success would depend on court approval of a clear strategy deploying existing military forces against considerable rebel power, Hou submitted a memorial entitled "The Current Situation among the Roving Bandits." He began by describing the history of the rebellion and its present influence over 70 to 80 percent of Henan, a crisis that had caused the Ming princes to cry out for help. These events, Hou suggested, had radically changed the situation in the region. In his words:

> In former days, the central plain was the heart, mind, and stomach of the world; today, it is a pulverized region. In the view of the territorial princes, only the towns are important; but in the view of those concerned about the world, the towns are not critical for the gods of grain and soil. I am the supreme commander of all armies with responsibility to pacify the bandits; how can I speak of giving up Bian and not going to its rescue? But the seven armies I command altogether do not exceed several tens of thousands of men, and four of them have yet to arrive. Even if I were to consider myself expend-

able, as an elder son it would not be appropriate for me to try to cross the river without boats. Such an effort would merely cause the bandits to look askance at us, and, realizing the emptiness of our threats, to play with the court.[55]

Like his client Zuo Liangyu, Hou Xun argued that the Ming lacked sufficient troops to impose a military solution in the central plain.

Unlike Zuo, however, Hou went on to propose a bold political strategy that he felt might yet save the situation for the Ming. He noted that the rebels consisted largely of starving people who robbed to survive but did not accumulate goods for the long term. They were good at moving quickly from place to place, but they did not occupy territory or secure the benefits of working the soil. Many of them, Hou thought, were ambivalent about rebellion; they hoped to avoid battles and might eventually return to the fold. There were tensions in the rebel leadership between Li Zicheng and Luo Rucai, each of whom aspired to be dominant, and Yuan Shizhong had already left. Hou recommended taking advantage of these conflicts by negotiating with the rebels, assuming responsibility for long-term political developments rather than counting on short-term military victories.

Hou Xun then proposed to abandon the central province and surround it with powerful armies to starve out the rebels. In his words:

> Using past experience to plan for the present and adopting a correct view, the best policy is to abandon Henan. The Baoding coordinator Yang Wenyue and the Shandong coordinator Wang Yongji should guard the river from the north; the Fengyang coordinator Ma Shiying and the Huai-Xuzhou coordinator Shi Kefa should keep the bandits from penetrating south; the Shaanxi commander Sun Chuanting should block Tongguan [to the west]. Meanwhile, I shall lead Zuo Liangyu to garrison Jing and Xiang. In this way, we shall cut off all of their escape routes.[56]

Confined to the famine-stricken central province, Hou explained, the myriad rebels would soon find insufficient resources to keep themselves and their horses alive. Meanwhile, based at Xiangyang, Hou would be able to mobilize the resources of Huguang to nourish the entire Ming army and would be able to control Zuo Liangyu's forces and coordinate them with those of Sun Chuanting.

To some extent, Hou's plan was but a variation on supreme commander Yang Sichang's earlier one calling for existing armies to encircle the central plain where the rebels were already strong. Unlike Yang's earlier proposal, however, Hou's envisioned no large striking force with which to attack the rebels and destroy them. In discussions leading up to the memorial, Hou Xun's son, Fangyu, had recommended punishing Xu Dingguo for his insubordination in failing to come to the rescue of Kaifeng. He had also called for mobilizing other local strongmen in Henan for a concerted attack on the forces of Li Zicheng. Hou Xun had rejected these proposals, however, and instead settled for reproducing the rebel strategy toward Kaifeng on a larger scale, confining the rebels to Henan and starving them into submission. In effect, Hou proposed giving up the central plain temporarily to gain it in the end. As he put it:

> If we do not adopt this plan and just worry about the central plain that we have already lost, we will forfeit the strategic points that we should be able to defend, snakes and

boars will impose bloody sacrifices on us, and I fear that the calamity will not be restricted to the territorial princes. This is a plan for the gods of grain and soil, not just some angling for petty success or failure.[57]

To the court's surprise, surely, Hou was recommending giving up his home region to the rebels in order to save the dynasty.

There were, of course, problems with the proposed strategy. If the rebels were allowed to continue to besiege Kaifeng, they might eventually take the city and use its cultural, political, and economic capital to enhance their control of the central plain and their claims to the mandate to succeed the Ming. If Kaifeng held and the rebels faced the prospect of starvation, they might break through the defenses to the north or west, thus coming within striking distance of Beijing without having to contend with Hou Xun's well-supplied troops at Xiangyang. The court must have worried that Hou's proposed negotiations with various rebel leaders might lead to a modus vivendi in Henan that would benefit the province at the expense of the Ming as well as of Li Zicheng. Finally, although Hou Xun professed willingness to sacrifice his home province for the dynasty, he was also offering a plan that would extricate himself from the dangerous confrontation in northeast Henan and enable him to withdraw to the relative safety of Huguang. Although the court's precise reasoning remains unknown, it expressed its skepticism by failing to make any reply to Hou's proposal. If it had responded, it might have argued that northeast Henan was too important a region to cede to the rebels without severe damage to the very gods of grain and soil that Hou claimed to be defending.

With Kaifeng unwilling to negotiate and the court unable to provide relief, the rebels tightened their siege. They moved their front lines closer to the city and dug a wide moat around it to control movement in and out (see Map 6.5). Within the city the price of wheat doubled from a quarter of a tael to half a tael per peck, and the price of hay doubled from two hundred to four hundred cash. Under such pressures, social tensions became more visible. Judge Huang Shu, unwilling to recognize that scarcity was the basic cause of inflation, arrested a grain broker for price gouging and had him beheaded in the marketplace. As prices continued to rise, the authorities allowed people to go outside the walls to forage for food. Some reportedly took advantage of the opportunity to establish contacts with the rebels. A woman who worked at the Zhou estate went outside the wall to look for sustenance and was captured by the rebels. She apparently informed them of conditions in the city and agreed to return to the city to encourage other women to go out. The rebels reportedly gave her four ingots of gold weighing forty ounces and two ingots of silver weighing one hundred ounces as advance payment for her services. When she returned to the city she was seized, charged with colluding with bandits, and executed in the marketplace. Others in the city may have tried to provide active support for the rebels. A metalworker allegedly made several hundred iron arrowheads to smuggle out of town to the rebels. When he was apprehended at the gate, he reportedly referred to the rebels as "revered heaven-sent troops." Although this report may have been based on a coerced confession, it was probably not entirely fabricated since its contents were so obviously damaging to public morale. The worker was charged with sympathy for the rebels, nailed to the city gate, and torn apart by a mob. In another incident, when government troops were sent out to drive the rebels back, some of the

像生先亮熙南

FIGURE 6.1. Li Guangtian. Source: White 1966: III frontispiece. Used with permission from the University of Toronto Press.

rank and file defected. In response, the officials closed the gates and forbade anyone to leave town for any purpose.[58]

In the middle, between nervous officials and wavering masses, members of the nobility, local elite, and middle strata cooperated to maintain the defenses of the city. Li Guangtian, the government student, was promoted to tributary student and placed in charge of collecting and distributing grain (see Figure 6.1). He purchased grain from hoarders at the market price and resold it to the needy at the same price, thereby eliminating the excess profits of speculators and getting more grain to more people. The community troops organized during the previous siege were revived and divided into five regiments with names taken from the *Chronicle of Zuo.* They included a "central authority" headed by two provincial graduates, "rear stalwarts" headed by two government students, a "front lance" commanded by two nobles, a "right wing" commanded by two other nobles, and a "left wing" led by a southerner in charge of merchants from Huizhou and Hangzhou. The total number of community troops, including local strongmen, reportedly reached ten thousand.[59]

On July 22, as if to remind the community troops of their ultimate loyalty to the Ming, Judge Huang Shu led them in making sacrifices to Guan Di, the god of war. Huang distributed special insignia and arms to the rank and file whose names were inscribed in the records. On July 31, the forces exercised in the northern part of the city. Two days later they expelled the rebels beyond the earthen wall, beheading forty-one; capturing twelve; and confiscating horses, tents, and weapons. They estimated the total enemy dead at three hundred and proclaimed victory; the next day they went out again and killed two hundred more. In this action, a government student was killed, one of the few Kaifeng residents to die in combat during the third siege.[60]

At this point, the Shandong commander Liu Zeqing led several thousand troops across the Yellow River from his base at Liuyuan and approached to within four kilometers of the city walls. The censor Wang Xie led other Ming troops across the river to the south bank in expectation that a local strongman would lead thirty thousand men north from Qi county to help relieve the siege. On August 9, however, rebel soldiers suddenly attacked advancing government troops. When the assistance from Qi failed to materialize, Liu and Wang lost heart and withdrew their forces back across the Yellow River. Thereafter they concentrated merely on fortifying the north bank to prevent any rebel advance toward Beijing.[61] The prospects for effective relief became more remote than ever.

The community leader Li Guangtian did not give up. On August 10, citing Sun Zi's *Military Methods*, a classic of the Warring States period, Li proposed building armored carts to defend a corridor from the city to the south bank of the Yellow River. This deployment would enable Ming troops to cross the river to supply the city without having to hold the entire south bank. The four-wheeled carts were designed as virtual tanks: eight feet long by eight feet high, covered with three-inch thick planks. Soldiers would look out from two small windows and shoot arrows from four slits. The carts would be equipped with hemp mats and water buckets for combating fire arrows. They would be pulled by four soldiers, manned by eight others, and armed with one small cannon and four blunderbusses. Li estimated that 2,400 carts would be needed to cover the distance with a double column extending from the northeast and northwest corners of the city wall. Li's proposed project apparently received enthusiastic approval from his chief patron, Judge Huang, who estimated that it could be managed by the community troops alone. With this provisional encouragement, Li Guangtian set to work building the carts.[62]

By August 26, Li and his men had assembled enough vehicles to conduct a demonstration for the authorities. Most officials seemed to favor the idea, but Grand Coordinator Gao Mingheng and Commander Chen Yongfu were skeptical. Gao wondered if the road to the river was smooth enough to accommodate such heavy vehicles, while Chen merely smiled and said nothing. When Li assured Gao about the terrain, Gao asked if the cannon could shoot far enough to prevent the rebels from overrunning the corridor. Li explained that cannons on the city wall could fire five kilometers, thus providing cover for the first part of the corridor, and cannons on the dikes of the Yellow River would be able to fire one and a half kilometers, thus covering the last section of the corridor. Gao noted that relief troops were on their way from the west, presumably under Sun Chuanting, and supplies were due to arrive from Beijing on the north bank of the Yellow River within two weeks. He therefore argued that the deployment of the carts should be postponed. Assuming rightly that this was a virtual veto of the project, Huang Shu stormed out of the meeting and exclaimed: "We might as well burn these carts and jump into the fire! Then at least our malevolent spirits could attack the bandits!" When prefect Wu Shijiang tried to console Judge Huang, noting that two weeks was not very long to wait, Huang replied that in two weeks no one in Kaifeng would be strong enough to execute the plan. Besides, he said, no relief was likely to arrive in the next two months. When the grand coordinator Gao came out of the meeting, he heard Huang's protestations but he did not change his mind. As a result, the project was effectively canceled. Li Guangtian recorded in his diary: "We baked for twenty days and ended up with only a picture of a cake."[63]

Whereas official discussion of Li Guangtian's plan for armored carts lasted two weeks, public debate over its significance would continue for two centuries. Zheng Lian criticized Li's proposal, writing that it was an "old method" that was no longer viable because "times had changed [from the Warring States period] and the nature of power was different." Zheng pointed out that if Gao had approved it, it would have required twelve men per cart, or a total of 28,800 men, some of whom would have had to have come from Commander Chen's official troops. Even if Huang and Li had taken sole responsibility for this mission, they could hardly have managed so many troops once they were spread out to the south bank of the Yellow River. Furthermore, Zheng noted, the rebels had destroyed Cao gate in the second siege like a pile of eggs and had kicked over Zhuxianzhen during the third siege like a rotten stump. Surely they would have made short work of this thinly spread corridor of carts. With the benefit of hindsight, Zheng Lian compared the confrontation of Li Guangtian's community troops with Li Zicheng's rebel army to a goat fighting a tiger; he compared the Ming troops on the north bank of the river to a praying mantis trying to stop a chariot. If the plan had been put into effect, he wondered who would have volunteered to enter the killing fields. This critical stance was shared by Ji Wenda, the editor of the Qing-sponsored *Annotated Bibliography of the Collectanea of the Four Treasuries* in the eighteenth century. Remarking that the late Ming "was not the Three Dynasties," he compared Li Guangtian with another Henanese scholar, Fang Guan, whose plan to suppress bandits in the mid-Tang had led to disaster.[64]

Other observers were more ambivalent and some even admired the plan. Zhou Sisheng, who visited Qi county in 1688 and read a copy of Li Guangtian's diary, wrote that the life and death of Bian affected the fortunes of the whole world. Invoking historical experience for his own purposes, Zhou compared Li Guangtian with one Du Tao, who had valiantly resisted the rebel Pang Xun toward the end of the Tang. Regarding Li's diary, Zhou wrote: "In reading this work one can know this man and grieve over his determination." Although this text is ambiguous, another version of the same preface included in the Kaifeng prefectural gazetteer reads more positively: "One can know the man and remember his achievement." In 1826, another scholar, after meeting a descendant of Li Guangtian in Yunnan, wrote a preface to a new edition of the diary. He pointed out that even if Gao Mingheng had approved Li's plan there was no guarantee that it would have succeeded in suppressing the rebels. But, he added, Gao had been too timid in refusing to try it, for "how can death by starvation be better than death in battle?" Finally, in 1898, another writer of a preface to Li's diary rejected Ji Wenda's association of Li Guangtian's proposal with Fang Guan's failure, observing that Li's plan, unlike Fang's, had never been put into effect. Even if Li's plan had been found wanting, the author argued, the result could not have been worse than what happened.[65]

The situation in Kaifeng in September 1642 was a virtual microcosm of late-Ming state-society relations. Having vetoed a plan to secure resources from outside, the grand coordinator now presided over the distribution of dwindling resources within. He mobilized clerks, soldiers, and community troops to collect grain from households that were hoarding it by demanding contributions, purchases, and requisitions. The available grain was used to feed the nobility, officials, and troops, not the middle strata and the masses. As one diarist recorded, the troops ate meat while the poor starved. In the growing crisis, abuses became rife. Official emissaries collected resources every day and plundered the households of those who resisted. The strong killed the weak and turned their corpses in as rebels to get monetary rewards. The price of food skyrocketed—wild herbs rose from fifty to five hundred cash—and the definition of food broadened to include almost everything. At first people ate such things as lotus seeds, tea leaves, and fungi that grew on fir trees. Then they turned to marsh grass, peony roots, pine cones, acorns, and bark. Some tried to prolong life by consuming insects, dung beetles, and red worms that were euphemistically called goldfish and sold for eight hundred cash per jin. The next step was often choking down leather, horse manure, organic soil, and mud, items that slackened hunger but hastened death. Rather than die of starvation, some residents of the city overcame their inhibitions and ate human flesh. Rewards for the heads of rebels gave way to payments for the heads of anyone and the price per head rose to three taels, then to four. By the middle of the month, hundreds of people were dying every day, affecting seven out of ten households. At first the streets were filled with corpses, then only the skeletons and hair were left. People stopped going out for fear of being killed and eaten by their neighbors. Finally, in the ultimate sign of desperation, people were reduced to eating members of their own families. Thus a disaster like that which had visited the countryside of Henan in the 1580s and 1590s arrived at the capital city of Kaifeng only a half-century later.[66]

In October 1642, the slow but inexorable destruction of the people of Kaifeng came to an end—in a sudden and even more devastating catastrophe. As discussed in Chapter 1, the late-Ming state had basically maintained the massive dikes constructed to keep the river on its standard course to the east. As a result, there were continual small leaks, including one fifteen kilometers northwest of Kaifeng in 1636, but no major breaks resulting in disastrous floods. After June 1642, however, repairs of the south bank were no longer possible because the rebels dominated the area. More ominous yet, as early as June 25, the rebels had warned the inhabitants of the city that they could be flooded out. The rebels were confident that they could starve the defenders into submission, however, and so they had not acted on that threat. In August, the defenders of the city, desperate in the absence of relief from outside, decided to try to use the force of the river against the rebels outside the city walls. According to Bai Yu, who was there, the residents of Kaifeng had initiated the idea. In his words:

> The people of Bian were well aware of the power of the river. They recalled that some years before it had broken through at Heigang and had inundated the area where the

rebels were now camped. It could therefore meet current needs. They secretly petitioned the grand coordinator Gao Mingheng, who subsequently sent agents across the river to instruct the regional inspector, Yan Yunjing, to undertake the matter. He [Yan] then sent [general] Bu Congshan and his men by boat bridge to the south shore where they began to dig. After a day and a night, the bandits became aware of him and sent troops to drive him away.[67]

"The people of Kaifeng," very likely including the prince and the local elite, initiated serious discussion of this tactic, and the officials were the first to try to put it into effect. But the rebels soon took up the idea. They broke the dike at Zhujiazhai, and directed a stream south in an effort to flood the city. But they succeeded merely in raising the water level in the moats three or four feet and, ironically, supplied the starving residents of the city with fish.[68]

These efforts in the late summer, ineffective in the short run, may have weakened the dikes enough to cause a catastrophic break when the monsoon came in the fall. The Ming and the rebels may also have tried to use the river against each other again in the early fall. According to Grand Coordinator Gao Mingheng's biography in the *Ming History*, the decision to use the river against the rebels was approved by the Zhou prince. The prince had recently fortified the walls of his estate and he apparently believed that they would withstand any floodwaters that entered the city. According to this version of events, after the Ming forces cut into the dike at Zhujiazhai, due north of Kaifeng, the rebels made a break at Majiazhai, ten kilometers upstream. Recent research suggests that these cuts may have been made in September or October as both sides became increasingly desperate. Whatever the precise dates of these events and the relative degrees of Ming and rebel responsibility, it would appear that both sides sought to use the river for their own ends and thus contributed to the disaster. Nature did the rest. In September and October the rains came, perhaps more heavily than usual. On October 7, in the middle of the night, one kilometer of dike gave way at Zhujiakou and five hundred meters of dike crumbled at Majiakou. The breaks produced loud roars that carried all the way to Kaifeng city. The two resulting streams soon converged in a single rampaging torrent that smashed into the north wall of Kaifeng.[69]

Despite both sides' efforts to cut the dikes and their shared responsibility for the result, no one apparently expected—let alone intended—the total destruction of the city. Early sources and recent studies agree that the final catastrophe was in part a natural one. When heavy rains broke the dikes and brought water rushing toward the city on October 8, some of the rebel forces outside the city saw it coming and decamped quickly to the south, but tens of thousands of others were trapped north of the city and drowned. On October 9, the flood waters broke through the gates of the city and flowed through the streets; survivors reported that it sounded like the tolling of tens of thousands of bells. By October 10, the entire city was submerged in a broad river that flowed southeast into the Guo River, raising its level by fifty feet. According to Zheng Lian, who probably heard reports from survivors,

> One could see standing alone in the waves only the drum and bell towers, the ridges of the homes of some princes, the top of the Xiangguo Temple, the peaks of the Zhou estate, and the upper stories of the Iron Pagoda.[70]

One might also have seen a couple dozen boats, manned by Wang Xie and Hou Xun among others, going in and out to rescue the Zhou prince and hundreds of his attendants. Other officials, such as Gao Mingheng and Huang Shu, saved some residents in boats, but most people who survived the initial inundation had to rely on floating debris to stay above the waves and navigate their way to safety. According to the best estimates, both then and now, 10 to 20 percent of the population had starved to death during the siege and some 70 to 80 percent of the rest died in the flood. Assuming there had been about 370,000 people in the city before the third siege, some fifty thousand may have perished in the famine and some 240,000 were drowned in the flood. The total number of survivors of the double calamity may therefore have been only eighty thousand.

The ultimate causes and consequences of the inundation of Kaifeng naturally inspired a great deal of discussion. Zheng Lian ascribed the pitiless third siege of the city to Li Zicheng's personal vendetta against Chen Yongfu for having put out his eye and to the heavy casualties suffered by the rebels during the first two sieges of the city. Zheng claimed that there was even a ditty in the rebel camp calling for the destruction of the city, including the lines:

> Kaifeng must be attacked and destroyed,
> Not a person should be left.
> This will be the sweeping away of the head,
> The body can then be chopped up with the sword.[71]

In the same vein, one might suppose that Niu Jinxing's animosity to his estranged relative by marriage, Wang Shijun, contributed to the rebels' uncompromising assault on the city. Yet Zheng Lian believed that Li Zicheng wished to occupy the city and turn it into the center of his movement, just as Liu Bang had used Feng and Pei as the early center of his rebellion to overthrow the Qin and found the Han. If so, the flooding of the city was more reminiscent of Qin-style tactics and an inappropriate way to go about taking the city. In the end, Li Zicheng and Luo Rucai were forced by the desolation of Kaifeng to set off in search of an entirely different region to serve as a base for their movement to overthrow the Ming.

The Ming court, meanwhile, tried to put the best face on events by bestowing promotions and rewards on the defenders of the city. It promoted Gao Mingheng to vice president of the ministry of troops and bestowed on him forty taels; it made Wang Han grand coordinator of Henan; it raised Huang Shu to censor; it jumped Commander Chen Yongfu up two ranks and awarded him thirty taels; and it moved Prefect Wu Shijiang up a rank, gave him twenty taels, and transferred him out of the province. But the court also fell into a prolonged debate over who was to blame for the policy of tampering with the dikes that had contributed to the destruction of the city. Since the nobility refused all responsibility, and the tactic of blaming the rebels was not yet in evidence, the focus was on Gao, Huang, and Yan.[72]

If the rebels could claim victory because they had destroyed the center of Ming authority in Henan, and the state could be pleased because they had denied Li Zicheng a potential base for his rebellion, the people of Kaifeng and northeast Henan may have been less satisfied with the outcome. To be sure, the metropolitan graduate from Xiangfu, Zhou Lianggong, who had passed the summer of the siege in Jiangnan, agreed with his fellow Henanese scholar-official Wang Duo that "The defense of Bian ranked with that of Suiyang in the past, and it was Bian's achievement that Jiangnan was able to sleep in peace." In other words, the uncompromising resistance at Kaifeng, like that at Suiyang in the mid-Tang, had been worth it because it had spared the lower Yangzi cities from the rebels' wrath. Perhaps Zhou could more readily express enthusiasm for the all-out defense of Kaifeng because his son Zaijun had survived the disaster to write a diary of the events. But another metropolitan graduate of Xiangfu, Liu Chang, who contributed to the defense of Kaifeng and barely survived its destruction, joined the chorus of criticism of regional inspector Yan Yunjing for having adopted a policy that resulted in calamity for the inhabitants. A third metropolitan graduate of Xiangfu, Wang Zishou, wrote a long prose poem to record the details of the hardships imposed on the city by the long siege and sudden flood.[73] Zheng Lian later drew heavily on that verse to construct his narrative. That account tended to indict both the rebels and the Ming for the shared obduracy that had led to the catastrophe.

The so-called hero of Kaifeng, Li Guangtian, whose organization of the urban militia had earned him a promotion to university student but whose plan for armored carts had been vetoed, may have acquiesced in the flooding strategy; he was later reported to have used the wood assembled for the armed carts to make boats. Even after the disaster he was recommended by Judge Huang for his contributions to the defense and was appointed a county magistrate by the court. Li apparently never assumed that post; instead he moved to Jiangnan where, brokenhearted, he dictated his diary to his son. Near the end of his account he acknowledged that the result of his efforts had been "unprecedented pain and disaster." His final, despairing words were "Now Bianliang has become a marshland; what more is there to say?"[74]

Some members of the middle strata and masses blamed the destruction of Kaifeng more on the Ming than on the rebels. The anonymous minor functionary who wrote *Record as From a Dream* had lived through the horror of the siege and flood. He prefaced his book with bitter criticism of the Ming officials and local elite who had tried to use the river against the rebels. Some residents of the city were rescued from the flood by the rebels and were later fired on by Ming troops. They too found it easy to blame the Ming, and some of them not only exonerated the rebels but joined them as well.[75] In the eyes of most people of northeast Henan, however, the third siege of Kaifeng was not a victory for the Ming, nor was it one for the rebels. It was rather a defeat for the people of the region and a stalemate in the ongoing struggle for the mandate to rule the central plain.

In sum, Li Zicheng took advantage of conflicts between Ming officials and the local elite to infiltrate rebel troops into Shangqiu and take the town with relative ease, but he failed to keep his troops from carrying out a massacre that undermined his effort to win popular support. He apparently learned from that experience and negotiated a more peaceful end to Ming authority in neighboring Xiayi. Li also exploited the failure of the Ming magistrate and local elite to defend Qi county and asserted his authority there in concert with a minor functionary, members of the local elite, government students, and some of the rural masses. In the absence of support from his erstwhile ally Yuan Shizhong, but with the encouragement of his chief advisor Niu Jinxing, Li then undertook a third attack on Kaifeng. He succeeded in isolating the city and destroying Ming authority there but at the cost of contributing to a process that consigned hundreds of thousands of people to famine and flood. Although Li badly damaged Ming authority in the northeastern region of the central province, he was unable to establish his own influence in its place.

During this period, Henan province fully earned its reputation as the place where armies had to contend for the mandate. The only points at issue between Li Zicheng and his advisor from Qi, and between the Ming and its commander from Shangqiu, were precisely when and how authority over this region should be asserted and maintained so as to ensure the legitimacy and long life of their respective polities. The cultural and political centrality of northeast Henan approached a zenith even as the region's social and economic fortunes neared a nadir.

In contending for the central plain, Li and his opponents continued to invoke various historical precedents. A Ming general-turned-rebel presumably knew what he was doing when he sent a subordinate who resembled the Curly Bearded Stranger, a literary hero associated with the founding of the Tang, to overawe the people of Shangqiu. The Shangqiu magistrate similarly tapped into a consensus among opponents of the rebels when he cited the example of Zhang Xun's uncompromising resistance to the mid-Tang rebel An Lushan in his call for all-out opposition to Li Zicheng. In Qi a government student pointed to the experience of Zhu Wen, who settled for the principality of Liang at the end of the Tang to urge Li Zicheng to form a regional government that might eventually inherit the mandate from the Ming. The rebel leaders, however, insisted on a third frontal assault on Ming authority in Kaifeng and failed to invoke any historical models—much less compelling ones—to win the inhabitants to their standard. It was left to a diarist in the city to draw an analogy, however far-fetched, between the involuntary starvation of tens of thousands of urban residents who remained loyal to the Ming and the voluntary fasting-to-death of two rural recluses who remained loyal to the Shang.

Later historians, including some from outside the region, also debated the meaning of the events of 1642 in terms of various historical analogies. In describing the massacre in Shangqiu, the editors of the local gazetteer alluded to the rebels' origins in Shaanxi (Qin) by comparing their excesses in Shangqiu to those of a famous Qin general who killed many thousands of prisoners of war in his quest for the central plain. In an account of the devastation of Kaifeng by famine and flood, however, a Shangqiu historian concluded that the rebels were unlikely to have willed it because they hoped to use the city as a political base much as Liu Bang had used Feng and Pei during his campaign against the Qin. An editor of the *Four Treasuries* compared Li Guangtian's ill-fated project of armored carts with an equally unsuccessful plan of a mid-Tang tactician. But another writer compared Li Guangtian favorably with a more successful late-Tang leader of the opposition to rebels. Thus continued to unfold in the central plain and elsewhere the association between the late-Ming rebellions and various Tang antecedents that would increasingly shape both history and historiography.

SEVEN

The Rise of the Shun, 1643–44

FACING STALEMATE IN THE CENTRAL PROVINCE in early 1643, Li Zicheng withdrew from Kaifeng in northeast Henan and moved his headquarters to Xiangyang in northwest Huguang. There he courted scholars, established a rudimentary administration, and appointed local officials in Huguang and Henan. He adopted measures to win broad popular support, eliminated rival rebels, and developed links with scholars and officials in Xiayi and Kaifeng that would later develop into metaphors for the rise and fall of his movement. Late in the year he returned in force to Henan, defeated a major Ming army sent from Shaanxi under Sun Chuanting, and went west to his native Shaanxi. There he seized his first provincial capital, Xi'an, and formally inaugurated a regional state. Clearly ambitious to found a new dynasty, he held examinations to recruit new personnel and appointed local officials in northern Henan. He then advanced through Shanxi and Beizhili to take Beijing in April 1644. During the next several weeks, he carried out reforms in the capital and extended his authority to Guide prefecture and much of the rest of the central plain.

Despite his success in dealing the Ming a blow that would eventually prove fatal, Li refrained from declaring himself son of heaven, apparently in an effort to placate erstwhile Ming officials in the capital and generals in the surrounding areas. But having passed up an opportunity to make a deal with the Qing state rising in the northeast, he now encountered the resistance of wealthy and powerful officials in Beijing and failed to win over the Ming general Wu Sangui at Shanhaiguan. On June 3 he finally ascended the throne and declared the Da Shun dynasty, but the very next day he was forced to vacate Beijing and retreat to Xi'an. In the three-way competition among the Ming, the Shun, and the Qing for the mandate to rule China, the Ming and the Shun both lost out, and the Qing, invoking historical precedents of its own, emerged the winner. But that is another story.

After Yuan Shizhong had split with Li Zicheng in Qi county on the eve of the third siege of Kaifeng, he had fled to the east with only a few cavalry. Thereafter, lured by the possibility of amnesty from the Ming, he returned to Guide where, according to Zheng Lian, "he refrained from killing people and simply collected resources and supporters." Indeed, in an apparent effort to regain the confidence of Ming officials and the populace, Yuan defeated a "local bandit" named Li Zhenhai and drove him from the area.[1]

Meanwhile the Ming commander Yang Wenyue, based in Xiayi at the head of several thousand troops, offered Yuan amnesty if he would agree to surrender and cooperate with the campaign to suppress Li Zicheng. When Yuan went to Xiayi in September 1642 to discuss terms, he became aware of the poor quality of Yang's troops and hesitated. Yuan's growing forces also clashed with those of the Zhending commander Liu Chao, the disgruntled military graduate from Yongcheng county who was nominally subordinate to Yang (see Chapter 3). Angry at what he considered to be bad faith, Yuan seized Yang's emissary, the magistrate of Xiayi, and had him publicly horsewhipped. Yang sent troops to rescue the hapless magistrate and chased Yuan away to Bozhou. In October the Ming commanders Huang Degong and Liu Liangzuo defeated Yuan in Yingshang and forced him to take refuge once again in the mountains (see Map 7.1).[2]

After the destruction of Kaifeng, Yuan distanced himself even more from the Ming. Although he had established an uneasy truce with Li Xu, a tributary student and militia head in Yingzhou, Nanzhili, he became increasingly suspicious of those who remained loyal to the dynasty. Yuan's subordinate, Li Kui, who had lost men to Li Xu in the past, openly urged Yuan to destroy the militia leader. Yuan finally agreed and adopted the classic method of inviting Li Xu to a banquet, plying him with drink, and having him killed.[3] By such measures, Yuan maintained a political position somewhere between the Ming and Li Zicheng.

Commander Liu Chao, meanwhile, had begun to carve out his own sphere of influence in Yongcheng. Unhappy with the rewards he had received for service in Guizhou and unsuccessful in pleading his case in Beijing, he had returned to Yongcheng as militia head. There he had soon encountered further trouble. According to one story, he had followed the example of Magistrate Liang in Shangqiu and had attempted to defend Yongcheng from bandits by exercising strict control over its inhabitants. When the relatives of a provincial graduate, Qiao Mingzhan, violated the rules by going outside the city walls, Liu threatened to punish them according to the law. A local metropolitan graduate, Wei Jingqi, dissuaded him and soon thereafter replaced him as head of the militia. Liu's resentment had grown. During the third siege of Kaifeng, he was authorized to lead six thousand local recruits to relieve the provincial capital and was named regional commander of Zhending. Once again he had encountered opposition from the Yongcheng local elite who had argued that he was not qualified for the post. In the end Liu neither assumed the post nor went to the aid of Kaifeng. Liu had also come into conflict with Yuan Shizhong, thereby impeding official efforts to bring that rebel back into the Ming fold. In November 1642 Liu was impeached for incompetence and for "having contacts with bandits," an ironic fate given his hostility to Yuan and Yuan's contacts with the Ming.[4]

Liu became enraged when he learned that the local scholars Wei and Qiao were behind the new charges. He first led his men to Wei's home and assassinated him along with twenty-nine of his relatives. He then rushed to Qiao's place and killed him, too.

MAP 7.1. The Rise of the Shun from Kaifeng to Xiangyangfu. Source: Tan 1975: 7: 80–83. Used with permission from The Chinese Map Society (Zhonghua ditu xueshe).

Aware that such crimes against members of the local elite would bring strict punishment, Liu sought advice from Lian Guoshi, the former Ming official and prominent member of the local elite. Lian scolded Liu and warned him he would never escape punishment after exterminating a whole family, but Lian was either too sympathetic or too frightened to take action against him. Liu Chao next confronted Hou Fangyu, who was passing through Yongcheng on his way to Nanjing, and sought his counsel. Hou urged Liu to volunteer to defend the court or to offer his services to his father, Hou Xun, who was still supreme commander. Liu rejected Hou's advice but released him and allowed him to proceed to Nanjing. Liu also consulted Ma Shiying, the regional commander at Fengyang, who advised him to redeem himself in the eyes of the Ming by killing some bandits and then submitting himself to the regular process of justice. Liu also ignored this advice, apparently believing that his close relations with Lian and past service in Ma's home province of Guizhou would deter the authorities from arresting him.[5]

In late 1642, in an obvious effort to regain control after the fiasco in Kaifeng, the Ming appointed a new set of officials to the region. Wang Han, who had distinguished himself as magistrate and censor, already held the top provincial post of grand coordinator. Su Jing, the erstwhile magistrate of Qi and supervisor of troops, became regional inspector. Li Yan, the former magistrate of Hua in Beizhili who had driven Yuan Shizhong from the county and had subsequently been considered for ministerial posts in Beijing, was made prefect of Kaifeng. Sang Kaidi, an official in the Kaifeng river conservancy, became prefect of Guide.[6]

The supreme commander Hou Xun, whose plan to give up Henan to save the Ming had been shelved, had initially been stationed in Fengqiu, north of the Yellow River. Soon he led a small band of retainers 150 kilometers east to Cao, the home county of Liu Zeqing. Hou's relations with Liu had long been volatile. Hou's chief lieutenant, Qiu Lei, and his undisciplined troops soon fell out with Liu Zeqing and his own ill-trained subordinates. When Liu sent government students to confront Hou Xun about his men's depredations, Hou was annoyed and had one of them beaten. Liu retaliated by marching on Hou's camp, ultimately driving him fifty kilometers farther to the east, to Dan county. Soon Hou was impeached by the Zhou prince for having failed to save Kaifeng and by Liu Zeqing for plundering Shandong. Hou's assistant Qiu Lei was arrested and sent to Huai'an, where he was executed.[7]

As Ming authority in northeast Henan gravitated into new hands, Li Zicheng and Luo Rucai left the region and headed south. Along the way they asserted, or recovered, their influence in many counties, including Sishui and Changge in Kaifeng, Mengjin and Gong in Henan, Jia and Baofeng in Ruzhou, and Xiping and Suiping in Runing (see Map 7.1). In November, the Shaanxi commander Sun Chuanting finally led Ming forces from Shaanxi into western Henan only to suffer defeat at the hands of the rebels in Nanyang. In December Li Zicheng and Luo Rucai gained the support of three other rebels, including one He Yilong. At the end of the year, the rebels assaulted Ruyang, the capital of Runing prefecture, killed the Ming commander Yang Wenyue, and captured the Chong prince, Zhu Youkui. In the first month of 1643, they marched south through Runing and Nanyang and entered Huguang.[8]

Establishing a Base: Xiangyang/Xiangjing

Unlike Kaifeng, Xiangyang was not a provincial capital, let alone a former capital of a major dynasty. But it was a well-known strategic town on a north-south highway and a commercial entrepôt located at the intersection of small rivers from southern Henan with the Han River, which then flowed southeast into the Yangzi. Control of the town had changed many times in recent years, but it had been occupied for the last six months by Zuo Liangyu. Although the site was quite defensible, Zuo, as usual, refused to risk his men to hold it. He departed before Li Zicheng arrived and hurried southeast to Jiujiang. Hou Fangyu, in Nanjing, wrote to Zuo imploring him to follow the example of Guo Ziyi and Li Guangbi, generals who had saved the Tang from An Lushan by upholding the Ming against Li Zicheng. Zuo responded by improving the discipline of his troops, but he refused to deploy them to stop Li Zicheng. The rebels therefore took Xiangyang on January 23, 1643, without firing a shot; some said they were welcomed by the people with offerings of meat and wine.[9]

On February 20 the rebels took Chengtian. When the Huguang grand coordinator refused to surrender, the rebels summarily killed him. The Huguang regional inspector, Li Zhensheng, whom they captured on the same day, was a different matter. Li Zhensheng had served as a magistrate in Yancheng, Henan, where he had suppressed a sectarian rebellion (see Chapter 4). But he was a metropolitan graduate from Mizhi, Li Zicheng's home county in northern Shaanxi. When Chengtian fell, Li Zhensheng neither fought to the death nor committed suicide. Li Zicheng believed that he might be won over to the rebel standard.[10]

Li Zicheng's wooing of Li Zhensheng illustrates both his eagerness to enlist support of Ming scholar-officials and the obstacles he faced in doing so. According to an eyewitness account, when Li Zhensheng was brought before Li Zicheng, the rebel leader pointed out that they shared the same surname and hailed from the same county. Li Zicheng addressed the former Ming official respectfully as "Censor Li" and "elder brother." Li Zhensheng rejected these ploys and demanded to know how he could be related to a bandit who had rampaged from Shaanxi to Huguang and who would soon be suppressed by government troops. Li Zicheng merely smiled and replied: "Elder brother is making a mistake." He offered his captive some wine, but Li Zhensheng poured it on the ground and said he was ready to die. The rebel leader then ordered that the scholar–official be kept under close guard so that nothing would happen to him.[11]

Li Zhensheng was thereafter well supplied with food and drink, but when he got drunk he would curse the rebels in a loud voice. When he heard that Li Zicheng was consulting diviners and organizing an administration, he declared that he could no longer live in the same world as the bandits and demanded to see their leader. Thinking that Li Zhensheng wished to advise him on the formation of his government, Li Zicheng arranged a banquet and a musical performance. Li Zhensheng, however, surprised his host by breaking into a discourse on the difference between loyalty and rebellion and announcing that he had come to offer his head. Li Zicheng was clearly annoyed but, once again, merely smiled and warned his captive to be careful. Li Zhensheng insisted that he would never rebel against the Ming and merely wanted to die, but Li Zicheng kept him at his headquarters under close guard "like an enemy state." Only when rumors arose that Li Zhensheng had secretly established contacts with Ming generals did Li Zicheng give up trying to win him over. In sadness as much as anger he finally ordered him to be taken outside the city wall and executed. According to an eyewitness, Li Zhensheng died heroically, announcing that he was not like the Henanese scholars Niu Jinxing and Kong Shangda, who had joined the rebels to save their skins. Rumors nonetheless arose that Li Zhensheng surrendered to Li Zicheng and later became vice president of the rebel ministry of troops in Beijing. The rebels may have encouraged those rumors as part of their efforts to win other literati to their movement. Although false, they were also widely accepted by historians who may have seen Li Zhensheng's surrender as a metaphor for growing links between the rebels and former Ming officials and elite.[12]

Although Li Zhensheng's dying words may have been apocryphal, they alluded accurately to Li Zicheng's success in winning over other literati, including several from northeast Henan. In addition to Niu Jinxing there was Kong Shangda, a sixty-fourth generation descendant of Kongzi, who hailed from Taikang county. Kong Shangda was the cousin of Kong Shangyue, who had called for an "equal fields" reform in 1640. Kong Shangda had obtained his provincial degree in 1639, the same year as Wu Boyi of Shangqiu, whose death at the hands of the rebels he had witnessed. Unlike Wu, Kong survived and appeared in the rebel camp in Xiangyang, although the existing records shed no light on his motives, activities, or fate. There were also two government students, Tian Zhujiao from Guide and Zhang Yuji from Kaifeng, who showed up at the rebel headquarters in Xiangyang and were appointed rebel prefects of Dean and Jingzhou in Huguang.[13]

Another government student, Chen Mingsheng from Shangqiu, witnessed the saga of Li Zhensheng in Xiangyang and later reported it to Zheng Lian. Chen had been captured during the battle of Shangqiu by a rebel named Jin Gang. Proud, strong, and a good talker, Chen reportedly found a niche in the rebel movement as a cook, a position he held in Xiangyang. Even after his patron Jin Gang died in battle in Henan in 1643, Chen stayed with the rebels and was promoted to advisor. Only after tiring of conflict among the leaders, perhaps as late as 1644, did Chen decide to leave the rebel movement and return home.[14]

In addition to wooing and winning over members of the elite and middle strata, the rebels at Xiangyang sought the support of the masses. When they took Huangbei county in Huangzhou prefecture they sought to exploit public resentment against the abuses of Ming troops by propagating the slogan "Suppress the troops and bring peace to the people." In 1641 they had promised to waive taxes for all who surrendered; in 1642 they reduced taxes 50 percent in some places and suspended them for three years in others. In 1643 they encouraged ditties, some of them ribald, to popularize these policies. For example, people were encouraged to chant:

> Wear his mother's, eat his mother's,
> Open the gates, welcome the brothers.
> When Dashing Prince comes,
> We'll have no tax bothers.

Another ballad went:

> Kill the swine, prepare the wine,
> Open the gates, form a welcome line,
> When Dashing Prince comes,
> We won't pay a dime.

The origin and date of these "popular" pieces of propaganda are difficult to determine. The songs seem to have become more numerous and widespread in Xiangyang in 1643. Presumably, they reflected the rebels' intensified efforts to win public sympathy more than any spontaneous outpouring of popular support for their movement.[15]

Li Zicheng's men had asserted their basic social ideology in the 1641 slogan "Pare the rich to succor the poor." Although they adopted no clear policy to redistribute land, they gained a reputation in northeast Henan for promoting some degree of social leveling. In 1642, for example, many wealthy and powerful families of Chenliu and Suizhou fled their homes, leaving their lands to poorer neighbors who had fewer reasons or occasions to depart. In Yanling, Xihua, Ningling, Shangqiu, and Luyi, lands for schools, temples, and shrines—normally managed by the local elite and landlords—fell into the hands of small holders and tenants. Although the rebels did not openly incite the poor against the rich, tenants in Yanling took advantage of the disorder to press claims against landlords. As a result, many landlords were killed or fled, allowing their property to pass into the hands of others. By the end of the rebellion, for example, 19 percent of the land in Linying and 37 percent of the land in Xihua was without owners or lay fallow. According to a diary of a government student, servants and tenants in Qi county, which was under strong rebel influence in 1643, evinced new confidence in dealing with their masters. In Xiangyang the rebels offered oxen and seed to poor farmers and provided grain to the landless. Such land transfers and relief measures may have given rise to rumors in 1643 that the rebels pursued a concerted policy of "equalizing fields" (*juntian*).[16]

From his base in Xiangyang, Li Zicheng called for assaults on prominent symbols of elite affluence in a time of mass penury. During the Wanli period, local officials and elite had erected many memorial arches for literati and chaste women, causing thoughtful scholars such as Lü Kun to warn that they imposed heavy burdens on the masses. Such admonitions, however, had been widely ignored and such structures continued to be constructed and repaired. By the end of the Ming, there were more than one hundred memorial arches in Yuzhou and more than seventy in Shangqiu. During the rebellions many were destroyed, in some cases by rebels who regarded them as symbols of wasteful conspicuous consumption, in others by militia who used the materials to build stockades. In 1641, for example, the rebels destroyed the Kongzi temple in Chenliu. In 1642 they razed temples, schools, and memorial arches in two counties of Kaifeng and three counties of Guide. In 1643 Li Zicheng formally authorized an all-out attack on such institutions. In line with this policy, a Kongzi temple in Yancheng that had been restored by Magistrate Li Zhensheng was destroyed along with shrines and memorial arches in four other counties of Kaifeng. These attacks may have been welcomed by some of the middle strata and masses who resented the use of temples to accumulate and perpetuate elite wealth. They probably also alienated some members of the local elite, middle strata, and masses who took pride in the achievements of local sons and daughters and who participated in the spiritual life of the shrines and temples. Significantly, Niu Jinxing, the chief elite advisor to the rebels, intervened to prevent the destruction of the Kongzi temple in his hometown, and even Li Zicheng issued instructions to protect the temples in his home province. As in the Cultural Revolution in more recent times, elite and commoner rebels alike tended to protect cultural institutions in their home regions and focus their iconoclasm on sites located elsewhere. However, it was a local rebel, not Li Zicheng, who destroyed a temple in Kaocheng as late as 1644.[17]

While destroying signs of the old order, the rebels adopted symbols of a new one. Li Zicheng assumed the more elevated title of "Great Civil and Military Commander Commissioned by Heaven to Promote Justice," and Luo Rucai took the title "Great Majestic and Virtuous General who Assists Heaven in Soothing the People." At this time, Li may also have begun using a new title, "New Prince of Accord" (*xin shunwang*). The term "accord" was perhaps an allusion to the "Great Accord" (*Da Shun*) reign at the end of the Tang; the term "prince" no doubt reflected incipient interest in establishing a territorial base. Niu Jinxing assumed the post of prime minister in the rebel regime, reviving an office that dated from Qin times but had been abolished in the early Ming. Niu's son, Quan, was appointed rebel prefect of Xiangyang. Li Zicheng's fellow provincial, Liu Zongmin, was made assistant commander in chief of the army.[18]

In March and April 1643, the rebels began to establish a bureaucracy based on that of the Ming but using "new" terms, significantly including some borrowed from the Tang. They set up the six ministries that had become standard since the Tang, simply replacing the term boards with the new term offices. They established regional civil and military officials, as in the Ming, but renamed them defense commissioners, as in the Tang. They appointed prefects after Ming practice but used Tang titles for the offices. They changed the names of departmental officials from *zhi*, used in the Ming, to *mu*, used for governors in the Tang. In another allusion to the Tang, they changed the term for county magistrates from *zhi*, used in the Ming, to *ling*, used in the Tang. The rebels followed the Ming military structure by establishing five guards located at Yuzhou, Runing, Xiangyang, Jingzhou, and Chengtian. They named the first and third ranks of their military officers after comparable positions in the Tang army and the fourth and fifth ranks after those of the Han.[19]

The rebels also changed place names to celebrate their achievements and highlight their ambitions. They altered Xiangyang to Xiangjing, to denote its new function as a capital, and renamed Xiangyang prefecture Changyi (literally, inaugurating justice), a concept already embedded in Li Zicheng's title. They changed Chengtian, originally named to commemorate the accession of a Ming prince to the throne, to Yangwu, signifying the rebels' military success. They changed the name of Dean prefecture to Anle, emphasizing happiness (*le*) over virtue (*de*). They promoted Yunmeng county to a department and renamed it Gu (fixed) to express the hope that their regime would prove durable.[20]

The rebels changed the names and statuses of places in Henan for a variety of reasons. They renamed Yuzhou (previously called Junzhou 鈞州 after the pottery made there) to the partially homophonous Junping (均平 peace and equality) to express their egalitarian ethos. They rewarded the residents of the town for their early support by promoting the department to a prefecture. In an apparent effort to replace devastated Kaifeng as the political center of the province, they gave Junping prefecture responsibility for no less than twenty-seven subordinate counties. They changed the name of Baofeng (precious and abundant; denoting the large amounts of iron it had produced in the Song) to the more simple and accurate Bao. They also promoted it to a department, probably to honor its native son Niu Jinxing. They reduced Yushi, which traced its name to the Song, to Yu, following the practice of the early Tang, and raised its status to department. They modified Shenqiu, first called that in the Tang, into Shenping, to retain the link to the Tang and add the values of peace and equality.

During what we may now call the Xiangjing period, the rebels also appointed local officials, of whom about half were sent to Henan. Of the Henan cohort, again, almost half were posted to the northeast region, suggesting that it remained an important part of the developing rebel base area (see Map 7.2). They created six prefectures, of which half were in Henan and one, Junpingfu, was in the northeast region. They sent magistrates to nineteen departments, including ten in Henan, of which four were in the northeast. They set up sixty-five counties, of which thirty-eight were in Henan, including fourteen in the northeast.[21] Thus, despite their failure to capture Kaifeng city and several neighboring counties, the rebels were able to assert their authority in some eighteen counties of southwestern Kaifeng prefecture.

In the early years in Henan, the rebels had appointed local men to administrative posts in Yiyang and Luoyang, but by 1643 they controlled enough territory to recruit and appoint men from outside the counties and provinces where they served. Of the thirteen men appointed to Henan whose origins are known, twelve were from Huguang and one was from Zhejiang. (Of course the heavy preponderance of Huguang men reflected the rebels' current, still quite restricted, base in that province.) Information about the rebel officials in northeast Henan is more limited, but of the five appointees whose origins are known, four (in Junping prefecture and Chen department) came from outside Henan and only one (in Yan county) came from within Henan. Of the nineteen rebel appointees to Henan during the period 1641 to 1643 whose credentials are known, one was a metropolitan graduate, nine were provincial graduates, two were university students, and seven were government students. Of the four known appointees to the northeast, one was a provincial graduate and three were government students. Many of the rebel officials' qualifications approximated those of Ming appointees in the region, but the presence of government students even in the important post of prefect of Junping suggested that the rebels had fewer members of the elite at their disposition or that they wished to bring more members of the middle strata into their administration. Some of the rebel officials whose backgrounds are obscure and whose names are unknown may also have been commoners, perhaps even members of the masses. Finally, three of the rebel appointees to northeast Henan were arrested—one was turned in by the local elite and one was captured as early as November 1643—suggesting that they were considered a serious threat to the Ming state and, at the same time, had only a tenuous grip on power.[22]

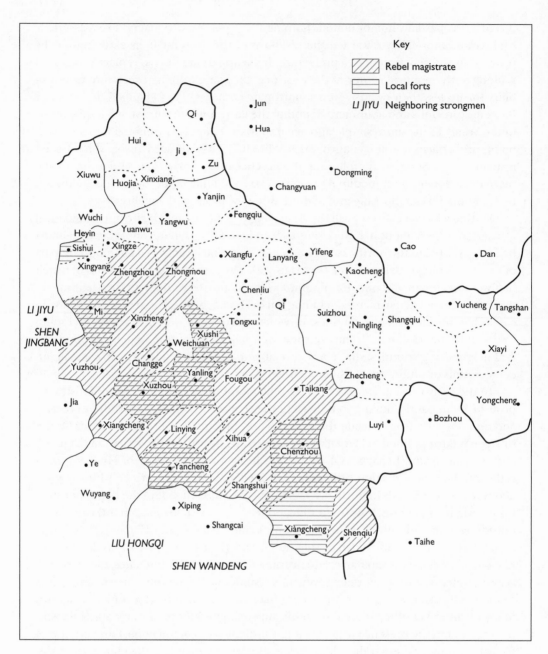

MAP 7.2. Counties and Departments of Kaifeng Prefecture, Including Locations of Rebel Magistrates, Local Forts, and Neighboring Strongmen, 1643. Source: based on data in Liu Yinan 1983: 334–42; Wang Xingya 1984b: 195–98.

Although Li Zicheng established a fledgling administration in Xiangjing by mid-1643, he continued to compete with other rebels for influence in the region between the Yellow and Yangzi Rivers. To the south, Zhang Xianzhong was setting up his own regime at Wuchang. Although Li had once cooperated with Zhang and sent him a congratulatory letter as late as 1643, he continued to treat him as a rival and thus forfeited any chance to ally with him against the Ming. Closer to home, Li Zicheng also became estranged from his erstwhile comrade-in-arms Luo Rucai. Li had always been more skilled in strategy, more sober in judgment, and more committed to establishing a base in the central plain than Luo. Luo was said to be more talented in fighting, more given to drink, and more determined to march directly to Beijing. During the last year, the two men had complemented each other and had subordinated their differences to the common task of challenging the Ming. During the third siege of Kaifeng, however, Li had learned that Luo had received an offer of amnesty from Grand Coordinator Gao Mingheng. He thereafter became suspicious of his lieutenant. Li was also reportedly jealous of Luo's close ties with the rebel leader He Yilong, who had joined them en route to Huguang. In March 1643, Li became even more concerned when one of his subordinates reported that Luo had had secret contacts with Zuo Liangyu. Although Li should have known that Zuo posed little real threat to the rebels and he had no proof that Luo contemplated surrender to the Ming, he worried about any sign of potential disloyalty as he prepared for a rematch with Sun Chuanting in Shaanxi. In late April, therefore, Li moved to prevent any divisions within his ranks by inviting Luo Rucai and He Yilong to a banquet and ruthlessly executing them.[23]

Li Zicheng's assassination of Luo Rucai and He Yilong had mixed consequences both in history and in historiography. On the one hand, Li was able to incorporate many of his erstwhile allies' forces into his own, thus greatly increasing the size of the army under his personal command. On the other hand, some of those men had fled and found sanctuary among the troops of Zuo Liangyu to the east and Sun Chuanting to the west, thus strengthening Li's adversaries. By these killings, Li demonstrated that he was brutal enough to be a new ruler, but he also frightened followers into paying closer attention to their own interests. The Shangqiu historian Zheng Lian, who had been a captive of Luo Rucai, acknowledged his contributions to the rebellion but decried his inconstancy. He suggested that Luo, although nicknamed Cao Cao, proved to be more akin to Lü Bu, the general who had finally been killed by his superior, the historical Cao Cao. Noting that Luo was naive in believing that "bandits do not kill bandits," Zheng shed few tears for his former captor. Perhaps reflecting more recent struggles between Mao Zedong and his subordinates, Chinese historians today are more critical of Li Zicheng and partial to Luo Rucai. Even those who recognize Li's need to "unify the rebel leadership" criticize his susceptibility to "landlord manipulation" (in other words, the efforts of officials and elite to encourage mutual suspicions among the rebels) and his "peasant methods" (brute force) in dealing with suspected rivals and opponents.[24]

While consolidating his personal control in Xiangjing, Li Zicheng had an opportunity to ally with Liu Chao, the regional commander in Yongcheng who had mutinied after quarreling with the local elite over the defense of the county. As discussed above, Liu had used contacts with other members of the local elite to stave off punishment. In

February 1643, however, Wang Han, the newly appointed grand coordinator of Henan, decided to lead forces from his headquarters in Huaiqing to put down Liu Chao's mutiny. Wang Han was the highest authority in the province and was known to be an effective official. When he arrived in Yongcheng, therefore, members of the local elite who had previously sheltered Liu Chao opened the gates. Wang Han then climbed the wall to appeal to the populace to abandon their support of Liu Chao. Liu had apparently made careful preparations for this moment, however, and his men suddenly attacked and killed Wang Han. The assassination of Grand Coordinator Wang Han sent shock waves through the province. Liu Chao knew that he would be executed if captured, and thus he became even bolder. He asserted direct control over all troops in Yongcheng and killed anyone who resisted.[25]

According to Zheng Lian, Liu Chao also considered leading his forces west to join Li Zicheng in a common front against the Ming. If Li Zicheng had reached out to Liu Chao at this time, he might have secured an important new ally. Li was preoccupied with eliminating a suspected rival in Xiangjing, however, and did not seize the opportunity. Liu Chao, for his part, was said to be having a problem with his foot that made it difficult for him to ride horseback. In any case, the Yellow River, now flowing southeast in a broad swath between Yongcheng and Runing, inhibited passage in either direction (see Map 7.1). Liu and his followers also apparently believed they stood the best chance of defending against further Ming assaults if they stayed in their home county. In the end, therefore, Liu Chao did not reach out to Li Zicheng.

Facing the most direct possible challenge to its authority in Henan, the Ming was determined to suppress Liu Chao once and for all. It ordered Chen Yongfu and his son Chen De, the stalwart defenders of Kaifeng against Li Zicheng, the eunuch commander Lu Jiude, who had long experience in the area, and the commanders Huang Degong and Liu Liangzuo, subordinates of Ma Shiying based in the Huai valley, to converge on Yongcheng to crush the mutiny. The court also authorized the regional commander Ma Shiying at Fengyang to negotiate with Liu Chao and to promise him anything to obtain his surrender. In the course of these discussions, Liu reportedly asked why he was being attacked when the robber Yuan Shizhong had long been allowed to cause trouble and go free. Ma replied that Liu was a Ming officer and had greater responsibilities than the bandit Yuan, but he hinted that Liu might yet be granted an amnesty after the law was restored in Yongcheng. In a last ploy, Liu asked Lian Guoshi and Ding Kuichu to write another letter guaranteeing his behavior if he were granted immunity from prosecution. Ma accepted the letter, granted Liu immunity, and persuaded him to surrender on those terms. When Liu Chao came out of the Yongcheng gate to give up, however, General Huang Degong denounced him as a "rebel official," pounced on him from behind, and slit his throat. Perhaps to obscure this treachery—which, of course, merely echoed Liu Chao's own—official reports claimed that Liu Chao was captured and sent to Beijing for trial where he was found guilty of rebellion and decapitated on July 26, 1643.[26]

After Li Zicheng neglected the chance to ally with Liu Chao to extend his sway to Guide, he might still have made up with Yuan Shizhong to expand his authority in Kaifeng. Unable to continue his usual practice of moving back and forth between Kaifeng and Guide, Yuan had settled down in the market towns of southern Qi county. According to Zheng Lian, he continued to refrain from killing people and setting fires and instead "devoted himself to engaging scholars, collecting grain, and winning the people's hearts and minds."[27] Three scholars from Qi advised Yuan, who treated them as guests. Although Zheng Lian reported that they invoked astronomical signs in efforts to persuade Yuan to leave the county, the rebel regarded them as supportive and made them his commanders and counselors. Yuan later engaged another local man, Yu Longmen (dragon gate Yu), as an advisor, and built up an army of ten to twenty thousand men. Still, with only two thousand horsemen, he was no match for Li Zicheng.

Yuan Shizhong had mistrusted Li Zicheng ever since Li had killed Yang Wenyue, the Ming commander who had once offered Yuan amnesty. He therefore continued negotiations with Ming officials. In January 1643, a government student was reported to have cajoled Yuan into surrendering to the Ming. When Manchu forces raided Shandong in the spring of 1643, Yuan was also said to have led troops to protect the Lu prince. Although the validity of these reports has been challenged, Yuan Shizhong was clearly still trying to please the Ming state, if only to ensure his own survival. Having once offered Grand Coordinator Wang Han assistance in suppressing Liu Chao, Yuan now volunteered to help Regional Inspector Su Jing avenge Wang Han's death by bringing Liu Chao to justice. In the course of discussions, however, Yuan indicated a desire to lead his forces north across the Yellow River. Since that route was away from any confrontation with Liu Chao, Su Jing suspected that Yuan was simply afraid of Li Zicheng and had no real intention of helping to put down Liu Chao. Su nonetheless offered amnesty to Yuan if he captured the strongman Li Jiyu, who was allied with Li Zicheng, and if he arrested the next emissary from Li Zicheng and turned him over to the Ming for punishment.[28]

Li Zicheng kept sending agents to win Yuan back, and thus Yuan had ample opportunity to carry out his part of the bargain. When Li's next emissary, a government student from Fugou county, arrived, Yuan promptly arrested him and sent him to Su Jing to be executed. Angered by Yuan's betrayal, Li Zicheng sent several hundred cavalry north to intimidate him. Yuan's men managed to kill one of Li's officers and took three others captive. He reported his "victory" to Su Jing and proudly depicted himself as a "suppressor of bandits." When Li Zicheng learned about Yuan's latest defiance, he sent a much larger force to besiege his camp. Perhaps because Yuan had yet to deliver Li Jiyu, or perhaps because Su's promises had been hollow from the beginning, Yuan's appeals to Su for assistance went unanswered. Yuan's diviners rightly proclaimed the signs inauspicious. Yuan refused to concede, however, and instead led his forces into battle. After suffering defeat, he retreated with a few hundred cavalry to the northern part of Yuzhen township. There he and his closest supporters were finally surrounded by Li's forces and exterminated. Some ten thousand (in other words, many) of Yuan's troops thereupon surrendered and joined the forces of Li Zicheng. Others went over to a Ming army under the erstwhile Qi county magistrate Lü Xiru and the regional inspector Su Jing. Little Yuan's Brigade, long a major ally and alternative to Li Zicheng in northeast Henan, was no more.[29]

Li Zicheng's elimination of Yuan Shizhong had mixed consequences. It strengthened Li's hand as the leading challenger to the Ming in the region. The local historian Zheng Lian compared Yuan with Xiang Yu, the aristocrat who ended the Qin but lost the civil war to Liu Bang, suggesting that Li Zicheng emerged from the confrontation as the clear winner. Historians in China today have little sympathy for Yuan Shizhong's recurrent negotiations with the Ming and his failure to distinguish friends such as Li Zicheng from enemies such as Su Jing. The possibility of a reconciliation between Li and Yuan had greatly worried the Ming, and Yuan's death brought that threat to an end, strengthening Ming authority in the area. Satō Fumitoshi has suggested that Yuan's support among the landed social strata and his participation in the Ming defense against the Manchus made him a kind of "nationalist" hero in contrast to Li Zicheng, the more "radical" leader of the masses against the state.[30] Whatever his ultimate historical role, Yuan Shizhong's elimination in the short term left the Ming and Li Zicheng as the main contenders for authority in northeast Henan.

Although Li Zicheng failed to ally with a leader from a middle stratum in Yongcheng and a rebel from the masses in Qi, he seems to have reached out to a member of the elite in Xiayi and possibly even to an official in Kaifeng. As discussed in Chapter 6, Li Zicheng had taken Xiayi in 1642 without a fight. He also faced little resistance from the last Ming prefect of Xiangyang, Wang Jiean, who happened to have been a 1634 metropolitan graduate from Xiayi. Li's positive connection to Xiayi was strengthened further in the person of one Peng Xialing. Born in Lushan county in 1616, Peng had become a government student at fifteen and had studied with Niu Jinxing. He had passed the provincial examinations in 1634 but had allegedly "violated the regulations." He was therefore put on the supplementary list, making him ineligible to receive his degree or hold office. The grand coordinator was aware of his talent and recommended him for a post, but the request was ignored by higher officials. In 1639 Peng retook the provincial examinations, but again he was placed on the supplementary list. As with the case of Hou Fangyu in the same year, Peng's failure likely had more to do with literary style and political opinion than with sheer incompetence or inadvertent error. Significantly, a similar offense had prevented Peng Xialing's uncle, Peng Yaoyu of Xiayi, from getting a provincial degree.[31]

After these setbacks in Lushan, Peng Xialing moved to Xiayi to live with his uncle Peng Yaoyu and his cousin Peng Shunling. When Grand Coordinator Wang Han was killed by Liu Chao's men in neighboring Yongcheng, his funeral cortege passed through Xiayi. Peng Yaoyu, a famous writer, drafted a poem to celebrate Wang Han's achievements and to mourn his death. The poem was copied and widely circulated in the region. According to Zheng Lian, someone changed the words of Peng's piece in a way that made it seem sympathetic to Liu Chao's revolt. Because the Pengs were close associates of Lian Guoshi, the metropolitan graduate and prominent literatus who had been remarkably tolerant of Liu's mutiny, Peng may well have used his verse to praise both Wang Han and Liu Chao, thus casting aspersions on the Ming, for whom they had both died. In any case, according to Zheng Lian, the regional inspector and censor Su Jing, who was involved in suppressing Liu Chao and courting Yuan Shizhong, charged Peng Yaoyu with calumny and imprisoned him along with his nephew Peng Shunling. When Peng Xialing complained to the Xiayi magistrate, he too was arrested and jailed. At this point,

Peng Xialing reportedly wrote to his former teacher, Niu Jinxing, and requested his help in getting out of jail. In return, Peng promised Niu, now the rebel prime minister, that he would do his best to help him in his current enterprise. Niu raised the matter with Li Zicheng, who was only too happy to send a small detachment to liberate all three Pengs. Li then reportedly invited Peng Xialing to an audience and offered him a high post in the rebel administration.[32]

As might be expected in a saga linking a literatus of northeast Henan to a rebel who ultimately failed to establish an enduring state, the times and places of these events are obscure. The Pengs may have been jailed in Xiayi and rescued there by Li Zicheng's men while Li was still in Xiangjing, or they may have been incarcerated in Huaiqing and released only later when Li's forces were based in Xi'an. As for Peng Xialing's subsequent relations with Li Zicheng, the only extant record is so romantic and fantastic as to strain credulity. According to it, Peng Xialing never took the proffered post in the rebel regime. Instead, having used his ties to his former teacher Niu Jinxing to get his family out of jail, he now recompensed him by trying to assassinate his boss, Li Zicheng. According to this story, when Li Zicheng was preparing to "cross the river and go north," presumably in late 1643, he called Niu and Peng to his tent for a drink. Peng reportedly flattered Li, saying:

> The times are critical. The officials are corrupt and bring harm to the people. The Great Prince has led a host of one million in a great uprising that has taken many towns and much territory. The Great Prince must soon become the monarch of all under heaven.[33]

Li Zicheng was reportedly pleased. Then, having lulled Li into insouciance, Peng took out a whip he had hidden in his sleeve and used it to beat Li. Taken completely by surprise, Li fell to the ground, but he managed to yell out "Xialing is trying to kill me!" Niu Jinxing and others then came to Li's rescue, but Peng managed to flee. According to the story in Peng's biography, he rode off on a horse (without benefit of saddle or bridle) and crossed the border into Shanxi. There is no record of Peng's later activities, but he apparently avoided both retribution from the rebels and prosecution by the Ming state. Given his experiences at the end of the Ming, however, he may have suffered physical harm or psychological trauma. According to his biography, he died in 1650 at the age of thirty-four.

Although some parts of this narrative are clearly fabulous, others may be based on facts. The story is of interest in any case as a metaphor. It seems quite possible that the Pengs of Xiayi were jailed for political reasons; that one or more of them were freed by the rebels in Xiayi, Huaiqing, or elsewhere; and that Peng Xialing spent some time in the rebel entourage under his former teacher, Niu Jinxing, and his recent benefactor, Li Zicheng. Like Su Gengsheng before him, the government student Peng Xialing could well have given the rebel leader some advice, although in this case it did not go beyond the need to declare himself the son of heaven. At the very least, the story suggests the value Li Zicheng attached to winning literati support and the interest some scholars showed in coming to terms with the rebellion as it gained in strength. Historiographically, the story is significant for the parallel it suggests, perhaps intentionally, between Li Zicheng, the general from Shaanxi (Qin), and King Zheng of the Qin, who survived a

similar assassination attempt before proclaiming himself the first emperor and unifying the realm in 221 BCE. Unfortunately, the date of origin of this story about Peng is
unknown. But it may have been quite early since it reflects the tendency of Li Zicheng's
adversaries to associate him with the Qin founder who had ruled China only briefly—
and allegedly tyrannically—from 221 to 206 BCE. The story may also be appreciated
somewhat more ironically as an allegory for those numerous literati who came to terms
with the rebel regime for their own reasons only to disengage themselves from it once
it had served their purposes.

If Li Zicheng's contacts with the elite of Xiayi remain obscure, his relations with an
official in Kaifeng are nonexistent—except insofar as they may be glimpsed obliquely
through another fantastic story. The death of Grand Coordinator Wang Han at the hands
of Liu Chao in February 1643 began a new cycle of personnel changes that, with few
exceptions, resulted in the decline of Ming authority in Kaifeng prefecture. The court
apparently appointed a new grand coordinator, Qin Suoshi, but he, like Wang Han, was
almost certainly not based in Kaifeng because that city was still largely under water. Indeed,
Qin's tenure was so tenuous that his name does not appear on the list of grand coordinators in the provincial gazetteer.[34] The regional inspector Su Jing remained in office,
but he was based outside Kaifeng, in Huaiqing prefecture to the west.

The new prefect of Kaifeng, Li Yan, was credited in his biography with "arduous
labor in planting the flag in Da Liang" and was promoted to vice commissioner of the
provincial surveillance office of the Kaifeng, Guide, and Henan tax circuit. Although
there is independent confirmation of Li Yan's appointment as prefect of Kaifeng, there
is no information concerning his promotion to the surveillance office nor any evidence
regarding his specific activities in this period. In fact, nothing may have become Li Yan
more in these posts than his leaving of them. On March 29, 1643, Qing troops overran
his hometown of Laiyang in Shandong and killed many people, including his father, Li
Zaibai. Li Yan therefore left his post in Henan and returned home to go into mourning. Perhaps it was at this time that rumors first arose that a Li Yan from Henan had
joined the rebellion of Li Zicheng. If so, these rumors seem to have circulated first in
an oral form among people who were unsure of Li Yan's identity. Later when the presumed rebel advisor Li Yan's personal name came to be written down, it was represented
by no less than five different characters, all pronounced Yan with variations only in tones:
嚴, 岩＝巖, 炎, 延, 兗.[35]

The rumors that the Laiyang man who had served as prefect of Kaifeng later joined
Li Zicheng's rebellion were almost certainly false. Although this historical Li Yan may have
communicated with Li Zicheng, if only to demand that he surrender or stay away from
Kaifeng, there is no evidence that he joined the rebel movement. Instead it seems clear
that he returned to Laiyang, where he went into mourning, most likely for the regulation twenty-seven months. There is a small chance (although again no evidence) that
this Li Yan had contacts with the rebels after they took Beijing. But it seems more likely
that, as his biography in the Laiyang gazetteer indicates, "after the change in dynasty,
he went into retreat at Lige village and chanted poetry to amuse himself."[36]

Whatever the relationship between the historical Li Yan, who served as prefect in
Kaifeng, and the storied Li Yan, who supposedly joined Li Zicheng as chief advisor, the

Li Yan from Laiyang was indeed the last Ming prefect of Kaifeng. Similarly, Sang Kaidi, who was appointed to Guide at this time, was to be the last Ming prefect there. Although Sang was to remain in office longer than Li Yan, his political loyalties were ultimately to become suspect, suggesting that the line between the Ming and the rebels was wearing thin. Meanwhile, on June 19, 1643, the Henan grand coordinator Qin Suoshi reported frankly, although with some exaggeration, on the decline of Ming authority in the province. He noted that "roving robbers" had devastated five prefectures and reduced eighty towns to rubble. He wrote that every ten days another town fell into rebel hands while "local bandits" controlled the province south of the river. They included Li Jiyu, Shen Jingbang, and Li Hao, each with ten thousand men and thousands of horses. They also included Li Kui, Liu Hongli, and the Little Yuan Brigade that alternated between submission and rebellion. To deal with these challenges, Qin had only two thousand troops, and his subordinates Chen Yongfu and Bu Congshan had fewer than four thousand each. These troops were busy dealing with Liu Chao's mutiny in Yongcheng and repairing the dikes along the Yellow River. Supplies were scarce because of the havoc wrought by the flood. The number of taxpayers had dropped by 60 percent, seriously reducing revenues. In the absence of the men and boys, who had gone off with the rebels or the army, women and girls were struggling to survive on their own. Officials were appointed but rarely went to their posts; instead they found safe havens and watched to see which way the wind was blowing. Noting that Henan was the heart and stomach of the realm, Qin called on Chongzhen to disburse funds from his personal treasury to provide relief. According to Zheng Lian, the ruler simply sighed and did not bother to reply. In the next two months Liu Chao and Yuan Shizhong were eliminated, but the situation scarcely improved. On September 2, with the fall of Chief Grand Secretary Zhou Yanru, Supreme Commander Hou Xun was dismissed, arrested, and sent back to jail.[37]

As Li Zicheng's influence waxed and Ming authority waned, Henanese potentates maneuvered to suppress the rebels and protect their interests. Some of them cast their lot with the rebels and were labeled "bandits." Li Jiyu of Dengfeng had allied with Li Zicheng in 1641, Shen Wandeng of Runing had gone over to rebellion in 1642, and Han Huamei and other stockade heads in Runing joined the insurrection in 1643 (see Map 7.2). Others in southwestern departments of Kaifeng prefecture, such as Xuzhou and Chenzhou, were named commanders by the Ming and presumably regarded the rebels as their main enemy. Strongmen in other counties leaned to one side or the other. In Yushi, a member of the local elite organized self-defense forces and then surrendered to Li Jiyu. In Mi, local elite and commoners in several forts fought repeatedly with Li Jiyu, perhaps because of his alliance with Li Zicheng or because of some local feud. Local rivalries seem to have generated conflicts among local elite, strongmen, and clans in the forts and villages of Xiàngcheng county. Finally, there are hints that one strongman, of Xiàngcheng, was predatory (he "robbed and plundered") and another, of Yanling, was defensive (he engaged in "self-defense and farming").[38]

In sum, the local strongmen of northeast Henan were a more varied lot than is suggested by Grand Coordinator Qin Suoshi's summary label "local bandits." But they did all share a modicum of wealth, power, and solidarity and a determination to defend themselves against all comers. Both the pragmatism of their goals and the difficulty of realizing them would become apparent in the months ahead.

Founding a State: Xi'an/Chang'an

As Li Zicheng and Zhang Xianzhong established bases in Huguang, the Ming court tried to mount a vigorous response. It offered rewards to those who killed rebel officials, captured rebel followers, and rescued rebel captives. It promised ten thousand taels of silver and noble rank for the capture of Li Zicheng and five thousand taels of silver and hereditary office for the capture of Zhang Xianzhong. Addressing long-standing appeals from local officials, it decreed a tax holiday of three years in the five prefectures of Henan south of the river. Although the court reincarcerated Hou Xun, it relied on his colleagues and clients to contain the rebels. It continued to press the Shaanxi grand coordinator Sun Chuanting to roll back rebel authority in Henan. In the summer of 1643, it named him concurrently president of the ministry of troops and supreme commander of the armies in seven provinces. The court instructed Zuo Liangyu to advance from Jiujiang into Huguang to put pressure on Zhang Xianzhong. It made Shi Kefa, the Xiangfu metropolitan graduate, president of the ministry of troops in Nanjing.[39]

After his defeat by the rebels in Henan in late 1642, Sun Chuanting had retreated to Shaanxi to plan revenge. He demanded supplies from the rich and recruited soldiers among the poor. He opened up military colonies, stockpiled grain, trained troops, and repaired weaponry. He even constructed twenty thousand "fire carts," virtual tanks like those proposed by Li Guangtian in Kaifeng, but in this case they were to be drawn by horses. In addition to transporting heavy armament, these carts could be turned sideways to block rebel cavalry charges. In August, Sun was still not ready to move into Henan, but he came under increasing pressure to do so. The court was impatient, and Sun, more conscientious than Zuo Liangyu, was embarrassed. In Beijing, scholar-officials from Shaanxi were more worried about Sun's demands on their province than about his likely prospect of defeat in Henan. They therefore implored the court to threaten Sun with punishment if he did not advance soon. Finally, the grand coordinator of Shaanxi held a farewell banquet to shame Sun into leaving.[40]

Sun Chuanting's reservations about moving into Henan may have been reinforced by a letter he received from Liu Lishun, the Qi county optimus of 1634 who was companion to the heir apparent in Beijing. Liu wrote that, if one really understood the "bandits," one could pacify them as easily as General Yue Fei had pacified the rebel Yang Ma in the Song. But Liu acknowledged the many difficulties of securing troops and supplies, unifying leadership and authority, and arranging cooperation and communication. He pointed out that Sun's mission pertained not just to Henan and Huguang but to the entire realm, and it entailed both opportunities and risks. There were opportunities because Luo Rucai's troops, now under Li Zicheng, remained resentful over the death of their leader, and some rebel officials were probably ambivalent about the course they were following. However, there were risks because the local strongmen Li Jiyu and Shen Jingbang were still lurking in the mountains and could cause trouble for the Ming. As always, Zuo Liangyu was unreliable and insubordinate. Liu noted that the Shaanxi local elite were aware of these problems but tended to overlook them in their desire to see Sun leave Shaanxi.[41]

In a second letter, Liu Lishun was a bit more optimistic. Invoking the parallel so dear to the Ming court and Henanese local elite, he reminded Sun that when the capable general Li Guangbi joined the army of Guo Ziyi in the mid-Tang, he was able to achieve great victories against the forces of the rebel An Lushan. He remarked on the recent suppression of the mutiny of Liu Chao and assured Sun that he could rely on Generals Bu Congshan and Chen Yongfu to confront Li Zicheng. Together they should be able to capture the rebel officials in Henan. As for supplies, Sun should be able to count on the fall harvest. Still, Liu warned that "the affairs of my home province cannot afford to be mismanaged again, and they are of great relevance to the general situation."[42] One of northeast Henan's most prominent sons thus gave Sun only mild encouragement to proceed against the rebels in the central province.

Knowing that Sun Chuanting was preparing to move into Henan, Li Zicheng reentered Henan in the summer of 1643 and established himself at Dengzhou, in Nanyang prefecture (see Map 7.3). He installed the families of his generals in Tang county and deployed troops in Jia and Baozhou to serve as a base in Ruzhou. Whereas Li regarded these moves as largely defensive, they were interpreted by the Ming court, authorities in Henan, and Sun Chuanting as evidence that the rebels intended to expand northward. On September 13, therefore, Sun conducted sacrifices at the Guan Di temple in Xi'an and set out for Henan. As supreme commander he supervised Generals Gao Jie, a former rebel, and Bai Guang'en, a former commander in northeast China. He instructed the Henan regional commanders Bu Congshan and Chen Yongfu to converge on Luoyang, and he ordered Regional Commander Zuo Liangyu to come north to Runing to put pressure on Li Zicheng from the rear. After a brief dispute with the Henan grand coordinator Qin Suoshi and regional inspector Su Jing, Sun prevailed on Bu and Chen to proceed to Luoyang as directed. There was, as usual, no response from Zuo Liangyu.[43]

When Li Zicheng heard that Sun's army had passed through Tongguan into western Henan, he established a military base in western Xiangcheng. His men constructed a long moat and a stout wall behind which they stationed the bulk of their cavalry. One half kilometer to the east of these ramparts they erected twenty smaller earthen walls, each with a lookout tower manned by four soldiers and defended by infantry using bows and arrows, swords and lances, and small cannons. Having secured this base, Li led light cavalry west to beyond Luoyang to confront Sun's advancing troops. Apparently, Li's strategy was to effect a series of retreats that would make Sun overconfident and would entice him to march deep into rebel territory. In any case, that is what happened. After the first encounter, Li fell back to Longmen gorge, south of Luoyang, allowing Sun to occupy the city on September 28. Some in Sun's party were in favor of tarrying there, strengthening the defenses, storing grain, and making it a secure base for later operations to the east. Under court orders to continue his advance and secure more victories, however, Sun pressed east, interpreting Li's retreat as a sign of weakness rather than as a tactic of deception.[44]

Li Zicheng's withdrawal entailed costs and risks. One of Luo Rucai's former gen-

MAP 7.3. The Rise of the Da Shun from Xiangyang to Xi'an, 1643. Source: Tan 1975: 82–83. Used with permission from The Chinese Map Society (Zhonghua ditu xueshe).

erals, now on the Ming side, persuaded one of Li's generals to surrender. The defector revealed the whereabouts of the rebel leaders' families in Tang county. When Sun reached Ruzhou, Li again sent light troops against him, and in the ensuing "defeat" lost another of his generals and one of the rebel flags. Sun then sent a detachment south to Tang county to wipe out the rebel generals' families. On October 24 the rebels were forced once again to give up Baozhou, Niu Jinxing's hometown and an important locus of rebel authority. As a result of that defeat, the rebels lost their local magistrate and his assistant along with several thousand troops and inhabitants of the town. The next day, Sun attacked nearby Jia, inflicting many casualties on the rebels. Li Zicheng was almost captured and the town was stripped of food.[45] Like most strategies, the one of drawing the enemy in deep could be a double-edged sword.

The Ming armies, however, had now greatly overextended their supply lines. During the attack on Jia county, rain had begun to fall, and the deluge continued without stop for six days. The entire region became a sea of mud, impassible for foot soldiers and horses let alone for the carts that provided the bulk of Sun's supplies and firepower. Li Zicheng tightened the noose by sending light cavalry to the north and west, intercepting whatever supplies were still making it through the downpour. Sun Chuanting placed the redoubtable Chen Yongfu in charge of holding Jia county while he attempted to break out of the encirclement. Unwilling to retreat to the west, Sun pushed on to the east. Meeting stiff resistance at the rebel fortifications in Xiangcheng, however, he was forced to turn back. Chen Yongfu's men, misinterpreting Sun's movement as flight, mutinied and began to disperse. Chen sought to hold his men together by executing deserters, but he soon lost control. On October 29, Sun's rear troops also collapsed at Ruzhou. Bai Guang'en counseled an orderly retreat to more defensible points, but Sun Chuanting and Gao Jie resolved to fight on against all odds. On November 3, Bai's recent recruits from Shaanxi broke ranks and fled; Sun's and Gao's men soon followed suit. At first the fire carts blocked the roads and slowed the retreat. After clearing the matériel from the carts, the routed Ming forces fled more than two hundred kilometers in a day. They lost an estimated forty thousand men and tens of thousands of weapons.[46]

The victory of the rebels in Jia county in central Henan was an important step in their rise to power. The Shangqiu historian Zheng Lian compared Li Zicheng's tactics, such as cutting off Sun Chuanting's overextended supply lines, with those of Zhou Yafu, the wise prime minister of the Western Han who won battles against the satrapies of Wu and Chu. Basing his account largely on firsthand observations by his uncle, Zheng Zhijun, who served as commissioner of grain transport under Sun Chuanting, Zheng also cited an editor of the Jia county gazetteer, who concluded that the failure of the capable Sun Chuanting to stem the rebels' advance was a sure sign that "heaven's mandate had already been lost." In fact, Zheng argued, the events in Jia were not a defeat but a collapse like that in Xiangzhou, northern Henan, during the campaigns against An Lushan. Then, alluding to battles of the Warring States period, Zheng suggested that the confrontation between Sun and Li was more like two rats struggling in a hole than a clear-cut victory worthy of the Han statesman Zhou Yafu. In other words, although Sun's campaign failed to save the Ming from Li Zicheng (as the Tang had been saved from An Lushan),

Li would eventually prove to be unable to establish his own enduring order (like the Han served by Zhou Yafu). Although Zheng rightly disagreed with the prominent early Qing historians Gu Yingtai and Wu Weiye over the dates of the Ruzhou battles, he equally rightly concurred with them—and with other historians—that those confrontations were an important part of the fall of the Ming and the rise of the rebels.[47]

More immediately, Li Zicheng's triumph over Sun Chuanting in central Henan led to his decision to march west to Xi'an. According to a widely accepted story, Li had already made that choice at a meeting in Xiangjing when he had ruled out the alternatives of going to Nanjing or to Beijing. Li Zicheng may well have considered those options, but Shaanxi was his home province and it had served as the political center of the Han and Tang orders on which he modeled his own developing regime. Yet, Li Zicheng was also establishing bases in Henan, including Junping in northeast Henan. As the historian Gu Cheng suggests, it is likely that the decision to go to Xi'an was not made at a dramatic meeting in Xiangjing but was rather arrived at later in Henan in light of the surprisingly complete rout of Sun Chanting's forces in Ruzhou.[48]

Li Zicheng pursued Sun as he retreated to the west. According to Zheng Lian, Sun had first gone north to Mengjin, on the south bank of the Yellow River, where he was so distraught at the sight of his men being killed that he tried to throw himself in the river. His subordinates intervened and prevailed on him to continue resisting the rebels. Zheng Lian also reports an unlikely story that Sun went to Shouyang mountain in Yanshi county, east of Luoyang, to pay respects to the Shang loyalists Bo Yi and Shu Qi, who had starved themselves to death rather than live under the Zhou. Although rightly skeptical of this account, Zheng emphasized that it could serve to symbolize the truth that Sun was willing to sacrifice himself for his state. Noting that the supreme commander from Shaanxi had been forced into a military confrontation with an army of one million against his will, Zheng also compared the sequence of events to that which had brought down the Qin dynasty and ushered in the Han. Such historical analogies were essential, he seemed to believe, to make his point that "the fall of the Ming was decided here." In fact, from Mengjin Sun had fled west to Wenxiang and Tongguan, where he rejoined Bai Guang'en. On November 12, Li Zicheng's forces took Wenxiang, and four days later they assaulted Tongguan, killing Sun Chuanting among other defenders. Gao Jie and Bai Guang'en fled further west.[49]

Installing a subordinate to garrison Tongguan, Li Zicheng proceeded west toward Xi'an, the capital of his home province. In the next four days his forces took four towns—Huayang, Huazhou, Weinan, and Lintong—meeting little resistance. In Weinan the magistrate and his brothers mounted the wall to defend the town, but a local provincial graduate opened the gates and welcomed the rebel army. The grand coordinator of Shaanxi, who was in nearby Shangzhou and Luonan, heard that the rebels were approaching Xi'an. He returned to the city, but he had few troops with which to defend it. The local Ming prince, for his part, refused to supply local troops with cotton-padded clothing despite the cold weather. This angered the local commander, who wrote to the rebels and promised them cooperation from within. When the rebels arrived at Xi'an on November 21, he opened the gates and surrendered the town. The grand coordinator died along with two other officials, but the prince surrendered to the rebels and was spared. There was little if any resistance among the local elite, middle strata, or masses. Li Zicheng installed himself in the estate of the deposed prince and set about the task of administering the first provincial capital he had won.[50]

From his new base in Xi'an, Li Zicheng sent subordinates to assert control over the rest of his home province. One general had already taken Shangzhou and Luonan in the southeast, and another campaigned south into Sichuan. Liu Zongmin pursued the Ming generals Bai Guang'en and Chen Yongfu west into Gansu and encouraged them to surrender in return for amnesty. Bai surrendered, but Chen was reluctant, reportedly arguing that Li Zicheng would not forgive him for having put out his eye. Only after Li Zicheng reassured him by taking an oath on a broken arrow, the story went, did Chen, the erstwhile stalwart defender of Kaifeng, surrender to the rebels. Indeed, unlike some who surrendered merely to survive, Chen seems to have had a change of heart. He soon became an important rebel general. Meanwhile, Li Guo had chased the Ming general Gao Jie north to Yan'an and then east into Shanxi. In November, Li Zicheng went north to his home county of Mizhi, where he supervised the repair of his ancestral graves. He sent Li Guo at the head of seventy thousand troops farther north to secure the Shaanxi frontier. Li Guo met some resistance. The battle for Yulin, for example, lasted three days and was won only after using explosives to blow up a section of the town wall. By the end of 1643, however, the rebel armies had taken control of Shaanxi. They began to move into neighboring Shanxi and Henan north of the Yellow River.[51]

Back in Xi'an, Li Zicheng and his officials took further steps to legitimate their state. Li wore a small yellow cap, symbolizing his status as leader, and was reportedly greeted by the people with spontaneous calls of "long life," a sign of his growing political stature. But he and his officials continued to wear blue cotton garments to emphasize their plebian origins and perhaps to symbolize the agent water that the rebels chose in an effort to overcome the agent fire associated with the Ming. (The radical for Shun was the character for river, and the radical for Ming was the sun). The rebels renamed Xi'an Chang'an (long peace) in an obvious effort to recall the glories of the capitals of the Han and Tang located there. They also called the city the Western Capital, leaving open the possibility of establishing one or more capitals elsewhere. The rebels deposed the Ming prince of Qin and, when he agreed to cooperate, installed him as a plenipotentiary general in charge of a Xin Shun (new accord) estate, terms reminiscent of the Tang. They renamed both Mizhi county and Xi'an prefecture Tianbao (heaven protected), terms homophonous with the famous Tianbao (heavenly treasure) reign of the Tang.

The Shun state in Chang'an adopted other measures that consciously or unconsciously recalled the atmosphere of the Tang. Officials rode on horseback, not in palanquins, and the elite were obliged to pay their taxes rather than claiming illegal exemptions. With respect to women, the rebels did not challenge foot binding but they discouraged concubinage and the treatment of women as mere social capital even while encouraging widow chastity. In one case that touched on these issues, a subordinate seeking favor with Li Zicheng offered him the talented widow of a deceased friend as a concubine. Li decided to make an example of the man and had him executed for showing disloyalty to his friend and disrespect for the woman. He then demonstrated his own intentions, consistent with Ming tokenism but perhaps a step toward a more serious attitude toward women exemplified in the Tang, by hiring the literate widow to tutor women in the families of his officials.[52]

In February 1644, at the end of the sixteenth year of the Chongzhen reign of the Ming dynasty, the rebels formally declared a new calendar to inaugurate a new order. In taking Pingyang in Shanxi, they announced that they had already liberated Chu, Yu, and Qin and were ready to liberate Jin and Yan. These names for Huguang, Henan, Shaanxi, Shanxi, and the Beijing region were conventional, of course, but their use underscored the rebels' argument that they were winning the mandate much as preceding dynasties had back at least to the Han. On February 8, Li Zicheng changed part of his personal name from *cheng* (becoming) to *sheng* (昇 extant splendor), and he formally adopted the title Shun Wang (prince of accord). The rebels also formally adopted Da Shun (great accord) as the name of their state and Yongchang (forever prosperous) as the name of the first reign. The dwarf diviner Song Xiance was appointed a military commander, and the provincial graduate Niu Jinxing was named a grand secretary (using a term for that office taken from the *Venerated Documents*). The rebels reaffirmed the administrative system outlined in Xiangjing and added more offices with names drawn from the Tang. For example, the Hanlin Academy was renamed the Institute for the Advancement of Literature, and the Office of Transmission was renamed the Office of the General Manager in accord with Tang practices.[53]

From its base in Xi'an (now Chang'an), the Shun confronted challenges to its authority in Henan. Local potentates south of the river had rallied to the Ming and attacked rebel magistrates even before Li Zicheng had left the region. For example, during the battle of Jia, Shen Wandeng had defected from Li Zicheng and allied with Sun Chuanting. He had then taken Runing and killed the rebel prefect Deng Lian, among others. Li Jiyu had nominally been allied with Li Zicheng, but his attitude was sufficiently ambiguous that Ming officials and local elite still tried to win his allegiance with titles. After Li Zicheng had left Henan for Shaanxi, Liu Hongqi and his brothers, who had once cooperated with Li in Xiping, made contact with Zuo Liangyu. They killed one rebel official in Ruzhou and plotted against others in Nanyang and Kaifeng. A ditty current at the time reflected the popular image of Liu Hongqi as a threat to the rebel areas:

> Raise high the lighted lamps,
> Boil more oil.
> Here comes Flathead Liu again,
> Our livelihood to spoil.

In January 1644, Commander Ding Qirui, based in Yongcheng, led troops to capture and behead no fewer than seventy-two rebel officers in Fugou, Kaifeng prefecture. At the same time, Li Jiyu was called upon to secure the surrender of eight forts that were presumably under rebel control. To fend off threats to his rear area, Li Zicheng sent General Yuan Zongdi from Shaanxi into southern Henan. With such military support, the Shun was able to reappoint magistrates to Baozhou and Neixiang.[54]

Meanwhile the Shun went on the offensive farther north. In January 1644, it sent three hundred crack cavalry into western Henan prefecture and installed magistrates in Wenxiang, Lingbao, Shaanzhou, and Mianzhi (see Map 7.3). Along the way, rebel troops chanted slogans such as "Killing a man is like killing my father, raping a woman is like raping my mother" to publicize their commitment to strict discipline. They encountered strong opposition from the Henan grand coordinator Qin Suoshi, who was based in Meng county, Huaiqing prefecture. Two months later, the rebel general Liu Fangliang led tens of thousands of rebel troops from Shanxi to Huaiqing, where he drove out the Ming prefect and captured a Ming prince. The magistrate of Henei county, the capital of Huaiqing prefecture, refused to surrender and was killed. The regional commander Chen De and the regional inspector Su Jing, who had once led the defense of Kaifeng and Jia from the rebels, now surrendered to the Shun.[55]

Since Chen De's father had already switched sides, his surrender was not very surprising, but the case of Su Jing was more complicated and interesting. Su was known as a hard-liner who had suppressed the *shibazi* uprising in Qi in 1638, punished the students of Shangqiu who supported Song Quan, imprisoned the Pengs of Xiayi for allegedly sympathizing with Liu Chao's mutiny, and maneuvered Yuan Shizhong into a fatal confrontation with Li Zicheng. According to Zheng Lian, however, Su Jing had failed to distinguish the guilty from the innocent and was highly unpopular in northeast Henan.[56] If that was true, the addition of Su to the Shun entourage would not do much to enhance its legitimacy among the people.

The rebels seem to have been aware of this for they dealt roughly with Su Jing. According to Zheng Lian, Su enjoyed killing and was in the habit of smiling just before he was about to strike. A student named Wang Jun from Shangqiu, who was skilled in the martial arts, had become Su's chief bodyguard. When Wang wrote a poem congratulating Su on his birthday, Su smiled and Wang became frightened. He soon crossed the Yellow River and joined the rebels. Wang (汪) subsequently dropped the water radical from his name, making it simply Wang (王), and he became known among the rebels as Man Tian Xing (the star that fills the heavens). When Chen De and Su Jing surrendered, Chen became a Shun general, but, according to Wang, Su was subject to the rebels' contempt. They criticized him for having harshly oppressed the people on the one hand and for having readily (if tardily) surrendered to the Shun on the other. According to Zheng Lian, who based his account on conversations with Wang, the rebels forced Su to change into women's clothing, powdered his face, decked his hair with flowers, and paraded him through the streets of Huaiqing on the back of a mule. Later they forced him to don the black garb of a *yamen* runner and to perform the duties of a servant. These efforts to humiliate Su, of course, reflected the rebels' own patriarchal and elitist assumptions as well as their concern to win popular support. Su Jing reportedly took them in stride, but, unlike the Chens who became active supporters of the rebellion, Su managed to sneak away when the rebels moved on. Zheng Lian, demonstrating a more egalitarian sense of gender as well as a surprisingly conventional view of loyalty, compared the former Ming official Su Jing unfavorably with some of the women of Henei who died rather than serve the rebels. He concluded with his favorite idea that "all people are endowed with the capacity for propriety," this time adding, with a refreshing lack of gender as well as class bias, that in this respect, "there is no difference between noble and base or man and woman."[57]

The Shun general Liu Fangliang installed a defense commissioner and prefect in

Huaiqing and county magistrates in Henei, Jiyuan, Xiuwu, Wuzhi, Meng, and Wen (see Map 7.3). On March 28, he and Chen Yongfu advanced northeast to Weihui and took Huojia, Xinxiang, Zucheng, Hui, and Qí counties. The Ming prince of Lu, Zhu Chaofang, fled to Jiangnan. On April 6, Liu Fangliang and another rebel general named Liu Rukui proceeded northeast to take Zhangde in Henan and Daming in Beizhili.[58]

From its base in Chang'an, the Shun continued to try to win Ming scholars to its standard but not always successfully. A Ming provincial graduate from Xihua county, Kaifeng prefecture, named Li Changhe, for example, had been so chagrined to share the family name of Li Zicheng (李) that he had decided to write it with a homophone (Li 理). The new name may have had the advantage of alluding to the idea of pattern (and thus to the idea of loyalty, perhaps) embraced by the Song ruists. At the same time, Li changed his personal name to Hanshi, meaning a scholar who does not take office. When Chang'an issued a call for scholars, the Shun magistrate of Xihua urged Li Changhe to respond. Li used many ploys to avoid service to the Shun state, including taking to his bed for long periods of time. A younger brother, Li Anhe, also changed his name. He forfeited the privileges of government student status to avoid service to the rebels. In the end, the Shun officials gave up trying to recruit these scholars who were determined to uphold the principle of serving only one dynasty.[59]

Instead, the Shun moved to recruit its own scholars to serve in such newly acquired regions as northeast Henan. In Xiangjing it had instructed its defense commissioners to reexamine Ming government students or select their own government students in the areas they controlled, including Nanyang and Runing in southern Henan. In Chang'an the rebels ordered their magistrates and prefects to hold lower-level examinations to select new government students who would be examined further in the capital before earning posts in the new government. The Shun retained the basic structure of the Ming examination system but made some changes in the processes of selection and appointment. It abolished the highly structured eight-legged essay that was sometimes blamed for stereotypical thinking among literati of the late Ming. Instead it emphasized the free essay form that had often been favored by reformers. It retained questions on the classics but stressed applications to current policy. In line with the practice of many previous regimes, it invited discussion of the defects of the faltering Ming and encouraged praise of the achievements of the rising Shun. The new government sought to reduce the barrier that had long separated officials from clerks and appointed both from the ranks of successful graduates. In January 1644, the Shun president of the ministry of personnel implemented these reforms in examinations held in Pingyang, Shanxi. Graduates from that examination were among the Shun local officials sent to Guide in April (see Map 7.4).[60]

The records indicate the names of Shun officials appointed to Kaifeng and Weihui prefectures but nothing about their origins and means of selection. There is more information on the Shun vice prefect and six of the nine Shun magistrates posted to Guide, including their names, origins, status, and times of appointment. These appointees were all from Shanxi, a current center of rebel authority. Indeed, four of the six magistrates were from Pingyang prefecture, of whom three were from Pu department, suggesting that Shun recruitment by examination was confined to a relatively small area.

MAP 7.4. Counties of Northeast Henan with Magistrates Appointed by the Rebel Shun State Based at Xi'an/Chang'an, 1643–44. Sources: based on data in Liu 1983: 232; Wang 1984b: 97–98.

Five of the six magistrates were young (twenties and early thirties), and all six passed the examinations held by the Shun in Pingyang prefecture. They were appointed along with the vice prefect in April 1644. As was the custom, the appointee with higher examination status (a provincial graduate) got the higher post (vice prefect), whereas those of lesser status (government students all) assumed the lesser posts (of magistrate). The use of government students probably reflected the continuing difficulty in attracting elite participation in the rebel movement as well as rebel interest in involving members of that middle stratum in their administration. The relative youth and lesser status of the appointees probably made them more vigorous, flexible, and sympathetic to the masses, but their comparative lack of experience almost certainly diminished their ability to cope with the challenges they faced. It would take them a full month to reach their posts, and they would not hold office for long.

Overturning the Ming: Beijing

Li Zicheng valued Xi'an as the capital of his home province and renamed it Chang'an after the capitals of the Han and Tang dynasties, but he was aware that Beijing had served as the primary capital of the last two dynasties. To consolidate the Shun state, if not to replace the Ming, he had to take the center of Ming authority in Beijing. In some ways, the signs were auspicious. The Shun had extended its influence over much of the central plain, and the Ming was preoccupied with the challenge to its authority coming from the Manchus in the northeast. The rebel momentum was such that Li Zicheng received a letter in February 1644 from Dorgon, the recently named prince regent of the Qing, offering to cooperate in wresting the central plain from the Ming.[61] But Li ignored the Qing initiative, thus forfeiting an opportunity to gain a powerful ally against the Ming and increasing the likelihood of strong competition in the effort to establish a successor state.

During the second month of the Yongchang reign (March–early April 1644), the Shun armies marched on Beijing along two routes (see Map 7.5). The first, under Li Zicheng, advanced to Taiyuan, the capital of Shanxi province. The Shanxi grand coordinator Cai Moude, who had once served in Henan, and the defense commissioner Mao Wenbing, who was from Zhengzhou, both died defending the town. But the erstwhile rebel and present Ming general Gao Jie fled rather than give his life on behalf of the Ming, and the local Ming prince and prefect surrendered on March 16. The victory at Taiyuan gave the Shun more leverage in its negotiations with the court and more reason to believe that it was winning the mandate. Ten days later, Li Zicheng took Xinzhou without a fight. He met more resistance at Daizhou, and particularly at Ningwu pass. Indeed, his forces were so badly battered there that he considered withdrawing to Xi'an to recuperate. At this point, however, the Ming regional commander at Datong, Jiang Xiang, surrendered. On April 7, Li Zicheng sent Li Guo and Liu Zongmin to take over the town, encountering only perfunctory resistance.[62]

Meanwhile the second Shun force under General Liu Fangliang pushed north from Henan to Guguan, which fell on March 24, and proceeded to Zhending, taken on March 31. A large detachment went east, winning Daming prefecture on April 5, and

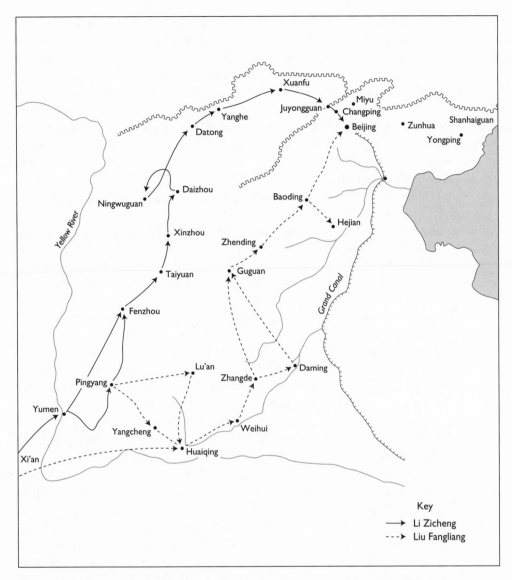

MAP 7.5. The Shun Advance on Beijing, Spring 1644. Sources: Based on data in Liu 1983: 258–59; Xie 1986: 322.

another detachment took Hejian five days later. These campaigns put military pressure on the Grand Canal nearby and discouraged the Ming court from moving south on the model of the Eastern Jìn and the Southern Song.[63] These forays also served as a forward defense for the newly established Shun administration in northeast Henan.

During the next two weeks, the Shun pincers closed quickly on the Ming capital. To the northwest, Li Zicheng took Yanghe, where the local commander, Jiang Xuan, the brother of Jiang Xiang, surrendered and joined the rebel forces. Li then moved toward Xuanfu and was met by the Ming commander, the eunuch Du Xun, who promptly surrendered. On April 21 the Shun army reached Juyongguan, where it was welcomed by the Ming regional commander Tang Tong. On the next day the rebels entered Changping, where a military mutiny had already shaken Ming authority. The Ming regional commissioner committed suicide, and the Shun forces humiliated the Ming by burning buildings at the twelve royal tombs. Meanwhile, to the south, Liu Fangliang led forces to attack Baoding, the provincial capital of Beizhili. Two months earlier the Shanxi-born metropolitan graduate and grand secretary Li Jiantai had volunteered to lead troops south to forestall the rebel advance. He had refused to go to the assistance of Taiyuan in his native province, however, and had failed to hold Zhending and Hejian in Beizhili. In April, as the rebels closed in on Baoding, the last major town before Beijing, all eyes turned to Li Jiantai.[64]

Chongzhen struggled to save his capital from the rebels. On March 29, he issued an apology for his deficiencies and offered an amnesty to the rebels, this time including even Niu Jinxing and other early supporters and excluding only Li Zicheng. He offered the rank of Tong marquis (*tonghou*), a title once held by Li Si, prime minister of the Qin, to anyone who would deliver the rebel leader's head to the court.[65] On April 11, as the Shun forces approached the capital, Chongzhen made Tang Tong "the earl who settles the west" and Wu Sangui "the earl who pacifies the east." He ordered them, among others, to come to the defense of the capital. Tang ignored the order and instead surrendered to Li Zicheng. Wu Sangui obeyed instructions by withdrawing his forces inside the wall at Shanhaiguan on April 19.[66]

Chongzhen now turned to his recently appointed minister of troops, Zhang Jinyan, to lead the defense of Beijing. Zhang was the metropolitan graduate from Xinxiang whose trenchant criticisms of Yang Sichang had cost him his censorial post in 1641, just as Li Zicheng was entering Henan (see Chapter 2). In November 1643 Zhang had been brought back to court, perhaps with the idea that he would help restore Ming authority in his home province. He had first been appointed vice president of the ministry of troops and then, in February 1644, was promoted to president. On the day Zhang assumed office, a secretary in the ministry, Zeng Yinglin, submitted a report deploring the growing gap between the rich and the poor. He noted specifically how the local elite had hoarded grain, only to lose it to the rebels in Xi'an and the Manchus in Laiyang. Zeng called for a policy of equal fields (*juntian*) to enable the state to recover revenues siphoned off by the elite and to assist cultivators in reclaiming lands engrossed by landlords. The court ignored Zeng's proposal, and it is impossible to determine the effect, if any, it had on Zhang Jinyan.[67] But it epitomized the reformist sentiment that had been around for decades and echoed some of the demands being made by the rebels advancing on Beijing.

Zhang Jinyan, in any case, soon fell out of favor with the court over strategies on dealing with the rebels. In one report he described the military devastation and harsh living conditions of the central plain, asking pointedly how their effects could possibly be limited to one region. He sent Li Jiantai to south Beizhili to deal with the rebel advance, but, when Li suffered a defeat at Zhending, Zhang disclaimed any knowledge of it. When Chongzhen learned of the setback and asked Zhang how he could be so uninformed, Zhang replied that, unlike more corrupt officials, he lacked the funds to send out private investigators. On April 13, Zhang came under sharp criticism for making unreliable statements; disregarding the reports of spies; knowing nothing about a mutiny in Baoding ten days after it happened; and, in general, for being weak, stupid, and devoid of any long-term strategy. Six days later, Chongzhen scolded Zhang again for lacking any plan for opposing the rebels, and Zhang offered to resign. The court rejected his resignation, so Zhang was at his post on April 22 when Changping fell to the Shun. Zhang reportedly ascribed the fall of Changping to mutinous troops and denied that it had been taken by rebels.[68] Although Zhang remained in his post as president of the ministry of troops, his behavior strongly suggested his sympathy with the rebels, or at least his inability to prevent their advance.

In the last days of his life, Chongzhen also relied on Li Guozhen, a curious figure loosely associated with northeast Henan. As the earl of Xiangcheng, Li was a member of the Ming nobility of merit, the group who enjoyed hereditary privileges and considerable wealth by virtue of their ancestors' contributions to the state. As was often the case with such men, Li Guozhen lacked the qualities of his forebears. He nonetheless retained the title that linked him, at least symbolically, with the county in Kaifeng prefecture that had been a major object of contention between the Ming and Li Zicheng. Although Li Guozhen's connection with Henan was symbolic, he was regarded by the Henanese historian Zheng Lian as "a Henan man." On April 8, despite the lack of any previous achievement, he was appointed military superintendent responsible for the defense of Beijing. Like Li Guangtian in Kaifeng, Li Guozhen in Beijing was expected to organize an urban militia that could substitute for feckless official troops in defending the city from the rebels. The authorities in Beijing, however, unlike those in Kaifeng, had no faith that the masses would participate loyally in the defense. As a result, they forbade the common people to mount the walls, from which they might only defect or flee, and they allowed only nobles like Li and officials like Zhang to man the ramparts. Li Guozhen was stationed at the Xizhi gate at the northwest corner of the wall when the rebels began to penetrate the suburbs on April 18. The court was in an uproar and could only close the gates to prevent people from going in and out. There was some talk of strengthening the forces on the outer wall, but it was vetoed for fear of weakening defense of the inner wall. A secretary in the ministry of rites criticized Li Guozhen for the lack of any plan.[69]

Suspicious of officials such as Zhang Jinyan and aristocrats such as Li Guozhen, Chongzhen turned to eunuchs. On March 29 he appointed ten eunuchs to supervise troops in Beizhili and Henan north of the river. Zhang Jinyan objected to these appointments on the grounds that they would divert limited resources from regularly appointed officials and officers, giving them a pretext for shirking their duties, but his views were ignored. The limitations of the policy became apparent with the surrender of the eunuch

Du Xun outside Xuanfu. Chongzhen also used eunuchs to try to extract money from wealthy nobles, such as the earl of Jiading, Zhou Kui. This effort foundered when Zhou refused to give up more than a small fraction of his wealth. On April 16, the eunuch Wang Cheng'en took charge of the defense of Beijing, and he was soon joined by another eunuch, Cao Huachun. A week later, when fifty to sixty rebel cavalry approached the city wall, the eunuch defenders fired on them, killing more than twenty. But when the Shun armies arrived in force at the Zhangyi gate, Li Guozhen's three battalions outside the wall collapsed. The men and their equipment were all added to the Shun forces. On April 24, when the rebels fired on the wall and called for surrender, the remaining defenders fled their posts.[70]

On the same day the Shun began to negotiate with the Ming for a peaceful transfer of authority. Stationed outside the Zhangyi gate and flanked by the surrendered princes of Qin and Jìn, Li Zicheng sent the surrendered eunuchs Du Xun and Shen Zhixiu to the wall, where they were received by the loyal eunuchs Wang Cheng'en and Cao Huachun. On the basis of such personal contacts, Du was admitted to an audience with Chongzhen. Du apparently proposed that Chongzhen abdicate the throne in return for Li Zicheng's promises of amnesty and favorable treatment. Chongzhen was loath to agree, but he instructed Zhang Jinyan to go to the wall and see what he could do. Zhang complied and observed the eunuchs engaged in discussions with the rebels. He reportedly criticized Wang and Cao for treason, but they turned away in annoyance. According to some sources, Zhang himself became intimately involved in these negotiations. During their course, the Shun may have offered to divide the realm with the Ming. In one version, they were said to have requested a subsidy of one million taels in return for assisting the Ming against the Qing and returning to their base in Henan province. These reports may reflect actual proposals or later suppositions or some combination of both.[71] Whatever the options and Zhang's role in weighing them, that same evening Chongzhen rejected any compromise. After lashing out with his sword at various female relatives in a final gesture of impotent patriarchy, Chongzhen and one loyal eunuch sneaked out of the palace. Together they climbed Coal Hill and hanged themselves from a tree. With that royal suicide, Ming authority in Beijing came to an end.[72]

The Shun governed Beijing—and much of the central plain—for forty days, from April 25 to June 4, 1644.[73] During the first half of this period, the new regime seemed to be gaining strength, winning over men from northeast Henan located in the capital and appointing officials to Guide prefecture. Although the link between the Shun and northeast Henan was less dramatic than the one that would later be depicted in the allegory of the supposed rebel advisor Li Yan, it nonetheless warrants close scrutiny as a case study revealing some of the achievements and limitations of Li Zicheng's rebellion.

After taking Beijing, Li Zicheng had to decide on the politically sensitive issue of dealing with the remains of Chongzhen. To handle this matter, he relied on Xu Zuomei, a 1640 metropolitan graduate and fellow townsman of Zhang Jinyan from Xinxiang. Xu had surrendered to the rebels and had been appointed a messenger in the Shun office of rites. Li instructed Xu to accompany the cortege of the deceased ruler and his consort to the tomb of his concubine in Changping. Following modest ceremonies paid for by local residents, Chongzhen and his consort were respectfully buried in the extant tomb. Li Zicheng was equally solicitous toward the Ming heir apparent, Zhu Zilang, who was enfeoffed as the prince of Song, and his younger brothers, Zhu Zijiong and Zhu Zihuan, who were accorded noble rank. Although princes seldom resided in the places they were named for, the Shun almost certainly had the historical model in mind when they assigned the Ming heir a title associated with the descendants of the first historical dynasty, the Shang. The Shun thus honored literally as well as figuratively its repeated vows to treat the heirs of the fallen Ming house in a civil fashion "according to the practices of Qi and Song."[74]

The rebels sought to consolidate broad support in Beijing by leaving open the precise nature of the new regime. Li Zicheng decreed that troops that killed civilians would be executed, and Prime Minister Niu Jinxing instructed the army to treat the population well. Several rebel soldiers who killed civilians were punished by decapitation. Former Ming officials who observed the rebel assumption of authority described it as largely peaceful. There were, to be sure, some predictable cases of theft, but many of the rumors of rape proved to be unfounded. After a brief period of uncertainty, merchants reopened their businesses. People in the streets carried signs inscribed "people of accord," indicating their acceptance of the new government. Li Zicheng reportedly continued to dress modestly and was largely indistinguishable from the other rebel leaders. Some people who saw him nonetheless shouted "Long Life!" a phrase connoting respect due to a virtual head of state. In taking over the Ming royal palaces, Li Zicheng had reportedly shot an arrow into the plaque over the "Chengtian Gate" (renamed Tiananmen in the Qing). Niu Jinxing pronounced it a good omen for the eventual establishment of a new dynasty. On May 8, Niu Jinxing, Song Xiance, and others began urging Li Zicheng to declare himself "son of heaven," and they suggested the date of May 22 for the ceremony. But Li Zicheng demurred. In addition to manifesting the expected trait of modesty, the Shun prince may have felt that the time was not yet ripe. Having already won many former Ming officials and generals to his standard, he apparently hoped and expected to negotiate a similar arrangement with the Ming general Wu Sangui stationed at Shanhaiguan. Once that was achieved there would be time enough to decide on the precise nature of the regime and to establish a broad-based and durable dynasty.[75]

To be sure, the Shun did not gain the support of all the people in the capital. Among officials who had served the Ming, there were some who refused to live under any successor regime. One of the most notable was Liu Lishun, the optimus from Qi who had been companion to the heir apparent in Beijing. When the rebels took Beijing, they sent agents to Liu's house in an effort to win his allegiance to the Shun state. Liu now realized that Li Zicheng's rebels transcended the Tang rebels An Lushan and Huang Chao with whom he and others had compared them and that they seemed likely to establish a new state of their own. As a lifelong advocate of the orthodox school of pattern, and inspired by Song-period concepts of loyalty, Liu resolved to follow the example of Wen Tianxiang, the optimus of the Southern Song who had died rather than serve the Mongol Yuan. According to Liu's biography, his wife and concubine followed the Ming tradition of loyal wives and chaste women, committing suicide first. Liu then took out his brush and wrote: "The tradition of Kongzi and Mengzi was to seek humanity and justice. Wen Tianxiang practiced it, so how can I not do likewise?" He then hanged himself. Liu's dramatic act became famous because, as a metropolitan graduate whose home county had played a key role in the rebellion, he might have held a high post in the new state. Moreover, two of his consorts and two of his sons as well as several of his servants supposedly died with him. Liu's suicide thus became one of the most dramatic expressions of loyalty to the Ming in the hour of its demise.[76]

The suicide of Liu Lishun and his concubine was significant. It illustrated the continuing force of Song notions of dynastic loyalty and Ming ideas of women's chastity. To celebrate these values, the Qing state later honored Liu with the posthumous title of Wenlie (cultured and loyal), set aside seventy mu of land to support annual sacrifices at his grave, and prescribed the items of sacrifice. The Shun had not only appealed to Liu to accept its rule but also expressed regret over the needless death of a great scholar of the central province. In doing so, it reminded people that the Shun remembered its early rise in Henan, respected the credentials of Ming scholar-officials, and remained eager to win literati of all kinds to its cause. One of Liu's sons, Liu Shengzhen, who had received his provincial degree in 1630, did not commit suicide and was protected by the Shun. He therefore survived the rebel interregnum and, together with four of his own sons, conducted sacrifices at his father's tomb in the Qing. Liu Lishun's suicide was also significant because it was exceptional. Out of the more than two thousand former Ming officials in the capital at the time, only three dozen committed suicide to express their loyalty to the old regime. Others, such as Jin Biaoce, a provincial graduate on the supplementary list of 1639 from Henan, showed their loyalty to the Ming in less dramatic ways by simply refusing to serve the Shun.[77]

The Shun, for its part, also turned away some men of northeast Henan who were ready to serve it. The aristocrat Li Guozhen not only surrendered to the rebel forces to save his life but also tried to please them in an effort to protect his property. When a Shun officer demanded that Li hand over a large proportion of his family fortune, he readily agreed in hopes of earning a post in the new government. Much to his dismay, however, he soon found that other rebels had already confiscated his family's holdings, and he was unable to provide the Shun with the resources he had promised. As a result, he not only failed to secure a position with the new regime but was arrested along with other nobles and officials and executed. Commenting on this case, Zheng Lian wrote with some amusement that Li Guozhen could hardly use the "Adu things" already taken by the rebel troops to satisfy their leaders' more formal demands. The reference was to the wife of Wang Yan, the last minister of the Jìn, whose fortune was reportedly so illgotten that even her corrupt husband used the neologism "Adu things" to refer to it.[78] Once again, Zheng alluded to the parallel between the late Ming and the late Western Jìn when elite decadence undermined the state and eventually opened the way to rule by a frontier minority people.

Zhang Jinyan was another former Ming servant from northeast Henan who accepted the Shun state but was rejected by it. Zhang's role in the fall of Beijing to the rebels had earned him insults from eunuchs and vilification by Ming loyalists; rebels also spurned him when he reportedly bared his shoulder in submission and sought a post in the Shun regime. Like Li Guozhen, Zhang Jinyan was then subjected to heavy financial exaction, but, unlike Li, he avoided arrest and death. Classed among the former Ming officials who were allowed to go home, he lingered in Beijing for a few weeks and then slipped away to Shanxi en route back to Henan.[79]

Though wary of using feckless aristocrats and controversial officials, the Shun welcomed the support of several other prominent members of the Henanese local elite. Prime Minister Niu Jinxing ordered all former Ming officials to burn their seals of office and invited all those of the fourth rank or lower who wished to be considered for posts to present themselves for selection. Niu divided the candidates into three groups: those to be punished, those to be sent home, and those worthy of service in the new state. Among the ninety-odd former Ming officials selected for service in the new government were several prominent Henanese who benefited from their provincial affinity with Niu as well as from their good reputations as officials. He Ruizheng, a descendant of He Jingming, one of the Seven Early Masters, was a metropolitan graduate from Xinyang county, Runing prefecture, who served as the junior supervisor of instruction for the Ming heir apparent. When the rebels entered Beijing, he promptly surrendered. On the recommendation of Niu Jinxing, he was appointed vice president of the office of rites and head of the documents section of the institute for the advancement of literature. He Ruizheng expressed his active support for the new government by taking down the Ming plaque over the door of his office and moving his family into his official quarters. He manifested his enthusiasm by recommending other scholars, such as Fang Yizhi, and urging Li Zicheng to ascend the throne as the son of heaven.[80]

Xue Suoyun was another prominent Henanese scholar-official who served the rebels. Xue was the metropolitan graduate from Meng county, Huaiqing prefecture, who had admired the writings of the Qi provincial graduate He Yinguang. When the rebels entered Beijing, he was director of the state university; he retained that position under the Shun. He demonstrated his active involvement in the new state by directing his students to write essays that would "lead Dashing [Li Zicheng] toward a better appreciation of scholarship." He was also said to have extended protection to Liu Lishun's son, thus allowing the young man to survive the rebel regime despite his father's famous suicide in protest against it. According to one early—hostile, but probably reliable—account by an eyewitness, Xue's servants "wore red and had silver stuffed into bands around their waists, revealing themselves to be nothing other than bandits."[81]

Niu Jinxing and Xue Suoyun together attracted other scholars from northeast Henan into the Shun administration. Liu Chang, the 1625 metropolitan graduate of Xiangfu county, Kaifeng prefecture, who had played an important role in the defense of Kaifeng from the rebels, blamed Ming officials for the destruction of the city. Although he subsequently returned to his old post in Beijing, he surrendered as soon as Li Zicheng arrived in the capital. Liu was recommended by Niu Jinxing and became vice minister of the Shun court of royal sacrifices. Another Henanese scholar-official from northeast Henan who made his peace with the rebels was Zhao Ying. Zhao was a 1627 provincial graduate and 1643 metropolitan graduate from Xiàngcheng county, Kaifeng prefecture. He was a bachelor in the Hanlin Academy when Beijing fell to the rebels. As a fellow provincial and classmate of Niu Jinxing, he was appointed a straight pointer (censor) in the Shun and wielded considerable influence. Wang Jiean, the 1634 metropolitan gradu-

ate from Xiayi who had been prefect of Xiangyang, had been jailed by the Ming for losing that town to the rebels. Wang was freed when the rebels reached Beijing. Wang later
reported that he had found many of his Xiayi colleagues kneeling at the Zhengyang
gate seeking office in the Shun state, and thus he joined them. Shi Kecheng, another
1643 metropolitan graduate and member of the Hanlin Academy, also appeared in the
Shun ranks at this time. Shi, who was from Xiangfu, was an important addition since
his cousin, Shi Kefa, was the Ming commander in Jiangnan.[82]

A fifth member of the local elite of northeast Henan who served the Shun in Beijing
was He Yinguang, the 1639 provincial graduate from Qi county. He had played a key
role in the strategy of "uniting with Bian," which had resulted in the fall of Qi to the
rebels in 1642. He had gone on to pass the metropolitan examination in 1643 and
became a bachelor in the Hanlin Academy in Beijing. According to his biography in
the county gazetteer edited by his brother, when the rebels arrived outside the capital,
He "climbed the wall in anger and submitted a six point memorial on how to defend
the city." He may have made such a report, but, if so, it elicited no response. Curiously,
not even a summary of its contents remains extant. According to other sources, He surrendered to the rebels and served the Shun state in an unspecified post.[83]

If He Yinguang represented Qi county's accommodation to the Shun, two even more
prominent Ming scholar-officials exemplified Shangqiu county's acceptance of that new
government. Hou Xun, the former Ming supreme commander who had recommended
giving up northeast Henan to maintain the rest of the realm, had been reimprisoned
in late 1643. When the rebels reached Beijing he was freed and together with other
such political prisoners was taken before Li Zicheng. Li expressed his sympathy for Hou
and the others but sent them all to Liu Zongmin for interrogation. Since Hou had held
Ming posts above the fourth rank, he was technically ineligible for a post under the Shun,
but the rebels courted him anyway. Perhaps the Shun, like the Ming, hoped to use Hou
to extend its influence over his unruly client Zuo Liangyu. During the course of his
interrogations, Hou reportedly received strong support from his previously inattentive
servant Guo, who was said to have showed surprising vigor and loyalty in his master's
hour of need. Hou's interrogator, however, was another servant with the family name
Wei (personal name unknown) who was said to have once worked in the household
of the Pengs of Xiayi. Wei had apparently joined the rebellion at the time of the fall
of Shangqiu and had served it as a local official in Daming, Beizhili, before coming to
Beijing. Wei had supervised the interrogation and execution of Li Guozhen. Now he
reportedly gave Hou Xun a choice between a high post in the Shun regime and death.[84]

As Hou Xun weighed his options, the Shun state adopted policies that seemed
designed to appeal to him. It offered the empress dowager Yi'an (née Zhang), a native
of northeast Henan and erstwhile patron of the Donglin, safe passage back to her home,
the estate of the Taikang earl Zhang Guoji. Although Lady Zhang refused to compromise herself by accepting favors from "bandits" and eventually committed suicide, Hou
Xun may well have been impressed by the Shun gesture, especially since he had only
recently billeted troops at Earl Zhang's estate north of Kaifeng. Hou Xun must also have
been impressed by the Shun's literal as well as figurative honoring of the traditions of
Qi and Song by its plan to enfeoff the Ming heir apparent as the prince of Song, the

Shang successor state located in Shangqiu. Finally in burying Chongzhen and his wife in an appropriate tomb in Changping, Li Zicheng had followed the advice of Zhou Zhong, a prominent member of the Fushe in Jiangnan. From this, Hou may well have concluded that the new rulers would continue to take advice from his old Donglin and Fushe associates. On the day after the enfeoffment of the Ming heir apparent in Song, the Shun court announced the appointment of Hou Xun as president of its ministry of troops.[85]

The other senior Ming scholar-official from Shangqiu who surrendered and took a post in the Shun was Song Quan. After making a deal with the rebels in Shangqiu, allowing him to cross the Yellow River with his mother, Song had been named Ming intendant in Daming prefecture, Beizhili. Then, on March 24, 1644, Song was appointed assistant censor in chief and grand coordinator, stationed at Miyun county, in Shuntian, the prefecture that included Beijing (see Map 7.5). On April 14 he was transferred to Zunhua county, farther east in the same prefecture, and on April 22 he was named assistant censor in chief and grand coordinator of Shuntian prefecture. Three days later, Beijing fell to Li Zicheng and the Shun began to appoint local officials to take charge of the area east of the capital. At this point, according to one early account, Song surrendered to the Shun and was named military commissioner of Shuntian. Other early accounts do not include this information, perhaps because they focus on the situation in Beijing and pay less attention to the countryside, or perhaps because they were more sensitive to political pressures in the early Qing (to which Song would eventually shift his allegiance). Given the actions of Song Quan's clan uncle, Song Xun, during the Shi Shangzhao revolt, and Song Quan's own response to Li Zicheng's assault on Shangqiu, however, a decision to acquiesce in the Shun state in Beijing was quite in character.[86]

The rebels also won over members of the middle strata and commoners from Henan. For example, the government student Li Xiaoyu, said to be from Xiangfu, appeared in the Shun ranks in Beijing. A commoner named Yao Qiying, identified only as being "from Henan," assisted the Shun in dealing with the former Ming literati from Jiangnan.[87]

Although these two commoners appeared in the records by name, there were undoubtedly many more nameless commoners from Henan who participated in the Shun regime in Beijing. The Shun state attempted to consolidate its standing in the eyes of members of all social strata by reducing the tax burden that had increased considerably in the last decades of the Ming. Even the Ming in its last days had rescinded the surcharges and suspended the taxes in Henan south of the Yellow River. The Shun implemented even more radical tax reductions and holidays during its long march from Huguang to Beijing. Instead of taxing the general population, the Shun adopted the policy of extracting resources from those who had become rich at the expense of the state and the masses.

In Beijing Liu Zongmin put pressure on nobles, eunuchs, and officials to "return stolen booty as contributions."[88] Demanding large "contributions"—the usual euphemism for forced payments—from the wealthy according to their ability to pay was scarcely a new or radical idea in China. Indeed, as the rebels had advanced on the capital, the Ming state itself had attempted to extract resources from the wealthy to supply the troops.

But Chongzhen had set a poor example by denying that he had any funds left in his private treasury. His father-in-law, the Jiading earl Zhou Kui, was just as stingy, offering only twelve thousand taels when his total wealth was estimated at more than one million. The Taikang earl, Zhang Guoji, had been slightly more generous, providing twenty thousand taels, but that, too, was a tiny fraction of his total resources. Some powerful eunuchs who had accumulated great wealth were also reluctant to share it with the state. One eunuch whose resources turned out to be 300,000 taels gave up only ten thousand. Officials gave even smaller amounts, ranging from tens to hundreds of taels. The Ming state thus raised an estimated total of only some 200,000 taels in contributions on the eve of the fall of Beijing to the rebels.[89]

With a strong political base outside Beijing and considerable support among the masses, the Shun state was determined to do better. It began with the royal treasury where, according to early diarists, it found thirty-seven million taels in silver and 1.5 million in gold. It then expropriated the entire royal clan, a political and social stratum that was destined for extinction, in any case. The Shun also targeted prominent nobles of the external clan, the families of royal consorts. Zhou Kui was forced to disgorge 600,000 taels, and Zhang Guoji was relieved of similar sums before he died. The Shun then went after the nobility of merit, including particularly men such as Li Guozhen, who unwittingly pledged more than he could produce. Wealthy eunuchs were also assessed heavily, up to 50 percent of their wealth in some cases. Whereas a few eunuchs were rewarded for their roles helping to smooth the political transition, many were forced to leave the city to find other work. The goal was a reduction of the total number of eunuchs in the capital to one thousand, a reform that occurred frequently in Chinese history at the beginning of new regimes. Officials too were to be assessed according to their income and wealth. Grand secretaries were to contribute 100,000 taels; high ministers and officers of the embroidered uniform guard between thirty and seventy thousand; supervising secretaries, censors, and officials of the ministry of personnel between thirty and fifty thousand; Hanlin scholars ten to twenty thousand; and lesser officials one thousand or less. The new regime also targeted rich merchants and large landlords.

The Shun's methods were varied but effective. The quotas were to be filled voluntarily if possible, by force if necessary, and by torture only in cases of extreme defiance. According to the *Ming History*, some 70 percent of the former Ming officials in the capital complied voluntarily and only 30 percent were subject to punishment up to and including death. According to recent scholarship, the Shun thereby appropriated some 30 percent of the resources of the nobility, eunuchs, rich merchants, and great landlords and some 20 percent of the wealth of other officials in the capital. Altogether, in a few weeks, the Shun collected an estimated seventy million taels, roughly comparable to the annual revenue of the late-Ming state.[90] The rebels thereby made good on their promise to redress the social and economic balance among the state, the elite, the middle strata, and the masses. At the same time they acquired sufficient funds to assert their political interests against their Ming and Qing rivals for the mandate.

Evaluations of the Shun policy of expropriating the rich rather than taxing the poor have naturally varied according to time and place, even in the minds of individual participants and observers. In general, early diarists who lived through the events and recent analysts in the People's Republic have tended to depict the policy as a reasonable response to the skewed distribution of wealth in the late Ming. They stress that the policy was carried out relatively nonviolently and lasted only a short period of time. Southern Ming, early Qing, and some twentieth-century historians, however, have regarded the policy as ill advised to begin with and increasingly abusive as it was put into effect.

Details are lacking on the experiences and perspectives of most of the people of northeast Henan regarding the policy of expropriation of property, but one account touches on the experience of one participant and includes a brief evaluation by one observer. Wang Jie'an, the metropolitan graduate from Xiayi who was jailed by the Ming, freed by the rebels, and served the Shun, later reported that he had fared well under the rebels because he had few resources to be expropriated. After the Shun failed, however, Wang returned home to Xiayi and expressed remorse for having served a regime that had violated his "principles," presumably by demanding too much from the elite, among other things. Zheng Lian, who reported on Wang's experiences and views, commented that those who had served the Shun but later expressed regrets should certainly not be prosecuted for consorting with rebels. Zheng thus implicitly recognized that the Shun might have appealed to members of the elite who were not rich. However, Zheng criticized Shun personnel who used torture to extract resources and coerce literati into submission. For example, he condemned the servant Wei from the Peng household of Xiayi, who, he wrote, had threatened to use the finger press to force Hou Xun to take a post in the Shun.[91]

Recent analysts have expressed similar ambivalence about the Shun's requisition policy in Beijing. Gu Cheng defends the policy as a reasonable effort to correct, however incompletely, the overconcentration of resources in the late Ming. But Gu also argues that Liu Zongmin expropriated too much property and amassed an excessive amount of revenue. Xie Chengren similarly points out that the original goal of raising revenue was reasonable, and Li Zicheng soon put an end to Liu Zongmin's excessive exactions. But he acknowledges that elements of personal revenge crept into the execution of the policy, as in the decision to take over the house of the Ming official Wu Xiang, father of Wu Sangui. This step, most scholars agree, was a grave error that contributed to the powerful Ming general's decision to oppose the Shun regime.[92] On balance, if the Shun had been able to establish an enduring order, they would have been able to produce a historiography justifying their initial expropriation of ill-gotten wealth as a step toward the creation of a more viable state and a more just society. Since they did not succeed in holding on to power, they were unable to control the history of their enterprise. Historians operating under other polities have therefore been free to conclude that the Shun's confiscation of wealth was excessive and that it ultimately contributed to their failure to retain the mandate.

During its brief tenure in Beijing, the Shun state carried out several other reforms, affecting the style of leadership, the names of offices, methods of recruitment, and policies toward land. Li Zicheng and his entourage continued to live modestly, rejecting the conspicuous consumption that had helped to undermine the authority of the late-Ming state. Symbolically, Niu Jinxing honored the tablets of the rustic and frugal Ming founder and destroyed those of all other Ming rulers. Li Zicheng reportedly took a lively personal interest in the affairs of state, meeting regularly with his advisors to develop policies and questioning local officials and elders on social conditions. For this reason, one scholar from Jiangnan compared Li favorably with Liu Bang, founder of the Han. The Shun continued to name regional and local offices in conformity with Tang practice, for example, by calling grand coordinators *jiedushi* and prefects *cishi*. In an effort to rectify the overemphasis on civil administration at the expense of the military during the Song and Ming, the Shun state rated military posts over civil ones. In conducting its civil service examinations, it reduced the Ming emphasis on the metropolitan degree and upgraded the status of provincial graduates and government students. Of seventy new provincial graduates passed by Niu Jinxing in Beijing, fifty were appointed directly to offices. All 150 new government students approved by the Shun prefect of Shuntian were assigned to posts pending provincial examinations planned for the fall. In the spirit of Tang Taizong, Li Zicheng reportedly changed a plaque in the capital— "Respect Heaven and Follow the Ancestors"—to read "Respect Heaven and Love the People." Although the Shun never formally called for a periodic redistribution of land ownership comparable to the equal fields system of the Tang, it condoned the redistribution of land to tenants and the landless, and it welcomed the support of former Ming officials associated with such policies.[93]

From its new headquarters in Beijing, the Shun further consolidated its influence in the central plain. On April 30, the Shun general Liu Fangliang secured the surrender of Li Jiantai at Baoding. Other officers established Shun authority in Tianjin and other towns of eastern Beizhili. A General Guo Sheng led troops to install local officials in Shandong, a General Dong Xueli proceeded along the Grand Canal to Anhui, and a General Lü Bizhou descended from Shangqiu to the Huai. Li Yutian, a former magistrate of Qi county who surrendered to the rebels, was sent to plant the Shun flag in Sichuan. At its height in early May, the Shun was able to send officials to their posts in Hebei, Shandong, and Henan without armed guards, suggesting a certain level of public acceptance in those provinces. The Shun also mobilized key personnel to appeal for support from their relatives and clients. Prime Minister Niu Jinxing drafted a letter for the former Ming official Wu Xiang to send to his son Wu Sangui, stationed at Shanhaiguan. The Hanlin bachelor Shi Kecheng wrote to his cousin Shi Kefa, who was stationed in the Huai valley. Minister of troops Hou Xun may have appealed to his sometime client, Zuo Liangyu, still in command of considerable troops in the middle Yangzi valley. In short, by the middle of May, using force and persuasion, the Shun state had established its authority in much of the central plain.[94]

The nature and extent of Shun authority at the local level can be glimpsed in the available records for northeast Henan. After failing to prevent the rebel march to Beijing, the last Ming grand coordinator of Henan, Qin Suoshi, "gave up his post" and disappeared. By March 1644 Wang Jun, the student from Shangqiu who served as bodyguard to Su Jing, had "annulled the regulations" (presumably the rule of avoidance) and "taken over the functions" of this office (grand coordinator of Henan). Later Wang broke with the Ming and joined the rebels as Man Tian Xing. Wang/Man had his differences with "Liu and Bai" (presumably Liu Zongmin and Bai Guang'en) as well as with an (unspecified) "old enemy" in Shangqiu, but he emerged as a leading Shun general in the Liang-

Song region. At one point, for example, he led one hundred cavalry to Cao county in Shandong to "collect seals" and meet with the "magistrate." Wang reportedly treated the local elite well, caused no disturbances, and departed. The local historian Zheng Lian, who provided this account, obviously knew Wang well. He described him as tall, cultivated in speech, and with one damaged ear. Like Yuan Shizhong before him, Wang seems to have been accepted by the local elite and middle strata of northeast Henan as a counterweight to the more external authority of Li Zicheng. Like Yuan, however, Wang also seems to have run into trouble by arousing the antipathy of Li Zicheng's nephew Li Guo, also known as Yi Zhi Hu (tiger). In a pattern by now all too familiar, Li Guo eventually had Wang killed and took over his forces.[95]

Whatever the local competition from the more genteel Wang Jun, the Shun magistrates installed in northeast Henan seem to have carried out the populist policies ordered by Beijing. According to Zheng Lian, Ming officials and most members of local elite families had already fled the towns of northeast Henan by the time Beijing fell to the rebels in early April. Many tried to hide in the villages, and some were killed, although nobody ever reported it. Only a few clerks remained in the prefectural and county offices when the Shun officials arrived on May 16, and they offered no resistance. In Guide, for example,

> The rebel officials were all scholars (*shiren*), but as soon as they got down from their carriages they began to press people for supplies. All of the respectable families (*fanyou shenjia*) were ruined. The local elite lineages (*yiguan zhizu*) could not live in peace, and many of them succumbed one after the other to the five punishments.[96]

At first people attributed the actions to the particular harshness of Assistant Prefect Jia Shimei, the highest Shun official in Guide. But soon it was reported that rebel generals were making the same demands in Changyuan and Shuntian in neighboring Beizhili. In fact, Shun local officials and officers seem to have remained true to their original promises to rule on behalf of the masses even at the expense of the local elite and middle strata. From the shared perspective of early diarists and recent historians, the Shun field administrators were relatively honest and "did not dare to oppress the people." As the historian Gu Cheng puts it: "The Da Shun authority established in the localities had a newly risen, energetic countenance, and it obtained the support of the poor masses and the small and middle-sized landowners."[97]

In Beijing, meanwhile, Li Zicheng addressed the last remaining obstacle to consolidating his authority and declaring himself a new son of heaven. Having rejected the option of negotiating with the Manchus, he now focused on securing the surrender of Wu Sangui. He may have thought the task would not be too difficult since he had gained the allegiance of the Ming generals Bai Guang'en in Shaanxi and Tang Tong in Beizhili. In any case, the former Ming officials who were now advising Li in Beijing must have favored a conciliatory approach to Wu Sangui. When Liu Zongmin took over Wu Xiang's (Wu Sangui's father) house in Beijing on April 30, Li immediately recognized the mistake and sent Niu Jinxing to regain Wu's trust. When it became obvious that Wu Sangui would not be moved merely to obtain his father's release from custody in Beijing, Li overruled Niu Jinxing and decided to lead troops to the east to put pressure on Wu. To indicate his good faith, Li continued to refuse official requests to ascend the throne.

He also took with him the Ming heir apparent, the princes of Qin and Jìn, and Wu Xiang. These men were all strong cards to be played in the negotiations with Wu Sangui over the nature of the emerging regime.

Wu Sangui, however, was unwilling to compromise with Li Zicheng, whom he continued to regard as a mere bandit. Sensing that his Ming force of forty thousand men would not be able to withstand the rebel army of sixty thousand, Wu Sangui invited Dorgon at the head of eighty thousand troops outside the wall to "unite" to take "the central state(s)." The Manchus respected the Shun armies for having succeeded in taking Beijing, something they had not been able to do. They therefore assembled some of their best cavalry to assist Wu Sangui in fighting them. Li Zicheng had unwisely left his best troops in Beijing. He therefore depended on recently surrendered Ming troops to back up his negotiations with Wu Sangui. On May 25, he surrounded part of Wu's forces near Shanhaiguan and demanded serious negotiations. When none occurred, Li ordered the encircled troops to surrender. On May 27, the combined Ming and Qing forces assaulted Li's army. They inflicted many casualties, wounded Liu Zongmin, and forced Li Zicheng to flee for his life. The next day, Li's forces suffered another defeat in Yongping prefecture. In retaliation, Li put Wu Xiang to death, thus foreclosing further negotiations with Wu Sangui. Upon his return to Beijing on June 3, moreover, Li Zicheng finally declared himself son of heaven. Recognizing that he would not be able to hold Beijing against the combined forces of Wu Sangui and Dorgon, however, he immediately ordered a retreat to the western capital of Chang'an (Xi'an). Li may well have hoped to make that city the capital of a regional state if not of all under heaven, but that was not to be. In retrospect, Li's early refusal to negotiate with Dorgon and his failure to win over Wu Sangui must be counted among the major reasons for his inability to replace the Ming with his own enduring dynasty.[98]

In sum, during 1643–44 the rebel Li Zicheng rose to power in northeast Henan and in the central plain in three main stages. During the first, he left Henan and established a fledgling regime in Huguang. There he courted supporters from various social strata, adopted egalitarian policies, eliminated rival leaders, contacted scholars and officials in Guide and Kaifeng, and appointed local officials in the counties of southwestern Kaifeng. In the second stage, Li returned to Henan and defeated the last major Ming army to be sent against him. He established a regional state in Shaanxi from which he fought a rearguard action against local militarists in central Henan and appointed officials in the counties of Weihui. In the third and final stage he led armies north to take Beijing, where he dealt the Ming a fatal blow. He recruited former Ming officials and members of the elite, middle strata, and masses; expropriated wealthy nobles, officials, and elite; and sent officials to administer similar reforms in Guide prefecture. To demonstrate his humility and to keep open the possibility of a deal with Ming loyalists, he refrained from declaring a new dynasty, but he clearly emerged as the leading authority in Beijing and in northeast Henan.

The rebels owed their success in part to influence in the central province and their skill in using history to buttress their claims to authority. By establishing an administration in Xiangjing and winning military victory in Henan, they effectively countered their adversaries' continuing efforts to depict them as analogous to the mid-Tang mutineer An Lushan and the late-Tang bandit Huang Chao. By creating a regional regime in Chang'an and sending officials to Weihui, they vitiated attempts to use their geographical origins and military excesses to identify them with the autocratic and short-lived Qin and Yuan. Instead, they claimed plebian origins and popular support on the model of the Western Han and used the Li family name and associated prophecies to assert their legitimacy in the fashion of the Tang. Li Zicheng appealed to scholar-officials who shared the Li surname, as the Tang founders had done; he adopted Tang terminology for offices and places; he named his capital Chang'an and his state Da Shun after Tang practices; and he encouraged his officials to perform in the manner of Tang antecedents. The Da Shun won support from scholars and officials from northeast Henan associated with public calls for equal fields, and it adopted tax, relief, and land policies that promoted a wider distribution of wealth than had been obtained in the late Ming.

In the end, Li Zicheng proved unable to establish his own enduring order to replace the Ming. It is clear that the rebels had certain weaknesses that complicated their effort to consolidate their grip on the mandate. Their hold on northeast Henan and on the central plain was always contested, and they were consistently better at taking towns than at governing them. Unlike the founder of the Han, Li Zicheng did not use men well, eventually killing his subordinates Luo Rucai, Yuan Shizhong, and Wang Jun, who might have helped him to replace the Ming in the central province. Unlike the founders of the Tang, Li did not take full advantage of his elite supporters, Liu Chang, Hou Xun, and Song Quan, who might have assisted him in confirming his authority in Beijing. His ostensible modesty in delaying his claim to the throne did not mask his reluctance to share power with Zhang Xianzhong, Dorgon, and Wu Sangui—a sure sign of weakness. His expropriation of the wealthy nobles, officials, and elite in Beijing was politically just and economically necessary, but he allowed it to be carried to excess and alienated some who might otherwise have cooperated in resisting the Qing. The rebels' ability to establish administrations in Xiangyang and Xi'an put them on the road to victory, but their failure to take and hold Kaifeng and Beijing portended their ultimate defeat. Still, the Da Shun might yet have succeeded if Ming loyalists and Qing founders had been less skilled in using the *habiti* of history to legitimate their own quests for the mandate. Thus the decline of the Shun must be reserved for another discussion that will include as well the demise of the Ming and the rise of the Qing.[99]

Conclusion:
Things Fall Apart, Can the Center Hold?

Turning and turning in the widening gyre
The falcon cannot hear the falconer;
Things fall apart; the center cannot hold;
Mere anarchy is loosed upon the world,
The blood-dimmed tide is loosed, and everywhere
The ceremony of innocence is drowned;
The best lack all conviction, while the worst
Are full of passionate intensity.

—W. B. Yeats in "The Second Coming," June 1919

When our country was founded it was given a fine name:
Zhonghua. *What does* Zhonghua *mean?*
Zhong *is what lies at the center of an area;*
but it is the duty of our generation's youth
to consider this zhong *not just from the point of view of space,*
as if China were the center of the world,
but also from the point of view of time.
Let us look at the history of the world:
so many changes from antiquity to now!

—Li Dazhao in "Spring," October 1916

CHINESE TODAY, AS DURING THE LAST FOUR THOUSAND YEARS, often use the term *zhongguo* (the central state or states) for China and the term *geming* (changing the mandate) for revolution. In this book, I have argued that the interaction between the idea of the center and the act of change—described in these old but still current terms—helps to explain the particular pattern of Chinese history. Anchored in *zhongyuan* (the central plain) and custodians of *zhonghua* (the central florescence), Chinese polities over the ages repeatedly returned to archetypal experiences of the center—or central experiences—to situate themselves in time and extend their influence in *tianxia* (all under heaven, in other words, the known world).

More particularly, I have suggested, *zhongzhou* (the central province) first appeared as a cultural center in the semilegendary Xia period and emerged as a political center in the fully historical Shang era. It was also the principal locus of the first verifiable political change in Chinese history, from the Shang to the Zhou. The province thereafter maintained its identity as an original and recoverable cultural and political center even as it competed with other such centers—often bolstered by social and economic power—that rose and fell around it. Through two millennia, this region—which finally acquired its present identity as Henan province in the Ming—was widely regarded by Chinese as the preeminent central place, where, for example, the four winds converged and the four armies contended.

During the Ming, the northeast region of Henan, boasting ancient symbolic sites such as Qi and Song and the erstwhile polity-wide, now provincial capital of Kaifeng, retained its status as the recognized center of the province. Many members of all social levels there, including officials, elite, women, various middle strata, a Jewish minority, and the masses, often returned to earlier historical experiences to situate themselves in time and to exert their influence in space. Over time, they arrived at an often tacit but widely discernible consensus that the Han was the most relevant model providing the most pertinent precedents for their own day. Thus, for example, officials drew on Han experience in managing the Yellow River, scholars took account of Han authorities in discussing cosmology and land reform, women were honored for virtue in ways initiated during the Han, students identified with predecessors of both the Former and Latter Han, Jews redated their arrival in China to the Han, and rebels promised a more literal return to the Han as an alternative to the Ming. For all the differences in the elements of the Han experience selected and interpreted over time, these people of northeastern Henan participated in what we may call a Han "discourse." They used that discourse to express their own current concerns and were in turn shaped by that discourse in what they were likely to think and do.

As pervasive as it was, Ming identification with the Han did not preclude interest in alternative models. Indeed, the people of Ming times drew on the entire range of previous history in their efforts to come to terms with the present and to shape the future. Thus, for example, the Ming state included posts inherited from the immediately preceding Yuan, the elite espoused philosophy developed in the Song and wrote poetry characteristic of the Tang, students adopted lifestyles reminiscent of the Jin, and rebels invoked associations with the Song and the Tang. In the late Ming, as the rebel Li Zicheng gained a following in Henan, his opponents attempted to associate him with a major mutineer of the mid-Tang and a roving bandit of the late Tang. Li Zicheng and his advisors responded by publicizing long-standing prophecies that a Li would take the throne and thereby designed a new regime based on the Tang model. They won support from some former Ming officials and members of the elite, middle strata, and masses in the central plain; gradually established the Shun state at Xiangyang, Xi'an, and Beijing; and finally extended their sway through much of the central plain. In short, the rebels helped to effect, and benefited from, a shift in the discourse from the Han to the Tang and thereby contributed to the fall of the Ming.

In Yeats's terms, then, "things fell apart" in China in the early seventeenth century—for the Ming and thus for the Han model on which it was largely based. As a preface to Zhang Jinyan's reports declared, referring to the Han as well as to the Ming: "People lost the ability to move from the old to the new and idleness eventually turned into decadence." Or as one of Hou Fangyu's friends in the Snow Garden Society exclaimed in 1640: "The world is heading toward chaos and there are no heroes who can save the situation." But if the Ming lost its flexibility and even loyalists could not save it, it is less clear that the center could not hold. Li Zicheng's Shun state took advantage of the "infinite capacity for generating products" characteristic of the habitus to claim authority in Beijing for a few short weeks in 1644 by invoking the Tang model. Insofar as the Shun state won official, elite, middle strata, and mass support for restoring peace and order and effecting social and economic reform, it can be said that "the center held" for China in 1644, as so many times before.

The bitter pessimism that the European poet Yeats expressed in the wake of the Russian revolution and before his flirtation with fascism, therefore, does not seem to fit the case of the rise of the Shun and the fall of the Ming in northeast Henan. More appropriate is the critical optimism of the Chinese intellectual Li Dazhao, who questioned the meaning of centrality from "the point of view of time" five years before joining with others to found the Chinese Communist Party. Li spoke of *zhonghua*, central florescence, a concept that arose along with that of the central province and was above all cultural. Over the centuries, central florescence was an independent variable that shaped as well as was shaped by political, social, and economic forces. As the recognized heart/mind as well as stomach of the polity, Henan may have been more intensely concerned with central florescence than any other single province. By the same token, the province may have been more representative of the entire polity than any other single province. If, as has been suggested, China manifested a fractal quality in which the whole was reflected in its various parts, further research may show that the perspectives from Henan explored here were shared by many people in other provinces.[1]

China's pretension to be the central florescence of the world, skeptically acknowledged by Li Dazhao, has usually been summarily dismissed by Westerners and strongly disavowed by Chinese, especially in recent times. Such critics typically assume or assert that, although perhaps once warranted, the Chinese quest for centrality became anachronistic with the rise of Europe and America in the last few centuries. In recent years, however, both Western and Chinese scholars, for various reasons, have become more averse to Euro-American centrism and more tolerant of sinocentrism in its various guises. American scholars have rejected the once hegemonic framework of "China's response to the West," called for a "China-centered" approach to Chinese history, revitalized the category of Western imperialism as the reality underlying modernization theory, and argued against the applicability of the European concept of "early modern" to the Ming and Qing on the grounds that those polities remained innocent of "transformations" like those that occurred in Europe and America.[2] Others have analyzed the Qing polity's process of "centering" foreign guests, the Peoples Republic's "core" problem in the wake of Tiananmen, and the general need to study China "from the center, looking out" to appreciate "the universe of Chinese experience."[3] Defenders of American global hegemony, members of the Chinese Diaspora, and Chinese advocates of "Saying no" all anticipate, albeit from different perspectives and with varying reactions, that China will take its "rightful place" in the world during the present century.[4]

At the same time, the various "post-" theories (postmodernism, poststructuralism, postcolonialism) as well as feminism have contributed much to the "de-centering" of the Western experience and to the production of more sensitive studies of the peoples and cultures of East Asia and other world regions. They have explored the role of power in shaping the production and reproduction of knowledge from the so-called "Enlightenment" to the present, and they have critiqued Orientalism, or the Euro-American effort to dominate Asia by controlling the creation and dissemination of knowledge about it. They have called for an end to the search for cultural essences transcending time and place, and they have rejected binary thinking implicit in such dualities as tradition and modernity, feudalism and capitalism, East and West, male and female, and self and other. They have questioned the value of central subjects, master narratives, complete theories, and premature presumptions of universalism. They have prompted awareness of the multiple meanings of words (heteroglossia) and the value of repressed narratives representing subordinate genders, classes, and ethnicities (subaltern studies).[5]

Although much of this critical theory is most valuable in dissolving the unsubstantiated certainties of more orthodox Marxists and modernizationists, I believe some of it goes too far in rejecting any claim to any kind of centrality. One writer argues that a sinocentric approach to China is tantamount to a quest to preserve a Chinese essence; she calls for the deconstruction of "centrisms such as 'communities' with their rings of monolithic closure." Others reject the "centralizing, statist narrative of History," said to be hegemonic in China since 1911, call for a "world that has no ordering center at all," seek to "unmask the will to power that lies at the very heart of modern rationality," and try "to de-center its epistemological and moral subject" on behalf of the rest of the world.[6] Some leading Chinese scholars in the Diaspora equate claims to centrality to pretensions to superiority and reject both. In the wake of the Tiananmen tragedy, some expatriate Chinese intellectuals argue that "cultural China," broadly defined to include all those throughout the world interested in China, has become the center of China, that one can be Chinese without being loyal to any "central state(s)," or that China should abandon its quest for centrality to become a "normal" nation-state in a supposed European or Western mode.[7]

Some contemporary critiques of centrality seem too sweeping. As I have suggested in this study, centrality may occur in different arenas—geographical, cultural, political, social, economic, and so on. Sites that establish their centrality in more than one arena or successfully assert the priority of one arena over others may become preeminent centers presiding over subordinate centers. Centrality may also be distinguished from the arguably cognate but readily distinguishable concepts of superiority, hegemony, and centralism. One could go further to argue that there are different types of centrality, both within a single culture and across cultures. For example, in the Chinese case, the Kongzian idea of the virtue (*de*) that attracts is different from the Daoist notion of the emptiness (*xu*) that empowers; they are both distinct from the Legalist concept of the force (*shi*) that coerces. The prevailing Chinese notions of center and periphery may differ considerably from the European notions that have asserted their universality in the last two centuries.[8]

Nor does centrality necessarily imply closure. An intellectual historian observes that the "Neo-Confucian self is a *center* of relationships, not an enclosed world of private thoughts and feelings." A social historian who uses the problematic term "empire" to describe the Chinese polity from early times to 1600 CE nonetheless acknowledges that it was an "open" one, receptive to foreign influences as well as intent on maintaining its centrality in the world.[9] The continuing "power of the center" (in Arnheim's phrase) leads even critical theorists to consider certain ideas as "central" to their work and to attempt to bring peripheral subjects into the "center" of discourse. Some theorists seem inconsistent in calling for an end to binaries while continuing to employ dichotomous and teleological terms such as "pre-modern," "late capitalism," and "the West and the rest." Even binaries can differ in kind and function: *yin* (shadow) and *yang* (sunlight) and *nei* (inner) and *wai* (outer) operate differently under different circumstances. Such polarities must also be distinguished from the dichotomies of light and darkness in Manichaeism and being and nothingness in Western thought.[10]

The Chinese concern with centrality is unusually explicit and enduring, but it is not unique. A wide variety of Western social scientists have emphasized the importance of centrality in various contexts. Edward Shils, focusing on the Western experience, pointed out that "society has a center . . . a phenomenon of the realm of values and beliefs." Claude Levi-Strauss, specializing in Latin America, argued that a culture, to be really itself and to produce something, must be convinced of its originality and even, to some extent, its superiority. Martin Buber, aware of Asian perspectives, suggests that the "essence of community" is that it "has a center," whether manifest or hidden. Clifford Geertz and others working on Southeast Asia have found that "exemplary centers" are sites that confer "charisma." Samuel Huntington, analyzing a supposed coming clash of cultures, points out that even a hegemonic center may welcome other "dominant centers" in the interest of reducing "instability" in the world.[11]

In the study of Chinese history, one needs to eschew Eurocentrism but not necessarily Sinocentrism, avoid teleology but not always entelechy (or the accumulating power of precedent), and problematize empire but not necessarily polity (a term that is broad enough to include culture-states). With Pierre Bourdieu, one must seek to transcend "the usual antinomies . . . of determinism and freedom, conditioning and creativity, consciousness and the unconscious, or the individual and society."[12] One needs to emphasize personalities as well as structures, ideas as well as socioeconomic forces, and historiography as well as history. Above all, one should take account of the perspectives of the people one is studying and arrive at a theory of history that does justice to them. As Felipe Fernández-Armesto has pointed out, "The course of history is influenced less by events as they happen than by the constructions—often fanciful, often false—which people put on them." Indeed, insofar as all things happen in time and space, and there may be no source of authority outside of history, it is difficult if not impossible to label any constructions as simply fanciful or false. As Umberto Eco puts it, "False tales are, first of all, tales, and tales, like myths, are always persuasive."[13] Whatever the general rule, since Chinese historical actors and observers have long attached—and continue to attach—much significance to the idea of the center, no serious student of Chinese history can afford to dismiss the power of that concept out of hand.

As we have seen, people from all walks of life in northeast Henan regarded history as a cultural storehouse of experiences and models they could invoke not only to defend the status quo but also to initiate effective change. The intensity with which people looked to, spoke about, and acted out past exemplars suggests the need for a theory of historical development that takes full account of these practices. If many of the people of this region and elsewhere arrived at a consensus that there were important parallels between the Ming polity and the Han, and if rebels and their supporters effectively challenged the Ming by establishing a system reminiscent of the Tang, we may well wish to ask what this tells us about the larger pattern of Chinese history. Having traced the precise steps by which one discourse turned into another in this case, we may now turn to the task of developing a theory of Chinese history that can make maximal sense of the occurrence and recurrence of such discourses over the ages.[14]

One opportunity is to update the insights and modify the scheme of the much analyzed but sometimes poorly understood late-Qing scholar Liang Qichao. At the inception of the twentieth century, Liang divided Chinese history into three cultural epochs. Retaining his labels but modifying his periodization to take account of more recent findings and events, we may describe the three periods as follows: first, "China in China," from earliest times through the Han; second, "China in Asia," from the Wei-Jin Nan-Bei-Chao through the Ming; and third, "China in the World," from the early Qing to the present.[15] These epochs are consistent with the findings of this study that the Chinese polity began with its main center in the central province and expanded gradually outward in a world that grew to include the rest of Asia and eventually the rest of the globe. According to this revised schema, the Han appears as the last polity in the early period of Chinese history and the Ming as the last polity in the middle period. Since the Tang appeared as an attractive alternative to the Ming at the beginning of the recent period, questions arise about what role the Tang played in the middle period and whether it had a predecessor in the early period.

In thinking along such lines, one is reminded of the worldview of Sima Qian, the "grand historian" of the Han period. Sima developed a historiographical theory based on the "Three Dynasties," the Xia, Shang, and Zhou, that were regarded by many early Chinese thinkers as normative.[16] In Sima's view, each of the three polities rose on the basis of certain distinctive strengths and fell because of certain related weaknesses. Once the Three Dynasty megacycle was completed, moreover, it recapitulated itself, with the Han fulfilling the function of the Xia, and so on. This kind of historical thinking was reflected also in the Han-period idea of the sequence of the five agents (earth, wood, metal, fire, and water) that was invoked to legitimate successive dynasties.[17] Given these historiographical archetypes, it is but a small step to consider the possibility that all of the major dynasties of Chinese history had certain distinctive characteristics and appeared and reappeared in certain discernible patterns. With the benefit of hindsight, is it possible to relate the Han to the Ming and the Tang to the Shun in a meaningful pattern of history?

One strategy might be to combine the insights of Liang Qichao, Sima Qian, and the five agents theory, to classify Chinese polities into a limited number of types, and to analyze their production and reproduction over time. Scanning the period from early times through the Ming, we find that there were in fact five sorts of polities, or phases, that emerged in the early epoch in a certain sequence. More surprisingly, these five phases seem to have reemerged in the middle period in the same sequence. Defining these polities or phases by their distinguishing but complementary characteristics, we may describe them provisionally. First, there was the monarchical unifying state in which a preeminent ruler brought previously unorganized, disparate, or contending peoples together under one political roof, as the Shang did in the early period and the Sui did in the middle. Next came the elitist-reformist order in which an aristocratic or aristogenic elite sought to shape society in accordance with inherited ideals and succeeded in establishing a durable state, the Zhou in the early period and the Tang in the middle. Then developed a phase of cultural crisis and political disorder in which old ideas and institutions were questioned and numerous states contended for power, the Spring and Autumn/Warring States period and the Five Dynasties/Liao/Song/Jin. This phase was followed by the autocratic centralizing state in which tough rulers used civil and military force to reimpose order on society, governing a large territory relatively briefly but leaving an enduring legacy, the Qin and the Yuan. Finally there was the populist-egalitarian state in which plebian founders established an ethos of concern for the ideas and interests of the broad masses of the population, the Han and the Ming.[18]

Whatever debates we may have over the particular nature and quality of this or that polity or phase, the larger pattern seems to work remarkably well for the first four millennia of Chinese history. It takes good account of some of the similarities and differences among successive polities, and it factors in both contemporary Chinese mentalities and retrospective Chinese interpretations that shaped the course of Chinese history. The question remains whether it has anything to tell us about the more recent period of Chinese history, from the late Ming to the present. Although this issue cannot be addressed in any depth here and must await fuller treatment elsewhere, it can be broached in a preliminary way to round out the analysis of the present work.

In the recent epoch of Chinese history, from the late Ming to the present, there appeared no monarchical unifying state, although Zhang Juzheng's effort to strengthen the polity to deal with internal and external challenges on the model of Yi Yin of the Shang may have been a faint reflection of that phase in the late sixteenth century.[19] Perhaps Chinese society was sufficiently integrated by this time that it "needed" no such state. But in light of the growing momentum of the pattern, the accelerating pace of change, and the increasing extent of territory evident in the second epoch of Chinese history, the Shun seems to have been on to something in attempting to replace the late Ming with a rather different type of order. Although the Shun would not prove to be an enduring state, it would clear the way for such a state modeled on the Tang and the Zhou.[20] When the Qing came to an end in the early twentieth century, it was succeeded by a republic and warlords that were themselves soon shaken by the New Culture and May Fourth Movements. Although these institutions and events were in some ways novel, they may also be viewed as reinstantiations of the political disorder and cultural crisis of the Spring and Autumn/Warring States and Five Dynasties/Liao/Song/Jin phases of earlier times. With the establishment of a more muscular Republic after 1927 and an even more powerful People's Republic after 1949, there was no neat recapitulation of the autocratic-centralizing state followed by the populist-egalitarian one that we found in the early and middle epochs of Chinese history. We may nonetheless readily discern the legacies of both types of polities in each of the two competing Chinese republics of the latter half of the twentieth century.

Such anomalies in, or variations on, the pattern are healthy reminders that this theory, like any other, is not a direct description of the historical process but rather a model—or a heuristic device—designed to bring maximal order to the continuities and changes visible in Chinese history when viewed from afar at the beginning of the twenty-first century. The exceptions to the pattern may also be interpreted as signs that China, now changing far more rapidly in a far larger world than ever before, is transcending some of the "robust processes" of the past to develop new cultural and political, as well as social and economic, forms for which fewer precedents may be found in the past. But if the symmetry of the pattern as played out in the first four millennia seems too neat to be "true," the irregularities of the pattern in the last three centuries should make it more credible to those who are convinced of the irreducible messiness of the past.[21]

In any case, I would suggest that we visualize the basic dynamics of this deep structure of Chinese history as a version of what Stephen Jay Gould has called "time's arrow and time's cycle," figures that may be combined rather easily into a spiral.[22] Recognition of the appearance and reappearance or, perhaps better, the construction and reconstruction of the five different kinds of polities through two—and perhaps even into three—epochs of Chinese history allows us to focus on the novelties of time, space, personality, and event, which make each gyre different from any other without becoming meaninglessly singular. Among the many forces governing the mix of continuity and change is historiography, broadly defined to include historical actors' as well as professional historians' interpretations and reinterpretations of the past in ways that enable them to address present needs and shape future developments.[23] Using more abstract terms, we may say that strands of historical events intertwine with strands of historiographical representation to produce a kind of double helix containing the DNA of Chinese history.[24] Insofar as that history may be conceived to have spiraled slowly outward from its center, replicating earlier forms while drawing on the periphery at an accelerated pace over an ever larger space, the structure of Chinese history might even be thought of as a cornucopia. Completing the metaphor, we may say that out of that structure emerged not just the material wealth of a vibrant economy but also the spiritual riches of a vital civilization.[25]

Whether this theory of Chinese history "works" will depend in part on further research, including work on the recent period since the seventeenth century. It is not possible to go into this issue here, but it is worth noting that much recent scholarship on the last three centuries seems consistent with the schema. The late Ray Huang, an influential analyst of China's macrohistory, used the concept of the spiral repeatedly in his work that linked all of the Chinese past to its present and likely future.[26] Specialists on rituals, institutions, law, architecture, and frontier policy have noted resonances among the Zhou, Tang, and Qing. Students of the early twentieth century have remarked on affinities among militarists of the late Zhou, late Tang, and late Qing. They have also recorded republican nationalists' interest in precedents found in the Han and Ming. Scholars inside and outside the field have noted parallels among the multistate systems of the Warring States, Five Dynasties/Liao/Song/Jin, and China in East Asia of the late 1930s. Others have recognized important homologies among the Han, Ming, and People's Republic.[27]

The theory may help us to formulate answers to general questions raised by other scholars. It can indicate quite specifically how "history is culturally ordered" and how "cultural schemes are historically ordered," how models from the past are chosen "to interpret the future," and how various "robust processes" reproduce themselves in China. It can explain why one can find throughout Chinese history "events, personalities, [and] moods that appear to echo the present in haunting ways." In fact, I would suggest, the recent history of China often resonates with the past in quite explicable ways, such as when Mao Zedong identified with Zhu Yuanzhang, who had looked back to Liu Bang. The spiral theory of Chinese history might be used by students of contemporary Chinese foreign relations to help determine "which of the remembered pasts . . . is likely to have the liveliest influence on policy." It might also help us to understand why the People's Republic of China ranked its nuclear-powered submarines using Han and Ming classifications. It might even help us understand under which conditions those vessels are likely to be deployed.[28]

The viability of this theory will also depend on how well it articulates with our developing understanding of what Li Dazhao called "the history of the world"—"the many changes from antiquity to now." As scholars in China and the rest of the world have begun to question Eurocentric and teleological paradigms, they have attempted to define and locate something they are bold enough to call the "center" of world history over time. Building on a rather narrow conception of civilization (as synonymous with writing, cities, and the like), some writers continue to imagine a single "central civilization" that supposedly began in Mesopotamia and spread gradually to pervade the entire world by the end of the twentieth century. Others argue for various series of civilizations based on different world regions over time.[29]

Whatever their various and particular merits, I believe we need some such models before we can even broach the question of whether China or any other world region was ever central to world history and, if so, in what sense or senses. Examining various forms of knowledge, Lewis Mumford long ago wrote:

> [In] the ecological approach, it is the whole that reveals the nature and function and purpose of the part. Though threads in the pattern may need to be replaced, a part of the pattern modified or completely redrawn as new evidence accumulates, it is important to take in the whole, even at the cost of sharp definition, and to carry the whole through time, since some of the transformations effected by time can only be experienced, not measured.[30]

In other words, the pattern of world history that we hold in our minds, consciously or unconsciously, will inevitably shape our interpretation of Chinese or any other "regional" history. We must therefore directly confront the issue of the pattern of world history if we are not simply, in Bourdieu's words, to "ascertain preconstructed facts" that are imposed on us because we are "not provided with the means of knowing the rules of their construction."[31]

Despite the limits of my knowledge and of the available space, I shall undertake to do that here, emboldened by Lytton Strachey's mischievous claim that "ignorance is the first requisite of the historian, ignorance which simplifies and clarifies, which selects and omits."[32] Working out shamelessly from the Chinese model, I would hypothesize a pattern of world history consisting of a sequence of five different kinds of centers that succeeded one another from earliest recorded times to the present. In this view, each of five world regions—what we might call Sub-Saharan Africa, the Middle East, East Asia, Europe, and the Americas—has made its own essential, distinctive, equal, and in some ways universal contributions to the construction of today's increasingly integrated global civilization.

Central Africa, it seems, was the principal—perhaps singular—locus of the origins of the human species and the earliest human cultures. It produced the basic gender roles; hunting and gathering economies; wood, reed, bone, and shell technologies; and oral, pictorial, musical, and performing arts that became in some ways universal and continue to nourish "high" as well as "popular" culture throughout the world. Mesopotamia, apparently, was the first region to give rise to agriculture, pastoralism, and cities; terra cotta, stone, and metal technologies; commerce, chariots, and scripts; states, nations, and empires; and interimperial exchanges, rivalry, and war. Contrary to what is often implied by the phrase "four thousand years of Chinese history," then, Chinese civilization actually reached its stride only later, in the middle, as it were, of the global sequence of cultural centers. That civilization emphasized cultural continuity and political change more than social and economic transformation. It focused on establishing the greatest possible degree of peace, order, and justice among diverse peoples in a large *oecumene*. It conceptualized centrality and change as well as devised script and bronze casting, refined rites and bureaucracies as well as invented acupuncture and paper, transmitted Buddhism from India to Japan as well as produced silk and porcelain, and centered East Asia as well as sent the compass, printing, fire powder, and large fleets to the West. By that time Europe had recovered its classical heritage in the Renaissance, reformed its religion in the Reformation, and broadened its culture in the Enlightenment to produce rational–empirical science, capitalism, nationalism, industrialism, and imperialism, eventually exploiting the wealth of the New World and developing military technology to extend its hegemony over the rest of the globe. In the last century, the Americas, building on indigenous cultures, states, and resources; absorbing immigrants, ideas, and institutions from the rest of the world; and developing their own forms of industrial, technological, and military power have established their own centrality in the world. It is on that foundation that the United States presently asserts its economic and military preeminence over the land, sea, and air of the globe, the world's only self-proclaimed and widely recognized superpower.[33]

Whatever its intrinsic value, this sketch of world history allows us to return to the related questions of the place of Henan province in the late Ming and the place of late-Ming China in the world. Just as Henan arguably retained its identity as the central province of China in the late Ming, so late-Ming China maintained its status—in its eyes and in others'—as a (perhaps *the*) central state in the world. But, I would suggest, the centrality in both cases was more cultural and political than social and economic. The people of northeast Henan, in any case, seemed more concerned about invoking relevant models to maintain or reestablish a legitimate polity than about transforming society or expanding the economy. As the similarity between the Chinese characters for centrality and history might suggest, many Chinese were intent on finding centrality in history and using history to recreate centrality. During the Ming, they typically sought centrality through identification with the Han; during the Shun, they attempted to recover it through association with the Tang. In the former case, they used Han models to sustain or reform the political status quo; in the latter, they used Tang models to destabilize the existing political order and to point the way toward a new one.

As an American student of Chinese history, finally, I would conclude with brief reflections on the theory's implications for the future of Sino-American relations. It suggests that Chinese and Americans who are concerned about greater China's growing wealth and power may want to look at the early Han and early Ming for indications of how that polity is likely to exert its influence in the world of the twenty-first century. Given the two Chinese republics' dual nature (combining authoritarianism with populism), observers might want to look back as well to the Qin and Yuan for guidance on what could occur if the former characteristic is provoked into prevailing over the latter. Given the general acceleration of history evident in China as in the world, we should probably also examine the post-Han and post-Ming periods for insights into what might happen if the People's Republic is overthrown or forced into disintegration. In light of the constant expansion of the world, extending now even into space, we might also want to consider China as merely one state among many in an international order (or disorder) reminiscent of the Warring States and Liao/Song/Jin eras. In view of the Chinese people's flexibility in selecting among past models and their current willingness to open themselves to the world, we should also recognize the appeal of the Zhou and Tang models of elite reform and cosmopolitan expansion.

In any event, the pattern of Chinese history suggests that the Chinese people will play an important role in the world of the twenty-first century while the American people will figure prominently in influencing the nature of that role as well as the context in which it is played out. Greater awareness of the pattern of the past might even foster a more positive relationship between the two peoples that together will do much to influence the fate of the planet. But Chinese and Americans, as well as others, will have to draw on the experience and wisdom of *all* of the world's peoples if they are to succeed in creating and maintaining a more peaceful, equitable, and sustainable world civilization.[34]

Appendixes

Estimated Surtaxes on Land and Other Properties and Commodities in the Late Ming

	China	Henan	Northeast Henan
Wanli registered land (in mu)	(1578) 600,000,000[a]	(1581) 94,949,374[a]	(1581) Kaifeng: 38,576,128[a,b,c] Qi: 2,186,179[f,g] Huaiqing: 5,489,792[c,d]
Wanli tax in grain (in shi)	(1578) 26,360,000[a,b] 28,360,000[e] (Tianqi) 25,790,000[e] (Chongzhen) 27,170,000[e]	(1578) 2,280,759[a,b] (late Ming) 2,751,970[b]	(late Ming) Kaifeng: 807,900[b,c] (1556) Huaiqing: 330,600[c,g]
Wanli tax in silver (liang)	27,000,000[a,b] (WL) 88,930,000[e] (TQ) 55,640,000[e] (CZ) 17,760,000[e]		Kaifeng: 270,033[a,b,c] Qi: 74,461[d,f]
Estimated rate of surtax per mu (in taels)	.0035[a,b] .009[e,h]	.0035[a,b] .009[e,h]	Kaifeng: .007[b] Huaiqing: .007[b]

Surtaxes in taels:
  Liaoxiang (in 1618)
  Liaoxiang (by 1631)
  Jiaoxiang 1637
  Lianxiang 1639
  total (1631+ 1637+ 1639)
	
	2,100,000[a,b]
	10,000,000[h1]
	2,800,000[h]
	7,300,000[h]
	20,100,000[a,b,h]		

Surtaxes in taels:
  Liaoxiang 1618
  +Jiaoxiang 1637 =
  +Lianxiang 1639 =
	
	5,200,000[e,h]
	7,590,000[e]
	24,290,000[e]
		
		332,323[a,b]
		854,544[e]
		667,422[b]
			Kaifeng:
			  (Liao) 270,033[a,b,c]
			  (Jiao) 18,861
			Huaiqing:
			  (Liao) 38,429[g]
			Henei:
			  (Jiao) 24,200[g]

Estimated percentage increase of surtaxes over original taxes	Liao: 8[a,b] Total: 77[a,b] Liao: 6[e] +Jiao: 14[e] +Lian: 137[e]		Qi: (total) 25[d,f]

NOTE: Key to sources: a Ray Huang 1974: 46, 163–b4, 312, 329; b Liang 1980: 358, 377; c Cong 1985: 11; d Du Baotian forthcoming: 11; e Henan Provincial Museum 1984; f Tian, Sun, and Asiha 1735: 21; g Zheng Lian 1749: 59; h Guo Songyi 1983: 222–29.

[1] This figure includes the results of repeated increases (from .0035 to .009) in the rate of the surtax on land after 1618 and 2,292,000 taels collected on other properties and commerce that became standard after 1623. Thus the Liaoxiang income reached almost five times its original amount by 1631. Guo 1983: 223, 225.

APPENDIX B

The Number and Distribution of Provincial Graduates in Northeast Henan During the Ming

Unit	Early Ming 1370–1468 thirty-one examinations				Middle Ming 1471–1570 thirty-four examinations				Late Ming 1573–1642 twenty-four examinations			
	No.	Av. per exam	% in pref.	Rank in pref.	No.	Av. per exam	% in pref.	Rank in pref.	No.	Av. per exam	% in pref.	Rank in pref.
Henan	2211	71.3			2480	72.9			1980	82.5		
NE	973				1203				921			
Kaifeng	744	24.0			854	25.1			548	22.8		
Xiangfu	211	6.8	28	1	233	6.9	27	1	136	5.7	25	1
Chenliu	18	.6			25	.7			15	.6		
Qi	44	1.4	6	4	75	2.2	8.8	3	70	2.9	12.8	2
Tongxu	26	.8			22	.7			7	.3		
Taikang	34	1.1	4.6	7	29	.9			36	1.5	6.6	4
Yushi	no data											
Weichuan	22	.7			6	.2			6	.3		
Yanling	21	.7			25	.7			14	.6		
Fugou	15	.5			30	.9	3.5	8	17	.7		
Zhongmou	27	.9			18	.5			9	.4		
Yangwu	incomplete				incomplete				incomplete			
Fengqiu	incomplete				incomplete				7	.3		
Lanyang	39	1.3	5.2	5	38	1.1	4.4	6	22	.9	4.	6
Yifeng	37	1.2	5.	6b	39	1.2	4.6	5	6	.3		
Yuanwu	incomplete				incomplete				incomplete			
Yanjin	13	.4			16	.5			17	.7	3.	7
Chenzhou	17	.6			22	.7			38	1.6	6.9	3b
Xihua	9	.3			21	.6			23	.96	4.2	5
Shangshui	7	.2			6	.2			3	.1		
Xiàngcheng	24	.8			6	.2			16	.7	2.9	8
Shenqiu	0				4	.12			1	.04		
Xuzhou	25	.8			24	.7			14	.58		
Linying	no data											
Xiangcheng	53	1.7	7		3	42	1.24	4.9	4	incomplete		

Unit	Early Ming 1370–1468 thirty-one examinations				Middle Ming 1471–1570 thirty-four examinations				Late Ming 1573–1642 twenty-four examinations			
	No.	Av. per exam	% in pref.	Rank in pref.	No.	Av. per exam	% in pref.	Rank in pref.	No.	Av. per exam	% in pref.	Rank in pref.
Yancheng	21	.68			16	.47			incomplete			
Changge	14	.45			7	.21			11	.46		
Yuzhou	61	2.	8	2	78	2.3	9.1	2	38	1.6	6.9	3a
Xinzheng	17	.55			19	.56			11	.46		
Mi	9	.29			3	.09			7	.29		
Zhenzhou	30	.97	4	8	32	.94	3.7	7	13	.54		
Xingyang	37	1.2	5	6a	10	.29			7	.29		
Xingze	14	.42			7	.21			3	.13		
Heyin	3	.10			7	.21			4	.17		
Sishui	13	.42			10	.29			4	.17		
Guide	160	5.2			184	5.4			293	12.2		
Shangqiu	35	1.1	22	2	44	1.3	24	2	85	3.5	40	1
Yucheng	12	.39	8	4	9	.26			16	.7		
Suizhou	47	1.5	29	1	70	2.06	38	1	66	2.75	32	2
Kaocheng	8	.3			8	.24			11	.46		
Zhecheng	11	.35			3	.09			11	.46		
Ningling	10	.32			15	.44			16	.67		
Luyi	18	.58	11	3	9	.26			25	1.04		
Xiayi	10	.32			19	.56	10	3	29	1.2	14	4
Yongcheng	9	.29			7	.21			34	1.4	16	3
Weihui	69	2.29			165?	4.85			80	3.3		
Ji	37	1.19	54	1	89	2.62	54?	1	19	.79	24	1a
Zucheng	9	.29			12?	.35?			9	.38		
Xinxiang	23	.74	33	2	18	.53	11?	2	15	.63	19	2
Huojia	12	.39			15	.44			19	.99	24	1
Qí	15	.48	22	3	13?	.38?			5	.21		
Hui	10	.32			18	.53	11	3	13	.54	16	3

NOTE: The totals for Henan province are based on Tian, Sun, and Asiha 1735: 46.1–7; for Kaifeng prefecture on Guan and Zhang 1695: 23.41ff; for Guide prefecture and Yucheng, Kaocheng, Zhecheng, Luyi, Xiayi, and Yongcheng counties on Chen and Zha 1754: 7.1–20; for Weihui on De and Xu 1788: 23.28a-29a, and for all other departments and counties on relevant departmental and county gazetteers. The variety of sources of varying quality result in some discrepancies among the totals even where information appears to be complete. Where some figures are illegible, a question mark has been appended to the total.

The Number and Distribution of Metropolitan Graduates in Northeast Henan During the Ming

Unit	Early Ming 1371–1469 thirty examinations			Middle Ming 1472–1571 thirty-four examinations			Late Ming 1574–1643 twenty-four examinations		
	Number	per exam	% /rank	Number	per exam	%/ rank	Number	per exam	%/ rank
Henan	339	11.30		700	20.59		643	26.79	
NE	170	5.70	50	308	9.00	44	303	12.60	47
Kaifeng	140	4.66	82 of NE Henan	235	6.90	75 of NE Henan	182	7.58	60 of NE Henan
Xiangfu	35	1.06	25/ 1	58	1.70	25/ 1	39	1.62	39/ 1
Chenliu	1	.03		5	.15		7	.29	
Qi	5	.16		18	.53	8/ 3	29	1.21	16/2
Tongxu	5	.16		4	.12		2	.08	
Taikang	5	.16		5	.15		10	.42	5/5
Yushi	1	.03		5	.15		2	.08	
Weichuan	2	.06		1	.03		1	.04	
Yanling	3	.10		8	.24		7	.29	
Fugou	3	.10		12	.35	5/ 4	6	.25	
Zhongmou	1	.10		3	.09		3	.13	
Yangwu	4	.13		2	.06		1	.04	
Fengqiu	3	.10		4	.12		2	.08	
Lanyang	5	.16		10	.29	4/ 5	7	.29	
Yifeng	8	.27	6/ 3	9	.26	4/ 6	1	.04	
Yuanwu	5	.16		3	.09		3	.13	
Yanjin	3	.10		9	.26	4/ 6	5	.21	
Chenzhou	1	.03		7	.21		11	.46	6/ 4
Xihua	1	.03		2	.06		7	.29	
Shangshui	3	.10		1	.03		0	0	
Xiàngcheng	6	.20		3	.09		7	.29	
Shenqiu	0	0		1	.03		0	0	
Xuzhou	6	.20		7	.21		3	.13	
Linying	1	.03		8	.24		0	0	
Xiangcheng	10	.33	7/2	5	.15		4	.17	

Unit	Early Ming 1371–1469 thirty examinations			Middle Ming 1472–1571 thirty-four examinations			Late Ming 1574–1643 twenty-four examinations		
	Number	per exam	% /rank	Number	per exam	%/ rank	Number	per exam	%/ rank
Yancheng	5	.16		4	.12		3	.13	
Changge	1	.16		0	0		2	.08	
Yuzhou	5	.16		20	.59	9/ 2	12	.50	7/ 3
Xinzheng	3	.10		3	.09		1	.04	
Mi	1	.03		0	0		0	0	
Zhengzhou	3	.10		7	.21		5	.21	
Xingyang	2	.06		2	.06		0	0	
Xingze	0	0		1	.03		0	0	
Heyin	0	0		2	.06		0	0	
Sishui	1	.03		1	.03		1	.04	
Guide	20	.67	12 % of NE Henan	42	1.24	13 % of NE Henan	93	3.88	31 % of NE Henan
Shangqiu	0	0		6	.18	14/ 2	23	.96	25/ 1
Yucheng	0	0		2	.06		5	.21	5/ 6
Suizhou	7	.23	35/ 1	18	.53	43/ 1	16	.67	17/ 3
Kaocheng	1	.03		3	.09		1	.04	
Zhecheng	1	.03		0	0		0	0	
Ningling	2	.06		4	.12	10/ 3	8	.33	13/ 4
Luyi	3	.10	15/ 2	1	.03		4	.17	
Xiayi	1	.03		3	.09		10	.42	11/ 5
Yongcheng	0	0		0	0		21	.88	23/ 2
Weihui	10	.33	6 % of NE Henan	31	.91	12 % of NE Henan	28	1.16	9 % of NE Henan
Ji	4	.13	40/ 1	17	.50	55/ 1	3	.13	11/ 3
Zucheng	0	0		2	.06		3	.13	
Xinxiang	2	.06	20/ 3	5	.15	16/ 2	6	.25	22/ 2
Huojia	1	.03		4	.12	13/ 3	11	.46	39/ 1
Qí	3	.10	30/ 2	1	.03		2	.08	
Hui	0	0		2.00	.06		3	.13	

NOTE Tian, Sun and Asiha 1735: 45.12b-46a.

Biographies of Notables in the Provincial Gazetteer
of Henan by Departments, Counties, and Reign Periods

Unit	HW	YL	XD	ZT	JT	TS	CH	HZ	ZD	JJ	LQ	WL	TQ	CZ
Xiangfu	9	2	2		1		3	2	1	3		5	1	
Chenliu							1	2			3			1
Qi					2					4		7		2
Tongxu				2								1		
Taikang	2	2										1		
Yushi	1											2		
Weichuan		1										1		
Yanling	2		1				2	1				3		
Fugou										1				
Zhongmou										1		1		
Yangwu	2					1	1			1	1			
Fengqiu	1													
Lanyang	1	1	1											2
Yifeng		1				1	1	1	2	2		1		
Yuanwu														
Yanjin														
Chenzhou	2											1		
Xihua	1											1		1
Shangshui														
Xiàngcheng									1					
Shenqiu														
Xuzhou	1													
Linying	2	1						1						
Xiangcheng	1				1								1	
Yancheng	1											1		
Changge														
Yuzhou	2	2			1							1	1	
Xinzheng							1			1	2			
Mi		2												
Zhengzhou	1													
Xingyang	1						1							

	HW	YL	XD	ZT	JT	TS	CH	HZ	ZD	JJ	LQ	WL	TQ	CZ
Xingze														
Heyin	1													
Sishui													1	
Shangqiu	3	1				1	1		1	1		6	3	3
Yucheng												2		
Suizhou							1	1				2		1
Kaocheng	1													
Zhecheng	1									1			1	
Ningling								1	1					
Luyi	1	1											1	1
Xiayi	2				1							2		
Yongcheng	1											2		
Ji	1					1	1	1		4		4		
Zuchen	1													
Xinxiang	1													
Qí	1													
Hui												1		1

NOTE: Tian, Sun, and Asiha 1735: 57.59a-79a, 58.12b-27a, 66b-72a. Personalities listed under the short Jianwen and Taichang reigns were active in the previous or succeeding reigns and have been included under them. Assignment among the Jiajing, Longqing, and Wanli reigns is sometimes arbitrary because the biographies lack dates.

APPENDIX E

Achievements of 434 Women of Northeast Henan During the Ming as Recorded in the Aligned Biography Section of the Henan Provincial Gazetteer

KEY: WL=widow loyalty, WS=widow suicide, BS=betrothed suicide, SR=suicide at rape, CT=cut thigh

	Early 1368–1464			Middle 1465–1572				Late 1573–1644			
	WL	WS	BS	WL	WS	BS	SR / CT	WL	WS	BS / SR	CT
Xiangfu		11		7	11			2	4		1
Chenliu					3			3			
Qi	2			7	4	2	1	4	4	1	1
Tongxu	1			1			4		2	3	3
Taikang	2			9	2						
Yushi							4	1	7		2
Weichuan	1			1				1	3	1	
Yanling	1			2						1	
Fugou	1									2	
Zhongmou				1							
Yangwu	2			4	5			2			
Fengqiu					1		3				
Lanyang				2	1						
Yifeng				3	3				1		6
Yuanwu											
Yanjin							3				
Chenzhou	3		1	1	2			1			
Xihua				5	4	1	9		7	1	
Shangshui					1						
Xiàngcheng	1				1	2					
Shenqiu					1	2					
Xuzhou	1			1							1
Linying											
Xiangcheng				5	1	1					
Yancheng	2				2						

	Early 1368–1464			Middle 1465–1572				Late 1573–1644			
	WL	WS	BS	WL	WS	BS	SR / CT	WL	WS	BS / SR	CT
Changge							1		4	6	2
Yuzhou	1			3		1	2	2	2		
Xinzheng		2		1		1	3				
Mi	2	1		3							
Zhengzhou	2			6					6		
Xingyang								1	2		
Xingze					1						
Heyin											
Sishui	1						1		1		
Shangqiu	3	2		5	8		2	2	12	25	
Yucheng				2	1		1				
Suizhou				4	5		1				
Kaocheng				1	3					2	10
Zhecheng				1	1		1				
Ningling				2	6			1			
Luyi				1	1	1	1	2			
Xiayi					2	1	1			1	
Yongcheng				1	2		1	1	6		
Ji	2			3				1	1		1
Zuchen	1			2							
Xinxiang	1	1		2	1			3			
Huojia				1				2	1	4	
Qi								1			
Hui				2	2			4			
Totals	30	17	1	89	75	12	38 2	24	55	9 59	23

NOTE Tian, Sun, and Asiha 1735: juan 67–71. The biographies are organized rigorously by prefecture and county but only loosely by reign period and year. During the first two-thirds of the Ming, the reigns and years when the women were recognized by the state are usually given, but during the last third of the dynasty there is less attention to dates.

The Correlation Between Academically Successful Males
and Morally Virtuous Females in Northeast Henan During the Ming Dynasty
in Top-Ranking and Lowest-Ranking Departments and Counties in Both Categories

Academically Successful Males (Rank Dept/County Prov. Degrees)		Virtuous Females (Rank Dept/County Biographies)	
Kaifeng Prefecture			
1. Xiangfu	586	1. Xiangfu	38
2. Yuzhou	144	2. Qi	29
3. Qi	104	3. Xihua	26
32. Shangshui	16	32. Yancheng	2
33. Heyin	14	33. Shangshui	1
34. Shenqiu	5	34. Heyin	0
Guide Prefecture			
1. Suizhou	192	1. Shangqiu	65
2. Shangqiu	157	2. Kaocheng	16
3. Xiayi	58	3. Yongcheng	11
7. Yucheng	37	7. Xiayi	5
8. Kaocheng	28	8. Yucheng	4
9. Zhecheng	25	9. Zhecheng	3
Weihui Prefecture			
1. Ji	145	1. Ji	9
2. Xinxiang	56	2. Huojia	9
3. Huojia	46	3. Xinxiang	8
4. Hui	41	4. Hui	8
5. Qí	33	5. Zucheng	3
6. Zucheng	30	6. Qí	1

NOTE: For provincial degrees, see Appendix B. For biographies of women, see
Appendix E.

Reference Matter

CHARACTER LIST

This is a selective list of the characters for relatively obscure persons, places, and terms that may not be widely known or easily located in standard sources.

Ai Jing　艾敬
Ai Jun　艾俊
Ai Tian　艾田
Ai Yingkui (Wensuo)　艾應奎（文所）
Anle　安樂
An San　俺三
Anchang　安昌
Andula　俺都剌
Bai Guang'en　白廣恩
Baoming　保明
Bu Congshan　卜從善
Cai Boguan　蔡伯貫
Cai Moude　蔡懋德
Cao (family of Nanyang)　曹
Cao Hua　曹華
Cao Huachun　曹化淳
Cao Wei　曹威
Chang Daoli　常道立
Chang Wejen　張維仁
Changping　長平
Changyi　昌義
Chen Biqian　陳必謙
Chen De　陳德

Chen Han　陳翰
Chen Menggong　陳孟公
Chen Mingsheng　陳明聖
Chen Taiqiu (Chen Shi)　陳太丘（陳實）
Chen Tianqing　陳天晴
Chen Wenshi　陳聞詩
Chen Yixin　陳意新
Chen Yongfu　陳永福
Chong (prince)　崇
Chongyang　重陽
Chu Cen　褚岑
Chu Taichu　褚泰初
Chu Taizhen　褚泰珍
Cui Zhihuai　崔植槐
Dabao　大寶
Dai Yi　戴逸
DaLiuzhai zhuang　大劉寨庄
Dan Anren　單安人
Dasheng Xingsheng　大乘興胜
De (prince)　德
Deng Lian　鄧璉

Desheng　德勝
Ding Moude　丁懋德
Ding Mouji　丁懋績
Ding Mouxun　丁懋勳
Ding Qirui　丁啓睿
Dong Sichen　董嗣諶
Dong Sipu　董嗣樸
Dong Xueli　董學禮
Dongping　東平
Dongwaxiang　洞瓦廂
Dongyuan gong　董園公
Du Tao　杜慆
Du Xun　杜勳
Duanli　端禮
Duan Xu　段續
Fan Liangyan　范良彦
Fan Mengdou　樊夢斗
Fan Pang　范滂
Fan Shuhua　樊書華
Fan Zuo　范左
Fang Guan　房琯
fanyou shenjia　凡有身家
Fei Cengmou　費曾謀
Fu Zhenlun　傅振倫

339

fulujiu 福祿酒

Gao Nian 高年

Gao Yingxiang 高迎祥

Gao Yuanheng (Chuangzi)
高元衡（闖子）

Gaoyang 高陽

Geng Yinggeng 耿應庚

Geng Yingzhang 耿應張

Gu Bingqian 顧秉謙

Guan Yongjie 關永杰

Guanhuayuan 關花園

Guo (river) 渦

Guo Shang 郭尚

Guo Sheng 郭陞

Guo Tai 郭泰

Haiyang 海陽

Han Huamei 韓華美

hanshi 寒石

He Chengxiang 何程祥

He Dengshan 何登山

He Dongsheng 何東升

He Guang 何廣

He Qian 何謙

He Ruizheng 何瑞徵

He Yilong 賀一龍

He Yinguang 何印光

He Yinzhen 何胤軫

Heigang 黑罡

Hengdipu 橫地鋪

Hesen 合森

Hou Fanglai 侯方來

Hou Fangxia 侯方夏

Hou Fangyan 侯方嚴

Hou Fangyue 侯方岳

Hou Fangzhen 侯方鎮

Hou Jin (Zideng) 侯進
（子登）

Hou Lü 侯慮

Hou Shu 侯恕

Hou Xie 侯緦

Hou Xing 侯性

Hou Yin 侯愔

Hou Yinglin 侯應璘

Hou Yingyu 侯應瑜

Hou Yu 侯瑀

Hou Yuzhao 侯于趙

Hou Zhigao 侯執羔

Hou Zhigong 侯執躬

Hou Zhigu 侯執穀

Hou Zhijie 侯執介

Hou Zhizhong 侯執中

Huang Shu 黃澍

Huangfu Gui 皇甫規

Ji Wenda 紀文達

Jia Kaizong 賈開宗

Jia Shimei 賈士美

Jia Sui 賈遂

Jia Yi (Changsha) 賈誼
（長沙）

Jiang Taigong 姜太公

Jiang Xiang 姜瓖

Jiang Xuan 姜瑄

Jiaoxiang 劉銅

Jin Biaoce 靳標策

Jin Gang 金剛

Jiyang 濟陽

Jing (prince) 景

Jing Liangtian 井良田

jinzhong Ligong 金鍾李公

Julu 鉅鹿

Junpingfu 均平府

Juyong 居庸

Ke (madame) 客氏

Kong Shangda 孔尚達

Kong Shangyue 孔尚鉞

Kou Xun 寇恂

li (pattern) 理

Li (for Levy) 李

Li Anhe 李安和

Li Changhe 李芑和

Li Chaowang 李朝網

Li Donglu 李東魯

Li Eryu 李爾育

Li Fuda 李福達

Li Gu 李固

Li Guanglu 李光閭

Li Guangtian 李光殿

Li Guo 李過

Li Guoyong 李國用

Li Guozhen 李國楨

Li Hao 李好

Li Hongji 李鴻基

Li Goupi 李狗皮

Li Jichun 李際春

Li Jiexuan 李潔軒

Li Jing 李靖

Li Jiyu 李際遇

Li Keda 李可大

Li Kui 李奎

Li Laibi 李來庇

Li Laiming 李來命

Li Laiqing 李來慶

Li Laixuan 李來宣

Li Laizhao 李來詔

Li Liang 李良

Li Liangyu 李良雨

Li Liangzhi 李良知

Li Linfu 李林甫

Li Mengchen 李夢辰

Li Mouchun 李茂春

Li Rong 李榮

Li Senxian 李森先

Li Shangyin 李商陰

Li Shenwu 李慎吾

Li Shizi 李氏子

Li Shouzhi 李守志

Li Tingsheng 李挺生

Li Tong 李同

Li Wu 李五, or 午

Li Xianfeng 李仙風

Li Xiangjun 李香君

Li Xiaoyu 李肖宇

Li Xin (Xiangfu physician)
李信

Li Xin (Luyi sectarian)
李新

Li Xu 李栩

Li Xueshu 李學恕

Li Yan 李嚴, or 李岩

Li Yao 李耀

Li Yiqi 酈食其

Li Ying 李膺

Li Yinglong 李應龍	Liu Liangzuo 劉良佐	Ma Zhifei 馬之騆
Li Yingqian 李應乾	Liu Lihua 琉璃滑	Ma Zhifu 馬之皁
Li Yuan (Huzi) 李原	Liu Lishun 劉理順	Majiakou 馬家口
（鬍子）	Liu Lun 劉輪	Majiazhai 馬家齋
Li Yuangong 李元共	Liu Qianjin 劉千斤	Mamuji 馬牧集
Li Yue 李鉞	Liu Qingyuan 劉清源	Mamuzhen 馬牧鎮
Li Yutian 黎玉田	Liu Rukui 劉汝魁	Man Tian Xing 滿天星
Li Zaibai 李再白	Liu Shengzhen 劉聖箴	Manla 滿喇
Li Zhen (official) 李真	Liu Tianxu 劉天緒	Mao Jiaqi 茅家琦
Li Zhen (rabbi) 李禎	Liu Tong 劉通	Mao Wenbing 毛文炳
Li Zhenhai 李振海	Liu Xiang 劉向	Matou 馬頭
Li Zhensheng 李振聲	Liu Xiangshun 劉向順	Meng Jiongsu 孟冏驌
Li Zhenzuo 李貞佐	Liu Xingshun 劉行順	Meng Nan 孟楠
Li Zhiyang 李支揚	Liu Xueting 劉學婷	Meng Ruhu 猛如虎
Li Zilong 李子龍	Liu Yan 劉晏	Meng Shaokang 孟紹康
Lian 練	Liu Zhongying 劉仲郢	Meng Shaoqian 孟紹謙
Lian Fan 廉范	Liu Zongmin 劉宗敏	Meng Shaoyi 孟紹伊
Lian Guoshi 練國事	Liuyuan 柳園	Meng Shaoyu 孟紹虞
Lianxiang 練餉	Longshan 龍山	Meng Yanghuo 孟養活
Liang Xiaowang 梁孝王	Lu (prince, Shanxi) 潞	Meng Yuanlao 孟元老
Liang Yizhang 梁以樟	Lu (prince, Shandong) 魯	Miao Henglun 苗恆淪
Liang Yungou 梁雲構	Lu Jiude 盧九德	Miao Sishun 苗思順
Liao Guolin 廖國遴	Lu Xiangsheng 盧象昇	Miao Wenying 苗文英
Liaoxiang 遼餉	Lu Zhi (Zhongxuan) 陸贄	Ni Heng 禰衡
Liewei 列微	（忠宣）	Ning Long 寧龍
Lige 李格	Lu Zongtai 盧宗泰	Niu Jinxing 牛金星
Lijiqianzhai 李繼遷寨	Lü (sect leader) 呂	Niu Quan 牛佺
Liu Bingshan 劉炳善	Lü Bizhou 呂弼周	Niweini 你尾尼
Liu Boyu 劉伯愚	Lü Desheng 呂德胜	Pan 潘
Liu Chang 劉昌	Lü Guan 呂官	Pan Fu 潘复
Liu Chao 劉超	Lü Hou 呂后	Pang Xun 龐勛
Liu Chen 劉宸	Lü Pusa (Bodhisattva)	Peng Shunling 彭舜齡
Liu Chong 劉寵	呂菩薩	Peng Xialing 彭遐齡
Liu Dashun 劉大順	Lü Zhenzhi 呂貞知	Peng Yaoyu 彭堯諭
Liu Dong 劉東	Lü Zhiwei 呂知畏	Ping Wang 平王
Liu Fangliang 劉方亮	Lü Xiru 呂翕如	Qi (state, county) 杞
Liu Fen 劉黃	Lü Zuqian 呂租謙	Qí (river, county) 淇
Liu Ge 劉格	Luo Rucai 羅汝才	Qi Bo 岐伯
Liu Hanchen 劉漢臣	Luo Wenying 羅文英	Qi Shirong 齊世榮
Liu Hao 劉浩	Ma Chengde 馬呈德	Qiao Hongqi 喬宏杞
Liu Hongli 劉洪禮	Ma Qi 馬顓	Qiao Jiabao 喬家保
Liu Hongqi 劉洪起	Ma Shiying 馬士英	Qiao Mingzhan 喬明旃
Liu Hui (San) 劉惠（三）	Ma Yuan 馬援	Qiao Sheng 喬生
Liu Hui 劉輝	Ma Zhichi 馬之馳	Qin Mengxiong 秦夢熊

Qin Moude　秦懋德

Qin Suoshi　秦所式

Qing Hong　慶鴻

Qinglonggang　青龍岡

Qingzhen　清青

Qiu Lei　邱磊

Rusong　如松

Sang Kaidi　桑開第

Saodi Wang　掃地王

Shang Jiong　尚絅

Shen Du　沈杜

Shen Han　沈瀚

Shen Jiayin　申佳印

Shen Jingbang　申靖邦

Shen Li　沈鯉

Shen Shi　沈試

Shen Wandeng　沈萬登

Shen Xuan　沈旋

Shen Yu　沈譽

Shen Zhixiu　申芝秀

Shenjiaji　沈家集

Sheng Shun　盛順

Shi (Jewish family)　石

Shi Kecheng　史可程

Shi Kefa　史可法

Shi Long (heshang)　石龍
（和尚）

Shi Shangzhao　師尚詔

Shi Shi　史仕

shiba haier zhu shenqi　十八
孩兒主神器

shibazi　十八子

Shoushan　首善

Shu Qi　叔齊

Song Cong　宋琮

Song Mei　宋玫

Song Xiance　宋獻策

Song Xun　宋繡

Song Yang　宋賜

Song Zhan　宋沾

Songfo Zhang　宋佛張

Su Gengsheng　蘇更生

Su Jing　蘇京

Suiyang　睢陽

Tang (prince)　唐

Tang Tong　唐通

Tang Xuan　唐鉉

Tian Sheng　田生

Tian Zhujiao　田助教

Tianbao (heaven protected)
天保

Tianbao (heavenly treasure)
天寶

tonghou　通侯

Wan Shi Jun (Shi Fen)
萬石君（石奮）

Wan Yuanji　萬元吉

Wang Cheng'en　王承恩

Wang Dao　王導

Wang Duo　王鐸

Wang Guoning　王國寧

Wang Han　王漢

Wang Haoxian　王好賢

Wang Hongjun　王宏鈞

Wang Jiean (Chenglu)
王介菴（承魯）

Wang Jing　王景

Wang Jun　汪濬

Wang Liang　王良

Wang Meng　王猛

Wang Qiaonian　王喬年

Wang Ruiping　王瑞平

Wang Sanshan　王三山

Wang Shijun　王士俊

Wang Shiqing　王世清

Wang Shixiu　王世琇

Wang Shulin　王樹林

Wang Zichao　王子超

Wang Tang　王堂

Wang Xian　王獻

Wang Xie　王燮

Wang Yan　王衍

Wang Yanfang　王彥方

Wang Yongji　王永吉

Wang Yuxin　王鈺欣

Wang Zhaojun　王昭君

Wang Zishou　王紫綬

Wang Zun　王尊

Wei (family name)　韋

Wei (servant from Xiayi)　魏

Wei Guangwei　魏廣微

Wei Jingqi　魏景琦

Wenduan　文端

Wenlie　文烈

Wenshu　文殊

Wu Boyi　吳伯裔

Wu Boyin　吳伯胤

Wu Shijiang　吳士講

Wu Qi　吳起

Wu Xueli　吳雪莉

Xiangjing　襄京

Xiao Qin Wang　小秦王

Xie An　謝安

Xie Chengren　謝承仁

Xifeizhai　西肥寨

Xihuayuan pu　西花園鋪

xin shunwang　新順王

Xing Shuen　邢樹恩

Xu Dingguo　許定國

Xu Lintang　徐鄰唐

Xu Yuan　許遠

Xu Zuolin　徐作霖

Xu Zuomei　許作梅

Xuan Mo (Yuan Mo)　玄默
（元默）

Xue Suoyun　薛所縕

xueyuan she　雪園社

Yan Yunjing　嚴雪京

Yan Zekong　顏則孔

Yang Cuihua　楊翠華

Yang Hu　楊虎

Yang Ma　楊麼

Yang Nianqun　楊念群

Yang Sijing　楊思敬

Yang Wenyue　楊文岳

Yang Youwen　楊右文

Yangwu　揚武

Yanlizhai　閻李寨

Yanqing　延慶

Yao Qiying　姚奇英

yiguan zhizu　衣冠之族

Yihe　義和

Yingcheng　應城

Yitiaolong　一條龍

Yizhihu　一隻虎

Yongchang　永昌

You and Yan　幽,燕

Youguo　祐國

Yu (Henan province)　豫

Yu (sage ruler)　禹

Yu (Qi county)　圉

Yu Longmen　余龍門

Yu Zhining　于志寧

Yuan Laoshan　袁老山

Yuan Shizhong　袁時中

Yuan Shu　袁框

Yuan Zongdi　袁宗第

Yudong　豫東

Yuzhen　圉鎮

Yuzhou　豫州

Zeng Yinglin　曾應遴

Zhang (Yi'an Huanghou)　張（懿安皇后）

Zhang Anshi　張安世

Zhang Changtui　張長腿

Zhang Deng　張登

Zhang Guoji　張國紀

Zhang Han　張瀚

Zhang Hefeng　張鶴峰

Zhang Hesheng　張和聲

Zhang Jinjian　張金監

Zhang Jinyan　張縉彥

Zhang Mengxi　張孟習

Zhang Panzi　張判子

Zhang Pingshan　張平山

Zhang Qing　張清

Zhang Renlong　張人龍

Zhang Shao　張劭

Zhang Wei　張溦

Zhang Weiyi　張唯一

Zhang Wenguang　張文光

Zhang Wenming　張問明

Zhang Wenren　張問仁

Zhang Xiu　張琇

Zhang Yao　張瑤

Zhang Yingfeng　張應奉

Zhang Yizhu　張一柱

Zhang Yongqi　張永祺

Zhang Yu　張輿

Zhang Yuji　張虞機

Zhang Xun　張巡

Zhang Zhong　張中

Zhangyi　彰義

Zhao Cheng　趙誠

Zhao Jinglong　趙景隆

Zhao Sui (Fengzi)　趙鐩（瘋子）

Zhao Ying　趙應

Zhao Ying (Xiàngcheng man)　趙穎

Zhaocunji　趙村集

Zheng Eryang　鄭二陽

Zheng Sanjun　鄭三俊

Zheng Xia　鄭俠

Zheng Yi　鄭鎰

Zheng Zhijun　鄭之俊

Zhengyang　正陽

Zhong Huamin　鍾化民

Zhongxing Fuliedi　中興福烈帝

Zhou (prince)　周

Zhou Kui　周奎

Zhou Lianggong　周亮工

Zhou Pu　周溥

Zhou Sheng　周生

Zhou Shipu　周試樸

Zhou Sisheng　周斯盛

Zhou Yu　周瑜

Zhou Zhong　周鍾

Zhu Bingnan　朱炳南

Zhu Changfang　朱常淓

Zhu Dadian　朱大典

Zhu Muyang　朱睦㮰

Zhu Weimin　朱維民

Zhu Yi　朱邑

Zhu Yiliu　朱翊鏐

Zhu Youkui　朱由檟

Zhujiakou　朱家口

Zhujiazhai　朱家寨

Zhujiazhuang　朱家庄

Ziweixing　紫微星

Zou Yang　鄒陽

Zuo Guoji　左國機

Zuo Moutai　左懋泰

Zuo Tang　左唐

NOTES

Introduction

1. Shanquan 1977: 1, 3; Henan huace 1984: 3, 6. Henan has a slightly higher percentage of arable land than China. The term "central plain" dates from an earlier era than the term "North China plain," reflecting the periodic rise of cultures in the Yangzi valley from the late Zhou on.

2. Chi 1936: 17–20; Shanquan 1977: 14; Skinner 1977: 211–49, map on 214–15; Tan Qixiang 1982: I: 20–21, 26–27; Lin and Chen 1983: 20–21; Geelen and Twitchett 1974: xxiii; Loewe and Shaughnessy 1999: 32. For other problems with the macroregional model, see von Glahn 1987: xx–xxii, 215–22; Heijdra 1994: 9–11; Gates 1996: 63–83. In 1988 a Chinese television miniseries used the Yellow River as a symbol of the alleged stasis of Chinese civilization (Su and Wang 1994). The river might equally well be seen as a symbol of the topographical dynamism of northeast Henan.

3. Geelen and Twitchett 1974: xxi.

4. Herrmann 1964: 9–10; Zhu 1972: 17; Huang Yizhu 1981: 3; Tan Qixiang 1982: I: 7–10; Lin and Chen 1983: 14; Henan huace 1984: 6; Shuili dianli bu 1984: 56; Loewe and Shaughnessy 1999: 47–59, 71–73, 648–49.

5. Herrmann 1964: 9; Chang Kwang-chih 1968: 226; Wheatley 1971: 10, 20, 30, 75, 114; Ho 1975; Huang Yizhu 1981: 3; Tan Qixiang 1982: I: 12–14; Keightley 1983; Kwang-chih Chang 1983: 508; Sage 1992: 219; Loewe and Shaughnessy 1999: 108, 269, 275–77, 281. Karl Wittfogel contrasted the Shang capitals' locations with those of Mesopotamian and Egyptian capitals in the midst of deserts. See Chi 1936: 28. For a recent summary of problems with Wittfogel's other theses on China, see Lewis and Wigen 1997: 94–96. For arguments against the centrality, extent, and even historicity of the Shang state, see Loewe and Shaughnessy 1999: 124–231.

6. Tan Qixiang 1982: I: 16; Huang Yizhu 1981: 4–5; Ebrey 1996: 31. For the Zhou's acceptance (or invention) of Shang assertions of centrality as a basis for their own, see Loewe and Shaughnessy 1999: 158, 230; for recognition of the Zhou's centrality even by the large peripheral state of Chu, see Ibid., 525.

7. Huang Yizhu 1981: 6; Tan Qixiang 1982: I: 33–34. For the importance of the Yellow River in defining the Warring States world, see Loewe and Shaughnessy 1999: 593, 597.

8. Chi 1936: 36; Herrmann 1964: 18–19; Tan Qixiang 1982: II: 7–8; Sage 1992: 2, 119.

9. Chi 1936: 85–86, 92, 93; Durand 1960: 249; Herrmann 1964: 22–23; Zhu 1972: 20–21; Huang Yizhu 1981: 7; Tan Qixiang 1982: II: 15–16, 19–20; Lin and Chen 1983: 62–63; Twitchett and Loewe 1986: 206–7, 241, 250–51; Sage 1992: 88–91. For the cultural centrality of Henan in this period, including bas-reliefs that set standards for other places, see Wu Hong 1989: 67.

10. Chi 1936: 101–7; Herrmann 1964: 25, 28–33; Geelen and Twitchett 1974: x; Huang Yizhu 1981: 8; Tan Qixiang 1982: III: 3–8, 35–38; IV: 3–4, 7–28, 46–49, 61–62, 65–66; Yang Hsüan-chih 1984: 113–22, 145–51, 173–74, 202–4, 230; Ebrey 1996: 104.

11. Chi 1936: 116–21; Durand 1960: 249; Herrmann 1964: 36; Twitchett 1979: 60, 72; Tan Qixiang 1982: V: 3–6, 15–16, 17–18; Lin and Chen 1983: 68–70.

12. Chi 1936: 116–21; Durand 1960: 249; Herrmann 1964: 36; Twitchett 1979: 60, 72; Tan Qixiang 1982: V: 3–6, 15–16, 17–18; Lin and Chen 1983: 68–70.

13. Chi 1936: 131; Miyakawa 1954–55; Elvin 1973; Hermann 1964: 41; Tan Qixiang 1982: V: 84–90; Ebrey 1996: 135.

14. Durand 1960: 249; Kracke 1975: 66; Mei 1975: 23; Huang Yizhu 1981: 9; Tan Qixiang 1982: VI: 12–17; Lin and Chen 1983: 77–79; Chao Kang 1986: 50.

15. Miyakawa 1954–55; Hartwell 1966, 1967, 1982; Shiba 1970; Laurence J. C. Ma 1971; Haeger 1975; McNeill 1982b: ch. 2; Frank 1998: 108.

16. Chi 1936: 130; Mei 1975: 30; Huang Yizhu 1981: 10; Tan Qixiang 1982: VI: 16–17, 52–53.

17. Yao Shao-yu 1942–43: 368; Chi 1936: 36; Herrmann 1964: 52; Perkins 1969: 198; Huang Yizhu 1981: 10; Tan Qixiang 1982: VII: 5–6, 34–35; Lin and Chen 1983: 78, 80; Jin and Liu 1984: 226; Chao Kang 1986: 203.

18. Shanquan 1977: 2; Wakeman 1985: 28–29; Brook 1998: 36.

19. The size of the prefectures is an estimate based on the size of their constituent counties. See Guan 1956: 81–86.

20. Chi 1936: 143–44; Van der Sprenkel 1953: 312–13; Zhu 1972: 25–26; Ho 1959: 258, 264; Durand 1960: 233–34, 248–49; Perkins 1969: 216; Elvin 1973: 255; Mei 1975: 52–53; Yim 1978: 15–18; Liang 1980: 218–21; Huang Yizhu 1981: 10; Lin and Chen 1983: 79–80; Cong 1985; Chao Kang 1986: 37; Brook 1985: 32; 1998: 28; Frank 1998: 168, 170; Lavely and Wong 1998: 739; Mote 1999: 745; Hansen 2000: 411. Given recent population estimates for China as a whole by 1600, Yim's figures for Henan seem plausible, but they may have been inflated by officials eager to claim achievements in administering relief. For the famine that led to those statistics, see Chapter 1.

21. Van der Sprenkel 1953: 312–13; Liang 1980: 218–21; Guan 1956: 80–86.

22. Tian, Sun, and Asiha 1735: 21–22; Wang Yü-ch'üan 1965; Perkins 1969: 16, 222–31; Ray Huang 1974: 164, 301; Wu Dange 1979; Liang 1980: 220–21, 332–33, 364; Cong 1985: 11; Wang Xingya 1984a: 37–42; Chao Kang 1986: 81–85; Gu Cheng 1986: 193–213; 1990: 200, 204, 207, 216–17; Twitchett and Mote 1998: 433.

23. Wang Yü-ch'üan 1936; Ray Huang 1974: 35–36, 164; Liang 1980: 357–58, 453–54; Skinner 1985: 279; Chao Kang 1986: 38–42; Perdue 1987: 62–64; Goldstone 1991: 368–75; Twitchett and Mote 1998: 105.

24. Bourdieu 1990: 54–55.

25. For these concepts, see Goldstone 1991: 36, 46–47, 54–60, 346; Wong 1997: 3, 196, 293.

Chapter 1

1. Zhang Tingyu 1739: 116: 3557; 127: 3769; Hucker 1958: 8; Farmer 1976: 76–79; Gu Cheng 1982: 92; Mote and Twitchett 1988: 121; Tong 1991: 174; Su Jinzi 1991: 41; Andrew and Rapp 2000: 22.

2. Zhang Tingyu 1739: 116: 3565–66; Farmer 1976: 43–45, 75; Goodrich and Fang 1976: 350. See also Chapter 3.

3. Zhang Tingyu 1739: 116: 3566–67; Goodrich and Fang 1976: 353–54, 380–81; T'ien 1988: 2–3.

4. Lo 1975: 28; Mei 1975: 59; Su 1991: 41–43.

5. Wang Shixing 1831: 1: 20a; Hucker 1958: 8–9; Lo 1975: 26–27; Mei 1975: 61, 62, 66; Gu Cheng 1982: 97–98, 100; Zhi 1990: 122–25. In general, concubinage among the nobility of Ming and Qing times may not have increased their fertility. See Dardess 1996: 90–91; James Lee 1997; Rawski 1998: 129; Lee and Wang 1999: 75–77.

6. Zhang Tingyu 1739: 116: 3568; Gu Yanwu 1811: 13: 76a–77a; Lo 1975: 26; Mei 1975: 62–63; Gu Cheng 1982: 98–99, 101; Tong 1991: 175; Twitchett and Mote 1998: 150; Rawski 1998: 94.

7. Wang Yü-ch'üan 1964: 219–305; Gu Cheng 1982: 107–8; Tong 1991: 172.

8. Su Derong 1984: 25–35, 39–40.

9. Ibid., 45–48.

10. Chang Moulai 1852: 4a–11b; Lo 1975: 29; Mei 1975: 37–39, 44–45, 64, 179–94. The Zhou prince undoubtedly held much of the 528,343 mu of noble land in Kaifeng prefecture reportedly taken over by the people in the early Qing. See Gugong bowuyuan 1979: 4: 182–86.

11. Su Derong 1984: 85–91.

12. Ibid., 3, 51–54, 55–56, 80–81, 82–84. For reasons to problematize the term "Confucian," derived from the term "Confucius" invented by the Jesuits, see Jensen 1997.

13. Ibid., 9–10, 13–18, 25, 52. For the idea of China as an "open empire," see Waley-Cohen 1999; Hansen 2000. Unlike Hansen, I see this openness as stemming from China's emphasis on cultural centrality over imperial control and lasting through the Ming.

14. Quotation from He Qiaoyuan, *Mingshan Zang*, 106 juan, 1640, cited in Mei 1975: 63–64; see also Su Derong 1984: 40–45, 86–87.

15. Zhang Tingyu 1739: 120: 3749–50; Goodrich and Fang 1976: 332–33. Precisely because the biography of Zhu Changxun corresponds so well to the stereotype of what we may call the "bad last prince," it should be evaluated critically. Unfortunately this topic lies largely outside this study, but it may be significant that the same sources that excoriate the Fu prince are evenhanded in discussing the Lu and Zhou princes.

16. Hucker 1985: 70–78. In general, I follow Hucker's translations but use "ministry of troops" instead of "war," "punishments" instead of "justice," "departments" instead of "subprefectures," and "counties" instead of "districts." For the censorate, see Hucker 1966 and 1969.

17. Tian, Sun, and Asiha 1735: 54: 27a–31b; 55: 16b–19b; Hucker 1985: 75–76.

18. Goodrich and Fang 1976: 1608; Tian, Sun, and Asiha 1735: 54: 22a; Zhang Tingyu 1739: 170: 4543–44; Ray Huang 1974: 104; Twitchett and Mote 1998: 488n212.

19. Zhang Tingyu 1739: 170: 4545, 4553; Tian, Sun, and Asiha 1735: 54: 22; Ray Huang 1974: 255; Goodrich and Fang 1976: 1609–11; Wolfgang Franke 1976.

20. Van der Sprenkel 1961: 308–15; Parsons 1969: 181–84; Ho 1962: 226–31; Tian, Sun, and Asiha 1735: 31: 7–9; 54: 33a.

21. Tian, Sun, and Asiha 1735: 31: 3a.

22. Needham, Wang, and Lu 1971: IV.3: 209 and facing map, fig. 859, table 69, 242–43; Greer 1979: 5, 22; Tan Qixiang 1982: IV: 17–18; Mote and Twitchett 1988: 39, 40, 46, 59, 60.

23. Tian, Sun, and Asiha 1735: 14: 1–2, 9a, 18a; Farmer 1976: 44; Goodrich and Fang 1976: 350; Zhou Kuiyi 1990: 320–21, 329.

24. Tian, Sun, and Asiha 1735: 14: 4b; Zhang Tingyu 1739: 153: 4204; Needham, Wang, and Lu 1971: 313–19; Goodrich and Fang 1976: 1224–25; Hoshi 1969: 6–9; Mote and Twitchett 1988: 252–53; Zhou Kuiyi 1990: 321.

25. Tian, Sun, and Asiha 1735: 14: 6b–9a; Hoshi 1969: 20; Hucker 1985: 521; Mote and Twitchett 1988: 311; Zhou Kuiyi 1990: 323–24.

26. Zhou Kuiyi 1990: 326–27.

27. Tian, Sun, and Asiha 1735: 14: 9a–13a; Zhou Kuiyi 1990: 328–29; Hoshi 1969: 23;

Hucker 1985: 224–25; Vermeer 1987: 38. This duty assignment was first called "supervisor of waterways" (*zongli hedao*), but those who assumed it were soon referred to more formally as "directors-general of waterways" (*hedao zongdu* or *zongdu hedao*).

28. Tian, Sun, and Asiha 1735: 14: 13a–14b; Tan Qixiang 1982: VII: 43, 46, 82–83; Zhou Kuiyi 1990: 329–30.

29. Tian, Sun, and Asiha 1735: 14: 16a–18a; Zhou Kuiyi 1990: 336–52; Goodrich and Fang 1976: 1107–9; Vermeer 1987: 44. Some scholars regret that the Ming never developed the sea route. See Wu 1961: 346–48; Goodrich and Fang 1976: 898–902. But Vermeer points out that the Ming, unlike contemporary European overseas trading companies, was concerned about the high loss of life on the sea. See Vermeer 1987: 43.

30. Tian, Sun, and Asiha 1735: 14: 20.

31. Ibid., 21b–22b.

32. Ibid., 23a.

33. Ibid., 14: 24a; 32: 18a; Needham, Wang, and Lu, 1971: 229; Goodrich and Fang 1976: 1110–11; Huanghe shuilibu 1986: 69; Vermeer 1987: 33, 35, 47, 59; Zhou Kuiyi 1990: 354, 373–74.

34. Tian, Sun, and Asiha 1735: 14: 24a–26; Vermeer 1987: 65.

35. Ming officials were classified in nine grades, each grade subdivided into two degrees, from 1a at the top to 9b at the bottom. See Hucker 1958: 11.

36. Ray Huang 1974: 26–29, 46–48; Liang 1980: 357–58; Dardess 1996: 140.

37. Zhu and Zhou 1788: 7: 1b–2a, 15b, 22a; Gu Yanwu 1811: 50: 23b.

38. Zhu and Zhou 1788: 7: 22b; Gu Yanwu 1811: 50: 24b. For the system of yellow registers, see Wei Qingyuan 1961.

39. Zhu and Zhou 1788: 21: 10b. One copy of this report substituted "equal lands" (*jundi*) for equal taxes. Ibid., 21: 22b. Another copy used the words "equal fields" (*juntian*). See Gu Yanwu 1811: 50: 24b. Since the principal tax was based on land, these phrases essentially all meant the same thing: equitable payment of taxes according to the amount of land held. They did not suggest an effort to equalize land holdings except insofar as that might be furthered by policies designed to limit tax fraud and the resulting inequalities in income that resulted in—and sustained—inequalities in landholding.

40. Zhu and Zhou 1788: 21: 10b; Tian, Sun, and Asiha 1735: 33: 4a–6b.

41. Gu Yanwu 1811: 50: 20a, 24; Ray Huang 1974: 108.

42. Gu Yanwu 1811: 50: 25a; Ray Huang 1974: 98; Du forthcoming: 8–9.

43. Zhu and Zhou 1788: 7: 22b–23a; Gu Yanwu 1811: 50: 25a–26b. See also Wakeman 1985: I: 97.

44. Tian, Sun, and Asiha 1735: 55: 21a; Zhu and Zhou 1788: 7: 3a, 6; Crawford 1970: 376–79; Ray Huang 1974: 110–11, 300, 329; Littrup 1981: ch. 5; Heijdra 1994: 201–3; Du forthcoming: 11.

45. Guo Songyi 1983: 220; Tong 1991: 122.

46. Ray Huang 1974: 308. This is true despite the museum's much higher estimate of the average surtax per mu (.009 taels as opposed to Huang's .0035). Thus, while the museum estimates a considerably higher total for the *Liaoxiang* (5.2 million taels as opposed to other scholars' 2.1 million taels), the figures for the *Jiaoxiang* and the *Lianxiang* must have been about the same (unfortunately we lack other scholars' calculations for them), resulting in a total at the museum only slightly higher than that of other observers. Incidentally, the museum's total, like Huang's, includes surtaxes on salt and commodities as well as on land.

47. Guo Songyi 1983: 229. For the complex issues of inflation and depression in this period, see Atwell 1986: 229; 1990: 675–77; Goldstone 1991: 374; Von Glahn 1996: chs. 4–6.

48. Guo Songyi 1983: 230–37.

49. Guo Songyi 1983: 228, 237–38; Liang 1980: 378; Tong 1991: 124.

50. Du forthcoming.

51. Will and Wong 1991: 10–11; Tong 1991: 125–26; Brook 1998: 192–93.

52. Tian, Sun, and Asiha 1735: 54: 32a–45a; 55: 17b–23a; Dunstan 1975: 9, 17, 29; Yim 1978: 1, 3, 25n14. For the difficulty of identifying the nature of epidemic diseases even in the nineteenth century, see Benedict 1996.

53. Yim 1978: 4; Goodrich and Fang 1976: 209.

54. For Yang, see Zhang Tingyu 1739: 241: 14a; Goodrich and Fang 1976: 209; for his report, see Yang Dongming 1688: 1a.

55. Yang Dongming 1688; Liu Yian 1982a: 31; I am grateful to Timothy Brook for his felicitous translation of the title of this work.

56. Yang Dongming 1688: 35b–36a.

57. Ibid., 2b–3a

58. Ibid., 3.

59. Ibid.,4a, 5a, 6a, 6b–8a.

60. Yim 1978: 19–20. The totals include gifts and loans from other unidentified individuals and units. See also Brook forthcoming for a discussion of Wanli's personal response to the album. Brook argues that Wanli was galvanized into action in part because of the shared memory of the disastrous famine of 1588 and in part because of the power of Yang's illustrated stories that conformed to a popular literary genre of the day.

61. Zhong 1595: 8; Zhang Tingyu 1739: 227: 5971; Will 1990: 12.

62. Zhong 1595: 1.

63. Ibid., 1, 3.

64. Ibid., 9.

65. Ibid., 9–10.

66. Ibid., 10; Yim 1978: 22.

67. Zhong 1595: 3–4, 10.

68. Ibid., 5–6, 7, 11, 12.

69. Ibid., 11, 12, 14. For the general decline in rural handicrafts in the late Ming, see Bray 1997: ch. 6. Zhong did not mention the possibility that cotton had displaced food crops, contributing to the severity of the famine. In the 1640s landlords who were aware of the subsistence crisis actually encouraged tenants to grow grain rather than cotton. See Twitchett and Mote 1998: 518.

70. Zhong 1595: 7–8.

71. Ibid., 14.

72. Ibid., 14.

73. Ibid., 15.

74. Ibid., 16.

75. Ibid., 16.

76. Zhang Tingyu 1739: 227: 5972. The report included eighteen illustrations, unfortunately no longer extant.

77. Zhong 1595: 5, 13.

78. Zhang Tingyu 1739: 227: 5972; Tian, Sun, and Asiha 1735: 54: 43b.

79. Grimm 1969: 130–31; Meskill 1982; Hucker 1985: 173.

80. Liu and Ye 1705: 3: 68; Zhang Tingyu 1739: 254: 6563; Chen and Zha 1754: 4: 1; 21: 11b; Tian, Sun, and Asiha 1735: 32: 2b–3b; 54: 35b–46a; 55: 19b–66a; Meskill 1982: 8, 140. For Fan, see James T. C. Liu 1957; Twitchett 1959.

81. Zhang Tingyu 1739: 254: 6563–64.

82. Ibid., 6565; Liu and Ye 1705: 8: 255.

83. Tian, Sun, and Asiha 1735: 31: 51b–52a; 54: 27a–31a, 39b, 40, 41a; Zhang Tingyu 1739: 185: 4909; Tan Qixiang 1975: VII 82–83; Li Shoukong 1968: 38; Zhao 1954: 138–39. The military system is treated in Chapter 3, the rebellions in Chapter 4.

84. Hucker 1985: 534.

85. Tian, Sun, and Asiha 1735: 31: 13a; 54: 47a; Zhang Tingyu 1739: 261: 6759–63; Zheng 1749: 1:12; 2:24, 29, 41–42; 4:79–80; Parsons 1970: 40–43, 54, 66.

86. Zhang Tingyu 1739: 250: 6511; Tian, Sun, and Asiha 1735: 31: 42b; Goodrich and Fang 1976: 1538–39; Guo Songyi 1983: 223; Wakeman 1985: 141–42.

87. Zheng 1749: 2:22; Yue, Hu, and Lü 1903: 11: 5.

88. Liu and Ye 1705: 5: 141; Sun 1986: 221.

89. Zhang Tingyu 1739: 262: 6785–89; Sun 1986: 1.

90. Yang Lien-sheng 1969: 13, 15. The remaining four posts were not accounted for.

91. Tian, Sun, and Asiha 1735: 33, 34. These are all estimates based on data for the last twenty magistrates, the average number serving between the years 1573 and 1644. For the general tendency to appoint higher degree holders to more demanding posts despite the lack of any clear indication that they were administratively more qualified and for the reliance on the drawing of lots to determine assignments, especially after 1595, see Nimick 1999: 42, 53.

92. Tian, Sun, and Asiha 1735: 33: 1–78; 34: 12–37.

93. Van der Sprenkel 1961: 334–35; Parsons 1969: 204–5. Exceptions that prove the rule were Kaocheng, a rather poor county that nonetheless had 29 percent of its magistrates from Shandong, and Suizhou, a prosperous county that had none from Shandong.

94. Zheng 1749: 3: 59–60; Guo Songyi 1983: 238–39.

95. Zheng 1749: 3: 60.

96. Ibid., 3: 60. While the gist of Wang's report has come down to us, the illustrations have not.

97. Zheng 1749: 2: 22–23; Tian, Sun, and Asiha 1735: 34: 27a.

98. Tian, Sun, and Asiha 1735: 34:31–33; Wang and Liang 1935: 31; Van der Sprenkel 1961: 335; Parsons 1969: 188–95.

99. Tan Qian 1653: 99: 5962.

100. Wang and Liang 1935: 32: 44; Tan Qian 1653: 99: 5962. According to Song Mei's biographies in the Henan provincial gazetteer, the *Ming History*, and, following that, the Laiyang gazetteer, he was posted to Yucheng county in Guide. See Tian, Sun, and Asiha 1735: 55: 23b; Zhang Tingyu 1739: 267: 6879; Wang and Liang 1935: 33: 15a. But the table on officials in the Henan provincial gazetteer and the biography in the Guide prefectural gazetteer as well as the Yongcheng gazetteer indicate he actually served in Yongcheng county. See Tian, Sun, and Asiha 1735: 33: 67b; Chen and Zha 1754: 21: 14a; Yue, Hu, and Lü 1903: 3: 12a; 11:5b.

101. Wang and Liang 1935: 33: 15a; Zhang Tingyu 1739: 267: 6879–80.

102. Zhu and Zhou 1788: 9: 48.

103. Wen early Qing a: 62; Zhang Tingyu 1739: 32: 51a.

104. Wen early Qing a: 185; Wang and Liang 1935: 33:15b.

Chapter 2

1. My definition of the Ming elite follows Ho 1962: 26–41 but includes officials living at home and excludes nontributary students at the universities who often purchased their status after 1449 and were less likely to obtain office. (For more on students, see Chapter 3). For continuing use of the term "gentry" to emphasize landholding and local activity as bases for elite status in the Ming, see Brook 1993 and 1998. For definitions of the elite in Qing and later times, see Spence 1966: 45, 77–81; Esherick and Rankin 1990: 1–24, 305–45. For the changing nature of the local elite in northeast and southwest Henan in the early Republican period analyzed within the parameters of the modernization paradigm, see Zhang 2000. For problems with estimates of the decline in population toward the end of the dynasty, see Wakeman 1985: 8; Heijdra 1994: 21; Lavely and Wong 1998: 738–39.

2. Ho 1962: 17, ch. 5, 227; Parsons 1969: 184.

3. Tian, Sun, and Asiha 1735: 45: 12b–56a; Liang 1980: 218–21. The prefectural percentage is based on a provincial total of 339, considerably more than indicated in Ho 1962: 227. If one used Ho's total, Kaifeng's percentage would increase to 51.

4. The 1585 and 1608 editions of the Xiangfu gazetteer were lost, the 1661 edition in

Beijing has only three fascicles (juan), and the 1739 edition at Harvard is so badly printed as to be unusable (whole pages are missing). I have not seen the 1871 edition but it is unlikely to include much, if anything, for the Ming period beyond what is in the 1898 edition. Liu and Geng 1990: shang 135–40. For the biographies, see Tian, Sun, and Asiha 1735: 57: 59a–60a; Shen and Huang 1898: 14: 52b, 91a; 15: 9b, 10a. For the concept of an aristogenic elite, see Brook 1990: 35.

5. Parsons 1969: 182–86, 188–89, 210.

6. Ji and Wang 1764: 10: 10a–11a.

7. Goodrich and Fang 1976: 510–13, 841–45, 877–81, 941–45, 1431–34; Yu 1997: 91. For a similar shift to scholarship in contemporary Taihe county, Jiangxi, see Dardess 1996: 2–3.

8. Henderson 1984: 159, 160, 197, 214. For a defense of Shao Yong's thought, see Wyatt 1996.

9. Tian, Sun, and Asiha 1735: 57: 68b–69a; Zhang Tingyu 1739: 194: 5156; Ji and Wang 1764: 10: 8a–9a; Goodrich and Fang 1976: 844–45, 1433; Yü 1976: 87–156; Henderson 1984: 139, 145.

10. Ge 1990: 26–27, 52, 54–57, 60–61, 73–101, 135–51, 137, 155, 211–23. For Liu, see Chen Jo-shui 1992.

11. Ge 1990: 37, 47, 59, 70, 211, 214–16.

12. Ibid., 27, 37, 38, 52, 54, 58, 60, 61–62, 63, 65, 212, 222, 223.

13. Ibid., 27, 51, 261, 299, 314; for the Hetu and Luoshu, see Robinet 1993.

14. Tian, Sun, and Asiha 1735: 58: 16a; Xiao and Lü 1911: 8: 188–89, 236, 247–51; 9: 304–5, 330–31; Handlin 1975, 1983; Goodrich and Fang 1976.

15. Xiao and Lü 1911: 8.210; Goodrich and Fang 1976: 1006; Lü 1986: 1: 23a, 26a, 43b–49b.

16. Xiao and Lü 1911: 6: 152, 158; Zheng Han 1985: 4, 5, 6; Lü 1986: 1: 25b, 61a, 70a. Lian and Qing were celebrated in the *History of the Latter Han*.

17. De Bary 1970: 145–248; Handlin 1975; Goodrich and Fang 1976: 1007; Li Mowry 1983; Handlin 1983: 106–7, 127, 131, 134, 139, 149–57; Zheng Han 1985: 3, 6–7, 26; Rey Chow 1991: 58–59; Bernhardt 1996: 46; Brook 1998: 153ff. For differences between Liu Xiang's and Ban Zhao's biographies of women and between Han and Ming treatment of women, see Raphals 1998.

18. Xiao and Lü 1911: 6: 133, 7: 170–71, 189; Zheng Han 1985: 7–8, 10, 13; Lü 1986: 1: 68a. For the gazetteer of 1566, no longer extant, see Liu and Geng 1990: 97–98; for the growth of autobiography, see Wu Pei-yi 1990; for the development of school libraries, see Brook 1996.

19. Xiao and Lü 1911: 8: 199; Zheng Han 1985: 13, 16–17, 22. For Zhang Juzheng's identification of himself with Yi Yin, the primordial prime minister and regent, see Ray Huang 1981: 36.

20. Zheng Han 1985: 11, 22; Lü 1986: 1: 25b–26a, 68b; Shen and Shen 1987: 45b, 54b.

21. Handlin 1983: 106; Zheng Han 1985: 24, 34; Twitchett and Mote 1998: 488–89.

22. Handlin 1983: 117–18, 124; Zheng Han 1985: 39, 61–63, 69.

23. Zhang Tingyu 1739: 226: 5936–43; Goodrich and Fang 1976: 208–11; Zheng Han 1985: 91–104, 110–11.

24. Handlin 1983: 110; Zheng Han 1985: 106–13, 121–22, 155.

25. Zheng Han 1985: 88–91, 113, 115, 116–17, 126–32, 138–43, 154, 171–73.

26. Goodrich and Fang 1976: 1009–10; Handlin 1983: 120; Zheng Han 1985: 4–5, 114, 117, 118, 134, 148–50, 166, 168. For Guan Zhong, see Rickett 1985.

27. Goodrich and Fang 1976: 1008–9; Handlin 1983: 218; Huang Tsung-hsi 1987: 218–20. For Lü's influence on a leading high Qing official Chen Hongmou, see Rowe 2001.

28. Goodrich and Fang 1976: 1546–47; Handlin 1983: ch. 6; Zhang Tingyu 1739: 241: 6070.

29. Yang Dongming 1624: 1: 6b–9a, 9b–11b; 2: 2, 3b–9a.

30. Yang Dongming 1624: 4: 18b–22a; 5; Li and Xi 1895: 6: 11a–12b, 15a.

31. Yang Dongming 1624: 1: 1a–4b; 3: 1; Li and Xi 1895: 3: 10b, 12b–13a; Hucker 1957: 152; Goodrich and Fang 1976: 1546.

32. Handlin 1983: 67, 68, 76–78, 82, 83.

33. Tian, Sun, and Asiha 1735: 58: 12b–27a.

34. Liu and Ye 1705: 6: 149, 156–57, 178–89; 9: 277; 10: 332; Zhang Tingyu 1739: 217: 5733; Shen 1986: 1: 41b, 42b–43a, 45; 3: 5b. For hereditary military households, see Chapter 3. For the Shi Chengzhao rebellion, see Chapter 4.

35. Liu and Ye 1705: 8: 247–49; Zhang Tingyu 1739: 213: 5638; 217: 5733; Crawford 1970: 367–414; Goodrich and Fang 1976: 53–61; Liu and Geng 1990: 525.

36. Zhang Tingyu 1739: 112: 3477–78. The Jianwen reign name was restored in 1595; the reevaluation of the Jingtai reign had to await the fall of the dynasty. Goodrich and Fang 1976: 297, 397; Elman 1997: 78–80.

37. Liu and Ye 1705: 12: 396–97; Zhang Tingyu 1739: 217: 5735; Goodrich and Fang 1976: 1180.

38. Liu and Ye 1705: 8: 249; Zhang Tingyu 1739: 217: 5735–37; Goodrich and Fang 1976: 768–70, 1181.

39. Even then, Shen Yu might never have merited a biography by Hou if he had not died in the rebel siege of Shangqiu in 1642. Liu and Ye 1705: 7: 191–94; Shen 1986: 1: 45b, 49b–50a, 54a; He and Wang 1992: 479–80.

40. Song Luo 1705: 3: 4b–5a; 5: 1a; Liu and Ye 1705: 6: 158; 8: 254. Further research would be necessary to establish the Songs' link to the Lius, if any. For more on the Lius, see Chapters 3 and 5.

41. Song Luo 1705: 5: 1a.

42. Liu and Ye 1705: 8: 245. The official Yu Qian had resisted similar pressures. See Chapter 1.

43. Liu and Ye 1705: 6: 150; 8: 245; Song Luo 1705: 5: 1–2a; Zhang Tingyu 1739: 224: 5889; Liu and Geng 1990: 2: 521.

44. Song Luo 1705: 5: 2b; Liu and Geng 1990: 2: 80.

45. Liu and Ye 1705: 8: 245; Zhang Tingyu 1739: 224: 5889–90. For Zhang's plans, see Crawford 1970: passim and especially 387–88; Ray Huang 1981: ch. 3; Mote and Twitchett 1988: 518–32; Twitchett and Mote 1998: 162–64, 447–53, 738–42. For Europe's use of American silver to take over Asian economies, see Frank 1998.

46. Song Luo 1705: 5: 2b–3a.

47. Liu and Ye 1705: 8: 234–35, 238–40, 245–46; 12: 397–98; Song Luo 1705: 5: 3b–4a; Zhang Tingyu 1739: 224: 5890; Goodrich and Fang 1976: 1312–14.

48. Liu and Ye 1705: 7: 192, 198, 220; 8: 246; 10: 340; Song Luo 1705: 5: 4b, 8a–9a, 13.

49. Song Luo 1705: 5: 6a–10a; Liu and Ye 1705: 10: 338. There was a prominent Tian family in Shangqiu, but it is not known if Song Yang's wife belonged to it.

50. Song Luo 1705: 5: 10a–12a; Liu and Ye 1705: 9: 281.

51. Song Luo 1705: 5: 6; Liu and Ye 1705: 11: 378. For the close bonds between widows and sons in the Ming and Qing, see Hsiung 1994.

52. Song Luo 1705: 6: 1a–2a; Liu and Ye 1705: 11: 378–80.

53. Song Luo 1705: 6: 2a; Liu and Ye 1705: 8: 262.

54. Song Luo Kangxi: Wenkang gong yiji, juan xia: 3a–9a. In 1570, the minister of personnel and chief grand secretary Gao Gong, who happened to be from Henan, had similarly called for the appointment of the highest degree holders to "distant posts" in the south and on the northern frontier. Nimick 1999: 53, 55.

55. Song Luo 1705: 5: 14a; 6:2b.

56. Hou Fangyue 1908: 2 zuputu: 1a–2a.

57. Hou Fangyue 1908: 2 zuputu: 2b–3a; Liu and Ye 1705: 6: 178–81; 7:220.

58. Liu and Ye 1705: 10: 338–39; Hou Fangyue 1908: 3 jia zhuan: 1–3a.

59. Liu and Ye 1705: 7: 220; 10: 339.

60. Liu and Ye 1705: 10: 339. For a variation on this encomium, see Hou Fangyue 1908: 2 muzhiming: 11a.

61. Hou Fangyue 1908: 3 jia zhuan: 2b.

62. Liu and Ye 1705: 7: 194; 10: 339; Hou Fangyue 1908: 3 jia zhuan: 4a–5b, 9a–10a.

63. Liu and Ye 1705: 8: 250; he also participated in one of Yang Dongming's societies. See Yang Dongming 1624: 1: 11b.

64. Hou Fangyue 1908: 3 jia zhuan: 4a–5b.

65. Liu and Ye 1705: 8: 251.

66. Liu and Ye 1705: 8: 252; He and Wang 1992: 574–75, 589.

67. Liu and Ye 1705: 6: 151, 161, 255, 256; Hou Fangyue 1908: 3 jia zhuan: 11a–14b; Liu and Geng 1990: 2: 522, 525.

68. Liu and Ye 1705: 11: 257; Hucker 1957; Mammitzsch 1968.

69. Liu and Ye 1705: 11: 257; Hou Fangyue 1908: 3 jia zhuan: 12b; He and Wang 1992: 576. For profiles of Yang Lian and Wei Zhongxian, see Tsai 1996: 1–6.

70. Hou Fangyue 1908: 3 jia zhuan: 16a.

71. Liu and Ye 1705: 11: 258; He and Wang 1992: 577; for the Fushe, see Atwell 1975; Dennerline 1981; see also Chapter 3.

72. Liu and Ye 1705: 11: 255; Hou Fangyue 1908: 2: 28b; Hummel 1943–44: 954–55; Goodrich and Fang 1976: 1313; Mote and Twitchett 1988: 593–94; He and Wang 1992: 574, 576, 578–79.

73. He and Wang 1992: 578–79.

74. Liu and Ye 1705: 11: 255; Hou Fangyue 1908: 2 muzhiming: 29b–30a; He and Wang 1992: 181–210, 582–84. For Hou's views on currency issues while serving at the ministry of revenue, see Von Glahn 1996: 168, 198.

75. Yang Dongming 1624: 4: 20b; Zhang Tingyu 1739: 260: 6738–40; Yue, Hu, and Lü 1903: 12: 2a, 6a, 26a; 19: 2b–4b, 9a–10a; 21: 2b–3a, 6b–7a; 22: 3b, 7.

76. Zhang Tingyu 1739: 260: 6742; Hummel 1943–44: 723; Yue, Hu, and Lü 1903: 19: 10b; 12: 25b–26a; 22: 4, 7a.

77. See Hummel 1943–44: 723, where, however, Ding Qirui's name is incorrectly romanized.

78. Tian, Sun, and Asiha 1735: 57: 59a–79a; 58: 12b–27a, 66b–72a.

79. For examples, see the Zhous and the Xus. Zhu and Zhou 1788: 10: 5b–8a; 14: 12a, 16a–17a, 25b–26a, 29b–30a; Tian, Sun, and Asiha 1735: 57: 72b.

80. Li and Li 1749: preface, yishi, sishi, qishi, bashi; Zhu and Zhou 1788: 10: 1a–8a; 11: 5a; 14: 12a; Guan and Zhang 1695: 23: 57; Tian, Sun, and Asiha 1735: 57: 71b. There were only three, not eleven, metropolitan graduates in this Li family in the late Ming. See Liu and Geng 1990: 2: 467. Compare Li Xiaosheng 1986: 53; and Li Xiaosheng 1987b: 40, where the term *jinshi* was misinterpreted and then mistranslated as "metropolitan graduate" rather than as "entered into the ranks of scholars."

81. Li and Li 1749: bashi; Zhu and Zhou 1788: 10: 6a, 19a; 14: 12.

82. Li and Li 1749: jiushi, shishi; Zhu and Zhou 1788: 10: 20a, 22b. It is not clear whether the town was Kaifeng or Qi.

83. Li and Li 1749: liushi through shisanshi. For an analysis, sometimes mistaking student status for degree holding, see Li Xiaosheng 1986: 53–56; Li 1987b: 49.

84. For the origins of the Hous, see Hou Shimei 1987: shixishu 2–3. There was a theory that the Hous originated in Hunan in the late Song and spread first to Jiading in Nanzhili and Kaifeng in Henan and then in three streams to Qi, Song, and Yingshan; but the genealogy concludes that there is insufficient evidence for it. For Yuzhao, see Ibid., shixishu: 5; Zhu and Zhou 1788: 14: 13b–15b; Tian, Sun, and Asiha 1735: 57: 71b; for the eighth generation, see Hou Shimei 1987: shixishu: 8–10; Zhu and Zhou 1788: 14: 27b–28a, 30b; 16: 9b–10a; for the ninth and tenth, see Hou Shimei 1987: shixishu: 12–13.

85. Ma Chaoqun 1780: yishi, jiushi, shishi; Zhu and Zhou 1788: 10: 23b; 14: 34, 35b–36a; 15: 6b–7a; 17: 8b.

86. Meng 1990: 4: 1–2, 4, 124, 138–39; Zhu and Zhou 1788: 14: 32a–34a.

87. Meng 1990: 4: 44–45; Zhu and Zhou 1788: 14: 40; 15: 16b; Liu and Geng 1990: 468.

88. Wen early Qing b: xia 77a/2083; Zhu and Zhou 1788: 14: 17; Liu and Geng 1990: 468.

89. Zhu and Zhou 1788: 22: 14b–16b.

90. Ibid., 14: 19b–20a.

91. Zhu and Zhou 1788: 2: 15b; 14: 18a; 17: 39b–42a.

92. Ibid., 9: 7b, 48b–49a; 23: 8b–10a; Wang Xingya 1984a: 270–71.

93. Zhu and Zhou 1788: 10: 8a, 23a; 14: 18b; 18: 4a; Meng 1990: 4: 138, 184, 316.

94. He Xinzhen 1987: 2: 25–30.

95. He Xinzhen 1987: 2: 32b; Zhu and Zhou 1788: 15: 4a–5a.

96. He Xinzhen 1987: 2: 31b, 33b–34a, 35a, 38b; Li and He 1693: 8: 8b; Zhu and Zhou 1788: 11: 7a; Han and Li 1920: 8: 13b–21a.

97. Zhu and Zhou 1788: 10: 23a; 16: 12a; Wang Zhonghan 1987: 79: 6543–44, 6599–6600; He Xinzhen 1987: 2: 34a. Wang Duo had received his metropolitan degree in 1622 and held high posts including lecturer to the ruler in 1638. Xue Suoyun had received his metropolitan degree in 1628 and served in provincial posts before becoming a compiler in the Hanlin Academy and director of studies in the state university in the early 1640s.

98. Liu Lishun 1658: shixi: 2b; Liu 1986: xu: 6–9.

99. Liu Lishun 1658: shixi: 3a.

100. Ibid., 12: 26a–28b.

101. Ibid., shixi: 4a; for Liu's poetry and correspondence, see Ibid., juan 3–6; for Luo, see 11: 15a–20a.

102. Ibid., benzhuan: 1a; 12: 1a–11b; Liu and Geng 1990: 2: 466. For *li* as pattern, see Graham 1989: 286; Munro 1988: 5.

103. Liu Lishun 1658: benzhuan: 1b; shixi: 3; 8: 30a; Zhang Tingyu 1739: 120: 3657–58; 266: 6859.

104. The complete phrase was: "To be humane is to control oneself and return to the rites." See Qian Mu 1964: 12/1: 397. For alternative translations, see Lau 1979: 12/1: 112; Waley 1938: 12/1: 162. Here again I use Kongzi rather than the Latinate Confucius to remind readers of some of the problems arising from the Jesuit interpretation of that strain of Chinese thought in the seventeenth century. See Jensen 1997.

105. Liu Lishun 1658: benzhuan: 1b; 1: 20a–25a, 29b–30a; 2: 28a–30a; for Xue Xuan, see Zhang Tingyu 1739: 69: 1689; Chan Wing-tsit 1970: 29–38; Goodrich and Fang 1976: 616–19. Tang and Wu were founders of the Shang and Zhou, respectively.

106. Liu Lishun 1658: 1: 19a, 30.

107. Ibid., 1: 32b, 33b; Chao Yang 1979: 110–11.

108. Liu Lishun 1658: ba: 2a; benzhuan: 1b; shixi: 3a; Zhang Tingyu 1739: 253: 6537–42; 266: 6859; Hummel 1943–44: 53; Goodrich and Fang 1976: 1474–78.

109. Liu Lishun 1658: 1: 13a–14a; for the date of this memorial, see Tan Qian 1653: 96: 5833.

110. Liu Lishun 1658: 1: 16a.

111. Ibid., 2: 10a–12b; 6: 22b; 7: 20b; 10: 5b; 11: 35a; 12: 32a; Burton Watson 1968: 2: 92–104, 481.

112. For Wang, see Liu Lishun 1658: 12: 19b. For Kou, see Ibid., 7: 10b. For Li's administration in Qi, see Zhu and Zhou 1788: 7: 7b; 9: 48b. Kou's name was later incorporated in an aphorism indicating popular satisfaction with a magistrate. For Shen, see Liu Lishun 1658: 8: 3a; Zhu and Zhou 1788: 12: 19b.

113. Liu Lishun 1658: 1: 33; 8: 9, 12a, 19a; 10: 9a–10b; Zhang and Wang 1987: 2.

114. Zhao and Chang 1747: 5, 30–31; 33: 11a; Zhang Shizhong 1870: jiuxu: 1a; shang: 16a; zhong: 1a, 2a–3b; Guo and Guo 1915; Liu and Geng 1990: 2: 487–88.

115. Zhang Shizhong 1870: shang: 13a, 16.

116. Ibid., zhong: 2a–5a.

117. Ibid., shang: 13; zhong: 2a–5a; Zhang and Wang 1987: 1, 71; Liu and Geng 1990: 2: 488.

118. Tan Qian 1653: 95: 5809, 5829; Zhao and Chang 1747: 33: 1b; Zhang Tingyu 1739: 257: 6641; Zhang and Wang 1987: 1–2; Wang Zhonghan 1987: 79: 6621–22.

119. Zhang and Wang 1987: 1–3. Although the prefaces are mostly undated, I have arrived at 1643 on the basis of internal evidence, including the title given to Zhang (*sima*) and the term used to describe the Manchus (*lu*). The pejorative term *caitiff* was uniformly blacked out of the original text that circulated in the early Qing. See Zhang Jinyan c. 1643: passim.

120. Zhang and Wang 1987: 1: 6–8, 13–14; 2: 62–63, 65–66, 72–76.

121. Ibid., 1: 11–12, 25–27; 2: 53–54. Zheng was from Yanling county in Kaifeng prefecture. For his proposals and appointment, see Tan Qian 1653: 96: 5836, 5837.

122. Zhang and Wang 1987: 1: 20; 2: 39–40, 40–46; these reports were perhaps in response to Yang Sichang's proposal of January 1639 to raise horses in Shandong and Henan. See Tan Qian 1653: 96: 5831.

123. Zhang and Wang, 1: 9–10.

124. Ibid., 1: 16.

125. Ibid., 1: 16.

126. Ibid., 1: 17.

127. Ibid., 2: 66–67.

128. Ibid., 1: 17–28, 33–34; 2: 47.

129. Zhang and Wang 1987: 2: 51–52, 58–59, 60–61. The figures on increased revenue may have referred to annual polity-wide increases in revenue from the surtaxes or to the increases in total revenues of some (unspecified) region. Compare data in Appendix A.

130. Ibid., Pan preface: 1–2; 2: 70–71, 245–46.

131. Ibid., Li preface: 1. The six arts were archery, charioteering, music, rites, mathematics, and literature.

132. Ibid.

133. Ibid., Li preface: 2.

134. Ibid., Zhang preface: 1.

135. For one of many analyses along these lines, see Chow Kai-wing 1994: 18–19; for a slightly different interpretation, see Brook 1998.

136. Zhang Tingyu 1739: 267: 6883. Gao had thus graduated the same year as Zhang Jinyan and followed a remarkably similar career path.

137. For Suizhou's success in winning degrees, see Appendixes B and C. For the Chus, see Ma and Gao 1987: 5: 138, 151, 161; Liu and Geng 1990: 2: 532.

138. Li and Xi 1895: 5: 4, 8a–11a, 13b–16a, 18a–21b, 23–24b; 6: 18a; 7: 3a, 20b; 8: 11b–15b; 9: 32a–35a, 62b; Liu and Geng 1990: 2: 528. For the lifestyle of such members of the elite in the late Ming, see Clunas 1991, 1996.

139. Li and Xi 1895: 6: 18a; see also Ibid., 8: 75b–79a, 82a–84a; Wang Xingya 1989: 108–10.

140. Li and Xi 1895: 6: 16, 18, 19a, 20b, 23b; 9: 63a, 65a; Liu and Geng 1990: 2: 91, 528.

141. Xiao and Lü 1911: 8: 189, 190, 199, 211; 9: 302–3.

142. Miao and Miao 1987: 1: 20a, 24b–25a, 27a–29b; Xiao and Lü 1911: 6: 135.

143. Miao and Miao 1987: 1: 32a–35b.

144. Tan Qian 1653: 95: 5818.

145. Ibid., 95: 5821.

146. Zheng 1749: 3: 61–62.

147. Zheng, for example, attributed many of Lü Kun's key ideas to Miao Wenying. See Miao and Miao 1987: 1: 23a.

148. Zheng 1749: 3: 62–63.

149. Ibid., 3: 63.

150. Ibid., 3: 61.

151. Ibid., 3: 61.

152. Ibid., 3: 63.

153. Ibid., 3: 63.

154. This identity had been clearly indicated to the elite in the first generation in the first answer on the civil service examination of 1371. However it was later contested by literati favoring Cheng-Zhu learning. See Elman 2000: 75–78, 121.

Chapter 3

1. For gender as a category of historical analysis, see Joan Scott 1996.

2. For pioneering studies in the history of women during the Ming and Qing, see Waltner 1981, 1996; Waltner and Hsu 1997; Elvin 1984; Ebrey 1993a; Furth 1986, 1987, 1994, 1998; Ko 1994; Mann 1997.

3. For the similarities and differences between Han and Ming biographies of women, see Raphals 1998: 21, ch. 5; for the "peasantization" of family law during the Ming, see Bernhardt 1996: 57; 1999.

4. For critiques of "Confucian" patriarchy, see Mon 1999; Tung 2000; Yü 2001; for hostility to women in popular culture, see Cole 1998; Cass 1999.

5. Li Yu-ning 1992; Lily Lee 1994; Wu Qingyun 1995; Widmer and Chang 1997; Chang and Saussy 1999; Lu 2001; Mann and Cheng 2001.

6. Zhang Tingyu 1739: 114: 3542; Chang Moulai 1852: 36b; Albert Chan 1982: 18–19, 152, 377–78; Tong 1991: 101, 231; Wu Qingyun 1995: 8; Hsieh 1999: 32–33, 37, 50. For the Ming founder's respect for his wife Ma, see Kutcher 1999: 38–39. For Madame Ke and the parallels between Han and Ming "grannies," see Cass 1999: 54–55. For the important role of Ming emperors and empress dowagers in patronizing the temples that shaped the development of Beijing, see Naquin 2000: 152–61. For the relatively high status of aristocratic women in the Qing, see Rawski 1998: ch. 4.

7. Zhang Tingyu 1739: 114: 3542; Hsieh 1999: 42–43.

8. Lee and Wang 1999: 47, 61.

9. T'ien 1988: 24–31; Ebrey 1993a: 52; 1993b: 37–43, 266–67, 269; Ko 1994: 148, 156; Dardess 1996: 82; Gates 1996: 46–54; Brook 1998: 97–98, 163. Once the bound foot became a focus of male erotic desire, it left the more specifically genital realms of the female body for the more important function of reproduction. Furth 1998: 131, 153; Cass 1999: 104. For a review of foreign (mainly Western) images of Chinese foot binding, see Ebrey 1999.

10. Bernhardt 1999: 4, 40–45, 47–48, 62–67.

11. T'ien 1988: 1, 39, 124–25; Ebrey 1993b: 188–203; Bernhardt 1999: 67; Hsieh 1999: 44.

12. T'ien 1988: 45, 46, 60–62, 149–61; Bernhardt 1996: 51; Yü 2001: 338–47.

13. Leung 1993:3n4.

14. If so, it was despite the charges by the late Ming physician Li Shizhen that the practice was inhumane and foolish. See Yü 2001: 340.

15. T'ien 1988: ch. 5.

16. Shen and Huang 1898: juan 18.

17. T'ien 1988: 39.

18. For the related phenomenon of love suicides in the late Ming, see Li Mowry 1983.

19. See Ko 1994 passim; Bernhardt 1996: 45; Bray 1997: chs. 5, 6; Mann 1997: ch. 6; Brook 1998: 202; Widmer and Chang 1997; Chang and Saussy 1999.

20. For the emerging concept of the middle class in Europe at the time, see Williams 1976: 45–48, 60–69.

21. Zhang Tingyu 1739: 69: 1686; Chang Moulai 1852: 58a; Ho 1962: 177–81; Atwell 1975: 338; Twitchett and Mote 1998: 715. For estimates of the population of the region in the late Ming, see the Introduction.

22. Ma Tai-loi 1975: 12–18, 22, 25, 27; Elman 2000: 150.

23. This conclusion is based on data in Zhang Tingyu 1739: 69: 1686; Ma Tai-loi 1975: 15; as well as all county gazetteers of the region except those of Tongxu, Weichuan, Yanjin, Yancheng, and Xingyang in which data are too incomplete to be useful.

24. Li, Wei, and Des Forges 1994: 85–122.

25. He and Wang 1992: 573. Although Hou Fangyu was not a typical government student, the lack of detailed information on other government students means that his case must serve as illustrative.

26. Ibid., 234–35, 576–77; Liu and Ye 1705: 9. 304–8.

27. Hummel 1943–44: 587; Ray Huang 1970: 418; He and Wang 1992: 577.

28. He and Wang 1992: 181–210, 311–29, 415–33.

29. Ibid., 580, 582. Zhang Anshi had held high posts under Han Wudi and succeeding reigns. Li Wenrao (better known as Li Deyu) had been prime minister under Tang Wuzong. For biographies of Chen, Xia, and Wu, see Hummel 1943–44: 102–3, 882–83, 896; and Atwell 1975. Wu Weiye had won high honors in the metropolitan examination of 1631. Wu Boyi's biographer in the county gazetteer attached some importance to the placing of Wu's name at the head of the list. Liu and Ye 1705: 9: 305.

30. He and Wang 1992: 583, 584.

31. Ibid., 586. Zhou had helped engineer the defeat of the late Latter Han general Cao Cao at the famous battle of Red Cliff; Wang's advice had been ignored by the Qin ruler Fu Jian who met defeat at the famous battle of Fei River.

32. Hummel 1943–44: 53, 82–83, 389–99; Wen early Qing b: xia: 74b; Atwell 1975: 353–54; He and Wang 1992: 586–87.

33. He and Wang 1992: 361–75. For the suggestion that Hou's infraction was minor and unintentional, see Liu and Ye 1705: 9: 309; Hummel 1943–44: 291 For a serious case in the Qing where that was true, see Pierre-Henri Durand 1992. For Lu Qi, see Twitchett 1979: 582–86. For other suggestions at the time favoring recommendations over examinations, including one by the grand coordinator of Henan and another citing the precedent of the Han, see Elman 2000: 214–19.

34. He and Wang 1992: 377, 379.

35. In 1637 the Fushe had won the first, second, and third places in the palace examination. Atwell 1975: 350; and Dennerline 1981: 30–38.

36. He and Wang 1992: 588.

37. Ibid., 6, 20–22, 267–70, 428, 588. The name of Hou's new society alluded to phrases from the *Book of Changes*, the *Rites of Zhou*, and a poem by Li Bai of the Tang. The object of Hou's allegory was Gu Bingqian, who had been the chief author of a 1626 document charging the Donglin partisans with crimes. Wen early Qing b: xia 70: 2069. For the Han analogy, see Liu and Ye 1705: 9: 308, 310.

38. He and Wang 1992: 262–64.

39. Idem and 114.

40. Ibid., 510–14. Fushe members from Henan have been estimated at as few as 1.2 percent and as many as 10 percent of the total membership of the society. Atwell 1975: 343; and Ono 1996: 433.

41. He and Wang 1992: 1–5, 588. For Song, see Chapter 2.

42. Ibid., 460–62, 588.

43. Ibid., 53–58, 235, 460–62; Liu and Ye 1705: 8. 258.

44. He and Wang 1992: 241, 486–87; Liu and Ye 1705: 9: 308.

45. Zhang Tingyu 1739: 288; He and Wang 1992: 242–46. Ni antagonized the strongman Cao Cao and died at the hands of one of his subordinates. Cao's son later brought the Han to an end and established the Wei.

46. For the comparison with the Ruans, see Liu and Ye 1705: 9: 310, 311. The Ruans, from Chenliu commandery, were fully historical. See Holzman 1976: 2. The seven worthies all hailed from the region around northern Henan but the location of the Bamboo Grove is

unclear, suggesting that the coherent group may have been a later construct of the Eastern Jìn designed to dramatize what had been only a loose association of contemporaries in the Western Jìn. See Liu and Mather 1976: 371–72. For Wang Dao, see Ibid., 175; He and Wang 1992: 62–65; for Jia and Ruan Ji, see ibid., 234–39.

47. Liu and Ye 1705: 9: 306; 10: 326–27; He and Wang 1992: 243; for Ma Zhou, see Birch 1958: 97–115.

48. Shen and Huang 1898: 4: 7a–9b, 24a, 28, 29a, 58b; 17: 7b–8a, 21b; William White 1966: III: 158; Li Yunlai n.d.: dazong pai.

49. Elvin 1973: ch. 15; Dennerline 1981: ch. 3; Grove and Daniels 1984; Heijdra 1994: 275, 277, 292–93.

50. Liu Tinggui 1929: 5: 2.

51. Wang Xingya 1982a: 34.

52. Dietrich 1972: 110–26; Nishijima 1984: 19; Fu 1984: 120; Cong 1985: 21–22; Tian, Sun, and Asiha 1735: 19: 6b; Heijdra 1994: 294.

53. Nishijima 1984: 45; Ma and Gao 1987: 1: 7; Zhu and Zhou 1788: 8: 6a; Liu and Ye 1705: 1: 43.

54. Liu and Ye 1705: 1: 42–43; Tian, Sun, and Asiha 1735: 27: 7b; 29: 6b; Mei 1975: 102.

55. Mei 1975: ch. 4.

56. Zhang Tingyu 1739: 288; Liu and Ye 1705: 10: 326–27.

57. See, for example, Rawski 1991: 85–88. For a critique of this Marxian-Weberian position, see Philip Huang 1991; for doubts about the whole concept of capitalism and an argument that China had a powerful commercial economy long before the Ming as well as during and after it, see Frank 1998. For a range of contemporary views of wealth during the Ming, see Brook 1998.

58. This translation follows Brook's with only minor modifications. See Brook 1981: 192.

59. Tong 1991: 151; Han 1991: 130; Brook 1998: 73–4; Twitchett and Mote 1998: 684.

60. Such measures, of course, were not always sufficient to prevent starvation. Brook 1998: 190–94.

61. Li Mowry 1983: 67–68; Fu 1958: 2: 36; Fu 1984: 120; Whelan 1979; Tong 1991: 146; Brook 1998: 210; Twitchett and Mote 1998: 506.

62. Zurndorfer 1989: 233–34; He and Wang 1992: 523.

63. For other examples, see Brook 1998: 128–29, 143, 213–17.

64. He and Wang 1992: 523.

65. Shen and Huang 1898: 16: 25b–27a; 17: 17b–18a.

66. Chang Moulai 1852: passim; Mei 1975: 72.

67. Mei 1975: 75, 76, 106, 110.

68. Chang Moulai 1852: 20b, 22a, 23a, 26b, 27b, 34a, 38b, 40a, 51b; Mei 1975: 111–12. A few businesses may have been managed by same-place associations that accommodated sojourners from places like Huizhou and Shanxi, but there is no evidence of such associations in Kaifeng in the late Ming. Ho 1966: passim.

69. Hucker 1958: 18; Watt 1972: 14–16. This definition of minor functionaries differs from some others by including some lower-ranked officials, but the line between ranked and unranked functionaries was porous and variable in any case. For details on such functionaries in the Qing period, see Reed 2000.

70. Shen and Huang 1898: 3: 21a; Zhu and Zhou 1788: 9: 12b, 20b–21a; Yue, Hu, and Lü 1903: 3: 15a; 11: 7a; Tian and Zhao 1928: 3: 13b, 36b.

71. Mayfair Mei-hui Yang 1994; Littrup 1981: chs. 2–4; Hucker 1958: 18; Albert Chan 1982: 292; Ch'ü 1962: 38; He and Wang 1992: 534.

72. He and Wang 1992: 534–56. Clerks in the Han dynasty had indeed been able to rise into the regular bureaucracy, but they were deprived of that chance in the Tang and Song. The Han system had been revived by the Ming founder but was shelved again under Yongle and his successors. See Albert Chan 1982: 26–28.

73. June Mei concurred that he was probably "a clerk or a secretary." See Mei 1975: 166–67.

74. Chang Moulai 1852: yuanxu: 1.

75. For Jiang, see ibid., 16b, 33b, 44b, 45b, 49a; Allan 1972–73; for Guan Yu, see Chang Moulai 1852: 14a, 16a, 36b, 39b; Duara 1988; Shelley Hsueh-lun Chang 1990: 37–40; Luo and Roberts 1991: 950–53; Wilson 1995: 108–10.

76. For Zhang and Xu, see Chang Moulai 1852: 53b–54a; Graff 1995; for Zhu and Zhao, see Chang Moulai 1852: 15b–16a, 25a, 35b.

77. For the Zhou estate, see Chang Moulai 1852: 4a, 4b, 6b, 8a, 9a, 11a; for other structures, see ibid., 18, 27a, 36a, 37b, 41b, 49, 52a, 53, 55a.

78. Ibid., 4b–5b; Shelley Hsueh-lun Chang 1990: 20.

79. Ibid., 20b, 42a, 47a, 48b, 53a. For Zhang, see Chan Hok-lam 1973.

80. For Zhu, see Chang Moulai 1852: 26a, 32b, 34b, 45b, 56b, 58b. For Yu and Liu, see ibid., 19b, 27a, 28a, 30a, 31a, 39a, 41b, 46b; Shen and Huang 1898: 4: 7b, 8, 22b; Guan and Zhang 1695: 26: 31a, 37b; Zhang Tingyu 1739: 186. In the late Ming, the icon was still standing guard on the northeast corner of the city's outer earthen wall. For Zuo, Zhang, and Li, see Chang Moulai 1852: 33b, 44b, 45b, 50b, 55b, 56; Zhang Tingyu 1739: 288: 7399–7400.

81. Chang Moulai 1852: 28, 38a. For the cult of the Taishan Goddess, see Pomeranz 1997.

82. Chang Moulai 1852: 18a, 19a, 25a, 37a, 38b, 50b.

83. Ibid., 52a.

84. Hucker 1958: 57–58; Liu 1992: 411.

85. Chang Moulai 1852: 17b; Tian, Sun, and Asiha 1735: 11: 1a; 31: 50a–52a.

86. Chang Moulai 1852: 1b, 16; Chen and Zha 1754: 13a–14a; Tan Qixiang 1975: 7: 82–83; Ma and Gao 1987: 118; Hucker 1958: 51–56.

87. Hucker 1958: 62–63; Ma and Gao 1987: 118; Liu 1992: 415–16.

88. Tian, Sun, and Asiha 1735: 52a; Chen and Zha 1754: 31: 15a; Shen and Huang 1898: 9: 36b; Hucker 1958: 57; Ma and Gao 1987: 427–28; Liu 1992: 416–20, 422–26, 429–36.

89. Liu 1992: 439–45.

90. Ibid., 1992: 436–38, 449–51, 455–58; Albert Chan 1982: 51–63.

91. Liu and Ye 1705: 10: 316; Ma and Gao 1987: 4: 118; 6: 239; Liu 1992: 434.

92. Ma and Gao 1987: 4: 118; Zhu and Zhou 1788: 16: 22; 18: 4a

93. Ma and Gao 1987: 9: 363; Liu 1992: 444.

94. Chang Moulai 1852: 1a–2a, 3b–4a, 16b, 29b, 51.

95. Ma and Gao 1987: 5: 182–88; 6: 237; Han and Li 1920: 8: 1a, 8b–9a; Shen and Huang 1898: 4: 61b–62a, 63a; Liu and Ye 1705: 7: 209–12; Zhu and Zhou 1788: 11: 30b; Yue, Hu, and Lü 1903: 24: 3a; Wang and Zhang 1923: 10: 57a; Zhou and Liu 1931: 9: 48a, 49a; Zhang and Shi 1914: 4: 49a; Tian and Zhao 1928: 2: 27b; Xiao and Lü 1911: 8: 236, 244.

96. Ma and Gao 1987: 4: 118; 6: 237; Liu and Ye 1705: 7: 211.

97. Liu Tinggui 1929: 3: 2a, 2b, 4b; 5: 8a.

98. Yue, Hu, and Lü 1903: 37: 1.

99. Needham, Wang, Lu, and Ho 1970: 269, 270–74, 380–81, 392; Needham 1981: 99; Loewe and Shaughnessy 1999: 830.

100. Chang Moulai 1852: 20a, 24a, 25b, 29b, 30a, 32a, 39a, 40a, 42b, 46a, 50a, 55a; Guan and Zhang 1695: 10: 7a–12a.

101. Tian, Sun, and Asiha 1735: 71: 1–17.

102. Guan and Zhang 1695: 30: 5a; Shen and Huang 1898: 17: 27.

103. Guan and Zhang 1695: 30: 5; Shen and Huang 1898: 17: 27b.

104. Guan and Zhang 1695: 30: 5b; Chang Moulai 1852: 33b; Shen and Huang 1898: 4: 9a, 29a; 16: 51b; 17: 27b–28a.

105. Tian, Sun, and Asiha 1735: 33.14b–16a; Zhu and Zhou 1788: 18.14b; Shen and Huang 1898: 17: 28a.

106. Chang Moulai 1852: 32b–33a; Dehergne 1957: 45–46; Mei 1975: 84–86, 127–28, 130–31.

107. William White 1966: II: 11, 37. The stele of 1489 listed only seventeen surnames (*xing*) but suggested that there were actually over seventy. The consensus of twentieth-century scholars has been that seventy was simply a mistake for seventeen, but this has recently been persuasively challenged with the argument that there were probably seventy or more original *families* (but perhaps not seventy separate family *names*) and they had dwindled to seventeen by the time the stele was inscribed. See Wei Qianzhi 1997: 29–31. ZhongXia probably referred to all of China but it was an archaism which, if interpreted literally, would refer more especially to the Henan region of China where the Xia culture had been concentrated and where the Northern Song capital of BianLiang was located. For the date of 998, see Shapiro 1984: 139–42; Wei Qianzhi 1993b: 38. Ni-wei stood for Levy; the *ne* may have denoted the common particle in spoken Chinese indicating a rest stop or a slight rhetorical interrogative. For the synagogue, see William White 1966: II: 11, 12, 21, 37; Leslie 1967b: 159; Wei Qianzhi 1993c: 4–5. The name Temple of Purity and Truth was later adopted by Muslims for their mosques in China.

108. William White 1966: II: 8–11, 12, 14–15, 24, 37; Leslie 1972: 25; Plaks 1991, 1998.

109. Fang 1965: 127, 128. For the prince's comedown, see the discussion of Princes in Chapter 1 and the discussion of minor functionaries above.

110. The original Chinese text is in William White 1966: II: 37; this translation departs considerably from White's (in ibid., 12–13) to take account of corrections in Fang 1965: 126–27 and the alternative in Shapiro 1984: 132.

111. Fang 1965.

112. Shapiro 1984: 136–38. Some medical specialists must certainly have assisted the prince in his projects but Li adduces no independent evidence that An Cheng was among them.

113. It is ironic that Fang's interpretation tends to rely on the royal *Veritable Records* while sympathizing with the dissident prince. He clearly shares the long Chinese intellectual traditions of respect for the royal records on the one hand and antipathy to Yongle for having usurped the throne and ruling in an authoritarian fashion on the other. Li relies on the more independent stele account while showing more sympathy for the ruler Yongle. He apparently shares the current enthusiasm in China for the use of a wide variety of sources combined with respect for Yongle's policy of "opening" to the world. For this view of Yongle, see also Wei Qianzhi 1993c: 1–2.

114. Leslie 1966, 1967a, 1967b; 1971: 5, Chao. A stele of 1679 established by Zhao Cheng's descendants hints that Zhao Cheng may have been honored by Yongle for the deeds of his *ancestors*, suggesting yet another interpretation of the An/Zhao case, but the text is too fragmentary to conclude anything from it. William White 1966: II: 98.

115. William White 1966: II: 13–14, 38; Shen and Huang 1898: 4: 18b, 44a; Leslie 1967b: 156–57.

116. William White 1966: II: 13, 14, 25, 27, 37, 38–39.

117. Chen Yuan 1923: 23–24; William White 1966: II: 47, 49; Leslie 1972: 28–29.

118. Chen Yuan 1923: 3, 6–9, 22; William White 1966: II: 42–46, 51–54; Leslie 1972: 5; Wei Qianzhi 1993b: 37; Farmer et al. 1988–89; Plaks 1991; Wilson 1995: 57–58.

119. William White 1966: II: 44–45, 46, 53–54.

120. Leslie 1966: 8, 25; Leslie 1972: 30.

121. Shen and Huang 1898: 4: 18b; Leslie 1967a: 21–22, 24. In getting the provincial degree, Ai Tian replicated the achievement of Ai Jun over a century earlier and he may have been from the same lineage. Leslie 1966: table between 14 and 15. For Ai Tian's office holding and inscription, see Chen Yuan 1923: 36. For contacts with Ricci, see Leslie 1966: 19; 1967: 46; Pollak 1980: 3–11.

122. William White 1966: I: 11, 34, 35; Leslie 1972: 35–36; Pollak 1980: xxii–xxiv.

123. Leslie 1967a: 31; Leslie 1967b: 158; Shen and Huang 1898: 4: 28b; 17c: 28; Chang Moulai 1852: 35b. Ai Tian had a son, named Uzziel, and a nephew, named Abdiel. Chen Yuan 1923: 36; Leslie 1966: chart between 14 and 15; 1967a: 24–25.

Chapter 4

1. David Keightley notes that the original character for *zhong* included two or three persons laboring under the sun and referred to people mobilized for service to the Shang state. He argues, however, that they were fewer in number than the people (*ren*) in general. If so, our use of the term here involves an expansion of its original meaning. See Keightley 1999: 282–84. For a Western philosophical meditation on the masses, see de Certeau 1984.

2. One may distinguish banditry from rebellion objectively—as smaller, more rural, and less political—and subjectively—as more violent, predatory, and arbitrary. I shall use both terms in the following discussion in an effort to reflect both the objective and subjective judgments of contemporaries and later observers, including me. For examples of early attempts to conceptualize the pattern of rebellion and revolution in Chinese history, see Des Forges 1979; Perry 1980. For more recent work, see Little 1989; Weller and Guggenheim 1989; Wou 1994; Wasserstrom and Perry 1994. For a thorough and persuasive overview of popular uprisings during the Ming based largely on prefectural-level records see Tong 1991. For covert forms of resistance, see James C. Scott 1990.

3. Zhu 1972: 25–26; Yao Shao-yu 1942–43: 375; Tong 1991: 46; Brook 1998: 17–85.

4. Yue, Hu, and Lü 1903: 15: 1; Han and Li 1920: 9: 2; Tong 1991: 79, 126; Seybolt 1996: 1–2; Brook 1998: 29, 269n23.

5. Li Shoukong 1968: 18, 27–30; Seidel 1969–70; Bingham 1941; Suzuki 1974: 92; Overmyer 1976: 98–100; Shen Dingping 1982: 292; Shek 1990: 92; Tong 1991, ch. 5; Ter Haar 1992: 114–30; Robinson 1995b: chs. 1–3.

6. Zhang Tingyu 1739: 172: 4596. Shi Long claimed to be related to Shi Heng, one of the most powerful officials and generals of the day. Ling, Lü, and Zhang 1938: 1: 10b. The numbers of adherents to rebellions, like the numbers of troops sent to suppress them, should always be viewed as approximate, indicating simply orders of magnitude. Even then, they were often exaggerated.

7. Li Shoukong 1968: 39; Overmyer 1976: 101.

8. Zhang Tingyu 1739: 172: 4596; Lai 1958: 257–60.

9. Shen Dingping 1982: 293; Zhang Tingyu 1739: 178: 4730; Lai 1958; Suzuki 1974: 96.

10. For eunuchs in general, see Mote and Twitchett 1988; Wang and Du 1989; Xu and Wang 1991; and Tsai 1996. For administrative decline, see Tong 1991: 108, 126–27, 184; Zhang 1992a; Wang Xingya 1993.

11. Mote and Twitchett 1988: 403–12; Tong 1991: 46, 48, 50, 52.

12. Liu and Ye 1703: 3: 76; Yue, Hu, and Lü 1903: 15: 1; Zhang Tingyu 1739: 185: 4909; Li Shoukong 1968: 38.

13. Gu Yingtai 1658: 45: 665–66; Zhao 1954: 135; Robinson 1995b: 1–16, 187–206, 252–54.

14. Liu and Ye 1705: 3: 84; Yue, Hu, and Lü 1903: 15: 1, 2a; Han and Li 1920: 9: 17; Robinson 1995b: 307–8.

15. Gu Yingtai 1658: 671; Zhao 1954: 136; Robinson 1995b: 326–31.

16. Gu Yingtai 1658: 673; Zhao 1954: 137–38; Guan and Zhang 1695: 39: 17, 18b; Robinson 1995b: 332–34.

17. Gu Yingtai 1658: 673; Zhao 1954: 137–38; Goodrich and Fang 1976: 1027–29.

18. Gu Yingtai 1658: 674; Goodrich and Fang 1976: 233–34; Robinson 1995b: 335–36, 342–43.

19. Gu Yingtai 1658: 677; Zhao 1954: 138; Robinson 1995b: 367–416.

20. Zhu and Zhou 1788: 2: 11b. Perhaps he suspended his revolt or was absorbed into the

Liu Liu-Liu Qi rebellion; perhaps there were two men named Wang Tang; or, most likely, the gazetteer stated the first year of Zhengde when it meant the first year of Jiajing.

21. Liu and Ye 1705: 3: 84; Yu, Hu, and Lü 1903: 15: 2a; Han and Li 1920: 9: 17b; Ma and Gao 1987: 12: 505; Robinson 1995b: 461–62.

22. Robinson 1995b: 461–64.

23. In his search for immortality, Jiajing has been compared with Han Wudi. See Albert Chan 1982: 109. For balanced accounts of the reign and of Yan Song, see Mote and Twitchett 1988: 486–87; Goodrich and Fang 1976: 1586–91; and Zhang Xiangqing 1992a.

24. Chen and Zha 1754: 34: 12b; Yue, Hu, and Lü 1903: 152b; Shen and Huang 1898: 23: 7b; Ma and Gao 1987: 12: 499.

25. Chen and Zha 1754: 31: 10b; Ma and Gao 1987: 12: 505.

26. Han and Li 1920: 9: 17b; Yue, Hu, and Lü 1903: 15: 2b.

27. Ma and Gao 1987: 12: 505.

28. Guan and Zhang 1695: 39: 17a–18a; Wang and Zhang 1923: 19: 5b; Ma and Gao 1987: 12: 505.

29. Chen and Zha 1754: 31: 10b; Ma and Gao 1987: 12: 505.

30. Chen and Zha 1754: 31: 11; Ma and Gao 1987: 12: 505; Yue, Hu, and Lü 1903: 15: 2b.

31. The Li Fuda affair was used by factions at court to discredit one another, and it led the Ming to apply the label "White Lotus religion" to all kinds of heterodox groups after 1525. See Ter Haar 1992: 155–72. For the role of a preacher Li in Jiangnan in the 1550s, see ibid., 182–95.

32. Shek 1980: 320–23, 346; Shen Dingping 1982: 295–97.

33. Zhu 1972: 26–31; Wakeman 1985: 3–7; Atwell 1977, 1990; Tong 1991: 127.

34. See Chapter 1; Elvin 1973: 310–12; and Dunstan 1975: 29.

35. Zhang Tingyu 1739: 226: 5937; Li Shoukong 1968: 43–44.

36. Ma and Gao 1987: 12: 505.

37. Shek 1980: 245–48; Shen Dingping 1982: 297; Ter Haar 1992: 216–17.

38. Li Shoukong 1968: 44; Shen Dingping 1982: 297; Zheng Han 1985: 134, 148–50; Ter Haar 1992: 218–19. For other alleged conspiracies of this time alluding to rebellions of the late Qin, the late Han, and the late Tang, see Ter Haar 1992: 213–15, 222.

39. Zhang Tingyu 1739: 257: 6621; Li Shoukong 1968: 45; Goodrich and Fang 1976: 587; Naquin 1986: 228. For the history behind the legend of Bodhisattva Lü, see Li and Naquin 1988: 135–36, 141, 144–45, 147, 149, 156–58, 168–73.

40. Noguchi 1963: 21: 44, 47; Goodrich and Fang 1976: 588; Shek 1980: 358–60.

41. Shek 1980: 361–67; Li Jixian 1982: 272.

42. For contemporary awareness of the parallel, see Ter Haar 1992: 222, 226.

43. Zhang Tingyu 1739: 207: 6940; Li Shoukong 1968: 46.

44. Zheng 1749: 1: 23–24; Li Shoukong 1968: 46; Ma and Gao 1987: 12: 506. The critical references to Dashing (Li Zicheng) and Cao (Luo Rucai) suggest that the note was written sometime after 1644 and before 1949.

45. Wu Sheng late Ming: 5: 6b–7a. For Wu's biography, see Goodrich and Fang 1976: 1494–95. I am grateful to Shen Dingping for providing me with copies of these reports and to Blaine Gaustad for pointing out the meaning of Ziweixing. The Ziweixing is a circumpolar constellation that protects the pole star (the metaphor for the son of heaven). See Schafer 1977: 47; Naquin 1981: 189–90n121.

46. Wu Sheng late Ming: 5: 7.

47. Ibid., 6: 16b.

48. Ibid., 6: 33a–34b. In fact, during the following decade, a Yuandun sect associated with Li Guoyong's group and under the leadership of a Gong-chang continued to be active in North China, including Kaifeng city. Although it organized no political activities, it emphasized magical charms and breathing exercises to deal with the multiple calamities of famine,

flood, and plague, which it associated with the coming of the kalpic transition. See Shek 1980: 287–306.

49. For preliminary and ongoing discussions of this hypothesis, see Des Forges 1984 and Des Forges in process.

50. Li Wenzhi 1948: 1–51; Li Guangtao 1965: 1–32; Taniguchi 1969: 99–108; Parsons 1970: 1–32; Gu Cheng 1984: 27–64.

51. Yuan Mo Kangxi: 1. Xuan's name was later written as "Yuan" to avoid using part of Kangxi's personal name, Xuanye.

52. Gu Yingtai 1658: 75: 1247–73; Peng early Qing: 2: 20–26; Xuan Kangxi: 1–15; Zheng 1749: 2: 30–31; Liu Yinan 1983: 50–52; Gu Cheng 1984: 53–60.

53. Peng early Qing: 2: 25–26; Li Wenzhi 1948: 206; Parsons 1970: 27, 31; Wang Chenmain 1999: ch. 3.

54. Zheng 1749: 2: 31–34.

55. Peng early Qing: 2: 27; Wang Xingya 1984b: 37–38; Parsons 1970: 37, 45.

56. Zhou and Liu 1931: 7: 5b, 58b, 16: 9a; Peng early Qing: 2: 27; Zheng 1749: 2: 40.

57. Peng early Qing: 2: 27–29; Wu Weiye 1674: 2; Li Wenzhi 1948: 57–58; Shen Dingping 1982: 300; Gu Cheng 1984: 74.

58. Wu Weiye 1674: 2: 10b; Zhang Tingyu 1739: 309: 7; Parsons 1970: 36–40. The name of the county where the meeting was supposedly held—Xingyang—is usually misread as "Rongyang" (or "Jung-yang") in Western sources.

59. Wang Xingya 1984a: 32–47; Gu Cheng 1984: 71–76.

60. Zheng 1749: 2: 35–36; the military abuse of "borrowing heads" later became so widespread that in 1640 the Ming court instructed the grand coordinator of Henan province that it was no longer necessary to present the heads of the enemy to prove they had been killed. Albert Chan 1982: 206–8.

61. Zheng 1749: 2: 36; for social banditry, see Hobsbawm 1959, 1969.

62. Zheng 1749: 2: 37; Han and Li 1920: 9: 18a.

63. Zheng 1749: 2: 36–37.

64. Ibid., 38; Liu and Ye 1705: 4: 104.

65. Zheng 1749: 2: 39.

66. Idem; Chen and Zha 1754: 31: 12a; Ma and Gao 1987: 5: 150, 162; 6: 208–9, 212; 12: 50.

67. For the assaults, see Li Wenzhi 1948: 207. For the paucity of records, see also Yue, Hu, and Lü 1903: 15: 3b; for the attack on Qi, see Zhu and Zhou 1788: 2: 15b. For Zheng's harsh appraisal, see Zheng 1749: 2: 36. For the four men who used the nickname Saodi Wang, see Yao Jiaji 1935: 2.2: 87–88; for the Saodi Wangs in the Huai and at Fengyang, see Gu Yingtai 1658: 75: 1272, 1274–75; Peng early Qing: 2: 25, 28. For the capture and killing of a Saodi Wang in 1636 and the surrender of a Saodi Wang named Li Jing in 1640, see Yao Jiaji 1935: 2.2: 87–88.

68. Zheng 1749: 2: 40; Li Wenzhi 1948: 62, 208.

69. Zheng 1749: 2: 40–44, 48, 51, 57; Zhang Tingyu 1739: 23: 321; Dunstan 1975: 56, 58; Wakeman 1985: 6; Goldstone 1991: 374; Atwell 1982, 1990: 674–77. For doubts about the role of the international economy, see Von Glahn 1996: 5, 139, 237–45. For a summary of the issues and a reaffirmation of the negative effects of a silver shortage in China in the 1630s and early 1640s, see Frank 1998: 237–48; Twitchett and Mote 1998: 407–11.

70. Zheng 1749: 43–44; Chen and Zha 1754: 31: 12a; Parsons 1970: 59, 60–68, 73.

71. Zheng 1749: 2: 46.

72. Ibid., 47; Li Wenzhi 1948: 47.

73. Zheng 1749: 2: 48; 3: 51; Yao Jiaji 1935: 88.

74. Zheng 1749: 3: 52–54; Zhou and Liu 1921: 10: 22b–24a, 14: 19b–23a.

75. Zheng 1749: 3: 54–55; Parsons 1970: 68–71.

76. Zheng 1749: 3: 55–56; Parsons 1970: 71–83; Albert Chan 1982: 196–97.

77. Zheng 1749: 3: 60–61.

78. Ibid., 61.

79. Idem; Wang Xingya 1982b: 3; Albert Chan 1982: 225.

80. Zheng 1749: 3: 57.

81. Ibid., 57–58; Tong 1991: 83. Song Jiang, of course, was a nickname drawn from the Ming novel, *Bandits of the Marsh*, which depicted a bandit gang of the Song period as being at least as upright as the officialdom of that era. For the influence of the novel on the rebellions of the late Ming, see Li Wenzhi 1948: 196–97; Albert Chan 1982: 397–400.

82. Zheng 1749: 3: 58.

83. Ibid., 58–59.

84. Ibid., 64; Zhu and Zhou 1788: 2: 16b; Ma and Gao 1987: 12: 506.

85. Zheng 1749: 3: 64; Zhu and Zhou 1788: 2: 16b. See the case of Xuzhou in Dunstan 1975: 13.

86. Wang Xingya 1982a: 5–6; Cong 1985: 23; Tong 1991: 144, 190; Heijdra 1994: 88.

87. Mei 1975: 76–80. We know that local firemen earned two fen a day to cover their food and living expenses.

88. Ibid., 77–79.

89. Albert Chan 1982: 88; Tong 1991: 189; Wang 1992: 5; Heijdra 1994: 147, 273.

90. He and Wang 1992: 483.

Chapter 5

1. Mote 1999: 1036n53; Elliott 2001: 46, 52, 65.

2. Li Wenzhi 1948: 97–98; Parsons 1970: 19; Shen Dingping 1982: 297–98; Liu Yinan 1983: 6–8; Li Dengdi 1986: 7–10; Xie 1986: 28.

3. Xie 1986: 29–30, 34–35; Liu Yinan 1983: 14.

4. Liu Yinan 1983: 28–32; Xie 1986: 30–31. Another widespread, but chronologically contradictory, story was that Li went off to serve in the army in Gansu and participated in a mutiny of unpaid troops in 1629.

5. Zheng 1749: 3: 65; Liu Yinan 1983: 32; Gu Cheng 1984: 36–37.

6. Li Wenzhi 1948: 99–102; Gu Cheng 1984: 54, 59, 99; Li Dengdi 1986: 28, 31–32.

7. Gu Cheng 1984: 156–57; Li Dengdi 1986: 71.

8. Zheng 1749: 3: 65; Wang Xingya 1984a: 66–73.

9. Luan 1982: 147–52; Luan 1986: 1–10, 39–42, 50–53.

10. For Wang, see Shen and Huang 1898: 4: 9a, 28b; Tian, Sun, and Asiha 1735: 34: 103a. For the dispute, see Zhao 1645?: 17; Zheng 1749: 3: 67; Luan 1982: 152–59; Luan 1986: 15–17.

11. Zheng 1749: 3: 66–67; Luan 1982: 152–59; Liu Yinan 1983: 14; Wang Xingya 1984a: 222–24; Li Dengdi 1986: 47; Luan 1986: 10–17.

12. Zheng 1749: 3: 66; Wang Xingya 1984a: 19, 192, 212; Gu Cheng 1984: 130; Xie 1986: 165.

13. Xie 1986: 165. The term "cannon" (*dapao*) covers a wide range of large weapons common in the Ming that used explosive powder to hurl different kinds of projectiles. The terms "Portugese" or "Western-style cannon" will be used when weapons using more finely bored bronze barrels and metal cannon balls are indicated in the sources. Unfortunately, in many cases no descriptions of the weapons are given, and no distinctions are made among the various kinds.

14. Zheng 1749: 3.65–66.

15. Ibid., 66; Gu Cheng 1984: 130; Xie 1986: 166; Li Dengdi 1986: 72.

16. Zheng 1749: 4: 73.

17. Ibid., 2: 33; 4: 73; Goodrich and Fang 1976: 1014–16; Gu Cheng 1984: 133; Xie 1986: 167. The Yi-Luo Society was named after the two rivers that flowed near Luoyang, which

had become symbols of the Ruism propagated by the brothers Cheng Yi and Cheng Hao, residents of Luoyang in the Northern Song.

18. Zheng 1749: 4: 73; Gu Cheng 1984: 133.

19. Zheng 1749: 4: 74–75; Parsons 1970: 81; Goodrich and Fang 1976: 1014–16; Gu Cheng 1984: 134; Xie 1986: 168.

20. Zheng 1749: 4: 73–74.

21. Gu Cheng 1984: 134; Wang Xingya 1984a: 192–93, 210.

22. Zheng 1749: 4: 76; Gu Cheng 1984: 134–35; Xie 1986: 189.

23. Zheng 1749: 4: 74–75; Gu Cheng 1984: 134–35; Xie 1986: 189.

24. Zheng 1749: 4: 75; Xie 1986: 189.

25. Li Guangtian 1644: 1; Zheng 1749: 4: 77.

26. Bai 1644: 4.

27. Li Guangtian 1644: 2; Zheng 1749: 4: 77; Parsons 1970: 94.

28. Zhou early Qing: 25–26; Burton Watson 1968: 67. For the growth, unraveling, and persistence of the story that Chen Yongfu shot out Li Zicheng's eye, see Liu Yinan 1983: 177; Gu Cheng 1984: 137; Xie 1986: 191; Li Dengdi 1986: 77.

29. Zhang Tingyu 1739: 293: 7520; Wang Xingya 1984a: 73.

30. Zhou early Qing: 35–36; Xie 1986: 192. Zicheng and Jiyu shared the same charismatic surname.

31. Zheng 1749: 4: 80–81, 83; Xie 1986: 192. For Ding's background, see Chapter 2.

32. Zheng 1749: 4: 84.

33. Ibid., 85.

34. Shen Dingping 1982: 301–2; Liu Yinan 1983: 171; Li Dengdi 1986: 79. The precise formulation of the prophecy attributed to Song was "*shiba haier zhu shenqi*" which means "the eighteenth child will master the sacred instruments." See Runzhou 1645: 5; Xi Wu 1660s: 4: 9a–11a; Ji Liuqi 1671: 17: 294; 23: 653; Wu Weiye 1674: 12; Zhou early Qing: 35–36; Zheng 1749: fanli 1.

35. Zheng 1749: 4: 86; Xie 1986: 193–94.

36. Xie 1986: 217–19.

37. Zheng 1749: 4: 87.

38. Ibid., 89.

39. Idem. For a prophecy by a Li that encouraged Wu Wang of the Zhou to attack the capital of Shang in Anyang, see Fong 1980: 198, 204.

40. Zheng 1749: 4: 90–92; Xie 1986: 219.

41. Zheng 1749: 4: 92. Gu argues the turncoats got what they deserved. See Gu Cheng 1984: 139.

42. Zheng 1749: 4: 91–94; Xie 1986: 220–21.

43. Liu San and Zhao Sui had gone to Xiangcheng. See Chapter 4. Xie 1986: 219–20. Geng Yinggeng ultimately refused Niu Jinxing's appeal and fled to Nanjing. Luan 1982: 150–51; Luan 1986: 8–9.

44. Zheng 1749: 4: 91; Xie 1986: 221.

45. Zheng 1749: 5: 106.

46. Ibid., 4: 90–91.

47. Ibid., 95; Liu Yinan 1983: 173; Xie 1986: 221.

48. Tian, Sun, and Asiha 1735: 33: 51b.

49. Zheng 1749: 4: 97.

50. Ibid., 94–96. The Han Gongyang school had celebrated an all-out defense of the Spring and Autumn state of Song that had resulted in cannibalism, perhaps providing a precedent for Ming scholar-officials' interest in the defense of the Tang town of Suiyang that had similar results. For the earlier case, see Queen 1996: 145–50.

51. Wang Xingya 1984a: 5.

52. Li Guangtian 1644: 4; Zheng 1749: 4: 78; Xie 1986: 189–90.

53. Li Guangtian 1644: 5.

54. Ibid., 4–5; Zheng 1749: 78.

55. Zheng 1749: 4: 98.

56. Bai 1644: 12–13; Zhou early Qing: 51–52. Zheng Lian opined that Li Goupi was lucky he was not beaten to death; Zheng 1749: 4: 103.

57. Li Guangtian 1644: 5–6; Zhou early Qing: 31–32; Zheng 1749: 4: 98; Leslie 1972: 37–38.

58. Li Guangtian 1644: 6–7; Bai 1644: 20–21; Zhou early Qing: 31.

59. Bai 1644: 19–20; Li Guangtian 1644: 7; Zhou early Qing: 49; Zheng 1749: 5: 103.

60. Li Guangtian 1644: 7; Zhou early Qing: 49; Zheng 1749: 5: 103. Whatever its earlier history, the symbolic use of sexuality in battle reappeared in rebellions in the late Qing. Naquin 1981: 101; Cohen 1997: 129–32.

61. Li Guangtian 1644: 7–9; Zhou early Qing: 50; Zheng 1749: 5: 103–4.

62. Bai 1644: 28; Li Guangtian 1644: 9–11; Zhou early Qing: 61–62; Zheng 1749: 15: 105. The round figures do not inspire confidence. Because Li was supposed to have had only thirty thousand soldiers to begin with, these casualty figures, if accurate, must have included many camp followers.

63. Bai 1644: 22–24; Zhou early Qing: 52–53; Xie 1986: 197. There is no mention of the provenance of this cannon, but there were two Jesuit missionaries in Kaifeng who may have brought it in or cast it in situ.

64. Bai 1644: 27; Li Guangtian 1644: 7, 11; Zheng 1749: 15: 105; Xie 1986: 198.

65. Liu Yinan 1983: 181–82; Li Dengdi 1986: 87; Xie 1986: 222.

66. Xie 1986: 222; Li Dengdi 1986: 89.

67. Li Dengdi 1986: 89; Xie 1986: 223–26.

68. Zheng 1749: 5: 107–8.

69. Ibid., 5: 108; Parsons 1970: 97. The rumors may have been inspired by the story in Sima Qian's *Historical Records* that Xiang Yu, the rebel who overthrew the Qin in the third century BCE, had massacred the entire population of Xiangcheng. The parallel was seemingly "confirmed" when Li Zicheng failed once again to take Kaifeng, a failure Xiang Yu had also experienced. Like Xiang Yu too, of course, Li Zicheng ultimately failed to establish his own enduring state, leading historians to emphasize his supposed brutality as part of the explanation for his failure. Burton Watson 1968: I: 86–87. Harsh punishments were of course not limited to Chinese rebels in this age. When Indians retaliated for Portugese plundering of their ships by killing all the Western traders in Calicut, Vasco da Gama cut off the hands, ears, and noses of eight hundred Moorish seamen in 1502 and sent the lot to the local Indian authorities "for their curry." See Wolpert 1997: 136.

70. Zheng 1749: 5: 106–10; Li 1915: 31: 9a–10a; 34: 11a–13a; Liu Yinan 1983: 226. The Suiyang thirty-six presumably referred to those who died in the defense of Shangqiu from An Lushan in the Tang.

71. Xie 1986: 226–27.

72. Wang Xingya 1984a: 70, 221.

73. Zheng 1749: 5: 110–12; Xie 1986: 227.

74. Wang and Ma 1932: wubei, Ming-Qing bingzhi: 32b–33a; 20: dashi, jishi; Satō 1978: 210–11, 219–23; Satō 1985: 25–26, 34–39; Wang Xingya 1984a: 318; Wakeman 1985: 155n216.

75. Zheng 1749: 4: 72.

76. Sato 1985: 26.

77. Zheng 1749: 4: 72; Sato 1985: 26. Further research might reveal whether this scholar was related to Hou Xun's mother, née Tian.

78. Wang Xingya 1984a: 320; Satō 1985: 27.

79. Zheng 1749: 5: 111; Xiao and Lü 1911: zhong: 516; Liu Yinan 1983: 198; Wang Xingya 1984a: 321–22; Satō 1985: 27.

80. For the original "between Chen and Cai," see Qian Mu 1964: 2: 363; Lau 1979: 106; for the time and place of the alliance, see Liu Yinan 1983: 198; and Wang Xingya 1984a: 321–22; for Little Yuan's Battalion, see Zheng 1749: 5: 111. The terms "little" and "old," of course, denoted affection and respect as well as relative status and age. For example, Yuan Laoshan (old mountain Yuan) was an honorific for Yuan Shizhong. See Wei Qianzhi 1993a; Li, Wei, and Des Forges 1994: 107–8.

81. Zheng 1749: 5: 112; Liu Yian 1982a: 198; Xie 1986: 227.

82. Zheng 1749: 113–14; Zhang Tingyu 1739: 264: 6825–26.

83. Zheng 1749: 114; Ma and Gao 1987: 6: 211–12.

84. Zheng 1749: 5: 114; Ma and Gao 1987: 6: 239; 12: 506.

85. Zheng 1749: 5: 114; Xiao and Lü 1911: 6: 135, 160; 7: 174.

86. Xiao and Lü 1911: 7: 189, 199–200; 9: 306, 328; Lü 1986: 1: 51b–52a.

87. Xiao and Lü 9: 308–9.

88. Zheng 1749: 5: 114; Xiao and Lü 1911: 8: 189, 199, 211, 212, 214, 247, 251; 10: 382–84; Qiao 1920: 2: 1a–2a; 3: 2b.

89. Miao and Miao 1987: 1: 39a. For the role of youth in the rebellion, see Wang Xingya 1984a: 121–29; for the role of youth in the English, French, and Chinese revolutions, see Goldstone 1991: 137–38, 247–48; Saich and van de Ven 1995: 183.

Chapter 6

1. Zheng 1749: 5: 112; Tian, Sun, and Asiha 1735: 32: 3b, 51b. For the prevalence of the Jin model among bon vivants of the late Ming, see Chapter 3 and Li Mowry 1983: 19, 56, 61; Plaks 1987: 153–54; Roy 1993: 12, 430; Meskill 1994: 45, 52, 139, 143, 173.

2. Zheng 1749: 5: 112.

3. Ibid., 113. According to the gazetteer, Hou Xing was the adopted son of Hou Zhijie in Hou Xun's lineage. Liu and Ye 1705: 10: 322. The Hou genealogy, however, disavowed him. Hou Fangyue 1908: fanli: 6.2a.

4. Zheng 1749: 5: 115.

5. Chen and Zha 1754: shou: 1b–2a.

6. Zheng 1749: 5: 115–16; Liu and Ye 1705: 6: 151; 7: 192; 8: 252–53. Cannons (*dapao*), in this case, would have been of the old variety that used explosive powder to deliver inert ammunition such as rocks or metal.

7. Zheng 1749: 5: 116. For the story of the Tang-period Curly Bearded Stranger, see Zhou 1927: 154–58; Edwards 1938: 2: 35–44.

8. Zheng 1749: 5: 117.

9. Ibid., 116–17.

10. Liu and Ye 1705: 4: 104–5.

11. Ibid., 4: 106–7; Shen and Shen 1987: 1: 53–54, 57b–59a, 60a–61b. The Shen genealogy lacks information on women and cannot be used to supplement and corroborate the gazetteer.

12. Liu and Ye 1705: 10: 339.

13. Ibid., 4: 107; 11: 370. Two other Hou women listed in the gazetteer as casualties may have belonged to other branches of the Hou lineage.

14. Liu and Ye 1705: 9: 304–6; 10: 327. Xu and a Jiangnan friend, Wen Zhenmeng, had been such outspoken critics of the late-Ming state that they had been compared by contemporaries with Zhufu Yan and Yan An, two courageous officials of the reign of Han Wudi. Four of the eight Lius who died at this time belonged to the other, more military Liu lineage that had vowed to resist the rebels in the manner of Zhang and Xu of the Tang. See Liu Tinggui 1929: 5: 8a–9a, 24a–25a. For Zhang Wei, see also He and Wang 1992: 30.

15. Liu and Ye 1705: 1: 12, 16, 28.

16. Ibid., 2: 78–79; Burton Watson 1993: 31. Li, of course, came from Shaanxi, also

known as Qin. For the context of the battle of Changping, see Loewe and Shaughnessy 1999: 628, 640.

17. Zheng 1749: 5: 117–18.

18. Ibid., 118–19.

19. Liu and Ye 1705: 8: 258; 10: 339; Zheng 1749: 5: 117, 119.

20. Zheng 1749: 5: 118.

21. Ibid., 117, 119.

22. Ibid., 116–20; Liu and Ye 1705: 8: 262; Song Luo 1705: 5: 14.

23. Zheng 1749: 5: 118; Song Luo 1705: 5: 14b.

24. Liu and Ye 1705: 9: 309.

25. Ibid., 305–9.

26. Zheng 1749: 5: 120.

27. Chen and Zha 1754: 24: 25b; Han and Li 1920: 6: 9a–12a.

28. For the Pengs' original status, see Han and Li 1920: 8: 54b; 8 xuanjubiaoxia. For Yaoyu and Shunling, see Ibid., 6: 21–23b, 19a–30a, 36a; 8: 11a, 16a, 19, 20b. For the lack of a strong magistrate, see ibid., 5: 16a; 5 xunliangzhuan: 6b.

29. Liu Yinan 1983: 198; Wang Xingya 1984a: 324; Xie 1986: 227; Li Dengdi 1986: 91; Chen and Zha 1754: 24: 25a–26a; Li and Xi 1895: 6: 23b–24a; Yu, Hu, and Lü 1903: 26: 2a–3b.

30. Ji and Wang 1764: 10: 32–33a; mo: 3b. Two other members of the Yifeng local elite died at the hands of rebels at other times and places. See Zheng 1749: 5: 121.

31. For those ties, see Chapter 2.

32. Zhu and Zhou 1788: 14: 18.

33. Ibid., 2: 16b; 9: 48a. Su was erroneously identified in the provincial gazetteer as a Shandong man. Tian, Sun, and Asiha 1735: 31: 13a; 33: 6b.

34. Liu Yian 1982a: 110; Li, Wei, and Des Forges 1994: 88–89.

35. Zhu and Zhou 1788: 2: 16b; 13: 16a; Meng 1990: passim. Even these men may have perished in confrontations with insurgents at other times and places.

36. Because Meng 1990 and Ma Chaoqun 1780 do not include information on deaths, those lineages are excluded from this discussion. He Xinzhen 1987: 2: 34b, 36b, 39a; Hou Shimei 1987: shixixu: 14–17.

37. Guan and Zhang 1695: 26: 36a; Zhu and Zhou 1788: 21: 61b–63b; Qin and Qin 1952: 1a, 5b–6a, 7b–8a, 10b.

38. Li Yunlai n.d.: 36a, 38a–59a, 87b, 92b–97a, 104b–6a, 108a–10a; Li Xiaosheng 1987b: 43–44. According to the genealogies, Qins continued to marry Lis, although perhaps not the Lis of Qinglonggang. At least one Li, in the fourteenth generation, married a Qin; many Li spouses are not indicated by name. Qin and Qin 1952: 7a–59b; Li Yunlai n.d.: shisishi.

39. For Meng Shaoqian, see Zhu and Zhou 1788: 18: 4b; Li 1915: 31: 7. While the former source, written in the Qing, depicts Meng as an intermediary between the Ming and Li Zicheng, the latter, written in the Republic, considers Meng to have been the rebels' man in Qi. Meng is missing from all existing lists of rebel magistrates; perhaps his authority in Qi was informal. Li and He 1693: 18: 4b; Zhu and Zhou 1788: 18: 4b; Li 1915: 2a–3a; Wang Xingya 1984a: 327–28.

40. Zheng 1749: 5: 121.

41. Li Guangtian 1644: 14; Zheng 1749: 5: 121–22; Wang Xingya 1984a: 327–28.

42. Zheng 1749: 5: 122.

43. Li Guangtian 1644: 32; Xie 1986: 201.

44. Bai 1644: 35; Li Guangtian 1644: 15; Zheng 1749: 5: 124; Xie 1986: 200.

45. Bai 1644: 35–36; Li Dengdi 1986: 92.

46. Li Guangtian 1644: 16.

47. Zheng 1749: 5: 124–25; Zhou and Liu 1931: 7: 58b.

48. Li Guangtian 1644: 15; Liu Yinan 1983: 186; Li Dengdi 1986: 92; Xie 1986: 203.

49. Bai 1644: 39; Liu Yian 1982a: 81–82; Liu Yinan 1983: 186–87; Li Dengdi 1986: 92–93.

50. Zheng 1749: 5: 127. Bai's version seems to contain a more explicit threat to "cut the dikes of the Yellow River." Bai 1644: 41. It is not clear which version of the document is earlier or more genuine.

51. Zheng 1749: 5: 126.

52. Ibid., 129; Liu Yian 1982a: 81–82; Liu Yinan 1983: 187.

53. Tan Qian 1653: 98: 5930; Liu and Ye 1705: 8: 255–56; Zheng 1749: 5: 127; Hummel 1943–44: 531–32; Goodrich and Fang 1976: 278.

54. Liu Yian 1982b: 77–78; Liu Yinan 1983: 187; Xie 1986: 203.

55. Tan Qian 1653: 98: 5937; Zheng 1749: 5: 128; He and Wang 1992: 176. The full original report, said to have been drafted by Hou's son, Hou Fangyu, is no longer extant. This excerpt and the following discussion is based on partial copies in these three sources.

56. Tan Qian 1653: 98: 5937; Zheng 1749: 5: 128; He and Wang 1992: 177.

57. Zheng 1749: 5: 129; He and Wang 1992: 592.

58. Bai 1644: 42–43, 45; Li Guangtian 1644: 17–18; Liu Yian 1982b: 83; Xie 1986: 203.

59. Li Guangtian 1644: 18–20; Zheng 1749: 6: 129–33; Liu Yian 1982b: 90.

60. Li Guangtian 1644: 20–22; Zheng 1749: 6: 133.

61. Li Guangtian 1644: 22; Zheng 1749: 6: 134; Xie 1986: 203.

62. Li Guangtian 1644: 22; Zheng 1749: 6: 134; Li 1915: 31: 8a–9b.

63. Li Guangtian 1644: 25–27; Zheng 1749: 6: 135–36.

64. Li Guangtian 1644: 41; Zheng 1749: 6: 136.

65. Li Guangtian 1644: 43–45, 48–50, 67–68.

66. Bai 1644: 47–50; Li Guangtian 1644: 27–28; Zheng 1749: 6: 136–37; Liu Yian 1982b: 108.

67. Bai 1644: 46; Xie 1986: 204.

68. Li Guangtian 1644: 18; Zheng 1749: 5: 129. Li and Zheng date this rebel effort earlier, to June, and make no mention of any official effort to use the river against the rebels. Most historians in the People's Republic adopt the opposite position that the rebels made no significant breaks in the dikes that were relevant to the final disaster.

69. Zheng 1749: 6: 137–38; Zhang Tingyu 1739: 276: 6884–85; Liu Yian 1982b: 112–19; Liu Yinan 1983: 203–4; Wang Xingya 1984a: 311–12; Xie 1986: 205.

70. Li Guangtian may have anticipated the disaster; according to his diary he started building boats on September 12. Li Guangtian 1644: 29; Liu Yian 1982b: 120. For the natural causes of the disaster, see Zheng 1749: 6: 138; Wang Xingya 1984a: 299, 312. For Zheng's description of the result, see Zheng 1749: 6: 138. For estimated casualties, see Liu Yian 1982b: 111–25.

71. Zheng 1749: 6: 138, 140.

72. Ibid., 144; Wang Xingya 1984a: 307; Xie 1986: 206. Yan was perhaps the most vulnerable since he had been in charge of cutting the dikes and was rumored to be a descendant of Yan Song, the much maligned grand secretary of the early sixteenth century.

73. For Zhou, see Bai 1644: 2; Zhou early Qing; Zheng 1749: 6: 139–40; Liu Yian 1982b. For Liu, see Guan and Zhang 1695: 26: 41b; Liu Yian 1982b: 115–16; Wang Xingya 1984a: 308. For Wang, see Zheng 1749: 6: 139–40.

74. Li Guangtian 1644: 33; Li and Li 1749: shishi; Li 1915: 31: 9b.

75. Chang Moulai 1852: yuanxu: 1b–2b; Liu Yian 1982b: 124; Xie 1986: 206, 216.

Chapter 7

1. Tian, Sun, and Asiha 1735: 32: 3b; Zheng 1749: 5: 123; Satō 1985: 28.

2. Zheng 1749: 6: 134–35; Han and Li 1920: 5: 16a; Wang Xingya 1984a: 331; Satō 1985: 28–29.

3. Pan and Wang 1752: 8: 71a–75a; 10: 29b; Satō 1985: 29.

4. Zheng 1749: 6: 152.

5. Yue, Hu, and Lü 1903: 3: 12b–13a; 11: 6a; 19: 5a–7a, 10; 37: 1a–5b; Wang Xingya 1984a: 331–32; Satō 1985: 29–30; He and Wang 1992: 593.

6. Tian, Sun, and Asiha 1735: 31: 9b, 13a; 32: 2b, 3b; Wang and Liang 1935: 31: 26a; Wang and Ma 1932: zhiguan, huanji, 24b.

7. Zheng 1749: 6: 142–43; Liu Yinan 1983: 190.

8. Zheng 1749: 6: 141–42; Liu Yinan 1983: 190–92; Xie 1986: 262.

9. Zheng 1749: 6: 147–49; Liu Yinan 1983: 193; He and Wang 1992: 119–24.

10. Zheng 1749: 6: 149–50; Li Dengdi 1986: 104.

11. Zheng 1749: 6: 149.

12. Ibid., 149–50; Liu Yinan 1983: 207; Gu Cheng 1984: 165, 177–78; Li Dengdi 1986: 104; Xie 1986: 264.

13. For Kong, see Jiang and Gao 1828: 4: 9b; Kong 1684: 5: 10b; Guoli zhongyang yanjiu yuan 1930–36: jia: 972; Zheng 1749: 6: 150; for Tian, see Liu Yinan 1983: 201; for Zhang, see Gu Cheng 1984: 360.

14. Zheng 1749: 6: 150–51.

15. Tan Qian 1653: 100: 6027; Ji Liuqi 1671 (1984): 19: 356; Peng 1670s: 6; Zhang Tingyu 1739: 263: 6802; Shih 1967: 374; Wang 1982: 37–47, 50; Liu Yinan 1983: 192, 207; Wang Xingya 1984a: 103; Xie 1986: 277; Li Dengdi 1986: 104–6.

16. Wang Xingya 1982a: 11–15, 16, 17, 18–21, 24, 109–12; Li, Wei, and Des Forges 1994: 111. Attribution of the equal fields slogan to the rebels first occurred in print, however, only in the 1670s. See Zha 1670s: 136: 223; Wang Shouyi 1962: 97–112; Liu Chongri 1962: 116–30; Des Forges 1982: 563; Wang Xingya 1982a: 1, 21, 35; Wang Xingya 1984a: 103.

17. Li Guangtian 1644: 10; Liu and Ye 1705: 4: 109–11; Wang Xingya 1984a: 130–52.

18. Liu Yinan 1983: 208, 226–27; Gu Cheng 1984: 173, 359; Xie 1986: 274.

19. Liu Yinan 1983: 210; Wang Xingya 1984a: 193–98, 203; Gu Cheng 1984: 172–73; Hucker 1985: 28–37, 210; Xie 1986: 274–79.

20. Wang Xingya 1984a: 166–71.

21. Liu Yinan 1983: 334–42; Wang Xingya 1984a: 195–98.

22. Wang Xingya 1984a: 195–98, 209; Liu Yinan 1983: 339–40; Gu Cheng 1984: 366–69, 378–83.

23. Xie 1986: 270–72, 283.

24. For the effects of the assassinations, see Wang Xingya 1984a: 333; Gu Cheng 1984: 171. For Zheng's view, see Zheng 1749: 7: 156–57. For recent views, see Liu Yinan 1983: 210–11, 227–28; Gu Cheng 1984: 162–71; Xie 1986: 273; Li Dengdi 1986: 107.

25. Zheng 1749: 6: 152; Yue, Hu, and Lü 1903: 37: 1, 4.

26. Tan Qian 1653: 99: 5979–80; Zheng 1749: 6: 153; Yue, Hu, and Lü 1903: 37: 5.

27. Zheng 1749: 6: 141.

28. Satō 1985: 30–31; for doubts that Yuan actually surrendered to the Ming, see Wang Xingya 1984a: 332.

29. Zheng 1749: 6: 140–41; Wang Xingya 1984a: 334–35; Satō 1985: 31, 33; Xie 1986: 283.

30. Liu Yinan 1983: 210–11; Gu Cheng 1984: 171–72; Wang Xingya 1984a: 324; Li Dengdi 1986: 107; Satō 1985: 34–39. Yuan's link with the landed strata has been demonstrated but his participation in the campaign against the Manchus has been questioned. See Xie 1986: 283.

31. Tian, Sun, and Asiha 1735: 45: 54a; Li 1915: 31: 1a.

32. Zheng 1749: 6: 152; 7: 170; Li 1915: 31: 1b.

33. Li 1915: 31: 1b.

34. Tan Qian 1653: 99: 5973; Tian, Sun, and Asiha 1735: 31: 9b.

35. Gu early Qing: 31a, 91b; Wang and Liang 1935: 31: 26b; Gu Cheng 1978: 63; Des Forges 1984: 419; Wang Xingya 1984a: 277.

36. Feng Menglong 1644: 6: 1–5; Zhang Tingyu 1739: 265: 6852–53; Tian, Sun, and Asiha 1735: 32: 2b, 3b; Wang and Liang 1935: 31: 26b, 33: zhong: 69a; Des Forges 1984: 418–19. Li Yan wrote pieces that were compiled in a volume titled *Collection of E Mountain*, but the work is no longer extant. We do not know the date of Li Yan's death. For work to date on the Li Yan question, see studies by Gu Cheng, Luan Xing, Wang Xingya, Des Forges, Li Xiaosheng, and Qin Xinlin.

37. Tan Qian 1653: 99: 5973–74, 5985; Zheng 1749: 6: 158–59. The place of his incarceration is not indicated, but subsequent events suggest that it was in Beijing. For the fall of Zhou Yanru, see Wakeman 1985: I: 146–56.

38. Chen 1987.

39. Liu Yinan 1983: 213; Gu Cheng 1984: 199; Xie 1986: 294.

40. Xie 1986: 294; Li Dengdi 1986: 112.

41. Zheng 1749: 7: 157–58.

42. Liu Lishun 1658: 9: 3a–6b.

43. Liu Yinan 1983: 211, 213–14; Xie 1986: 295–96.

44. Zheng 1749: 7: 159–60; Liu Yinan 1983: 215; Gu Cheng 1984: 201; Li Dengdi 1986: 113; Xie 1986: 296.

45. Liu Yinan 1983: 215; Xie 1986: 296–97.

46. Xie 1986: 297–98.

47. Zheng 1749: 161–64.

48. Gu Cheng 1984: 203–4. Like the legend of the Xingyang meeting of 1635, the story of the strategy session in Xiangyang (Xiangjing) began among early-Qing historians from Jiangnan and has been transmitted in many accounts down to today. Liu Yinan 1983: 218; Li Dengdi 1986: 110; Xie 1986: 281.

49. Zheng 1749: 7: 161–65. In an elegy to Sun, Wu Weiye invoked the parallel of the Han founding and he alluded to the Red Eyebrows who had helped to end Wang Mang's Xin state and thus cleared the way for the restoration of the Han under Liu Xiu. Ibid., 167; Xie 1986: 298–99.

50. Zheng 1749: 7: 168; Gu Cheng 1984: 205; Xie 1986: 299.

51. Liu Yinan 1983: 219; Xie 1986: 300–305.

52. Liu Yinan 1983: 232; Xie 1986: 300–302. For an extended critique of the idea that women enjoyed higher status in the Tang, however, see Tung 2000.

53. Gu Cheng 1984: 209–10; Hucker 1985: 184, 265; Xie 1986: 305.

54. Tan Qian 1653: 99: 6005; Liu Yinan 1983: 219–20; Gu Cheng 1984: 207; Wang Xingya 1984a: 199, 208.

55. Tan Qian 1653: 100: 6025; Zheng 1749: 7: 170; Gu Cheng 1984: 220; Wang Xingya 1984a: 96; Xie 1986: 303.

56. Zheng 1749: 7: 170.

57. Idem.

58. Gu Cheng 1984: 220; Wang Xingya 1984a: 97–100, 201; Liu Yinan 1983: 233, 257.

59. Zheng 1749: 7: 82; Li 1915: 33: 25; Wang Xingya 1984a: 156, 208–10.

60. For the eight-legged essay, see Nivison 1960; Elman 1994: 115; for the Shun examinations, see Tan Qian 1653: 100: 6026–27; Wang Xingya 1984a: 97–98, 161, 202, 211; Liu Yinan 1983: 232. Thus it is not quite precise to say simply that the rebels conducted examinations "on the Ming model." See Elman 2000: 219.

61. Liu Yinan 1983: 233; Li Dengdi 1986: 124–25.

62. Tan Qian 1653: 100: 6023, 6027, 6032; Zheng 1749: 7: 174; Liu Yinan 1983: 349; Li Dengdi 1986: 125–26; Xie 1986: 324.

63. Wakeman 1979: 47–49; Gu Cheng 1984: 234–35; Xie 1986: 320–27.

64. Tan Qian 1653: 100: 6035; Zheng 1749: 7: 173–74; Liu Yinan 1983: 236; Li Dengdi 1986: 123–24, 126, 128–30.

65. This offer, which might have been a step toward restoring the prime ministership abol-

ished by the Ming founder, was ironic insofar as some adversaries of Li Zicheng tried to cast him as another authoritarian and short-lived claimant to the throne like Qinshi huangdi, who had also issued from Shaanxi (Qin).

66. Tan Qian 1653: 100: 6034–36; Zheng 1749: 172–73; Gu Cheng 1984: 222–23; Li Dengdi 1986: 128, 130.

67. Tan Qian 1653: 100: 5994, 6013; a fuller copy of Zeng's report appears in Wan early Qing: 61–62.

68. Tan Qian 1653: 100: 6018, 6027, 6033, 6036, 6039, 6040.

69. Tan Qian 1653: 100: 6033, 6034, 6039; Zheng 1749: 7: 175, 176.

70. Tan Qian 1653: 100: 6029, 6036, 6038, 6041, 6042–43; Gu Cheng 1984: 242.

71. Liu 1958: 6: 47; Liu Yinan 1983: 237; Gu Cheng 1984: 267n10; Xie 1986: 339.

72. Li Dengdi 1986: 132.

73. Wakeman 1979: 41–76; 1985: ch. 4.

74. Tan Qian 1653: 100: 6026; Zheng 1749: 7: 179; Li 1915: 1: 17a–20a; Liu Yinan 1983: 237; Gu Cheng 1984: 244, 245, 269n33.

75. Liu Yinan 1983: 232, 243–44; Gu Cheng 1984: 252, 268; Wakeman 1985: 237, 267; Li Dengdi 1986: 132, 135–36; Xie 1986: 312.

76. Zhang Tingyu 1739: 266: 6859–60; Zheng 1749: 7: 175. In fact, it appears that only one concubine accompanied Liu in Beijing and committed suicide with him there; his wife remained at home in Qi. Luan 1986: 127–31.

77. Yang Shicong 1644: 36; Tan Qian 1653: 100: 6079; Liu Lishun 1658: yiji; Gu Cheng 1984: 247; Xie 1986: 344; Liu and Liu 1986: 2: 4a. Jin refused the Shun post of defense commissioner and retreated into the hills of Yuzhou (Junping). Guan and Zhang 1695: 26: 40; 35: 39b–40b.

78. Zhao early Qing: 11; Tan Qian 1653: 100: 6954; Zheng 1749: 7: 175–76.

79. Qian early Qing: 59, 76; Tan Qian 1653: 100: 6055; Zheng 1749: 7: 175.

80. Yang Shicong 1644: 17b–18a, 31b–32a; Qian early Qing: 70, 72; Tan Qian 1653: 100: 6055–60, 6074, 6078; Wang Xingya 1984a: 236. Fang Yizhi later denied that he took office under the rebels. Peng 1670s: 10: 1b; Xu Zi 1861: 213; Li Wenzhi 1948: 213; Peterson 1979: 158n36.

81. Yang Shicong 1644: 10b, 17b; Qian early Qing: 82; Tan Qian 1653: 100: 6056, 6060; Feng and Chou 1790: 6 shang, renwu, xia, kegong: 2a; Wang Zhonghan 1987: 79: 6599–6600.

82. For Liu, see Qian early Qing: 82; Shen and Huang 1898: 4: 8b; Liu Yinan 1983: 355; Wang Xingya 1984a: 308; Wang Zhonghan 1987: 79: 6595–97. For Zhao, see Qian early Qing: 78; Ji Liuqi 1671: 22: 609; Guan and Zhang 1695: 23: 34a; Zhang and Shi 1914: 4: 9b–10a. For Wang, see Zheng 1749: 7: 176. For Shi, see Qian early Qing: 70; Wakeman 1985: 280, 381–82.

83. Tan Qian 1653: 100: 6056; Ji Liuqi 1671: 22: 43a; Zhang Tingyu 1739: 275: 7044. Oddly, Qian early Qing, usually quite reliable on such matters, does not include He among the rebel officials.

84. Tan Qian 1653: 100: 6056; Zheng 1749: 7: 179; Liu Yinan 1983: 241; Li Dengdi 1986: 137; He and Wang 1992: 483–84.

85. Tan Qian 1653: 100: 6057–60; Qian early Qing: 73; Zhang Tingyu 1739: 275: 7044; Xu Zi 1861: 146; Luan 1986: 131–37.

86. Tan Qian 1653: 100: 6027, 6060; Qian early Qing: 83; Song 1705: 5: 14b; Liu and Ye 1705: 8: 262–63; Li 1915: 1: 1; Wang Zhonghan 1987: 78: 6484.

87. Zhao 1645?: 17; Tan Qian 1653: 100: 6076.

88. Gu Cheng 1984: 248.

89. The Taicang treasury was apparently empty. Parsons 1970: 127; Wakeman 1979: 44; 1985: 13–14. But the ruler's personal funds may have been far from exhausted. Gu Cheng 1984: 236–37. Even a Ming loyalist remarked that at the time "no one was willing to respond with the amount he could afford." Struve 1993: 11.

90. Liu Yinan 1983: 241–42; Gu Cheng 1984: 248, 252–53; Wakeman 1985: 289; Xie 1986: 348.

91. Zheng 1749: 7: 176, 179.

92. Liu Yinan 1983: 244; Gu Cheng 1984: 253–54, 259; Wakeman 1985: 290; Xie 1986: 348, 359.

93. Liu Yinan 1983: 240, 243; Gu Cheng 1984: 249, 251, 254–57; Struve 1984: 6; Xie 1986: 356; Li Dengdi 1986: 138, 141; see also Brook 1998: 224–44.

94. Ji Liuqi 1671: 22: 607; Liu Yinan 1983: 239, 242; Gu Cheng 1984: 251–52.

95. Tan Qian 1653: 100: 6032; Zheng 1749: 7: 170–71. Man Tian Xing was a popular name among rebel leaders. Liu Yinan 1983: 383, 385.

96. Zheng 1749: 7: 179.

97. Liu Yinan 1983: 242; Gu Cheng 1984: 249–51.

98. Liu Yinan 1983: 244–46; Gu Cheng 1984; 257–65; Li Dengdi 1986: 142–45; Xie 1986: 361–63. For this reason, the saga of Li Zicheng's failure to win over Wu Sangui was subject to elaboration and romanticization at the hands of Ming loyalist historians such as Wu Weiye. See Hsi 1975; Wakeman 1985: 292.

99. For a preview, see Des Forges in process.

Conclusion

1. Wang 1997: 284.

2. Cohen 1984; Marks 1985; Philip Huang 1991.

3. Link 1993; Hevia 1995; Spence 1999: xxi. For other works taking the Chinese quest for centrality seriously, see Bernstein 1982; Mancall 1984; Hu 2000.

4. Bernstein and Munro 1997; Nathan and Ross 1997; Chen Jian 1994, 1995; Ci 1994; Tang 1996; Song, Zhang, and Qiao 1996; Peng, Yang, and Xu 1996; Song, Zhang, Qian, Tang, and Gu 1996. For East Asia as a center, see Cohen 2000.

5. Foucault 1972: 10; Said 1978, 1993: 14, 56; for central subjects, see Hull 1975; for quite different critiques of "false universalism," see Paz 1985: 101; Miyoshi 1991: 2, 42, 56, 72, 107; Huntington 1996: 20, 310–11; for feminism, see Scott 1986; Wolf 1992; Mann 2000.

6. Rey Chow 1991: 26, 29; Duara 1995: 6; Miyoshi 1991: 5, 92, 243; Chatterjee 1993: xi.

7. Tu 1991: 12; Tu, Hejtmanek, and Wachman 1992: 47–48; Yü 1991a, 1991b, 1994.

8. Zheng 1999; Dirlik and Zhang 2000: chs. 2–4; Des Forges and Xu 2001.

9. Tu 1985: 99, 114, 133; Hansen 2000. For confusion of centrality with nationalism, racism, centralization, and superiority, see Blum and Jensen 2002: xiv, 3–9, 12, 18, 23, 167–70, 174, 177, 181.

10. Arnheim 1988; Miyoshi 1991: 15, 17, 35, 92, 188, 215, 238; Rey Chow 1991: 27–29, 32, 35, 61, 76, 82–83, 86; Jameson 1991 passim; Said 1993: xi, xxv, 79; Chatterjee 1993: 8; Duara 1995: 8, 27, 33, 78, 232, 234–35; Raphals 1998: chs. 6, 7; Dirlik and Zhang 2000: introduction; Blum and Jensen 2002: xix, 10, 15, 17, 18, 43, 247, 272, 299, 305, 313, 324.

11. Wheatley 1971: 431; Shils 1975: 3–4; Tambiah 1976: 102–31; Levi-Strauss 1979: 20; Geertz 1980: 11–18, 1983: 122–23, 146; Gesick 1983b: 93; Errington 1983; Buber 1992: 98; Winichakul 1994: 22; Huntington 1996: 264.

12. Bourdieu 1990: 55.

13. Fernández-Armesto 1995: 19; Eco 1998: 19.

14. In thinking about the nature and necessity of theory in general as well as about the requirements and limitations of any particular theory, I was originally inspired by the observations of Carr 1964: 13, 32; Moore 1967: 520–21; Horton 1970: 132; Bourdieu 1968: 695; and Thomas Kuhn 1970: 25. More recently I have benefited from reading White 1973, 1978; Feyerabend 1978; Trompf 1979; McNeill 1982a, 1986; Lynn Hunt 1989; and Goldstone 1991.

15. Zhongguo tongshi jilun bianji xiaozu 1972: 6–8; for similar schemes by Li Siquang and Lei Haizong, see Meskill 1965: ch. 4; for a different tripartite division of Chinese history, see Tu Wei-ming 1987. The major change I am making in Liang's scheme is to end the second

epoch in the seventeenth century rather than in the nineteenth century. While there are numerous studies of Liang's thought that mention this scheme in passing, none examines it as a potential basis for periodizing Chinese history today. For a recent example, see Duara 1995.

16. Burton Watson 1968: 1: 118–19. Again, while several scholars have analyzed Sima Qian's historiography in recent years, none has taken this particular scheme seriously as a basis for understanding the cultural and political dynamics of early Chinese history. See, for example, Durrant 1995.

17. Hok-lam Chan 1984.

18. I outlined this theory in 1979 and I have weighed its utility in subsequent publications. See Dai Fushi 1987; Des Forges 1988, 1993, 1997.

19. Ray Huang 1981: 38; Mote 1999: 724–34.

20. See Des Forges in process.

21. For doubts about excessive symmetry, see Tu 1985: 39–40; William McNeill personal communication of 22 March 1987; for similarities and differences among myths, models, and paradigms, see Thomas Kuhn 1970; Barbour 1976; Hayden White 1973, 1978; McNeill 1982a, 1986; Eco 1998.

22. Gould 1987.

23. Vaughn 1985.

24. James D. Watson 1968.

25. Despite popular usage that associates the spiral with a loss of control, many observers have recognized the utility of the spiral as a way of incorporating continuity as well as linear and cyclical change into a single model. For spirals in nature, see Stevens 1974: 81–91; Chaisson 1987: 142; in the growth of knowledge, Mao 1965: 3: 117–22; Mote 1971: 4; Wakeman 1973: 231; Capra 1975: 5–6; Wang Fusan 1980; in literature, myth, and art, Yeats 1937; Levi-Strauss 1963: 229; Fong 1980: 8, 31, 212, 231, 243; Huber 1983: 182–84; Girardot 1983: 246; Robertson 1983: 182–84; Schipper and Wang 1986: 193; Chün-fang Yü 2001: 159; in academic and narrative strategies, Ching 1976: xiv, 181; Girardot 1983: 16; McNeill 1986: 25; Soja 1989: 136–44; Sakai 1997: xiv; in Chinese history and historiography, Fan 1954–65: 1: 33; Chang Hao 1971: 172; Hong 1981: 109; Wu Hong 1989: 162, 219; Mayfair Yang 1994: 110; Ko 1994: 110; in frontier studies, Lattimore 1962: 252–53; in Indian religion and history, Basham 1975: 86; Thapar 1996: 8, 39; in Western historiography, Hayden White 1973: 120–31, 173, 344, 418, 421; Braudel 1973: 244; François 1974; Leo Ou-fan Lee 1977: 179; Hayden White 1978: 60; Trompf 1979: chs. 1–2; Breisach 1983: 208, 241, 330; Schlesinger 1986: 24, 44; in world system history, Frank and Gills 1993: 90, 122, 189; in petty capitalist accumulation, Gates 1996: 118.

26. Ray Huang 1988: 19, 23, 47, 56, 102, 264–66; see also Huang 1999. Huang did not, however, take the spiral as an organizing principle of either history or historiography.

27. Paz 1985: 89, 112; Spence 1999: 426; Bartlett 1990: 137–38, 270, 339nn2, 4; Philip Kuhn 1990: 85; Link 1993: 203–4; Duara 1995: 32–33, 187; Fernández-Armesto 1995: 44, 147; Zito 1996: 80; Hevia 1996: 472; Howland 1996: 197, 200–201, 224–26; Crossley 1999: 133; Brook 1997: 400n25; Brook 1998: xvii; Millward 1998: 25; Mote 1999: xv.

28. Sahlins 1987: vii; Goldstone 1991: 54–60; Habermas 1994: 66; Spence 1999: xxiv; Michael H. Hunt 1996: 26; Bernstein and Munro 1997: 188; Nathan and Ross 1997: 21; Andrew and Rapp 2000: 5. For an effort in this direction, see Des Forges and Xu 2001.

29. For Chinese interest in tracing the centers of world history, see Zhongguo shixuehui 1985: 127; for past difficulties encountered in integrating Chinese into world history, see Littrup 1987, 1989; for a recent interpretation of China's place in world history, see Adshead 1988; for efforts to describe the evolution of a single central civilization or world system, see Frank and Gills 1993; for the value of the concept of world regions as opposed to continents, see Lewis and Wigen 1997.

30. Mumford 1970: 389.

31. Bourdieu 1968: 695. For recent world histories that acknowledge some of China's

claims to centrality but largely on the basis of criteria emphasized by the West since 1500 CE, see Fernández-Armesto 1995; Wong 1997; Frank 1998; Pomeranz 2000.

32. Cited in Carr 1964: 13; see also McNeill 1986, who claims that forgetting many details is especially essential to doing world history.

33. For Africa, I have drawn on Leakey and Lewin 1977; for Mesopotamia, Mumford 1966; for China, Gernet 1985 and Ebrey 1996; for Europe, McNeill 1963, 1982, 1986; for the United States, Chomsky 1991 and Johnson 2000.

34. For contrasting American views of the present world order, see Fukuyama 1992; and Chomsky 1994. For recent Chinese views, see Kim 1989; Dittmer and Kim 1993; and Zheng Yongnian 1999. For contemporary Sino-American and Asian-American relations, see Vogel 1997; Cumings 1999. For Chinese occidentalism and American paranoia, see Chen Xiaomei 1996; and Gertz 2000. For the views of some contemporary Chinese youth, see Des Forges 1999; and Des Forges and Xu 2001. For environmental issues, see Marks 1998; Tucker and Berthrong 1998; Elvin and Liu 1998. For a French view, see Boublil 1997.

BIBLIOGRAPHY

Abrams, M. H. 1979. *The Norton Anthology of English Literature: Volume 2*. Fourth edition. New York: W. W. Norton and Co.

Adshead, S. A. M. 1988. *China in World History*. London: Macmillan.

Allan, Sarah. 1972–73. "The Identities of Taigong Wang in Zhou and Han Literature." *Monumenta Serica* 30: 57–99.

Andrew, Anita M., and John A. Rapp. 2000. *Autocracy and China's Rebel Founding Emperors: Comparing Chairman Mao and Ming Taizu*. Boulder, Colorado: Rowman and Littlefield.

Arnheim, Rudolf 1988. *The Power of the Center: A Study of Composition in the Visual Arts: The New Version*. Berkeley: University of California Press.

Atwell, William S. 1975. "From Education to Politics: The Fushe." In William Theodore de Bary et al. *The Unfolding of Neo-Confucianism* (New York: Columbia University Press): 333–68.

———. 1977. "Notes on Silver, Foreign Trade, and the Late Ming Economy." *Ch'ing-shih wen-t'i* 8.3: 1–33.

———. 1982. "International Bullion Flows and the Chinese Economy circa 1530–1650." *Past and Present* 95: 68–90.

———. 1986. "Some Observations on the 'Seventeenth-Century Crisis' in China and Japan." *Journal of Asian Studies* 45.2: 223–44.

———. 1990. "A Seventeenth-Century 'General Crisis' in East Asia?" *Modern Asian Studies* 24.4: 661–82.

Bai, Yu 白愚. 1644. *Bianwei shijin lu* 汴圍濕襟錄 [Emotional record of the siege and flooding of Bian]. In Liu Yian 1982.

Barbour, Ian G. 1976. *Myths, Models, and Paradigms*. New York: Harper and Row.

Bartlett, Beatrice. 1990. *Monarchs and Ministers: The Grand Council in Mid-Ch'ing China, 1723–1820*. Berkeley: University of California Press.

Basham, A. L. 1975. *A Cultural History of India*. Oxford: Clarendon Press.

Benedict, Carol. 1996. "Framing Plague in China's Past." In Hershatter, Honig, Lipman, and Stross 1996: 27–41.

Bernhardt, Kathryn. 1996. "A Ming-Qing Transition in Chinese Women's History? The Perspective from Law." In Hershatter, Honig, Lipman, and Stross 1996: 42–58.

———. 1999. *Women and Property in China, 960–1949*. Stanford: Stanford University Press.

Bernstein, Richard. 1982. *From the Center of the Earth: The Search for the Truth about China.* Boston: Little, Brown.

———, and Ross H. Munro. 1997. *The Coming Conflict with China.* New York: Knopf.

Bingham, Woodbridge. 1941. "The Rise of Li in a Ballad Prophecy." *Journal of the American Oriental Society* 61: 272–80.

Birch, Cyril. 1958. *Stories from a Ming Collection: Translations of Chinese Short Stories Published in the Seventeenth Century.* New York: Grove Press.

Blum, Susan D., and Lionel M. Jensen, eds. 2002. *China off Center: Mapping the Margins of the Middle Kingdom.* Honolulu: University of Hawaii Press.

Boublil, Alain. 1997. *Le Siècle des Chinois.* Monaco: Editions du Rocher.

Bourdieu, Pierre. 1968. "Structuralism and the Theory of Sociological Knowledge." *Social Research* 35.4: 681–706.

———. 1990. *The Logic of Practice.* Stanford: Stanford University Press. Translation of *Le sens pratique* (Paris: Éditions de Minuit, 1980).

Braudel, Fernand. 1973. *Capitalism and Material Life, 1400–1800.* London: George Weidenfeld and Nicolson Ltd. Translation of *Civilisation Matérielle et Capitalisme* (Paris: Librairie Armand Colin, 1967).

Bray, Francesca. 1997. *Technology and Gender: Fabrics of Power in Late Imperial China.* Berkeley: University of California Press.

Breisach, Ernst. 1983. *Historiography: Ancient, Medieval, and Modern.* Chicago: University of Chicago Press.

Brook, Timothy. 1981. "The Merchant Network in Sixteenth Century China: A Discussion and Translation of Zhang Han's 'On Merchants.'" *Journal of the Economic and Social History of the Orient* 24.2: 165–214.

———. 1985. "The Spatial Structure of Ming Local Administration." *Late Imperial China* 6.1: 1–55.

———. 1990. "Family Continuity and Cultural Hegemony: The Gentry of Ningbo, 1368–1911." In Esherick and Rankin 1990: 27–50.

———. 1993. *Praying for Power: Buddhism and the Formation of Gentry Society in Late Ming China.* Cambridge: Harvard University Press.

———. 1996. "Edifying Knowledge: The Building of School Libraries in Ming China." *Late Imperial China* 17.1: 93–119.

———. 1997. "At the Margin of Public Authority: The Ming State and Buddhism." In Huters et al., eds. 1997: 161–81.

———. 1998. *The Confusions of Pleasure.* Berkeley: University of California Press.

———. Forthcoming. "Famished Bodies for the Emperor's Gaze: Yang Dongming's Representation of the 1594 Famine in Henan." Paper prepared for the workshop "Medicine in China: Techniques and Social History," Institut des Hautes Études Chinoises, Collège de France, 17–19 June 2000.

Buber, Martin. 1992. *On Intersubjectivity and Cultural Creativity.* Edited and with an introduction by S. N. Eisenstadt. Chicago: Chicago University Press.

Capra, Fritjof. 1975. *The Tao of Physics.* New York: Bantam Books.

Carr, Edward H. 1964. *What is History?* New York: Knopf.

Cass, Victoria. 1999. *Dangerous Women: Warriors, Grannies, and Geishas of the Ming.* New York: Rowman and Littlefield.

Chaisson, Eric. 1987. *The Life Era: Cosmic Selection and Conscious Evolution.* New York: The Atlantic Monthly Press.

Chan, Albert. 1982. *The Glory and Fall of the Ming Dynasty.* Norman: University of Oklahoma.

Chan, Hok-lam. 1973. "Chang Chung and his Prophecy: The Transmission of the Legend of an Early Ming Taoist." *Oriens Extremus* 15.1: 65–102.

———. 1984. *Legitimation in Imperial China: Discussions under the Jurchen-Chin Dynasty (1115–1234).* Seattle: University of Washington Press.

Chan, Wing-tsit. 1970. "The Ch'eng-Chu School of the Early Ming." In de Bary 1970: 29–52.

———. 1982. "Chu Hsi and Yüan Neo-Confucianism." In Hok-lam Chan and William Theodore de Bary. *Yüan Thought: Chinese Thought and Religion Under the Mongols* (New York: Columbia University Press): 197–232.

Chang, Hao. 1971. *Liang Ch'i-ch'ao and the Intellectual Transition in China, 1890–1907.* Cambridge: Harvard University Press.

Chang, Kwang-chih. 1968. *The Archaeology of Ancient China.* New Haven: Yale University Press.

———. 1983. "Sandai Archaeology and the Formation of States in Ancient China: Processual Aspects of the Origins of Chinese Civilization." In David N. Keightley, ed. *The Origins of Chinese Civilization* (Berkeley: University of California Press), 495–523.

Chang, Kang-I Sun, and Haun Saussy. 1999. *Women Writers of Traditional China.* Stanford: Stanford University Press.

Chang Moulai 常茂徠. 1852. *Ru Meng Lu* 如薨錄 [Record as from a Dream]. 1 juan. Kaifeng: Henan shengli tushu guan; 1921 reprint.

Chang, Shelley Hsueh-lun. 1990. *History and Legend: Ideas and Images in the Ming Historical Novels.* Ann Arbor: University of Michigan Press.

Chao, Kang. 1986. *Man and Land in Chinese History: An Economic Analysis.* Stanford: Stanford University Press.

Chao Yang chubanshe bianjibu 朝陽出版社編輯部 1979. *Zhongguo lishi renwu cidian* 中國歷史人物辭典 [Dictionary of Chinese historical personalities]. Hong Kong: Chao Yang chubanshe.

Chatterjee, Partha. 1993. *The Nation and Its Fragments: Colonial and Postcolonial Histories.* Princeton: Princeton University Press.

Chen, Jian. 1994. *China's Road to the Korean War: The Making of the Sino-American Confrontation.* New York: Columbia University Press.

———. 1995. "China's Involvement in the Vietnam War, 1964–69." *China Quarterly* 142 (June): 356–87.

Chen, Jo-shui. 1992. *Liu Tsung-yuan and Intellectual Change in T'ang China, 773–819.* Cambridge: Cambridge University Press.

Chen Lianying. 陳連營 1987. "Mingmo nongmin zhanzheng qijian Henan dizhu tuzhai shitan" 明末農民戰爭期間河南地主土寨試探 [A preliminary investigation of landlord forts in Henan during the farmers' wars of the late Ming]. Unpublished paper presented at Dierci quanguo Mingmo nongmin zhanzheng shi xueshu taolunhui 第二次全國明末農民戰爭史學術討論會 [Second national scholarly convention on the farmers' wars at the end of the Ming].

Chen, Xiaomei. 1996. *Occidentalism: A Theory of Counter-Discourse on Post-Mao China.* Oxford: Rowman and Littlefield.

Chen Xilu 陳錫輅 and Zha Changqi 查昌岐, comps. 1754. *Guide fuzhi* 歸德府志 [Gazetteer of Guide Prefecture]. 36 juan.

Chen Yuan 陳垣. 1923. "Kaifeng Yicileye jiao kao" 開封一賜樂業教考 [An examination of the Israelite religion of Kaifeng]. Shanghai: Shangwu yinshuguan, Dongfang wenku, 72.

Chi, Ch'ao-ting. 1936. *Key Economic Areas in Chinese History.* London: Allen & Unwin.

Ching, Julia. 1976. *To Acquire Wisdom, the Way of Wang Yang-ming.* New York: Columbia University Press.

Chomsky, Noam. 1994. *World Orders Old and New.* New York: Columbia University Press.

———. 1991. *Deterring Democracy.* London: Verso.

Chow, Kai-wing. 1994. *The Rise of Confucian Ritualism in Late Imperial China: Ethics, Classics, and Lineage Discourse.* Stanford: Stanford University Press.

Chow, Rey. 1991. *Woman and Chinese Modernity.* Minneapolis: University of Minnesota Press.

Ch'ü, T'ung-tsu. 1962. *Local Government in China under the Ch'ing.* Cambridge: Harvard University Press.

Ci, Jiwei. 1994. *Dialectic of the Chinese Revolution: From Utopianism to Hedonism.* Stanford: Stanford University Press.

Clunas, Craig. 1991. *Superfluous Things: Material Culture and Social Status in Early Modern China.* Cambridge: Polity Press.

———. 1996. *Fruitful Sites: Garden Culture in Ming Dynasty China.* Durham: Duke University Press.

Cohen, Paul. 1984. *Discovering History in China: American Historical Writing on the Recent Chinese Past.* New York: Columbia University Press.

———. 1997. *History in Three Keys: The Boxers as Event, Experience, and Myth.* New York: Columbia University Press.

Cohen, Warren. 2000. *East Asia at the Center: Four Thousand Years of Engagement with the World.* New York: Columbia University Press.

Cole, Alan. 1998. *Mothers and Sons in Chinese Buddhism.* Stanford: Stanford University Press.

Cong Hanxiang 從翰香. 1985. "Shisi shiji mo zhi shiliu shiji zhong Huabei pingyuan nongcun jingji fazhan de kaocha" 十四世紀末至十六世紀中華北平原農村經濟發展的考查 [An Investigation into the economic development of villages on the north China plain from the end of the fourteenth century to the middle of the sixteenth century]. A paper presented at the First International Conference on Ming History held at Huangshan, Anhui, 1–30.

Crawford, Robert. 1970. "Chang Chu-cheng's Confucian Legalism." In de Bary 1970: 367–414.

Crossley, Pamela Kyle. 1999. *A Translucent Mirror: History and Identity in Qing Imperial Ideology.* Berkeley: University of California Press.

Cumings, Bruce. 1999. *Parallax Visions: Making Sense of American-East Asian Relations at the End of the Century.* Durham: Duke University Press.

Dai Fushi (Roger Des Forges). 1987. "Zhongguo lishi leixing: yizhong luoxuan lilun" 中國歷史類型：一种螺旋理論 [The pattern of Chinese history: A spiral theory], Liu Dong 劉東 and Xie Weihe 謝維和, trans. *Zouxiang weilai* 走向未來 [Toward the future] 2.1 (Mar.): 72–81.

Dardess, John W. 1996. *A Ming Society: T'ai-ho County, Kiangsi, Fourteenth to Seventeenth Centuries.* Berkeley: University of California Press.

———. 2002. *Blood and History: The Donglin Faction and Its Repression, 1620–1624.* Honolulu: University of Hawaii Press.

de Bary, William Theodore, ed. 1970. *Self and Society in Ming Thought* (New York: Columbia University Press).

de Certeau, Michel. 1984. *The Practice of Everyday Life.* Steven Rendall, trans. Berkeley: University of California Press.

Dehergne, Joseph. 1957. "Les chrétientés de Chine de la période Ming (1581–1650)." *Monumenta Serica* 16: 1–136 plus map.

Dennerline, Jerry. 1981. *The Chia-ting Loyalists: Confucian Leadership and Social Change in Seventeenth-Century China.* New Haven: Yale University Press.

Des Forges, Roger. 1979. "Rebellion and Revolution in Chinese History: Definitions, Theories, and Hypotheses." Unpublished paper presented to the Workshop on Rebellion and Revolution in North China, Late Ming to the Present, sponsored by American Council of Learned Societies, held at the Fairbank Center, Harvard University.

———. 1982. "The Story of Li Yen: Its Growth and Function From the Early Qing to the Present." *Harvard Journal of Asiatic Studies* 42.2: 535–87.

———. 1984. "The Legend of Li Yen: Its Origins and Implications for the Study of the Ming-Ch'ing Transition in Seventeenth Century China." *Journal of the American Oriental Society* 104.3: 411–36.

———. 1988. "Zhongguo jindai shi shi cong shenma shihou kaishi de?" 中國近代史是從甚麻時侯開始的 [When does recent Chinese history begin?] *Jindai Zhongguo shi yanjiu tongxun* 近代中國史研究通訊 [Newsletter for Modern Chinese History] 6: 152–63.

———. 1993. "Democracy in Chinese History." In Roger Des Forges, Luo Ning, and Wu Yenbo, eds. *Chinese Democracy and the Crisis of 1989: Chinese and American Reflections* (Albany: State University of New York Press): 21–52.

————. 1997. "States, Societies, and Civil Societies in Chinese History." In Timothy Brook and Bernard Frolic, eds. *China and Civil Society* (Armonk, N. Y.: M. E. Sharpe, Inc.): 68–95.

————. 1999. "The People's Republic of China and the United States of America: Which is the Hegemon?" *The Literary Review of Canada*, 7.4: 9–13.

————. In process. "Toward Another Tang or Zhou? Views from the Central Plain During the Shunzhi Reign (1644–1661)." Chapter for conference volume edited by Lynn Struve, titled *In the Mean-time: Temporalities of the Ming-Qing Transition.*

————, and Luo Xu. 2001. "China as a Non-Hegemonic Superpower? The Uses of History Among the *China Can Say No* Writers and Their Critics." *Critical Asian Studies* 33.4: 483–507.

Dietrich, Craig. 1972. "Cotton Culture and Manufacture in Early Ch'ing China." In W. E. Willmott, ed. *Economic Organization in Chinese Society* (Stanford: Stanford University Press): 109–35.

Dirlik, Arif, and Xudong Zhang, eds. 2000. *Postmodernism and China.* Durham and London: Duke University Press.

Dittmer, Lowell, and Samuel S. Kim. 1993. *China's Quest for National Identity.* Ithaca: Cornell University Press.

Du, Baotian 杜寶田. Forthcoming. "'Jin Qixian' de laili" 金杞縣的來歷 [The origins of the expression "Golden Qi county"]. Qi County: Qixian difang shizhi zongbian shi.

Duara, Prasenjit. 1988. "Superscribing Symbols: The Myth of Guandi, Chinese God of War." *Journal of Asian Studies* 47.4: 778–95.

————. 1995. *Rescuing History from the Nation: Questioning Narratives of Modern China.* Chicago: University of Chicago Press.

Dunstan, Helen. 1975. "The Late Ming Epidemics: A Preliminary Survey." *Ch'ing-shih wen-t'i* 3: 1–59.

Durand, John D. 1960. "The Population Statistics of China, A.D. 2–1953." *Population Studies* 13: 209–58.

Durand, Pierre-Henri. 1992. *Lettrés et pouvoirs: Un procès littéraire dans la Chine impériale.* Paris: Éditions de l'École des Hautes Études en Sciences Sociales.

Durrant, Stephen W. 1995. *The Cloudy Mirror: Tension and Conflict in the Writings of Sima Qian.* Albany: State University of New York Press.

Ebrey, Patricia. 1993a. *Chinese Civilization: A Sourcebook.* New York: The Free Press.

————. 1993b. *The Inner Quarters: Marriage and the Lives of Chinese Women in the Sung Period.* Berkeley: University of California Press.

————. 1996. *Cambridge Illustrated History of China.* Cambridge: Cambridge University Press.

————. 1999. "Gender and Sinology: Shifting Western Interpretations of Footbinding, 1300–1890." *Late Imperial China* 20.2: 1–34.

Eco, Umberto. 1998. *Serendipities: Language and Lunacy.* William Weaver, trans. New York: Harcourt Brace and Co.

Edwards, E. D. 1938. *Chinese Prose Literature of the T'ang Period, A.D. 618–906.* 2 vols. London.

Elliott, Mark. 2001. *The Manchu Way: The Eight Banners and Ethnic Identity in Late Imperial China.* Stanford: Stanford University Press.

Elman, Benjamin A. 1994. "Changes in Confucian Civil Service Examinations from the Ming to the Ch'ing Dynasty." In Benjamin Elman and Alexander Woodside, eds. *Education and Society in Late Imperial China, 1600–1900* (Berkeley: University of California Press, 1994): 111–49.

————. 1997. "The Formation of 'Dao Learning' as Imperial Ideology During the Early Ming Dynasty." In Huters et al. 1997: 58–82.

————. 2000. *A Cultural History of Civil Examinations in Late Imperial China.* Berkeley: University of California Press.

Elvin, Mark. 1973. *The Pattern of the Chinese Past.* Stanford: Stanford University Press.

————. 1984. "Female Virtue and the State in China." *Past and Present* 104: 111–52.

————, and Liu Ts'ui-jung, eds. 1998. *Sediments of Time: Environment and Society in Chinese History*. Cambridge: Cambridge University Press.

Errington, Shelley. 1983. "The Place of Regalia in Luwu." In Gesick 1983: 194–241.

Esherick, Joseph and Mary Rankin 1990. *Chinese Local Elites and Patterns of Dominance*. Berkeley: University of California Press.

Fan Wenlan 範文瀾. 1954–65. *Zhongguo tongshi jianbian* 中國通史簡編 [A simplified edition of the comprehensive history of China]. 4 vols. Beijing: Renmin chubanshe.

Fang, Chaoying. 1965. "Notes on the Chinese Jews of Kaifeng." *Journal of the American Oriental Society* 85.2: 126–28.

Farmer, Edward L. 1976. *Early Ming Government: The Evolution of Dual Capitals*. Cambridge: Harvard University Press.

————, et al. 1988–89. "Symposium on Fifteenth-Century China." "Part One," *Ming Studies* 26 (fall 1988): 1–60; "Part Two," *Ming Studies* 27 (spring 1989): 1–66.

Feng Menglong 馮夢龍. 1644. *Jiashen jishi* 甲申紀事 [Record of 1644]. 14 juan. Reprinted in Zheng Zhenduo 鄭振鐸, ed. *Xuanlan tang congshu, chuji* 玄覽堂叢書, 初集 [Collectaneum of the Xuanlan Hall first series] (Shanghai, 1941) ce 107–18.

Feng Minchang 馮敏昌 and Chou Ruhu 仇汝瑚. 1790. *Meng xianzhi* 孟縣志 [Gazetteer of Meng County]. 10 juan.

Fernández-Armesto, Felipe. 1995. *Millennium: A History of the Last Thousand Years*. New York: Scribner.

Feyerabend, Paul. 1978. *Against Method: Outline of an Anarchist Theory of Knowledge*. London: Verso.

Fong, Wen. 1980. *The Great Bronze Age of China: An Exhibition from the People's Republic*. New York: Knopf.

Foucault, Michel. 1972. *The Archaeology of Knowledge and The Discourse on Language*. New York: Harper and Row.

François, Martha Ellis. 1974. "Revolts in Late Medieval and Early Modern Europe: a Spiral Model." *Journal of Interdisciplinary History* 5: 19–43.

Frank, André Gunder. 1998. *ReOrient: Global Economy in the Asian Age*. Berkeley: University of California Press.

————, and Barry K. Gills, eds. 1993. *The World System: Five Hundred Years or Five Thousand?* London and New York: Routledge.

Franke, Wolfgang. 1976. "Historical Precedent or Accidental Repetition of Events? K'ou Chun in 1004 and Yü Ch'ien in 1449." *Sung Studies in Memoriam Etienne Balazs*, ed. Francoise Aubin, ser. I, pt. 3 (Paris): 199–206.

Fu Yiling 傅衣凌. 1958. "Ming-Qing shidai Henan Wuan shangren kaolue" 明清時代河南武安商人考略 [Research on the merchants of Wuan, Henan in the Ming-Qing period]. *Xueshu luntan* 學術論壇 [Scholarly Discussions] 2: 36–38.

————. 1984. "Mingdai jingjishi shang de Shandong yu Henan" 明代經濟史上的山東與河南 [Shandong and Henan in the Economic History of the Ming]. *Shehui kexue zhanxian* 社會科學戰線 [Social Science Battlefront] 3: 119–27.

Fukuyama, Francis. 1992. *The End of History and the Last Man*. New York: Avon Books.

Furth, Charlotte. 1986. "Blood, Body, and Gender: Medical Images of the Female Condition in China." *Chinese Science* 7: 53–65.

————. 1987. "Concepts of Pregnancy, Childbirth, and Infancy in Ch'ing Dynasty China." *Journal of Asian Studies* 46.1: 7–35.

————. 1994. "Rethinking van Gulik: Sexuality and Reproduction in Traditional Chinese Medicine." In Christina K. Gilmartin, Gail Hershatter, Lisa Rofel, and Tyrene White, eds. *Engendering China: Women, Culture, and the State* (Cambridge: Harvard University Press):125–46.

————. 1998. *A Flourishing Yin: Gender in China's Medical History, 960–1665*. Berkeley: University of California Press.

Gates, Hill. 1996. *China's Motor: A Thousand Years of Petty Capitalism.* Ithaca: Cornell University Press.

Ge Rongjin 葛榮晉. 1990. *Wang Tingxiang he Mingdai qixue* 王廷相和明代氣學 [Wang Tingxiang and the Study of Qi in the Ming Period]. Beijing: Zhonghua shuju.

Geelan, P. J. M., and D. C. Twitchett 1974. *The Times Atlas of China.* Edinburgh: John Bartholomew and Son Ltd.

Geertz, Clifford. 1980. *Negara: The Theatre State in Nineteenth-Century Bali.* Princeton: Princeton University Press.

——. 1983. *Local Knowledge: Further Essays in Interpretive Anthropology.* New York: Basic Books.

Gernet, Jacques. 1985. *A History of Chinese Civilization.* Cambridge: Cambridge University Press.

Gertz, Bill. 2000. *The China Threat: How the People's Republic Targets America.* Washington, D. C.: Regnery Publishing, Inc.

Gesick, Lorraine. 1983a. *Centers, Symbols, and Hierarchies: Essays on the Classical States of Southeast Asia.* New Haven: Yale University Southeast Asia Studies.

——. 1983b. "The Rise and Fall of King Taksin: A Drama of Buddhist Kingship." In Gesick 1983: 87–105.

Girardot, N. J. 1983. *Myth and Meaning in Early Taoism.* Berkeley: University of California Press.

Goldstone, Jack A. 1991. *Revolution and Rebellion in the Early Modern World.* Berkeley: University of California Press.

Goodrich, L. Carrington, and Chaoying Fang, eds. 1976. *Dictionary of Ming Biography, 1368–1644.* 2 vols. New York: Columbia University Press.

Gould, Stephen Jay. 1987. *Time's Arrow, Time's Cycle: Myth and Metaphor in the Discovery of Geological Time.* Cambridge: Harvard University Press.

Graff, David A. 1995. "Meritorious Cannibal: Chang Hsun's Defense of Sui-yang (757) and the Exaltation of Loyalty in an Age of Rebellion." In Association for Asian Studies, Inc. *Abstracts of the 1995 Annual Meeting* (April 6–9, 1995) (n.p.: no publisher): 33.

Graham, A. C. 1989. *Disputers of the Tao: Philosophical Argument in Ancient China.* La Salle, Illinois: Open Court.

Greer, Charles. 1979. *Water Management in the Yellow River Basin of China.* Austin: University of Texas.

Grimm, Tilemann. 1969. "Ming Education Intendants." In Hucker 1969: 129–48.

Grove, Linda, and Christian Daniels, eds. *State and Society in China: Japanese Perspectives on Ming-Qing Social and Economic History.* Tokyo: University of Tokyo Press, 1984.

Gu Cheng 顧誠. 1978. "Li Yan zhiyi" 李巖質疑 [Doubts about Li Yan]. *Lishi yanjiu* 歷史研究 [Historical Research] 5: 62–75.

——. 1982. "Mingdai de zongshi" 明代的宗氏 [The Royal Lineage of the Ming Period]. *MingQing shi guoji taolun hui lunwen ji* 明清史國際討論會論文集 [Collected Papers of the International Ming-Qing History Conference]: 89–111.

——. 1984. *Mingmo nongmin zhanzheng shi* 明末農民戰爭史 [A history of the farmers' wars at the end of the Ming]. Beijing: Zhongguo shehui kexue chubanshe.

——. 1986. "Ming qianqi gengdi shu xintan" 明前期耕地數新探 [A new appraisal of the amount of land under cultivation in the early Ming], *Zhongguo shehui kexue* 中國社會科學 [Chinese Social Sciences], 4: 193–213.

——. 1990. "New Observations on Farmland Statistics in the Earlier Period of the Ming Dynasty." *Social Sciences in China* (spring): 197–224.

Gugong bowuyuan MingQing dang'anbu 故宮博物院明清檔案部 [The Ming-Qing Archives of the Palace Museum] 1979. *Qingdai dang'an shiliao congbian* 清代檔案史料叢編 [Collected historical materials from the Qing archives] 4. Beijing: Zhonghua shuju.

Gu Yanwu 顧炎武. Early Qing. *Mingji shilu* 明季實錄 [A true record of the late Ming]. 1 juan. In *Mingji baishi xubian.* Shanghai: Shangwu yinshuguan, 1912; reprinted, Taipei: Guangwen shuju, 1968.

———. 1811. *Tianxia junguo libing shu* 天下君國利病書 [A Study of the Chief Characteristics of all Provinces under Heaven]. Preface 1662. Sibu congkan ed. 120 juan.

Gu Yingtai 谷應泰. 1658. *Mingshi jishi benmo* 明史紀事本末 [A topical history of the Ming]. 80 juan. Guangya shuju, 1887. Also consulted in the 1977 edition printed in Beijing by Zhonghua shuju, 4 vols.

Guan Jiezhong 管竭忠 and Zhang Mu 張沐. 1695. *Kaifeng fuxhi* 開封府志 [Gazetteer of Kaifeng Prefecture]. 40 juan.

Guan Weilan 官蔚藍. 1956. *Zhonghua minguo xingzheng quhua ji tudi, renkou tongji biao* 中華民國行政區劃及土地人口統計表 [Tables of Population and Land in the Administrative Regions of the Republic of China]. Taibei: Beikai chuban she.

Guo Quanjie 郭荃階 and Guo Qingyun 郭慶雲. 1915. *Xinxiang Guoshi zupu* 新鄉郭氏族譜 [Genealogy of the Guo lineage of Xinxiang]. 12 juan.

Guo Songyi 郭松義. 1983. "Mingmo sanxiang jiapai" 明末三餉加派 [The Three Tax Surcharges for Supplies at the End of the Ming]. In Zhongguo shehui kexue yuan lishi yanjiu suo Mingshi yanjiu shibian 中國社會科學院歷史研究所明史研究室編 [Ming History Section, History Institute, Chinese Academy of Social Sciences, ed.], *Mingshi yanjiu luncong* 明史研究論叢 [Collected articles on research in Ming history] (Suzhou: Jiangsu renmin chubanshe) 2: 220–45.

Guoli zhongyang yanjiuyuan lishi yuyan yanjiu suo 國立中央研究院歷史語言研究所. 1930–36. *MingQing shiliao* 明清史料 [Ming-Qing Historical Materials]. Jia 甲, yi 乙, bing 丙 series, 30 vols. Shanghai: Commercial Press.

Habermas, Jürgen. 1994. *The Past as Future*. (Interviewed by Michael Haller). Lincoln: University of Nebraska.

Haeger, John Winthrop, ed. 1975. *Crisis and Prosperity in Sung China*. Tucson: University of Arizona Press.

Han Dacheng 韓大成. 1991. *Mingdai chengshi yanjiu* 明代城市研究 [A Study of Ming Cities]. Beijing: Zhongguo renmin daxue chubanshe.

Han Shixun 韓世勛 and Li Defen 黎德芬. 1920. *Xiayi xianzhi* 夏邑縣志 [Gazetteer of Xiayi county]. 9 juan, head juan.

Handlin, Joanna F. 1975. "Lü K'un's New Audience: The Influence of Women's Literacy on Sixteenth-Century Thought." In Margery Wolf and Roxane Witke, eds., *Women in Chinese Society* (Stanford: Stanford University Press): 13–38.

———. 1983. *Action in Late Ming Thought: The Reorientation of Lü K'un and other Scholar-Officials*. Berkeley: University of California Press.

Hansen, Valerie. 2000. *The Open Empire: A History of China to 1600*. New York: W. W. Norton.

Hartwell, Robert. 1966. "Markets, Technology, and the Structure of Enterprise in the Eleventh Century Chinese Iron and Steel Industry." *Journal of Economic History* 26: 29–58.

———. 1967. "A Cycle of Economic Change: Coal and Iron in Northeast China, 750–1350." *Journal of the Economic and Social History of the Orient* 10: 102–59.

———. 1982. "Demographic, Political, and Social Transformations of China, 750–1550." *Harvard Journal of Asiatic Studies* 42.2: 365–442.

He Fazhou 何法周 and Wang Shulin 王樹林. 1992. *Hou Fangyu ji jiaojian* 侯方域集校箋 [Annotated edition of the writings of Hou Fangyu]. Zhengzhou: Zhongzhou guji chubanshe.

He Xinzhen 何心貞. 1987. *Heshi zupu* 何氏族譜 [Genealogy of the He lineage]. Originally 2 volumes (ben), plus charts.

Heijdra, Martinus Johanne. 1994. "The Socio-Economic Development of Ming Rural China (1368–1644): An Interpretation." Princeton University doctoral dissertation.

Henan huace bianji weiyuan hui "河南" 畫冊編輯委員會 [Henan Map Editorial Committee]. 1984. *Henan* 河南 [Henan]. N.p.: Henan huace bianji weiyuan hui.

Henan Provincial Museum. 1984. Exhibition of Surtaxes in Henan in the Late Ming, Part of the Permanent Exhibit on the History of Henan Province. Zhengzhou.

Henderson, John. 1984. *The Development and Decline of Chinese Cosmology.* New York: Columbia University Press.

Herrmann, Albert. 1964. *Historical and Commercial Atlas of China.* Taipei: Literature House, Ltd.; reprint.

Hershatter, Gail, Emily Honig, Jonathan N. Lipman, and Randall Stross, eds. 1996. *Remapping China: Fissures in Historical Terrain.* Stanford: Stanford University Press.

Hevia, James. 1995. *Cherishing Men From Afar: Qing Guest Ritual and the Maccartney Embassy of 1793.* Durham: Duke University Press.

———. 1996. "Imperial Guest Ritual." In Lopez 1996: 471–87.

Ho, Ping-ti. 1959. *Studies on the Population of China, 1368–1953.* Cambridge: Harvard University Press.

———. 1962. *The Ladder of Success in Imperial China, Aspects of Social Mobility, 1368–1911.* New York: John Wiley and Sons, Inc.

———. 何炳棣 1966. *Zhongguo huiguan shi lun* 中國會館史論 [A Historical Survey of Landmanschaften in China]. Taibei: Xuesheng shuju.

———. 1975. *The Cradle of the East.* Chicago: University of Chicago Press.

Hobsbawm, Eric J. 1959. *Primitive Rebels: Studies in the Archaic Forms of Social Movement in the Nineteenth and Twentieth Centuries.* New York: Norton Press.

———. 1969. *Bandits.* New York: Delacorte Press.

Holzman, Donald. 1976. *Poetry and Politics: The Life and Works of Juan Chi, A.D. 210–263.* Cambridge: Cambridge University Press.

Hong Huanchun 洪煥椿. 1981. "Ming-Qing feng jian zhuanzhi zhengquan dui zibenzhuyi mengya de zu'ai" 明清封建專制政權對資本主義萌芽的阻礙 [Ming and Qing feudal authoritarianism as an obstacle to the sprouts of capitalism]. *Lishi yanjiu* 歷史研究 [Historical Research], Translation in *Social Sciences in China* 3: 193–219.

Horton, Robin. 1970. "African Traditional Thought and Western Science." In Bryan R Wilson, ed., *Rationality* (New York: Harper and Row): 131–71.

Hoshi, Ayao. 1969. *The Ming Tribute Grain System.* Mark Elvin, trans. Ann Arbor: The University of Michigan Center for Chinese Studies.

Hou Fangyue 侯方岳. 1908. *Shangqiu Houshi jiacheng* 商邱侯氏家乘 [Genealogy of the Hou Lineage of Shangqiu]. 5 juan.

Hou Shimei 侯世梅. 1987. *Houshi zupu* 侯氏族譜 [Genealogy of the Hou Lineage]. Not divided by juan.

Howland, D. R. 1996. *Borders of Chinese Civilization: Geography and History at Empire's End.* Durham and London: Duke University Press.

Hsi, Angela. 1975. "Wu San-kuei in 1644: A Reappraisal." *Journal of Asian Studies* 24.2: 443–53.

Hsieh, Bao Hua. 1999. "From Charwoman to Empress Dowager: Serving-Women in the Ming Palace." *Ming Studies* 42 (fall): 26–80.

Hsiung, Ping-chen. 1994. "Constructed Emotions: The Bond Between Mothers and Sons in Late Imperial China." *Late Imperial China* 15.1: 87–117.

Hu, Ying. 2000. *Tales of Translation: Composing the New Woman in China, 1898–1918.* Stanford: Stanford University Press.

Huang, Philip. 1991. "The Paradigmatic Crisis in Chinese Studies: Paradoxes in Social and Economic History." *Modern China* 17.3: 299–341.

Huang, Ray. 1970. "Ni Yüan-lu: 'Realism' in a Neo-Confucian Scholar-Statesman." In de Bary 1970: 415–49.

———. 1974. *Taxation and Governmental Finance in Sixteenth-Century Ming China.* Cambridge: Cambridge University Press.

———. 1981. *1587: A Year of No Significance: The Ming Dynasty in Decline.* New Haven: Yale University Press.

———. 1988. *China: A Macro History.* Armonk, N. Y.: M. E. Sharpe, Inc.

———. 1999. *Broadening the Horizons of Chinese History: Discourses, Syntheses, and Comparisons.* Armonk, N. Y.: M. E. Sharpe, Inc.

Huang, Tsung-hsi. 1987. *The Records of Ming Scholars.* A selected translation edited by Julia Ching and Chaoying Fang. Honolulu: University of Hawaii Press.

Huang Yizhu 黃以柱. 1981. "Henan chengzhen lishi dili chutan" 河南城鎮歷史地理初探 [A Preliminary Inquiry into the Historical Geography of the Towns of Henan]. *Shixue yuekan* 史學月刊 [Historical Monthly] 1: 1–13.

Huanghe shuili weiyuanhui Huanghe zhi zongbian jishi 黃河水利委員會黃河志總編輯室. 1986. *Henan Huanghe zhi* 河南黃河志 [Gazetteer of the Yellow River in Henan]. Zhengzhou: Huanghe shuili weiyuanhui.

Huber, Louisa G. Fitzgerald. 1983. "The Relationship of the Painted Pottery and Lung-shan Cultures." In David Keightley, ed. *The Origins of Chinese Civilization* (Berkeley: University of California Press): 177–216.

Hucker, Charles O. 1957. "The Tung-lin Movement of the Late Ming Period." In John K. Fairbank, ed. *Chinese Thought and Institutions.* (Chicago: University of Chicago Press): 132–62.

———. 1958. "Governmental Organization of the Ming Dynasty." *Harvard Journal of Asiatic Studies* 21: 1–66; reprinted in John L. Bishop, ed. *Studies of Governmental Institutions in Chinese History* (Cambridge: Harvard University Press, 1968): 57–151.

———. 1966. *The Censorial System of Ming China.* Stanford: Stanford University Press.

———. 1969. *Chinese Government in Ming Times.* New York: Columbia University Press.

———. 1985. *A Dictionary of Official Titles in Imperial China.* Stanford: Stanford University Press.

Hull, David L. 1975. "Central Subjects and Historical Narratives." *History and Theory* 14: 253–74.

Hummel, Arthur. 1943–44. *Eminent Chinese of the Ch'ing Period, 1644–1912.* Washington: United States Government Printing Office.

Hunt, Lynn, ed. 1989. *The New Cultural History.* Berkeley: University of California Press.

Hunt, Michael H. 1996. *The Genesis of Chinese Communist Foreign Policy.* New York: Columbia University Press.

Huntington, Samuel. 1996. *The Clash of Civilizations and the Remaking of World Order.* New York: Simon and Schuster.

Huters, Theodore, R. Bin Wong, and Pauline Yu, eds. 1997. *Culture and State in Chinese History: Conventions, Accommodations, and Critiques.* Stanford: Stanford University Press.

Jameson, Frederic. 1991. *Postmodernism, Or, The Cultural Logic of Late Capitalism.* Durham: Duke University Press.

Jensen, Lionel. 1997. *Manufacturing Confucianism: Chinese Traditions and Universal Civilization.* Durham: Duke University Press.

Ji Huangzhong 紀黃中 and Wang Ji 王繢. 1764. *Yifeng xianzhi* 儀封縣志 [Gazetteer of Yifeng County]. 12 juan, head and tail juan.

Ji Liuqi 計六奇. 1671. *Mingji beilue* 明季北略 [Outline record of the late Ming in the north]. 24 juan. In *Zhongkuo fanglue congshu* 中國方略叢書 [Collectanea on Chinese strategy]. 3 vols. (Taibei: Chengwen chuban she; reprint 1969). Another edition was published by Zhonghua shujü in Beijing in 1984; 2 vols.

Jiang Lian 江練 and Gao Song 高松. 1828. *Taikang xianzhi* 太康縣志 [Gazetteer of Taikang County]. 11 juan.

Jin Guantao 金觀濤 and Liu Qingfeng 劉青峰. 1984. *Xingsheng yu weiji: lun Zhongguo fengjian shehui de chaowending jiegou* 興盛與危机論中國封建社會的超穩定結構 [Prosperity and crisis: the hyper-stable structure of Chinese feudal society]. Changsha: Hunan renmin chubanshe.

Johnson, Chalmers. 2000. *Blowback: The Costs and Consequences of American Empire.* New York: Henry Holt and Co.

Kaifeng shi difang shizhi biancuan weiyuanhui 開封市地方史志編纂委員會. 1988. *Kaifeng jianzhi* 開封簡志 [A Simplified Record of Kaifeng]. Kaifeng: Henan renmin chuban she.

Keightley, David N. 1983. *The Origins of Chinese Civilization.* Berkeley: University of California Press.

———. 1999. "The Shang: China's First Historical Dynasty." In Loewe and Shaughnessy 1999: 232–91.

Kim, Samuel S. 1989. *China and the World: New Directions in Chinese Foreign Relations.* Boulder, Colorado: Westview Press.

Ko, Dorothy. 1994. *Teachers of the Inner Chambers: Women and Culture in Seventeenth-Century China.* Stanford: Stanford University Press.

Kong Shangren 孔尚任. 1684. *Kongzi shi jiapu* 孔子氏家譜 [Family Genealogy of Kongzi (Confucius)]. 24 juan.

Kracke, E. A., Jr. 1975. "Sung K'ai-feng: Pragmatic Metropolis and Formalistic Capital." In John Winthrop Haeger, ed. *Crisis and Prosperity in Sung China* (Tucson: University of Arizona Press): 49–78.

Kuhn, Philip. 1990. *Soulstealers: The Chinese Sorcery Scare of 1768.* Cambridge: Harvard University Press.

Kuhn, Thomas. 1970. *The Structure of Scientific Revolutions.* Second edition. Chicago: University of Chicago Press.

Kutcher, Norman. 1999. *Mourning in Late Imperial China: Filial Piety and the State.* Cambridge: Cambridge University Press.

Lai Jiadu 賴家度. 1958. "Ming zhongye Jing-Xiang shanqu Liu Tong, Li Yuan suo lingdao de liumin da qiyi" 明中葉荊襄山區劉通 李原所領導的流民大起義 [The great uprisings of migrants led by Liu Tong and Li Yuan in the mountainous region of Jing and Xiang in the mid-Ming]. In Li Guangbi 李光璧, Qian Junhua 錢君嘩, Lai Xinxia 來新夏, eds. *Zhongguo nongmin qiyi lunji* 中國農民起義論集 [Collected articles on Chinese farmer's uprisings] (Beijing: Sanlian): 252–66.

Lattimore, Owen. 1962. *Studies in Frontier History.* London: Oxford University Press.

Lau, D. C., trans. and introd. 1979. *Confucius: The Analects (Lun-yü).* London: Penguin.

Lavely, William, and R. Bin Wong. 1998. "Revising the Malthusian Narrative: The Comparative Study of Population Dynamics in Late Imperial China." *The Journal of Asian Studies* 57.3 (August): 714–48.

Leakey, Richard E., and Roger Lewin. 1977. *Origins: What New Discoveries Reveal About the Emergence of Our Species and its Possible Future.* New York: E. P. Dutton.

Lee, James. 1997. "Historical Demography of Late Imperial China: Recent Research Results and Implications." In Frederic Wakeman and Wang Xi, eds. *China's Quest for Modernization* (Berkeley: University of California Press): 65–86.

———, and Wang Feng. 1999. *One Quarter of Humanity: Malthusian Mythology and Chinese Realities, 1700–2000.* Cambridge: Harvard University Press.

Lee, Leo Ou-fan. 1977. "Genesis of a Writer: Notes on Lu Xun's Educational Experience, 1881–1909." In Merle Goldman, ed. *Modern Chinese Literature in the May Fourth Era* (Cambridge: Harvard University Press): 161–88.

Lee, Lily. 1994. *The Virtue of Yin: Essays in Chinese Women.* Honolulu: University of Hawaii Press.

Leslie, Donald. 1965. "The Chinese-Hebrew Memorial Book of the Jewish Community of K'aifeng." Part I. *Abr-Nahrain* IV (1963–64): 19–49.

———. 1966. "The Chinese-Hebrew Memorial Book of the Jewish Community of K'aifeng." Part II. *Abr-Nahrain* V (1964–65): 1–28.

———. 1967a. "The Chinese-Hebrew Memorial Book of the Jewish Community of K'aifeng." Part III. *Abr-Nahrain* VI (1965–66): 1–52.

———. 1967b. "The K'aifeng Jew Chao Ying-ch'eng and His Family." *Toung pao* 53: 147–79.

———. 1971. "Chao" In Cecil Roth, ed. *Encyclopaedia Judaica* 5. New York: MacMillan.

———. 1972. *The Survival of the Chinese Jews: The Jewish Community of Kaifeng.* Leiden: E. J. Brill.

Leung, Angela Ki Che. 1993. "To Chasten Society: The Development of Widow Homes in the Qing." *Late Imperial China* 14.2: 1–32.

Levi-Strauss, Claude. 1963. *Structural Anthropology*. New York: Basic Books.

———. 1979. *Myth and Meaning*. New York: Schocken Books.

Lewis, M., and K. Wigen. 1997. *The Myth of Continents: A Critique of Metageography*. Berkeley: University of California.

Li, Dazhao. 1995. "Spring (poem)." Claudia Pozzana, trans. and annot. *positions: east asia cultures critique* 3.2 (fall): 306–28; this translation is preceded by Claudia Possana's essay "Spring, Temporality, and History in Li Dazhao," in Ibid.: 283–305.

Li Dengdi 李登弟. 1986. *Li Zicheng nianpu* 李自成年譜 [A chronological biography of Li Zicheng]. Xi'an: San Qin chuban she.

Li Guangtao 李光濤. 1965. *Mingji liukou shimo* 明季流寇始末 [The roving bandits at the end of the Ming from their beginning to their end]. Taibei: Zhongyang yanjiu yuan lishi yuyan yanjiu so.

Li Guangtian 李光殿. 1644. *Shou Bian rizhi* 守汴日志 [Diary of the Defense of Bian]. Wang Xingya 王興亞, ed. Zhengzhou: Zhongzhou guji chubanshe, 1987.

Li Jilie 李繼烈 and He Yiguang 何彝光. 1693. *Qixian zhi* 杞縣志 [Gazetteer of Qi county]. 3–20 juan.

Li Jixian 李濟賢. 1982. "Xu Hongru qiyi xintan" 徐鴻儒起義新探 [A new investigation of the Xu Hongru uprising]. In Zhongguo shehui kexueyuan lishi yanjiusuo Mingshi yanjiu shi bian 中國社會科學院歷史研究所明史研究室編 [Ming History Section of the Institute of History of the Chinese Academy of Social Sciences], ed. *Mingshi yanjiu luncong* 明史研究論叢 [Collected articles on Ming history] (Nanjing: Jiangsu renmin chubanshe): 265–89.

Li Minxiu 李敏修. 1915. *Zhongzhou xianzhe zhuan* 中州先哲傳 [Biographies of Former Scholars of the Central Province]. 35 juan. Kaifeng: Jingchuan Library.

Li Mowry, Hua-yuan. 1983. *Chinese Love Stories from "Ch'ing-shih."* Hamden: The Shoe String Press.

Li Qi 李淇 and Xi Qingyun 席慶雲. 1895. *Yucheng xianzhi* 虞城縣志 [Gazetteer of Yucheng County]. 10 juan.

Li Shiyu 李世瑜 [Thomas Shiyu Li] and Susan Naquin. 1988. "The Baoming Temple: Religion and the Throne in Ming and Qing China." *Harvard Journal of Asiatic Studies* 48.1: 131–88.

Li Shoukong 李守孔. 1968. "Mingdai Bailian jiao kaolue" 明代白蓮教考略 [A study of the White Lotus religion in the Ming period]. Originally published in *Taida wenshi zhexue bao* 臺大文史哲學報 [Journal of literature, history, and philosophy of Taiwan University] 4 (1952). In Bao Zunpeng, ed. *Mingdai zongjiao* 明代宗教 [Religion in the Ming Period] (Taibei: Taiwan xuesheng shuju, 1968): 17–47.

Li Weisan 李畏三 and Li Lesan 李樂三. 1749. *Lishi zongpu* 李氏宗譜 [Genealogy of the Li lineage]. Not divided by juan.

Li Wenzhi 李文治. 1948. *Wan Ming minbian* 晚明民變 [Popular Uprisings of the Late Ming]. Shanghai: Zhonghua shuju.

Li Xiaosheng 李肖胜. 1984. "Qixian 'Lishi zupu' shang faxian Li Yan qiren" 杞縣 "李氏族譜" 上發現李岩其人 [The discovery of Li Yan in the "Li clan genealogy" of Qi county]. *Wenshi hanshou* 文史函授 [Literary and Historical Newsletter] 2: 39–42.

———. 1986. "Cong Qixian 'Li shi zupu' kan Li Yan qi ren" 從杞縣 "李氏族譜" 看李岩其 [The question of Li Yan as seen from the *Genealogical Records of the Li Clan* of Qi county]. *Henan Daxue Xuebao* 河南大學學報 [Journal of Henan University] 1: 53–5.

———. 1987a. "Cong xiangtu ziliao kan Li Yan qiren" 從鄉土資料看李岩其人 [Looking at the person Li Yan from the standpoint of local materials]. Paper delivered at Dierci quanguo Mingmo nongmin zhanzhengshi xueshu taolunhui 第二次全國明末農民戰爭史學術討論會 [Second national conference on the study of farmers' wars at the end of the Ming], 1–16, fubiao 1–8.

———. 1987b. "The Question of Li Yan as Seen from *The Genealogical Records of the Li Clan of Qi County*," *Ming Studies* 24 (fall): 39–57.

———, Wei Qianzhi, and Roger Des Forges. 1994. "Li Tingsheng's *A Record of Hardship*:

A Recently Discovered Manuscript Reflecting Literati Life in North Henan at the End of the Ming, 1642–44." *Late Imperial China* 15.2: 85–122.

Li, Yu-ning. 1992. *Chinese Women through Chinese Eyes.* Armonk, N.Y.: M. E. Sharpe, Inc.

Li Yunlai 李允萊. n.d. *Lishi zupu* 李氏族譜 [Genealogy of the Li Clan]. Collected by Li Xiaosheng 李肖胜 and Wang Yisha 王一沙 in Qi county, 1988.

Lian Chengxian 崇成显. 1998. *Mingdai huangce yanjiu* 明代黄冊研究 [Research on the yellow registers of the Ming dynasty]. Beijing: Zhongguo shehui kexue chubanshe.

Liang Fangzhong 梁方仲. 1980. *Zhongguo lidai hukou, tiandi, tianfu tongji* 中國歷代戶口, 田地, 田賦統計 [Statistics on registered population, cultivated land, and land taxes in China through the ages]. Shanghai: Remin chuban she.

Lin Furui 林富瑞 and Chen Daiguang 陳代光. 1983. *Henan renkou dili* 河南人口地理 [The Demography and Geography of Henan]. N.p.: Henan renmin chubanshe.

Ling Jialiang 凌甲糧, Lü Yingnan 呂應南, and Zhang Jiamou 張嘉謀. 1938. *Xihua xian xuzhi* 西華縣續志 [Gazetteer of Xihua county, continued]. 14 juan, head juan.

Link, Perry. 1993. "China's 'Core' Problem." *Daedalus* 122.2 (spring): 189–206.

Little, Daniel. 1989. *Understanding Peasant China: Case Studies in the Philosophy of Social Science.* New Haven: Yale University Press.

Littrup, Leif. 1981. *Subbureaucratic Government in China in Ming Times: A Study of Shandong Province in the Sixteenth Century.* Oslo: The Institute for Comparative Research in Human Culture.

———. 1987. "China and World History." In Yu-ming Shaw, ed. *Reform and Revolution in Twentieth-Century China* (Taipei: Institute of International Relations, no. 29): 16–29.

———. 1989. "World History with Chinese Characteristics." *Culture and History* 5: 39–64.

Liu Chongri 劉重日. 1962. "'Juntian' kouhao zhiyi de zhiyi" '均田田'口號質疑的質疑 [Doubts about the Doubts about the Equal Field Slogan]. *Lishi yanjiu* 歷史研究 [Historical Research] 2: 97–112.

Liu Dechang 劉德昌 and Ye Yun 葉澐, eds. 1705. *Shangqiu xianzhi* 商邱縣志 [Gazetteer of Shangqiu county]. 20 juan. Zhengzhou: Zhongzhou guji chubanshe; 1989 reprint.

Liu Huaizhong 劉懷忠 and Liu Huaizhang 劉懷章. 1986. *Liushi zupu* 劉氏族譜 [Genealogy of the Liu lineage]. 2 juan. Qi county.

Liu I-ch'ing and Richard B. Mather, author and translator. 1976. *Shih-shuo Hsin-yü: A New Account of Tales of the World.* Minneapolis: University of Minnesota Press.

Liu, James T. C. 1957. "An Early Sung Reformer: Fan Chung-yen." In John K. Fairbank, ed. *Chinese Thought and Institutions* (Chicago: Chicago University Press): 105–31.

———. 1959. *Reform in Sung China: Wang An-shih (1021–1086) and his New Policies.* Cambridge: Harvard University Press.

Liu Lishun 劉理順. 1658. *Liu Wenlie gong quanji* 劉文烈公全集 [Complete works of Master Liu Wenlie]. 12 juan.

Liu, Tinggui 劉廷桂. 1929. *Shangqiu Liushi jiacheng* 商邱劉氏家乘 [Genealogy of the Liu clan of Shangqiu]. 9 juan.

Liu Yian 劉益安. 1982a. *Bianwei shijin lu jiaozhu* 汴圍濕襟錄校注 [An annotated Emotional Record of the Siege and Flooding of Bian]. Henan: Zhongzhou shuhua she.

———. 1982b. *Da Liang shoucheng ji jianzheng* 大梁守成記箋証 [A critically annotated Record of the Defense of Da Liang]. Zhengzhou: Zhongzhou shuhua she.

Liu Yinan 柳義南. 1983. *Li Zicheng jinian fukao* 李自成紀年附考 [An Annotated Chronicle of Li Zicheng]. Beijing: Zhonghua shuju chuban.

Liu Yongzhi 劉永之 and Geng Ruiling 耿瑞玲, eds. 1990. *Henan difangzhi tiyao* 河南地方志提要 [A Guide to Henan Gazetteers]. 2 vols. Kaifeng: Henan daxue chuban she.

Liu Zhan 劉展. 1992. *Zhongguo gudai junzhi shi* 中國古代軍制史 [A history of China's ancient military system]. N.p.: Junshi kexue chubanshe.

Lo, Winston W. 1975. "A Seventeenth Century Chinese Metropolis K'ai-feng." *Chinese Culture* 16.1: 23–46.

Loewe, Michael, and Edward L. Shaughnessy. 1999. *The Cambridge History of Ancient China: From the Origins of Civilization to 221 B.C.* Cambridge: Cambridge University Press.

Lopez, Donald S., Jr., ed. 1996. *Religions of China in Practice*. Princeton: Princeton University Press.

Lu, Tina. 2001. *Persons, Roles, and Minds: Identity in* Peony Pavilion *and* Peach Blossom Fan. Stanford: Stanford University Press.

Lü Sizhou 呂思周. 1986. *Ningling Lüshi jiapu* 寧陵呂氏家譜 [Genealogy of the Lü Lineage of Ningling]. 6 juan.

Luan Xing 欒星. 1982. "Niu Jinxing shiji kaobian," shang, xia. 牛金星事跡考辨,上,下 [An inquiry into the activities of Niu Jinxing]. *Wenxian* 文獻 [Documentation] 14: 144–65; 15: 153–65.

———. 1983. "Li Yan chuanshuo de yubo" 李岩的俺说的餘波 [More waves from the story of Li Yan]. *Zhongzhou jingu* 中州金古 [Past and present in the central province] 4: 10–14.

———. 1986. *Li Yan zhi mi: Jiashen shi shang* 李巖之迷: 甲申史商 [The puzzle of Li Yan: a discussion of 1644]. Xuchang, Henan: Zhongzhou guji chubanshe.

Luo, Guanzhong, and Moss Roberts. 1991. *Three Kingdoms: A Historical Novel*. Berkeley: University of California Press.

Ma Chaoqun 馬超群. 1780. *Qixian Mashi zupu* 杞縣馬氏族譜 [Genealogy of the Ma Lineage of Qi county]. Not divided by juan.

Ma Junyong 馬俊勇 and Gao Yusheng 高玉生. 1987. *Suizhou zhi* 睢州志 [Gazetteer of Suizhou]. 12 juan.

Ma, Laurence J. C. 1971. *Commercial Development and Urban Change in Sung China*. Ann Arbor: University of Michigan Department of Geography.

Ma, Tai-loi. 1975. "The Local Education Officials of Ming China, 1368–1644." *Oriens Extremus* 22.1: 11–27.

Mammitzsch, Ulrich Hans-Richard. 1968. "Wei Chung-hsien (1568–1628): A Reappraisal of the Eunuch and the Factional Strife at the Late Ming Court." University of Hawaii doctoral dissertation.

Mancall, Mark. 1984. *China at the Center: 300 Years of Foreign Policy*. London: The Free Press.

Mann, Susan. 1997. *Precious Records: Women in China's Long Eighteenth Century*. Stanford: Stanford University Press.

———. 2000. "Presidential Address: Myths of Asian Womanhood." *Journal of Asian Studies* 59.4: 835–62.

———, and Yu-yin Cheng, eds. 2001. *Under Confucian Eyes: Writings on Gender in Chinese History*. Berkeley: University of California Press.

Mao Tse-tung. 1965. *Selected Works of Mao Tse-tung*. 4 vols. Beijing: Foreign Languages Press.

Marks, Robert. 1985. "The State of the China Field, or the China Field and the State." *Modern China* 11: 461–509.

———. 1998. *Tigers, Rice, Silk & Silt: Environment and Economy in Late Imperial South China*. Cambridge: Cambridge University Press.

McNeill, William. 1963. *The Rise of the West: A History of the Human Community*. Chicago: The University of Chicago Press.

———. 1982a. "The Care and Repair of Public Myth." *Foreign Affairs* 61.1: 1–13.

———. 1982b. *The Pursuit of Power: Technology, Armed Force, and Society since A.D. 1000*. Chicago: University of Chicago Press.

———. 1986. *Mythistory and Other Essays*. Chicago: University of Chicago Press.

Mei, June Yuet Mei. 1975. "Kaifeng, A Chinese City in the Ming Dynasty." Harvard University doctoral dissertation, Department of History and East Asian Languages.

Meng Xiangju 孟祥居. 1990. *Mengzi shijia liuyu Qixian zhipu* 孟子世家流寓杞縣支譜 [Genealogy of the branch of the descendants of Mencius resident in Qi county]. 5 ce.

Meskill, John. 1965. *The Pattern of Chinese History: Cycles, Development, or Stagnation?* Lexington, Mass.: D. C. Heath and Co.

————. 1982. *Academies in Ming China: A Historical Essay.* Tucson: The University of Arizona Press.

————. 1994. *Gentlemanly Interests and Wealth on the Yangtze Delta.* Ann Arbor: Association for Asian Studies, Inc., Monograph and Occasional Paper Series, Number 49.

Miao Zaixian 苗在賢 and Miao Youzhi 苗尤志. 1987. *Miaoshi jiapu* 苗氏家譜 [Genealogy of the Miao family]. 3 juan in 4 ce.

Millward, James A. 1998. *Beyond the Pass: Economy, Ethnicity, and Empire in Qing Central Asia, 1759–1864.* Stanford: Stanford University Press.

Miyakawa, Hisayuki. 1954–55. "An Outline of the Naito Hypothesis and Its Effects on Japanese Studies of China." *Far Eastern Quarterly* 2: 533–52.

Miyoshi, Masao. 1991. *Off Center: Power and Culture Relations Between Japan and the United States.* Cambridge: Harvard University Press.

Mon, Sherry T. 1999. *Presence and Presentation: Women in the Chinese Literati Tradition.* New York: St. Martin's Press.

Moore, Barrington, Jr. 1967. *Social Origins of Dictatorship and Democracy: Lord and Peasant in the Making of the Modern World.* Boston: Beacon Press.

Mote, Frederick W. 1971. *Intellectual Foundations of China.* New York: Knopf.

————. 1999. *Imperial China, 900–1800.* Cambridge: Harvard University Press.

————, and Denis Twitchett, eds. 1988. *The Cambridge History of China, Vol. 7: The Ming Dynasty, 1368–1644, Part I.* Cambridge: Cambridge University Press.

————. 1998. *The Cambridge History of China, Vol. 8: The Ming Dynasty, 1368–1644, Part II.* Cambridge: Cambridge University Press.

Mumford, Lewis. 1966. *The Myth of the Machine: Technics and Human Development.* New York: Harcourt Brace Jovanovich.

————. 1970. *The Myth of the Machine: The Pentagon of Power.* New York: Harcourt Brace Jovanovich.

Munro, Donald. 1988. *Images of Human Nature: A Sung Portrait.* Princeton: Princeton University Press.

Naquin, Susan. 1981. *Shantung Rebellion: The Wang Lun Uprising of 1774.* New Haven: Yale University Press.

————. 1986. "Two Descent Groups in North China: The Wangs of Yung-p'ing Prefecture, 1500–1800." In Patricia Buckley Ebrey and James L. Watson, eds. *Kinship Organization in Late Imperial China, 1000–1940* (Berkeley: University of California Press): 210–44.

————. 2000. *Peking: Temples and City Life, 1400–1900.* Berkeley: University of California.

Nathan, Andrew J., and Robert S. Ross. 1997. *The Great Wall and the Empty Fortress: China's Search for Security.* New York: Norton and Company.

Needham, Joseph, Wang Ling, Lu Gwei-djen, and Ho Ping-yü. 1970. *Clerks and Craftsmen in China and the West.* Cambridge: Cambridge University Press.

Needham, Joseph, Wang Ling, and Lu Gwei-djen. 1971. *Science and Civilization in China, Vol. 4: Physics and Physical Technology, Part III: Civil Engineering and Nautics.* Cambridge: Cambridge University Press.

Needham, Joseph. 1981. *Science in Traditional China: A Comparative Perspective.* Cambridge: Harvard University Press.

Nimick, Thomas. 1999. "The Placement of Local Magistrates in Ming China." *Late Imperial China* 20.2: 35–60.

Nishijima, Sadao. 1984. "The Formation of the Early Chinese Cotton Industry." In Linda Grove and Christian Daniels, ed. and trans. *State and Society in China: Japanese Perspectives on Ming-Qing Social and Economic History* (Tokyo: University of Tokyo Press): 17–77.

Nivison, David S. 1960. "Protest against Conventions and Conventions of Protest." In Arthur F. Wright, ed. *The Confucian Persuasion.* Stanford: Stanford University.

Noguchi, Tetsuro 野口鐵郎. 1963. "Tenkei Jokō-ju no ran" 天啓徐鴻儒の亂 [The rebellion of Xu Hongru in the Tianqi period]. *Tōhō shūkyo* 東方宗教 [Eastern Religions], Part 1, 20: 35–50; Part 2, 21: 41–50.

Ono, Kazuko 小野和子著. 1996. *Minki tōshako—Tōlintō to Fukusha* 明季黨社考—東林黨と復社[A study of parties and societies at the end of the Ming—the Donglin party and the Fushe]. Kyoto: Dohosha.

Overmyer, Daniel. 1976. *Folk Buddhist Religion: Dissenting Sects in Late Traditional China*. Cambridge: Harvard University Press.

Pan Yuxin 潘遇莘 and Wang Lianfu 王斂福, eds. 1752. *Yingzhou fuzhi* 潁州府志 [Gazetteer of Yingzhou Prefecture]. 10 juan.

Parsons, James. 1969. "The Ming Dynasty Bureaucracy: Aspects of Background Forces." In Hucker 1969: 175–231.

———. 1970. *Peasant Rebellions of the Late Ming Dynasty*. Tucson: University of Arizona Press.

Paz, Octavio. 1985. *One Earth, Four or Five Worlds: Reflections on Contemporary History*. New York: Harcourt, Brace and Jovanovich.

Peng Qian 彭謙, Yang Mingjie 楊明杰, and Xu Deren 徐德任. 1996. *Zhongguo weishenma shuo bu—lengzhan hou Meiguo dui Hua zhengce de wuqu* 中國為甚麻説不?冷戰後美國對華政策的誤區 [Why does China say No?—Mistakes in American Policy Toward China after the Cold War]. Beijing: Xinshijie chubanshe.

Peng Sunyi 彭孫貽. Early Qing. *Liukou zhi* 流寇志 [Record of the roving robbers]. 14 juan. Hangzhou: Zhejiang renmin chuban she; 1983 reprint.

———. 1670s. *Pingkou zhi* 平寇志 [Record of the pacification of the robbers]. 12 juan. National Library of Peking; reprint, 1931.

Perdue, Peter. 1987. *Exhausting the Earth: State and Peasant in Hunan, 1500–1850*. Cambridge: Council on East Asian Studies and Harvard University.

Perkins, Dwight H. 1969. *Agricultural Development in China, 1368–1968*. Chicago: Aldine Publishing Company.

Perry, Elizabeth J. 1980. *Rebels and Revolutionaries in North China, 1845–1945*. Stanford: Stanford University Press.

Peterson, Willard J. 1979. *Bitter Gourd: Fang I-chih and the Impetus for Intellectual Change*. New Haven: Yale University Press.

Plaks, Andrew. 1987. *The Four Masterworks of the Ming Novel: Ssu ta ch'i-shu*. Princeton: Princeton University Press.

———. 1991. "The Confucianization of the Chinese Jews: Interpretations of the Kaifeng Stelae Inscriptions." *Sino-Judaica: Occasional Papers of the Sino-Judaic Institute* 1: 47–62. A revised version of this article is included in Jonathan Goldstein (1998), *The Jews of China, Volume I: Historical and Comparative Perspectives* (Armonk, N.Y.: M. E. Sharpe, Inc.): 36–49.

Pollak, Michael. 1980. *Mandarins, Jews, and Missionaries: The Jewish Experience in the Chinese Empire*. Philadelphia: The Jewish Publication Society of America.

Pomeranz, Kenneth. 1997. "Power, Gender, and Pluralism in the Cult of the Goddess of Taishan." In Huters, Wong, and Yu 1997: 182–204.

———. 2000. *The Great Divergence: China, Europe, and the Making of the Modern World Economy*. Princeton: Princeton University Press.

Qian Mu 錢穆. 1964. *Lunyu xinjie* 論語新解 [A renewed interpretation of the Analects]. 2 vols. Hong Kong: Xinhua yinshua gufen gongsi.

Qian Xing 錢性. Early Qing. *Jiashen chuanxin lu* 甲申傳信錄 [A credible record of 1644]. In *Zhongguo neiluan waihuo lishi congshu* 中國內亂外禍歷史叢書 [Collectaneum of histories of internal chaos and external disasters in China], ce 12. Shanghai: Shenzhou guoguangshe, 1940.

Qiao Fangyi 喬方沂. 1920. *Ningling Qiaoshi zupu* 寧陵喬氏族譜 [Clan genealogy of the Qiaos of Ningling]. 4 juan. Reprint of the 1980s.

Qin Fuling 秦富嶺 and Qin Xingren 秦興仁. 1952. *Qixian Qinshi jiapu* 杞縣秦氏家譜 [Genealogy of the Qin family of Qi county]. Not divided by juan. Manuscript copy made in Kaifeng, 1990.

Qin Xinlin 秦新林. 1995. "Shilun *Jiao Chuang Xiaoshuo* yu Li Yan xing xiang de guanxi" 試論 "剿闖小説"與李巖形象的關系 [A discussion of *The Novel about the suppression of Dashing* and the Li Yan phenomenon] *Beijing shifan daxue xuebao, Shehui kexue ban* 北京師範大學學報,社會科學版 [Journal of Beijing Normal University, Social Science Edition] Cengkan: 70–75.

———. 1996a. "Qixian Lishizupu zhi Li Yan yi bian" 杞縣 "李氏族譜" 之李巖疑辨 [Doubts about the Li Yan in the Li family genealogy of Qi county], *Henan daxue xuebao, Shehui kexueban* 河南大學學報,科學版 [Journal of Henan University, Social Science Edition] 36.2: 77–82.

———. 1996b. "Li Yan zaijing shishi zhiyi" 李巖在京史實質疑 [Doubts about the historical truth of Li Yan in Beijing], *Shi xue yuekan* 史學月刊 [Historical Monthly] 3: 29–33.

Queen, Sarah A. 1996. *From Chronicle to Canon: The Hermeneutics of the Spring and Autumn, According to Tung Chung-shu.* Cambridge: Cambridge University Press.

Raphals, Lisa. 1998. *Sharing the Light: Representations of Women and Virtue in Early China.* Albany: State University of New York Press.

Rawski, Evelyn S. 1991. "Research Themes in Ming-Qing Socioeconomic History—The State of the Field." *Journal of Asian Studies* 50.1: 84–111.

———. 1998. *The Last Emperors: A Social History of Qing Imperial Institutions.* Berkeley: University of California Press.

Reed, Bradly W. 2000. *Talons and Teeth: County Clerks and Runners in the Qing Dynasty.* Stanford: Stanford University Press.

Rickett, W. Allyn. 1985. *Guanzi, Political, Economic, and Philosophical Essays from Early China.* Princeton: Princeton University Press.

Robertson, Maureen. 1983. "Periodization in the Arts and Patterns of Change in Traditional Chinese Literary Theory." In Susan Bush and Christian Murch, eds. *Theories of the Arts in China* (Princeton: Princeton University Press): 3–26.

Robinet, Isabelle. 1993. *Taoist Meditation: The Mao-shan Tradition of Great Purity.* Albany: State University of New York Press.

Robinson, David 1995a. "Notes on eunuchs in Hebei during the mid-Ming period." *Ming Studies* 34: 1–16.

———. 1995b. "Banditry and Rebellion in the Capital Region During the Mid-Ming (1450–1525)." Princeton University doctoral dissertation; Department of East Asian Studies.

Rowe, William T. 2001. *Saving the World: Chen Hongmou and Elite Consciousness in Eighteenth-Century China.* Stanford: Stanford University Press.

Roy, David Tod, trans. 1993. *The Plum in the Golden Vase: or Chin P'ing Mei, Volume 1: The Gathering.* Princeton: Princeton University Press.

Runzhou Huludaoren 潤州葫蘆道人 [The Calabash Daoist of Runzhou]. 1645? *Guo Chuang xiaoshi* 馘闖小史 [Little history of cutting off the left ear of Dashing]. This is part of Xiwu 1645? Manuscript edition photo-offprinted in *Xuanlan chuji* 玄覽初集 [First collection of Xuanlan (Hall)], ce 119–20.

Sage, Steven F. 1992. *Ancient Sichuan and the Unification of China.* Albany: State University of New York Press.

Sahlins, Marshall. 1987. *Islands of History.* Chicago: University of Chicago Press.

Saich, Tony, and Hans van de Ven, eds. 1995. *New Perspectives on the Chinese Communist Revolution.* Armonk, N. Y.: M. E. Sharpe.

Said, Edward. 1978. *Orientalism.* New York: Random House.

———. 1993. *Culture and Imperialism.* New York: Knopf.

Sakai, Naoki. 1997. *Translation and Subjectivity: On "Japan" and Cultural Nationalism.* Minneapolis: University of Minnesota Press.

Sato, Fumitoshi 佐騰文俊. 1978. "Minmatsu Yenjichū no ran ni tsuite" 明末袁時中の亂について [Concerning the revolt of Yuan Shizhong in the late Ming]. In Hoshi Ayao sensei taiken kinen jigyokai, eds. *Hōshi hakushi taikan kinen Chūgokushi ronshu* 星博士退官記念中國史論集 [Studies in Chinese history dedicated to Dr. Hoshi on his retirement] (Yamagata: Yamagata University): 209–26.

———. 1985. *Minmatsu nōmin hanran no kenkyu* 明末農民反亂の研究 [Research on the farmer's uprisings of the late Ming]. Tokyo: Kenbun Shuppan.

Schafer, Edward. 1977. *Pacing the Void: T'ang Approaches to the Stars.* Berkeley: University of California Press.

Schipper, Kristofer, and Wang Hsin-huei. 1986. "Progressive and Regressive Time Cycles in Taoist Ritual." In J. T. Fraser, N. Lawrence, and F. C. Haber, eds. *Time, Science, and Society in China and the West* (Amherst: University of Massachusetts Press): 185–205.

Schlesinger, Arthur M., Jr. 1986. *The Cycles of American History.* Boston: Houghton Mifflin Co.

Scott, James C. 1990. *Domination and the Arts of Resistance: Hidden Transcripts.* New Haven: Yale University Press.

Scott, Joan Wallach. 1996. "Gender: A Useful Category of Historical Analysis." In Joan Wallach Scott, ed. *Feminism and History* (Oxford: Oxford University Press): 152–80.

Seidel, Anna. 1969–70. "The Image of the Perfect Ruler in Early Taoist Messianism." *History of Religion* 9.2–3: 216–47.

Seybolt, Peter J. 1996. *Throwing the Emperor from his Horse: Portrait of a Village Leader in China, 1923–1995.* Boulder, Colorado: Westview Press.

Shanquan 山泉 1977. *Henan* 河南 [Henan]. Hong Kong: Zhonghua shuju.

Shapiro, Sidney, ed. 1984. *Jews in Old China: Studies by Chinese Scholars.* New York: Hippocrene Books.

Shek, Richard Hon-chun. 1980. "Religion and Society in Late Ming: Sectarianism and Popular Thought in Sixteenth and Seventeenth Century China." University of California, Berkeley, doctoral dissertation.

———. 1990. "Sectarian Eschatology and Violence." In Jonathan N. Lipman and Stevan Harrell, eds. *Violence in China: Essays in Culture and Counterculture* (Albany: State University of New York Press): 87–114.

Shen Dingping 沈定平. 1982. "Mingmo 'shibazi zhushenqi' yuanliu kao" 明末'十八子主神器'源流考 [An investigation of the origins and spread of the saying that a shibazi (Li) would take the throne]. In Zhongguo shehui kexue yuan lishi yanjiu so Mingshi yanjiu shi bian 中國社會科學院歷史研究所明史研究室編 [Ming history section of the Institute of History of the Chinese Academy of Social Sciences, ed.], *Mingshi yanjiu luncong* 明史研究論叢 [Collected articles on Ming history]. (Nanjing: Jiangsu renmin chubanshe): 290–306.

Shen Xiande 沈顯德 and Shen Qizeng 沈其曾. 1987. *Shenshi jiapu* 沈氏家譜 [Genealogy of the Shen lineage]. 4 juan. Suizhou.

Shen Zhuanyi 沈傳義 and Huang Shubing 黃舒昺. 1898. *Xinxiu Xiangfu xianzhi* 新修祥符縣志 [New Edition of the Xiangfu County Gazetteer]. 24 juan, 1 head juan.

Shiba, Yoshinobu. 1970. *Commerce and Society in Sung China.* Mark Elvin, trans. Ann Arbor: University of Michigan Center for Chinese Studies.

Shih, Vincent. 1967. *The Taiping Ideology.* Seattle: University of Washington Press.

Shils, Edward. 1975. *Center and Periphery: Essays in Macrosociology.* Chicago: University of Chicago Press.

Shuili dianli bu Huanghe shuili weiyuanhui zhi Huang yanjiu zu 水利電力部黃河水利委員會治黃研究組. 1984. *Huanghe de zhili yu kaifa* 黃河的治理和開發 [The Management and Development of the Yellow River]. Shanghai: Shanghai jiaoyu chuban she.

Skinner, G. William. 1977. "Regional Urbanization in Nineteenth-Century China." In G. William Skinner, ed. *The City in Late Imperial China* (Stanford: Stanford University Press): 211–49.

———. 1985. "Presidential Address: The Structure of Chinese History." *Journal of Asian Studies* 44.2 (February): 271–92.

Soja, Edward. 1989. *Postmodern Geographies: The Reassertion of Space in Critical Social Theory.* London: Verso.

Song Luo 宋犖 ed. Kangxi. *Shangqiu Songshi sanshi yiji* 商邱宋氏三世遺集 [Inherited collected writings of three generations of the Song family of Shangqiu]. 1 juan.

———. 1705. *Shangqiu Songshi jiacheng* 商邱宋氏家乘 [Genealogy of the Song lineage of Shangqiu]. 14 juan.

Song Qiang 宋強, Zhang Zangzang 張藏藏, and Qiao Bian 僑邊. 1996. *Zhongguo keyi shuobu: lengzhan hou shidai di zhengzhi yu qinggan jueze* 中國可以説不:冷戰後時代的政治與情感抉擇 [China can say no: political and emotional choices in the post-Cold War era]. Beijing: Zhonghua gongshang lianhe chubanshe.

———, Zhang Zangzang 張藏藏, Qiao Bian 僑邊, Tang Zhengyu 湯正宇 and Gu Qingsheng 古清生. 1996. *Zhongguo haishi neng shuo bu* 中國還是能説不 [China can still say no]. Beijing: Zhongguo wenlian chubanshe.

Spence, Jonathan D. 1966. *Ts'ao Yin and the K'ang-hsi Emperor: Bondservant and Master.* New Haven: Yale University Press.

———. 1999. *The Search for Modern China.* New York: Norton.

Struve, Lynn A. 1984. *The Southern Ming, 1644–1662.* New Haven: Yale University Press.

———. 1993. *Voices from the Ming-Qing Cataclysm: China in Tigers' Jaws.* New Haven: Yale University Press.

Struve, Peter S. *Patterns in Nature.* Boston: Little, Brown and Co.

Su Derong 蘇德榮, ed. 1984. *Lu Wang ziliao huibian* 潞王資料匯編 [Collected materials on the Lu prince]. Xinxiang: Henan sheng Xinxiang shi bowuguan Lu Wang fen wenwu guanli suo.

Su Jinzi 蘇晉子. 1991. "Henan fanfu jia tianxia: Mingdai Henan fanwang shulun zhi yi" 河南藩府甲天下—明代河南藩王述論之一 [The feudatories of Henan were first under heaven: an essay on the Ming period princes enfeoffed in Henan]. *Shixue yue kan* [Historical Monthly] 5: 40–45.

Su Xiaokang and Wang Luxiang. 1994. *Deathsong of the River: A Reader's Guide to the Chinese TV Series Heshang.* Richard W. Bodman and Pin P. Wan, trans. Ithaca: East Asia Program, Cornell University.

Sun Jurong 孫居容. 1986. *Sunshi zupu* 孫氏族譜 [Genealogy of the Sun Family].

Sun Wenliang 孫文良 and Li Zhiting 李治亭. 1983. *Qing Taizong quanzhuan* 清太宗全傳 [A complete biography of Qing Taizong]. Changchun: Jilin renmin chubanshe.

Suzuki Chūsei 鈴木中正. 1974. *Chūgokushi ni okeru kakumei to shūkyo* 中國史における革命と宗教 [Revolution and religion in Chinese History]. Kyoto: Kyōto daigaku shupan kai.

Tambiah, S. J. 1976. *World Conqueror and World Renouncer: A Study of Buddhism and Polity in Thailand Against a Historical Background.* Cambridge: Cambridge University Press.

Tan Qian 談遷. 1653. *Guoque* 國榷 [An Assessment of the Dynasty]. 104 juan. Original manuscript of 1653, edited and published in Beijing: Guji chubanshe, 1958, in 10 vols.

Tan Qixiang 譚其驤, ed. 1975/1982. *Zhongguo lishi ditu ji* 中國歷史地圖集 [Historical Maps of China]. 7 vols. Shanghai: Ditu chuban she. [I have used the original, hardbound edition of volume 7 and the reprinted, softbound edition of volumes 1–6.]

Tang, Xiaobing. 1996. *Global Space and the Nationalist Discourse of Modernity: The Historical Thinking of Liang Qichao.* Stanford: Stanford University Press.

Taniguchi Kikuo 谷口規矩雄. 1969. "Minmatsu kyōhei gigun ni tsuite—Minmatsu seikyoku ichisaku" 明末郷兵義軍について　明末政局一齣 [Concerning the Local Troops and Just Armies of the Late Ming—An Aspect of Late Ming Politics]. *Kenkyu* 研究 [Research] (Kobei daigaku bungakubu) 43: 99–122.

Ter Haar, B. J. 1992. *The White Lotus Teachings in Chinese Religious History.* Leiden: E. J. Brill.

Thapar, Romila. 1996. *Time as a Metaphor of History: Early India.* Delhi: Oxford University Press.

Tian Jinqi 田金祺 and Zhao Dongjie 趙東階. 1928. *Sishui xianzhi* 汜水縣志 [Gazetteer of Sishui County]. 12 juan.

396   *Bibliography*

Tian Wenjing 田文鏡, Sun Hao 孫灝, and Asiha 呵思哈. 1735. *Henan tongzhi, xu tongzhi* 河南通志續通志 [Comprehensive Gazetteer of Henan and a Continuation]. 80 juan. (Taipei: Huawen shuju; 1969 reprint, 5 vols.)

T'ien, Ju-k'ang. 1988. *Male Anxiety and Female Chastity: A Comparative Study of Chinese Ethical Values in Ming-Ch'ing Times.* Leiden: E. J. Brill.

Tong, James W. 1991. *Disorder under Heaven: Collective Violence in the Ming Dynasty.* Stanford: Stanford University Press.

Trompf, G. W. 1979. *The Idea of Historical Recurrence in Western Thought from Antiquity to the Reformation.* Berkeley: University of California Press.

Tu Wei-ming. 1985. *Confucian Thought: Selfhood as Creative Transformation.* Albany: State University of New York Press.

———. 杜維明. 1987. "Ruxue disanqi fazhan de qianjing wenti" 儒學第三期發展的前景問題 [The question of the foreground to the development of Confucianism in the third period]. *Wenhua: Zhongguo yu shijie* 文化:中國與世界 [Culture: China and the World] (Beijing: Sanlian shudian): 100–40.

———. 1991. "Cultural China: the Periphery as the Center." *Daedalus* 120.2 (spring): 1–32.

———, Milan Hejtmanek, and Alan Wachman. 1992. *The Confucian World Observed: A Contemporary Discussion of Confucian Humanism in East Asia.* Honolulu: The University of Hawaii Press.

Tucker, Mary Evelyn, and John Berthrong, eds. 1998. *Confucianism and Ecology: the Interrelationship of Heaven, Earth, and Humans.* Cambridge: Harvard University Press.

Tung, Jowen R. 2000. *Fables for the Patriarchs: Gender Politics in Tang Discourse.* New York: Rowman and Littlefield.

Twitchett, Denis C. 1959. "The Fan Clan's Charitable Estate, 1050–1760." In David S. Nivison and Arthur F. Wright, eds. *Confucianism in Action* (Stanford: Stanford University Press): 97–133.

———. 1979. *The Cambridge History of China, Volume 3: Sui and T'ang China, 589–906, Part I.* Cambridge: Cambridge University Press.

———, and Frederick W. Mote, eds. 1998. *The Cambridge History of China, Volume 8: The Ming Dynasty, 1368–1644, Part 2.* Cambridge: Cambridge University Press.

———, and Michael Loewe, eds. 1986. *The Cambridge History of China, Volume 1: The Ch'in and Han Empires, 221 B.C.–A.D. 220.* Cambridge: Cambridge University Press.

Van der Sprenkel, Otto Berkelbach. 1953. "Population Statistics of Ming China." *Bulletin of the School of Oriental and African Studies* 15.2: 289–326.

———. 1961. "The Geographical Background of the Ming Civil Service" *Journal of the Economic and Social History of the Orient* 4.3: 302–36.

Vaughn, Stephen, ed. 1985. *The Vital Past: Writings on the Uses of History.* Athens: University of Georgia Press.

Vermeer, E. B. 1987. "P'an Chi-hsün's Solutions for the Yellow River Problems of the Late Sixteenth Century." *T'oung Pao* LXXIII 7.3: 33–67.

Vogel, Ezra F. 1997. *Living with China: U.S.-China Relations in the Twenty-first Century.* New York: W. W. Norton and Company.

Von Glahn, Richard. 1987. *The Country of Streams and Grottoes: Expansion, Settlement, and the Civilizing of the Sichuan Frontier in Song Times.* Cambridge: Council on East Asian Studies, Harvard University Press.

———. 1996. *Fountain of Fortune: Money and Monetary Policy in China, 1000–1700.* Berkeley: University of California Press.

Wakeman, Frederic, Jr. 1973. *History and Will: Philosophical Perspectives of Mao Tse-tung's Thought.* Berkeley: University of California Press.

———. 1979. "The Shun Interregnum of 1644." In Jonathan D. Spence and John E. Wills, Jr., eds. *From Ming to Ch'ing: Conquest, Region, and Continuity in Seventeenth-Century China* (New Haven: Yale University Press): 34–76.

———. 1985. *The Great Enterprise: The Manchu Reconstruction of Imperial Order in Seventeenth-Century China.* 2 vols. Berkeley: University of California Press.

Waley, Arthur, trans. and annot. 1938. *The Analects of Confucius.* New York: Random House.

Waley-Cohen, Joanna. 1999. *Sextants of Beijing: Global Currents in Chinese History.* New York: Norton and Co.

Waltner, Ann. 1981. "Widows and Remarriage in Ming and Early Qing China." In Richard W. Guisso and Stanley Johannesen, eds. *Women in China: Current Directions in Historical Scholarship* (Youngstown, N. Y.: Philo Press): 129–46.

———. 1991. *Getting an Heir: Adoption and the Construction of Kinship in Late Imperial China.* Honolulu: University of Hawaii Press.

———. 1996. "Breaking the Law: Family Violence, Gender and Hierarchy in the Legal Code of the Ming Dynasty." *Ming Studies* 36: 29–43.

———, and Pi-ching Hsu. 1997. "Lingering Fragrance: The Poetry of Tu Yaose and Shen Tiansun." *Journal of Women's History* 8.4 (winter): 28–53.

Wan Yan 萬言. Early Qing. *Chongzhen changbian* 崇楨長編 [Documents from the Chongzhen reign]. 2 juan. *Taiwan wenxian congkan* 台灣文獻叢刊 [Collectaeneum of materials in Taiwan, 1969].

Wang, Chen-main. 1999. *The Life and Career of Hung Ch'eng-ch'ou (1593–1665): Public Service in a Time of Dynastic Change.* Ann Arbor: Association for Asian Studies.

Wang Chunyu 王春瑜 and Du Wanguan 杜婉官. 1989. *Mingchao huanguan* 明朝宦官 [Eunuchs of the Ming Dynasty]. Beijing: Zijin cheng chubanshe.

Wang Fusan 王復三. 1980. "Lun renshi shi jinsi luoxuan de quxian" 論認識是近似螺旋的曲線 [The history of human consciousness approximates the curve of a spiral]. *Wenshizhe* 文史哲 [Literature, History and Philosophy] 4: 73–8.

Wang Pixu 王丕煦, comp., and Liang Bingkun 梁秉錕, ed. 1935. *Laiyang xianzhi* 萊陽縣志 [Gazetteer of Laiyang County]. 10 juan.

Wang Puyuan 王蒲園 and Ma Zikuan 馬子寬. 1932. *Huaxian zhi* 滑縣志 [Gazetteer of Hua county]. 20 juan, one head juan.

Wang Shixing 王士性. 1831. *Yu zhi* 豫志 [Record of Yu]. 1 juan.

Wang Shouyi 王守義. 1962. "Mingmo nongmin jun 'juntian' kouhao zhiyi" 明末農民軍 '均田' 口號質疑 [Doubts about the Slogan "Equal Fields" in the Farmers' Army at the End of the Ming]. *Lishi yanjiu* 歷史研究 [Historical Research] 2: 97–112.

Wang Xingya 王興亞. 1973. *Li Chuang Wang zai Henan* 李闖王在河南 [The Dashing Prince Li in Henan]. Zhengzhou: Henan renmin chubanshe.

———. 1982a. "Zheng Lian he ta de *Yubian jilue*" 鄭廉和他的 '豫變紀略' [Zheng Lian and his *Outline Record of the Changes in Yu*]. *Zhengzhou daxue xuebao* 鄭州大學學報 [Journal of Zhengzhou University] 3: 34–43.

———. 1982b. *Li Zicheng jingji zhengce yanjiu* 李自成經濟政策研究 [A study of Li Zicheng's economic policies]. Zhengzhou: Henan renmin chuban she.

———. 1984a. "Ming chu qian Shanxi min dao Henan kaoshu" 明初遷山西民到河南考述 [An investigation of the migration of Shanxi people to Henan at the beginning of the Ming]. *Shixue yuekan* 史學月刊 [Historical Monthly] 4: 36–43.

———. 1984b. *Li Zicheng qiyi shishi yanjiu* 李自成起義史事研究 [Studies of the Historical Events of Li Zicheng's Uprising]. Zhengzhou: Zhongzhou guji chubanshe.

———. 1989. "Mingdai zhonghouqi Henan shehui fengshang de bianhua" 明代中後期河南社會風尚的變化 [Changes in the prevailing customs in Henan society during the middle and late Ming]. In *Zhongzhou xuekan* 中州學刊 [Journal of the Central Province] 2: 107–10.

———. 1993. "Mingdai guanli kaohe zhidu lunlue" 明代官吏考核制度論略 [A discussion of the Ming system for evaluating officials]. Paper presented at the International Conference on Ming History in Xi'an.

———. 1996. "Luelun Henan gudai jingji you xianjin dao luohou de zhuanbian" 略論河南古

代經濟由先進到落後的轉變 [The transformation of Henan's economy from an advanced to a backward one in ancient times]. *Zhongzhou xuekan* 中州學刊 [Journal of the central province] 3: 103–7.

Wang Xiuwen 王修文 and Zhang Tingfu 張庭馥. 1923. *Xuchang xianzhi* 許昌縣志 [Gazetteer of Xuchang county]. 20 juan.

Wang, Yü-ch'üan. 1936. "The Rise of the Land Tax and the Fall of Dynasties in Chinese History." *Pacific Affairs* 9.2 (June): 201–20.

———. 王毓銓. 1964. "Mingdai de wangfu zhuangtian" 明代的王府庄田 [Princely estates during the Ming]. Reprinted in Wang's collected works, *Laiwu ji* 萊蕪集 [Collection from Laiwu] (Beijing: Zhonghua shuju, 1983): 110–241.

———. 1965. *Mingdai de juntun* 明代的軍屯 [Military farms during the Ming]. Beijing: Zhonghua shuju.

Wang Zhonghan 王鍾翰. 1987. *Qingshi liezhuan* 清史列傳 [Aligned biographies of Qing history]. (Beijing: Zhonghua shuju chubanshe; reprint of early Republican period original, 80 juan in 20 vols.).

Wasserstrom, Jeffrey N., and Elizabeth Perry, eds. 1994. *Popular Protest and Political Culture in Modern China*. Boulder, Colorado: Westview Press.

Watson, Burton, trans. 1968. *Records of the Grand Historian of China: Translated from the Shih chi of Ssu-ma Ch'ien*. 2 vols. New York: Columbia University Press.

———. 1993. *Records of the Grand Historian: Qin Dynasty*. Hong Kong: The Chinese University of Hong Kong and Columbia University Press.

Watson, James D. 1968. *The Double Helix: A Personal Account of the Discovery of the Structure of DNA*. New York: Atheneum.

Watt, John R. 1972. *The District Magistrate in Late Imperial China*. New York: Columbia University Press.

Wei Qianzhi 魏千志. 1991. "*Jinantu* de shiliao jiazhi" 紀南圖的史料價質 [The value of the *Record of Hardship* as a historical source]. *Zhongzhou xuekan* 中州學刊 [Journal of the Central Province] 6: 113–16.

———. 1993a. "Cong *Jinantu* kan Mingmo ji ge wenti" 從紀南圖看明末幾個問題 [Several questions regarding the end of the Ming as seen from the *Record of Hardship*]. In *Dierjie Ming-Qingshi guoji xueshu taolunhui lunwenji* 第二屆明清史國際學術討論會論文集 [Collected essays from the Second International Conference on Ming-Qing History] (Tianjin: Tianjin renmin chuban she): 176–88.

———. 1993b. "Zhongguo Youtairen dingju Kaifeng shijian kao" 中國猶太人定居開封時間考 [An examination of the date when the Chinese Jews settled in Kaifeng]. *Shixue yuekan* [Historical Monthly] (Kaifeng) 5: 36–41.

———. 1993c. "Ming-Qing shiqi Zhongguo Youtairen de lishi gongxian" 明清時期中國猶太人的歷史貢獻 [Historical contributions of the Chinese Jews in the Ming-Qing period]. Paper presented at China's Fifth International Conference on Ming History.

———. 1997. "Zhongguo gudai Youtairen xingshi bianhua kao" 中國古代猶太人姓氏變化考 [An examination of changes in the names of the Jews in Chinese history]. *Shixue yuekan* 史學月刊 [Historical Monthly] (Kaifeng) 2: 29–35.

———. 2000. "An Investigation of the Date of Jewish Settlement in Kaifeng." In Jonathan Goldstein, ed. *The Jews of China, Volume Two: A Sourcebook and Research Guide* (Armonk: M. E. Sharpe): 14–25.

Wei Qingyuan 衛慶遠. 1961. *Mingdai huangce zhidu*. 明代黃冊制度 [The Ming yellow register system]. Beijing: Zhonghua shuju.

Weller, Robert P., and Scott E. Guggenheim, eds. 1989. *Power and Protest in the Countryside: Studies of Rural Unrest in Asia, Europe, and Latin America*. Durham: Duke University Press.

Wen Bing 文秉. Early Qing a. *Liehuang xiaoshi* 烈皇小事 [Small matters concerning the reign of Liehuang]. 8 juan. Reprinted in Taibei: *Taiwan wenxian congkan* 台灣文獻叢刊, 263: 1–230.

————, Early Qing b. *Xianbo zhishi* 先撥志始 [A record of those disposed of]. 2 juan. Reprinted in Taibei: *Ming-Qing shiliao huibian chuji mulu, di sice* 明清史料彙編初集目錄第四冊, 1767–2144. (Also reprinted in Zhongguo lishi yanjiu ziliao congshu 中國歷史研究資料叢書 [Collection of Chinese historical materials] (Shanghai: Shanghai shudian, 1982).

Wheatley, Paul. 1971. *The Pivot of the Four Quarters: A Preliminary Inquiry into the Origins and Character of the Ancient Chinese City.* Edinburgh: Edinburgh University Press.

Whelan, T. S. 1979. *The Pawnshop in China.* Ann Arbor: Center for Chinese Studies, The University of Michigan.

White, Hayden 1973. *Metahistory: The Historical Imagination in Nineteenth-Century Europe.* Baltimore: Johns Hopkins University Press.

————. 1978. *Tropics of Discourse, Essays in Cultural Criticism.* Baltimore: The Johns Hopkins University Press.

White, William Charles. 1966. *Chinese Jews: A Compilation of Matters Relating to the Jews of K'ai-feng Fu.* 3 vols. Toronto: University of Toronto Press.

Widmer, Ellen, and Kang-I Sun Chang. 1997. *Writing Women in Late Imperial China.* Stanford: Stanford University Press.

Will, Pierre-Étienne. 1990. *Bureaucracy and Famine in Eighteenth-Century China.* Stanford: Stanford University Press. A translation of *Bureaucratie et famine en Chine au 18e siècle* (Paris: Mouton, 1980).

————, and R. Bin Wong (with James Lee). 1991. *Nourish the People: The State Granary System in China, 1650–1850.* Ann Arbor: Center for Chinese Studies, University of Michigan.

Williams, Raymond. 1976. *Keywords: Vocabulary of Culture and Society.* New York: Oxford University Press.

Wilson, Thomas A. 1995. *Genealogy of the Way: The Construction and Uses of the Confucian Tradition in Late Imperial China.* Stanford: Stanford University Press.

Winichakul, Thongchai. 1994. *Siam Mapped: A History of the Geo-Body of a Nation.* Honolulu: University of Hawaii Press.

Wolpert, Stanley. 1997. *A New History of India.* New York: Oxford University Press.

Wolf, Margery. 1992. *A Thrice-Told Tale: Feminism, Postmodernism, and Ethnographic Responsibility.* Stanford: Stanford University Press.

Wong, R. Bin. 1997. *China Transformed: Historical Change and the Limits of European Experience.* Ithaca: Cornell University Press.

Wou, Odoric 1994. *Mobilizing the Masses: Building Revolution in Henan.* Stanford: Stanford University Press.

Wu, Dange 伍丹戈. 1979. "Mingdai de guantian yu mintian" 明代的官田與民田 [State land and civilian land during the Ming]. In *Zhonghua wenshi luncong* 中華文史論叢 [Essays on Chinese literature and history] 1: 1–80.

Wu, Hong. 1989. *The Wu Liang Shrine: The Ideology of Early Chinese Pictorial Art.* Stanford: Stanford University Press.

Wu, Jihua 吳緝華. 1961. *Mingdai haiyun ji yunhe de yanjiu* 明代海運及運河的研究 [Sea and canal transport in the Ming period]. Taibei: Zhongyang yanjiu yuen lishi yanjiu suo.

Wu, Pei-yi. 1990. *The Confucian's Progress: Autobiographical Writings in Traditional China.* Princeton: Princeton University Press.

Wu, Qingyun. 1995. *Female Rule in Chinese and English Literary Utopias.* Syracuse: Syracuse University Press.

Wu, Sheng 吳牲生. Late Ming. *Huainan Wu Chaian shuji* 淮南吳柴菴疏集 [The collected reports of Wu Chaian of Huainan]. 20 juan. (Taibei: Weiwengang shu chubanshe, 1976, 3 vols.).

Wu Weiye 吳偉業. 1674. *Suikou jilue* 綏寇紀略 [Outline Record of the Pacification of Robbers]. 12 juan. In *MingQing shiliao huibian sanji* 明清史料彙編三集 [Three collections of Ming-Qing historical materials] (Taibei reprint, Wenhai chuban she, 1969).

Wu, Yenna. 1995a. *The Chinese Virago: A Literary Theme.* Cambridge: Harvard University Press.

———. 1995b. *The Lioness Roars: Shrew Stories from Late Imperial China.* Ithaca: Cornell University Press.

Wyatt, Don J. 1996. *The Recluse of Loyang: Shao Yung and the Moral Evolution of Early Sung Thought.* Honolulu: University of Hawaii Press.

Xiao Jinan 蕭濟南 and Lü Jingzhi 呂敬之. 1911. *Ningling xianzhi* 寧陵縣志 [Gazetteer of Ningling County]. 12 juan, 1 head and 1 tail juan. Zhengzhou, 1989.

Xie Chengren 謝承仁. 1986. *Li Zicheng xinzhuan* 李自成新傳 [A new biography of Li Zicheng]. Shanghai: Shanghai renmin chuban she.

Xi Wu landaoren 西吳懶道人 [Lazy Daoist of Western Wu]. 1660s. *Xinbian jiao chuang tongsu xiao shuo* 新編剿闖通俗小說 [New edition of the popular novel on the suppression of Dashing]. Preface by Wu Jing 無競 (Wang Weilie 王維烈). 10 hui. Naikaku Bunko microfilm, Harvard-Yenching Library.

Xu Daling 許大齡 and Wang Tianyou 王天有. 1991. *Mingchao shiliu di* 明朝十六帝 [Sixteen rulers of the Ming dynasty]. Beijing: Zijin cheng chubanshe.

Xu Zi 徐鼒. 1861. *Xiaotian jinian fukao* 小腆紀年附考 [Annals of an age of lesser prosperity with supplementary annotations]. 20 juan. Annotated by Wang Chongwu 王崇武. Reprinted in *Taiwan wenxian congkan* 台灣文獻叢刊 [Collection of Materials from Taiwan] (Taibei: Bank of China, 1963) 134: 1–5.

Xuan, Mo 玄. Kangxi. See Yuan Mo. Kangxi.

Yang Dongming 楊東明. 1624. *Shanju gongke* 山居功課 [Lessons of Shanju]. 10 juan.

———. 1688. *Jimin tushuo* 飢民圖說 [Album of the Famished]. Unique copy, Henan sheng bowuguan, Zhengzhou.

Yang, Hsüan-chih. 1984. *A Record of Buddhist Monasteries in Lo-yang.* Yi-t'ung Wang, trans. Princeton: Princeton University Press.

Yang, Lien-sheng. 1969. "Ming Local Administration." In Hucker 1969, 1–22.

Yang, Mayfair Mei-hui. 1994. *Gifts, Favors, and Banquets: The Art of Social Relationships in China.* Ithaca: Cornell University Press.

Yang Shicong 楊士聰. 1644. *Jiashen hezhenlue* 甲申核真略 [An investigation of the truth of 1644]. In Zheng Zhenduo 鄭振鐸, ed. *Mingji shiliao congshu* 明季史料叢書 [Collectanea of historical materials of the end of the Ming]. Shanghai: Shengzeyuan, 1944.

Yao Jiaji 姚家積. 1935. "Mingji yiwen kaobu" 明季遺聞考補 [Annotated edition of hearsay of the late Ming]. *Shixue nianbao* 史學年報 [Annual of historical studies] 2.2: 69–200.

Yao, Shao-yu. 1942–43. "The Geographical Distribution of Floods and Droughts in Chinese History, 206 B.C.–A.D. 1911." *Far Eastern Quarterly* 2: 357–78.

Ya xindi xueshe 亞新地學社 [Study Society for a New Geography of Asia]. 1923. *Henan fenxian xiangtu* 河南分縣詳圖 [Detailed maps of the counties of Henan]. Wuchang: n.p.

Ye Gongchuo 葉恭綽. 1930. *Qingdai xuezhe xiang zhuan diyi ji* 清代學者象傳第一集 [First collection of portraits and biographies of scholars of the Qing period]. 4 ce. Shanghai: Shangwu yinshuguan.

Yeats, W. B. 1937. *A Vision.* New York: Collier Books.

Yim, Shui-yuen. 1978. "Famine Relief Statistics as a Guide to the Population of Sixteenth-Century China: A Case-Study of Honan Province." *Qing-shih wen-t'i* 3.9: 1–30.

Yü, Chün-fang. 2001. *Kuan-yin: The Chinese Transformation of Avalokitesvara.* New York: Columbia University Press.

Yu, Pauline. 1997. "Canon Formation in Late Imperial China." In Huters et al., eds. 1997: 83–104.

Yü Ying-shih 余英時. 1976. *Lishi yu sixiang* 歷史與思想 [History and thought]. Taibei: Lianjing chuban shiye gongsi.

———. 1991a. "The Radicalization of China in the Twentieth Century." *Daedalus* 122.2: 125–50.

———. 1991b. "Clio's New Cultural Turn and the Rediscovery of Tradition in Asia." Keynote

Address of the Twelfth Conference of the International Association of Historians of Asia, University of Hong Kong, 10–30.

———. 1994. "Changing Conceptions of National History in Twentieth-Century China." In Eric Lönnroth, Karl Molin, and Ragnar Björk, eds. *Conceptions of National History. Proceedings of Nobel Symposium 78* (Berlin: Walter de Gruyter): 155–74.

Yuan Mo 元默. Kangxi. *Jiaozei tuji* 剿賊圖記 [Illustrated record of the suppression of the bandits]. Beijing Library rare book.

Yue Tingkai 岳廷楷, Hu Zanlai 胡贊來, and Lü Yonghui 呂永輝. 1903. *Yongcheng xianzhi* 永城縣志 [Gazetteer of Yongcheng county]. 38 juan.

Yuan, Tsing. 1979. "Urban Riots and Disturbances." In Jonathan D. Spence and John E. Wills, Jr., eds. *From Ming to Ch'ing: Conquest, Region, and Community in Seventeenth Century China* (New Haven: Yale University Press): 279–311.

Zha Jizuo 查繼左. 1670s. *Zuiwei lu xuanji* 罪惟錄選輯 [Selections from the record of criminal reflections]. In *Taiwan wenxian congkan* 台灣文獻叢刊 [Collectanea of materials from Taiwan], vol. 136. Taibei: Bank of Taiwan, 1962.

Zhang Jinyan 張縉彥. c. 1643. *Luju wenji* 蘽居文集 [Collected works of the Lentil residence]. Includes *Luju fengshi*, 2 juan (see Zhang and Wang 1987) and *Luju shiji* 蘽居詩集 [Collected poems of the Lentil residence], 1 juan. The table of contents in this juan of poetry includes a supplement (*fu*) of two songs (*ge*) and a history (*shi*) that are missing from this copy. Consulted at the Tōyō Bunko in Tokyo.

———, comp., and Wang Xingya 王興亞, ed. 1987. *Luju fengshi* 蘽居封事 [Sealed reports of the Lentil residence]. 2 juan. Zhengzhou: Zhongzhou guji chubanshe.

Zhang Shizhong 張時中. 1870. *Zhangshi zupu* 張氏族譜 [Genealogy of the Zhang lineage]. 3 juan. (Shang and zhong juan extant; xia juan missing.)

Zhang Tingyu 張廷玉. 1739. *Mingshi* 明史 [History of the Ming]. 332 juan. Beijing: Zhonghua shuju, 1974.

Zhang Xianqing 張顯清. 1992a. "Lun Mingdai guanshen youmian maolan zhi bi" 論明代紳優免冒濫之弊 [A discussion of the abuses of officials and elite who expanded their privileges illicitly during the Ming]. *Zhongguo jingji shi yanjiu* 中國經濟史研究 [Research in the economic history of China] 4: 17–28.

———. 1992b. *Yan Song zhuan* 嚴嵩傳 [Biography of Yan Song]. Hefei: Huangshan shushe.

Zhang, Xin. 2000. *Social Transformation in Modern China: The State and Local Elites in Henan, 1900–1937*. Cambridge: Cambridge University Press.

Zhang Zhenfang 張鎮芳 and Shi Jingshun 施景舜. 1914. *Xiàngcheng xianzhi* 項成縣志 [Gazetteer of Xiàngcheng county]. 32 juan.

Zhao Kaiyuan 趙開元 and Chang Jun 暢俊. 1747. *Xinxiang xianzhi* 新鄉縣志 [Gazetteer of Xinxiang county]. 34 juan.

Zhao Lisheng 趙儷生. 1954. "Mingdai Zhengde jian jici nongmin qiyi de jingguo he tedian" 明代正德間幾次農民起義的經過和特點 [The experience and special characteristics of several farmers' uprisings in the Zhengde period]. *Wenshi zhe* 文史哲 [Literature, history and philosophy] 12; reprinted in Zhao Lisheng and Gao Zhaoyi 高昭一 1954. *Zhongguo nongmin zhanzheng shi lunwen ji* 中國農民戰爭史論文集 [Collected articles on Chinese farmers' wars]. Shanghai: Xinzhishi chubanshe, 1955: 134–53.

Zhao Shijin 趙士錦. 1645? *Jiashen jishi* 甲申紀事 [Record of 1644]. Reprinted in *Wan-Ming shiliao congshu* 晚明史料叢書 [Collectanea of Late Ming Historical Materials]. Beijing: Zhonghua shuju, 1962.

Zheng Han 鄭涵. 1985. *Lü Kun nianpu* 呂坤年譜 [Chronological Biography of Lü Kun]. Zhengzhou: Zhongguo guji chubanshe.

Zheng Lian 鄭廉. 1749. *Yubian jilue* 豫變紀略 [Outline record of the changes in Yu]. 8 juan. Wang Xingya 王興亞, ed. Hangzhou: Zhejiang guji chubanshe, 1984.

Zheng, Yongnian. 1999. *Discovering Chinese Nationalism in China: Modernization, Identity, and International Relations*. Cambridge: Cambridge University Press.

Zhi, Fucheng 智夫成. 1990. "Mingdai zongshi renkou de xunmeng zengzhang yu jiezhi cuoshi" 明代宗室人口的迅猛增長與节制措施 [The rapid growth in the population of the Ming royal lineage and efforts to limit it]. *Zhongzhou xuekan* 中州學刊 [Journal of the central province] 4: 121–26.

Zhong Huamin 鍾化民. 1595. *Zhen Yu jilue* 賑豫紀略 [A record of relief in Yu]. Shoushange edition.

Zhongguo shixuehui 中國史學會. 1985. *Zhongguo lishixue nianjian* 中國歷史學年監 [Yearbook of Chinese Historical Studies]. Vol. 5. Beijing: Renmin chubanshe.

Zhongguo tongshi jilun bianji xiaozu 中國通史集論編輯小組 [Editorial group of collected essays in the comprehensive history of China]. 1972. *Zhongguo tongshi jilun* 中國通史集論 [Collected essays on the comprehensive history of China]. Taibei: Changchunshu shufang.

Zhou Bingyi 周秉彝 and Liu Ruilin 劉瑞璘. 1931. *Zhengxian zhi* 鄭縣志 [Gazetteer of Zheng county]. 18 juan.

Zhou Kuiyi 周魁一 et al. annot. 1990. *Ershiwu shi hequ zhi zhushi* 二十五史河渠志注釋 [Annotations and explanations of the records of rivers and canals in the twenty-five histories]. Beijing: Zhongguo shudian.

Zhou Shuren 周樹人 (Lu Xun 魯迅), ed. 1927. *Tang-Song chuanqi ji* 唐宋傳奇集 [Collected tales of the Tang and Song]. 8 juan. Shanghai. Beijing: Wenxue guji kanxingshe, 1958.

Zhou Zaijun 周在浚. Early Qing. *Da Liang shoucheng ji* 大梁守城記 [Record of the defense of Da Liang]. 1 juan. In Liu 1982b.

Zhu Kezhen 竺可楨. 1972. "Zhongguo jin wuqian nian lai qihou biangqian de chubu yanjiu" 中國近五千年來气候變遷的初步研究 [A preliminary study of changes in the climate of China during the last five thousand years]. *Kaogu xuebao* 考古學報 [Journal of Archaeology]: 15–38.

Zhu Xuan 朱璇, comp., and Zhou Ji 周璣, ed. 1788. *Qixian zhi* 杞縣志 [Gazetteer of Qi County]. 24 juan.

Zito, Angela. 1996. "City Gods and Their Magistrates." In Lopez 1996: 72–81.

Zurndorfer, Harriet T. 1989. *Change and Continuity in Chinese Local History: The Development of Hui-chou Prefecture, 800–1800*. Leiden: E. J. Brill.

INDEX

Africa, 20, 321
agriculture, 1–2, 4, 6, 10, 321; commercial, 138–39; elite and, 107–8, 110; middle strata and, 127; rebellion and, 168, 176; taxes and, 28. *See also* land
Ai family (Kaifeng), 161
Ai Jing, 160
Ai Jun, 160
Ai Tian, 161–62
Ai Yingkui, 162
Aisin Gioro family, 205. *See also* Manchus
Album of the Famished (Yang Dongming), 35, 37–51, 76
all under heaven (*tianxia*), xiii, 3, 312
An Bangyan, 90, 154
An Cheng, 159
An Lushan, 149, 169; Li Zicheng and, 222, 224, 234, 236, 268, 273, 287, 289, 301, 311
An San, 159
Analects (Kongzi), 71, 102, 231
Ao (Shang capital), 2
aristocrats. *See* nobility
Arnheim, Rudolf, 316
artisans, 139–40, 163–64; in Kaifeng, 143–44; organizations of, 143
Asiatic mode of production, xvii
An Assessment of the Dynasty (Tan Qian), 114

Ba state, 3
Bai Guang'en, 287, 289–91, 308–9
Bai Yu, 213, 224, 226; on Kaifeng siege, 254, 264–65

Baiquan Academy, 61, 110
Ban Zhao, 72
banditry: causes of, 54, 132, 183, 196, 199–200, 252; in central plain, 133, 186; in countryside, 251; elite response to, 78, 80–81, 90–92, 94, 97–98, 106–8, 112–13, 182, 185, 187, 189–91, 197, 199, 203; grand coordinators and, 182–83, 194; Li Zicheng and, 207, 216; magistrates and, 64; map of, 188; masses and, 165–66, 199–200, 202–3; military and, 104, 152–54; militia and, 181, 185, 189, 196–97; officials and, 193–94, 197, 199, 203, 216–17; rebellion and, 169, 173, 198, 203, 230; sects and, 182, 194; state finances and, 104, 176; successes against, 193–98; supreme commanders and, 58–60; women as victims of, 124–26, 191; Xingyang conference and, 186–87, 191; Zheng Lian on, 186, 189–90, 197–98, 200, 216–17
Bandits of the Marsh, 171
Bao Zheng, 157
Baoding (Beizhili), 298–99, 308
Baofeng (Ruzhou), 38, 277
baojia system, 145
Beijing (Beizhili), 7, 14; defense of, 299–300; Kaifeng siege and, 260, 262; Li Zicheng and, 269, 279, 310; Manchus in, 136; map of Shun advance on, 297; Mongols in, 25; proposed move of capital from, 22; river conservancy and, 24–25; under Shun, 292, 311, 313–14; Shun advance on, 296–310

Yan Zhenqing, 234, 236
Yan Zhitui, 87
Yancheng (Kaifeng prefecture; Henan),
226–27
Yang Dongming, 35, 37–51, 62, 73, 76–77,
112, 129, 155, 218
Yang He, 58
Yang Hu, 169
Yang Lian, 56, 89
Yang Ma, 286
Yang Sichang, 58–60, 92, 107, 194,
196–200, 216, 259, 298; critics of, 103–4
Yang Sijing, 177–78
Yang Wenyue, 214, 217–18, 226, 253, 256,
272; Kaifeng siege and, 257–59; Yuan
Shizhong and, 270, 281
Yang Youwen, 245
Yangshao culture, 2
Yangzi River valley, 5. *See also* Jiangnan
region
Yanjin county (Kaifeng prefecture; Henan),
61, 138, 200
Yanling (Kaifeng prefecture; Henan), 200,
275
Yao Qiying, 305
Yeats, W. B., 312–14
Yellow Emperor, 154
Yellow Lord's Classic of Corporeal Medicine,
154–55
Yellow River: conservancy of, 23–28, 149;
course changes of, 137, 200; flooding of,
6–7, 35, 255, 264–66, 268; frozen, 183–
84, 230; Grand Canal and, 65–66; Henan
and, 1–2; historical models and, 66, 313;
Kaifeng siege and, 6, 255, 264–66; masses
and, 166; merchants and, 142; rebels and,
230, 280, 285; taxable land and, 30
Yellow Turbans, 179
Yi Yin, 73, 75, 318
Yifeng county (Kaifeng prefecture; Henan),
67, 69–71, 249
Yi-Luo Society, 211
Yim, Shui-yuen, 10
Yingtian (Song capital), 5
Yingtian Academy, 55
yinyang duality, 70, 316
Yitiao Long (a dragon), 187, 199–200, 230,
252
Yongcheng county (Guide prefecture;
Henan), 77, 138, 154; bandits in, 180–
81; elite of, 91–92, 118; Liu Chao in,
270, 279–80; natural disasters in, 35,

173–74; rebels in, 168–69, 174, 249;
White Lotus in, 217
Yongle (Zhu Di; Ming emperor), 16, 24, 121,
149, 159
Yongning county (Henan), 209–10
Yu (ancient region), 2
Yu department (Henan), 10, 277
Yu Longmen, 281
Yu Qian, 22–23, 34, 149, 157
Yu Zhining, 107
Yuan Chonghuan, 90
Yuan dynasty, 7, 61, 157, 166; centralization
of, 15; five-phase theory and, 318; floods
in, 23–24, 27; Li Zicheng and, 226, 311; as
model, 301, 313; Sino-American relations
and, 322; women in, 122–23
Yuan Shizhong, 247, 251, 269–70, 272, 285,
309; defection of, 253, 259; fall of, 280–
82, 285; Li Zicheng and, 229–35, 267, 311;
Liu Chao and, 280; in Shangqiu, 240; Su
Jing and, 293
Yuan Shu, 191
Yuan Zongdi, 292
Yucheng county (Guide prefecture; Henan),
50–51, 139, 187; elite of, 76–77, 112–13,
118, 129
Yue Fei, 157, 286
Yulin, battle of, 291
Yuzhou (Kaifeng prefecture; Henan), 139,
221, 276–77

Zeng Yinglin, 298
Zhang, Lady (empress dowager Yi'an;
mother of Tianqi), 121, 150, 304
Zhang Anshi, 130
Zhang Deng, 106
Zhang family (Kaifeng), 161
Zhang family (Suizhou), 116–17, 233
Zhang Fengyi, 186
Zhang Guoji, 150, 258, 304, 306
Zhang Han, 140
Zhang Heng, 70
Zhang Hesheng, 227
Zhang Jinjian, 105; writings of, 107–9
Zhang Jinyan, 105–11, 142, 298–300,
302–3, 313
Zhang Juzheng, 26, 32, 55, 143, 176, 318;
clients of, 72–73; opponents of, 78, 81,
93–94
Zhang Mengxi, 199
Zhang Pingshan, 150, 156
Zhang Pu, 131